Praise for the Cook's Illustrated series

THE COOK'S ILLUSTRATED BAKNG BOOK

"This book is a comprehensive, no-nonsense guide. . .a well-thought-out, clearly explained primer for every aspect of home baking."
—*Wall Street Journal*

"It's safe to say that with *The Cook's Illustrated Baking Book*, you need never buy another basic baking cookbook again. This book has it all."
—The Kitchn

THE COOK'S ILLUSTRATED MEAT BOOK

"Carnivores with an obsession for perfection will likely have found their new bible in this comprehensive collection."
—*Publishers Weekly* (starred review)

THE SCIENCE OF GOOD COOKING

"*The Science of Good Cooking* is a one-volume kitchen seminar, addressing in one smart chapter after another the sometimes surprising whys behind a cook's best practices.... You get the myth, the theory, the science and the proof, all rigorously interrogated as only America's Test Kitchen can do."
—*National Public Radio*

"The 400 recipes and 50 in-depth techniques are enough to grab the interest of even the most experienced cook."
—*New York Times*

"It's a kitchen education between hard covers."
—*Boston Globe*

THE COOK'S ILLUSTRATED COOKBOOK

"*The Cook's Illustrated Cookbook* is the perfect kitchen home companion."
—*Wall Street Journal*

"Revered by serious chefs as well as aspiring home cooks, this book is the bible of basic (and not-so-basic) kitchen knowledge. It focuses as much on technique (how to trim asparagus spears or frost a layer cake) as it does on recipes (roasted sesame green beans and chocolate cream pie)."
—*USA Today*

THE COOK'S ILLUSTRATED BAKING BOOK

COOK'S ILLUSTRATED

baking book

BAKING DEMYSTIFIED WITH 450 FOOLPROOF RECIPES FROM AMERICA'S MOST TRUSTED FOOD MAGAZINE

THE EDITORS AT AMERICA'S TEST KITCHEN

America's Test Kitchen
21 Drydock Avenue, Boston, MA 02210

Library of Congress Cataloging-in-Publication Data

The Cook's illustrated baking book : baking demystified : 450 recipes from America's most trusted food magazine / the editors of America's Test Kitchen.
    pages cm
Includes index.
ISBN 978-1-936493-58-6
1. Baking. 2. Cooking, American. I. America's test kitchen (Television program) II. Cook's illustrated.
TX765.C634 2013
641.5973--dc23
                        2013016858

ISBN 978-1-945256-81-3 (color edition)

Printed in Canada
10 9 8 7 6 5 4

Distributed by Penguin Random House Publisher Services
Tel: 800-733-3000

EDITORIAL DIRECTOR, BOOKS: Elizabeth Carduff
EXECUTIVE EDITOR: Lori Galvin
ASSOCIATE EDITOR: Alyssa King
DESIGN DIRECTOR: Amy Klee
ART DIRECTOR: Greg Galvan
ASSOCIATE ART DIRECTOR: Beverly Hsu
DESIGNER: Taylor Argenzio
ILLUSTRATION: John Burgoyne
ADDITIONAL PHOTOGRAPHY: Carl Tremblay and Keller + Keller
STAFF PHOTOGRAPHER: Daniel J. van Ackere
PRODUCTION DIRECTOR: Guy Rochford
SENIOR PRODUCTION MANAGER: Jessica Quirk
SENIOR PROJECT MANAGER: Alice Carpenter
PRODUCTION AND TRAFFIC COORDINATOR: Brittany Allen
WORKFLOW AND DIGITAL ASSET MANAGER: Andrew Mannone
SENIOR COLOR AND IMAGING SPECIALIST: Lauren Pettapiece
PRODUCTION AND IMAGING SPECIALISTS: Heather Dube, Lauren Robbins
COPYEDITOR: Cheryl Redmond
PROOFREADER: Debra Hudak
INDEXER: Elizabeth Parson

CHIEF CREATIVE OFFICER: Jack Bishop
EXECUTIVE EDITORIAL DIRECTORS: Julia Collin Davison and Bridget Lancaster

PICTURED ON FRONT OF JACKET: Profiteroles (page 450)
PICTURED ON BACK OF JACKET: Popovers (page 63)

Contents

Welcome to America's Test Kitchen

This book has been tested, written, and edited by the folks at America's Test Kitchen, where curious cooks become confident cooks. Located in Boston's Seaport District in the historic Innovation and Design Building, it features 15,000 square feet of kitchen space including multiple photography and video studios. It is the home of *Cook's Illustrated* magazine and *Cook's Country* magazine and is the workday destination for more than 60 test cooks, editors, and cookware specialists. Our mission is to empower and inspire confidence, community, and creativity in the kitchen.

We start the process of testing a recipe with a complete lack of preconceptions, which means that we accept no claim, no technique, and no recipe at face value. We simply assemble as many variations as possible, test a half-dozen of the most promising, and taste the results blind. We then construct our own recipe and continue to test it, varying ingredients, techniques, and cooking times until we reach a consensus. As we like to say in the test kitchen, "We make the mistakes so you don't have to." The result, we hope, is the best version of a particular recipe, but we realize that only you can be the final judge of our success (or failure). We use the same rigorous approach when we test equipment and taste ingredients.

All of this would not be possible without a belief that good cooking, much like good music, is based on a foundation of objective technique. Some people like spicy foods and others don't, but there is a right way to sauté, there is a best way to cook a pot roast, and there are measurable scientific principles involved in producing perfectly beaten, stable egg whites. Our ultimate goal is to investigate the fundamental principles of cooking to give you the techniques, tools, and ingredients you need to become a better cook. It is as simple as that.

To see what goes on behind the scenes at America's Test Kitchen, check out our social media channels for kitchen snapshots, exclusive content, video tips, and much more. You can watch us work (in our actual test kitchen) by tuning in to *America's Test Kitchen* or *Cook's Country* on public television or on our websites. Listen to *Proof*, *Mystery Recipe*, and *The Walk-In* (AmericasTestKitchen.com/podcasts) to hear engaging, complex stories about people and food. Want to hone your cooking skills or finally learn how to bake—with an America's Test Kitchen test cook? Enroll in one of our online cooking classes. And you can engage the next generation of home cooks with kid-tested recipes from America's Test Kitchen Kids.

Our community of home recipe testers provides valuable feedback on recipes under development by ensuring that they are foolproof. You can help us investigate the how and why behind successful recipes from your home kitchen. (Sign up at AmericasTestKitchen.com/recipe_testing.)

However you choose to visit us, we welcome you into our kitchen, where you can stand by our side as we test our way to the best recipes in America.

facebook.com/AmericasTestKitchen

instagram.com/TestKitchen

youtube.com/AmericasTestKitchen

tiktok.com/TestKitchen

twitter.com/TestKitchen

pinterest.com/TestKitchen

AmericasTestKitchen.com
CooksIllustrated.com
CooksCountry.com
OnlineCookingSchool.com
AmericasTestKitchen.com/kids

Baking Basics

Core Ingredients

Each year, the test kitchen goes through, on average, 2,500 pounds of flour, 2,000 pounds of sugar, 600 pounds of butter, and 850 dozen eggs for our recipe development and testing. In addition to running up an impressive grocery bill, we have developed some well-formed opinions about these ingredients. Here's what you need to know. (See our Shopping Guide on page 486 for more information on rounding out your baking pantry, including information on our top-rated brands.)

Flour

Bakers should really keep three flours—all-purpose, cake, and bread—on hand. Why? The protein content varies significantly among the three. Therefore, these flours will absorb water differently—the same amount of water might make a soupy batter with a cup of cake flour but a nice, firm dough with bread flour. Protein content also affects gluten development. More protein leads to more gluten, which, in turn, can translate to coarseness, chewiness, toughness, or crispness. Depending on the recipe, these traits might be desirable or not. Note that your choices of flour are not just limited to three.

ALL-PURPOSE FLOUR is by far the most versatile flour available. Its protein content (10 to 11.7 percent, depending on the brand: King Arthur is close to 11.7 percent, Pillsbury and Gold Medal around 10.5 percent) provides enough structure to make good sandwich bread, yet it's light enough to use for cakes of a medium-to-coarse crumb. We prefer unbleached flour. Bleached flours in our tests did not perform as well as the unbleached flours and were sometimes criticized for tasting flat or carrying off-flavors.

CAKE FLOUR has a low protein content—about 6 to 8 percent—and thus yields cakes and pastries with less gluten, which translates to a finer, more delicate crumb. We use cake flour for light cakes, such as pound cake and angel food cake. One note: Most cake flour is bleached, which affects the starches in flour so that it can absorb greater amounts of liquid and fat. Most cakes have so much sugar and fat it's very hard to detect any off-notes in the flour caused by the bleaching process. It is possible to approximate 1 cup of cake flour by using 2 tablespoons of cornstarch plus ⅞ cup of all-purpose flour.

BREAD FLOUR has a protein content of about 12 percent to 14 percent, meaning it develops a lot of gluten to provide strong, chewy structure for rustic breads. For sandwich breads we prefer using all-purpose flour for a softer crumb.

WHOLE-WHEAT FLOUR is made from all three parts of the wheat kernel—the endosperm as well as the fiber-rich bran, or outer shell, and the tiny, vitamin-packed germ. The presence of the germ and bran in whole-wheat flour makes it not only more nutritious and more flavorful, but also more dense and less able to rise. We generally don't like breads or baked goods made with 100 percent whole-wheat flour; they are more dense and can be sour-tasting. Instead, we rely on a combination of all-purpose flour and whole-wheat flour in most recipes.

OTHER SPECIALTY FLOURS

PASTRY FLOUR is a soft wheat flour with a protein content between that of all-purpose flour and cake flour. It is often used in pie crusts, tart pastry, scones, and other similarly buttery baked goods (such as biscuits and shortbread). While it performs well in these applications, we don't think it's worth stocking pastry flour unless you are a professional baker.

SELF-RISING FLOUR contains a leavener and is made from a soft flour that brings it closer to cake flour than all-purpose. We've found the convenience of self-rising flour to be pretty minor and recommend using cake flour in recipes that call for self-rising flour and adding the baking powder and salt yourself. The formula is 1½ teaspoons of baking powder and ½ teaspoon of salt for every cup of flour.

Refined flours, including all-purpose, bread, and cake flour, can be stored in airtight containers in your pantry for up to one year. Whole-wheat flour and others made from whole grains contain more fat than refined flours and can turn rancid quickly at room temperature. For this reason, we recommend storing these flours in the freezer. In various tests, we found that using flour straight from the freezer inhibited rise and yielded denser baked goods. Therefore, it's important to bring chilled flour to room temperature before baking. To quickly accomplish this, spread the flour in a thin layer on a baking sheet and let it sit for about 30 minutes.

STORING BAGGED FLOUR: A widemouthed plastic container allows you to scoop out what you need without making a floury mess of your countertop. Make sure the container can hold the entire contents of a 5-pound bag. A tight-fitting lid is also essential.

STORING BOXED FLOUR: Transfer the flour from the box to a large zipper-lock bag. Seal the bag, then store it in the original box. When you need some flour, simply lift the bag out of the box and drop the measuring cup right in.

The way you measure flour can make a big difference in your recipe. Too little flour can turn out baked goods that are flat, wet, or lacking in structure. Too much flour can result in tough, dry baked goods. For the ultimate in accuracy, nothing beats weighing flour, but our research has shown that the dip-and-sweep method is also reliable. (You might be surprised to learn that if you are spooning your flour into a measuring cup and then leveling it off, you could end up with 20 percent less flour than the dip-and-sweep method.)

WEIGHING FLOUR: We also weigh sugar, as well as many other dry baking ingredients. You can certainly weigh baking ingredients on a piece of parchment or a bowl, but we like to use a brown paper bag because the bag stands open on the scale, is deep enough to hold a lot with no overflow, and pours neatly.

THE DIP-AND-SWEEP METHOD: Spooning flour into a measuring cup simply isn't accurate (see above). We prefer to dip the measuring cup into the container of flour and sweep away the excess with a straight-edged object like the back of a butter knife. For information on measuring cups, see page 15.

Sifting flour is a chore, but sometimes it is important. When making a delicate cake like a sponge cake or genoise that requires flour to be folded into beaten eggs and sugar, sifted flour can be added quickly and distributed evenly (because sifting aerates the flour), thereby reducing the risk of deflating the batter.

Sifting reduces the overall amount of flour (in weight) that goes into the recipe. Because of the aeration, 1 cup of sifted cake flour weighs in at about 3 ounces, whereas 1 cup of cake flour measured straight from the bin using the dip-and-sweep method weighs around 4 ounces. As a result, if you don't follow recipe directions regarding sifting, you will end up with way too much (or too little) flour.

To guarantee you're using the proper amount of flour, for recipes that read "1 cup sifted flour," sift the flour directly into a measuring cup set on top of parchment paper and then level off the excess. For recipes reading "1 cup flour, sifted," measure the flour first using the dip-and-sweep method (see above) and then sift it. Of course, a scale makes all of this much simpler and more accurate, which is why our baking recipes give both weight and volume.

Place the flour in a fine-mesh strainer and sift directly into a measuring cup set on a piece of parchment paper.

Leaveners help all manner of baked goods rise—from quick breads, yeast breads, rolls, and biscuits to cookies and cakes. Yeast is a biological leavener, and the others, including baking soda, baking powder, and cream of tartar, fall under the category of chemical leaveners.

YEAST is commonly available in two forms. In the test kitchen, we prefer instant yeast, also called rapid-rise yeast, because it's faster-acting and easy to use. It does not need to be "proofed" in warm water and can simply be added to dry ingredients. Regular dry yeast can be substituted for instant yeast, although you will need to use more of it. Note that both types of yeast come in packets, each of which contains 2¼ teaspoons of yeast. To compensate for the greater quantity of inactive yeast cells in active dry yeast, simply use 25 percent more of it (for example, if the recipe calls for 1 teaspoon of instant yeast, use 1¼ teaspoons of active dry). The inverse holds true as well—use about 25 percent less instant yeast in a recipe that calls for active dry. Also, don't forget to dissolve active dry yeast in a portion of the water from the recipe, heated to 110 degrees. Then let it stand for 5 minutes before adding it to the remaining wet ingredients.

Never mix any yeast with water hotter than 120 degrees or the yeast will die. Yeast should be stored in a cool environment, either in the fridge or the freezer. Because yeast is a living organism, the expiration date on the package should be observed.

BAKING SODA is an alkali, and therefore requires an acidic ingredient in the batter or dough, such as buttermilk or sour cream, in order to produce the leavening gas (carbon dioxide). The leavening action happens as soon as the baking soda is mixed with acidic liquid ingredients, so you should be ready to bake soon after mixing. In addition to leavening, baking soda also promotes browning in baked goods.

BAKING POWDER is a mixture of baking soda (about one-quarter to one-third of the total makeup), a dry acid, and double-dried cornstarch. The cornstarch absorbs moisture and keeps the baking soda and dry acid apart during storage, preventing premature production of gas. Baking powder works in two stages: when it comes into contact with a liquid and again in response to heat. Once opened, baking powder will lose its effectiveness after six months. Baking powder should be stored in a place that is cool and dry (the latter rules out the refrigerator, which is a source of moisture).

To replace 1 teaspoon of baking powder, mix ¼ teaspoon of baking soda with ½ teaspoon of cream of tartar and use immediately.

CREAM OF TARTAR is a dry acid, and when mixed with baking soda and a liquid, it will produce carbon dioxide bubbles that leaven baked goods. Because of its acidic nature, cream of tartar is sometimes also used when whipping egg whites. It makes the whites more stable and allows them to obtain greater volume.

BAKING SODA AS DEODORIZER?

To test whether baking soda can indeed absorb or neutralize odors from the refrigerator or freezer, we placed equal amounts of sour milk, stinky cheese, and spoiled fish into two airtight containers, then added an open box of baking soda to one container and left the second alone. We sealed the samples and let them sit overnight at room temperature. Finally, we asked a panel of "sniffers" to smell each container after 24 hours and again after 48 hours, removing the boxes of baking soda each time. The results were inconclusive, with some sniffers claiming they couldn't detect much difference and others swearing they could.

What does science tell us? While baking soda does neutralize acids, the likelihood of gaseous molecules from acidic sour milk migrating through the refrigerator and interacting with the baking soda is slight. But don't rule out baking soda altogether. When this alkaline powder comes into direct contact with smells, it can make a difference. We recently tested different approaches to removing garlic and onion smells from a cutting board and found scrubbing with a paste of 1 tablespoon baking soda and 1 teaspoon water to be the most effective.

Sugar

Sugar not only adds sweetness to baked goods, it influences texture too. For example, the amount or type of sugar can make a cookie crisp or chewy. Here are the most common types of sugar we use in baking.

WHITE GRANULATED SUGAR made either from sugar cane or sugar beets, is the type of sugar used most often in our recipes. It has a clean flavor and its evenly ground, loose texture ensures that it incorporates well with butter when creaming and dissolves easily into batters.

SUPERFINE SUGAR is finely processed and has extra-small crystals that dissolve quickly. Superfine sugar promotes a melt-in-the-mouth texture in delicate cookies such as shortbread and butter cookies. (And because it dissolves easily in liquid, it's a must for iced tea, iced coffee, and other cold beverages.) To make your own superfine sugar, simply process granulated sugar in a food processor for about 30 seconds.

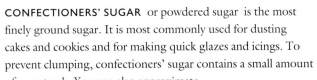

Superfine sugar can often be found in the baking or cocktail mixer aisle of the supermarket.

CONFECTIONERS' SUGAR or powdered sugar is the most finely ground sugar. It is most commonly used for dusting cakes and cookies and for making quick glazes and icings. To prevent clumping, confectioners' sugar contains a small amount of cornstarch. You can also approximate confectioners' sugar with this method: For 1 cup of confectioners' sugar, process 1 cup granulated sugar with 1 tablespoon of cornstarch in a blender (not a food processor) until fine, 30 to 40 seconds.

The cornstarch in confectioners' sugar prevents clumping and makes it ideal for dusting over a cake or dissolving in a glaze.

TURBINADO AND DEMERARA SUGAR are also referred to as "raw" sugar. The large crystals of these sugars do not readily dissolve—a reason to avoid them in dough. Instead, we like to sprinkle them on muffin tops to create crunch or to form the caramel crust on crème brûlée.

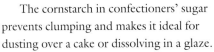

BROWN SUGAR is granulated white sugar that has been combined with molasses. (When necessary, our ingredient list will indicate "light" or "dark" brown sugar. If either can be used, we simply list "brown sugar.") Store brown sugar in an airtight container to prevent it from drying out.

To approximate 1 cup of light brown sugar, pulse 1 cup of granulated sugar with 1 tablespoon of mild molasses in a food processor until blended. Use 2 tablespoons molasses for dark brown sugar.

MEASURING SUGAR

White sugar should be measured by weight or by using the dip-and-sweep method (see page 3). Brown sugar, on the other hand, is so moist and clumpy that it must be packed into the measuring cup in order to get an accurate measurement.

NO-FUSS MEASURING FOR BROWN SUGAR: Fill the correct dry measure with brown sugar and use the next smallest cup to pack it down. For instance, if you need ⅓ cup packed brown sugar, use the bottom of the ¼-cup measure to pack it down. In addition to firmly packing the sugar down, the flat bottom of the smaller cup also helps to obliterate any hard clumps that may have developed in the bag. When properly packed 1 cup of brown sugar should weigh the same as 1 cup of granulated sugar: 7 ounces.

REVIVING HARDENED BROWN SUGAR: If your brown sugar dries out, place the sugar in a zipper-lock bag, add a slice of bread, and set it aside overnight until the sugar is soft again. Or, quicker yet, put the brown sugar in a microwave-safe bowl with the bread and tightly cover with plastic wrap. Microwave until the sugar is moist, 15 to 30 seconds.

Butter

Perhaps 95 percent of the recipes in this book contain butter. Butter not only adds flavor and richness to countless baking recipes, it affects texture as well, whether it's creamed in a velvety Bundt cake or cut with flour into a flaky pastry crust.

BUTTER, SALTED OR UNSALTED?

In the test kitchen, we use unsalted butter almost exclusively and add our own salt to recipes. Why? First, the amount of salt in salted butter (on average, ⅓ teaspoon per stick) varies from brand to brand, which makes offering a universal conversion impossible. Second, salted butter almost always contains more water, which can influence gluten development—particularly important in baking. (Biscuits made with salted butter were noticeably mushy.) Third, salt masks butter's naturally sweet, delicate flavors; in butter-specific recipes like buttercream frosting, we found the extra salt to be overwhelming.

PLAIN OR PREMIUM?

While you hear a lot about the higher fat content in premium butters, our tasters had trouble telling the difference, even when they tasted the butters plain. Regular unsalted butter contains 81 to 82 percent fat; premium brands have 83 to 86 percent fat. Because higher-fat butter remains solid over a wider temperature range, we like it when making croissant dough and other recipes where rapid softening of the butter would cause problems. The real distinction between plain and premium butters is culturing—the process of fermenting the cream before churning it that builds tangy, complex flavors. That said, these nuances are subtle in most cooked applications, so we save the expensive cultured stuff for spreading on toast.

WHAT ABOUT WHIPPED BUTTER?

Whipped butter, made by beating air into butter, makes a creamy spread but isn't always a good alternative to stick butter for cooking. While testers couldn't tell the difference in baked goods, they found the aerated butter "foamy" and "plastic-like" in uncooked applications such as frosting. If you want to use whipped butter, base your substitution on weight, not volume. (Adding air increases the volume, not the weight.) A standard tub of whipped butter weighs 8 ounces, equal to two sticks of butter.

MEASURING BUTTER ACCURATELY

We've noticed that the tablespoon increment measures on butter wrappers often don't line up correctly with the stick of butter. If this is the case, unwrap the butter, mark the halfway point in the stick and then mark the midpoint of each half, dividing the stick into quarters (each quarter is equal to 2 tablespoons, or 1 ounce). If necessary, mark the midpoint of each quarter, dividing the stick into eighths (each eighth is equal to 1 tablespoon, or ½ ounce). Alternatively, use a scale to weigh the butter, keeping in mind that 1 tablespoon equals ½ ounce.

STORING BUTTER

Placed in the back of the fridge where it's coldest (not in the small door compartment), butter will keep for 2½ weeks. In tests we've found that any longer and it can turn rancid as its fatty acids oxidize. For longer storage (up to four months), move it to the freezer. Also, since butter quickly picks up odors and flavors, we like to slip the sticks into a zipper-lock bag.

BUTTER PACKAGING

Ever wonder why butter is packaged in two different styles? The Elgin, or Eastern-pack, style of packaging butter creates the long, skinny sticks available in most regions of the United States. They are 4¾ inches long by 1¼ inches wide and are stacked two by two in their boxy containers. The Western-pack style makes for the short, stubby sticks that measure 3⅛ inches long by 1½ inches wide and are packed side by side in their flat, rectangular boxes. No matter what the style, one stick contains 8 tablespoons.

Elgin-style sticks (named for a once-prominent dairy in Elgin, Illinois) are the standard choice east of the Rockies. At some point, dairy farms in the West began using different butter printers (the machinery used to cut and package butter sticks) that produced shorter, wider sticks. We find both styles easy to use in the kitchen. The biggest difference may come down to your butter dish—most dishes are shaped to fit Elgin-style sticks.

The temperature of butter makes a difference in many recipes and can dramatically affect the texture of finished baked goods. For example, pie dough made with warm or room-temperature butter rather than chilled butter will be nearly impossible to roll out and the resulting crust will be hard and tough rather than tender and flaky. On the other hand, cakes and cookies require softened butter, which is crucial for creaming; softened butter blends easily with the sugar and this action incorporates air into the dough or batter, creating tender baked goods.

CHILLED (about 35 degrees)
Method: Cut butter into small pieces; freeze until very firm, 10 to 15 minutes.
How to Test It: Press with a finger—it should be cold and unyielding.
Why It Matters: Cold butter melts during baking, leaving behind small pockets of air that create flaky layers in recipes like pie dough and croissants.

SOFTENED (65 to 67 degrees)
Method: Let refrigerated butter sit at room temperature for about 30 minutes.
How to Test It: The stick will easily bend without breaking and will give slightly when pressed.
Why It Matters: Softened butter is flexible enough to be whipped but firm enough to retain the incorporated air—vital to making cakes with a tender crumb.

MELTED AND COOLED (85 to 90 degrees)
Method: Melt butter in a small saucepan or microwave-safe bowl; let cool about 5 minutes.
How to Test It: The butter should be fluid and slightly warm.
Why It Matters: Butter is roughly 16 percent water; when it's melted, the water breaks from the emulsion and helps create gluten for chewier cookies.

TWO WAYS TO SOFTEN BUTTER QUICKLY

A. Place cold butter in a plastic bag and use a rolling pin to pound it to the desired consistency in a matter of seconds.

B. Cut butter into small pieces. By the time you've preheated the oven and measured the remaining ingredients, the pieces should be near 65 degrees.

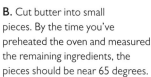
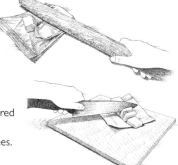

SOFTENING BUTTER IN THE MICROWAVE

Using the microwave to soften butter can be risky business. A few seconds too long and the butter can melt and your cakes or cookies might not rise properly. If you're going to soften butter in the microwave, here's how to keep it from melting:

For 4 tablespoons of butter, place the butter in one piece on a small microwave-safe plate. Place the plate in the microwave and heat for 1 minute at 10 percent power. Press on the butter with your finger to see if it is sufficiently softened; if not, heat for an additional 20 seconds at 10 percent power. This method also works with whole sticks.

The idea is to increase the second microwave time by 10 seconds for each additional 2 tablespoons of butter. For example, a whole stick should be microwaved for 1 minute, checked, and then microwaved for 40 seconds, if necessary. For a lower-wattage microwave (we tried an 800-watt oven), you will need to heat the 4 tablespoons of butter for 1½ minutes at 10 percent, check it, then heat for another 30 seconds at 10 percent power, if necessary. Either way, the butter should be about 67 degrees—perfectly softened and ready to be creamed.

RESCUING OVERSOFTENED BUTTER

The fat in butter is partially crystalline and highly sensitive to temperature changes. When butter is properly softened to 65 or 70 degrees, the tiny crystals can effectively surround and stabilize the air bubbles that are generated during creaming. When heated to the melting point, however, these crystals are destroyed. They can be reestablished but only if the butter is rapidly chilled. (Returning it to the refrigerator will cool it too slowly and fail to reestablish the tiny crystals.) To quickly cool down partially melted butter, we mixed in a few ice cubes. After less than a minute of stirring, the butter had cooled to a softened stage—right below 70 degrees—so we extracted the ice and prepared sugar cookies and buttercream frosting.

Sugar cookies made with our rehabilitated butter were nearly identical to those made with properly softened butter, and the frosting was also acceptable, if slightly softer than a control batch.

As primal to baking as flour, butter, or sugar, eggs contribute flavor, structure, richness, and texture to baked goods from velvety pound cakes to a smooth crème caramel.

FARM-FRESH AND ORGANIC

In our taste tests, farm-fresh eggs were standouts. The large yolks were bright orange and sat high above the comparatively small whites. Their flavor was rich and complex. Organic eggs followed in second place, while eggs from hens raised on a vegetarian diet came in third and standard supermarket eggs last. Differences were easily detected in egg-based dishes but not in cakes or cookies.

EGG SIZES AND WEIGHTS

Theoretically, eggs come in three grades (AA, A, and B), six sizes (from peewee to jumbo), and a rainbow of colors. But the only grade we could find in the market was grade A, the only colors were brown and white, and the only sizes were jumbo, extra-large, large, and medium. After extensive tasting, we could not discern any consistent flavor differences among egg sizes or colors. For consistency's sake, however, the size (and volume) of the eggs used in recipes is important, particularly when baking. Thus, in all of our recipes, we use large eggs.

MEDIUM	LARGE	EXTRA-LARGE	JUMBO
1.75 ounces	2 ounces	2.25 ounces	2.50 ounces

You can use this chart to make accurate calculations when substituting egg sizes. For example, four jumbo eggs are equivalent to five large eggs because their weight (10 ounces) is the same.

STORING EGGS

Although perishable, properly stored eggs will last up to three months, but both the yolks and the whites will become looser and their flavor will begin to fade. To be sure that you have fresh eggs, check the sell-by date on the side of the carton. By law, the sell-by date must be no more than 30 days after the packing date. To ensure freshness, store eggs in the back of the refrigerator (the coldest area), not in the door (which is actually the warmest part of your refrigerator), and keep them in the carton. It holds in moisture and keeps eggs from drying out; the carton also protects the eggs from odors.

WHAT ABOUT FREEZING EGGS?

Egg whites can be frozen, but in our tests we found that their rising properties were compromised. Frozen whites are best used in recipes that call for small amounts (like an egg wash) or recipes that don't depend on whipping the egg whites (such as an omelet). Egg yolks, however, can't be frozen as is; the water forms ice crystals that disrupt the protein network. Adding sugar syrup (2 parts sugar to 1 part water) allows yolks to be frozen. Stir a scant ¼ teaspoon of syrup per yolk into yolks before freezing. Defrost and use in custards.

GETTING A CLEAN BREAK

Many baking recipes call for bringing eggs to room temperature before they are separated. But this can be a tricky business, as the warm egg yolk can easily leak into the white (a recipe for failure if you are looking for fluffy, whipped whites). Separating each egg over a smaller bowl before adding the yolk or white to another bowl is always a safe measure, but we have found that we have much better luck when we separate the eggs while they are still chilly from the fridge. Yolks are more taut and less apt to break into the whites when cold. If a recipe calls for the eggs to be brought to room temperature, simply separate the eggs while cold, cover both bowls with plastic wrap (make sure the wrap touches the surface of the eggs to keep them from drying out), and let sit on the counter until they've lost their chill.

CRACKING EGGS

Here's our preferred method for cracking eggs.

Tap egg on flat surface, such as countertop, rather than edge of mixing bowl. This results in cleaner break through shell and inner membrane, which translates to fewer pieces of shattered shell in your bowl.

Nuts

We use all manner of nuts in this book. For many recipes we toast nuts before baking to intensify their flavor. And some nuts are covered in skins which should be removed before being used in a recipe. Here's what you need to know.

STORING NUTS

All nuts are high in oil and will become rancid rather quickly. In the test kitchen, we store all nuts in the freezer in sealed freezer-safe zipper-lock bags. Frozen nuts will keep for months and there's no need to defrost before toasting or chopping.

TOASTING NUTS

What is the best way to toast nuts? A quick straw vote in the test kitchen revealed a divided camp on this issue. To settle the matter once and for all, we toasted a range of different-size nuts (slivered almonds, sliced almonds, walnut halves, pecan halves, and whole pine nuts) in a 10-inch skillet over medium heat and on a baking sheet in a 350-degree oven. After comparing the cooled nuts, we found no flavor differences. As for technique, toasting nuts on the stovetop requires more attention from the cook: Frequent stirring is a necessity. Another strike against the stovetop is that large amounts of nuts can crowd a skillet, preventing thorough toasting. The bottom line: For more than 1 cup of nuts (or if you happen to have the oven on already), use your oven. For smaller quantities, pull out a skillet; just remember to stir the nuts often to prevent them from burning.

TOASTED NUTS AT THE READY

If you use toasted nuts in recipes such as cookies or brownies, but become impatient when it comes to toasting small amounts for each dish, use this method to ensure that you always have toasted nuts at the ready.

Toast several cups of nuts on a rimmed baking sheet in a 350-degree oven for 3 to 5 minutes. When the nuts are cool, transfer them to a zipper-lock bag, then freeze them. Do not use pretoasted frozen nuts for recipes in which a crisp texture is desired, such as salads.

SKINNING NUTS

The skins from some nuts such as walnuts and hazelnuts can impart a bitter flavor in some dishes.

To remove the skins, rub the hot toasted nuts inside a clean dish towel.

BLANCHING ALMONDS

Most of the time, you'll be able to buy almonds already blanched. But if you don't want to make a special trip to the store, try this method using raw almonds.

1. Place 1 cup almonds in medium heatproof bowl and cover with 2 cups boiling water. Let almonds stand for 2 minutes, then drain and rinse them under cold running water.

2. Press each almond between your thumb and index finger to slip off skin.

3. To dry and lightly toast skinned nuts, place them on baking sheet in 350-degree oven for 7 to 10 minutes.

CHOPPING ROUND NUTS NEATLY

Wet a dish towel, grasp both ends, and twist them in opposite directions to form a tight rope. Place the rope on the cutting board in a ring around the nuts. Leave enough room in the center of the ring to fit the knife, and chop away.

Chocolate

All chocolate begins as cacao beans, which are seeds found in large pods that grow on cacao trees in regions around the equator. These beans are fermented, dried, and roasted and then the inner meat (or nib) of the bean is removed from the shell and ground into a paste. This paste is called chocolate liquor (although it contains no alcohol) and consists of cocoa solids and cocoa butter. Chocolate liquor is then further processed and mixed with sugar and flavorings to make the various types of chocolate. White chocolate is made from just the cocoa butter and doesn't contain any cocoa solids. Sweet, semisweet, and bittersweet chocolate go through a refining process known as conching where the chocolate liquor and the other ingredients are smeared against rollers until smooth. This conching action also drives off some of the volatile compounds responsible for chocolate's natural bitterness. Since unsweetened chocolate is rarely conched, it has a coarse texture and bitter flavor.

Using the right type and brand of chocolate in baking can make a big difference in something as simple as Ultimate Chocolate Chip Cookies (page 183) or as complex as Ultimate Flourless Chocolate Cake (page 325). After tasting and cooking with hundreds of pounds of chocolate in the test kitchen, we came up with what you really need to know. For information on our top-rated brands see our Shopping Guide on page 496.

COCOA POWDER is chocolate liquor that is fed through a press to remove all but 10 to 24 percent of the cocoa butter. Cocoa powder comes in natural and Dutched versions. Dutching, which was invented in the 19th century by Dutch chemist and chocolatier Coenraad Van Houten, raises the powder's pH, which neutralizes its acids and astringent notes and rounds out its flavor. (It also darkens the color). In the test kitchen, we often "bloom" cocoa powder in a hot liquid such as water or coffee. This dissolves the remaining cocoa butter and disperses water-soluble flavor compounds for a deeper, stronger chocolate flavor.

UNSWEETENED CHOCOLATE is the traditional choice for recipes in which a bold hit of chocolate flavor is more important than a smooth or delicate texture (think brownies).

If you don't have unsweetened chocolate, you can replace 1 ounce of unsweetened chocolate with 3 tablespoons of cocoa powder and 1 tablespoon of butter or oil. This substitution, however, is best for small quantities, because it ignores the many important differences between butter, oil, and cocoa butter. A pan of fudgy brownies made with cocoa powder and butter will usually turn out cakelike and dry.

SEMISWEET AND BITTERSWEET CHOCOLATES also called dark chocolate, must contain at least 35 percent chocolate liquor (a combination of chocolate solids and cocoa butter), although most contain more than 55 percent and some go as high as 99 percent. Although many brands have distinctive flavors that tasters liked in particular desserts, two brands, Ghirardelli 60% Cacao Bittersweet Chocolate Premium Baking Bar and Callebaut Intense Dark Chocolate, L-60-40NV, consistently produced great results in all types of baked goods. Note that both of these chocolates contain 60 percent cacao—the type most recipes calling for dark chocolate have been developed to use. (Chocolates containing 70 percent or more cacao usually require recipe adjustments to get good results.)

Can you substitute for bittersweet and semisweet chocolate? We found that you can replace 1 ounce of bittersweet or semisweet chocolate with ⅔ ounce of unsweetened chocolate and 2 teaspoons of granulated sugar, yet because the unsweetened chocolate has not been conched it will not provide the same smooth, creamy texture as bittersweet or semisweet chocolate. Also, while the same weight of chocolate chips can be substituted in many recipes, we don't think they work as well in sauces or puddings.

MILK CHOCOLATE must contain at least 10 percent chocolate liquor (a mix of chocolate solids and cocoa butter) and 12 percent milk solids, with sweeteners and flavorings making up the balance. The result is a mellow, smooth, milky flavor. Yet because of its relatively weak chocolate flavor (milk chocolate is usually more than 50 percent sugar), we don't use it in very many recipes. We reserve milk chocolate for frostings and for eating out of hand. Don't confuse sweet chocolate with milk chocolate. Sweet chocolate is extremely sweet and doesn't contain the milk solids found in milk chocolate.

WHITE CHOCOLATE White chocolate is technically not chocolate since it contains no cocoa solids. Authentic white chocolate contains at least 20 percent cocoa butter (along with milk solids and sugar), which gives this product its meltingly smooth texture. Note that many brands rely on palm oil in place of some or all of the cocoa butter and can't be labeled "chocolate." If the product is called "white chips" or "white confection," it is made with little or no cocoa butter. That said, since both styles derive their flavor from milk and sugar, not the fat, we find this distinction makes little difference in recipes.

DARK CHOCOLATE CHIPS contain far less cacao, about 42 to 47 percent, than bar chocolate, which start at about 60 percent. This means that chocolate chips will be less fluid when melted, making it easier for the chips to hold that classic teardrop shape on the production line. In our testing, tasters picked up big differences among brands in creaminess, awarding extra points to brands that were especially smooth melters. Our winning brand, Ghirardelli 60% Premium Baking Chips, had the highest percentage of cacao in the lineup, comparable to bar chocolate—and the most cocoa butter by far (44 percent, minus a tiny amount of milk fat). It was also wider and flatter than a standard chip, which enhanced its ability to melt into thin strata throughout the cookie.

STORING CHOCOLATE

Never store chocolate in the refrigerator or freezer, as cocoa butter can easily pick up off-flavors from other foods. If chocolate is exposed to rapid changes in humidity or temperature, sugar or fat may dissolve and migrate, discoloring the surface. This condition, known as bloom, is cosmetic and not harmful—bloomed chocolate is safe to eat and cook with.

To extend the shelf life of chocolate, wrap it tightly in plastic wrap and store it in a cool, dry place. Milk and white chocolates should last for six months to a year; dark chocolates will last for several years.

Some chocolate is sold in large, thick bars, which can make chopping difficult. We found two techniques that help make the task easier.

TWO WAYS TO CHOP CHOCOLATE

WITH A KNIFE: To chop a large block of chocolate, hold a large knife at a 45-degree angle to one of the corners and bear down evenly. After cutting about an inch from the corner, repeat with the other corners.

WITH A LARGE FORK: Alternatively, use a sharp two-tined meat fork to break the chocolate into smaller pieces.

MELTING CHOCOLATE

When melting chocolate, it is best to be gentle because chocolate can easily burn or separate and become greasy. We've found two methods to be the best for melting chocolate: using a double boiler or microwaving it at 50 percent power.

TWO WAYS TO MELT CHOCOLATE

STOVETOP: Chop the chocolate (so it melts evenly) and place it in a heatproof bowl set over a pot of barely simmering water, but be sure the bowl is not touching the water or the chocolate could scorch. Stir occasionally.

MICROWAVE: Microwave chopped chocolate at 50 percent power for 2 minutes. Stir the chocolate and continue heating until melted, stirring once every additional minute.

Equipping Your Kitchen

With a well-equipped kitchen, you can tackle almost any baking project. But the sheer number of equipment choices on the market can be positively overwhelming. How do you know which items are really essential? Or which loaf pan to buy when there are dozens of options? Not to worry—we've done the work for you and cut through the confusion. For more information on equipping your kitchen, see our Shopping Guide on pages 486–499.

A NOTE ON BAKING MATERIALS

Though its manufacturers are loath to admit it, choosing quality bakeware is pretty simple. All the usual jargon about clad aluminum cores and anodized coatings remains in full force, but a dozen years of testing have left us even more skeptical than usual about bells and whistles when it comes to shopping for cake pans and cookie sheets. Here's what to look for—and what to avoid.

TEMPERED, OVENPROOF GLASS Better known by the brand name Pyrex, thick tempered glass retains plenty of heat, so pans made from it ensure deep and even browning. They also make it easy to monitor the browning as it develops. Because Pyrex is scratch-resistant, you can cut and serve right from the pan with sharp knives and metal spatulas. What's not to like? Just the occasional explosion, a manageable risk as long as you take precautions (see "Handling Pyrex" below).

DARK FINISHES When it comes to metal pans, neither the type of metal nor its thickness matters much. What does matter is the color of the pan. Dark nonstick pans allow metal to absorb more heat inside the oven than reflective, lighter-colored materials. The result: darker browning of baked goods, which is almost always a good thing. Combine that with the clean release and easy cleanup of nonstick, and pans in this category are often the ones to beat.

LIGHT-COLORED FINISHES A well-browned crust releases more easily from a pan than a pale crust. Because light gold colored pans brown more slowly than dark pans, they bake goods evenly without overbrowning them. And a nonstick coating also makes for an easy release. Controlled browning can be an advantage, such as when baking cookies. (Because only the bottom of a cookie is in contact with the metal, it can easily burn before the rest of the cookie bakes through.)

INSULATED To protect against overbrowning (not usually a problem for us), insulated pans incorporate a layer of air sandwiched between two sheets of metal. Unfortunately, this "insulation" works all too well: The pans produce pale, underdeveloped crusts. The interior chamber also becomes waterlogged if submerged in water during cleanup. What a pain.

CAST-IRON We don't use cast-iron bakeware often because acidic ingredients such as lemon juice can release some of the metal molecules from the pan surface, causing foods to have a metallic or "off" taste. That said, we recommend a cast-iron skillet for quickbreads like Southern-Style Cornbread (page 31) and Skillet Irish Soda Bread (page 34), where its superior heat-retaining properties help yield a browned, crunchy crust. Likewise, an enameled or regular cast-iron Dutch oven is the baking pan of choice for our Almost No-Knead Bread (page 139). For information on seasoning and caring for cast iron, see page 34.

SILICONE We have tested a half-dozen types of silicone bakeware and have yet to find something we can recommend. These flexible, rubbery pans are the most useless things to appear in the kitchen since salad shooters. These "pans" don't brown well, and getting them into the oven when loaded down with batter is awkward.

HANDLING PYREX

Pyrex pie plates and baking dishes had been standard issue in the test kitchen, but over the years we've learned that they are prone to shattering when exposed to sudden and extreme temperature changes. Naturally, this prohibits their use under a broiler or over direct stovetop heat, but the tempered glass bakeware is also vulnerable to sudden drops in temperature, known in the industry as downshock. Downshock would result from adding cold liquid to a hot Pyrex dish or from placing a hot dish directly on a cold or wet surface. It is considered safe, however, to transfer a Pyrex dish directly from the refrigerator or freezer to a hot oven, provided the oven has been properly preheated— some ovens use the broiler element to heat up to the desired temperature.

BAKING PANS We use these pans in the test kitchen for everything from fruit crisps to sticky buns. We like sturdy Pyrex because it's dishwasher-safe, scratch-resistant, and has handy handles for easy maneuvering in and out of the oven. The thick tempered glass retains plenty of heat to ensure deep, even browning and lets you see exactly how brown (or burned) the food is on the bottom. A 13 by 9-inch pan is the best all-around option, but the 8-inch and 9-inch square pans are good for smaller batches. For baked goods with squared off edges like cornbread, brownies, and bar cookies, we like straight-sided metal pans with a nonstick finish.

CAKE PANS We use our cake pans to bake not only cakes, but deep-dish pizza, too. And we've also encountered a few hidden uses, like serving as a shallow dish when rolling cookies in sugar, or for small baking tasks like toasting a few nuts in the oven. It's best to have two sets of cake pans, preferably two 8-inch pans and two 9-inch pans. Look for pans with high, straight sides. Pans with short sides have a hard time accommodating tall cakes, such as an upside-down cake, and flared sides produce cakes with uneven sides that are more difficult to frost and harder to slice into layers. In general, we prefer aluminum or tinned-steel pans, preferably with a nonstick coating.

SPRINGFORM PANS A springform pan is essential for a variety of cakes that would be impossible to remove from a standard cake pan. We like pans with light-colored nonstick finishes and raised bases, which made it easier to cut and remove slices. The disappointing truth we've found in our testing is that even the best springform pans leak to some degree, so we recommend double-wrapping the pan with aluminum foil when using a water bath. Or you can place the springform pan inside a larger standard cake pan before setting it in the water bath.

BUNDT PANS Bundt pans were introduced by Nordic Ware in the 1950s, based on the traditional cast-iron kugelhopf molds of Eastern Europe (used for a yeasted bread common to much of Europe). These fluted baking pans eventually gained widespread popularity, largely thanks to a slew of Bundt cake mixes marketed by Pillsbury. Look for clearly defined ridges, a 15-cup capacity, and heavyweight cast aluminum with a nonstick surface for even browning and an easy release—though we also recommend greasing and flouring the pan before baking.

TUBE PANS Tube pans (or angel food cake pans) are not just for looks. The tube also helps cakes bake faster and more evenly by providing more surface area in which to heat the thick batter quickly. When choosing a tube pan, the three variables that matter most are weight, finish, and a removable bottom. Heavier pans retain heat for even browning; darker pans produce similar results by absorbing rather than reflecting heat. Finally, a heavy-bottomed pan is important to create a leak-free seal. We also find pans with feet on the top rim handy for elevating the upturned pan during cooling.

COOKIE SHEETS Cookie sheets come in many materials, sizes, thicknesses, and finishes, insulated or not, with rims or not. After testing numerous cookie sheets, we found that we liked thick sheets; thin sheets baked unevenly, ran hot, and tended to warp, as did insulated sheets. We also preferred light finishes—the dark nonstick cookie sheets we tested consistently overbrowned the bottoms of cookies. Aluminum sheets have better, more even heat transference than steel sheets. As for rims, raised edges provide a useful handhold, but we prefer sheets with at least one rimless edge, which easily allows us to slide a sheet of cookies on parchment paper onto a cooling rack. Pans with two raised edges on the short sides handled best.

BAKING SHEETS In the test kitchen, we use baking sheets for baking everything from cookies to jelly rolls and tarts. When buying baking sheets, look for ones that are light and thick. A light-colored surface will heat and brown evenly, making for perfectly browned baked goods. And a pan that isn't thick enough can buckle or transfer heat too intensely, burning the food. We prefer pans that are 18 by 13 inches with a 1-inch rim all around. Note that a traditional jelly roll pan is smaller than these industrial-size baking sheets. And because they have so many different uses, we recommend having more than one.

PIE PLATES In our testing, we have found that neither ceramic nor clear glass pie plates turn out evenly browned crusts as reliably as our favorite light gold nonstick metal pie dish. Crusts bake without overbrowning and produce crisp and flaky bottom crusts. A wide nonfluted lip is essential; it makes the plate easier to move in and out of the oven and allows for maximum crust-crimping flexibility. Also, when the crust edge rests on the pie plate lip, it helps prevent it from slipping down during baking.

FLUTED TART PANS The fluted edges and false bottoms of tart pans allow even a novice baker to turn out elegant-looking desserts without much effort. Avoid pans without removable bottoms as well as the generic tinned-steel pans with a traditional finish. We prefer darker nonstick models with deep grooves for impressive edges. (There's so much fat in buttery tart dough that it wouldn't stick to flypaper, much less a pan.) Our tart recipes are generally developed to fit a 9-inch pan, but 11-inch models are also common.

LOAF PANS A good loaf pan will evenly brown quick breads, such as banana bread, as well as yeast breads. Loaves should release cleanly, and the pans should be easy to get in and out of the oven. When testing loaf pans, we've found that light-colored metal loaf pans browned breads more evenly than dark-colored metal pans. Most of the metal pans were lined with a nonstick coating that also made the release of baked breads especially easy (though even with the nonstick coating, we recommend greasing and flouring your loaf pan to ensure easy release). We prefer pans that are 8½ by 4½ inches for loaves with tall, rounder tops. Many recipes yield two loaves, so it's good to have at least two pans. One of the heavier, more expensive pans in our testing was the favorite.

MUFFIN TINS Muffin tins appear in a variety of shapes and sizes, from the typical light, coated aluminum models to heavy-gauge "professional" models. We've found that the heavier-gauged aluminum tins are much more expensive than other tins, weigh twice as much, and do not produce superior muffins. Their heft may make them durable, but unless you bake commercially, the lighter-weight models will last a lifetime. The two big issues with muffins are browning and sticking, but we've found that as long as you liberally spray your tin with vegetable oil spray, sticking is not a problem. Browning, however, is a different story. A good tin will brown muffins evenly; a bad one will leave them pallid and underbaked on the bottom. Lighter coated metals, which brown more slowly, do the best job of perfect browning, producing muffins and cupcakes that not only brown better but also rise higher and sport more nicely domed tops. As for muffin papers, skip them. We have found that they inhibit browning, and bits of muffin inevitably stick to them (though they can be helpful for cupcakes).

DRY MEASURING CUPS As a kitchen staple, a set of measuring cups must be durable. Look for heavy, well-constructed, evenly weighted stainless-steel models—plastic cups can warp in the dishwasher or melt easily. The measurement markings should be easy to read even once the cup is full; cups with measurement markings on the handles are the most common and most practical. Dry ingredients like flour and sugar should always be measured in dry measuring cups; in a wet measuring cup, it is impossible to level the surface of the contents to obtain an exact measurement. When measuring ingredients, we prefer the dip-and-sweep method for the greatest accuracy. An extra-long 4-inch handle is helpful when dipping into a bin of flour or sugar; a short, awkward handle can make dipping difficult, and a shoddy, thin handle will bend under pressure. Also avoid cups with heavy handles that tilt when set down. Handles that are straight and flush with the rim of the measuring cups make it easy to scrape off any excess ingredient for a level, accurate measure.

LIQUID MEASURING CUPS The simple Pyrex cup with red lines and a pour spout is the industry standard, with good reason. It is easy to use, accurate, and durable. We prefer glass models to plastic because the lines tend to wear off the latter. The measurement markings should be clear and easy to read from the outside of the cup, even when full of a dark-colored ingredient, and should cover a range of gradations, including in-between sizes. To read the cup properly, make sure the cup is on a flat surface and you're at eye level with the meniscus (the concave surface of the liquid); otherwise it may be too little or too much. Since liquid measuring cups cost just a few dollars, it makes sense to own at least two; we find the 2-cup and 4-cup sizes most useful, but a 1-cup measure is worth having on hand for measuring small amounts. The very best cups are just an inch or two wider than a spatula, with rounded bottoms instead of sharp corners. This design will trap less honey or other sticky ingredients and allow you to swipe away what's left behind with a rubber spatula.

MEASURING SPOONS These spoons are vital for measuring ingredients like salt, baking soda, and spices as well as herbs and small amounts of many other ingredients. We prefer heavy, well-constructed stainless steel models with long, sturdy, well-designed handles. Plastic models, no matter how thick, feel flimsy and are more likely to break, bend, crack, warp, or melt. Long, slim spoons have an easier time reaching into tall, narrow jars, plus their slim metal handles make for compact storage. As with dry measuring cups, these spoons should have a flat rim and handle so that dry ingredients can be easily leveled. We prefer spoons with deeper bowls as opposed to those with narrow and elongated or wide and shallow bowls. Shallow bowls allowed more liquid to spill as the result of a slight misstep or unsteady hand. Also, the spoons should be comfortable to use on their ring and easy to remove from it.

DIGITAL SCALE Baking is an exacting art, and nothing is more accurate than weighing ingredients. If you bake frequently, we strongly recommend that you purchase a good kitchen scale. There are two basic types of kitchen scales: electronic and mechanical. We strongly prefer electronic scales. Their digital displays are much easier to read than the measures on most mechanical scales, where the lines on the ruler are so closely spaced it's impossible to nail down the precise weight. Among the electronic scales we've tested, we've found that readability is key. Look for an easy-to-read display that isn't obscured when a big bowl is placed on the weighing platform. The larger the weight range (we like scales that measure from ¼ ounce up to 7 pounds at least), the more versatile your scale is and the more you'll turn to it in the kitchen. If your scale can be zeroed, you can automatically subtract the weight of the weighing vessel to measure only the ingredients and you can make incremental additions to your mixing bowl. A large weighing platform that detaches for easy cleaning is another plus. Last, we prefer electronic scales that display weight increments in decimals rather than fractions; the former are more accurate and easier to work with when scaling a recipe up or down.

INSTANT-READ THERMOMETER Sight, touch, and experience are age-old ways to gauge when food is done, but for consistent results, nothing is as reliable as taking the food's internal temperature. An instant-read thermometer makes it easier to tell if your loaf of bread is fully cooked or still doughy on the inside before you cut into it. There are two types of commonly sold hand-held thermometers: digital and dial face. They both take accurate readings, but while pocket-size dial-face thermometers are less expensive than digital models, they are much less legible, and most have narrower effective temperature ranges than digitals (look for a thermometer with a wide temperature range, at least -10 to 425 degrees). We prefer digital models because they register temperatures faster and are easier to read. The size of the thermometer stem can also make a big difference. A long stem (one that measures at least 4 inches) is necessary to reach the center of large loaves of bread. Water-resistant thermometers are helpful as they're easier to clean and less likely to be damaged by spills.

HOW TO CALIBRATE AN INSTANT-READ THERMOMETER

You should check your instant-read thermometer's accuracy when you first buy it and then again periodically. To calibrate it, put a mixture of ice and cold tap water in a glass or bowl; allow this mixture to sit for 2 minutes to let the temperature stabilize. Put the probe in the slush, being careful not to touch the sides or bottom of the glass or bowl. On a digital thermometer, press the "calibrate" button to 32 degrees; on a dial-face thermometer, turn the dial to 32 degrees (the method differs from model to model; you may need to use pliers to turn a small knob on the back).

OVEN THERMOMETER Unless you have your oven routinely calibrated, there is a good chance that its temperature readings may be off. We tested 16 home ovens of friends and colleagues and found many that varied as much as 50 degrees in either direction. Inaccurate temperatures will dramatically impact your baked goods, leaving them doughy on the inside or overbrowned and tough. To avoid such problems, we recommend purchasing an inexpensive oven thermometer and checking it once the oven is preheated. Look for a thermometer that mounts securely in the oven and has clearly marked numbers that make it easy to read quickly.

PARCHMENT PAPER AND ALUMINUM FOIL We use parchment paper for a variety of baking needs, such as lining baking sheets, cake pans, and pie dough for blind baking. We even use parchment for improvising a pastry bag. Parchment is paper that has been treated with sulfuric acid and then coated with silicone, and the result is a nonstick surface that is impervious to grease and moisture. We also turn to aluminum foil for many baking needs. It is especially handy when lining the baking pan for brownies, bar cookies, and some snack cakes. We line the baking pan with enough foil to overhang the edges of the pan. Once baked, the brownies can be lifted from the pan using the foil "handles" and cut into tidy squares (see page 234).

ROLLING PIN If you're looking to buy a rolling pin, you have quite an array of choices, from nonstick coatings to marble to ergonomic handles. We've tried a wide range of rolling pins, from traditional American style (rolling on bearings) to French "stick" style to a couple of real oddities (aluminum?). We prefer a classic straight-barrel wood rolling pin without handles, which easily turns and pivots and allow you to feel the thickness of the dough and apply pressure as needed—plus they're economical to boot. Look for a pin that measures about 20 inches long, a suitable length for any task.

RUBBER SPATULAS A rubber spatula is invaluable for scraping bowls clean, stirring batters, and folding egg whites. As a general rule, we prefer larger-bladed spatulas. Large heads minimize the amount of folding necessary, keeping batters light and fully aerated. Thin, flexible edges aid in agility and scraping ability, making it easy to get the last traces of batter from a bowl or honey from a measuring cup. We've found that both silicone and rubber are reasonably heat resistant, despite the claimed superiority of the silicone. While a spatula's blade is the most important element, stiff, relatively long handles with round edges are the most comfortable and efficient to use.

WHISKS The market is loaded with different types of whisks; long or short, narrow or balloon-shaped, thick wires or thin, and even some gyroscopic ones. We find traditional models to be the best choice. It's best to have at least two whisks. A large balloon whisk is designed to add volume to ingredients, and it quickly and easily whips egg whites and cream. Choose a fairly long-handled balloon whisk with at least 10 thin, flexible wires for efficient aeration. For whisking items in a pan, such as when you're emulsifying pan sauces or making pastry cream, a smaller flat-style whisk is best. Look for one with thicker, sturdier wires and about 11 or 12 inches in total length to keep your hand safe from the heat.

BENCH SCRAPERS Invaluable for countless baking tasks, a metal bench scraper is the chef's knife of the baking world. We use it to mix and fold soft dough, to cut through plump rounds of yeast bread or biscuit dough, and to scrape sticky dough loose from the counter. As a general rule, look for scrapers with a fairly sharp edge and a comfortable handle. Some models come stamped with rulers on the bottom—always a bonus for accurate baking. We also like inexpensive, flexible plastic bowl scrapers, also called dough scrapers, for certain tasks.

BAKING STONE Baking stones (also called pizza stones) are prized for their ability to retain heat and lessen the effects of hot spots and temperature fluctuations in home ovens. They simulate a brick oven in your home oven, absorbing moisture and radiating intense, consistent heat to produce crispier, golden-brown pizza, calzones, and bread. If you like to bake bread, we strongly recommend that you own a baking stone. Look for a model made of clay or stone (avoid composite cement stones) and one that can comfortably accommodate a large pizza. Elevated feet are nice for easier lifting.

WIRE RACKS Most baked goods need a cooling-down period. Left to sit directly on a countertop, a cake's bottom will overcook, a pie's crust can turn gummy, and chewy cookies will turn brittle. By resting the pans or trays on a wire cooling rack, air can freely circulate underneath, allowing baked goods to dry properly. A good rack should be sturdy with plenty of supportive feet, able to withstand a hot broiler, and clean up without warping or damage. It should also fit inside a standard 18 by 13-inch baking pan.

HAND-HELD MIXER Although we like the hands-free operation of a stand mixer, we realize that its high price tag makes it a luxury item, especially for the occasional baker. A hand-held mixer will perform all the same baking tasks (minus kneading bread) and at a fraction of the cost. Although cream and egg whites may require a few extra seconds to whip, we have found that there is no real difference between cookies and cakes prepared in hand-held and stand mixers. The weight of a mixer can affect how fatiguing it is to use. Look for a mixer that is comfortable to hold and easy to maneuver around a bowl. Also, don't get a mixer with a "bowl rest" (a lip for leaning the mixer on the bowl rim)—it prevents the beaters from reaching the bottom of the mixing bowl. We prefer simple, slim beaters that don't have a central post. Traditional beaters have flat metal strips around a center post, which is a good spot for batter to collect, inhibiting mixing. To remove the beaters, we like separate ejector buttons, which ensure you won't accidentally turn the mixer on when removing the beaters.

STAND MIXER If you plan on serious baking, a stand mixer is virtually essential. From mixing heavy doughs and batters to lightly whipping cream and egg whites, it does it all. The combination of its hands-free operation, numerous attachments, and strong mixing arm make a stand mixer a truly significant and versatile, albeit expensive, piece of equipment. The best mixers are quiet, powerful workhorses. Heft matters (a heavy mixer won't shimmy around the counter) as does a strong motor that can knead stiff dough with ease. We highly recommend getting a mixer that uses planetary action (the mixing attachment moves around a stationary bowl). It is more effective because the attachment reaches the sides as well as the center of the bowl and gathers ingredients quickly; mixers with a rotating bowl and two stationary beaters are much more likely to miss ingredients or get clogged up on stiff doughs. Look for a slightly squat bowl that holds at least 4.5 quarts. If the bowl is too tall or too large, small batches of batter won't get mixed properly and scraping down the sides of the bowl will be impossible to do without getting your sleeves dirty. Look for a stand mixer that includes a flat paddle, dough hook, and metal whisk. We prefer spiral-shaped dough hooks to the classic C-shaped hook because their design pushes the dough back down into the bowl where it can be kneaded. We also recommend picking up an extra mixing bowl—it can expedite many baking tasks and is especially helpful in recipes that call for beating egg whites in a clean bowl.

FOOD PROCESSOR A food processor can't knead very stiff dough or whip egg whites, but it can whip together pizza and pie dough in a flash. Not to mention its importance for kitchen tasks outside of baking. Still, pick the wrong processor and suddenly this great convenience leaves you worse off than when you started. Less expensive food processors (under $150) can't perform the most basic tasks very well. It seems like it should be a given, but not all food processors come with sharp blades. Blades with deep serrations tend to mangle food like bad steak knives. We prefer blades that are smooth or have mini-serrations. Just as important is the blade's location in the workbowl. The gap between the blade and the workbowl should be as small as possible, preferably less than ⅛ inch. Look for a workbowl that has a capacity of at least 11 cups. Smaller models can't knead bread dough or make pie dough and you will be forced to work in batches when shredding vegetables. And many models have a small feed tube that requires trimming food extensively—in which case you might as well use a chef's knife for the entire job. Our favorite models have an oval feed tube that's just wide enough to fit a russet potato as well as a smaller round tube insert for carrots and celery. A heavy base keeps the food processor in place, even when handling tough jobs like mixing dough. You don't move a food processor around the kitchen so don't worry about buying a model that's too heavy.

Ten Tips for Better Baking

It doesn't matter where you learned to bake. Mistakes are inevitable. Whether you learned how to bake at the elbow of your grandmother, in a rigorous cooking school, or in the Cook's Illustrated test kitchen, mistakes happen. Of course, our testing process is designed so we can learn from these mistakes. In fact, some of our most important baking discoveries have occurred by accident. That said, a mistake is a mistake, and no one is happy with a lopsided layer cake or tough biscuits. Here are some general mistakes that we find are at the root of many baking problems. Follow our suggestions and you'll be well on your way to baking with confidence.

1. PREHEAT YOUR OVEN It takes at least 15 minutes for a standard oven to reach the desired temperature. Baked goods, especially biscuits, scones, and pizzas, need that immediate blast of high heat in order to rise and develop a crisp exterior. Also, make sure the oven racks are set to the correct position. A pie crust that browns properly on the lower rack will emerge pale and unappealing if baked on the middle rack.

2. PAY ATTENTION TO TEMPERATURE An oven that is not calibrated properly will ruin many baked goods and leave you wondering what you are doing wrong. It pays to use an oven thermometer. In addition, ingredients at the wrong temperature will often cause problems in baked goods. Butter that is too cold or too warm can result in a flat, dense cake. Water that is too warm can kill yeast and prevent dough from rising. Use an instant-read thermometer to avoid these kinds of problems.

3. CHOOSE THE RIGHT MEASURING CUPS Liquids must be measured in liquid measures (glass or plastic cups with pour spouts and handles) and dry ingredients must be measured in dry measures (handled cups with straight edges so ingredients can be leveled off). For more about measuring, see pages 3 and 5.

4. USE GOOD INGREDIENTS Old eggs don't have the rising properties of fresh eggs. Baking powder can lose its punch after six months. Butter can pick up off-flavors after a few weeks in the refrigerator. A gritty, low-quality chocolate can ruin a flourless chocolate cake. See pages 2–11 for information about buying and handling common baking ingredients. And see our Shopping Guide on pages 486–499 for information on our top-rated brands of baking ingredients.

5. PREP YOUR BAKING PANS IN ADVANCE While some pans may require little or no prep, others may need to be greased, floured, and lined with parchment paper. Don't let your cake batter deflate in the mixing bowl because you're looking for scissors to cut out parchment for your pan.

6. USE THE RIGHT EQUIPMENT If you bake cake layers in 8-inch pans but the recipe specifically calls for 9-inch pans, the batter is likely to rise right out of the pans (and onto the floor of your oven). And if you bake cake layers in pans that are too large, the cakes will bake faster and turn out dense and squat. See pages 13–14 for information about essential baking equipment.

7. SLOW DOWN AND DOUBLE-CHECK YOUR INGREDIENT LIST We recommend doing this as you make your way through each step. It sounds like common sense, but even in the test kitchen, we've endured the frustrations of popping a pan of biscuits into the oven only to realize that we had forgotten to add the baking powder to the dough.

8. TAKE CARE WHEN MAKING SUBSTITUTIONS Recipes are often complex chemical formulas with a precise balance of acids and leaveners and if you change one ingredient the formula may no longer work. Read the recipe through before you begin baking and make sure that you have all the ingredients and equipment on hand. We do offer some substitutions in this book, but working with the ingredients called for is best.

9. TIME YOUR KITCHEN WORK PROPERLY Many baking recipes contain multiple components that must come together in a specific order. Pastry cream, for example, must be well chilled before being spread in a tart shell, so it makes sense to prepare the pastry cream first. Many recipes are also best served at specific temperatures, such as cheesecakes, which should be cooled and then refrigerated until thoroughly chilled before serving.

10. WATCH THE MIXING BOWL OR OVEN, NOT THE CLOCK Most baking recipes, including those in this book, are filled with times for mixing and baking. The times are merely guidelines, so pay attention to visual cues. In many cases, cream may form "soft peaks" well before a recipe says so. Likewise, a toothpick may emerge from brownies "with a few moist crumbs attached" well before the end of the stated baking time.

ZUCCHINI BREAD

Quick Breads, Muffins, Biscuits, and Scones

Quick breads and muffins often rely on a quick and easy mixing method for producing baked goods with a tender crumb. Generally, the method works as follows:

1. Whisk together dry ingredients—sugar, flour, leavener, and spice—in bowl until evenly combined.

2. In separate bowl, whisk together wet ingredients—dairy, melted butter, eggs, extracts, and pureed fruit—until evenly combined. (Note that some recipes may rely on the food processor to mix wet ingredients).

3. Make well in dry ingredients and pour wet ingredients into well. Gently stir with rubber spatula until just combined. You should be able to see some streaks of flour in batter. (Overmixing will make the baked good tough.)

Cranberry-Nut Bread

✔ WHY THIS RECIPE WORKS

This simple bread is often subpar; too heavy, or so overly sweetened that the contrast between the tart berries and what should be a slightly sweet, cakelike bread is lost. We were looking for a crust that was golden brown and evenly thin all the way around and an interior texture that was somewhere between a dense breakfast bread and a light, airy cake. Taming the puckery tart of the cranberries was one route to delivering an above-average loaf.

USE THE QUICK-BREAD METHOD
Creaming, where butter is aerated with sugar, produced a loaf that was too light, so we turned to the quick-bread method. We combine the liquid ingredients and dry ingredients separately, then stir them together. And like the name says, this method is quick, which makes it even more convenient to whip up a loaf.

USE TWO LEAVENERS The best breads we found in our testing use both baking powder and baking soda—baking powder enhances the flavor, while baking soda supports the structure and promotes browning.

BALANCE THE SWEET AND TART Yes, tart cranberries require sugar to help make them palatable, but some breads we tried were overly sweet. We use just 1 cup sugar to 1½ cups cranberries to give us a sweet, but not-too-sweet loaf. As for the cranberries, we found no difference between fresh and frozen berries in our bread.

REACH FOR ORANGE ZEST PLUS JUICE TO BRIGHTEN FLAVORS Orange and cranberries are often partnered together and we can see why. The sweet, bright, citrusy flavor of orange offsets the puckery tang of cranberries. Orange juice alone doesn't add much flavor, but zest increases the presence of orange and the flecks of the zest also add a hint of color to the interior of the bread.

CRANBERRY-NUT BREAD
MAKES I LOAF

Fresh or frozen cranberries (not thawed) will work here. See page 9 for information on toasting nuts. The test kitchen's preferred loaf pan measures 8½ by 4½ inches; if you use a 9 by 5-inch loaf pan, start checking for doneness 5 minutes earlier than advised in the recipe.

- ⅔ cup buttermilk
- 6 tablespoons unsalted butter, melted and cooled
- 1 tablespoon grated orange zest plus ⅓ cup juice
- 1 large egg, lightly beaten
- 2 cups (10 ounces) all-purpose flour
- 1 cup (7 ounces) sugar
- 1 teaspoon salt
- 1 teaspoon baking powder
- ¼ teaspoon baking soda
- 5¼ ounces (1½ cups) fresh or frozen cranberries, chopped coarse
- ½ cup pecans or walnuts, toasted and chopped coarse

1. Adjust oven rack to middle position and heat oven to 350 degrees. Grease 8½ by 4½-inch loaf pan. Stir together buttermilk, melted butter, orange zest and juice, and egg in small bowl. Whisk together flour, sugar, salt, baking powder, and baking soda in second large bowl. Stir liquid ingredients into dry ingredients with rubber spatula until just moistened. Gently stir in cranberries and pecans (do not overmix).

2. Scrape batter into loaf pan and spread with rubber spatula into corners of pan. Bake until golden brown and toothpick inserted in center of loaf comes out clean, 55 minutes to 1¼ hours, rotating pan halfway through baking. Let loaf cool in pan for 10 minutes, then turn out onto wire rack and let cool for 1 hour before serving.

Date-Nut Bread

✔ WHY THIS RECIPE WORKS

The dense texture and unmitigated sweetness of most date breads are overwhelming. Even worse, dates can bake up hard and chewy. We wanted to make a quick bread rich with soft, sweet dates and a moist, tender crumb. One of our secrets turned out to be baking soda—and we don't just use it in the way you might think.

SOFTEN YOUR DATES Hard chunks of dates can mar the bread's texture; soaking them in hot water and baking soda softens the dates by breaking down their fibers. Adding the soaking liquid to the batter gives the bread even more flavor.

CHOOSE DARK BROWN SUGAR OVER WHITE SUGAR Dark brown sugar (preferred over light brown sugar) complements the flavor of the dates and gives our loaf an appealingly rich, dark color.

ADD BUTTERMILK FOR TANG Buttermilk brings a tanginess to our loaf that balances the sweetness of the dates.

DON'T FORGET NUTS Chopped toasted nuts (pecans or walnuts) add further flavor and some crunch to our loaf.

DATE-NUT BREAD
MAKES 1 LOAF

To make chopping the dates easier, coat the blade of your knife with a thin film of vegetable oil spray. Soaking the dates in boiling water and baking soda helps to soften their tough skins. For an accurate measurement of boiling water, bring a full kettle of water to a boil, then measure out the desired amount. See page 9 for information on toasting nuts. The test kitchen's preferred loaf pan measures 8½ by 4½ inches; if you use a 9 by 5-inch loaf pan, start checking for doneness 5 minutes earlier than advised in the recipe.

10 ounces (1⅔ cups) pitted dates, chopped coarse
1 cup boiling water
1 teaspoon baking soda
2 cups (10 ounces) all-purpose flour
1 teaspoon baking powder
½ teaspoon salt
¾ cup packed (5¼ ounces) dark brown sugar
⅔ cup buttermilk
6 tablespoons unsalted butter, melted and cooled
1 large egg
1 cup pecans or walnuts, toasted and chopped coarse

1. Adjust oven rack to middle position and heat oven to 350 degrees. Grease 8½ by 4½-inch loaf pan.

2. Stir dates, water, and baking soda together in medium bowl. Cover and set aside until dates have softened, about 30 minutes.

3. Whisk flour, baking powder, and salt together in large bowl. In medium bowl, whisk brown sugar, buttermilk, melted butter, and egg together until smooth, then stir in date mixture until combined. Gently fold buttermilk mixture into flour mixture with rubber spatula until just combined (do not overmix). Gently fold in pecans.

4. Scrape batter into prepared pan and smooth top. Bake until golden brown and toothpick inserted in center of loaf comes out with few crumbs attached, 55 minutes to 1 hour, rotating pan halfway through baking.

5. Let loaf cool in pan for 10 minutes, then turn out onto wire rack and let cool for 1 hour before serving.

CHOPPING DRIED FRUIT

Dried fruit, especially dates, very often sticks to the knife when you try to chop it. To avoid this problem, coat the blade with a thin film of vegetable oil spray just before you begin chopping. The chopped fruit won't cling to the blade and the knife stays relatively clean.

Ultimate Banana Bread

✓ WHY THIS RECIPE WORKS

Our ideal banana bread is simple enough—a moist, tender loaf that really tastes like bananas. We discovered that doubling the dose of bananas in our favorite test recipe was both a blessing and a curse. The abundance of fruit made for intense banana flavor, but the weight and moisture sank the loaf and gave it a cakelike structure. We wanted to add banana flavor without excess moisture for a truly exceptional loaf.

START WITH RIPE BANANAS It's important to use very ripe bananas for the best flavor—there are no shortcuts.

SQUEEZE IN MORE BANANAS After increasing the number of bananas in our recipe, we knew we needed to lighten the loaf by ridding our bananas of some of their moisture. Roasting the bananas helps drive off moisture but it takes too long and the end result is still too wet. We tried simmering mashed bananas, as well as dicing and sautéing them. But the best technique turned out to be the same one we use to remove excess moisture from eggplant: We microwave them. We then reduce the liquid and use that concentrated banana juice in place of some of the dairy in the batter for super banana flavor.

TWEAK THE FLAVOR We exchange the typical sugar for light brown sugar, finding that the latter's molasses notes better complement the bananas. A teaspoon of vanilla rounds out the bananas' faintly boozy, rum-like flavor. Don't forget the salt.

REPLACE OIL WITH BUTTER We replaced the traditional oil in our banana bread recipe with butter. Butter gives our bread a nutty, rich flavor that we prefer.

SEPARATE, THEN FOLD To make the batter, we combine the wet ingredients (including the brown sugar), and then add them to the bowl with the dry ingredients and fold gently. Make sure that you fold the batter gently enough that flour streaks remain. (And be sure to mash the bananas well before they even hit the dry ingredients.)

TOP WITH MORE BANANAS We slice one final banana and shingle it on top of the batter. A sprinkle of granulated sugar helps the buttery slices to caramelize and gives the loaf an enticingly crisp, crunchy top. To ensure an even rise, place the banana slices along the long sides of the loaf pan and leave a 1½-inch-wide space down the center.

ULTIMATE BANANA BREAD
MAKES I LOAF

Be sure to use very ripe, heavily speckled (or even black) bananas in this recipe. This recipe can be made using five thawed frozen bananas; since they release a lot of liquid naturally, they can bypass the microwaving in step 2 and go directly into the fine-mesh strainer. Do not use a thawed frozen banana in step 4; it will be too soft to slice. Instead, simply sprinkle the top of the loaf with sugar. See page 9 for information on toasting nuts. The test kitchen's preferred loaf pan measures 8½ by 4½ inches; if you use a 9 by 5-inch loaf pan, start checking for doneness 5 minutes earlier than advised in the recipe. The texture is best when the loaf is eaten fresh, but it can be stored (let cool completely first), covered tightly with plastic wrap, for up to three days.

1¾	cups (8¾ ounces) all-purpose flour
I	teaspoon baking soda
½	teaspoon salt
6	large very ripe bananas (2¼ pounds), peeled
8	tablespoons unsalted butter, melted and cooled
2	large eggs
¾	cup packed (5¼ ounces) light brown sugar
I	teaspoon vanilla extract
½	cup walnuts, toasted and chopped coarse (optional)
2	teaspoons granulated sugar

MAKING BANANAS LAST

Most people store bananas on the countertop, and we wondered if chilling the fruit could slow ripening. To find out, we left 12 pounds of bananas at room temperature for three days until they were perfectly ripe (signified by a firm but yielding texture). We then moved half of the bananas into the refrigerator, leaving the remainder at room temperature.

After four days, the room-temperature fruit became markedly soft and mushy, while the refrigerated fruit remained firm, despite blackened skins. We continued to taste the refrigerated bananas after the room-temperature samples had been discarded and were delighted to discover that they lasted an additional five days (so, almost two weeks after purchase).

The explanation is simple: As a banana ripens, it emits a gas called ethylene and develops acids that aid in ripening. Cool temperatures slow down this process, thereby decelerating ripening. Note that refrigeration also causes the cell walls of the peel to break down, releasing enzymes that cause the formation of black-brown pigments.

1. Adjust oven rack to middle position and heat oven to 350 degrees. Spray 8½ by 4½-inch loaf pan with vegetable oil spray. Whisk flour, baking soda, and salt together in large bowl.

2. Place 5 bananas in separate bowl, cover, and microwave until bananas are soft and have released liquid, about 5 minutes. Transfer bananas to fine-mesh strainer over medium bowl and allow to drain, stirring occasionally, for 15 minutes (you should have ½ to ¾ cup liquid).

3. Transfer liquid to medium saucepan and cook over medium-high heat until reduced to ¼ cup, about 5 minutes. Remove pan from heat, stir reduced liquid into bananas, and mash with potato masher until mostly smooth.

Whisk in melted butter, eggs, brown sugar, and vanilla.

4. Pour banana mixture into dry ingredients and stir until just combined, with some streaks of flour remaining. Gently fold in walnuts, if using. Scrape batter into prepared pan. Slice remaining banana diagonally into ¼-inch-thick slices. Shingle banana slices on top of loaf in 2 rows, leaving 1½-inch-wide space down center to ensure even rise. Sprinkle granulated sugar evenly over loaf.

5. Bake until toothpick inserted in center of loaf comes out clean, 55 minutes to 1¼ hours, rotating pan halfway through baking. Let loaf cool in pan for 10 minutes, then turn out onto wire rack and let cool for 1 hour before serving.

Zucchini Bread

✔ WHY THIS RECIPE WORKS

It can be difficult to muster enthusiasm for a slice of zucchini bread, especially if the bread is your typical bland loaf. We wanted a zucchini bread worth making and eating, one that boasted a moist, but not wet, crumb and offered great summery zucchini flavor.

SHRED, SUGAR, AND WRING We found some recipes that suggest shredding and squeezing the zucchini to rid it of its excess moisture. We came up with an even better solution—sugaring the shredded zucchini before squeezing it dry. We typically salt porous vegetables like eggplant to extract their bitter liquid. Sugar acts in a similar manner—it both softens the zucchini and draws moisture from the vegetable. We toss the shredded zucchini with a few tablespoons of sugar and then let it drain. Then we squeeze the drained zucchini dry between paper towels. This step not only prevents a gummy, dense loaf, but also intensifies the zucchini flavor for a better-tasting bread.

CHOOSE BUTTER AND GO FOR YOGURT Many zucchini bread recipes use oil, but we found that butter makes for a richer, sweeter bread. For the dairy, we passed on sour cream because it made our loaf too heavy and rich. Buttermilk gave our bread a pleasant tang, but for a thick, rich batter that baked into a tender crumb, yogurt won out.

KEEP FLAVORINGS TO A MINIMUM We tried our loaf with a variety of spices, but except for the lemon juice and nuts, we found flavorings out of place in our relatively light, brightly flavored quick bread.

ZUCCHINI BREAD

MAKES 1 LOAF

Small zucchini have smaller, drier seeds than large zucchini and are preferred in this recipe. If you are using a large zucchini, cut it in half lengthwise and use a spoon to scrape out and discard the seeds before shredding. See page 9 for information on toasting nuts. The test kitchen's preferred loaf pan measures 8½ by 4½ inches; if you use a 9 by 5-inch loaf pan, start checking for doneness 5 minutes earlier than advised in the recipe.

1	pound zucchini, ends trimmed, cut into 1-inch pieces
¾	cup (5¼ ounces) sugar
2	cups (10 ounces) all-purpose flour
1	teaspoon baking soda
1	teaspoon baking powder
½	teaspoon salt
¼	cup plain whole-milk or low-fat yogurt
2	large eggs, lightly beaten
1	tablespoon lemon juice
6	tablespoons unsalted butter, melted and cooled
½	cup pecans or walnuts, toasted and chopped coarse

1. Adjust oven rack to middle position and heat oven to 375 degrees. Grease 8½ by 4½-inch loaf pan.

2. Pulse zucchini and 2 tablespoons sugar in food processor until zucchini is coarsely shredded, about 15 pulses. Transfer mixture to fine-mesh strainer set at least 2 inches over bowl and allow to drain for 30 minutes. (Alternatively, halve zucchini, shred it on large holes of box grater, toss with 2 tablespoons sugar, and drain.)

3. Whisk flour, baking soda, baking powder, and salt until combined. Set aside.

4. Whisk together remaining ½ cup plus 2 tablespoons sugar, yogurt, eggs, lemon juice, and melted butter in 2-cup glass measure until combined. Set aside.

5. Squeeze shredded zucchini between several layers of paper towels to absorb excess moisture. Stir zucchini, yogurt mixture, and nuts into flour mixture until just moistened.

6. Scrape batter into prepared pan and smooth top. Bake until golden brown and toothpick inserted in center of loaf comes out with few crumbs attached, 55 minutes to 1 hour, rotating loaf pan halfway through baking.

7. Let loaf cool in pan for 10 minutes, then turn out onto wire rack and let cool for 1 hour before serving.

SHREDDING, SUGARING, AND DRAINING ZUCCHINI

1. If you don't have a food processor, halve zucchini and shred it on large holes of box grater. Toss shredded zucchini with 2 tablespoons sugar and drain it in fine-mesh strainer set at least 2 inches over bowl.

2. Transfer drained zucchini to several layers of paper towels and squeeze out excess liquid.

Pumpkin Bread

✔ WHY THIS RECIPE WORKS

Although most recipes for pumpkin bread are pleasantly sweet and spicy, they're nothing to write home about. We wanted a bread that had just the right texture—neither too dense nor too cakey—and a rich pumpkin flavor that was properly tempered with sweetness and gently enhanced rather than obscured by spices. Our plan started with a can, a can of pumpkin, that is.

PUMP UP THE FLAVOR OF CANNED PUMPKIN We wanted to skip roasting and pureeing canned pumpkin because after all, this is supposed to be a "quick" bread. Canned pumpkin has a raw flavor though, a problem we easily remedy by cooking it on top of the stove just until it begins to caramelize. This yields loaves with full pumpkin flavor.

MOISTEN WITH BUTTERMILK Cooking the canned pumpkin improves its flavor but also drives off moisture. The resulting loaves taste great, but are dense and dry. To restore that moisture, we add buttermilk.

BALANCE SWEETNESS WITH CREAM CHEESE Caramelizing the puree also increases its sweetness, throwing off the balance of flavors. Tangy cream cheese, stirred into the batter, restores balance and adds richness.

TOP WITH STREUSEL We liked toasted walnuts added to the batter, but we still wanted something to complement the bread's crumb and flavor. Sprinkled on just before baking, a simple streusel gives the perfect amount of sweet crunch to each slice. As a bonus, the topping prevents the surface of the loaf from getting soggy when stored overnight, so our bread is just as delicious the next day.

PUMPKIN BREAD
MAKES 2 LOAVES

The test kitchen's preferred loaf pan measures 8½ by 4½ inches; if you use 9 by 5-inch loaf pans, start checking for doneness 5 minutes earlier than advised in the recipe.

TOPPING

5	tablespoons packed (2¼ ounces) light brown sugar
1	tablespoon all-purpose flour
1	tablespoon unsalted butter, softened
1	teaspoon ground cinnamon
⅛	teaspoon salt

BREAD

2	cups (10 ounces) all-purpose flour
1½	teaspoons baking powder
½	teaspoon baking soda
1	(15-ounce) can unsweetened pumpkin puree
1	teaspoon salt
1½	teaspoons ground cinnamon
¼	teaspoon ground nutmeg
⅛	teaspoon ground cloves
1	cup (7 ounces) granulated sugar
1	cup packed (7 ounces) light brown sugar
½	cup vegetable oil
4	ounces cream cheese, cut into 12 pieces
4	large eggs
¼	cup buttermilk
1	cup walnuts, toasted and chopped fine

1. FOR THE TOPPING: Using your fingers, mix all ingredients together in bowl until well combined and topping resembles wet sand; set aside.

2. FOR THE BREAD: Adjust oven rack to middle position and heat oven to 350 degrees. Grease two 8½ by 4½-inch loaf pans. Whisk flour, baking powder, and baking soda together in bowl.

3. Combine pumpkin puree, salt, cinnamon, nutmeg, and cloves in large saucepan over medium heat. Cook mixture, stirring constantly, until reduced to 1½ cups, 6 to 8 minutes. Remove pot from heat; stir in granulated sugar, brown sugar, oil, and cream cheese until combined. Let mixture stand for 5 minutes. Whisk until no visible pieces of cream cheese remain and mixture is homogeneous.

4. Whisk eggs and buttermilk together. Add egg mixture to pumpkin mixture and whisk to combine. Fold flour mixture into pumpkin mixture until combined (some small lumps of flour are OK). Fold walnuts into batter. Scrape batter into prepared pans. Sprinkle topping evenly over top of each loaf. Bake until toothpick inserted in center of loaf comes out clean, 45 to 50 minutes, rotating pan halfway through baking. Let loaves cool in pans on wire rack for 20 minutes. Remove loaves from pans and let cool for at least 1½ hours. Serve warm or at room temperature.

PUMPKIN BREAD WITH CANDIED GINGER

Substitute ½ teaspoon ground ginger for cinnamon in topping. Fold ⅓ cup minced crystallized ginger into batter after flour mixture has been added in step 4.

All-Purpose Cornbread

WHY THIS RECIPE WORKS

Cornbread can be sweet and cakey (the Northern version) or savory and light (the Southern version). We wanted a combination of the two. And most important, we wanted our cornbread to be bursting with corn flavor. The secret turned out to be pretty simple: Use corn, not just cornmeal.

DOUBLE THE CORN FLAVOR For this cornbread, we use widely available degerminated yellow cornmeal. The best texture comes from using a ratio of 3 parts flour to 2 parts cornmeal—but this also limits the corn flavor in our bread. The solution? We add frozen corn, ground up in the food processor to release its full flavor. With pureed corn in the mix, we need to cut back on the dairy (we prefer the flavor of buttermilk to whole milk).

BROWN SUGAR IS BEST Regular white granulated sugar makes good cornbread but in this recipe a little brown sugar adds pleasing molasses notes.

DRIZZLE IN THE BUTTER We add the butter to our batter last. This creates subtle streaks of unmixed butter in the batter, but, as the bread bakes, the butter rises to the surface and creates a more deeply browned top crust and a stronger butter flavor. (And we add a lot of butter—a whole stick.)

USE A HOT OVEN For cornbread that's moist and tender with a crunchy crust, use a hot oven.

ALL-PURPOSE CORNBREAD
SERVES 6

Before preparing the baking dish or any of the other ingredients, measure out the frozen kernels and let them stand at room temperature until needed. When corn is in season, fresh cooked kernels can be substituted for the frozen corn. This recipe was developed with Quaker yellow cornmeal; a stone-ground whole-grain cornmeal will work but will yield

a drier and less tender cornbread. We prefer a Pyrex glass baking dish because it yields a nice golden-brown crust, but a metal baking pan (nonstick or traditional) will also work. Serve with a flavored butter (page 31).

1½	cups (7½ ounces) all-purpose flour
1	cup (5 ounces) cornmeal
2	teaspoons baking powder
¼	teaspoon baking soda
¾	teaspoon salt
¼	cup packed (1¾ ounces) light brown sugar
¾	cup frozen corn, thawed
1	cup buttermilk
2	large eggs
8	tablespoons unsalted butter, melted and cooled

1. Adjust oven rack to middle position and heat oven to 400 degrees. Spray 8-inch square baking dish with vegetable oil spray. Whisk flour, cornmeal, baking powder, baking soda, and salt in medium bowl until combined; set aside.

2. In food processor or blender, process brown sugar, corn kernels, and buttermilk until combined, about 5 seconds. Add eggs and process until well combined (corn lumps will remain), about 5 seconds longer.

3. Using rubber spatula, make well in center of dry ingredients; pour wet ingredients into well. Begin folding dry ingredients into wet, giving mixture only a few turns to barely combine. Add melted butter and continue folding until dry ingredients are just moistened. Pour batter into prepared baking dish and smooth surface with rubber spatula.

4. Bake until cornbread is deep golden brown and toothpick inserted in center comes out clean, 25 to 35 minutes, rotating pan halfway through baking. Let cool in pan on wire rack for 10 minutes, then invert onto wire rack,

1. Cut pepper in half with knife.

2. Cut off core with small melon baller scoop.

3. Starting opposite stem end, run edge of scoop down inside of pepper, scraping up seeds and ribs.

turn right side up, and let cool until warm, about 10 minutes longer. Serve. (Leftover cornbread can be wrapped in aluminum foil and reheated in a 350-degree oven for 10 to 15 minutes.)

SPICY JALAPEÑO-CHEDDAR CORNBREAD

Reduce salt to ½ teaspoon. Add ⅜ teaspoon cayenne pepper, 1 seeded and finely chopped jalapeño chile, and ½ cup shredded cheddar cheese to flour mixture and toss well to combine. Reduce brown sugar to 2 tablespoons and sprinkle ½ cup shredded cheddar cheese over batter in dish just before baking.

BLUEBERRY BREAKFAST CORNBREAD

Reduce salt to ½ teaspoon. Reduce buttermilk to ¾ cup and add ¼ cup maple syrup to food processor along with buttermilk in step 2. Add 1 cup fresh or frozen blueberries with melted butter in step 3. Sprinkle 2 tablespoons granulated sugar over batter in baking dish just before baking.

Golden Northern Cornbread

✔ WHY THIS RECIPE WORKS

We set out to make a classic Northern version of cornbread. It needed to be slightly sweet, light in texture, and on the thicker side (compared to Southern versions which are often only about 1 inch thick).

FLOUR-CORNMEAL RATIO MATTERS Traditionally, Northern cornbread recipes combine white flour and yellow cornmeal, and we found that a 1:1 ratio works best for good corn flavor and light texture.

WATCH THAT SUGAR We wanted our cornbread to be sweet but not like dessert; we tested recipes with honey, molasses, and light brown sugar, but in the end settled on granulated sugar. Just 4 teaspoons lends the right hint of sweetness.

DON'T MAKE IT TOO TANGY Southern cornbreads are often made with all buttermilk. For our Northern bread, we use equal amounts of milk and buttermilk to provide rich flavor and a slight but not overwhelming tang.

GOLDEN NORTHERN CORNBREAD
SERVES 9

Use stone-ground cornmeal for the best taste and texture.

- 1 cup (5 ounces) stone-ground cornmeal
- 1 cup (5 ounces) all-purpose flour
- 4 teaspoons sugar
- 2 teaspoons baking powder
- ½ teaspoon baking soda
- ½ teaspoon salt
- 2 large eggs
- ⅔ cup buttermilk
- ⅔ cup whole milk
- 2 tablespoons unsalted butter, melted and cooled

1. Adjust oven rack to middle position and heat oven to 425 degrees. Grease 9-inch square baking pan. Stir cornmeal, flour, sugar, baking powder, baking soda, and salt in large bowl to combine. Make well in center of dry ingredients.

2. Crack eggs into well and stir gently with wooden spoon. Add buttermilk and milk, then quickly stir wet ingredients into dry ingredients, stirring until almost combined. Add melted butter and stir until ingredients are just combined.

3. Pour batter into prepared pan. Bake until top is golden brown and lightly cracked and edges have pulled away from sides of pan, about 25 minutes.

4. Transfer to wire rack to let cool slightly, 5 to 10 minutes, and serve.

GOLDEN NORTHERN CORNBREAD WITH CHEDDAR

Omit sugar. After adding butter to batter, quickly fold in 1 cup shredded cheddar cheese.

GOLDEN NORTHERN CORNBREAD WITH JALAPEÑOS

One jalapeño lends mild heat to the cornbread. For bolder heat, use up to 2 jalapeños, with seeds.

Omit sugar. After adding butter to batter, quickly fold in 1 small seeded and minced jalapeño chile.

GOLDEN NORTHERN CORNBREAD WITH BACON

Cook 8 slices finely chopped bacon over medium-high heat until crisp, about 5 minutes. Transfer to paper towel–lined plate and let cool. Omit sugar. After adding butter to batter, quickly fold in bacon.

Southern-Style Cornbread

✓ WHY THIS RECIPE WORKS

Traditionally, Southern-style cornbread is made from white cornmeal and has only trace amounts of sugar and flour. We wanted to perfect the proportions of ingredients and come up with our own crusty, savory Southern-style cornbread and we'd reach for our cast-iron skillet to get started.

CHOOSE YELLOW CORNMEAL Departing from tradition, we chose yellow cornmeal over white—cornbreads made with yellow cornmeal consistently had a more potent corn flavor than those made with white cornmeal.

MIX UP A MUSH FOR MOISTNESS Combining part of the cornmeal with boiling water to create a cornmeal "mush" gives us a cornbread with great corn flavor, and it also produces a fine, moist crumb. In addition, buttermilk lends good tang, and just a small amount of sugar enhances the natural sweetness of the corn.

GET YOUR SKILLET HOT We pour the batter into a hot, greased cast-iron skillet to bake until crusty and fragrant.

SOUTHERN-STYLE CORNBREAD
SERVES 8 TO 10

Cornmeal mush of just the right texture is essential to this bread. Make sure that the water is at a rapid boil when it is added to the cornmeal. For an accurate measurement of boiling water, bring a kettle of water to a boil, then measure out the desired amount. Though we prefer to make cornbread in a preheated cast-iron skillet, a 9-inch round cake pan or 9-inch square baking pan, greased lightly with butter and not preheated, will also produce acceptable results if you double the recipe and bake the bread for 25 minutes.

FLAVORED BUTTERS FOR QUICK BREADS

Each recipe makes about ½ cup and can be stored in the refrigerator for about 1 week.

MOLASSES-PECAN BUTTER

Using stand mixer fitted with whisk, whip 8 tablespoons softened butter on medium speed until smooth, about 30 seconds. Add ¼ cup toasted and chopped pecans, 4 teaspoons light molasses, 2 teaspoons sugar, ¼ teaspoon vanilla extract, and pinch salt and whip until combined, about 15 seconds, then increase speed to high and whip until very light and fluffy, about 2 minutes, scraping down bowl as needed.

SWEET ORANGE BUTTER

Using stand mixer fitted with whisk, whip 8 tablespoons softened butter on medium speed until smooth, about 30 seconds. Add 2 teaspoons sugar, 1 teaspoon orange zest, ⅛ teaspoon vanilla, and pinch salt and whip until combined, about 15 seconds, then increase speed to high and whip until very light and fluffy, about 2 minutes, scraping down bowl as needed.

WHIPPED HONEY BUTTER

Using stand mixer fitted with whisk, whip 8 tablespoons softened butter on medium speed until smooth, about 30 seconds. Add 1 tablespoon honey and pinch salt and whip until combined, about 15 seconds, then increase speed to high and whip until very light and fluffy, about 2 minutes, scraping down bowl as needed.

4　teaspoons bacon drippings or
　　I tablespoon melted unsalted butter
　　plus I teaspoon vegetable oil
I　cup (5 ounces) stone-ground cornmeal
2　teaspoons sugar
I　teaspoon baking powder
¼　teaspoon baking soda
½　teaspoon salt
⅓　cup boiling water
¾　cup buttermilk
I　large egg, lightly beaten

1. Adjust oven rack to lower-middle position and heat oven to 450 degrees. Add bacon drippings to 8-inch cast-iron skillet and place skillet in oven while oven heats.

2. Place ⅓ cup cornmeal in medium bowl and set aside. Mix remaining ⅔ cup cornmeal, sugar, baking powder, baking soda, and salt in small bowl; set aside.

3. Pour boiling water over reserved ⅓ cup cornmeal and stir to make stiff mush. Gradually whisk in buttermilk, breaking up lumps until smooth. Whisk in egg. When oven is up to temperature and skillet is very hot, stir dry ingredients into mush mixture until just moistened. Carefully remove skillet from oven. Pour hot bacon fat from skillet into batter and stir to incorporate, then quickly pour batter into heated skillet. Bake until golden brown, about 20 minutes. Immediately turn cornbread out onto wire rack; let cool for 5 minutes, then serve.

SOUTHERN-STYLE CORN STICKS
MAKES ABOUT 12 CORN STICKS

Corn stick pans have anywhere from 7 to 12 molds. If your pan has fewer than 12 molds, you will need to bake the sticks in two batches.

Substitute heavy-gauge corn stick pan for cast-iron skillet; heat pan in oven as directed, omitting fat. Remove hot pan from oven, brush molds generously with bacon fat, then fill almost to rim with batter. Bake until cornbread is golden brown, 18 to 20 minutes. Turn sticks onto rack to cool. If making second batch, wipe crumbs from molds and reheat pan in oven for 5 minutes before brushing with additional fat and filling with remaining batter.

Classic Irish Soda Bread

✓ WHY THIS RECIPE WORKS
American-style Irish soda bread adds eggs, butter, and sugar along with caraway seeds, raisins, and a multitude of other flavorings to the traditional Irish recipe. Meanwhile, authentic Irish soda bread is less sweet and more simple, often relying on only flour, baking soda, salt, and buttermilk. We started with a cast-iron skillet to turn out a loaf closer in line with traditional soda breads and ditched the kitchen-sink approach.

ADD CAKE FLOUR FOR LIGHTNESS
All-purpose flour produces doughy, heavy bread with a thick crust. To soften the crumb, we add some cake flour (using just cake flour creates a loaf that is too delicate to hold the structure of the bread and turned out squat).

BRING ON THE BUTTER AND SUGAR
The most austere recipes turn out bread that's a bit tough and lacking in flavor. Fortunately, tradition allows for small amounts of butter and sugar. A modest 3 tablespoons of butter softens the dough without making it overly rich, and 2 tablespoons of sugar adds flavor without calling attention to itself.

COOL BEFORE SLICING This bread will be gummy if sliced straight out of the oven. Let it cool for at least 30 minutes and serve slightly warm.

SCORING IRISH SODA BREAD

Use serrated knife to cut cross shape in top of dough before baking. Each score should be 5 inches long and ¾ inch wide.

SKILLET IRISH SODA BREAD
SERVES 8 TO 10

If you do not have a cast-iron skillet, the bread can be baked on a baking sheet, although the crust won't be quite as crunchy. Soda bread is best eaten on the day it is baked but does keep well wrapped in plastic wrap and stored at room temperature for a couple of days, after which time it will become dry.

3	cups (15 ounces) all-purpose flour
1	cup (4 ounces) cake flour
2	tablespoons sugar
1½	teaspoons baking soda
1½	teaspoons cream of tartar
1½	teaspoons salt
2	tablespoons unsalted butter, softened, plus 1 tablespoon melted for brushing loaf
1¾	cups buttermilk

1. Adjust oven rack to middle position and heat oven to 400 degrees. Whisk all-purpose flour, cake flour, sugar, baking soda, cream of tartar, and salt together in large bowl. Add softened butter and use your fingers to rub it into flour until completely incorporated. Make well in center of flour mixture and add 1½ cups buttermilk. Work buttermilk into flour mixture using fork until dough comes together in large clumps and there is no dry flour in bottom of bowl, adding up to ¼ cup more buttermilk, 1 tablespoon at a time, until all loose flour is just moistened. Turn dough onto lightly floured counter and pat together to form 6-inch round; dough will be scrappy and uneven.

2. Place dough in 12-inch cast-iron skillet. Score deep cross, about 5 inches long and ¾ inch deep, on top of loaf and place in oven. Bake until nicely browned and knife inserted in center of loaf comes out clean, 40 to 45 minutes. Remove from oven and brush with melted butter. Let cool at least 30 minutes before serving.

SKILLET WHOLE-WHEAT SODA BREAD

This variation is known as brown bread in Ireland. The dough will be sticky and you may need to add a small amount of flour as you mix it.

Reduce all-purpose flour to 1½ cups and cake flour to ½ cup and increase sugar to 3 tablespoons. Add 1½ cups whole-wheat flour and ½ cup toasted wheat germ to dry ingredients.

SEASONING CAST IRON

For years we've seasoned cast-iron cookware in the test kitchen by placing it over medium heat and wiping out the pan with coats of vegetable oil until its surface turns dark and shiny. When a pan starts to look patchy, we simply repeat the process. But when we heard about a new method that creates a slick surface so indestructible that touch-ups are almost never necessary, we were intrigued. Developed by blogger Sheryl Canter, the approach calls for treating the pan with multiple coats of flaxseed oil between hour-long stints in the oven.

We carried out Canter's approach on new, unseasoned cast-iron skillets and compared them with pans treated with vegetable oil—and the results amazed us. The flaxseed oil so effectively bonded to the skillets, forming a sheer, stick-resistant veneer, that even a run through our commercial dishwasher with a squirt of degreaser left them totally unscathed. But the vegetable oil–treated skillets showed rusty spots and patchiness when they emerged from the dishwasher, requiring reseasoning before use.

Why did the new treatment work so well? Flaxseed oil is the food-grade equivalent of linseed oil, used by artists to give their paintings a hard, polished finish, and it boasts six times the amount of omega-3 fatty acids as vegetable oil. Over prolonged exposure to high heat, these fatty acids combine to form a strong, solid matrix that polymerizes to the pan's surface.

Although lengthy, seasoning with flaxseed oil is a mainly hands-off undertaking. We highly recommend the treatment:

1. Warm an unseasoned pan (either new or stripped of seasoning*) for 15 minutes in a 200-degree oven to open its pores.

2. Remove the pan from the oven. Place 1 tablespoon flaxseed oil in the pan and, using tongs, rub the oil into the surface with paper towels. With fresh paper towels, thoroughly wipe out the pan to remove excess oil.

3. Place the oiled pan upside down in a cold oven, then set the oven to its maximum baking temperature. Once the oven reaches its maximum temperature, heat the pan for one hour. Turn off the oven; let the pan cool in the oven for at least two hours.

4. Repeat the process five more times, or until the pan develops a dark, semimatte surface.

* To strip a cast-iron pan of seasoning, spray it with oven cleaner, wait 30 minutes, wash with soapy water, and thoroughly wipe with paper towels.

Boston Brown Bread

✔ WHY THIS RECIPE WORKS

Boston brown bread can be heavy and dense. We wanted a lighter loaf; moist, not dry, and flavored with molasses. And while the traditional method of baking this bread in a coffee can is charming, we saw little sense in this since coffee is sold not just in cans, but in a variety of packaging. In short, we would be making our Boston brown bread using a standard loaf pan.

SCALE BACK WHOLE-WHEAT FLOUR To achieve our goals, we cut back on the amount of whole-wheat and rye flour that is typically called for and added some all-purpose flour in its place, dramatically improving the bread by lightening up its texture and flavor balance.

CHOOSE DARK MOLASSES FOR BEST FLAVOR We use "robust," or dark, molasses for the deep color and bold, bittersweet flavor that it adds to the loaves.

LIGHTEN THE LOAF WITH BUTTER-MILK We opt for buttermilk rather than milk because its tanginess complements the other flavors in the bread and its acidity reacts with the baking soda already in the batter to provide greater lift.

LOSE THE CAN Instead of the traditional but less-convenient coffee can, we use a loaf pan. After filling it with batter, we cover the pan tightly with foil, place it in a Dutch oven with water reaching halfway up the sides of the pan, and cook it on the stovetop, which steams the loaf perfectly.

BOSTON BROWN BREAD

MAKES 1 LOAF

Don't use blackstrap molasses here; if you can't find robust molasses, substitute light molasses. The test kitchen's preferred loaf pan measures 8½ by 4½ inches; if you use a 9 by 5-inch loaf pan, start checking for doneness 5 minutes earlier than advised in the recipe.

½	cup (2½ ounces) yellow cornmeal
½	cup (2¾ ounces) rye flour
¼	cup (1⅓ ounces) whole-wheat flour
¼	cup (1¼ ounces) all-purpose flour
1	teaspoon baking soda
½	teaspoon salt
1	cup buttermilk
⅓	cup robust or full molasses
½	cup raisins

1. Grease 8½ by 4½-inch loaf pan. Fold piece of heavy-duty aluminum foil into 12 by 8-inch rectangle, and grease center portion of one side.

2. Whisk cornmeal, rye flour, whole-wheat flour, all-purpose flour, baking soda, and salt together in large bowl. Stir in buttermilk and molasses until combined and uniform. Stir in raisins. Scrape batter into prepared pan and smooth top. Wrap with prepared foil, greased side facing batter, sealing edges tightly.

3. Set loaf pan in Dutch oven and fill pot with enough water to reach halfway up sides of loaf pan. Bring to simmer over medium heat, then reduce heat to low, cover pot, and cook until toothpick inserted in center of loaf comes out clean, 50 minutes to 1 hour. (Check water level every 20 minutes to make sure water still reaches halfway up sides of loaf pan; add more water if necessary.)

4. Let loaf cool in pan for 10 minutes, then turn out onto wire rack and let cool for 1 hour before serving.

PREPARING BOSTON BROWN BREAD

1. Fold 16 by 2-inch piece of aluminum foil in half to yield rectangle that measures 12 by 8 inches. Liberally grease center portion of foil.

2. Scrape batter into loaf pan, place foil greased side down over batter, and then seal edges tightly.

Quick Cheese Bread

SHREDDING CHEESE CLEANLY

Soft and semisoft cheeses will tend to mash onto the grater and clog its holes. Here's how to shred cheese neatly.

1. Spray grater with vegetable oil spray before beginning.

2. Cheese will shred cleanly without sticking to grater.

✔ WHY THIS RECIPE WORKS

Run-of-the-mill cheese bread is at once dry and greasy, with almost no cheese flavor at all. We wanted a rich, moist loaf topped with a bold, cheesy crust.

ADD DAIRY FOR A MOIST BASE We start with all-purpose flour and add whole milk and sour cream for a clean, creamy flavor and rich, moist texture.

BE CAREFUL WITH THE BUTTER Just a few tablespoons of butter adds enough richness without greasiness, and using less fat makes the texture heartier and less cakelike.

FORGET SHREDDED CHEESE Most recipes for cheese bread call for shredded cheese. We prefer our cheese (cheddar or Asiago), cut into small chunks, which, when mixed into the dough and baked, create luscious, cheesy pockets throughout the bread.

ADD MORE CHEESE, PLEASE For added cheesy flavor and a crisp, browned crust, we coat the pan and sprinkle the top of the loaf with grated Parmesan.

QUICK CHEESE BREAD
SERVES 10

A mild Asiago, crumbled into ¼- to ½-inch pieces, can be used instead of the cheddar. Aged Asiago that is as firm as Parmesan is too sharp and piquant. If, when testing the bread for doneness, the toothpick comes out with what looks like uncooked batter clinging to it, try again in a different, but still central, spot; if the toothpick hits a pocket of cheese, it may give a false indication. The texture of the bread improves as it cools, so resist the urge to slice the loaf while it is piping hot. Do not use skim milk for this bread. We developed this recipe using a loaf pan that measures 8½ by 4½ inches; if you use a 9 by 5-inch loaf pan, start checking for doneness 5 minutes earlier than advised in the recipe.

3   ounces Parmesan cheese, grated on large holes of box grater (1 cup)
2½ cups (12½ ounces) all-purpose flour
1   tablespoon baking powder
1   teaspoon salt
⅛   teaspoon cayenne pepper
⅛   teaspoon pepper
4   ounces extra-sharp cheddar cheese, cut into ½-inch cubes (1 cup)
1   cup whole milk
½   cup sour cream
3   tablespoons unsalted butter, melted and cooled
1   large egg, lightly beaten

1. Adjust oven rack to middle position and heat oven to 350 degrees. Spray 8½ by 4½-inch loaf pan with vegetable oil spray, then sprinkle ½ cup Parmesan evenly in bottom of pan.

2. In large bowl, whisk flour, baking powder, salt, cayenne, and pepper to combine. Using rubber spatula, mix in cheddar, breaking up clumps, until cheese is coated with flour. In medium bowl, whisk together milk, sour cream, melted butter, and egg. Using rubber spatula, gently fold wet ingredients into dry ingredients until just combined (batter will be heavy and thick; do not overmix). Scrape batter into prepared loaf pan; spread to sides of pan and level surface with rubber spatula. Sprinkle remaining ½ cup Parmesan evenly over surface.

3. Bake until loaf is deep golden brown and toothpick inserted in center of loaf comes out clean, 45 to 50 minutes, rotating pan halfway through baking. Let cool in pan on wire rack for 5 minutes, then invert loaf onto wire rack. Turn right side up and let cool until warm, about 45 minutes. Serve. (To freeze, wrap cooled loaf tightly with double layer of aluminum foil and freeze for up to 3 months.

Trying to remove steaming
hot muffins from a tin straight
out of the oven never
works—they are too delicate
and will break apart. Instead,
be sure to let the muffins cool
in the tins for the amount of
time specified, so the muffins
can set up and be easier to
remove. If you still need some
extra help, see our tips on
page 42.

When ready to serve, adjust oven rack to middle position and heat oven to 375 degrees. Bake wrapped loaf until it yields under gentle pressure, 8 to 10 minutes. Remove foil and continue to bake until exterior is crisp, about 5 minutes longer. Let loaf cool on wire rack for 15 minutes before serving.)

QUICK CHEESE BREAD WITH BACON, ONION, AND GRUYÈRE

Cook 5 slices bacon, cut into ½-inch pieces, in 10-inch nonstick skillet over medium heat, stirring occasionally, until crisp, 5 to 7 minutes. Transfer bacon to paper towel–lined plate and pour off all but 3 tablespoons fat from skillet. Add ½ cup minced onion to skillet and cook, stirring frequently, until softened, about 3 minutes; set skillet with onion aside. Substitute 4 ounces Gruyère, cut into ½-inch cubes, for cheddar and omit butter. Add bacon and onion to flour mixture with cheese in step 2.

QUICK CHEESE MUFFINS
MAKES 12 MUFFINS

Adjust oven rack to middle position and heat oven to 375 degrees. Reduce Parmesan cheese to 2 ounces and cut cheddar into ¼-inch cubes (or crumble mild Asiago into ¼-inch pieces). Spray 12-cup muffin tin with vegetable oil spray, then sprinkle each muffin cup with about 1 teaspoon grated Parmesan cheese, tapping and shaking pan so that cheese evenly coats sides and bottom of each cup. Prepare batter as directed. Using ice cream scoop or large spoon, divide batter evenly among prepared muffin cups, dropping batter to form mounds (do not level or flatten batter). Sprinkle remaining Parmesan evenly over surface of batter. Reduce baking time to 20 to 25 minutes, rotating muffin tin halfway through baking. Let muffins cool in tin for 5 minutes, then transfer to wire rack and continue to let cool until warm, about 30 minutes.

Bakery-Style Muffins

✓ WHY THIS RECIPE WORKS

Jumbo bakery-size muffins should boast a rich, full flavor and a thick, crisp crust protecting their fragile, tender crumb. We wanted to develop such a version that was also versatile enough that it would taste great on its own or work with add-ins like dried fruit, citrus zest, nuts, and even chocolate chips.

CHOICE OF FLOUR MATTERS Muffin batter made with cake flour was incredibly loose, resulting in muffins that were squat, wet, and greasy. They also lacked a distinct crisp outer crust. Instead we use all-purpose flour for shapely, tender muffins with a nice contrast between crust and crumb.

THICKEN IT UP We tested all manner of dairy in our muffins and found that thin liquids like milk and half-and-half produce thin batters that bake into smooth-topped muffins reminiscent of cupcakes. Thicker liquids, such as buttermilk, sour cream, and yogurt, deliver thicker batters and muffins with rounded, textured tops.

CREAM THE BUTTER AND SUGAR We prefer the more tender, cakey crumb of muffins made using the creaming method.

BATTER UP For jumbo-size muffins, we increase all the ingredients to ensure there is enough batter to fill the muffin cups to the brim.

FORGET PAPER LINERS Paper liners sure save on cleanup, but when you peel back the paper, it takes some of the muffin with it. Instead, take a minute to grease your muffin tin and you'll be able to enjoy every crumb.

SIMPLE BAKERY-STYLE MUFFINS

MAKES 12 MUFFINS

If you are short on time, you can melt the butter, mix it with the eggs, and stir it into the dry ingredients. When thoroughly mixed, beat in the yogurt and proceed with the recipe. To cinnamon-coat the muffin tops, dip warm muffins in melted butter, then in a mixture of ½ cup granulated sugar and 2 teaspoons cinnamon. Serve these plain muffins warm with jam.

3	cups (15 ounces) all-purpose flour
1	tablespoon baking powder
½	teaspoon baking soda
½	teaspoon salt
10	tablespoons unsalted butter, softened
1¾	cups (12¼ ounces) plus 3 tablespoons sugar
2	large eggs
1½	cups plain low-fat yogurt

1. Adjust oven rack to lower-middle position and heat oven to 375 degrees. Spray 12-cup muffin tin with vegetable oil spray. Mix flour, baking powder, baking soda, and salt in medium bowl and set aside.

2. Using stand mixer fitted with paddle, beat butter and sugar on medium-high speed until pale and fluffy, about 3 minutes. Add eggs, one at a time, and beat until combined. Reduce speed to low and add dry ingredients in 3 additions, alternating with yogurt in 2 additions, scraping down bowl as needed. Give batter final stir by hand.

3. Using ice cream scoop or large spoon, divide batter evenly among prepared muffin cups. Bake until muffins are golden brown and toothpick inserted in center of muffin comes out with few crumbs attached, 25 to 30 minutes, rotating muffin tin halfway through baking. Let muffins cool in tin for 5 minutes, then transfer to wire rack and let cool for 5 minutes before serving.

LEMON–POPPY SEED MUFFINS

Add 3 tablespoons poppy seeds to flour mixture and 1 tablespoon grated lemon zest to butter-sugar mixture. While muffins are baking, heat ¼ cup sugar and ¼ cup lemon juice in small saucepan until sugar dissolves and mixture forms light syrup, 3 to 4 minutes. Brush warm syrup over warm muffins.

MOCHA CHIP MUFFINS

Dissolve 3 tablespoons instant espresso powder in yogurt before adding to batter and fold 1 cup semisweet chocolate chips into finished batter.

APRICOT-ALMOND MUFFINS

Cream 1 ounce almond paste with butter and sugar and fold 1½ cups dried apricots, chopped fine, into finished batter. Sprinkle batter with ½ cup sliced almonds before baking.

RASPBERRY-ALMOND MUFFINS

We like raspberry jam here but any jam will work.

Cream 1 ounce almond paste with butter and sugar. In step 3, spoon half-portion of batter into each muffin cup, then with small spoon make well in center of each portion of batter. Spoon about 1 teaspoon raspberry jam into each well. Fill cups with remaining batter and proceed as directed.

LEMON-BLUEBERRY MUFFINS

Add 1 teaspoon grated lemon zest to butter-sugar mixture and fold 1½ cups blueberries into finished batter.

BANANA-WALNUT MUFFINS

Substitute 1 cup packed light brown sugar for granulated sugar. Add ½ teaspoon ground nutmeg to flour mixture in step 1, and fold 3 small bananas, chopped fine (about 1½ cups), and ¾ cup walnuts, chopped, into finished batter.

MUFFIN TIN MYTH BUSTER

Did your mother or grandmother ever tell you that if you're baking a half batch of muffins using a 12-cup tin, you should fill the empty cups with water? Proponents of this practice contend that filling empty cups with water serves two functions: preventing the pan from warping and acting as a "heat sink" to ensure that muffins next to empty cups heat evenly (avoiding stunted growth or spotty browning).

We tested this theory by baking one muffin tin completely filled with batter, one tin in which only half of the 12 cups were filled with batter and the remaining six with water, and one tin in which six of the cups were filled with batter and the other six left empty. The results? All muffins had the same height, texture, and color, and none of the tins warped.

On reflection, the results made sense: In a full 12-cup muffin tin, all but the two center muffins are directly exposed to the oven's heat on at least one side to no ill effect. Furthermore, if your muffin tin warps, that's a sign that you need to find a better quality pan.

Blueberry Swirl Muffins

✔ WHY THIS RECIPE WORKS

Ultimate blueberry muffins should be packed with blueberry flavor and boast a moist crumb. But too often, the blueberry flavor is fleeting, thanks to the fact that the berries in the produce aisle have suffered from long-distance shipping. We wanted blueberry muffins that put the berry flavor at the forefront and would taste great with blueberries of any origin, even the watery supermarket kind. To achieve this goal, we make our own low-sugar blueberry jam and fold our batter rather than using the creaming method.

USE MORE BERRIES—DIFFERENTLY Adding more blueberries to a muffin batter can make the muffins soggy and heavy. We cook some of the berries down into a jam, evaporating excess moisture and concentrating the flavor. (Commercial jam is too sweet.) Adding this jam to our muffin batter gives us muffins with great texture and pure blueberry flavor. We add some fresh blueberries, too.

FOLD, DON'T CREAM Instead of creaming the butter and sugar as if we were making a cake, we fold the batter, as we do for quick breads. This yields a slightly coarser crumb, which we prefer for these muffins. It's important to fold the wet and dry ingredients gently; the batter will be slightly lumpy and have spots of flour.

USE BUTTER AND OIL To achieve the supremely moist muffins we sought, we examined the fat in the recipe. While butter contributes lots of flavor, we knew that oil has a propensity for making baked goods moist and tender. Unlike butter, oil contains no water and is able to completely coat flour proteins and restrict them from absorbing liquid to develop gluten. We swapped some butter for oil for a moist, tender texture.

SWIRL IN JAM After scooping the batter into the muffin tin, we place 1 teaspoon of our homemade berry jam in the center of each batter-filled cup Then, using a chopstick or a skewer, we swirl the jam—very gently, using a "figure-eight" motion—to spread berry flavor throughout the muffin.

ADD LEMON SUGAR To get a good crust on our muffins, we bake them on the upper-middle rack of a 425-degree oven. We sprinkle lemon-scented sugar on top of the batter just before baking. The oven melts the sugar slightly, which then hardens as it bakes to create an irresistibly crunchy shell.

BLUEBERRY SWIRL MUFFINS
MAKES 12 MUFFINS

If buttermilk is unavailable, substitute ¾ cup plain whole-milk or low-fat yogurt thinned with ¼ cup milk.

LEMON-SUGAR TOPPING
- ⅓ cup (2⅓ ounces) sugar
- 1½ teaspoons grated lemon zest

MUFFINS
- 10 ounces (2 cups) blueberries
- 1⅛ cups (7¾ ounces) plus 1 teaspoon sugar
- 2½ cups (12½ ounces) all-purpose flour
- 2½ teaspoons baking powder
- 1 teaspoon salt
- 2 large eggs
- 4 tablespoons unsalted butter, melted and cooled
- ¼ cup vegetable oil
- 1 cup buttermilk
- 1½ teaspoons vanilla extract

1. FOR THE TOPPING: Stir together sugar and lemon zest in small bowl until combined and set aside.

You can use either fresh or frozen blueberries in our muffins. When blueberries are ripe during the summer, it's a no-brainer what you'd choose. But these days, you can find fresh berries in your supermarket almost year-round.

Last winter, the test kitchen tried fresh berries from Chile as well as five frozen brands in a cobbler. The frozen wild berries easily beat the fresh imported berries as well as the other frozen contenders. (Compared with cultivated berries, wild berries are smaller, more intense in color, firmer in texture, and more sweet and tangy in flavor.) While frozen cultivated berries trailed in the tasting, all but one brand received decent scores.

Why did frozen wild berries beat fresh berries? The imported berries are picked before they have a chance to fully ripen to help them survive the long trip north. As a result, they are often tart and not so flavorful. Frozen berries have been picked at their peak—when perfectly ripe—and are then individually quick frozen (IQF) at -20 degrees. The quick freezing preserves their sweetness, letting us enjoy them year-round.

2. FOR THE MUFFINS: Adjust oven rack to upper-middle position and heat oven to 425 degrees. Spray 12-cup muffin tin with vegetable oil spray. Bring 1 cup blueberries and 1 teaspoon sugar to simmer in small saucepan over medium heat. Cook, mashing berries with spoon several times and stirring frequently, until berries have broken down and mixture is thickened and reduced to ¼ cup, about 6 minutes. Transfer to small bowl and let cool to room temperature, 10 to 15 minutes.

3. Whisk flour, baking powder, and salt together in large bowl. Whisk remaining 1⅛ cups sugar and eggs together in medium bowl until thick and homogeneous, about 45 seconds. Slowly whisk in melted butter and oil until combined. Whisk in buttermilk and vanilla until combined. Using rubber spatula, fold egg mixture and remaining 1 cup blueberries into flour mixture until just moistened. (Batter will be very lumpy with few spots of dry flour; do not overmix.)

4. Using ice cream scoop or large spoon, divide batter evenly among prepared muffin cups (batter should completely fill cups and mound slightly). Spoon 1 teaspoon of cooked berry mixture into center of each mound of batter. Using chopstick or skewer, gently swirl berry filling into batter using figure-eight motion. Sprinkle lemon sugar evenly over muffins.

5. Bake until muffins are golden brown and toothpick inserted in center of muffin comes out with few crumbs attached, 17 to 19 minutes, rotating muffin tin halfway through baking. Let muffins cool in tin for 5 minutes, then transfer to wire rack and let cool for 5 minutes before serving.

BLUEBERRY SWIRL MUFFINS WITH FROZEN BLUEBERRIES

Substitute 1⅔ cups frozen blueberries for fresh blueberries. Cook 1 cup blueberries as directed in step 2. Rinse remaining berries under cold water and dry well. Proceed with recipe from step 3 as directed.

BLUEBERRY SWIRL MUFFINS WITH STREUSEL TOPPING

Omit Lemon-Sugar Topping. Instead combine 3 tablespoons granulated sugar, 3 tablespoons packed dark brown sugar, pinch salt, and ½ cup plus 3 tablespoons all-purpose flour in small bowl. Drizzle with 5 tablespoons warm, melted unsalted butter and toss with fork until evenly moistened and mixture forms large chunks with some pea-size pieces throughout. Proceed with recipe as directed, sprinkling streusel topping over muffins before baking.

BLUEBERRY SWIRL MUFFINS WITH ORANGE GLAZE

Turbinado sugar is often sold as Sugar in the Raw.

Omit Lemon-Sugar Topping. Add 2 teaspoons grated orange zest to egg mixture. Proceed with recipe as directed, sprinkling 4 teaspoons turbinado sugar over muffins before baking. While muffins cool, whisk together 1 cup confectioners' sugar and 1½ tablespoons orange juice until smooth. Drizzle each cooled muffin with 2 teaspoons glaze before serving.

BLUEBERRY SWIRL MUFFINS WITH ALMOND CRUNCH TOPPING

Turbinado sugar is often sold as Sugar in the Raw.

Omit Lemon-Sugar Topping. Instead combine ⅓ cup finely ground almonds and 4 teaspoons turbinado sugar in step 1 for topping and set aside. Add ⅓ cup finely ground almonds to flour mixture. Proceed with recipe as directed, adding 1 teaspoon almond extract to batter with vanilla extract and sprinkling almond topping over muffins before baking.

MUFFIN-TIN GREASING WITHOUT THE MESS

Spraying a muffin tin with vegetable oil spray inevitably means some of the spray will end up on your kitchen floor or counter. Instead, open your dishwasher door, place the muffin tin on the door and spray away. Any excess or overspray will be cleaned off the door the next time you run the dishwasher. Spraying your muffin tin over your sink or trash barrel works too.

Classic Blueberry Muffins

1. Spray large serving spoon with vegetable oil spray and spoon even amounts of batter into each cup of muffin tin. Batter will slide easily from spoon into muffin cups.

2. The thin, slightly curved blade of a grapefruit knife is particularly well suited to getting under stubborn muffins with little risk of tearing muffins apart.

✔ WHY THIS RECIPE WORKS

Old-fashioned blueberry muffins can be too sweet, too rough, too dense, or just plain bland, with little to no real blueberry flavor. We wanted delicate muffins, with a balanced fresh blueberry flavor.

MELTED BUTTER YIELDS DELICATE TEXTURE For a muffin with a delicate texture, we decided to forget creaming the butter and sugar; instead we whisk the sugar with melted butter.

INCLUDE SOUR CREAM FOR RICHNESS Sour cream gives our sweet muffins a bit of tang and lush richness.

BLUEBERRIES? GO WILD Using frozen wild blueberries means we can enjoy these muffins year-round, and when we want to make these muffins extra special, we found that coating the tops with a frosty sugar glaze ensures these muffins would disappear as quickly as we could make them.

CLASSIC BLUEBERRY MUFFINS
MAKES 12 MUFFINS

This recipe does not require a stand mixer, but when making the batter, be sure to whisk vigorously in step 2, then fold carefully in step 3. There should be no large pockets of flour in the finished batter, but small occasional spots may remain. Do not overmix the batter. These muffins are great unadorned, but for an extra flourish, dip warm muffins in melted butter, then in mixture of ½ cup granulated sugar and 2 teaspoons cinnamon.

2	cups (10 ounces) all-purpose flour
1	tablespoon baking powder
½	teaspoon salt
1	large egg
1	cup (7 ounces) sugar
4	tablespoons unsalted butter, melted and cooled
1¼	cups sour cream
6	ounces (1½ cups) frozen blueberries, preferably wild

1. Adjust oven rack to middle position and heat oven to 350 degrees. Spray 12-cup muffin tin with vegetable oil spray.

2. Whisk flour, baking powder, and salt in medium bowl until combined. Whisk egg in second medium bowl until well combined and light-colored, about 20 seconds. Add sugar and whisk vigorously until thick and homogeneous, about 30 seconds. Add melted butter in 2 or 3 additions, whisking to combine after each addition. Add sour cream in 2 additions, whisking until just combined.

3. Add blueberries to dry ingredients and gently toss to combine. Add sour cream mixture and carefully fold with rubber spatula until batter comes together and berries are evenly distributed, 25 to 30 seconds (small spots of flour may remain and batter will be thick). Do not overmix.

4. Using ice cream scoop or large spoon, divide batter evenly among prepared muffin cups. Bake until muffins are golden brown and toothpick inserted in center of muffin comes out with few crumbs attached, 25 to 30 minutes, rotating muffin tin halfway through baking. Let muffins cool in tin for 5 minutes, then transfer to wire rack and let cool for 5 minutes before serving.

CLASSIC BLUEBERRY MUFFINS WITH LEMON GLAZE OR GINGER GLAZE

While muffins are baking, mix 1 teaspoon grated lemon zest or grated fresh ginger and ½ cup sugar in small bowl and set aside. Bring ¼ cup lemon juice and ¼ cup sugar to simmer in small saucepan over medium heat and simmer until mixture is thick and syrupy and reduced to about 4 tablespoons. After muffins have cooled for 5 minutes, brush tops with glaze, then, working one at a time, dip tops in lemon-sugar or ginger-sugar. Set muffins upright on wire rack and serve.

Oatmeal Muffins

✔ WHY THIS RECIPE WORKS

What should be a satisfying breakfast treat is often a dry, chewy cause for regret. We were after a muffin that boasted all the comforting appeal of a great bowl of oatmeal. We quickly discovered that choosing the proper oats and treating them right were key.

TOAST YOUR OATS Ever notice how nutty oats smell when you toast them for granola? We followed suit for our oat muffins by toasting the oats in a skillet. We tried toasting them dry, but the oats were even better—rich and complex—when sautéed with a little butter.

PROCESS 'EM Old-fashioned rolled oats boast great flavor but when stirred into muffin batter, they never fully hydrate, so our muffins baked up with a dry, chewy crumb. Quick oats, which are precooked and rolled into thin flakes before processing, produced a muffin with a great texture, but faint oat flavor. The solution? We process our flavorful rolled oats into fine oat flour, which we mix with all-purpose flour.

GIVE IT A REST Our home-ground oat flour absorbs liquid much more slowly than wheat flour does, leading to a thin muffin batter that needs to be poured into the cups and spreads when baked. To fix this problem, we give the batter a 20-minute rest after mixing so it fully hydrates, thereby ensuring that it is thick enough to scoop.

WIELD YOUR WHISK The oat flour can develop a few large clumps that stubbornly refuse to hydrate and dissolve into the batter during baking, leaving dry, floury pockets in the finished muffins. Vigorous stirring results in a crumb with a tough texture—a repercussion of overworking the oat starch and gluten. To remedy this problem, we employ a lesser-known technique called whisk folding. In this method, a whisk is gently drawn down and then up through the batter before being tapped lightly against the side of the bowl to knock any clumps back into the mixture.

The wires of the whisk exert very little drag and thus develop minimal gluten, while the tapping action helps rupture pockets of dry ingredients.

CRISP IT UP Just as one might top a bowl of oatmeal with crunchy nuts or chewy, sweet raisins, we wanted a contrasting adornment on our muffins that featured crunch and a bit of sweetness. A fruit crisp–like topping was the answer. We crumble a crisp-inspired topping of oats, finely chopped pecans, brown sugar, flour, melted butter, salt, and a hint of cinnamon evenly over the muffin batter before baking. The topping bakes into a proud crown of crunchy, chewy, sweet, and salty oats and nuts—the perfect accent to the rich crumb of our oat muffins.

OATMEAL MUFFINS
MAKES 12 MUFFINS

Do not use quick or instant oats in this recipe. Walnuts may be substituted for the pecans. The easiest way to grease and flour the muffin tin is with baking spray with flour.

TOPPING

½	cup (1½ ounces) old-fashioned rolled oats
⅓	cup (1⅔ ounces) all-purpose flour
⅓	cup pecans, chopped fine
⅓	cup packed (2⅓ ounces) light brown sugar
1¼	teaspoons ground cinnamon
⅛	teaspoon salt
4	tablespoons unsalted butter, melted

MUFFINS

2	tablespoons unsalted butter, plus 6 tablespoons melted
2	cups (6 ounces) old-fashioned rolled oats
1¾	cups (8¾ ounces) all-purpose flour
1½	teaspoons salt

Even finely ground oats create lumps. To minimize lump size without overworking the oat starch and gluten—and thus toughening the crumb—draw a whisk gently down and then up through the batter. Tap the whisk against the bowl to release clumps.

¾ teaspoon baking powder

¼ teaspoon baking soda

1⅓ cups packed (9⅓ ounces) light brown sugar

1¾ cups milk

2 large eggs, beaten

1. FOR THE TOPPING: Combine oats, flour, pecans, sugar, cinnamon, and salt in medium bowl. Drizzle melted butter over mixture and stir to thoroughly combine; set aside.

2. FOR THE MUFFINS: Grease and flour 12-cup muffin tin. Melt 2 tablespoons butter in 10-inch skillet over medium heat. Add oats and cook, stirring frequently, until oats turn golden brown and smell like popcorn, 6 to 8 minutes. Transfer oats to food processor and process into fine meal, about 30 seconds. Add flour, salt, baking powder, and baking soda to oats and pulse until combined, about 3 pulses.

3. Stir 6 tablespoons melted butter and sugar together in large bowl until smooth. Add milk and eggs and whisk until smooth. Using whisk, gently fold half of oat mixture into wet ingredients, tapping whisk against side of bowl to release clumps. Add remaining oat mixture and continue to fold with whisk until no streaks of flour remain. Set aside batter for 20 minutes to thicken. Meanwhile, adjust oven rack to middle position and heat oven to 375 degrees.

4. Using ice cream scoop or large spoon, divide batter evenly among prepared muffin cups (about ½ cup batter per cup; cups will be filled to rim). Evenly sprinkle topping over muffins (about 2 tablespoons per muffin). Bake until toothpick inserted in center of muffin comes out clean, 18 to 22 minutes, rotating muffin tin halfway through baking.

5. Let muffins cool in tin for 10 minutes, then transfer to wire rack and serve warm.

Better Bran Muffins

✓ WHY THIS RECIPE WORKS

Classic bran muffins rely on unprocessed wheat bran, but our supermarket survey showed that few stores carry this specialized ingredient. We wanted to make a moist, hearty muffin redolent of bran's rich, earthy flavor without tracking down unprocessed bran. Using a mixture of pulverized and whole twig bran cereal turned out to be just one simple step in our path to a truly great bran muffin.

PICK THE RIGHT CEREAL Bran is the outer layer of the wheat grain that is removed during milling. Bran cereal can come in various forms, including flakes, buds, and twigs. Here's how they stack up in muffins: Bran flakes are often made with whole wheat in addition to bran and give muffins very little flavor. Small bran buds make dense muffins

with almost no bran flavor. Cereal made of bran twigs (like All-Bran), however, give muffins the most robust flavor.

CRUSH THE BRAN The twigs provide a deep bran flavor, but getting them to bend to our will is another matter. Twigs don't easily dissolve in the batter, and presoaking them only makes the muffins as dense as hockey pucks. But we found that grinding half of the cereal into a fine powder and leaving the other half in twig form creates muffins with an even, but not heavy, texture. We like mixing all-purpose flour and whole-wheat flour to reinforce the flavor of the bran.

USE YOGURT We found that more than 6 tablespoons of butter makes these muffins greasy, so we looked elsewhere for additional

Greek-style yogurt is made by allowing the watery whey to drain from yogurt, giving it a smooth, thick texture. American-style yogurt still contains whey, so it has more moisture and a thinner, runnier consistency. We weren't surprised, then, with our findings when we baked batches of bran muffins and peach cobbler (with a biscuit topping) using these two different types of yogurt. In both instances, the samples made with Greek yogurt tasted slightly drier than those made with American yogurt.

To come up with a formula to compensate for the difference in moisture content, we drained 1 cup each of plain whole-milk, low-fat, and fat-free yogurt in a fine-mesh strainer lined with cheesecloth; after 2 hours, ⅓ cup of liquid had been exuded from each sample. Armed with these results, we went back into the test kitchen, reducing the amount of Greek yogurt used in our recipes by one-third and making up the difference with water. The results? Tasters found the muffins and cobblers nearly identical.

So to substitute Greek-style yogurt for American-style yogurt in baked goods, remember this rule: Use only two-thirds of the amount of Greek yogurt called for in the recipe and make up the difference with water.

richness and tenderness. Swapping the milk in most recipes for sour cream was overkill. Buttermilk was an improvement over plain milk, but whole-milk yogurt was the tasters' first choice. And replacing the baking powder with baking soda gives us a coarser crumb that tasters likewise enjoyed.

COMBINE BROWN SUGAR AND MOLASSES We use both light brown sugar (the classic recipe uses granulated sugar) and molasses to provide malty, caramel sweetness to match with the bran and whole-wheat flour.

PLUMP THE RAISINS After complaints that the raisins didn't soften enough during baking, we began plumping them in the microwave with a little water. Works like a charm.

FILL THOSE CUPS For big, hearty muffins, fill the muffin cups to the rim. And for nicely domed tops, mound the batter in the cups and don't level it off.

BETTER BRAN MUFFINS
MAKES 12 MUFFINS

We prefer Kellogg's All-Bran Original cereal in this recipe. Dried cranberries or dried cherries may be substituted for the raisins.

1	cup raisins
1	teaspoon water
2¼	cups (5 ounces) All-Bran Original cereal
1¼	cups (6¼ ounces) all-purpose flour
½	cup (2¾ ounces) whole-wheat flour
2	teaspoons baking soda
½	teaspoon salt
1	large egg plus 1 large yolk
⅔	cup packed (4⅔ ounces) light brown sugar
3	tablespoons molasses
1	teaspoon vanilla extract
6	tablespoons unsalted butter, melted and cooled
1¾	cups plain whole-milk yogurt

1. Adjust oven rack to middle position and heat oven to 400 degrees. Spray 12-cup muffin tin with vegetable oil spray. Line plate with paper towel. Combine raisins and water in small bowl, cover, and microwave for 30 seconds. Let stand, covered, until raisins are softened and plump, about 5 minutes. Transfer raisins to prepared plate to cool.

2. Process 1 cup plus 2 tablespoons cereal in food processor until finely ground, about 1 minute. Whisk all-purpose flour, whole-wheat flour, baking soda, and salt in large bowl until combined and set aside. Whisk egg and yolk together in medium bowl until well combined and light-colored, about 20 seconds. Add sugar, molasses, and vanilla to bowl with eggs and whisk until mixture is thick, about 30 seconds. Add melted butter and whisk to combine. Add yogurt and whisk to combine. Stir in processed cereal and remaining 1 cup plus 2 tablespoons unprocessed cereal. Let mixture sit until cereal is evenly moistened (there will still be some small lumps), about 5 minutes.

3. Add wet ingredients to dry ingredients and mix gently with rubber spatula until batter is just combined and evenly moistened (do not overmix.) Gently fold raisins into batter. Using ice cream scoop or large spoon, divide batter evenly among prepared muffin cups, dropping batter to form mounds (do not level or flatten batter).

4. Bake until muffins are dark golden and toothpick inserted in center of muffin comes out with few crumbs attached, 16 to 20 minutes, rotating muffin tin halfway through baking. Let muffins cool in tin for 5 minutes, then transfer to wire rack and let cool for 10 minutes before serving.

Cranberry-Pecan Muffins

✔ WHY THIS RECIPE WORKS

Cranberry-nut muffins are fraught with problems: The berries' ultra-sour burst can overwhelm their delicate flavor, the nuts' toasty flavor washes away in the oven, and the mix-ins are always unevenly distributed. We wanted a muffin that would feature a moist crumb with plenty of its own flavor, punctuated by zingy but not harsh cranberries and rich-tasting, crunchy nuts. First we found that biting into a whole cranberry was a recipe for disaster.

CHOP, SUGAR, AND SALT THE BERRIES To tame the harsh bite of the cranberries found in most cranberry-nut muffins, we chop the cranberries in a food processor and toss them with confectioners' sugar and a little salt (which we often use to tame the bitterness in eggplant).

PUMP UP THE PECAN FLAVOR To underscore the flavor of the pecans in our muffins, we take a cue from cakes made with nut flour and augment some of the all-purpose flour with pecan flour (made by grinding pecans in a food processor).

REST THE BATTER Because ground pecans are used in place of some of the flour, muffins tend to spread rather than baking up tall and self-contained. We fix the problem by letting the batter rest for 30 minutes. This allows what flour there is to become more hydrated, resulting in a properly thickened batter that bakes up perfectly domed. To replace the missing crunch of the nuts, we simply top the muffins with a pecan streusel.

CRANBERRY-PECAN MUFFINS
MAKES 12 MUFFINS

If fresh cranberries aren't available, substitute frozen cranberries and microwave on high power until they are partially thawed, 30 to 45 seconds. See page 9 for information on toasting nuts.

STREUSEL TOPPING

3   tablespoons all-purpose flour
1   tablespoon packed light brown sugar
4   teaspoons granulated sugar
2   tablespoons unsalted butter, cut into ½-inch pieces, and softened
    Pinch salt
½   cup pecans

MUFFINS

1⅓   cups (6⅔ ounces) all-purpose flour
1½   teaspoons baking powder
1   teaspoon salt
1¼   cups pecans, toasted and cooled
1   cup (7½ ounces) plus 1 tablespoon granulated sugar
2   large eggs
6   tablespoons unsalted butter, melted and cooled
½   cup whole milk
8   ounces (2 cups) fresh cranberries
1   tablespoon confectioners' sugar

1. Adjust oven rack to upper-middle position and heat oven to 425 degrees. Spray 12-cup muffin tin with vegetable oil spray.

2. FOR THE TOPPING: Process flour, brown sugar, granulated sugar, softened butter, and salt in food processor until mixture resembles coarse sand, 4 to 5 pulses. Add pecans and process until pecans are coarsely chopped, about 4 pulses. Transfer to small bowl; set aside.

3. FOR THE MUFFINS: Whisk flour, baking powder, and ¾ teaspoon salt together in bowl; set aside.

4. Process toasted pecans and granulated sugar until mixture resembles coarse sand, 10 to 15 seconds. Transfer to large bowl and whisk in eggs, melted butter, and milk until combined. Whisk flour mixture into egg mixture until just

FREEZING FRESH CRANBERRIES

You can't always find frozen cranberries in the freezer case, so when they're available fresh in the fall (the cranberry harvest happens just after Labor day), buy a few extra bags and store them in the freezer so you can enjoy these muffins and other baked goods relying on cranberries any time of year.

moistened and no streaks of flour remain. Set batter aside for 30 minutes to thicken.

5. Pulse cranberries, remaining ¼ teaspoon salt, and confectioners' sugar in food processor until very coarsely chopped, 4 to 5 pulses. Using rubber spatula, fold cranberries into batter. Using ice cream scoop or large spoon, divide batter evenly among prepared muffin cups (batter should completely fill cups and mound slightly). Evenly sprinkle streusel topping over muffins, gently pressing into batter to adhere.

6. Bake until toothpick inserted in center of muffin comes out clean, 17 to 18 minutes, rotating muffin tin halfway through baking. Let muffins cool in tin for 10 minutes, then transfer to wire rack and let cool for 10 minutes before serving.

Corn Muffins

✓ WHY THIS RECIPE WORKS

A corn muffin shouldn't be as sweet and fluffy as a cupcake, nor should it be dense and "corny" like cornbread. It should taste like corn, but not overpoweringly, and should be moist with a tender crumb and a crunchy top. Our mission was to come up with a recipe that struck just the right balance in both texture and flavor.

USE STONE-GROUND CORNMEAL Degerminated cornmeal just doesn't have enough corn flavor for our muffins. A fine-ground, whole-grain meal provides better flavor and texture.

CHOOSE THREE TYPES OF DAIRY Butter, sour cream, and milk provide the moisture, fat (for richness), and acidity (for its tenderizing effect) that we wanted in our muffin.

EMPLOY QUICK-BREAD METHOD FOR BEST CRUMB We tried mixing together our muffin batter with both the quick-bread and creaming methods; not only is the quick-bread method much easier, but it also results in less airy, cakey muffins.

OVEN TEMPERATURE MATTERS We tested oven temperatures from 325 to 425 degrees and found that 400 degrees delivers the crunchy, crispy, golden crust we were looking for.

CORN MUFFINS
MAKES 12 MUFFINS

We prefer stone-ground cornmeal because it has a full flavor. Serve with jam or honey.

2	cups (10 ounces) all-purpose flour
1	cup (5 ounces) stone-ground cornmeal
1½	teaspoons baking powder
1	teaspoon baking soda
½	teaspoon salt
2	large eggs
¾	cup (5¼ ounces) sugar
8	tablespoons unsalted butter, melted and cooled
¾	cup sour cream
½	cup whole milk

1. Adjust oven rack to middle position and heat oven to 400 degrees. Spray 12-cup muffin tin with vegetable oil spray.

2. Whisk flour, cornmeal, baking powder, baking soda, and salt together in medium bowl. Whisk eggs in second medium bowl until well combined and light-colored, about 20 seconds. Add sugar to eggs and whisk vigorously until thick and homogeneous, about 30 seconds. Add melted butter in 3 additions,

whisking to combine after each addition. Add 6 tablespoons sour cream and ¼ cup milk and whisk to combine, then whisk in remaining 6 tablespoons sour cream and remaining ¼ cup milk until combined.

3. Add wet ingredients to dry ingredients and mix gently with rubber spatula until batter is just combined and evenly moistened (do not overmix). Using ice cream scoop or large spoon, divide batter evenly among prepared muffin cups, dropping batter to form mounds (do not level or flatten batter).

4. Bake until muffins are light golden brown and toothpick inserted in center of muffin comes out clean, about 18 minutes, rotating muffin tin halfway through baking. Let muffins cool in muffin tin for 5 minutes, then transfer to wire rack, let cool 5 minutes longer, and serve warm.

CORN AND APRICOT MUFFINS WITH ORANGE ESSENCE

While our regular corn muffins can be served with jam or honey, these bright fruit-filled muffins taste just right on their own.

TOPPING

⅔ cup granulated sugar
1½ teaspoons grated orange zest

MUFFINS

1½ cups (8 ounces) dried apricots
½ teaspoon grated orange zest plus ⅔ cup juice (2 oranges)
2 cups (10 ounces) all-purpose flour
1 cup (5 ounces) stone-ground cornmeal
1½ teaspoons baking powder
1 teaspoon baking soda
½ teaspoon salt
2 large eggs
½ cup (3½ ounces) granulated sugar
¼ cup packed (1¾ ounces) dark brown sugar
8 tablespoons unsalted butter, melted and cooled
¾ cup sour cream
½ cup whole milk

1. Adjust oven rack to middle position and heat oven to 400 degrees. Spray 12-cup muffin tin with vegetable oil spray.

2. FOR THE TOPPING: In food processor, process sugar and orange zest until pale orange, about 10 seconds. Transfer to small bowl and set aside.

3. FOR THE MUFFINS: Pulse apricots in food processor until chopped fine, about 10 pulses. Transfer to medium bowl, add orange juice, cover, and microwave until simmering, about 1 minute. Let apricots stand, covered, until softened and plump, about 5 minutes. Strain apricots; discard juice.

4. Whisk flour, cornmeal, baking powder, baking soda, and salt together in medium bowl. Whisk eggs in second medium bowl until well combined and light-colored, about 20 seconds. Add granulated sugar and brown sugar to eggs and whisk vigorously until thick and homogeneous, about 30 seconds. Add melted butter in 3 additions, whisking to combine after each addition. Add 6 tablespoons sour cream and ¼ cup milk and whisk to combine, then whisk in remaining 6 tablespoons sour cream and remaining ¼ cup milk until combined. Stir in orange zest and strained apricots.

5. Add wet ingredients to dry ingredients and mix gently with rubber spatula until batter is just combined and evenly moistened (do not overmix). Using ice cream scoop or large spoon, divide batter evenly among prepared muffin cups, dropping batter to form mounds (do not level or flatten batter). Sprinkle each muffin with orange-sugar topping.

6. Bake until muffins are light golden brown and toothpick inserted in center of muffin comes out clean, about 18 minutes, rotating muffin tin halfway through baking. Let muffins cool in tin for 10 minutes; serve warm.

THE BEST CORNMEAL FOR MUFFINS

To find our favorite cornmeal, we made corn muffins with three different brands; we were surprised to discover how much the flavor and grind can vary among different brands. Some muffins had a barely perceptible corn flavor and a dusty texture, while others had a clean, pure flavor and gritty bite.

Our winning whole-grain cornmeal, **Whole-Grain Arrowhead Mills Cornmeal,** had a texture resembling slightly damp, fine sand. It made muffins with deep corn flavor and a delicate crumb. The second whole-grain cornmeal produced great flavor, but the texture was coarser (akin to kosher salt), making muffins that were too coarse. The degerminated cornmeal had a fine texture (similar to table salt) but made muffins that were bland and dry.

Our conclusion? For the best corn muffins, look for more finely ground whole-grain cornmeal. Degerminated cornmeal doesn't supply enough flavor, and if the cornmeal is ground too coarsely, your muffins will be too heavy.

For Rounds

1. Pat dough on lightly floured counter into ¾-inch-thick circle.

2. Punch out dough rounds with biscuit cutter. Push together remaining pieces of dough, pat into ¾-inch-thick round, and punch out several more dough rounds. Discard remaining scraps.

For Wedges

1. Press dough into 8-inch cake pan, then turn dough out onto lightly floured counter.

2. With sharp knife or bench scraper, cut dough into 8 wedges.

Quick and Easy Cream Biscuits

✓ WHY THIS RECIPE WORKS

We wanted a quick biscuit (no cutting butter into flour) that came together quickly and easily but still boasted rich flavor and a light and tender crumb. Surprisingly, we found a little kneading went a long way toward a high and fluffy biscuit.

REPLACE THE BUTTER WITH CREAM We tried various forms of dairy including yogurt, sour cream, and a combination of milk and butter. But nothing came close to heavy cream, which contains all the richness of butter, but is far easier to incorporate into the dough, since it requires just a stir.

KNEAD THE DOUGH SLIGHTLY Most biscuit recipes warn against overhandling the dough. Kneading the dough encourages the formation of gluten, a protein that gives baked products structure but when overdeveloped can also make them tough. But because cream biscuits are less sturdy than those made with butter and become soft and "melt" during baking, a little kneading can do them some good. We found that kneading the dough slightly gives the dough structure so the biscuits bake up higher and fluffier than dough that has not been kneaded.

PAT AND STAMP OR CUT INTO WEDGES You can cut the biscuit dough into rounds using a traditional biscuit cutter or pat the dough into a cake pan to form a circle, then simply cut it into wedges.

BAKE THE BISCUITS IMMEDIATELY Shaped biscuits that sit out before baking spread in the oven, resulting in biscuits with bottoms that are too wide and tops that are too narrow. For evenly risen biscuits, we bake them right away.

QUICK AND EASY CREAM BISCUITS
MAKES 8 BISCUITS

These biscuits come together in a flash.

- 2 cups (10 ounces) all-purpose flour
- 2 teaspoons sugar
- 2 teaspoons baking powder
- ½ teaspoon salt
- 1½ cups heavy cream

1. Adjust oven rack to upper-middle position and heat oven to 450 degrees. Line baking sheet with parchment paper.

2. Whisk flour, sugar, baking powder, and salt together in medium bowl. Stir in cream with wooden spoon until dough forms, about 30 seconds. Turn dough out onto lightly floured counter and gather into ball. Knead dough briefly until smooth, about 30 seconds.

3. FOR ROUNDS: Shape dough into ¾-inch-thick circle and cut dough into 8 rounds with 2½-inch biscuit cutter.

4. FOR WEDGES: Press dough into 8-inch cake pan, turn out onto lightly floured counter and use sharp knife or bench scraper to cut dough into 8 wedges. Place rounds or wedges on prepared sheet. Bake until golden brown, about 15 minutes, rotating sheet halfway through baking. Serve.

QUICK AND EASY CREAM BISCUITS WITH CHEDDAR CHEESE

Stir 2 ounces sharp cheddar cheese, cut into ¼-inch pieces, into flour along with sugar, baking powder, and salt. Increase baking time to 18 minutes.

QUICK AND EASY CREAM BISCUITS WITH CRYSTALLIZED GINGER

Add 3 tablespoons minced crystallized ginger to flour along with sugar, baking powder, and salt. Before baking, brush tops of biscuits with 1 tablespoon heavy cream and sprinkle with 1 tablespoon sugar.

QUICK AND EASY CREAM BISCUITS WITH FRESH HERBS

Any herb or combination of herbs will work here.

Whisk 2 tablespoons minced fresh herbs into flour along with sugar, baking powder, and salt.

Tall and Fluffy Buttermilk Biscuits

✔ WHY THIS RECIPE WORKS

We wanted a rustic "mile-high" buttermilk biscuit recipe that would produce extra-fluffy, moist, tender rolls with crisp, golden-brown tops. We found a wet dough was one strategy that helped us meet our goal.

DOUBLE UP ON THE BUTTERMILK We found that a very wet dough, made by using twice as much buttermilk for the same volume of flour, yielded a fluffy, high rise. It turns out that the extra moisture in the dough converts to steam in the oven, which causes the biscuits to swell to great heights.

CHOOSE ALL-PURPOSE FLOUR Tasters assumed they'd prefer biscuits made with cake flour, which is lower in protein and as a result, yields a tender crumb. Wrong. They actually preferred the biscuits made with all-purpose flour. These biscuits had more flavor, the crust was crispier, and the crumb was moist and light without being cakey or gummy.

SCOOP AND BAKE To make forming the biscuits easier, we rely on a greased measuring cup to scoop the dough onto a flour-lined baking sheet, so the balls of dough can be rolled in the flour to help them keep their shape. A brush of melted butter over the

biscuits before they go into the oven lends them more flavor and encourages a browned, crisp crust.

USE TWO OVEN TEMPERATURES Baking the biscuits at 475 degrees yielded a good rise, but 500 was even better. The problem was that the tops browned too quickly. We found that by starting the oven at 500 degrees and turning the heat down to 450 after 15 minutes, we could maximize the rise and turn out perfectly baked golden-brown biscuits.

GIVE 'EM A REST Most biscuits are best hot from the oven, but our high-moisture biscuits need a few minutes' rest to allow some of the steam to escape.

TALL AND FLUFFY BUTTERMILK BISCUITS

MAKES 12 BISCUITS

We prefer to use low-fat buttermilk in these biscuits, but nonfat buttermilk will work as well (though the biscuits will be a little lighter in texture and flavor).

2 cups (10 ounces) all-purpose flour, plus 1 cup (5 ounces) all-purpose flour, distributed in rimmed baking sheet

SHAPING TALL AND FLUFFY BUTTERMILK BISCUITS

1. Using greased ¼-cup measure, scoop 12 level portions of dough onto floured baking sheet. Lightly dust top of each biscuit with flour.

2. With floured hands, gently pick up piece of dough, coating outside with flour, shaping it into ball, and shaking off excess flour.

3. Place 9 biscuits snugly around perimeter of cake pan, then arrange last 3 in center.

1	tablespoon baking powder
1	tablespoon sugar
1	teaspoon salt
½	teaspoon baking soda
4	tablespoons unsalted butter, cut into ¼-inch pieces and chilled plus 2 tablespoons unsalted butter, melted for brushing biscuits
1½	cups buttermilk, chilled

1. Adjust oven rack to middle position and heat oven to 500 degrees. Grease 9-inch round cake pan; set aside.

2. In food processor, pulse flour, baking powder, sugar, salt, and baking soda to combine, about 6 pulses. Scatter chilled butter evenly over dry ingredients; pulse until mixture resembles pebbly, coarse cornmeal, 8 to 10 pulses. Transfer mixture to medium bowl. Add buttermilk to dry ingredients and stir with rubber spatula until just incorporated (dough will be very wet and slightly lumpy).

3. Generously spray inside and outside of ¼ cup dry measuring cup. Working quickly, scoop level amount of dough; drop dough from measuring cup into flour on baking sheet (if dough sticks to cup, use small spoon to pull it free). Repeat with remaining dough, forming 12 evenly sized mounds. Dust tops of each piece of dough with flour from baking sheet. With floured hands, gently pick up piece of dough and coat with flour; gently shape dough into rough ball, shake off excess flour, and place in prepared cake pan. Repeat with remaining dough, arranging 9 rounds around perimeter of cake pan and 3 in center. Brush rounds with melted butter, taking care not to flatten them. Bake 5 minutes, then reduce oven temperature to 450 degrees; continue to bake until biscuits are deep golden brown, about 15 minutes. Let cool in pan 2 minutes, then invert biscuits onto clean dish towel; turn biscuits right side up and break apart. Let cool 5 minutes longer and serve.

FREEZING BUTTERMILK

Buttermilk is typically sold in quarts, which can be a pain if you're only using a small amount. Here's an easy way to freeze buttermilk in ready-to-use portions.

1. Place small paper cups on tray and fill each with ½ cup buttermilk.

2. Place tray in freezer.

3. Once buttermilk has frozen, wrap each cup with plastic wrap and store them in large zipper-lock bag. Defrost amount you need in refrigerator before you bake.

Easy Buttermilk Drop Biscuits

✔ WHY THIS RECIPE WORKS

We wanted a drop biscuit recipe that would offer a no-nonsense alternative to traditional rolled biscuits, with the same tenderness and buttery flavor. Too many drop biscuits are dense, gummy, and doughy or lean and dry; we wanted a biscuit that could be easily broken apart and eaten piece by buttery piece.

CHOOSE ALL-PURPOSE FLOUR Super-soft cake or pastry flours don't work here. Since the dough is not kneaded or rolled, the biscuits need a little gluten for structure. We use all-purpose; it has more protein than softer flours, so it can develop more gluten.

PICK BUTTERMILK Buttermilk provides much-needed flavor and it also allows us to add baking soda (along with baking powder). The baking soda reacts with the acid in the buttermilk and gives the biscuits a crispier, browner exterior and fluffier middle.

CLUMP THE BUTTER Usually, properly combining melted butter with buttermilk (or any liquid) requires that both ingredients be at just the right temperature; if they aren't, the melted butter clumps in the cold buttermilk. This may look like a mistake, but it actually mimics the chunks of fat in a

A greased ¼ cup measure is the perfect tool to scoop and drop our biscuit dough.

BETTER FLOUR DUSTER

When rolling out biscuits, pie pastry, or pizza dough, avoid covering your counter with drifts of wasted flour. Instead, fill a clean, dry cheese shaker (like the kind at a pizza parlor) with flour and sprinkle just what you need.

classic biscuit recipe. The result is a surprisingly better biscuit, slightly higher and with better texture. It turns out that the water in the lumps of butter turn to steam in the oven, helping create additional height.

EASY BUTTERMILK DROP BISCUITS
MAKES 12 BISCUITS

A ¼-cup portion scoop can be used to portion the batter. To refresh day-old biscuits, heat them in a 300-degree oven for 10 minutes.

    2   cups (10 ounces) all-purpose flour
    2   teaspoons baking powder
    ½   teaspoon baking soda
    1   teaspoon sugar
    ¾   teaspoon salt
    1   cup buttermilk, chilled
    8   tablespoons unsalted butter, melted
        and cooled slightly, plus 2 tablespoons
        melted

1. Adjust oven rack to middle position and heat oven to 475 degrees. Line rimmed baking sheet with parchment paper. Whisk flour, baking powder, baking soda, sugar, and salt in large bowl. Combine buttermilk and 8 tablespoons melted butter in medium bowl, stirring until butter forms small clumps.

2. Add buttermilk mixture to flour mixture and stir with rubber spatula until just incorporated and batter pulls away from sides of bowl. Using greased ¼-cup dry measure and working quickly, scoop level amount of batter and drop onto prepared sheet (biscuits should measure about 2¼ inches in diameter and 1¼ inches high). Repeat with remaining batter, spacing biscuits about 1½ inches apart. Bake until tops are golden brown and crisp, 12 to 14 minutes, rotating sheet halfway through baking.

3. Brush biscuit tops with remaining 2 tablespoons melted butter. Transfer sheet to wire rack and let cool for 5 minutes before serving.

Flaky Buttermilk Biscuits

✔ WHY THIS RECIPE WORKS
Truly flaky biscuits have become scarce, while their down-market imitators (think supermarket "tube" biscuits) are alarmingly common. We wanted to achieve a really flaky—not fluffy—biscuit, with a golden, crisp crust surrounding striated layers of tender, buttery dough. While ingredients (lard versus butter, buttermilk versus milk, and so on) influence texture and flavor, we discovered that the secret to the fluffy/flaky distinction is how the ingredients are handled: Flaky butter equals flaky biscuits.

MAKE LARGE FLAKES When we make pie crusts, we usually cut the butter into cubes, and then put them in the food processor along with the other dry ingredients, turning the butter into small pebbles. The pebble shape is ideal for the small, irregular flakes in a pie crust but not for the pronounced layers we need in a biscuit. Instead, we get "flaky" butter by abandoning the food processor, slicing the butter into very thin squares, and—instead of cutting the squares into the flour with a pastry blender, pressing each piece into the flour with our fingers, breaking them into flat, flaky pieces about the size of a nickel.

ADD SHORTENING Swapping out some butter for some shortening has a tenderizing effect. Why? For one, butter contains 16 to 18 percent water while shortening is all fat. The use of shortening, then, reduces the level of hydration in the biscuits. Less hydration means less gluten formation and a more tender biscuit.

USE TWO LEAVENERS We use both baking soda and baking powder to leaven our biscuits. The baking soda reacts with the acidic buttermilk in the dough, producing carbon dioxide and helping the biscuits to rise immediately. The baking powder adds its leavening power as soon as the biscuits hit the heat of the oven.

CHILL WELL Don't let the flakes of butter melt. If they soften and mix with the flour during the series of folds, the result will be biscuits that are short and crumbly instead of crisp and flaky. We don't have the luxury of resting our dough in the refrigerator to firm up the butter because the baking soda in the dough begins reacting the moment the liquid and dry ingredients come together. Chilling the mixing bowl and all of the ingredients (instead of just the butter) before mixing buys us the time needed to complete all of the necessary turns with the cold butter intact.

CREATE A NONSTICK COUNTER Biscuit dough is a Catch-22. It needs to be wet—a dry dough makes a dry biscuit—but it also needs to be rollable. We don't want to scatter too much flour on the surface of the counter, because then the wet dough will absorb the extra flour and no longer be wet. The solution? We give the counter a quick blast from a can of vegetable oil spray. It helps the flour adhere more evenly to the counter, letting our dough release easily, and without much flour sticking to it.

PRESS, DON'T TWIST To cut the biscuits, flour your biscuit cutter, dipping it back into the flour after each cut. We invert the biscuits onto the baking sheet with the flat underside on top so that they will rise more evenly. Do not twist the biscuit cutter as you cut the dough. Twisting can seal the edges of the biscuit and prevent it from rising. Press gently.

FLAKY BUTTERMILK BISCUITS
MAKES 12 BISCUITS

The dough is a bit sticky when it comes together and during the first set of turns. Note that you will use up to 1 cup of flour for dusting the counter, dough, and rolling pin to prevent sticking. Be careful not to incorporate large pockets of flour into the dough when folding it over. When cutting the biscuits, press down with firm, even pressure; do not twist the cutter.

2½	cups (12½ ounces) all-purpose flour
1	tablespoon baking powder
½	teaspoon baking soda
1	teaspoon salt
2	tablespoons vegetable shortening, chilled and cut into ½-inch chunks
8	tablespoons unsalted butter, chilled, lightly floured, and cut into ⅛-inch slices, plus 2 tablespoons melted and cooled
1¼	cups buttermilk, chilled

1. Adjust oven rack to lower-middle position and heat oven to 450 degrees. Whisk flour, baking powder, baking soda, and salt in large bowl.

2. Add shortening to flour mixture; break up chunks with your fingertips until only small, pea-size pieces remain. Working with a few chilled butter slices at a time, drop butter slices into flour mixture and toss to coat. Pick up each slice of butter and press between well-floured fingertips into flat, nickel-size pieces. Repeat until all butter is incorporated, then toss to combine. Freeze mixture (in bowl) until chilled, about 15 minutes, or refrigerate for about 30 minutes.

3. Spray 24-inch-square area of counter with vegetable oil spray; spread spray evenly across surface with clean dish towel or paper towel. Sprinkle ⅓ cup flour across sprayed area, then gently spread flour across counter with palm to form thin, even coating. Add 1 cup plus 2 tablespoons buttermilk to flour mixture. Stir briskly with fork until

GAUGING WHEN BUTTERMILK HAS GONE BAD

It's easy enough to know when regular milk has gone bad—it will simply smell bad. But what about buttermilk? Our experience has shown that refrigerated buttermilk won't turn truly bad (signified by the growth of blue-green mold) until at least three weeks after opening. That it can last this long is not surprising, since buttermilk is high in lactic acid, which is hostile to the growth of harmful bacteria. That said, we wondered if the flavor of buttermilk changes the longer it's stored.

To find out, we held a series of tastings, comparing pancakes made with freshly opened buttermilk with those made with buttermilk that had been refrigerated for one week, two weeks, and three weeks. We found that as time went on, the pancakes tasted bland.

Here's why: The bacteria in buttermilk produce lactic acid and diacetyl, a flavor compound that gives buttermilk its characteristic buttery aroma and taste (diacetyl is also the dominant flavor compound in butter). As time passes, the buttermilk continues to ferment and becomes more acidic. The abundance of acid kills off virtually all of the bacteria that produce the buttery-tasting diacetyl. So three-week-old buttermilk will retain its tartness (from lactic acid) but lose much of its signature buttery taste, giving it less dimension. The good news is that there is a way to prolong the shelf life and preserve the flavor of buttermilk: Freeze it. See our tip on page 53 for freezing it in ready-to-use portions.

1. Cut butter (coated in flour to prevent sticking) into ⅛-inch-thick slices.

2. Pinch butter slices between well-floured fingertips into flat, nickel-size pieces.

3. With bench scraper or metal spatula, fold dough into thirds (like business letter).

4. Fold dough into thirds again, rotate 90 degrees, roll out, and repeat process.

ball forms and no dry bits of flour are visible, adding remaining 2 tablespoons buttermilk as needed (dough will be sticky and shaggy but should clear sides of bowl). With rubber spatula, transfer dough to center of prepared counter, dust surface lightly with flour, and, with floured hands, bring dough together into cohesive ball.

4. Pat dough into approximate 10-inch square, then roll into 18 by 14-inch rectangle about ¼ inch thick, dusting dough and rolling pin with flour as needed. Use bench scraper or metal spatula to fold dough into thirds, brushing any excess flour from surface of dough. Lift short end of dough and fold in thirds again to form approximate 6 by 4-inch rectangle. Rotate dough 90 degrees, dusting counter underneath with flour, then roll and fold dough again, dusting with flour as needed.

5. Roll dough into 10-inch square about ½ inch thick. Flip dough over and cut nine 3-inch rounds with floured 3-inch biscuit cutter, dipping cutter back into flour after each cut. Carefully invert and transfer rounds to ungreased baking sheet, spacing them 1 inch apart. Gather dough scraps into ball and roll and fold once or twice until scraps form smooth dough. Roll dough into ½-inch-thick round and cut 3 more 3-inch rounds and transfer to sheet. Discard excess dough.

6. Brush biscuit tops with melted butter. Bake, without opening oven door, until tops are golden brown and crisp, 15 to 17 minutes. Let cool on sheet for 5 to 10 minutes before serving.

FLAKY BUTTERMILK BISCUITS WITH PARMESAN

Add ¼ cup finely grated Parmesan cheese, ¼ teaspoon pepper, and ⅛ teaspoon cayenne pepper to flour mixture in step 1. Sprinkle dough rounds with another ¼ cup finely grated Parmesan after brushing with melted butter in step 6.

Blueberry Scones

✔ WHY THIS RECIPE WORKS

For our ultimate blueberry scone recipe, we wanted to bring together the sweetness of a coffeehouse confection, the moist freshness of a muffin, the richness of clotted cream and jam, and the super-flaky crumb of a good biscuit. Taking a hint from puff pastry was one strategy to achieving an puffed, tender scone.

FOLD THE DOUGH In puff pastry, the power of steam is used to separate super-thin layers of dough into striated flakes. In a standard puff pastry recipe, a piece of dough will be turned, rolled, and folded about five times. With each fold, the number of layers of butter and dough increases exponentially. Upon baking, steam forces the layers apart and then escapes, causing the dough to puff up and crisp. We found that adding a few quick folds to our recipe allows the scones to gently rise and puff.

GRATE THE BUTTER A good light pastry depends on distinct pieces of butter distributed throughout the dough that melt during baking and leave behind pockets of air. For this to happen, the butter needs to be as cold and solid as possible until baking. We find that freezing sticks of butter and grating them on the large holes of a box grater works best. We start with two sticks of butter, but then, using the wrapper to hold the frozen butter, grate only 4 tablespoons from each.

GET THE FLAVOR RIGHT Starting with traditional scone recipes, we increase the amounts of sugar and butter to add sweetness and richness; a combination of whole milk and sour cream lends more richness as well as tang.

ADD BLUEBERRIES Adding the blueberries to the dry ingredients means they get mashed when we mix the dough, but when we add them to the already-mixed dough, they ruin our pockets of butter. The solution is pressing the berries into the dough, rolling the dough into a log, then pressing the log into a rectangle and cutting the scones. You can use fresh or frozen berries.

CREATE A CRISP TOP We brush the tops of the scones with melted butter, and sprinkle them with sugar, before baking to help form a crisp top.

BLUEBERRY SCONES
MAKES 8 SCONES

It is important to work the dough as little as possible—work quickly and knead and fold the dough only the number of times called for or else the scones will turn out tough, rather than tender. The butter should be frozen solid before grating. In hot or humid environments, chill the flour mixture and mixing bowls before use. While this recipe calls for two whole sticks of butter, only 10 tablespoons are actually used (see step 1). If fresh berries are unavailable, an equal amount of frozen berries, not thawed, can be substituted. An equal amount of raspberries, blackberries, or strawberries can be used in place of the blueberries. Cut larger berries into ¼- to ½-inch pieces before incorporating. Serve with Homemade Clotted Cream (recipe follows), if desired.

16	tablespoons unsalted butter, each stick frozen
7½	ounces (1½ cups) blueberries
½	cup whole milk
½	cup sour cream
2	cups (10 ounces) all-purpose flour
½	cup (3½ ounces) plus 1 tablespoon sugar

2	teaspoons baking powder
¼	teaspoon baking soda
½	teaspoon salt
1	teaspoon grated lemon zest

1. Adjust oven rack to middle position and heat oven to 425 degrees. Line baking sheet with parchment paper. Remove half of wrapper from each stick of frozen butter. Grate unwrapped ends (half of each stick) on large holes of box grater (you should grate total of 8 tablespoons). Place grated butter in freezer until needed. Melt 2 tablespoons of remaining ungrated butter and set aside. Save remaining 6 tablespoons butter for another use. Place blueberries in freezer until needed.

2. Whisk milk and sour cream together in medium bowl; refrigerate until needed. Whisk flour, ½ cup sugar, baking powder, baking soda, salt, and lemon zest in medium bowl. Add frozen grated butter to flour mixture and toss with your fingers until butter is thoroughly coated.

3. Add milk mixture to flour mixture and fold with rubber spatula until just combined. Using spatula, transfer dough to liberally floured counter. Dust surface of dough with flour and with floured hands knead dough 6 to 8 times, until it just holds together in ragged ball, adding flour as needed to prevent sticking.

4. Roll dough into approximate 12-inch square. Fold dough into thirds like business letter, using bench scraper or metal spatula to release dough if it sticks to counter. Lift short ends of dough and fold into thirds again to form approximate 4-inch square. Transfer dough to plate lightly dusted with flour and chill in freezer 5 minutes.

5. Transfer dough to floured counter and roll into approximate 12-inch square again. Sprinkle blueberries evenly over surface of dough, then press down so they are slightly embedded in dough. Using bench scraper or metal spatula, loosen dough from counter. Roll dough into cylinder, pressing to form tight log. Arrange log seam side down

FOLDING AND SHAPING BLUEBERRY SCONES

1. Fold dough into thirds (like business letter).

2. Fold in ends of dough to form 4-inch square. Chill dough.

3. Reroll dough into 12-inch square. Press berries into dough. Roll dough into jelly roll–like log to incorporate blueberries.

4. Lay log seam side down and press into even 12 by 4-inch rectangle.

5. Cut dough into 8 triangular pieces.

Recipes for scones sometimes provide a make-ahead option that involves refrigerating the dough overnight so it can simply be shaped and then popped into the oven the next day. But now we've found that resting the dough overnight has another benefit: It makes for more symmetrical and attractive pastries.

Rested dough is far easier to shape cleanly than unrefrigerated dough is, and it bakes up noticeably taller, smoother, and with crispier edges. The explanation is simple: As with other doughs, including pizza dough, resting lets scone dough's gluten relax completely, so that it doesn't snap back during shaping or baking. Does this mean that from now on we'll always rest our scone dough? Not necessarily. But it's nice to know that when we do, our scones will only improve.

and press into 12 by 4-inch rectangle. Using sharp, floured knife, cut rectangle crosswise into 4 equal rectangles. Cut each rectangle diagonally to form 2 triangles and transfer to prepared baking sheet.

6. Brush tops with melted butter and sprinkle with remaining 1 tablespoon sugar. Bake until tops and bottoms are golden brown, 18 to 25 minutes, rotating sheet halfway through baking. Transfer to wire rack and let cool for at least 10 minutes before serving.

TO MAKE AHEAD: After placing scones on baking sheet in step 5, either refrigerate them overnight or freeze for up to 1 month. When ready to bake, for refrigerated scones, heat oven to 425 degrees and follow directions in step 6. For frozen scones, do not thaw, heat oven to 375 degrees and follow directions in step 6, extending cooking time to 25 to 30 minutes.

HOMEMADE CLOTTED CREAM
MAKES 2 CUPS

Ultrapasteurized heavy cream can be substituted but the resulting cream will be not as flavorful and tangy. This recipe can be halved or doubled as needed.

- 1½ cups pasteurized (not ultrapasteurized) heavy cream
- ½ cup buttermilk

Combine cream and buttermilk in jar or measuring cup. Stir, cover, and let stand at room temperature until mixture has thickened to the consistency of softly whipped cream, 12 to 24 hours. Refrigerate; cream will continue to thicken as it chills. (Clotted cream can be refrigerated for up to 10 days.)

Classic Cream Scones

✓ WHY THIS RECIPE WORKS
Traditional British scones seem to be a rarity in the U.S. They are essentially fluffy biscuits. These scones should be sweet, but not too sweet, so that they can be enjoyed with jam and perhaps clotted cream.

GO ALL-PURPOSE For a light tender texture, we tried cake flour, but it made gummy scones. All-purpose flour, on the other hand, gives us light, feathery scones.

REIN IN THE SUGAR A modest amount of sugar keeps the sweetness level in check and there was no question we would rely on butter over shortening for best flavor. Heavy cream gives our scones a rich, not-too-dry character.

PULL OUT YOUR FOOD PROCESSOR A food processor makes quick work of incorporating the butter into the flour; we stir in the cream by hand and then lightly knead the dough before cutting it into wedges.

CLASSIC CREAM SCONES
MAKES 8

Resist the urge to eat the scones hot out of the oven, as letting them cool for at least 10 minutes firms them up and improves their texture.

- 2 cups (10 ounces) all-purpose flour
- 3 tablespoons sugar
- 1 tablespoon baking powder
- ½ teaspoon salt
- 5 tablespoons unsalted butter, cut into ¼-inch pieces and chilled
- ½ cup dried currants (optional)
- 1 cup heavy cream

1. Adjust oven rack to middle position and heat oven to 450 degrees. Line baking sheet with parchment paper.

KEEPING THE CHILL IN CHILLED PASTRY

Here's a trick for keeping pastry dough—and the butter it contains—as cold as possible as you roll it out, which helps ensure the flakiest biscuits, scones, and pie crusts.

1. Cut sheet of cotton canvas (available at fabric stores) into 16-inch square; launder and dry.

2. Fold canvas, place it in zipper-lock bag, and freeze.

3. When you're ready to use it, unfold canvas and lay it on countertop, sprinkle it with flour, and place dough on top to roll.

2. Pulse flour, sugar, baking powder, and salt together in food processor to combine, about 3 pulses. Scatter butter evenly over top and continue to pulse until mixture resembles coarse meal with some slightly larger pieces of butter, about 12 more pulses. Transfer mixture to large bowl and stir in currants, if using. Stir in cream until dough begins to form, about 30 seconds.

3. Turn dough and any floury bits out onto floured counter and knead until rough, slightly sticky ball forms, 5 to 10 seconds. Pat dough into 9-inch round and cut into 8 wedges.

4. Place wedges on prepared sheet, spacing wedges about 2 inches apart. Bake until tops of scones are lightly golden brown, 12 to 15 minutes, rotating sheet halfway through baking. Transfer baking sheet to wire rack and let cool for at least 10 minutes. Serve warm or at room temperature.

CLASSIC GINGER CREAM SCONES

Substitute ½ cup coarsely chopped crystallized ginger for currants.

CLASSIC CRANBERRY-ORANGE CREAM SCONES

Add 1 teaspoon grated fresh orange zest with butter and substitute ¾ cup dried cranberries for currants.

CLASSIC MAPLE-PECAN CREAM SCONES

Omit sugar and substitute ½ cup coarsely chopped pecans for currants. Whisk 3 tablespoons maple syrup into heavy cream before adding to flour mixture. While scones bake, whisk 6 tablespoons confectioners' sugar and 2 tablespoons maple syrup together in bowl to make glaze. Drizzle glaze over cooled scones before serving.

Oatmeal Scones

✓ WHY THIS RECIPE WORKS

The oatmeal scones served in a typical coffeehouse are so dry and leaden that they seem like a ploy to get people to buy more coffee to wash them down. We wanted rich toasted oat flavor in a tender, flaky, not-too-sweet scone.

CHOOSE THE RIGHT OATS AND TOAST Whole rolled oats and quick oats perform better than instant or steel-cut oats, and toasting the oats brings out their nutty flavor.

EMBRACE DAIRY AND EGG Our recipe includes plenty of butter—more than a stick. Cutting the cold butter into the flour, instead of using melted butter, gives the scones a lighter texture. We also include a mixture of milk and heavy cream, which provides richness without making these scones too heavy. And for ultimate richness, we add an egg.

GET YOUR OVEN HOT A very hot oven makes these scones rise spectacularly and gives them a craggy appearance. A higher baking temperature also means less time in the oven and therefore less time to dry out.

RICH AND TENDER OATMEAL SCONES
MAKES 8 SCONES

Rolled oats will give the scones a deeper oat flavor, but the quick-cooking oats will create a softer texture; either type will work here. Half-and-half is a suitable substitute for the milk and cream combination.

1½ cups (4½ ounces) old-fashioned rolled oats or quick oats
¼ cup whole milk
¼ cup heavy cream

1 large egg

1½ cups (7½ ounces) all-purpose flour

⅓ cup (2⅓ ounces) plus 1 tablespoon sugar

2 teaspoons baking powder

½ teaspoon salt

10 tablespoons unsalted butter, cut into ½-inch cubes and chilled

1. Adjust oven rack to middle position and heat oven to 375 degrees. Spread oats evenly on baking sheet and toast in oven until fragrant and lightly browned, 7 to 9 minutes; let cool on wire rack. Increase oven temperature to 450 degrees. When oats are cooled, measure out 2 tablespoons for dusting counter and set aside. Line second baking sheet with parchment paper.

2. Whisk milk, cream, and egg in large measuring cup until incorporated. Reserve 1 tablespoon in small bowl for glazing and set aside.

3. Pulse flour, ⅓ cup sugar, baking powder, and salt in food processor until combined, about 4 pulses. Scatter butter evenly over dry ingredients and pulse until mixture resembles coarse cornmeal, 12 to 14 pulses. Transfer mixture to medium bowl and stir in cooled oats. Using rubber spatula, fold in liquid ingredients until large clumps form. Mix dough by hand in bowl until dough forms cohesive mass.

4. Dust counter with 1 tablespoon reserved oats, turn dough out onto counter, and dust top with remaining 1 tablespoon reserved oats. Gently pat dough into 7-inch circle about 1 inch thick. Using bench scraper or chef's knife, cut dough into 8 wedges and place on prepared sheet, spacing wedges about 2 inches apart. Brush tops with reserved egg mixture and sprinkle with remaining 1 tablespoon sugar.

Bake until golden brown, 12 to 14 minutes, rotating sheet halfway through baking. Let scones cool on sheet on wire rack for 5 minutes, then transfer to wire rack and let cool to room temperature, about 30 minutes. Serve.

TO MAKE AHEAD: After placing scones on baking sheet in step 4, either refrigerate them overnight or freeze for up to 1 month. When ready to bake, bake as directed. For frozen scones, do not thaw; heat oven to 375 degrees, increasing baking time to 25 to 30 minutes.

CINNAMON-RAISIN OATMEAL SCONES

Add ¼ teaspoon cinnamon to food processor with flour and ½ cup raisins to flour-butter mixture with toasted oats.

GLAZED MAPLE-PECAN OATMEAL SCONES

Toast ½ cup chopped pecans with oats in step 1. Omit sugar and whisk ¼ cup maple syrup into milk mixture. When scones are cool, whisk 3 tablespoons maple syrup and ½ cup confectioners' sugar until combined, then drizzle over scones.

APRICOT-ALMOND OATMEAL SCONES

Reduce oats to 1 cup and toast ½ cup slivered almonds with oats in step 1. Add ½ cup chopped dried apricots to flour-butter mixture with toasted oats and almonds.

OATMEAL SCONES WITH DRIED CHERRIES AND HAZELNUTS

Reduce oats to 1¼ cups and toast ¼ cup chopped hazelnuts with oats in step 1. Stir ½ cup chopped dried tart cherries into flour-butter mixture with toasted oats.

MAKING OATMEAL SCONES

1. Pour liquid ingredients into dry ingredients and combine with rubber spatula. Dough will be very chunky.

2. Gently knead dough in bowl until all dry bits are incorporated and dough forms cohesive mass.

3. Turn out dough onto counter dusted with oats, sprinkle with remaining oats, and gently pat into 7-inch circle.

4. Cut dough into 8 wedges, place on prepared baking sheet, brush with milk-cream mixture, and sprinkle with sugar.

Popovers

✓ WHY THIS RECIPE WORKS

The perfect popover soars to towering heights, but only if you get the baking magic just right. We wanted to create a foolproof recipe that would produce tall popovers with a crisp exterior and custardy interior.

INCREASE THE BATTER Popovers are made with a pancakelike batter of milk, eggs, flour, and melted butter. The most common formulas we found in our research made for skimpy popovers, so our first move was to double the recipe to fill the same 6-cup popover pan.

BUILD STRUCTURE WITH BREAD FLOUR High-protein bread flour yields popovers with the highest rise and crispiest crust. The downside is that bread flour is so sturdy it sometimes sets up too quickly, which impedes rise. Resting the batter for an hour before baking gives the proteins in the flour time to relax and prevents the popovers from setting up too quickly.

GO LOW-FAT FOR A HIGHER RISE We had been using whole milk in our recipes as tradition dictated, but the fat was weighing down our popovers. Low-fat milk fixed the problem. A pinch of salt and sugar helps with flavor.

GIVE 'EM A POKE Popovers will collapse like leaking tires as they cool, so we poke a hole in the top of the popovers toward the end of baking and then again once out of the oven. This slowly releases the steam and keeps the crisp structure intact.

POPOVERS
MAKES 6 POPOVERS

Greasing the pans with shortening ensures the best release, but vegetable oil spray may be substituted; do not use butter. To gauge the popovers' progress without opening the oven door, use the oven light during baking. Bread flour makes for the highest and sturdiest popovers, but an equal amount of all-purpose flour may be substituted.

3   **large eggs**
2   **cups low-fat milk, heated to 110 degrees**
3   **tablespoons unsalted butter, melted and cooled slightly**
2   **cups bread flour**
1   **teaspoon salt**
1   **teaspoon sugar**

1. Adjust oven rack to lower-middle position and heat oven to 450 degrees. Grease 6-cup popover pan with vegetable shortening, then dust lightly with flour. Whisk eggs in medium bowl until light and foamy. Slowly whisk in milk and melted butter until incorporated.

2. Combine flour, salt, and sugar in large bowl. Whisk three-quarters of milk mixture into flour mixture until no lumps remain, then whisk in remaining milk mixture. Transfer batter to large measuring cup, cover with plastic, and let rest at room temperature for 1 hour. (Alternatively, batter can be refrigerated for 1 day. Bring to room temperature before proceeding with recipe.)

3. Whisk batter to recombine, then pour into prepared popover pan (batter will not quite reach top of cups). Bake until just beginning to brown, about 20 minutes. Without opening oven door, decrease oven temperature to 300 degrees and continue to bake until popovers are golden brown all over, 35 to 40 minutes longer. Poke small hole in top of each popover with skewer and continue to bake until deep golden brown, about 10 minutes longer. Transfer popover pan to wire rack. Poke again with skewer and let cool for 2 minutes. Turn popovers out onto wire rack. Serve.

TO MAKE AHEAD: Once popovers have cooled completely, they can be stored at room temperature in zipper-lock bag for 2 days. To serve, adjust oven rack to middle position and heat oven to 400 degrees. Heat popovers on rimmed baking sheet until crisp and heated through, 5 to 8 minutes.

POPOVER PANS

Only tangentially related to muffin tins, popover pans are composed of heavyweight steel cups affixed to one another with thick steel wire. The open design maximizes heat transfer, which is crucial to high-rising popovers. Very few companies manufacture popover pans these days; in fact, most cookware stores carry only one—the **Chicago Metallic 6-Cup Popover Pan**. We found these pans, glazed with a dark nonstick coating, brown popovers well and release them easily. Popover pans typically have six cups.

BAKING POPOVERS IN A MUFFIN TIN

If you don't have a popover pan, you can bake the popovers in a nonstick 12-cup muffin tin—with a sacrifice in stature. To ensure even cooking, fill only the 10 outer cups to ¼ inch from the top (you may have some batter left over). Reduce initial baking time in step 3 to 15 minutes, and reduce secondary baking time to 20 to 25 minutes after oven temperature has been lowered. Poke popovers as directed and continue to bake for another 10 minutes.

STICKY BUNS WITH PECANS

Sweet Rolls, Doughnuts, and Coffee Cakes

Buttermilk Doughnuts

MAKING BUTTERMILK DOUGHNUTS

1. Roll out dough to ½-inch thickness on lightly floured counter and then stamp out rounds as close together as possible. Gather scraps, press them into disk, and repeat rolling and stamping.

2. Slip doughnuts into hot fat, four or five at a time. As doughnuts rise to surface, turn them over with skimmer, slotted spoon, or tongs.

✓ WHY THIS RECIPE WORKS

We wanted great old-fashioned country-style doughnuts that were crunchy on the outside, tender yet sturdy on the inside, laced delicately with the flavor of nutmeg, and as greaseless as fried doughnuts could be.

INCLUDE BUTTERMILK FOR A BETTER BATTER Buttermilk proved superior to regular milk in our doughnuts. The doughnuts made with milk were dense, firm, and less crisp, while the doughnuts made with buttermilk fried up light and tender and boasted a crunchy exterior.

CHOOSE BOTH BAKING POWDER AND BAKING SODA FOR LIFT For our quicker non-yeasted doughnuts, we went with both baking powder and baking soda. Using just one leavener makes for a denser doughnut. And in addition to creating lift, baking soda encourages browning.

ADD AN EXTRA YOLK FOR TENDERNESS Our working recipe relied on two whole eggs. When we added an additional yolk, the dough was moister and the extra fat resulted in a more tender dough.

AVOID VANILLA While we like vanilla in many baked goods, the flavoring overwhelms nutmeg, which is so essential in an old-fashioned doughnut, so it was out.

TAKE CARE WHEN ROLLING AND CUTTING When rolling out the dough, we found that it should be ½ inch thick. Thinner doughs make for doughnuts that are squat, with insufficient height to provide contrast between the exterior and interior. Dough rolled too thick produces bloated cakes with undercooked interiors.

SHORTEN THE FRYING TIME Although some recipes called for cooking times as long as 2½ minutes, we found that the longer the doughnuts cooked, the greasier they got. Cooking for about 50 seconds per side is ideal.

BUTTERMILK DOUGHNUTS
MAKES 15 TO 17 DOUGHNUTS

If you don't have a doughnut cutter, you can improvise with two biscuit cutters: Use a standard-size cutter (about 2½ inches) for cutting out the doughnuts and a smaller one (about 1¼ inches) for cutting out the holes. For a chewier doughnut with a less crisp exterior, add ¼ cup flour. The dough can also be made by hand, using a large bowl with a wooden spoon. Doughnuts rolled from scraps will be a little drier and less crisp than those cut from the first roll. You will need at least a 6-quart Dutch oven for this recipe. These doughnuts are best eaten very warm, as soon out of the pot as possible.

3½	cups (17½ ounces) all-purpose flour
1	cup (7 ounces) sugar
2	teaspoons baking powder
½	teaspoon baking soda
1½	teaspoons ground nutmeg
1	teaspoon salt
¾	cup buttermilk
4	tablespoons unsalted butter, melted and cooled
2	large eggs plus 1 large yolk
6	cups vegetable shortening

1. Line baking sheet or wire rack with paper towels. Using stand mixer fitted with paddle, beat 1 cup flour, sugar, baking powder, baking soda, nutmeg, and salt on low speed to combine.

2. Mix buttermilk, melted butter, and eggs and yolk in 2-cup liquid measuring cup. Add wet ingredients to dry ingredients and beat on medium speed until smooth, about 30 seconds. Decrease speed to low, gradually add remaining 2½ cups flour, and mix until just combined, about 30 seconds. Stir batter once or twice with wooden spoon or rubber spatula to ensure all liquid is incorporated. (Dough will be moist and tacky, a cross between cake batter and cookie dough.)

3. Heat shortening in large Dutch oven over medium-high heat to 375 degrees. Meanwhile, turn out dough onto lightly floured counter. Roll out dough with heavily floured rolling pin to ½-inch thickness. Cut out dough rings with heavily floured 2½- or 3-inch doughnut cutter, reflouring between cuts. Transfer dough rounds to baking sheet or large wire rack. Gather scraps and gently press into disk; repeat rolling and stamping process until all dough is used. (Cut doughnuts can be covered and stored at room temperature for up to 2 hours.)

4. Carefully slip dough rings, four or five at a time, into hot shortening. Turn doughnuts as they rise to surface with tongs, wire skimmer, or slotted spoon, frying doughnuts until golden brown, about 50 seconds per side. Remove doughnuts and drain on prepared baking sheet or wire rack. Repeat frying, returning shortening to temperature between each batch. Serve.

CINNAMON-SUGARED BUTTERMILK DOUGHNUTS

Mix 1 cup sugar with 1½ tablespoons cinnamon in small bowl. Let fried doughnuts cool for about 1 minute, then toss in cinnamon sugar to coat.

SUGARED BUTTERMILK DOUGHNUTS

We found that regular confectioners' sugar broke down into a gummy glaze on the doughnuts, but that Snow White Non-Melting Sugar made a long-lasting coating.

Let fried doughnuts cool for about 1 minute, then toss in 1 cup nonmelting sugar to coat.

Yeasted Doughnuts

✔ WHY THIS RECIPE WORKS

The yeasted doughnuts found in chain shops always seem to look more impressive than they taste, and the flavor always seems to fall short, but it's those killer calories that stop us in our tracks. We set out to develop the ultimate yeasted doughnut and to make every calorie count. What we wanted was a lightly sweetened doughnut that was tender on the inside and lightly crisp on the outside.

CHOOSE ALL-PURPOSE OVER BREAD FLOUR Yeasted doughnuts are simply enriched bread dough, rolled and cut into circles and fried. When we compared bread flour with all-purpose, we found that bread flour makes the doughnut too dense and chewy, almost like a deep-fried bagel. All-purpose flour is the better choice, making a doughnut with a lighter interior.

REIN IN THE SUGAR AND BUTTER Because we wanted the doughnut to complement fillings and glazes, we didn't want the doughnut itself to be excessively sweet. And another factor we took into consideration was browning. Too much sugar could cause the doughnuts to brown too quickly in the hot oil. As a result, we use just a modest amount of sugar. Likewise, too much butter results in an overly rich, greasy doughnut, so we keep our butter to under a stick.

USE A STAND MIXER TO KNEAD Doughnut dough is made with softened butter. Mixing and kneading the dough by hand makes the dough wet and greasy, a result of warm hands melting the butter. A food processor doesn't knead this soft dough properly. The best results are achieved with a stand mixer, which thoroughly kneads the dough while allowing it to remain cool.

STORING USED FRYING OIL

After frying up a batch of doughnuts you might be tempted to store the frying oil for another use, but does how you store the oil matter?

Generally, storing used cooking oil in a cool, dark cupboard is fine for the short term, since exposure to air and light hastens oil's rate of oxidative rancidification and the creation of off-flavors and odors. But for long-term storage (beyond one month), we found that the cooler the storage temperature the better.

To test this theory, we fried chicken in vegetable oil and then divided the oil (strained first) among three containers and stored them in various locations: in a cool, dark cupboard; in the refrigerator; and in the freezer.

Two months later, we sautéed chunks of white bread in each sample and took a taste. Sure enough, the oil from the cupboard had turned fishy and unpleasant and the refrigerated sample only somewhat less so, while the oil kept in the freezer tasted remarkably clean.

Why? Though an absence of light is important, very cold temperatures are most effective at slowing oxidation and the production of peroxides, which are the source of rancid oil's unpleasant taste and smell. That's why storing oil in the super-cold, dark freezer is your best bet for keeping it fresh.

1. Place dough on floured counter and, using rolling pin, roll out to thickness of ½ inch.

2. Cut dough using 2½- or 3-inch doughnut cutter, gathering scraps and rerolling them as necessary.

3. Place rings and holes carefully in hot fat, four or five at a time.

4. Using skimmer, slotted spoon, or tongs, remove doughnuts from hot fat and drain on paper towel–lined baking sheet or wire rack.

YEASTED DOUGHNUTS

MAKES ABOUT 16 DOUGHNUTS AND DOUGHNUT HOLES

If you don't have a doughnut cutter, you can improvise with two biscuit cutters: Use a standard-size cutter (about 2½ inches) for cutting out the doughnuts and a smaller one (about 1¼ inches) for cutting out the holes. Don't try to make this dough by hand or in a food processor; your hands or the metal blade will heat the butter too much and make the dough greasy. These doughnuts are best eaten the day they are made.

3–3¼	cups (15 to 16¼ ounces) all-purpose flour
6	tablespoons (2⅔ ounces) sugar, plus 1 cup for rolling
2¼	teaspoons instant or rapid-rise yeast
½	teaspoon salt
⅔	cup whole milk, room temperature
2	large eggs, lightly beaten
6	tablespoons unsalted butter, cut into 6 pieces, softened but still cool
6	cups vegetable shortening

1. In bowl of stand mixer, whisk together 3 cups flour, 6 tablespoons sugar, yeast, and salt. Fit stand mixer with dough hook, add milk and eggs, and mix on low speed 3 to 4 minutes, or until ball of dough forms.

2. Add butter piece by piece, waiting about 15 seconds after each addition. Continue mixing for about 3 minutes longer, adding remaining flour 1 tablespoon at a time if necessary, until dough forms soft ball.

3. Place dough in lightly oiled medium bowl and cover with plastic wrap. Let dough rise at room temperature until nearly doubled in size, 2 to 2½ hours. Turn dough out onto floured counter and, using rolling pin, roll out to thickness of ½ inch. Cut dough using 2½- or 3-inch doughnut cutter, gathering scraps and rerolling them as necessary. Place doughnut rings and holes on floured baking sheet. Loosely cover with plastic wrap and let rise at room temperature until slightly puffy, 30 to 45 minutes.

4. Meanwhile, heat shortening in large Dutch oven over medium-high heat to 375 degrees. Line baking sheet or wire rack with paper towels. Place rings and holes carefully into hot fat four or five at a time. Fry until golden brown, about 30 seconds per side for holes and 45 to 60 seconds per side for doughnuts, turning doughnuts as they rise to surface with wire skimmer, slotted spoon, or tongs. Remove doughnuts from hot fat and drain on prepared baking sheet or wire rack. Repeat with remaining doughnuts, returning fat to temperature between batches.

5. Let doughnuts cool until cool enough to handle, about 10 minutes. Place remaining 1 cup sugar in medium bowl or pie plate and roll doughnuts in sugar. Serve warm or at room temperature.

VANILLA-GLAZED DOUGHNUTS

Omit 1 cup sugar for rolling. While doughnuts are cooling, whisk together ½ cup half-and-half, 3 cups confectioners' sugar, sifted, and 1 teaspoon vanilla extract in medium bowl until combined. When doughnuts have cooled, dip 1 side of each doughnut into glaze, shake off any excess, and transfer to wire rack to set glaze.

CHOCOLATE-GLAZED DOUGHNUTS

Omit 1 cup sugar for rolling. While doughnuts are cooling, place 4 ounces finely chopped semisweet or bittersweet chocolate in small bowl. Add ½ cup hot half-and-half and whisk together to melt chocolate. Add 2 cups confectioners' sugar, sifted, and whisk until no lumps remain. When doughnuts have cooled, dip 1 side of each doughnut into glaze, shake off any excess, and transfer to wire rack to set glaze.

CINNAMON SUGAR–GLAZED DOUGHNUTS

Mix 1 cup sugar for rolling with 1 tablespoon ground cinnamon in medium bowl or pie plate. In step 5, roll doughnuts in cinnamon sugar to coat.

Quick Cinnamon Buns

✓ WHY THIS RECIPE WORKS

A tender, fluffy bun with a sweet cinnamon filling and rich glaze is a treat no one can turn down. Most recipes, though, require yeast, which makes cinnamon buns time-consuming to make. We wanted a superbly satisfying cinnamon bun we could enjoy in minutes, not hours.

TRADE IN YEASTED BUNS FOR BISCUITS Yeasted buns are out since a yeasted dough would need time to rise. Buttermilk biscuits, however, make sense as a base for cinnamon buns, since they're leavened with quick-acting baking powder and baking soda.

KNEAD JUST A BIT These quick buns benefit from a brief knead that encourages gluten formation and a good rise.

FILL 'ER UP No one likes a cinnamon bun with skimpy filling. We cover our rolled-out dough with a rich, well-seasoned mix of brown and granulated sugars, cinnamon, cloves, and salt; melted butter helps the mixture adhere to the dough.

ASSEMBLE AND BAKE We simply roll up the dough, cut the buns, and place the buns snugly together in a nonstick baking pan to bake. The nonstick pan means that the buns will easily release from the pan. Keeping the buns close together ensures they bake up with soft and tender exteriors—just like an old-fashioned cinnamon bun.

KEEP THE GLAZE SIMPLE A quick, but rich, glaze of confectioners' sugar, buttermilk, and cream cheese makes the perfect crowning touch to our easy cinnamon buns.

QUICK CINNAMON BUNS WITH BUTTERMILK ICING

MAKES 8 BUNS

Melted butter is used in both the filling and the dough and to grease the pan; it's easiest to melt the total amount (8 tablespoons) at once and measure it out as you need it. The finished buns are best eaten warm. For our yeasted cinnamon buns, see page 71.

1 tablespoon unsalted butter, melted

FILLING
¾ cup packed (5¼ ounces) dark brown sugar
¼ cup (1¾ ounces) granulated sugar
2 teaspoons ground cinnamon
⅛ teaspoon ground cloves
⅛ teaspoon salt
1 tablespoon unsalted butter, melted

DOUGH
2½ cups (12½ ounces) all-purpose flour
2 tablespoons granulated sugar
1¼ teaspoons baking powder
½ teaspoon baking soda
½ teaspoon salt
1¼ cups buttermilk
6 tablespoons unsalted butter, melted

ICING
2 tablespoons cream cheese, softened
2 tablespoons buttermilk
1 cup (4 ounces) confectioners' sugar

1. Adjust oven rack to upper-middle position and heat oven to 425 degrees. Butter 9-inch nonstick cake pan. Spray wire rack with vegetable oil spray; set aside.

2. FOR THE FILLING: Combine brown sugar, granulated sugar, cinnamon, cloves, and salt in small bowl. Add melted butter and stir with fork or your fingers until mixture resembles wet sand; set aside.

3. FOR THE DOUGH: Whisk flour, sugar, baking powder, baking soda, and salt in large bowl. Whisk buttermilk and 2 tablespoons melted butter in measuring cup or small bowl. Add wet ingredients to dry ingredients and stir with wooden spoon until liquid is absorbed (dough will look very shaggy), about 30 seconds. Transfer dough to lightly floured counter and knead until just smooth and no longer shaggy.

1. Pat dough into 12 by 9-inch rectangle and brush with melted butter. Sprinkle filling evenly over dough, leaving ½-inch border. Press filling firmly into dough.

2. Using bench scraper or metal spatula, loosen dough from counter. Starting at long side, roll dough, pressing lightly, to form tight cylinder. Pinch seam to seal.

3. Arrange cylinder seam side down and cut into 8 equal pieces. With your hand, slightly flatten each piece of dough to seal open edges and keep filling in place.

4. Place 1 roll in center of prepared pan, then place remaining 7 rolls around perimeter.

4. Pat dough with your hands into 12 by 9-inch rectangle. Brush dough with 2 tablespoons melted butter, then sprinkle evenly with filling, leaving ½-inch border around edges, and press filling firmly into dough to adhere. Using bench scraper or metal spatula, loosen dough from counter. Starting at long side, roll dough, pressing lightly, to form tight cylinder. Pinch seam to seal. Arrange cylinder seam side down and cut into 8 equal pieces. With 1 hand, slightly flatten each piece of dough to seal open edges and keep filling in place. Place 1 roll in center of prepared pan, then place remaining 7 rolls around perimeter of pan. Brush with remaining 2 tablespoons melted butter.

5. Bake until edges are golden brown, 23 to 25 minutes, rotating pan halfway through baking. Using offset metal spatula, loosen buns from pan; without separating, slide buns out of pan onto prepared wire rack. Let cool about 5 minutes before icing.

6. FOR THE ICING: While buns are cooling, line rimmed baking sheet with parchment paper and set rack with buns over baking sheet. Whisk cream cheese and buttermilk together in large bowl until thick and smooth (mixture will look like cottage cheese at first). Sift sugar over and whisk until smooth glaze forms, about 30 seconds. Spoon glaze evenly over buns; serve immediately.

Ultimate Cinnamon Buns

✔ WHY THIS RECIPE WORKS

Sweet, gooey, softball-size cinnamon buns are worth every last calorie. This mammoth breed of cinnamon bun is distinguished from its leaner, more diminutive cousins by its size, yes, but also by the richness of the soft, buttery yeasted dough, the abundance of cinnamon-sugar filling, and the thickness of the sticky cream cheese glaze.

BASE ON BRIOCHE FOR AN ULTRARICH BUN Dough for brioche, an eggy, buttery white sandwich bread, makes the perfect soft and tender base for our buns.

ADD A LITTLE TENDERNESS We had been using all-purpose flour in our dough, but thought swapping in cake flour would make an even more tender dough. But buns made with cake flour came out of the oven heavy and squat. Sometimes we approximate cake flour by cutting all-purpose flour with a little cornstarch. It turns out that adding just a bit less cornstarch to all-purpose flour gives us a tender, soft dough that holds its structure once baked.

USE BROWN SUGAR FOR A RICHER FILLING For a filling with a hint of caramel flavor, we combine a good amount of cinnamon with brown sugar, rather than white sugar. Softened butter helps keep the filling from spilling out as we roll up the dough. Baked together, the butter and cinnamon sugar turn into a rich, gooey filling.

TOP WITH A THICK, RICH GLAZE No bun would be complete without a thick spread of icing. We spread the buns with a tangy glaze of cream cheese, confectioners' sugar, and milk.

ULTIMATE CINNAMON BUNS
MAKES 8 BUNS

For smaller cinnamon buns, cut the dough into 12 pieces in step 3.

DOUGH
¾ cup whole milk, heated to 110 degrees
2¼ teaspoons instant or rapid-rise yeast
3 large eggs, room temperature
4¼–4½ cups (21¼ to 22½ ounces) all-purpose flour
½ cup cornstarch
½ cup (3½ ounces) granulated sugar
1½ teaspoons salt
12 tablespoons unsalted butter, cut into 12 pieces and softened

FILLING
1½ cups packed (10½ ounces) light brown sugar
1½ tablespoons ground cinnamon
¼ teaspoon salt
4 tablespoons unsalted butter, softened

GLAZE
1½ cups (6 ounces) confectioners' sugar
4 ounces cream cheese, softened
1 tablespoon whole milk
1 teaspoon vanilla extract

1. FOR THE DOUGH: Make foil sling for 13 by 9-inch baking pan by folding 2 long sheets of aluminum foil; first sheet should be 13 inches wide and second sheet should be 9 inches wide. Lay sheets of foil in pan perpendicular to each other, with extra foil hanging over edges of pan. Push foil into corners and up sides of pan, smoothing foil flush to pan. Grease foil. Whisk milk and yeast together in liquid measuring cup until yeast dissolves, then whisk in eggs.

2. Adjust oven rack to middle position and place loaf or cake pan on bottom of oven. Using stand mixer fitted with dough hook, mix flour, cornstarch, sugar, and salt on low speed until combined. Add warm milk mixture in steady stream and mix until dough comes together, about 1 minute. Increase speed to medium and add butter, 1 piece at a time, until incorporated. Continue to mix until dough is smooth and comes away from sides of bowl, about 10 minutes (if dough is still wet and sticky, add up to ¼ cup flour, 1 tablespoon at a time, until it releases from bowl). Turn dough out onto counter and knead to form smooth, round ball. Transfer dough to medium greased bowl, cover with plastic wrap, and transfer to middle rack of oven. Pour 3 cups boiling water into loaf pan in oven, close oven door, and let dough rise until doubled in size, about 2 hours.

3. FOR THE FILLING: Combine sugar, cinnamon, and salt in small bowl. Remove dough from oven and turn out onto lightly floured counter. Roll dough into 18-inch square and, leaving ½-inch border around edges, spread butter over dough, then sprinkle evenly with sugar mixture and lightly press sugar mixture into dough. Starting with edge closest to you, roll dough into tight cylinder, pinch lightly to seal seam, and cut into 8 pieces. Transfer pieces, cut side up, to prepared pan. Cover with plastic and let rise in oven until doubled in size, about 1 hour.

4. FOR THE GLAZE: Remove buns and water pan from oven and heat oven to 350 degrees. Whisk all glaze ingredients together in medium bowl until smooth. Remove plastic and bake buns until deep golden brown and filling is melted, 35 to 40 minutes, rotating pan halfway through baking. Transfer to wire rack, top buns with ½ cup glaze, and let cool for 30 minutes. Using foil overhang, lift buns from pan and top with remaining glaze. Serve.

TO MAKE AHEAD: Skip step of letting buns rise in step 3. Place buns in pan, cover with plastic wrap, and refrigerate for up to 1 day. To bake, let sit at room temperature for 1 hour. Remove plastic and proceed with step 4.

Sticky Buns with Pecans

✓ WHY THIS RECIPE WORKS

Sticky buns are often too sweet, too big, too rich, and just too much. We wanted a bun that was neither dense nor bready, with a crumb that was tender and feathery and a gently gooey and chewy glaze.

SOFTEN THE GLAZE WITH CREAM To keep the sticky bun glaze from hardening into a tooth-pulling, taffylike shell, we add a couple of tablespoons of heavy cream, which keeps the glaze supple.

BALANCE BUTTERMILK WITH SWEETNESS We make our dough with a basic mix of flour, yeast, and salt and add buttermilk, which gives the buns a complex flavor and a little acidity that balances the sweetness. Butter and eggs enrich the dough further.

LIGHTEN UP WITH LIGHT BROWN SUGAR Most recipes for cinnamon buns rely on molasses-rich dark brown sugar for both glaze and filling. Dark brown works fine in the filling but it makes for an unappealingly dark (and burnt-looking) glaze. To keep things simple we stick with light brown sugar.

BAKE ON A STONE We found that setting the pan on a baking stone in the oven helps the bottoms of the buns (which will end up on top) bake and brown evenly.

BE PATIENT Rolls turned out of the pan right out of the oven lose most of their glaze to the plate because the glaze is very hot and fluid. Letting the buns rest in the pan for a few minutes allows the glaze to cool down a bit and thicken.

TOAST NUTS TO GUARANTEE CRUNCH We like nuts with our sticky buns but many recipes we tried turned out buns with soggy nuts—mostly because the nuts were incorporated in the filling or under the glaze, where they steamed and lost their crunch. To preserve the crispness of the nuts, we toast them in a lightly sweetened glaze and spoon the mixture over the baked buns.

STICKY BUNS WITH PECANS
MAKES 12 BUNS

Although the ingredient list may look long, note that many ingredients are repeated. If you don't have a baking stone, bake the rolls on an overturned and preheated rimmed baking sheet set on the lowest oven rack.

DOUGH
- 3 large eggs, room temperature
- ¾ cup buttermilk, room temperature
- ¼ cup (1¾ ounces) granulated sugar
- 2¼ teaspoons instant or rapid-rise yeast
- 1¼ teaspoons salt
- 4¼ cups (21¼ ounces) all-purpose flour
- 6 tablespoons unsalted butter, melted and cooled

GLAZE
- 6 tablespoons unsalted butter
- ¾ cup packed (5¼ ounces) light brown sugar
- 3 tablespoons corn syrup
- 2 tablespoons heavy cream
- Pinch salt

FILLING
- ¾ cup packed (5¼ ounces) light brown sugar
- 2 teaspoons ground cinnamon
- ¼ teaspoon ground cloves
- Pinch salt
- 1 tablespoon unsalted butter, melted and cooled

TOPPING
- ¼ cup packed (1¾ ounces) light brown sugar
- 3 tablespoons unsalted butter
- 3 tablespoons light corn syrup

MAKING STICKY BUNS

1. Spread hot glaze in baking pan.

2. Sprinkle dough with filling, leaving ¾-inch border along top edge. If you don't leave border, it will be harder to get dough to stick together when forming cylinder. Roll dough into tight cylinder.

3. Firmly pinch seam to seal.

4. Using serrated knife and gentle sawing motion, cut cylinder into 12 buns.

5. Arrange buns in prepared pan over glaze.

Pinch salt

1   teaspoon vanilla extract

¾   cup pecans, toasted and chopped coarse

1. FOR THE DOUGH: In bowl of stand mixer, whisk eggs to combine; add buttermilk and whisk to combine. Whisk in sugar, yeast, and salt. Add 2 cups flour and melted butter; stir with wooden spoon or rubber spatula until evenly moistened and combined. Fit stand mixer with dough hook, add all but ¼ cup remaining flour, and knead at low speed for 5 minutes. Check consistency of dough (dough should feel soft and moist but not wet and sticky; add more flour, if necessary, 1 tablespoon at a time); knead for 5 minutes longer (dough should clear sides of bowl but stick to bottom). Turn dough onto lightly floured counter; knead by hand for about 1 minute to ensure dough is uniform (dough should not stick to counter; if it does stick, knead in additional flour 1 tablespoon at a time).

2. Transfer dough to large, lightly greased bowl, spray dough lightly with vegetable oil spray, cover bowl, and set in warm, draft-free spot until doubled in volume, 2 to 2½ hours.

3. FOR THE GLAZE: Combine all ingredients in small saucepan and cook over medium heat, whisking occasionally, until butter is melted and mixture is thoroughly combined. Pour mixture into nonstick metal 13 by 9-inch baking pan. Using rubber spatula, spread mixture to cover surface of pan; set aside.

4. FOR THE FILLING: Combine sugar, cinnamon, cloves, and salt in small bowl and mix until thoroughly combined, using your fingers to break up sugar lumps; set aside.

5. Turn dough out onto lightly floured counter. Gently shape dough into rough rectangle with long side nearest you. Lightly flour dough and roll to 16 by 12-inch rectangle.

Brush dough with melted butter, leaving ½-inch border along top edge; brush sides of baking dish with butter remaining on brush. Sprinkle filling mixture over dough, leaving ¾-inch border along top edge; smooth filling in even layer with your hand, then gently press mixture into dough to adhere. Starting at long side, roll dough, pressing lightly, to form tight cylinder. Firmly pinch seam to seal. Very gently stretch to form cylinder of even diameter and 18-inch length, pushing ends in to create even thickness. Using serrated knife and gentle sawing motion, slice cylinder in half, then slice each half in half again to create evenly sized quarters. Slice each quarter evenly into thirds, yielding 12 buns (end pieces may be slightly smaller).

6. Arrange buns cut side down in prepared baking pan, cover, and set in warm, draft-free spot until puffy and pressed against one another, about 1½ hours. Meanwhile, adjust oven rack to lowest position, place baking stone on rack, and heat oven to 350 degrees.

7. Place baking pan on baking stone and bake until rolls are golden brown, 25 to 30 minutes, rotating pan halfway through baking. Let cool on wire rack for 10 minutes; invert onto rimmed baking sheet, large rectangular platter, or cutting board. With rubber spatula, scrape any glaze remaining in baking pan onto buns; let cool while making pecan topping.

8. FOR THE TOPPING: Combine sugar, butter, corn syrup, and salt in small saucepan and bring to simmer over medium heat, whisking occasionally to thoroughly combine. Off heat, add vanilla and pecans and stir until pecans are evenly coated. Using soupspoon, spoon heaping 1 tablespoon nuts and topping over center of each sticky bun. Continue to let cool until sticky buns are warm, 15 to 20 minutes. Pull apart or use serrated knife to cut apart buns and serve.

Sticky buns can be prepared and shaped the night before and then refrigerated. Setting the baking dish in a warm-water bath the next morning speeds the dough's rise.

After forming and arranging buns in baking pan in step 6, cover pan and refrigerate for 10 to 14 hours. Place baking pan in warm-water bath (about 120 degrees) in kitchen sink or large roasting pan for 20 minutes. Remove from water bath and let stand at room temperature until buns look slightly puffy and are pressed against one another, about 1½ hours. About an hour before baking, adjust oven rack to lowest position, place baking stone on rack, and heat oven to 350 degrees. Proceed with step 7 as directed.

This make-ahead version makes sticky buns possible during hectic times, like the holidays.

After buns have risen 1½ hours, place baking pan, covered tightly with plastic wrap, in freezer and store for up to 1 month. To bake, adjust oven rack to middle position and heat oven to 350 degrees. Remove buns from freezer, remove plastic wrap, wrap pan tightly with aluminum foil, and set on baking sheet. Bake buns for 30 minutes, then remove foil and continue to bake until golden brown and center of dough registers about 180 degrees, about 20 minutes longer. Proceed with cooling buns and making topping as directed in step 8.

New York–Style Crumb Cake

✔ WHY THIS RECIPE WORKS

The essence of this cake is the balance between the tender, buttery cake and the thick, lightly spiced crumb topping. Starting with our favorite yellow cake recipe, we realized we needed to reduce the amount of butter or the richness would be overwhelming. We also wanted our crumb topping to be soft and cookielike, not a crunchy streusel.

REDUCE BUTTER AND ADD BUTTERMILK A yellow butter cake is a good base for this crumb cake. But combined with all those buttery crumbs, the cake is a bit too rich. Cutting back on the butter necessitates adding more milk to keep the cake from becoming dry, but this makes the batter too thin to support the heavy crumbs. Our solution is to substitute buttermilk for the milk. We also use one less egg white so the cake won't be rubbery.

USE CAKE FLOUR Even though the cake layer has to support a heavy layer of crumbs, don't think about switching to all-purpose flour. Yes, the cake layer will be sturdy but it will also be dry.

MAKE CRUMBS, NOT STREUSEL For really big crumbs you have to make a dough and then break that dough apart by hand. Melted butter, two kinds of sugar, and flour are essential. You need more butter than you do when making streusel—the overall effect is

more like cookie dough, with more substance than streusel and less sweetness.

SHAPE AND DISTRIBUTE THE CRUMBS Using both hands, break apart the crumb dough, rolling the broken dough between your thumb and forefinger to form crumbs about the size of large peas. Sprinkle the crumbs evenly over the cake batter, breaking apart any larger chunks. Spread the crumbs from the outside of the cake toward the center so as to not make the center too heavy.

BAKE IN A LOW OVEN Reducing the oven temperature to a gentle 325 degrees, lengthening the baking time, and placing the cake in the upper part of the oven all help to crisp the crumb topping.

NEW YORK–STYLE CRUMB CAKE
SERVES 8 TO 10

Don't be tempted to substitute all-purpose flour for the cake flour, as doing so will make a dry, tough cake. If you can't find buttermilk, you can substitute an equal amount of plain low-fat yogurt. When topping the cake, take care to not push the crumbs into the batter. This recipe can be easily doubled and baked in a 13 by 9-inch baking pan. If doubling, increase the baking time to about 45 minutes.

CRUMB TOPPING

8	tablespoons unsalted butter, melted
⅓	cup (2⅓ ounces) granulated sugar
⅓	cup packed (2⅓ ounces) dark brown sugar
¾	teaspoon ground cinnamon
⅛	teaspoon salt
1¾	cups (7 ounces) cake flour

CAKE

1¼	cups (5 ounces) cake flour
½	cup (3½ ounces) granulated sugar
¼	teaspoon baking soda
¼	teaspoon salt

6	tablespoons unsalted butter, cut into 6 pieces and softened
⅓	cup buttermilk
1	large egg plus 1 large yolk
1	teaspoon vanilla extract
	Confectioners' sugar

1. Adjust oven rack to upper-middle position and heat oven to 325 degrees. Make foil sling for 8-inch baking pan by folding 2 long sheets of aluminum foil so each is 8 inches wide. Lay sheets of foil in pan perpendicular to each other, with extra foil hanging over edges of pan. Push foil into corners and up sides of pan, smoothing foil flush to pan.

2. FOR THE TOPPING: Whisk melted butter, granulated sugar, brown sugar, cinnamon, and salt together in medium bowl to combine. Add flour and stir with rubber spatula or wooden spoon until mixture resembles thick, cohesive dough; set aside to cool to room temperature, 10 to 15 minutes.

3. FOR THE CAKE: Using stand mixer fitted with paddle, mix flour, sugar, baking soda, and salt on low speed to combine. With mixer running, add softened butter 1 piece at a time. Continue beating until mixture resembles moist crumbs, with no visible butter chunks remaining, 1 to 2 minutes. Add buttermilk, egg and yolk, and vanilla and beat on medium-high speed until light and fluffy, about 1 minute, scraping down bowl as needed.

4. Transfer batter to prepared pan. Using rubber spatula, spread batter into even layer. Break apart crumb topping into large pea-size pieces and spread in even layer over batter, beginning with edges and then working toward center. Bake until crumbs are golden and toothpick inserted in center of cake comes out clean, 35 to 40 minutes, rotating pan halfway through baking. Let cool on wire rack for at least 30 minutes. Remove cake from pan by lifting foil overhang. Dust with confectioners' sugar just before serving.

1. Reserve 1¼ cups batter, then fill pan with remaining batter; smooth top.

2. Beat ¼ cup reserved batter with filling ingredients; spoon filling evenly over batter.

3. Top filling with remaining cup reserved batter; smooth top. Using figure-eight motion, swirl filling into batter. Tap pan on counter.

4. Sprinkle lemon sugar–almond topping onto batter, then gently press to adhere.

Cream Cheese Coffee Cake

✔ WHY THIS RECIPE WORKS

This coffee cake is fraught with pitfalls, from bland cake to lackluster fillings. We wanted a rich, moist cake that could support a tangy swirl of cream cheese filling.

START WITH A STURDY, BUT TENDER CAKE BASE A batter of flour, granulated sugar, salt, butter, eggs, whole milk, and baking powder turns out a cake that's full of flavor and capable of supporting our cheese filling—but it's also a bit dry.

RESTORE MOISTURE We replace the milk with tangy and rich sour cream and increase the amount of butter. Our cake now has a lush texture as well as subtle acidity.

LEAVEN WITH BAKING SODA With sour cream in the mix, we add more leavener—baking soda—which reacts with and neutralizes the acidic sour cream. Baking soda also promotes browning, which makes this cake a perfect backdrop for the cheese filling.

ADD DIMENSION TO THE FILLING A filling made with sweetened cream cheese is good, but adding lemon juice and vanilla makes it even better. Incorporating some of the cake batter into the cheese mixture prevents graininess and helps the filling fuse seamlessly with the cake. A lemon-almond topping provides the crowning touch.

CREAM CHEESE COFFEE CAKE

SERVES 12 TO 16

Leftovers should be stored in the refrigerator, covered tightly with plastic wrap. For the best texture, allow the cake to return to room temperature before serving.

TOPPING

¼	cup sugar
1½	teaspoons grated lemon zest
½	cup sliced almonds

CAKE

2¼	cups (11¼ ounces) all-purpose flour
1⅛	teaspoons baking powder
1⅛	teaspoons baking soda
1	teaspoon salt
10	tablespoons unsalted butter, softened but still cool
1⅛	cups (7¾ ounces) plus 5 tablespoons sugar
1	tablespoon grated lemon zest plus 4 teaspoons juice
4	large eggs
5	teaspoons vanilla extract
1¼	cups sour cream
8	ounces cream cheese, softened

1. FOR THE TOPPING: Adjust oven rack to middle position and heat oven to 350 degrees. Spray 10-inch tube pan with vegetable oil spray. Stir sugar and lemon zest in small bowl until combined and sugar is moistened. Stir in almonds; set aside.

2. FOR THE CAKE: Whisk flour, baking powder, baking soda, and salt together in medium bowl; set aside. Using stand mixer fitted with paddle, beat butter, 1⅛ cups sugar, and lemon zest on medium-high speed until pale and fluffy, about 3 minutes. Add eggs, one at a time, and beat until combined. Add 4 teaspoons vanilla and mix to combine. Reduce speed to low and add flour mixture in 3 additions, alternating with 2 additions of sour cream, scraping down bowl as needed. Give batter final stir by hand.

3. Reserve 1¼ cups batter and set aside. Spoon remaining batter into prepared pan and smooth top. Return now-empty bowl to mixer and beat cream cheese, remaining 5 tablespoons sugar, lemon juice, and remaining 1 teaspoon vanilla on medium speed until smooth and slightly lightened, about

1 minute. Add ¼ cup reserved batter and mix until incorporated. Spoon cream cheese mixture evenly over batter, keeping filling about 1 inch from edges of pan; smooth top. Spread remaining 1 cup reserved batter over filling and smooth top. With butter knife or offset spatula, gently swirl filling into batter using figure-eight motion, being careful to not drag filling to bottom or edges of pan. Firmly tap pan on counter 2 or 3 times to dislodge any bubbles. Sprinkle sugar topping evenly over batter and gently press into batter to adhere.

4. Bake until top is golden and just firm, and skewer inserted in cake comes out clean (skewer will be wet if inserted in cream cheese filling), 45 to 50 minutes, rotating pan halfway through baking. Remove pan from oven and firmly tap on counter 2 or 3 times (top of cake may sink slightly). Let cake cool in pan on wire rack for 1 hour. Gently invert cake onto rimmed baking sheet (cake will be topping side down); remove tube pan, place wire rack on top of cake, and invert cake sugar side up. Let cool to room temperature, about 1½ hours, before serving.

SOFTENING CREAM CHEESE

When you need softened cream cheese in hurry, you can speed things up by submerging the foil-wrapped package in a bowl of warm water for about 10 minutes, or until softened.

Sour Cream Coffee Cake

✔ WHY THIS RECIPE WORKS

Sour cream coffee cakes should be buttery and rich, but not heavy and greasy like many versions tend to be. We wanted a pleasantly rich cake with lots of streusel on top and throughout.

BUILD A THICK, RICH BATTER All-purpose flour gives us a better texture than the cake flour specified. For richness, we use plenty of butter, sour cream, and eggs.

REINFORCE THE RISE A good dose of baking powder, along with baking soda, is necessary to make this hefty batter rise.

REVERSE CREAM FOR THE BEST CRUMB Rather than creaming the butter and sugar, which makes the cake too light and airy, we cut softened butter and some of the sour cream into the dry ingredients, then add the eggs and the rest of the sour cream; the result is a tighter but still tender crumb.

STREUSEL INSIDE AND OUT In addition to the streusel in the middle of the cake, we wanted more on top, so we divide the mixture, using some for the interior streusel layers (which we sweeten further with more brown sugar) and the rest for the topping. To the topping portion, we add pecans and butter for texture and richness.

SOUR CREAM COFFEE CAKE WITH BROWN SUGAR–PECAN STREUSEL

SERVES 12 TO 16

A fixed-bottom, 10-inch tube pan (with a 10-cup capacity) is best for this recipe. Note that the streusel is divided into two parts—one for the inner swirls, one for the topping.

STREUSEL

- ¾ cup (3¾ ounces) all-purpose flour
- ¾ cup (5¼ ounces) granulated sugar
- ½ cup packed (3½ ounces) dark brown sugar
- 2 tablespoons ground cinnamon
- 2 tablespoons unsalted butter, cut into 2 pieces and chilled
- 1 cup pecans, chopped

CAKE

- 12 tablespoons unsalted butter, cut into ½-inch cubes and softened but still cool, plus 2 tablespoons softened for greasing pan
- 4 large eggs
- 1½ cups sour cream
- 1 tablespoon vanilla extract

STORING CAKE FLOUR

Bakers who make cakes infrequently may not have a covered storage container especially for cake flour. Because cake flour typically comes in a box, we recommend transferring the flour to a zipper-lock bag and then slipping the bag back in the original box. When you need flour, simply lift the bag out of the box, open it up wide, and dip the cup measure right in. No more spills from pouring flour out of the box.

LAYERING COFFEE CAKE BATTER AND STREUSEL

1. Using rubber spatula, spread 2 cups batter in bottom of prepared pan, smoothing surface.

2. Sprinkle evenly with ¾ cup streusel filling.

3. Repeat steps 1 and 2 with 2 cups batter and remaining streusel filling.

4. Spread remaining batter over filling, then sprinkle with streusel topping.

2¼ cups (11¼ ounces) all-purpose flour
1¼ cups (8¾ ounces) granulated sugar
1 tablespoon baking powder
¾ teaspoon baking soda
¾ teaspoon salt

1. FOR THE STREUSEL: Process flour, granulated sugar, ¼ cup brown sugar, and cinnamon in food processor until combined, about 15 seconds. Transfer 1¼ cups of flour-sugar mixture to small bowl and stir in remaining ¼ cup brown sugar; set aside for streusel filling. Add butter and pecans to mixture in food processor and pulse until nuts and butter resemble small pebbly pieces, about 10 pulses. Set aside for streusel topping.

2. FOR THE CAKE: Adjust oven rack to lowest position and heat oven to 350 degrees. Grease and flour 10-inch tube pan with 2 tablespoons softened butter. Whisk eggs, 1 cup sour cream, and vanilla in medium bowl until combined.

3. Using stand mixer fitted with paddle, mix flour, sugar, baking powder, baking soda, and salt on low speed for 30 seconds to combine. Add remaining 12 tablespoons butter and remaining ½ cup sour cream and mix until dry ingredients are moistened and mixture resembles wet sand, with few large butter pieces remaining, about 1½ minutes. Increase speed to medium and beat until batter comes together, about 10 seconds; scrape down sides of bowl with rubber spatula. Lower speed to medium-low and gradually add egg mixture in 3 additions, beating for 20 seconds after each and scraping down sides of bowl. Increase speed to medium-high and beat until batter is light and fluffy, about 1 minute.

4. Using rubber spatula, spread 2 cups batter in bottom of prepared pan and smooth surface. Sprinkle evenly with ¾ cup streusel filling. Repeat with another 2 cups batter and remaining ¾ cup streusel filling.

Spread remaining batter over filling, then sprinkle with streusel topping.

5. Bake until cake feels firm to touch and skewer inserted in center comes out clean (bits of sugar from streusel may cling to skewer), 50 minutes to 1 hour, rotating pan halfway through baking. Let cake cool in pan on wire rack for 30 minutes. Gently invert cake onto rimmed baking sheet (cake will be streusel side down); remove tube pan, place wire rack on top of cake, and invert cake streusel side up. Let cool to room temperature, about 2 hours, before serving.

SOUR CREAM COFFEE CAKE WITH CHOCOLATE CHIPS

Sprinkle ½ cup chocolate chips over bottom layer of batter before sprinkling with streusel and another ½ cup chocolate chips over middle layer of batter before sprinkling with streusel.

LEMON-BLUEBERRY SOUR CREAM COFFEE CAKE

Toss 1 cup frozen blueberries with 1 teaspoon grated lemon zest in small bowl. Sprinkle ½ cup blueberries over bottom layer of batter before sprinkling with streusel and remaining ½ cup blueberries over middle layer of batter before sprinkling with streusel.

APRICOT-ALMOND SOUR CREAM COFFEE CAKE

Substitute 1 cup slivered almonds for pecans in streusel and ½ teaspoon almond extract for vanilla extract in cake batter. Spoon six 2-teaspoon mounds apricot jam over bottom layer of batter before sprinkling with streusel and another six 2-teaspoon mounds jam over middle layer of batter before sprinkling with streusel.

Almond Ring Coffee Cake

✔ WHY THIS RECIPE WORKS

Why buy inferior boxed versions when you can make a better coffee cake at home—one with buttery layers of dough, a sweet almond filling, and a smooth glaze of white frosting?

CUT THE BUTTER FOR A MORE TENDER CAKE Most yeasted coffee cakes rely on a rich dough made with milk, butter, and eggs, Because we were filling this cake with a rich almond filling, we wanted a lighter dough. To that end, we cut the butter in half.

SWEETEN WITH HONEY We thought we'd be using granulated sugar or brown sugar in our dough, as most recipes do, but once we started testing other sweeteners, we found that honey gave the cake a slight caramel flavor and made the cake moister.

REACH FOR ALMOND PASTE For the filling, most recipes enrich cream cheese with ground almonds and sugar, but this makes a soft mixture that can leak out of the dough. In addition, the almond flavor is barely perceptible. We had better luck with almond paste, which is sold in tubes in the supermarket baking aisle. When mixed with a little cream cheese, it is thick enough to stay put in the dough and has a rich, nutty flavor.

ALMOND RING COFFEE CAKE
MAKES 2 RINGS, EACH SERVING 6

Note that you will need three eggs, but that the yolks and whites are used separately. Feel free to bake both cakes at the same time or freeze one for another time (see the make-ahead instructions on page 83). For alternative fillings, see page 83.

FILLING

1	(7-ounce) tube almond paste
4	ounces cream cheese, softened
½	cup (2 ounces) confectioners' sugar

DOUGH

1⅓	cups warm whole milk, (110 degrees)
8	tablespoons unsalted butter, melted and cooled
⅓	cup honey
3	large egg yolks
2	teaspoons vanilla extract
5	cups (25 ounces) all-purpose flour
2¼	teaspoons instant or rapid-rise yeast
2	teaspoons salt
	Vegetable oil spray

TOPPING

3	large egg whites, lightly beaten
½	cup sliced almonds
1½	cups (6 ounces) confectioners' sugar
2	ounces cream cheese, softened
2	tablespoons milk
½	teaspoon vanilla extract

1. FOR THE FILLING: Using stand mixer fitted with paddle, beat almond paste, softened cream cheese, and sugar together on medium speed until smooth. Cover with plastic wrap and refrigerate until ready to use.

2. FOR THE DOUGH: Whisk milk, melted butter, honey, egg yolks, and vanilla together in large liquid measuring cup. Using clean, dry mixer bowl and dough hook, mix 4¾ cups flour, yeast, and salt together on low speed. Add milk mixture and knead until dough comes together, about 2 minutes.

3. Increase mixer speed to medium and knead until dough is smooth and shiny, 5 to 7 minutes. If after 5 minutes more flour is needed, add remaining ¼ cup flour, 1 tablespoon at a time, until dough clears side of bowl but sticks to bottom.

4. Turn dough out onto lightly floured counter and knead by hand to form smooth, round ball. Place dough in lightly oiled bowl and wrap tightly with plastic. Let rise in warm, draft-free place until doubled in size, 1 to 1½ hours.

5. Line 2 baking sheets with parchment paper. On lightly floured counter, divide dough into 2 equal pieces. Roll 1 piece dough into 18 by 9-inch rectangle. Spread half of filling in 1-inch-wide strip just above bottom edge of dough.

6. Loosen dough from counter using bench scraper (or metal spatula), roll dough into tight log, and pinch seam closed. Transfer log, seam side down, to prepared sheet. Repeat with the remaining dough and filling.

7. Shape each log into a ring. Make about 11 cuts around outside of dough with sharp knife or scissors, and twist each piece cut side up. Mist rings with oil spray, wrap loosely in plastic, and let rise in a warm place until they have nearly doubled in size and spring back slowly when indented with your finger, 1 to 1½ hours.

8. FOR THE TOPPING: Adjust oven racks to upper-middle and lower-middle positions and heat oven to 375 degrees. Brush rings with egg whites and sprinkle with almonds. Bake cakes until deep brown, about 25 minutes, switching and rotating sheets halfway through baking.

9. Let cakes cool for 1 hour. Whisk together sugar, cream cheese, milk, and vanilla in small bowl until smooth, then drizzle it over cakes before serving.

TO MAKE AHEAD: Shape and cover cakes as directed in step 7, but do not let them rise. Refrigerate for up to 12 hours; let cakes return to room temperature for about 1 hour, then bake as directed. Alternatively, unbaked cakes can be frozen for up to 1 month; let cakes rise in step 7, then wrap tightly with greased plastic wrap followed by aluminum foil and freeze. Let frozen cakes thaw in refrigerator for 12 hours, then return them to room temperature for about 1 hour and bake as directed.

APRICOT-ORANGE RING COFFEE CAKE

The filling can be refrigerated in an airtight container for up to 3 days.

Omit almond filling. Bring 2 cups dried apricots, 1 cup water, and 3 tablespoons sugar to boil in medium saucepan over medium-high heat. Reduce heat to medium and boil gently, stirring occasionally, until apricots are soft and water has nearly evaporated, 16 to 18 minutes. Transfer warm apricots to food processor. Add 3 tablespoons grated orange zest, 3 tablespoons orange juice, and 2 tablespoons rum (optional) and process until smooth, about 1 minute. Let mixture cool to room temperature before spreading over dough in step 5.

BERRY RING COFFEE CAKE

The filling can be refrigerated in an airtight container for up to 3 days.

Omit almond filling. Stir together 2½ cups fresh or frozen raspberries, blueberries, or blackberries, 3 tablespoons sugar, 2 tablespoons lemon juice, 2 tablespoons water, 1½ tablespoons cornstarch, and pinch salt in medium saucepan. Bring to boil over medium heat and cook, stirring occasionally, until mixture is thick and shiny, about 2 minutes. Let mixture cool to room temperature before spreading on dough in step 5.

MAKING ALMOND RING COFFEE CAKE

1. After rolling dough into 18 by 9-inch rectangle, spread 1-inch-wide strip of filling about 1 inch above bottom edge of dough.

2. Loosen dough from counter with bench scraper (or metal spatula) and carefully roll dough into even cylinder. Pinch seam to seal.

3. Transfer dough log to parchment-lined baking sheet and shape into ring. Make about 11 cuts around outside of ring using sharp knife or scissors, spacing them 1 to 1½ inches apart.

4. Twist each piece of dough cut side up.

BLUEBERRY PANCAKES

Griddle Cakes, Waffles, and Granola

"Clabbered" milk is widely recommended as a substitute for buttermilk in baked goods. The usual approach is to stir lemon juice into milk (1 tablespoon per cup) and let the mixture sit for 10 minutes to "clabber" (or thicken). But after following this method and closely observing what transpired, we discovered that clabbering milk doesn't give it the smooth, thick consistency of buttermilk. Small curds formed almost instantly, but after a 10-minute rest, most of the milk had not thickened at all. And more waiting didn't help.

It turns out that when lemon juice is added to milk, the citric acid changes the electrical charge on the dairy's casein proteins, causing them to coagulate tightly into clumps. On the other hand, the Lactobacillus bacteria added to milk to produce commercial buttermilk remove some of the sugar molecules bonded to the proteins, allowing them to form a gel that gradually becomes thicker over time.

To find out if waiting after clabbering milk impacts its baking properties, we made multiple batches of biscuits and buttermilk pancakes: one set with clabbered milk that had rested for 10 minutes and one set in which we mixed the milk into the batter immediately after adding the lemon juice. All of the biscuits and pancakes were virtually identical in appearance, flavor, and texture.

Our conclusion: You can safely skip the resting time when using clabbered milk.

Best Buttermilk Pancakes

✓ WHY THIS RECIPE WORKS

Too often, buttermilk pancakes lack true tang, and they rarely have the light and fluffy texture we desire. We wanted buttermilk pancakes with a slightly crisp, golden crust surrounding a fluffy, tender center with just enough structure to withstand a good dousing of maple syrup. We achieve this with a sour cream substitution, the use of two leaveners, and some techniques to keep the pancakes nice and tender.

START WITH BUTTERMILK When our forebears set out to make pancakes enriched with the sweet tang of buttermilk, they had a built-in advantage: real buttermilk. Instead of using the thinly flavored liquid processed from skim milk and cultured bacteria that passes for buttermilk today, earlier Americans turned to the fat-flecked byproduct of churning cream into butter. The switch from churned buttermilk to cultured buttermilk accounts for the lack of true tang in most modern-day buttermilk pancakes. We have to use other methods to obtain tang.

SUPPLEMENT WITH SOUR CREAM We wanted more tang in our pancakes, but using more buttermilk didn't work. More buttermilk means a greater concentration of acid in the mix, which in turn causes the baking soda to bubble too rapidly. The result: pancakes that overinflate when they first cook, then collapse like popped balloons, becoming dense and wet by the time they hit the plate. A little sour cream, on the other hand, adds a ton of flavor but doesn't radically affect the consistency of the batter. With the extra fat from the sour cream, we found it best to trim the butter back to just 3 tablespoons.

USE TWO LEAVENERS Both baking soda and baking powder are essential in our pancakes. Baking soda responds to the acid in the buttermilk, producing carbon dioxide gas that aerates the pancakes, while baking powder reacts to the heat of the pan to release more carbon dioxide. Baking soda also helps promote a nice brown color on the pancakes, boosting flavor through the Maillard reaction.

KEEP IT TENDER Three techniques help us to get our pancakes as tender as possible. First, we use a lower-protein all-purpose flour like Gold Medal or Pillsbury. Second, we fold the batter very minimally to prevent too much gluten from forming. And finally, we let the batter rest for 10 minutes before cooking. Why? Even with minimal mixing, some gluten develops in the pancake batter. During a 10-minute rest, the gluten relaxes and the end result is tender pancakes. Don't worry that the leavening will dissipate. Remember that baking powder is double acting and will provide plenty of lift when the batter hits the hot pan.

BEST BUTTERMILK PANCAKES

MAKES SIXTEEN 4-INCH PANCAKES,
SERVING 4 TO 6

The pancakes can be cooked on an electric griddle. Set the griddle temperature to 350 degrees and cook as directed. The test kitchen prefers a lower-protein all-purpose flour like Gold Medal or Pillsbury for this recipe. If you use an all-purpose flour with a higher protein content, like King Arthur, you will need to add an extra tablespoon or two of buttermilk. Serve with warm maple syrup.

2	cups (10 ounces) all-purpose flour
2	tablespoons sugar
1	teaspoon baking powder
½	teaspoon baking soda
½	teaspoon salt
2	cups buttermilk
¼	cup sour cream
2	large eggs
3	tablespoons unsalted butter, melted and cooled
1–2	teaspoons vegetable oil

1. Adjust oven rack to middle position and heat oven to 200 degrees. Spray wire rack set in rimmed baking sheet with vegetable oil spray; place in oven. Whisk flour, sugar, baking powder, baking soda, and salt together in medium bowl. In second medium bowl, whisk together buttermilk, sour cream, eggs, and melted butter. Make well in center of dry ingredients and pour in wet ingredients; gently stir until just combined (batter should remain lumpy, with few streaks of flour). Do not overmix. Let batter sit for 10 minutes before cooking.

2. Heat 1 teaspoon oil in 12-inch nonstick skillet over medium heat until shimmering. Using paper towels, carefully wipe out oil, leaving thin film of oil on bottom and sides of pan. Using ¼-cup measure, portion batter into pan in 4 places. Cook until edges are set, first side is golden brown, and bubbles on surface are just beginning to break, 2 to 3 minutes. Using thin, wide spatula, flip pancakes and continue to cook until second side is golden brown, 1 to 2 minutes longer. Serve pancakes immediately, or transfer to wire rack in preheated oven. Repeat with remaining batter, using remaining oil as necessary.

Blueberry Pancakes

✓ WHY THIS RECIPE WORKS

Blueberry pancakes are too often tough, rubbery, tasteless, and short on real berry flavor. We wanted light and fluffy pancakes, studded with juicy bursts of blueberry.

FAKE THE BUTTERMILK Buttermilk gives pancakes a tangy flavor and contributes to their fluffy texture, but what if you don't have any on hand? We find that milk mixed with lemon juice boasts a tang similar to buttermilk. And the acid in the lemon juice is enough to react with the leaveners and provide lift.

SWEETEN UP We like our blueberry pancakes on the sweet side so our question wasn't whether we'd add sugar to the batter, but how much. We settled on 2 tablespoons since we planned on sweetening our hotcakes further with warm maple syrup.

USE A LIGHT TOUCH Mixing the batter until smooth will produce tough, dense pancakes because mixing encourages the formation of gluten in the batter. We mix our batter until just combined for pancakes with a light and fluffy texture.

BRING ON THE BLUEBERRIES Does the type of blueberry matter in your pancakes? If you like sweet berries, go for small, wild berries (either fresh or frozen). As for mixing in the blueberries, we skip that step because the blueberries break into the batter causing mottled gray hotcakes. Instead, we ladle the batter onto the hot skillet and sprinkle the berries over the top.

BLUEBERRY PANCAKES

MAKES SIXTEEN 4-INCH PANCAKES, SERVING 4 TO 6

The pancakes can be cooked on an electric griddle. Set the griddle temperature to 350 degrees and cook as directed. To make sure frozen blueberries don't bleed, rinse them under cool water in a fine-mesh strainer until the water runs clear, then spread them on a paper towel–lined plate to dry. If you have buttermilk on hand, use 2 cups instead of the milk and lemon juice. Serve with warm maple syrup.

2   cups whole milk
1   tablespoon fresh lemon juice
2   cups (10 ounces) all-purpose flour
2   tablespoons sugar
2   teaspoons baking powder
½   teaspoon baking soda

½ teaspoon salt

I large egg

3 tablespoons unsalted butter, melted
and cooled

1–2 teaspoons vegetable oil

5 ounces (I cup) fresh or frozen
blueberries, rinsed and dried

We wondered how far in
advance we could mix up
pancake batter. Sometimes,
say for a brunch or during the
holidays, it can be convenient
to have batter premixed.

To determine how far in
advance we could make pancake batter, we mixed up a
few batches of basic pancake
batter and held them for different lengths of time before
cooking: I hour, 2 hours, and
3 hours. Holding the batter
for I hour had no detrimental
effect on the pancakes. After
2 and 3 hours, however, the
batter spread out too easily,
producing thin, floppy cakes
that were much less appealing
than the ones made from
fresh batter.

Here's why: In fresh pan-
cake batter, baking powder
reacts quickly, releasing most
of its gas in a short period of
time. The longer the batter
sits, the fewer bubbles there
are left when it's time to
cook, increasing the likelihood
of flat flapjacks.

1. Adjust oven rack to middle position and heat oven to 200 degrees. Spray wire rack set in rimmed baking sheet with vegetable oil spray; place in oven. Whisk milk and lemon juice together in large measuring cup. Whisk flour, sugar, baking powder, baking soda, and salt together in medium bowl.

2. Add egg and melted butter to milk mix-ture and whisk until combined. Make well in center of dry ingredients; pour in milk mixture and whisk very gently until just combined (few lumps should remain). Do not overmix.

3. Heat 1 teaspoon oil in 12-inch nonstick skillet over medium heat until shimmering. Using paper towels, carefully wipe out oil, leaving thin film of oil on bottom and sides of pan. Using ¼-cup measure, portion bat-ter into pan in 4 places. Sprinkle 1 tablespoon blueberries over each pancake. Cook pancakes until large bubbles begin to appear, 1½ to 2 minutes. Using thin, wide spatula, flip pan-cakes and cook until second side is golden brown, 1 to 1½ minutes longer. Serve pan-cakes immediately or transfer to wire rack in preheated oven. Repeat with remaining batter, using remaining oil as necessary.

LEMON-CORNMEAL BLUEBERRY PANCAKES

Add 2 teaspoons grated lemon zest to milk along with lemon juice and substitute 1½ cups stone-ground yellow cornmeal for 1 cup flour.

Multigrain Pancakes

✔ WHY THIS RECIPE WORKS

Bland, dense, and gummy, most multigrain pancakes are more about appeasing your diet than pleasing your palate. We wanted flavorful, fluffy, and health-ful flapjacks. After testing lots of grains, we found that muesli had all the ingredients and flavor we wanted in one convenient package—raw whole oats, wheat germ, rye, barley, toasted nuts, and dried fruit. But pancakes made with whole muesli are too chewy and gummy. We solve this problem by converting muesli into a flour and combining it with some other flour options, as well as using two leaveners.

LIGHTEN TEXTURE WITH CLABBERED MILK When testing our multigrain pan-cakes, we found that using buttermilk made them taste too sour when combined with grains. But if we did away with the butter-milk entirely, we would have to rethink our leaveners. (After all, baking soda needs acid

to react.) But what if we simply used a less acidic-tasting blend of milk and lemon juice as we do in our Blueberry Pancakes? The milk and lemon juice mixture makes for a surpris-ingly cleaner, richer-tasting pancake with an even lighter texture.

MAKE INSTANT MULTIGRAIN FLOUR
Some multigrain pancake recipes load up on unprocessed grains—great for flavor but bad for texture. To avoid gummy, chewy pancakes, we make our own multigrain "flour" by pro-cessing store-bought muesli cereal in a food processor. To give our pancakes a subtle hint of that hearty whole-grain texture, we add a few tablespoons of unprocessed muesli to the batter, too.

USE TWO LEAVENERS Many chemi-cally leavened pancake recipes include both baking powder and baking soda—especially when they're bulked up with heavy grains. The combination makes for fail-safe leavening and thorough browning. (After all, baking soda is a browning agent.)

LET THE BATTER REST To get light, fluffy pancakes, it's important to let the batter rest while the pan heats (a full 5 minutes). The flour needs this time to absorb all the liquid, thus ensuring that the batter sets up properly. Skip this step and the pancakes will run together in the pan and cook up flat, not to mention misshapen. Properly rested batter will maintain its shape when poured into the pan and will produce tall and fluffy pancakes.

MULTIGRAIN PANCAKES

MAKES SIXTEEN 4-INCH PANCAKES,
SERVING 4 TO 6

The pancakes can be cooked on an electric griddle. Set the griddle temperature to 350 degrees and cook as directed. Familia brand no-sugar-added muesli is the best choice for this recipe. If you can't find Familia, look for Alpen or any no-sugar-added muesli. (If you can't find muesli without sugar, muesli with sugar added will work; reduce the brown sugar in the recipe to 1 tablespoon.) Mix the batter first and then heat the pan. Letting the batter sit while the pan heats will give the dry ingredients time to absorb the wet ingredients; otherwise, the batter will be runny. Serve with warm maple syrup or our fruit and nut topping or flavored syrup (recipes follow).

2	cups whole milk
4	teaspoons fresh lemon juice
1¼	cups (6 ounces), plus 3 tablespoons no-sugar-added muesli
¾	cup (3¾ ounces) all-purpose flour
½	cup (2¾ ounces) whole-wheat flour
2	tablespoons packed brown sugar
2¼	teaspoons baking powder
½	teaspoon baking soda
½	teaspoon salt
2	large eggs
3	tablespoons unsalted butter, melted and cooled
¾	teaspoon vanilla extract
1–2	teaspoons vegetable oil

1. Adjust oven rack to middle position and heat oven to 200 degrees. Spray wire rack set in rimmed baking sheet with vegetable oil spray; place in oven. Whisk milk and lemon juice together in large measuring cup; set aside.

2. Process 1¼ cups muesli in food processor until finely ground, 2 to 2½ minutes; transfer to large bowl. Add remaining 3 tablespoons unground muesli, all-purpose flour, whole-wheat flour, brown sugar, baking powder, baking soda, and salt; whisk to combine.

3. Add eggs, melted butter, and vanilla to milk mixture and whisk until combined. Make well in center of dry ingredients; pour in milk mixture and whisk very gently until just combined (batter should remain lumpy with few streaks of flour). Do not overmix. Allow batter to sit while pan heats.

4. Heat 1 teaspoon oil in 12-inch nonstick skillet over medium heat until shimmering. Using paper towels, carefully wipe out oil, leaving thin film of oil on bottom and sides of pan. Using ¼-cup measure, portion batter into pan in 4 places. Cook until small bubbles begin to appear evenly over surface, 2 to 3 minutes. Using thin, wide spatula, flip pancakes and cook until second side is golden brown, 1½ to 2 minutes longer. Serve pancakes immediately or transfer to wire rack in preheated oven. Repeat with remaining batter, using remaining oil as necessary.

APPLE, CRANBERRY, AND PECAN TOPPING

SERVES 4 TO 6

We prefer semifirm apples, such as Fuji, Gala, or Braeburn, for this topping. Avoid very tart apples, such as Granny Smith, and soft varieties like McIntosh. This syrup will keep for a week, refrigerated. Reheat gently before serving.

3½	tablespoons unsalted butter, chilled
1¼	pounds apples, peeled, cored, and cut into ½-inch pieces
	Pinch salt

BLEMISH-FREE PANCAKES

We've all experienced the annoying phenomenon of having the first batch of pancakes turn out splotched with brown spots, while subsequent batches come out evenly golden.

Here's why: When fresh oil hits a hot pan, the surface tension of the oil causes it to bead together into little droplets, leaving some of the pan bottom without a coating. Since bare metal conducts heat better than oil, when you ladle your batter into the pan, the spots directly in contact with uncoated metal will cook faster than those touching oil. By the time you get to your second batch of pancakes, the oil has undergone chemical changes that make the molecules less prone to clustering. What's more, the first batch of pancakes has absorbed much of the oil, leaving only a thin film that's more likely to be evenly distributed across the pan.

For spot-free pancakes from the get-go, start by applying oil to an unheated pan or griddle. Allow the oil to heat up over medium heat for at least 1 minute, then use a paper towel to wipe away all but a thin, barely visible layer to prevent sticking. The pancakes should cook up golden brown from the first batch to the last.

We tried several methods to determine how to hold pancakes before serving, from stacking up the pancakes on a heated plate to covering them with aluminum foil or placing the plate of stacked pancakes in a warm oven. All of these methods did the job as far as keeping the pancakes warm. When the last batch of pancakes was coming off the griddle, the temperature of the earliest batch still registered between 145 and 150 degrees. But these pancakes were compressed from being stacked, and they steamed from the heat and became very rubbery.

We found the best method was to spread the pancakes on a large wire rack placed on a baking sheet. (Be sure to spray the rack with vegetable oil spray to save yourself from stuck pancakes). Place the pan and the rack in a 200-degree oven and place your pancakes on the rack in a single layer, uncovered, for up to 20 minutes (any longer and they will start to dry out). The warm oven keeps the pancakes hot enough to melt a pat of butter, and leaving the pancakes uncovered keeps them from becoming soggy.

1 cup apple cider
½ cup dried cranberries
½ cup maple syrup
1 teaspoon lemon juice
½ teaspoon vanilla extract
¾ cup pecans, toasted and chopped coarse

Melt 1½ tablespoons butter in 12-inch skillet over medium-high heat. Add apples and salt; cook, stirring occasionally, until softened and browned, 7 to 9 minutes. Stir in cider and cranberries; cook until liquid has almost evaporated, 6 to 8 minutes. Stir in maple syrup and cook until thickened, 4 to 5 minutes. Add remaining 2 tablespoons butter, lemon juice, and vanilla; whisk until sauce is smooth. Serve with toasted nuts.

BUTTER-PECAN MAPLE SYRUP
SERVES 6 TO 8

This syrup will keep for a week, refrigerated. Reheat gently before serving.

1½ cups maple syrup
½ cup pecans, toasted and chopped
2 tablespoons unsalted butter
¼ teaspoon vanilla extract
  Pinch salt

Simmer all ingredients together in small saucepan over medium-low heat until slightly thickened, about 5 minutes. Serve.

German Apple Pancake

✔ WHY THIS RECIPE WORKS

German apple pancakes combine the best qualities of a popover and a pancake, but this old-world classic is prone to numerous pitfalls: insufficient rise, leaden texture, and eggy flavor. The perfect pancake should have crisp, lighter-than-air edges and a custardlike center, with buttery sautéed apples baked right into the batter. A hot skillet, the right apple, and the way we pour the pancake batter into the skillet all contribute to a pancake worthy of a celebratory brunch.

REACH FOR HALF-AND-HALF We tried a variety of liquid additions before we got our batter right. Heavy cream makes a pancake that's rich, but awfully heavy. Milk and sour cream make a pancake that's simply too tangy. Half-and-half, however, has just enough butterfat to make a rich, but not leaden, pancake.

GET IT HOT Like a popover, a German apple pancake relies on steam for rise so it's important to have your oven at the right temperature and to have the pan hot before you pour in the batter. Starting the pancake in a hot oven gives the batter the quick rise it needs; we then reduce the heat to a more moderate temperature, which cooks the pancake to perfection.

PRECOOK THE APPLES We prefer tart Granny Smiths in our pancake. They hold their shape better and won't turn to mush in the oven. There isn't enough time for the apples to cook through in the oven, so we sauté the apples (sliced ½ inch thick) before adding the batter.

CUSHION THE FRUIT After sautéing the apples, we pour the batter directly into the pan, but we start around the perimeter of the skillet—this builds a bit of a barrier that prevents apple slices from popping out of the pan once it hits the oven.

1. Pour batter around edge of pan, then over apples.

2. Loosen edges of pancake with heatproof rubber spatula.

3. Invert pancake onto serving platter.

GERMAN APPLE PANCAKE
SERVES 4

A 10-inch ovensafe skillet is necessary for this recipe; we highly recommend using a nonstick skillet for the sake of easy cleanup, but a regular skillet will work as well. If you prefer tart apples, use Granny Smiths; if you prefer sweet ones, use Braeburns. For serving, dust the apple pancake with confectioners' sugar and pass warm maple syrup or Caramel Sauce (recipe follows) separately, if desired.

½	cup (2½ ounces) all-purpose flour
1	tablespoon granulated sugar
½	teaspoon salt
2	large eggs
⅔	cup half-and-half
1	teaspoon vanilla extract
2	tablespoons unsalted butter
1¼	pounds Granny Smith or Braeburn apples, peeled, cored, quartered, and cut into ½-inch-thick slices
¼	cup packed brown sugar
¼	teaspoon ground cinnamon
1	teaspoon lemon juice
	Confectioners' sugar

1. Adjust oven rack to upper-middle position and heat oven to 500 degrees.

2. Whisk flour, granulated sugar, and salt together in medium bowl. In second medium bowl, whisk eggs, half-and-half, and vanilla until combined. Add liquid ingredients to dry ingredients and whisk until no lumps remain, about 20 seconds; set aside.

3. Melt butter in 10-inch ovensafe nonstick skillet over medium-high heat. Add apples, brown sugar, and cinnamon; cook, stirring frequently, until apples are golden brown, about 10 minutes. Off heat, stir in lemon juice.

4. Working quickly, pour batter around and over apples. Place skillet in oven and immediately reduce oven temperature to 425 degrees. Bake until pancake edges are brown and puffy and have risen above edges of skillet, about 18 minutes.

5. Carefully remove skillet from oven and loosen pancake edges with heatproof rubber spatula; invert pancake onto serving platter. Dust with confectioners' sugar, cut into wedges, and serve.

CARAMEL SAUCE
MAKES ABOUT 1½ CUPS

When the hot cream mixture is added in step 3, the hot sugar syrup will bubble vigorously (and dangerously), so don't use a smaller saucepan. If you make the caramel sauce ahead, reheat it in the microwave or a small saucepan over low heat until warm and fluid.

½	cup water
1	cup sugar
1	cup heavy cream
⅛	teaspoon salt
½	teaspoon vanilla extract
½	teaspoon lemon juice

1. Place water in 2-quart saucepan. Pour sugar in center of pan, taking care not to let sugar touch sides of pan. Cover and bring mixture to boil over high heat; once boiling, uncover and continue to boil until syrup is thick and straw-colored and registers 300 degrees, about 7 minutes. Reduce heat to medium and continue to cook until syrup is deep amber and registers 350 degrees, 1 to 2 minutes.

2. Meanwhile, bring cream and salt to simmer in small saucepan over high heat (if cream boils before sugar reaches deep amber color, remove cream from heat and cover to keep warm).

3. Remove sugar syrup from heat. Very carefully pour about one-quarter of hot cream into syrup (mixture will bubble vigorously) and let bubbling subside. Add remaining cream, vanilla, and lemon juice; whisk until sauce is smooth. (Sauce can be refrigerated for up to 2 weeks.)

French Toast

✓ WHY THIS RECIPE WORKS

French toast just isn't worth the trouble if the result is soggy, too eggy, or just plain bland. We wanted crisp French toast with a custardy and moist, but not mushy, interior.

GET THE BREAD RIGHT Can you use just any bread for French toast? Absolutely not. French and Italian breads make French toast that's too chewy. White sandwich bread works—depending on which variety you reach for. It comes in regular and hearty varieties; choose hearty for crisp toast. And if you have challah, that works great, too.

START WITH DRY BREAD Even with hearty sandwich bread, it's necessary to dry it out some to prevent it from becoming soggy after a dip in the egg and milk mixture. Many recipes advocate letting the bread go stale overnight. Normally, exposing bread to air causes its starch molecules to bond and recrystallize, leading to a harder texture, but most breads now include stabilizers that slow down this process. In the test kitchen, we've determined that leaving bread out to stale isn't nearly as effective as drying it in the oven, which hardens it by actually removing moisture. Drying the bread in a low oven produces French toast that is crisp on the outside and velvety on the inside, with no trace of sogginess.

HOLD THE WHITES To prevent our French toast from tasting like scrambled eggs, we tried a yolks-only approach. Using just egg yolks yields French toast that tastes rich and custardlike. Research revealed that most of the flavor in eggs comes not from the yolk but from the sulfur compounds in the white. These are the same compounds that lead to the offensive odors of an overdone hard-cooked egg.

DON'T FORGET THE FLAVORINGS Cinnamon, vanilla, and brown sugar give our French toast just the right balance of warm, sweet flavor. And for nutty butter flavor, we incorporate melted butter.

FRENCH TOAST
SERVES 4

To prevent the butter from clumping during mixing, warm the milk in a microwave or small saucepan until warm to the touch (about 80 degrees). The French toast can be cooked all at once on an electric griddle, but may take an extra 2 to 3 minutes per side. Set the griddle temperature to 350 degrees and use the entire amount of butter (4 tablespoons) for cooking. Serve with warm maple syrup.

8	large slices hearty white sandwich bread or challah
1½	cups whole milk, warmed
3	large egg yolks
3	tablespoons packed light brown sugar
2	tablespoons unsalted butter, plus 2 tablespoons melted
1	tablespoon vanilla extract
½	teaspoon ground cinnamon
¼	teaspoon salt

1. Adjust oven rack to middle position and heat oven to 300 degrees. Place bread on wire rack set in rimmed baking sheet. Bake bread until almost dry throughout (center should remain slightly moist), about 16 minutes, flipping slices halfway through baking. Remove bread from rack and let cool for 5 minutes. Return baking sheet with wire rack to oven and reduce temperature to 200 degrees.

2. Whisk milk, egg yolks, sugar, 2 tablespoons melted butter, vanilla, cinnamon, and salt in large bowl until well blended. Transfer mixture to 13 by 9-inch baking pan.

3. Soak bread in milk mixture until saturated but not falling apart, 20 seconds per side. Using firm slotted spatula, pick up 1 bread slice and allow excess milk mixture to drip off; repeat with remaining slices. Place soaked bread on another baking sheet or platter.

4. Melt ½ tablespoon butter in 12-inch skillet over medium-low heat. Using slotted

KEEPING MAPLE SYRUP WARM

To keep maple syrup from getting cold during breakfast, pour freshly warmed syrup into a coffee carafe or thermos. This is especially helpful if you're entertaining since you can warm up the syrup ahead of time.

spatula, transfer 2 slices soaked bread to skillet and cook until golden brown, 3 to 4 minutes. Flip and continue to cook until second side is golden brown, 3 to 4 minutes longer. (If toast is cooking too quickly, reduce temperature slightly.) Transfer to baking sheet in oven. Wipe out skillet with paper towels. Repeat cooking with remaining bread, 2 pieces at a time, adding ½ tablespoon of butter for each batch. Serve warm.

PECAN-RUM FRENCH TOAST

Substitute 8 large slices cinnamon-raisin bread for hearty white sandwich bread. Process ½ cup pecans, 1 tablespoon packed light brown sugar, and ¼ teaspoon ground cinnamon in food processor until coarsely ground, 12 to 15 pulses (you should have about ½ cup). Add 2 teaspoons dark rum to milk mixture in step 2. Sprinkle 1 tablespoon nut mixture over 1 side of each slice of soaked bread. Cook as directed in step 4, starting with nut mixture side down.

EXTRA-CRISP FRENCH TOAST

Process 1 slice hearty white sandwich bread or challah, torn into 1-inch pieces, 1 tablespoon packed light brown sugar, and ¼ teaspoon ground cinnamon in food processor until finely ground, 8 to 12 pulses (you should have about ½ cup). Sprinkle 1 tablespoon breadcrumb mixture over 1 side of each slice of soaked bread. Cook as directed in step 4, starting with crumb mixture side down.

ALMOND-CRUSTED FRENCH TOAST

Process ½ cup slivered almonds and 1 tablespoon packed light brown sugar in food processor until coarsely ground, 12 to 15 pulses (you should have about ½ cup). Add 1 tablespoon triple sec and 1 teaspoon grated orange zest to milk mixture in step 2. Sprinkle 1 tablespoon nut mixture over 1 side of each slice of soaked bread. Cook as directed in step 4, starting with nut mixture side down.

Yeasted Waffles

✓ WHY THIS RECIPE WORKS

Raised waffles are barely on the current culinary radar, and that's a shame. They sound old-fashioned and do require an ounce of advance planning, but they are crisp, tasty, and easy to prepare. We wanted to revive this breakfast treat with yeasted waffles that were creamy and airy, tangy and salty, refined and complex. We settled on all-purpose flour, found the right amount of yeast to provide a pleasant tang, and added a full stick of melted butter for rich flavor. Refrigerating the batter overnight keeps the growth of the yeast under control and produces waffles with superior flavor. Even better, all you have to do in the morning is heat up the iron.

LET RISE OVERNIGHT The concept for yeasted waffles is simple enough. Most of the ingredients (flour, salt, sugar, yeast, milk, melted butter, and vanilla) are combined the night before and left to rise on the counter. The next day, eggs and baking soda are added and the batter is baked off. But older recipes call for the batter to be left out at room temperature, which causes the batter to rise and then fall, and turn sour rather than tangy. We find that slowing down the fermentation in the fridge ensures that flavors don't overdevelop. Also, this way we don't need to wait to add the eggs in the morning.

DON'T ADD BUTTERMILK We think buttermilk is the key to great pancakes and waffles made à la minute. (See Best Buttermilk Pancakes, page 86, and Buttermilk Waffles, page 96.) Unfortunately, most cooks don't have buttermilk in the fridge and many markets don't even carry it. The good news about this recipe: It works best with regular milk. The yeast provides plenty of tang. Buttermilk would be overkill.

FORGET THE BAKING SODA Many older recipes call for baking soda to be added with the eggs just before baking. In our recipe, this isn't necessary. The baking soda is needed for lift in those recipes because the batter is left out overnight, which results in dead yeast in the morning. In our waffles, the yeast has plenty of leavening power the next morning because the batter has been refrigerated; as a result, the baking soda is redundant.

USE A HOT IRON Not all waffle irons are the same—you want to use a hot iron. The best irons produce waffles that are evenly cooked and consistently browned from the beginning to the end of a batch—and in the promised shade of light to dark. Look for models with thick heating coils extending under most of the cooking surface, which cook efficiently, helping to ensure uniformly golden waffles.

YEASTED WAFFLES

MAKES SEVEN 7-INCH ROUND OR
FOUR 9-INCH SQUARE WAFFLES

While the waffles can be eaten as soon as they are removed from the waffle iron, they will have a crispier exterior if rested in a warm oven for 10 minutes. (This method also makes it possible to serve everyone at the same time.) This batter must be made 12 to 24 hours in advance. We prefer the texture of the waffles made in a classic waffle iron, but a Belgian waffle iron will work, though it will make fewer waffles.

1¾   cups milk
8   tablespoons unsalted butter, cut into
      8 pieces
2   cups (10 ounces) all-purpose flour

1   tablespoon sugar
1½   teaspoons instant or rapid-rise yeast
1   teaspoon salt
2   large eggs
1   teaspoon vanilla extract

1. Heat milk and butter in small saucepan over medium-low heat until butter is melted, 3 to 5 minutes. Let mixture cool until warm to touch.

2. Meanwhile, whisk flour, sugar, yeast, and salt together in large bowl. Gradually whisk warm milk mixture into flour mixture; continue to whisk until batter is smooth. Whisk eggs and vanilla in small bowl until combined, then add egg mixture to batter and whisk until incorporated. Scrape down bowl with rubber spatula, cover bowl with plastic wrap, and refrigerate for at least 12 hours or up to 24 hours.

3. Adjust oven rack to middle position and heat oven to 200 degrees. Set wire rack in rimmed baking sheet; place in oven. Heat waffle iron according to manufacturer's instructions. Remove batter from refrigerator when waffle iron is hot (batter will be foamy and doubled in size). Whisk batter to recombine (batter will deflate). Bake waffles according to manufacturer's instructions (use about ½ cup for 7-inch round iron and about 1 cup for 9-inch square iron). Transfer waffles to wire rack in preheated oven; repeat with remaining batter. Serve.

BLUEBERRY YEASTED WAFFLES

We found that frozen wild blueberries—which are smaller—work best here. Larger blueberries release too much juice, which burns and becomes bitter when it comes in contact with the waffle iron.

After removing waffle batter from refrigerator in step 3, gently fold 1½ cups frozen blueberries into batter using rubber spatula. Bake waffles as directed.

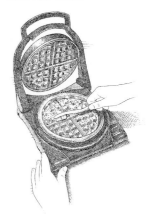

CLEANING A WAFFLE IRON

While most waffle irons and panini presses feature an easy-to-clean nonstick cooking surface, food still gets stuck in the deep ridges. A firm bristle toothbrush is perfect for this cleaning task. The bristles are stiff enough to remove stubborn stuck-on food yet soft enough for a nonstick surface. You can also use cotton swabs to get in the nooks and crannies.

Buttermilk Waffles

KEEPING WAFFLES WARM AND CRISP

We experimented with several methods of keeping waffles warm and crisp before finding one that worked well. First, we set the waffles on a baking sheet in a 200-degree oven, which was just hot enough to keep them warm without actually cooking them. But by the time the last batch was done, the ones that had been waiting in the oven the longest had lost their crispness.

Next, we placed the waffles on a wire rack set in a baking sheet. This method improved matters dramatically by allowing hot air to circulate underneath and keep the waffles crisp as if they had just come from the waffle iron.

✓ WHY THIS RECIPE WORKS

Most "waffle" recipes are merely repurposed pancake recipes that rely on butter and maple syrup to mask the mediocre results. And even those designed specifically for a waffle iron are time-consuming affairs that complicate this would-be simple breakfast. We found that a tip from Japanese tempura batter (yes, you read that right) set us on the course to fuss-free waffles.

INCREASE THE TANG We start with our recipe for Best Buttermilk Pancakes (page 86), but for waffles with a distinct tang, we supplement the buttermilk with rich sour cream.

BATTER UP For a light, crisp waffle, we took a cue from the Japanese and their method of making tempura. In tempura batters, seltzer or club soda is often used in place of still water. The idea is that the tiny bubbles of carbon dioxide released from the water will inflate the batter the same way as a chemical leavener—minus the metallic taste. Instead of the typical buttermilk, we use powdered buttermilk and seltzer.

BAKING SODA FOR BROWNING Because there is seltzer water in our batter, we wondered if we could omit the baking soda. Waffles made without baking soda emerged from the waffle iron with sufficient lift, but they were pale. Baking soda promotes browning, which in turn promotes better flavor, so we keep it in our recipe.

OIL ENCOURAGE CRISPNESS Straight out of the iron, our waffles were delightfully crisp, but as we ate them, we noticed that they quickly became soft. It turns out the interior moisture was making its way to the surface, causing our waffles to lose their crisp texture. We had been making our waffles with butter, which contains some water. Because fat repels moisture, we traded the butter for pure fat in the form of vegetable oil. Waffles made with oil stay significantly crispier than those made with melted butter. For the flavor of butter, simply add a pat to your hot waffles.

BUTTERMILK WAFFLES
MAKES ABOUT EIGHT 7-INCH ROUND WAFFLES

While the waffles can be eaten as soon as they are removed from the waffle iron, they will have a crispier exterior if rested in a warm oven for 10 minutes. Buttermilk powder is generally located in supermarkets near the dried-milk products or in the baking aisle. Leftover buttermilk powder can be kept in the refrigerator for up to a year. Seltzer or club soda gives these waffles a light texture that would otherwise be provided by whipped egg whites. (Avoid sparkling water such as Perrier—it's not bubbly enough.) Use a freshly opened bottle for maximum lift. Serve these waffles with butter and warm maple syrup.

2	cups (10 ounces) all-purpose flour
½	cup (2½ ounces) buttermilk powder
1	tablespoon sugar
¾	teaspoon salt
½	teaspoon baking soda
½	cup sour cream
2	large eggs
¼	teaspoon vanilla extract
¼	cup vegetable oil
1¼	cups seltzer water

1. Adjust oven rack to middle position and heat oven to 200 degrees. Set wire rack in rimmed baking sheet; place in oven. Whisk flour, buttermilk powder, sugar, salt, and baking soda together in large bowl. Whisk sour cream, eggs, vanilla, and oil together in medium bowl to combine. Gently stir seltzer into wet ingredients. Make well in center of dry ingredients and pour in wet ingredients. Using a rubber spatula, gently stir until just combined (batter should remain lumpy with few streaks of flour).

2. Heat waffle iron and bake waffles according to manufacturer's instructions (use about ⅓ cup for 7-inch round iron). Transfer waffles to wire rack in preheated oven; repeat with remaining batter. Serve.

Almond Granola

✓ WHY THIS RECIPE WORKS

The slow baking and frequent stirring that most do-it-yourself granola recipes recommend often result in a loose, granular texture—not the distinct clusters we were after. Our ideal granola would be markedly crisp yet tender enough to shatter easily when bitten.

START WITH THE RIGHT FOUNDATION We like whole rolled oats in our granola. Instant and quick oats make insubstantial, powdery granola. By contrast, steel-cut oats make eating granola akin to eating gravel. Some recipe add nuts whole, but we like them chopped for more even distribution.

SWEETEN IT Honey and maple syrup are the most common choices for granola. We find honey too distinct even in small amounts. Maple syrup, along with light brown sugar, gives our granola just the right level of sweetness.

ADD FAT FOR FLAVOR AND MOISTURE Granola recipes often add oil or butter. Intrigued by fat-free varieties of granola on the market, we tried leaving the fat out and the result was dry, powdery granola that no amount of milk or yogurt could rescue. It turns out that fat is essential for likable crispness. Why? When the water in a viscous liquid sweetener (like the maple syrup in our recipe) evaporates in the heat of the oven, the sugars left behind develop into a thin coating on the oats and nuts. But without any fat, the sugar coating will become brittle and dry. Butter burned in the heat of the oven, so we use vegetable oil in our granola.

PRESS, BAKE, AND THEN BREAK For granola with crisp, substantial chunks, we press the granola into the pan so it forms a solid sheet (as if we were making granola bars). We then bake the granola undisturbed (no stirring!) so it solidifies. Finally, we cool the baked granola and break it into pieces as large or small as we prefer.

FINISH WITH FRUIT We like dried fruit such as raisins, apples, or cranberries in our granola but baking the fruit turns it dry, even if you plump the fruit in water before mixing it in. The best method is to keep the fruit away from heat altogether—simply stir it into the granola after you've broken it up into pieces.

ALMOND GRANOLA WITH DRIED FRUIT

MAKES ABOUT 9 CUPS

Chopping the almonds by hand is best for superior texture and crunch. If you prefer not to hand chop, substitute an equal quantity of slivered or sliced almonds. Use a single type of your favorite dried fruit or a combination. Do not substitute quick oats. We especially like this granola served with our home-made Greek-style Yogurt (recipe follows).

- ⅓ cup maple syrup
- ⅓ cup packed (2⅓ ounces) light brown sugar
- 4 teaspoons vanilla extract
- ½ teaspoon salt
- ½ cup vegetable oil
- 5 cups old-fashioned rolled oats
- 2 cups (10 ounces) raw almonds, chopped coarse
- 2 cups (10 ounces) raisins or other dried fruit, chopped

1. Adjust oven rack to upper-middle position and heat oven to 325 degrees. Line rimmed baking sheet with parchment paper.

2. Whisk maple syrup, sugar, vanilla, and salt together in large bowl. Whisk in oil. Fold in oats and almonds until thoroughly coated.

3. Transfer oat mixture to prepared baking sheet and spread across sheet into thin, even layer (about ⅜ inch thick). Using stiff metal spatula, compress oat mixture until very compact. Bake until lightly browned, 40 to 45 minutes, rotating sheet halfway through baking. Remove granola from oven and let cool on wire rack to room temperature, about 1 hour. Break cooled granola into pieces of desired size. Stir in dried fruit. (Granola can be stored in airtight container for up to 2 weeks.)

PECAN-ORANGE GRANOLA WITH DRIED CRANBERRIES

Add 2 tablespoons finely grated orange zest and 2½ teaspoons ground cinnamon to maple syrup mixture in step 2. Substitute coarsely chopped pecans for almonds. Use 2 cups dried cranberries for dried fruit.

SPICED WALNUT GRANOLA WITH DRIED APPLE

Add 2 teaspoons ground cinnamon, 1½ teaspoons ground ginger, ¾ teaspoon ground allspice, ½ teaspoon ground nutmeg, and ½ teaspoon pepper to maple syrup mixture in step 2. Substitute coarsely chopped walnuts for almonds. Use 2 cups chopped dried apple for dried fruit.

TROPICAL GRANOLA WITH DRIED MANGO

Reduce vanilla extract to 2 teaspoons and add 1½ teaspoons ground ginger and ¾ teaspoon ground nutmeg to maple syrup mixture in step 2. Substitute coarsely chopped macadamias for almonds and 1½ cups unsweetened shredded coconut for 1 cup oats. Use 2 cups chopped dried mango or pineapple for dried fruit.

HAZELNUT GRANOLA WITH DRIED PEAR

Substitute coarsely chopped skinned hazelnuts for almonds. Use 2 cups chopped dried pear for dried fruit.

GREEK-STYLE YOGURT

MAKES 2 CUPS

Making your own yogurt takes a little time—you must start this recipe a day ahead—but the results are outstanding. Mix with granola or enjoy drizzled with fruit and/or honey. Be sure to use pasteurized and not ultrapasteurized or UHT milk in this recipe.

4	cups 2 percent low-fat milk
¼	cup nonfat dry milk powder
¼	cup plain 2 percent Greek Yogurt

1. Adjust oven rack to middle position. Place fine-mesh strainer over large glass bowl, then set bowl in larger bowl filled with ice water. Heat milk in large saucepan over medium-low heat (do not stir while heating), until milk registers 185 degrees. Remove pot from heat, gently stir in milk powder, and let cool to 160 degrees, 7 to 10 minutes. Strain milk through prepared strainer and let cool, gently stirring occasionally, until milk registers 110 to 112 degrees; remove from ice bath.

2. In small bowl, gently stir ½ cup warm milk into yogurt until smooth. Stir yogurt mixture back into milk. Cover tightly with plastic wrap and poke several holes in plastic. Place bowl in oven and turn on oven light, creating a warm environment of 100 to 110 degrees. Let yogurt sit undisturbed until thickened and set, 5 to 7 hours. Transfer to refrigerator until completely chilled, about 3 hours.

3. Set clean fine-mesh strainer over large measuring cup and line with double layer of coffee filters. Transfer yogurt to prepared strainer, cover with plastic, and refrigerate until about 2 cups of liquid have drained into measuring cup, 7 to 8 hours. Transfer strained yogurt to jar with tight-fitting lid, discarding drained liquid. Yogurt can be refrigerated for up to 1 week.

TWO WAYS TO SKIN HAZELNUTS

The most common way to remove the skins from toasted hazelnuts is to rub them off with a dish towel. Here are two other methods that contain the mess.

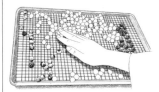

A. This method works best with a wire rack with a crosshatch design. Place nuts on a wire rack set in a rimmed baking sheet, then lightly toast them in a 350-degree oven for 10 to 15 minutes. Once hazelnuts are cool enough to touch, rub them against the rack, letting their skins fall the sheet below.

B. Place nuts on a rimmed baking sheet and lightly toast them in a 350-degree oven for 10 to 15 minutes. Place freshly toasted nuts in a mesh strainer and, once nuts have cooled slightly, rub them back and forth against rough mesh. Most of the skins sift through the strainer and it's easy to extract the skinned nuts from the remaining loose skins.

RUSTIC DINNER ROLLS

Yeasted Rolls and Loaves

Nine Bread Myths You Shouldn't Believe

Bread making is shrouded in mystery and plagued by misinformation and myths. After years of kitchen testing, we're ready to set the record straight.

MYTH #1: Bread Flour Is Best
FACT: All-Purpose Flour Is Fine

We have found that unbleached all-purpose flour is the best choice in most bread recipes. Bread flour (which has more protein than all-purpose) is necessary only for rustic breads with a really sturdy crumb and thick crust.

MYTH #2: Tap Water Is Fine
FACT: Bottled Water Is Best

Water from the tap can contain many minerals and additives that adversely affect the flavor of bread. In our experience, bread made with bottled water has a sweeter, fuller flavor than bread made with tap water. If your tap water has an off-taste or is particularly hard or soft, we recommend using bottled water.

MYTH #3: Salt Is Optional
FACT: Salt Is Essential

If salt comes in direct contact with yeast, it will kill the yeast. Therefore, salt should be added to the dough after the yeast has been mixed with the flour. Because salt controls the activity of yeast, strengthens gluten, and accents the bread's flavor, it should never be omitted.

MYTH #4: Yeast Must Be Proofed
FACT: Proofing Is Unnecessary

Older cookbooks tell you to sprinkle yeast over warm water and wait five minutes before proceeding. This process, called proofing the yeast, is no longer necessary. Our test kitchen relies on instant yeast (also labeled rapid-rise yeast) and most of the time we add the yeast directly to the dry ingredients.

MYTH #5: Always Start with a Sponge
FACT: Some Breads Don't Require a Sponge

A sponge is made by mixing a portion of the flour, water, and yeast before the dough is made. This sponge (also called a *biga* or pre-ferment) is then allowed to ferment for several hours or overnight before the dough is prepared. Although a sponge does impart a great deal of flavor to rustic breads, it isn't necessary with higher-fat loaf breads, for which all of the ingredients are usually just combined in a bowl.

MYTH #6: Hand Kneading Is Better
FACT: You Should Use a Stand Mixer

In the test kitchen, kneading in a stand mixer is the technique of choice. This method ensures that we don't add too much flour to the dough (which can happen with hand kneading and leads to dry, tough loaves). A stand mixer is especially suited for kneading wet or sticky dough. Once dough is kneaded, it may require a brief kneading by hand on the counter to form a cohesive ball. Of course, you needn't own a stand mixer and for most of our recipes, hand kneading is still an option.

MYTH #7: You Can't Overknead
FACT: Too Much Kneading Leads to Flavor Loss

Many bakers assume that the longer you knead bread, the better. However, prolonged kneading will overoxidize the dough, which leads to flavor loss. When properly kneaded, dough should have a smooth, almost shiny appearance. If you pull the dough, it should feel very stretchy and quickly spring back into place.

MYTH #8: Rising Times Are Flexible
FACT: Rising Times Should Be Followed

While there is some flexibility in the first rise (fermentation), we have found that it is important to pay close attention to the dough during the second rise (proofing). If underproofed, there is a chance that the dough will rise too much when baked, causing splitting and tearing. If overproofed, the dough may collapse when baked. A reliable way to test the dough's progress during proofing is to press it gently with a lightly moistened finger.

MYTH #9: Baked Bread Will Sound Hollow
FACT: Thermometers Are Helpful

Many recipes instruct bakers to tap the bottom of the loaf to check the bread's doneness—if it sounds hollow, then it's done. In our experience, we have found that it is much better to combine visual signs (the bread is properly browned) with the use of an instant-read thermometer. Rustic breads should be baked to an internal temperature of 200 to 210 degrees, while richer breads are done at 190 to 195 degrees.

Bread Making at a Glance

Here's a brief overview of the steps you must follow to make most breads.

1. MEASURE: Carefully measuring ingredients is crucial to success. Because the ratio of flour to water greatly impacts the end result, we recommend weighing the ingredients before making bread.

2. MIX: Mixing distributes the ingredients, hydrates the flour, and starts the development of gluten.

3. AUTOLYSE: Once the ingredients are fully combined, a 20-minute rest (called autolyse) allows the flour to completely absorb the moisture and makes kneading quicker and easier.

4. KNEAD: Kneading develops the gluten strands in the dough, which in turn provide the bread's structure. Resist the temptation to add excess flour, which will make the baked loaf dry.

5. FERMENT: Fermentation is the process in which the starches in the flour break down to feed the yeast, which then releases carbon dioxide, which gives the bread lift. We like to ferment dough in a clear, straight-sided container. It is also helpful to mark the height of the dough by placing a rubber band around the container.

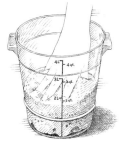

6. PUNCH DOWN: Punching down helps to redistribute the yeast and allows it to find new food. This increases the yeast activity, ultimately leading to bread with a better texture. Punching down bread should not be violent. The simplest way is to pull the edges of the dough toward the center or push down gently on the dough.

7. SHAPE: Form the dough into the desired shape on an unfloured work surface, which allows the dough to grip the counter, thus facilitating shaping.

8. PROOF: Proofing is the dough's final rise before baking. When properly proofed, dough will have enough energy to provide the yeast with one last burst of activity (called oven spring) in the hot oven.

9. SLASH: Slashing the proofed loaf with a sharp paring knife or razor allows the crust to expand and prevents the bread from splitting in the oven.

10. ADD WATER: Misting the loaf delays the formation of a crust, allowing the bread to fully expand without tearing or splitting. The steam also promotes a crisp, glossy crust.

11. BAKE: A baking stone will help keep the oven temperature steady and promote a thicker, crispier crust on free-form loaves.

12. COOL: Cooling on a rack allows moisture to escape and keeps the bottom crust from becoming damp and soggy.

SHAPING DINNER ROLLS

1. Pat dough into 12 by 10-inch rectangle.

2. Roll dough to form even cylinder, stretching to 18-inch length.

3. Using bench scraper or chef's knife, cut cylinder into 16 pieces.

4. Using circular motion, gently form dough pieces into rounds.

5. Arrange rounds in pan, one in center, seven around edge.

Best American Dinner Rolls

✔ WHY THIS RECIPE WORKS

Quick recipes for dinner rolls produce rolls that aren't much better than what you buy at the supermarket because they don't allow enough time for the dough to develop much flavor. But homemade rolls—made right—are often too bothersome for an overextended home cook. We wanted to develop a largely make-ahead recipe that would deliver rich, soft, tender, airy, semisweet, pull-apart all-American dinner rolls.

DON'T BE SHY WITH THE BUTTER AND EGGS Plenty of butter contributes richness and flavor to our rolls. The same goes for eggs. Most recipes use a single egg, but we added an extra egg for more flavor and better texture.

INCLUDE SUGAR AND SALT We found that typical recipes for soft dinner rolls contain downright skimpy amounts of sugar and salt. For best flavor, we significantly bumped up both ingredients.

SCALD YOUR MILK Years ago, milk was scalded to destroy potentially dangerous bacteria. With the pasteurization process scalding is moot. But in bread baking, milk is often scalded because it breaks down a reducing agent, glutathione, that can weaken gluten. If cold milk is added to the dough, the bread will bake up coarse and dense. (For more on this process, see "Scalding Milk" on page 108.) To that end, we heat the milk when making our dough for soft, well-risen rolls.

RISE, RISE, AND RISE AGAIN The queen mother of rich breads, brioche, traditionally undergoes several rises, including a slow, cool rise in the fridge that gives the flavors time to develop. We apply the same magic to our rolls. This technique also has the advantage of allowing the bulk of the work to be completed a day (or even two days) in advance.

BEST AMERICAN DINNER ROLLS
MAKES 16 ROLLS

If you don't have a stand mixer, you can mix the dough by hand following the instructions on page 115. For this recipe, the dough is made and the rolls are shaped and refrigerated a day or two before being baked and served. Be sure to plan accordingly, as the refrigerated rolls require about 6 hours to rise before they're ready for baking. If your cake pans have a dark nonstick finish, bake the rolls in a 375-degree oven to moderate the browning. This dough should be moister than most; resist the urge to add more flour than is needed to keep the dough from sticking to your hands. Made on a humid day, the dough may require more flour than if made on a dry day.

- ¾ cup whole milk
- 8 tablespoons unsalted butter, melted
- 6 tablespoons sugar
- 1½ teaspoons salt
- 2 large eggs, room temperature
- 2¼ teaspoons instant or rapid-rise yeast
- 3 cups (15 ounces) all-purpose flour, plus extra as needed

1. Bring milk to boil in small saucepan over medium heat; let stand off heat until skin forms on surface, 3 to 5 minutes. Transfer milk to bowl of stand mixer and add 6 tablespoons melted butter, sugar, and salt; whisk to combine and let mixture cool. When mixture is just warm to touch (90 to 100 degrees), whisk in eggs and yeast until combined.

2. Transfer bowl to stand mixer fitted with dough hook, add flour, and mix on low speed until combined, 1 to 2 minutes. Increase speed to medium-low and knead about 3 minutes; when pressed with finger, dough should feel tacky and moist but should not stick to finger.

Evaporated milk is made by slowly heating milk to remove about half of its water—a process that gives the milk a light golden color and mildly sweet flavor. Nestlé states that Carnation evaporated milk can be substituted in a 1:1 ratio for regular whole milk. To test this claim, we opened a few cans to make sponge cake, vanilla pudding, and Parker House rolls, and compared the results with the same recipes made with regular whole milk. The results with evaporated milk were inferior across the board. The evaporated-milk cake exhibited a firmer structure than the cake made with regular milk. And although the consistency of the evaporated-milk pudding was acceptable, its delicate vanilla flavor was marred by caramel undertones. The Parker House rolls made with evaporated milk emerged from the oven more stunted and much darker than rolls made with regular milk.

The bottom line: Evaporated milk is a poor substitute for regular milk. The reason? It contains about 6.6 percent fat and 10 percent caramelized lactose (milk sugar), versus the 3.3 percent fat and 4.5 percent lactose in regular milk—differences significant enough to interfere with flavor and with proper structure in baked goods.

(If dough is sticky, add another 1 to 3 tablespoons flour.) Continue to knead until cohesive, elastic dough has formed (it should clear sides of bowl but stick to bottom), 4 to 5 minutes longer. Transfer dough to lightly floured counter and knead by hand until very soft and moist but not overly sticky, 1 to 2 minutes. (If dough sticks excessively to hands and work surface, knead in flour 1 tablespoon at a time until dough is workable.) Place dough in large, lightly greased bowl; cover tightly with plastic wrap and let rise at room temperature until doubled in size, 2 to 3 hours.

3. Grease two 9-inch round cake pans. Transfer dough to lightly floured counter and press into rough 12 by 10-inch rectangle, with long side facing you. Roll dough toward you into firm cylinder, keeping roll taut by tucking it under itself as you go. Using your palms, roll dough (seam side down) from center outward until cylinder measures 18 inches. Using bench scraper, cut cylinder into 16 equal pieces. Working with 1 piece of dough at a time, loosely cup hand around dough (not directly over it) and, without applying pressure, move hand in small circular motions to form smooth, taut round. Arrange shaped rolls in prepared pans (one in center and seven spaced evenly around edges); loosely cover cake pans with lightly greased plastic, then cover pans securely with aluminum foil. Refrigerate for at least 24 or up to 48 hours.

4. Remove foil (but not plastic) from cake pans; let rolls rise at cool room temperature until doubled in size (rolls should press against each other), 6 to 7 hours. Thirty minutes before baking, adjust oven rack to lower-middle position and heat oven to 400 degrees. Brush rolls with remaining 2 tablespoons melted butter and bake until deep golden brown, 14 to 18 minutes. Let rolls cool in pans on wire rack for about 3 minutes, then invert onto rack; reinvert rolls and let cool for 10 to 15 minutes longer. Break rolls apart and serve warm. (Rolls can be placed in zipper-lock bag and stored at room temperature for up to 3 days. Wrapped with foil before placing in bag, rolls can be frozen for up to 1 month.)

Parker House Rolls

✓ WHY THIS RECIPE WORKS

These thin-crusted, fluffy-crumbed American rolls are pillowy soft, a little sweet, and packed with butter. They owe their name to Boston's famed Parker House, a hotel that has been a bastion of Brahmin hospitality since the middle of the 19th century. For our version, we wanted a simple, rich roll.

GIVE THE DOUGH A RELATIVELY SHORT KNEAD With a soft, billowy, tender crumb as our goal, we tried kneading times of 4 to 10 minutes (in a stand mixer at medium speed) and were most pleased with a 8-minute knead, followed by a scant minute of hand kneading. Eight minutes builds just enough gluten for support but not enough to detract from the airy crumb.

ROUND THE ROLLS After we divide the dough, we round the individual portions on the counter until they develop a smooth, tight skin and perfect globe shape. Rounding relies on the friction created between the moisture in the dough and the work surface, and this process helps the dough rise by redistributing the yeast and sugars and expunging the carbon dioxide.

SHAPE CAREFULLY The best way to shape the dough is to lightly flatten each piece of dough with your palms and then roll it into an oval shape with a small French-style rolling pin or short dowel. It is important to keep the edges thicker than the center so that they will adhere to each other when the dough is folded and not puff open during baking.

BRUSH WITH BUTTER AND RISE After folding and spacing the rolls on a baking sheet, we give them a light brushing of butter and allow them to rise. Traditional recipes suggest dunking the formed rolls in melted butter, but we consider that too much of a good thing.

BAKE THE ROLLS ON A BAKING SHEET While we liked the height of the rolls baked in a dish, the rolls in the middle were gummy long after the outer rolls were perfectly baked. A metal baking sheet delivers even heat and gets the rolls out of the oven in about 20 minutes.

PARKER HOUSE ROLLS

MAKES 24 ROLLS

If you don't have a stand mixer, you can mix the dough by hand following the instructions on page 115. You will need about 6 tablespoons of melted butter to brush over the dough during shaping, and over the rolls before baking.

1¼	cups warm whole milk (110 degrees)
8	tablespoons (1 stick) unsalted butter, melted and cooled, plus extra for brushing
1	large egg
4–4½	cups (20 to 22½ ounces) all-purpose flour
2	tablespoons sugar
2¼	teaspoons instant or rapid-rise yeast
1½	teaspoons salt
	Vegetable oil spray

1. Whisk milk, melted butter, and egg together in 4-cup liquid measuring cup. Combine 4 cups flour, sugar, yeast, and salt in stand mixer fitted with dough hook. With mixer on low speed, add milk mixture and mix until dough comes together, about 2 minutes.

2. Increase mixer speed to medium-low and knead until dough is smooth and elastic, about 8 minutes. If after 4 minutes more flour is needed, add remaining ½ cup flour,

2 tablespoons at a time, until dough clears sides of bowl but sticks to bottom.

3. Turn dough out onto lightly floured counter and knead to form smooth, round ball. Place dough in large, lightly oiled bowl and cover with greased plastic wrap. Let rise in warm place until doubled in size, 1 to 1½ hours.

4. Line 2 large baking sheets with parchment paper. Turn dough out onto clean counter, divide it into 2 equal pieces, and using your hands, stretch each piece into an even 12-inch log. Cut each log of dough into 12 equal pieces and cover with greased plastic. Working with 1 piece of dough at a time (keep remaining pieces covered), round dough into smooth, taut balls.

5. Use your hands and small rolling pin to flatten and roll each piece of dough into oval with a depressed middle. Brush oval-shaped pieces of dough with melted butter, then fold into traditional Parker House shape, pressing lightly on edges to seal. Lay rolls on prepared sheets, spaced about 2 inches apart. Mist rolls with vegetable oil spray, cover loosely with plastic, and let rise in warm place until nearly doubled in size and dough barely springs back when poked with knuckle, 45 minutes to 1¼ hours.

6. Adjust oven racks to upper-middle and lower-middle positions and heat oven to 350 degrees. Brush rolls lightly with melted butter, then spray lightly with water. Bake until golden, 20 to 25 minutes, switching and rotating sheets halfway through baking. Let rolls cool on pans for 10 minutes, then serve warm.

TO MAKE AHEAD: In step 3, do not let dough rise, but refrigerate it overnight or up to 16 hours; let dough sit at room temperature for 30 minutes then continue with step 4. Alternatively, unbaked rolls can be frozen for up to 1 month; let rolls rise in step 5, then freeze. Transfer frozen rolls to large zipperlock bag for easy storage. To bake, transfer frozen rolls to 2 parchment-lined baking sheets and let sit at room temperature for 30 minutes while heating oven; bake as directed, increasing baking time to 25 to 30 minutes.

SHAPING PARKER HOUSE ROLLS

1. After dividing dough into 24 pieces (cover with greased plastic wrap), use cupped palm to roll each piece of dough into smooth, tight ball and then loosely cover it with plastic.

2. Beginning with ball rounded first (because dough has relaxed), use palm of your hand to flatten ball of dough into ½-inch-thick circle.

3. With small rolling pin or thick dowel, floured to prevent sticking, flatten out center of dough until circle becomes rough oval. Make sure to keep edges thicker than middle.

4. Lightly brush dough with melted butter, then fold in half and gently seal edges. Place roll on prepared baking sheet. Repeat recipe steps 4 through 6 with remaining balls of dough, making sure to space rolls evenly on sheet.

Crescent Rolls

SCALDING MILK

Once upon a time, scalding milk—bringing milk to just shy of a boil—was necessary to kill off bacteria that could interfere with thickening, as in a custard or béchamel. Nowadays, however, modern pasteurization makes this unnecessary.

However, many recipes still call for scalded milk for two reasons. One: It raises the temperature of the other ingredients. For instance, yeast thrives and causes maximum rise in a warm environment of about 80 degrees. While most cooks focus on the temperature of the kitchen, the temperature of the dough is equally important. If cold butter, eggs, and milk are used to make a yeast bread, the dough will be well below room temperature, thus slowing the rising process. Two: Scalding breaks down a reducing agent in milk, glutathione, that can weaken gluten and thus result in coarse, dense bread.

For this reason, many recipes call for warm (usually about 110 degrees) or scalded liquids. Note that scalding is relatively imprecise. *The Joy of Cooking* defines "scalding" as the temperature at which tiny bubbles form around the edge of the pan, or about 180 degrees. Other sources define scalding as just below 212 degrees or when a thick skin develops on the milk surface. In either case, very hot milk will kill active yeast cells if not first combined with cooler ingredients.

✔ WHY THIS RECIPE WORKS

Crescent rolls from the supermarket are artificial-tasting and stale quickly, but making them at home is time-consuming. We were determined to come up with a recipe for rich, tender, flaky crescent rolls that could fit into an already-hectic holiday cooking schedule. A lot of butter and a little patience add up to rolls that are worlds better than ready-to-roll crescents out of a tube.

ADD BUTTER The dough for our crescent rolls differs from rustic bread and pizza doughs—it has a lot of fat. This family of bread dough (which includes American sandwich bread, brioche, and challah) calls for eggs, milk, and butter on top of flour, water, and yeast. With all of that fat, however, the dough can be incredibly sticky and hard to handle. This is why chilling it is essential. (Chilling also gives the gluten time to relax so that you can stretch the dough easily into crescents.)

CHILL WELL Not only is a chilled dough easier to handle, but the texture of the final rolls made from chilled dough is better, too. These rolls are flaky and flavorful with a blistery, snappy crust. The process of retarding (or chilling for a long time) allows acetic acid to build up in the dough, which is responsible for a richer flavor as well as a blistered crust.

STRETCH, CUT, AND ROLL To turn a lump of dough into 16 crescent rolls, first roll the dough into a 20 by 13-inch rectangle. Use a pizza wheel to trim the edges. Cut the dough in half lengthwise, and then cut each length into eight triangles. Elongate each triangle of dough before rolling the crescent, stretching it an additional 2 to 3 inches in length. And then, starting at the wide end, gently roll up the dough, ending with the pointed tip on the bottom.

START IN A HOT OVEN We start our crescent rolls in a 425-degree oven for an initial bake, and then lower the oven temperature to 350 degrees just when the rolls are starting to color. Why? This improves the rolls' oven spring, or the dramatic increase in size caused by that initial blast of heat from the oven. The high heat makes the rolls larger and loftier. Lowering the oven temperature allows the rolls to bake through without burning.

CRESCENT ROLLS
MAKES 16 ROLLS

If you don't have a stand mixer, you can mix the dough by hand following the instructions on page 115. We developed this recipe using lower-protein flour such as Gold Medal or Pillsbury. If using a higher-protein flour such as King Arthur, reduce the flour amount to 3½ cups (17½ ounces).

16 tablespoons unsalted butter, cut into 16 pieces
¾ cup skim milk
¼ cup (1¾ ounces) sugar
3 large eggs
4 cups (20 ounces) all-purpose flour, plus extra as needed
1 teaspoon instant or rapid-rise yeast
1½ teaspoons salt
1 large egg white, beaten with 1 teaspoon water

1. Microwave butter, milk, and sugar in 4-cup liquid measuring cup until butter is mostly melted and mixture is warm (110 degrees), about 1½ minutes. Whisk to melt butter and blend in sugar. Beat eggs lightly in medium bowl; add about one-third of warm milk mixture, whisking to combine.

When bottom of bowl feels warm, add remaining milk mixture, whisking to combine.

2. Using stand mixer fitted with paddle, mix flour and yeast together on low speed until combined, about 15 seconds. Add egg mixture in steady stream and mix until loose, shiny dough forms (you may also see satiny webs as dough moves in bowl), about 1 minute. Increase speed to medium and beat for 1 minute; add salt slowly and continue beating until stronger webs form, about 3 minutes longer. (Dough will remain loose rather than forming neat, cohesive mass.) Transfer dough to large, lightly greased bowl; cover tightly with plastic wrap and let rise at room temperature until dough doubles in size and surface feels tacky, about 3 hours.

3. Line rimmed baking sheet with plastic. Sprinkle dough with flour (no more than 2 tablespoons) to prevent sticking and press down gently to deflate. Transfer dough to floured counter and press into rough rectangle shape. Transfer rectangle to prepared sheet, cover with plastic, and refrigerate for 8 to 12 hours.

4. Transfer dough rectangle to lightly floured counter and line sheet with parchment paper. Roll dough into uniform 20 by 13-inch rectangle. Cut dough in half lengthwise, then cut each rectangle into 8 triangles, trimming edges as needed to make uniform triangles. Before rolling crescents, elongate each triangle of dough, stretching it an additional 2 to 3 inches in length. Starting at wide end, gently roll up dough, ending with pointed tip on bottom, and push ends toward each other to form crescent shape. Arrange crescents in 4 rows on

prepared sheet, wrap sheet with plastic, and refrigerate for at least 2 hours or up to 3 days.

5. Remove sheet with chilled rolls from refrigerator, unwrap, and slide sheet into large clean garbage bag; seal to close. Let crescents rise until they feel slightly tacky and soft and have lost their chill, 45 minutes to 1 hour.

6. Thirty minutes before baking, adjust oven racks to lower-middle and lowest positions, place second rimmed sheet on lower rack, and heat oven to 425 degrees. Bring 1 cup water to boil on stovetop. Lightly brush risen crescent rolls with egg-white mixture. Working quickly, place sheet with rolls on upper rack, then pour boiling water onto rimmed sheet on lower rack and quickly close oven door. Bake for 10 minutes, then reduce oven temperature to 350 degrees and continue baking until tops and bottoms of rolls are deep golden brown, 12 to 16 minutes longer. Transfer rolls to wire rack, let cool for 5 minutes, and serve warm. (Rolls can be placed in zipper-lock bag and stored at room temperature for up to 3 days. Wrapped with aluminum foil before placing in bag, rolls can be frozen for up to 1 month.)

TO MAKE AHEAD: Rolls can be partially baked and frozen until ready to serve. Begin baking rolls as instructed, but let them bake at 350 degrees for only 4 minutes, or until tops and bottoms brown slightly. Remove them from oven and let cool to room temperature. Place partially baked rolls in single layer inside zipper-lock bag and freeze. When ready to serve, defrost rolls at room temperature and place in preheated 350-degree oven for 12 to 16 minutes.

SHAPING CRESCENT ROLLS

1. Roll dough to 20 by 13-inch rectangle; Use pizza wheel to trim edges. Cut dough in half lengthwise, then cut each into 8 triangles for a total of 16.

2. Before rolling crescents, elongate each triangle of dough, stretching it an additional 2 to 3 inches in length.

3. Starting at wide end, gently roll up each crescent, ending with pointed tip on bottom and push ends toward each other to form crescent shape.

Rustic Dinner Rolls

✔ WHY THIS RECIPE WORKS

The remarkably crisp crust of European-style dinner rolls keeps them in the domain of professionals, who use steam-injected ovens to expose the developing crust to moisture. We wanted a reliable recipe for rustic dinner rolls with a crisp crust and chewy crumb as good as any from an artisanal bakery. Among our discoveries, we found that making a wetter dough and letting it sit for 30 minutes (a process called autolyse) are the best fixes.

USE A WET DOUGH Our first tests left us with unimpressive dinner rolls. As a result, we began playing with hydration to fix the dense crumb. After all, during baking, the water within the dough turns to steam, which then rushes to escape, making hollow pockets within. The more water, the airier the crumb. Determining that our original recipe gave us a dough with 60 percent hydration, we assembled several batches of dough with varying amounts of water. Sure enough, increasing hydration opened the crumb considerably. Working our way up, we found about 72 percent hydration to be optimal; more than that and the dough started to get too wet to shape into rolls.

ADD HONEY AND WHEAT As in our Olive-Rosemary Bread (page 131), we swap some of the bread flour for whole wheat and add a bit of honey. This gives us rolls with subtle earthiness and just enough sweetness to leave the rolls' savory profile intact.

HANDLE GENTLY Using more water improves the finished rolls but also makes the dough extremely sticky, oozy, and hard to shape. In fact, the very process of forming rolls sometimes causes the delicate dough to deflate, making its texture too dense. To solve this problem, we forgo shaping altogether and instead use a bench scraper to divide the dough into rough (but equal) pieces. With less handling, these rolls retain far more of the open texture we take such pains to achieve. But to keep the soft dough from spreading and baking into a squat shape we begin by crowding them in a cake pan, coated lightly with flour. To keep the spots that rest against each other from staying soft, we remove the rolls from the oven halfway through baking, pull them apart, and return them to the oven spaced out on a baking sheet. With this two-stage baking method, they finish uniformly golden and crisp.

START HIGH For a shatteringly crisp crust, we start the rolls at a higher temperature, then reduce the heat to finish them. This initial blast of heat makes all the difference between a so-so crust and one with real crackling crispness. It has another advantage, too—boosting the oven spring (the rise that yeasted dough experiences when it first hits the heat of the oven), so the crumb is even airier than before. Misting the rolls with water before baking (mimicking steam-injected ovens) makes the crust even crispier.

RUSTIC DINNER ROLLS
MAKES 16 ROLLS

Because this dough is sticky, keep your hands well floured when handling it. We do not recommend mixing this sticky dough by hand.

1½	cups plus 1 tablespoon water, room temperature
2	teaspoons honey
1½	teaspoons instant or rapid-rise yeast
3	cups plus 1 tablespoon (16½ ounces) bread flour, plus extra as needed
3	tablespoons whole-wheat flour
1½	teaspoons salt

1. Whisk water, honey, and yeast together in bowl of stand mixer until well combined, making sure no honey sticks to bottom of bowl. Transfer bowl to stand mixer fitted with dough hook. Add bread flour and whole-wheat flour and mix on low speed until cohesive dough is formed, about 3 minutes; cover bowl tightly with plastic wrap and let sit at room temperature for 30 minutes.

2. Sprinkle salt evenly over dough and knead on low speed for 5 minutes, scraping down bowl and dough hook as needed. Increase speed to medium and continue to knead until dough is smooth and slightly tacky, about 1 minute. If dough is very sticky, add 1 to 2 tablespoons flour and continue mixing for 1 minute. Transfer dough to large, lightly greased bowl; cover tightly with plastic and let rise at room temperature until doubled in size, about 1 hour.

3. Spray rubber spatula or bowl scraper with vegetable oil spray. Fold partially risen dough over itself by gently lifting and folding edge of dough toward middle. Turn bowl 90 degrees; fold again. Rotate bowl again and fold once more. Cover with plastic and let rise for 30 minutes. Repeat folding, replace plastic, and let dough rise until doubled in size, about 30 minutes longer.

4. Grease two 9-inch round cake pans. Transfer dough to floured counter and sprinkle top with more flour. Using bench scraper, cut dough in half and gently stretch each half into 16-inch log. Cut each log into 8 equal pieces and dust top of each piece with more flour. With floured hands, gently pick up each piece and roll in palms to coat with flour, shaking off excess. Arrange rolls in prepared pans, placing one in center and seven spaced evenly around edges, with long side of each roll running from center of pan to edge and making sure cut side faces up. Loosely cover pans with lightly greased plastic and let rolls rise until doubled in size, about 30 minutes. (Dough should barely spring back when poked with knuckle.)

5. Thirty minutes before baking, adjust oven rack to middle position and heat oven to 500 degrees. Spray rolls lightly with water, bake until tops of rolls are brown, about 10 minutes, then remove them from oven. Reduce oven temperature to 400 degrees; using dish towels or oven mitts, invert rolls from both cake pans onto rimmed baking sheet. When rolls are cool enough to handle, turn them right side up, pull apart, and space evenly on sheet. Continue to bake until rolls develop deep golden-brown crust and sound hollow when tapped on bottom, 10 to 15 minutes, rotating sheet halfway through baking. Transfer rolls to wire rack and let cool to room temperature, about 1 hour, before serving. (Rolls can be placed in zipper-lock bag and stored at room temperature for up to 3 days. Wrapped with aluminum foil before placing in bag, rolls can be frozen for up to 1 month. To recrisp crust, thaw rolls at room temperature, if frozen, and place unwrapped rolls in 450-degree oven for 6 to 8 minutes.)

Potato Buns

WHY THIS RECIPE WORKS

Potato roll recipes abound, but they're inconsistent. Almost none specify what type of potato to use, and some use so much potato that the bread gets weighed down by the load. We wanted a potato roll that delivered the same soft tenderness of a classic American dinner roll but without its richness. What's more, our dough should work equally well for burger buns.

REACH FOR RUSSETS We opted for peeled russet potatoes, figuring that their floury texture would serve us best. Initial testing showed that the more we upped the potato the more we had to decrease the flour in order to keep our rolls light and fluffy. How is it that a food almost synonymous with stodge has the ability to bestow such a light, soft character on bread? When potatoes are boiled, their starch granules swell with water. When these swollen starches are mixed into bread dough, they physically interfere with the flour proteins' ability to link together and form gluten, thus weakening the dough's structure so that it bakes up softer and more tender.

ADD MORE POTATOES FOR A SHORTER RISE We also discovered that the more potato we used the less time the dough needed to rest. We chalked that up to the dispersal of more warm potato throughout the dough, since yeast thrives in a warm environment. But we later learned that there was a more potato-specific reason behind the faster rise: The potassium in potatoes activates yeast, and the more of it there is the quicker and more vigorous the rise.

USE THE POTATO COOKING WATER TOO When potatoes are boiled, they leach almost half of their potassium into the cooking water—helping to explain why so many recipes add it to the dough. We found that when we switched from using 5 tablespoons

of milk to the same amount of potato cooking water, the rising times dropped still more.

BUILD STRUCTURE WITH BREAD FLOUR We had been using all-purpose flour in our dough, but with the increased potato, our rolls fell flat. The protein in all-purpose flour couldn't provide enough muscle to support all the freeloading potato starch, so we switched to higher-protein bread flour. This simple swap increases the protein and provides just enough stable yet tender structure to support the potatoes, yielding rolls that are not only perfectly risen but also light and airy.

POTATO BURGER BUNS
MAKES 9 BUNS

These rolls are ideal for both burgers and sandwiches. If you don't have a stand mixer, you can mix the dough by hand following the instructions on page 115. Don't salt the cooking water for the potatoes. A pound of russet potatoes should yield just over 1 very firmly packed cup (½ pound) of mash. To ensure optimum rise, your dough should be warm; if your potatoes or potato cooking water are too hot to touch, let cool before proceeding with the recipe. This dough looks very dry when mixing begins but will soften as mixing progresses. If you prefer, you may portion the rolls by weight in step 5 (2.75 ounces of dough per roll).

1	pound russet potatoes, peeled and cut into 1-inch pieces
2	tablespoons unsalted butter, cut into 4 pieces
2¼	cups (12⅓ ounces) bread flour
1	tablespoon sugar
2	teaspoons instant or rapid-rise yeast
1	teaspoon salt
2	large eggs, 1 lightly beaten with 1 teaspoon water and pinch salt
1	tablespoon sesame seeds (optional)

MASHING POTATOES

For the fluffiest mashed potatoes, the goal is to use the gentlest touch possible to avoid bursting the potatoes' swollen starch granules. Once released, the sticky gel inside will turn the mash gluey. We've found that the vigorous action of a food processor guarantees glueyness—and although a potato masher is fine for producing a rustic chunky texture, it yields a mash that's far from fluffy. In tests, we've zeroed in on the ricer as the best tool for producing a fluffy texture. But is a ricer really the top choice if your goal is not only a fluffy mash, but a supremely smooth one as well? We made two identical batches of mashed potatoes, putting one through a ricer and the other through a food mill. While tasters found the riced potatoes a tad fluffier, they were also a bit grainy. The potatoes that passed under the food mill's sweeping blade were almost as fluffy and boasted a far smoother texture. We still stand by the ricer as the most effective tool for fluffy potatoes, but there's no need to rush out and buy one if you have the more versatile food mill in your cabinet. And if all else fails, a standard potato masher and some elbow grease will also get the job done, but not as smoothly.

1. Place potatoes in medium saucepan and add water to just cover. Bring to boil over high heat; reduce heat to medium-low and simmer until potatoes are cooked through, 8 to 10 minutes.

2. Transfer 5 tablespoons potato cooking water to bowl to cool; drain potatoes. Return potatoes to saucepan and place over low heat. Cook, shaking pot occasionally, until any surface moisture has evaporated, about 1 minute. Remove from heat. Process potatoes through ricer or food mill, or mash well with potato masher. Measure 1 very firmly packed cup potatoes and transfer to bowl. Reserve any remaining potatoes for another use. Stir in butter until melted.

3. Combine flour, sugar, yeast, and salt in bowl of stand mixer. Add warm potato mixture to flour mixture and mix with your hands until combined (some large lumps are OK). Add 1 egg and reserved potato cooking water; mix with dough hook on low speed until dough is soft and slightly sticky, 8 to 10 minutes.

4. Shape dough into ball and place in lightly greased container. Cover tightly with plastic wrap and allow to rise at room temperature until almost doubled in volume, 30 to 40 minutes.

5. Turn out dough onto counter, dusting with flour only if dough is too sticky to handle comfortably. Pat gently into 8-inch square of even thickness. Using bench knife or chef's knife, cut dough into 9 pieces (3 rows by 3 rows). Separate pieces and cover loosely with plastic.

6. Working with 1 piece of dough at a time and keeping remaining pieces covered, form dough pieces into smooth, taut rounds. (To round, set piece of dough on unfloured work surface. Loosely cup your hand around dough and, without applying pressure to dough, move your hand in small circular motions. Tackiness of dough against work surface and circular motion should work dough into smooth, even ball, but if dough sticks to your hands, lightly dust fingers with flour.) Cover rounds with plastic and allow to rest for 15 minutes.

7. Line 2 rimmed baking sheets with parchment paper. On lightly floured surface, firmly press each dough round into 3½-inch disk of even thickness, expelling large pockets of air. Arrange on prepared sheets. Cover loosely with plastic and let rise at room temperature until almost doubled in size, 30 to 40 minutes. While rolls rise, adjust oven racks to middle and upper-middle positions and heat oven to 425 degrees.

8. Brush rolls gently with egg wash and sprinkle with sesame seeds, if using. Bake rolls until deep golden brown, 15 to 18 minutes, rotating and switching sheets halfway through baking. Transfer sheets to wire racks and let cool for 5 minutes. Transfer rolls from sheets to wire racks. Serve warm or at room temperature.

POTATO DINNER ROLLS
MAKES 12 ROLLS

If you don't have a stand mixer, you can mix the dough by hand following the instructions on page 115. Don't salt the cooking water for the potatoes. A pound of russet potatoes should yield just over 1 very firmly packed cup (½ pound) of mash. To ensure optimum rise, your dough should be warm; if your potatoes or potato cooking water are too hot to touch, let cool before proceeding with the recipe. Bread flour is best for this recipe; do not attempt to substitute all-purpose flour. This dough looks very dry when mixing begins, but resist the urge to add more cooking water; the dough will soften as mixing progresses. If you prefer, you may portion the rolls by weight in step 5 (2 ounces of dough per roll).

- 1 pound russet potatoes, peeled and cut into 1-inch pieces
- 2 tablespoons unsalted butter, cut into 4 pieces
- 2¼ cups (12⅓ ounces) bread flour

2 teaspoons instant or rapid-rise yeast
1 tablespoon sugar
1 teaspoon salt
2 large eggs, 1 lightly beaten with
    1 teaspoon water and pinch salt

1. Place potatoes in medium saucepan and add water to just cover. Bring to boil over high heat; reduce heat to medium-low and simmer until potatoes are cooked through, 8 to 10 minutes.

2. Transfer 5 tablespoons potato cooking water to bowl to cool; drain potatoes. Return potatoes to saucepan and place over low heat. Cook, shaking pot occasionally, until any surface moisture has evaporated, about 1 minute. Remove from heat. Process potatoes through ricer or food mill, or mash well with potato masher. Measure 1 very firmly packed cup potatoes (8 ounces) and transfer to bowl. Reserve any remaining potatoes for another use. Stir in butter until melted.

3. Combine flour, yeast, sugar, and salt in bowl of stand mixer. Add warm potato mixture to flour mixture and mix with your hands until combined (some large lumps are OK). Add 1 egg and reserved potato cooking water; mix with dough hook on low speed until dough is soft and slightly sticky, 8 to 10 minutes.

4. Shape dough into ball and place in lightly greased container. Cover tightly with plastic wrap and allow to rise at room temperature until almost doubled in volume, 30 to 40 minutes.

5. Turn out dough onto counter, dusting with flour only if dough is too sticky to handle comfortably. Pat gently into 8-inch square of even thickness. Using bench knife or chef's knife, cut dough into 12 pieces (3 rows by 4 rows). Separate pieces and cover loosely with plastic.

6. Line rimmed baking sheet with parchment paper. Working with 1 piece of dough at a time and keeping remaining pieces covered, form dough pieces into smooth, taut rounds. (To round, set piece of dough on unfloured work surface. Loosely cup your hand around dough and, without applying pressure to dough, move your hand in small circular motions. Tackiness of dough against work surface and circular motion should work dough into smooth, even ball, but if dough sticks to your hands, lightly dust fingers with flour.) Arrange rolls on prepared sheet. Cover loosely with plastic and let rise at room temperature until almost doubled in size, 30 to 40 minutes. While rolls rise, adjust oven rack to upper-middle position and heat oven to 425 degrees.

7. Brush rolls gently with egg wash. Bake rolls until deep golden brown, 12 to 14 minutes, rotating sheet halfway through baking. Transfer sheet to wire rack and cool for 5 minutes. Transfer rolls from sheet to wire rack. Serve warm or at room temperature.

POTATO DINNER ROLLS WITH CHEDDAR AND MUSTARD

In step 3, add ½ cup shredded cheddar cheese and 1 teaspoon ground mustard to stand mixer with dry ingredients. In step 7, sprinkle each roll with 1 teaspoon shredded cheddar (¼ cup total).

POTATO DINNER ROLLS WITH PARMESAN AND BLACK PEPPER

In step 3, add ½ cup grated Parmesan cheese and 1 teaspoon pepper to stand mixer with dry ingredients. In step 7, sprinkle each roll with 1 teaspoon grated Parmesan (¼ cup total).

HAND-MIXING METHOD FOR YEAST BREADS AND ROLLS

We prefer to mix dough with a stand mixer fitted with a dough hook because it's effortless and produces great bread. However, if you don't own one you can mix dough by hand following the instructions below. Note that there are some recipes in this chapter for which a stand mixer is necessary because the dough is too sticky or wet.

Whisk the liquid ingredients together in a medium bowl. In a large bowl, whisk the dry ingredients together. Stir the liquid mixture into the dry ingredients until the dough comes together and looks shaggy. Turn the dough out onto a clean counter and knead to form a smooth, round ball, 15 to 25 minutes, adding extra flour as needed to prevent the dough from sticking to the counter. Transfer to a large, lightly oiled bowl, cover with greased plastic wrap, and let rise as directed.

American Loaf Bread

✓ WHY THIS RECIPE WORKS

Many people who might enjoy making terrific sandwich bread at home don't even try it because they think it takes most of a day. We wanted a good, solid sandwich bread recipe that could be prepared in 2 hours, start to finish, including baking time.

KNEAD WITH A STAND MIXER OR FOOD PROCESSOR Our dough can be sticky and this hands-off method helped us resist the temptation to add extra flour. More flour tends to make the dough denser and less flavorful; it also makes it rise less. Another reason to knead in a machine—it's faster.

REACH FOR RAPID-RISE YEAST It sounds like a no-brainer, but instant or rapid-rise yeast works well in this bread in less time with no adverse affect on flavor.

INCLUDE MILK, BUTTER, AND HONEY Most American loaf breads contain fat in the form of milk and melted butter. We found we liked a sweetener as well. Honey produces a just-sweet-enough loaf.

ADD STEAM FOR A CRISP CRUST Professional bread bakers use steam-injected ovens. But we found that we could improvise with a loaf pan filled with boiling water. Why bother? The steam moistens the exterior of the loaf and allows for it to expand more and develop a crisp crust during baking.

AMERICAN LOAF BREAD

MAKES 1 LOAF

All-purpose flour can be used if bread flour is unavailable. If you don't have a stand mixer, you can mix the dough by hand following the instructions on page 115. If you don't have a baking stone, bake the bread on an overturned and preheated rimmed baking sheet set on the lowest oven rack.

1	cup warm whole milk (110 degrees)
⅓	cup warm water (110 degrees)
3	tablespoons honey
2	tablespoons unsalted butter, melted

3½	cups (19¼ ounces) bread flour
2¼	teaspoons instant or rapid-rise yeast
2	teaspoons salt

1. Adjust oven rack to lowest position and heat oven to 200 degrees. Once oven temperature reaches 200 degrees, maintain heat for 10 minutes, then turn off oven.

2. Whisk milk, water, honey, and melted butter together in 4-cup liquid measuring cup. Using stand mixer fitted with dough hook, combine flour, yeast, and salt on low speed. Slowly add milk mixture and let dough come together, about 2 minutes. Increase speed to medium and knead until dough is smooth and satiny, about 10 minutes, scraping down dough from bowl and hook as needed. Transfer dough to lightly floured counter and knead by hand to form smooth, round ball, about 15 seconds. Place dough in large, lightly greased bowl; cover tightly with plastic wrap and let rise in warm oven until doubled in size, 40 to 50 minutes.

3. Grease 9 by 5-inch loaf pan. Transfer dough to lightly floured counter and press into rectangle about 1 inch thick and no longer than 9 inches, with long side facing you. Roll dough toward you into firm cylinder, keeping roll taut by tucking it under itself as you go. Turn loaf seam side up and pinch it closed. Place loaf seam side down in prepared pan, pressing gently into corners. Cover loaf loosely with greased plastic and let rise at room temperature until nearly doubled in size, 20 to 30 minutes. (Dough should barely spring back when poked with knuckle.)

4. One hour before baking, place baking stone on lowest rack, place empty loaf pan or other heatproof pan on baking stone, and heat oven to 350 degrees. Bring 2 cups water to boil on stovetop. Working quickly, pour boiling water into empty loaf pan in oven and set loaf in pan on baking stone. Bake until crust is golden brown and loaf registers 195 degrees,

40 to 50 minutes. Transfer pan to wire rack and let cool for 5 minutes. Remove loaf from pan, return to rack, and let cool to room temperature, about 2 hours, before slicing and serving. (Bread can be wrapped in double layer of plastic wrap and stored at room temperature for up to 3 days. Wrapped with additional layer of aluminum foil, bread can be frozen for up to 1 month.)

BUTTERMILK LOAF BREAD

Substitute 1 cup buttermilk, heated to 110 degrees, for whole milk. Increase first rise to 50 minutes to 1 hour.

OATMEAL LOAF BREAD

Do not substitute instant oats in this recipe. To turn this loaf into oatmeal-raisin loaf bread, knead ¾ cup raisins, tossed with 1 tablespoon all-purpose flour, into the dough after it comes out of the mixer.

Omit warm water from wet ingredients. Bring ¾ cup water to boil in small saucepan. Stir in ¾ cup old-fashioned rolled oats or quick oats and cook until softened slightly, about 90 seconds. Decrease flour to 2¾ cups and combine cooked oatmeal with flour and salt in mixer before adding milk mixture.

Whole-Wheat Bread

✓ WHY THIS RECIPE WORKS

Most recipes for whole-wheat sandwich bread lead to one of two pitfalls. They either pay lip service to being "whole wheat," yielding loaves containing so little of the whole-grain stuff that they resemble the fluffy, squishy bread you find at the supermarket, or they call for so much whole wheat that the loaves bake up coarse and dense, crumbling as soon as you slice into them. (The challenge when making whole-wheat bread is that the very thing that gives it character and distinguishes it from white bread—the presence of bran—is also an impediment to gluten development.) We wanted a sandwich bread with a full-blown nutty (but not bitter) taste and a hearty yet soft crumb that sliced neatly.

INCREASE THE WHOLE WHEAT AND SOAK Using bread flour, with its extra gluten-forming ability, in place of all-purpose flour allows us to increase the amount of whole-wheat flour from 40 to 50 percent. But to up the percentage even more, we have to soak. A prolonged soaking of the whole-wheat flour accomplishes three things: First and foremost, it softens the grain's bran, thereby preventing the sharp edges from puncturing

and deflating the dough. Second, the hydrating effect also prevents the grains from robbing moisture from the dough, which would toughen the crumb. Third, steeping the grains activates the wheat's enzymes, converting some starches into sugars and, in turn, reducing bitterness and coaxing out a sweet flavor. Using a soaker, we can get our whole wheat up to 60 percent, producing a considerably wheatier final product.

ADD WHEAT GERM To bring our already wheaty wheat bread up to the next level, we add extra wheat germ, which is removed along with the bran during the milling process for refined flour and is a significant source of not only the whole grain's nutrition but also its sweet flavor. To add even more flavor to our bread, we add some honey for a complex sweetness and cut back on the fat, swapping some of the butter for oil, for a hearty yet soft-textured loaf.

USE A SPONGE The difference between a good-tasting loaf and one that offers the most robust, well-developed flavor can boil down to the use of a sponge. When left to sit

When developing our recipe for Whole-Wheat Bread, our goal was to cram as much whole wheat into the dough as possible to create a seriously wheaty sandwich loaf. Fifty percent whole wheat wasn't enough to get us to this goal—but any more and the bread got too heavy and developed off-flavors. Would giving the whole-wheat flour a long soak before creating the final dough allow us to bump up its amount?

We baked two loaves, each with a 3:2 ratio of whole-wheat to refined bread flour. We soaked the whole-wheat flour in the first batch overnight in the milk from our recipe before combining it with the other ingredients. In the second batch, we didn't give the whole-wheat flour any special treatment and proceeded with the recipe as usual.

The texture and flavor of the bread made with the soaked flour were markedly better than those of the loaf in which we didn't soak the whole wheat. Soaking has a twofold effect on the final loaf. First, it dulls the flour's hard, fibrous bran, blunting its ability to disrupt gluten development and produce a denser crumb. Soaking also activates enzymes in the flour that convert some of the starches into sugars, thereby sweetening the bran's natural bitterness. The technique allowed us to pack our bread with roughly 50 percent more whole wheat than most recipes call for and still create a loaf with earthy-sweet flavor and a soft yet hearty crumb.

overnight, this mixture of flour, water, and yeast develops a full range of unique flavors that give bread even more character. Because we are already soaking the whole-wheat flour overnight, we make our sponge at the same time and let it ferment overnight.

TURN, SLASH, AND STEAM This recipe relies on many of the usual tricks: We turn the dough midway through the first rise in order to remove large gas bubbles and promote even fermentation. We slash the top of the dough before baking to make it easier for the dough to rise suddenly in the oven. And before putting the bread in the oven, we pour boiling water into an empty loaf pan that we positioned on the bottom rack. This supplies steam—a common bread baker's technique that prevents the crust from drying out before the loaves have fully expanded.

WHOLE-WHEAT SANDWICH BREAD
MAKES 2 LOAVES

If you don't have a stand mixer, you can mix the dough by hand. To do this, stir the wet and dry ingredients together along with the soaker and sponge with a stiff rubber spatula until the dough comes together and looks shaggy. Transfer the dough to a clean counter and knead by hand to form a smooth, round ball, 15 to 25 minutes, adding additional flour, if necessary, to prevent the dough from sticking to the counter. Proceed with the recipe as directed. The test kitchen's preferred loaf pan measures 8½ by 4½ inches; if you use a 9 by 5-inch loaf pan, start checking for doneness 5 minutes earlier than advised in the recipe. If you don't have a baking stone, bake the bread on an overturned and preheated rimmed baking sheet set on the middle oven rack.

SPONGE
2 cups (11 ounces) bread flour
1 cup warm water (110 degrees)
½ teaspoon instant or rapid-rise yeast

SOAKER
3 cups (16½ ounces) whole-wheat flour
½ cup wheat germ
2 cups whole milk

DOUGH
6 tablespoons unsalted butter, softened
¼ cup honey
2 tablespoons instant or rapid-rise yeast
2 tablespoons vegetable oil
4 teaspoons salt

1. FOR THE SPONGE: Combine flour, water, and yeast in large bowl and stir with wooden spoon until uniform mass forms and no dry flour remains, about 1 minute. Cover bowl tightly with plastic wrap and let sit at room temperature for at least 8 hours or up to 24 hours.

2. FOR THE SOAKER: Combine flour, wheat germ, and milk in separate large bowl and stir with wooden spoon until shaggy mass forms, about 1 minute. Transfer dough to lightly floured counter and knead by hand until smooth, 2 to 3 minutes. Return soaker to bowl, cover tightly with plastic, and refrigerate for at least 8 hours or up to 24 hours.

3. FOR THE DOUGH: Tear soaker apart into 1-inch pieces and place in bowl of stand mixer fitted with dough hook. Add sponge, butter, honey, yeast, oil, and salt and mix on low speed until cohesive mass starts to form, about 2 minutes. Increase speed to medium and knead until dough is smooth and elastic, 8 to 10 minutes. Transfer dough to lightly floured counter and knead by hand to form smooth, round ball, about 1 minute. Place dough in large, lightly greased bowl. Cover tightly with plastic and let rise at room temperature for 45 minutes.

4. Gently press down on center of dough to deflate. Spray rubber spatula or bowl scraper with vegetable oil spray; fold partially risen dough over itself by gently lifting and folding edge of dough toward middle. Turn bowl 90 degrees; fold again. Turn bowl and fold dough 6 more times (total of 8 folds). Cover tightly with plastic and allow to rise at room temperature until doubled in size, about 45 minutes.

5. Grease two 8½ by 4½-inch loaf pans. Transfer dough to well-floured counter and divide in half. Press 1 piece of dough into

1. Starting at farthest end, roll dough piece into log. Keep roll taut by tucking it under itself as you go.

2. To seal loaf, pinch seam gently with thumb and forefinger.

3. Place loaf seam side down in greased loaf pan, pressing gently into corners.

17 by 8-inch rectangle, with short side facing you. Roll dough toward you into firm cylinder, keeping roll taut by tucking it under itself as you go. Turn loaf seam side up and pinch it closed. Place loaf seam side down in prepared pan, pressing gently into corners. Repeat with second piece of dough. Cover loaves loosely with greased plastic and let rise at room temperature until nearly doubled in size, 1 to 1½ hours (top of loaves should rise about 1 inch over lip of pan).

6. One hour before baking, adjust oven racks to middle and lowest positions, place baking stone on middle rack, place empty loaf pan or other heatproof pan on bottom rack, and heat oven to 400 degrees. Bring 2 cups water to boil on stovetop. Using sharp serrated knife or single-edge razor blade, make one ¼-inch-deep slash lengthwise down center of each loaf. Working quickly, pour boiling water into empty loaf pan in oven and set loaves in pans on baking stone. Reduce oven temperature to 350 degrees. Bake until crust is dark brown and loaves register 200 degrees, 40 to 50 minutes, rotating loaves front to back and side to side halfway through baking. Transfer pans to wire rack and let cool for 5 minutes. Remove loaves from pans, return to rack, and let cool to room temperature, about 2 hours, before slicing and serving. (Bread can be wrapped in double layer of plastic wrap and stored at room temperature for up to 3 days. Wrapped with additional layer of aluminum foil, bread can be frozen for up to 1 month.)

Multigrain Bread

✔ WHY THIS RECIPE WORKS

Often multigrain bread either has great flavor but is as dense and as heavy as a brick, or it has a nice, light sandwich-style texture but so little grain it might as well be white bread. We wanted a multigrain bread with both great flavor and balanced texture.

ADD ALL-PURPOSE FLOUR FOR A LESS DENSE LOAF Early tests showed that the whole grains impede the development of gluten, the protein that gives baked goods structure. Bread flour, with its high protein content, would seem the ideal candidate to combat this problem, but we found that it only made the bread chewier, not less dense. We switched to all-purpose flour.

EMPLOY AUTOLYSE FOR A LIGHTER TEXTURE While the purist mode of some multigrain recipes requires kneading the dough by hand, we wanted to avoid a full workout. We do employ a stand mixer, but there's another strategy that kickstarts gluten development—an autolyse, a resting period that gives the flour time to hydrate. After our first knead, we let the dough rest for 20 minutes, then gave it a good knead and rise and then once shaped, another rise. When we kneaded the bread without an autolyse, the bread had a crumbly texture. With the autolyse, our loaf bakes up light yet chewy without being tough.

SHOP THE CEREAL AISLE We wanted a multidimensional flavor profile for our bread, but we didn't want to drive all over town, collecting grains. We started with what we found in the supermarket: cornmeal, rolled oats, and rye flour, but this abridged grain mixture produced a loaf that was more of a muddy-tasting rye than a sweet, earthy multigrain bread. Back in the supermarket, we spied a package of seven-grain hot cereal near the rolled oats. To soften the grains, we made a thick porridge with the cereal before adding it to the dough. And sure enough, our bread now sported complexity—from the nutty flaxseed to the tangy rye and sweet wheat.

ADD CRUNCH TO THE LOAF The seven-grain cereal mix gave our bread terrific flavor but we wanted some crunch too, so we turned to seeds. Poppy and sesame were too small and got lost in the mix of grains. Sunflower and pumpkin seeds were better able to distinguish themselves from the crowd and added richness as well. In addition to incorporating the seeds in the dough, we take the final step of rolling the shaped loaves in oats to yield a finished, professional look.

MULTIGRAIN BREAD
MAKES 2 LOAVES

If you don't have a stand mixer, you can mix the dough by hand following the instructions on page 115. Don't confuse seven-grain hot cereal mix with boxed cold breakfast cereals that may also be labeled "seven-grain." Our favorite brands of seven-grain mix are Bob's Red Mill and Arrowhead Mills. Do not substitute instant oats in this recipe. For an accurate measurement of boiling water, bring a full kettle of water to a boil, then measure out the desired amount.

1¼	cups (6¼ ounces) seven-grain hot cereal mix
2½	cups boiling water
3	cups (15 ounces) all-purpose flour, plus extra as needed
1½	cups (8¼ ounces) whole-wheat flour
¼	cup honey
4	tablespoons unsalted butter, melted and cooled
2½	teaspoons instant or rapid-rise yeast
1	tablespoon salt
¾	cup unsalted pumpkin seeds or sunflower seeds
½	cup (1½ ounces) old-fashioned rolled oats or quick oats

1. Place cereal mix in bowl of stand mixer fitted with dough hook and pour boiling water over it; let stand, stirring occasionally, until mixture cools to 100 degrees and resembles thick porridge, about 1 hour. Whisk all-purpose flour and whole-wheat flour together in separate bowl.

2. Once grain mixture has cooled, add honey, butter, and yeast and mix on low speed until combined. Add flour mixture, ½ cup at a time, and knead until cohesive mass starts to form, 1½ to 2 minutes; cover bowl tightly with plastic wrap and let dough rest for 20 minutes. Add salt and knead on medium-low speed until dough clears sides of bowl, 3 to 4 minutes (if it does not clear sides, add 2 to 3 tablespoons additional all-purpose flour and knead until it does); continue to knead dough for 5 more minutes. Add seeds and knead for another 15 seconds. Transfer dough to lightly floured counter and knead by hand until seeds are dispersed evenly and dough forms smooth, round ball. Place dough in large, lightly greased bowl; cover tightly with plastic and let rise at room temperature until nearly doubled in size, 45 minutes to 1 hour.

3. Grease two 9 by 5-inch loaf pans. Transfer dough to lightly floured counter and divide in half. Press 1 piece of dough into 9 by 6-inch rectangle, with short side facing you. Roll dough toward you into firm cylinder, keeping roll taut by tucking it under itself as you go. Turn loaf seam side up and pinch it closed. Repeat with second piece of dough. Spray loaves lightly with water or vegetable oil spray. Spread oats on rimmed baking sheet. Roll each loaf in oats to coat evenly and place seam side down in prepared pans, pressing gently into corners. Cover loaves loosely with greased plastic and let rise at room temperature until nearly doubled in size, 30 to 40 minutes. (Dough should barely spring back when poked with knuckle.)

COATING YOUR LOAF

Spread oats on rimmed baking sheet. Roll moistened loaf back and forth, pressing dough gently against oats to ensure that they stick.

We commonly advise check-
ing the internal temperature
of a loaf of bread before
making the decision to pull
it from the oven. A properly
baked loaf should register
a temperature between
195 and 210 degrees on an
instant-read thermometer,
depending upon the type of
bread. But is internal temperature by itself sufficient proof
that bread is fully baked?

We placed temperature
probes in the center of two
loaves of Rustic Italian Bread
(page 127) and monitored
them as they baked. Halfway
into the baking time, the
internal temperature of
the loaves had already
passed 200 degrees, and
they reached the optimal
210 degrees a full 15 minutes before the end of the
recommended baking time.
We pulled one loaf from the
oven as soon as it neared
210 degrees and left the other
in the oven for the recommended baking time. (The
temperature of the longer-
baked loaf never rose above
210, because the moisture
it contains, even when fully
baked, prevents it from going
past the boiling point of
water, or 212 degrees.) The
differences between the two
loaves were dramatic: The
loaf removed early had a pale,
soft crust and a gummy interior, while the loaf that baked
the full hour had a nicely
browned, crisp crust and a
perfectly baked crumb.

The takeaway? Internal
temperature matters but in
conjunction with a browned
crust.

4. Thirty minutes before baking, adjust
oven rack to middle position and heat oven
to 375 degrees. Bake until loaves register 200 degrees, 35 to 40 minutes. Transfer
pans to wire rack and let cool for 5 minutes.
Remove loaves from pans, return to rack, and
let cool to room temperature, about 2 hours,
before slicing and serving. (Bread can be
wrapped in double layer of plastic wrap and
stored at room temperature for up to 3 days.
Wrapped with additional layer of aluminum
foil, bread can be frozen for up to 1 month.)

MULTIGRAIN DINNER ROLLS
MAKES 18 ROLLS

This recipe also works with a 13 by 9-inch baking dish.

1. After dough has nearly doubled in size in
step 2, grease two 9-inch square baking dishes.
Transfer dough to lightly floured counter and
divide in half. Cut each half into thirds, then
into thirds again, to make 18 equal pieces of
dough. Loosely cup hand around each piece
of dough (not directly over it) and, without
applying pressure, move hand in small circular motions to form smooth, taut round, then
roll 1 side of ball in oats. Arrange 9 rolls in
each prepared baking dish, cover lightly with
greased plastic wrap, and let rise until nearly
doubled in size, 30 to 40 minutes. (Dough
should barely spring back when poked
with knuckle.)

2. Thirty minutes before baking, adjust
oven rack to middle position and heat oven
to 375 degrees. Bake until rolls register
200 degrees, 30 to 35 minutes. Transfer
dishes to wire rack and let cool for 5 minutes.
Remove rolls from dishes, return to rack, and
let cool to room temperature, about 2 hours,
before serving.

French Baguette

✓ WHY THIS RECIPE WORKS

*Is it possible to make an outstanding baguette at
home? We wanted ours to have a thin, golden-brown
crust, an airy texture, moist crumb, and fully developed flavor.*

START WITH A SPONGE Looking for
the best way to rise the dough, we found that
the sponge method (using a small amount
of yeast to rise some of the dough for several hours) made loaves with superior flavor
and texture than commercial yeast alone. As
in many of our rustic breads, we also employ
autolyse to allow better flavor development—
this means allowing the mix of flour, water,
and yeast to rest briefly so the flour becomes
hydrated, before adding the sponge.

KNEAD IN A STAND MIXER This
dough can be hand-kneaded, but we prefer
the ease of the stand mixer. During our testing, we read about "windowpaning," which
is the point at which the dough is properly
kneaded—it should be able to stretch thin
enough so that it's almost translucent. You
don't need to do this in our recipe, but it
doesn't hurt.

FOLD THE DOUGH As in our Rustic
Italian Bread (page 127), we fold the dough
to gently bring the sheets of gluten into
alignment for a loaf with a more consistent
structure.

SHAPE AND BAKE Shaping the loaves is
simple: Pat out the dough and fold the bottom and top halves up like a business letter,
press the edges to seal, make a crease down
the middle of the dough, pinch the crease
shut, then roll the dough back and forth to

form a traditional baguette shape. We put the loaves in a hot (500-degree) oven, but immediately turn it down to 425 degrees for a crisp crust and moist crumb.

BAKERY-STYLE FRENCH BAGUETTES
MAKES 2 BAGUETTES

If you don't have a stand mixer, you can mix the dough by hand following the instructions on page 115. If you don't have a baking stone, bake the bread on an overturned and preheated rimmed baking sheet set on the lower-middle oven rack. Don't forget to reduce the oven temperature to 425 degrees immediately after putting the loaves in the oven. For slow-rise baguettes (made by letting the shaped loaf rise overnight) see the variation (page 124).

SPONGE
½   cup (2¾ ounces) bread flour
½   cup warm water (110 degrees)
½   teaspoon instant or rapid-rise yeast

DOUGH
3–3½   cups (16½ to 19¼ ounces) bread flour
¾   teaspoon instant or rapid-rise yeast
1½   cups warm water (110 degrees)
1½   teaspoons salt
     Vegetable oil spray

GLAZE
1   large egg beaten with 2 tablespoons water

1. FOR THE SPONGE: Stir all ingredients together in medium bowl until combined. Cover with plastic wrap and let sit at room temperature until sponge has risen and fallen, at least 6 hours or up to 24 hours.

2. FOR THE DOUGH: Using stand mixer fitting with dough hook, combine 3 cups flour and yeast. With mixer on low speed, add water and mix until dough comes together, about 2 minutes. Stop mixer, cover bowl with plastic wrap (no need to remove bowl from mixer), and let sit at room temperature for 20 minutes.

3. Remove plastic, add sponge and salt, and knead dough on medium-low speed until it is smooth and elastic, about 8 minutes. If after 4 minutes more flour is needed, add remaining ½ cup flour, 2 tablespoons at a time, until dough clears sides of bowl, but sticks to bottom.

4. Turn dough out onto lightly floured counter and knead by hand to form smooth, round ball. Place dough in large, lightly oiled bowl and cover tightly with greased plastic. Let rise in warm place until doubled in size, about 1 hour.

5. Slide a plastic bench scraper or rubber spatula under side of dough; gently lift and fold one-third of dough toward center. Repeat with opposite side of dough. Finally fold dough in half, perpendicular to first folds, so dough is rough square. Cover, let rise for 30 minutes more, then repeat folding process. Cover and let rise until dough has doubled in size, about 30 minutes longer.

6. Top pizza peel with parchment paper. Turn dough out onto lightly floured counter and divide it into 2 equal pieces. Working with 1 piece of dough at a time, gently pat dough into rough 8 by 6-inch rectangle. Gently fold bottom third of dough up to center and press to seal. Gently fold bottom of dough up to top and press to seal. Make indentation along length of dough with side of your outstretched hand. Working along length of dough, press your thumb against dough while folding and rolling upper edge down with other hand. Repeat 5 times until upper edge meets lower edge. Using your fingertips, press seam to seal. Roll dough cylinder seam side down; gently and evenly roll and stretch dough until it measures 15 inches long by 2½ inches wide and lay it seam side down on the prepared peel, spaced about 5 inches apart. Mist baguettes with vegetable oil spray, cover loosely with plastic, and let rise in warm place until nearly doubled in size and dough barely springs back when poked with knuckle, 1 to 1½ hours.

7. One hour before baking, adjust oven rack to lower-middle position, place baking stone on rack, and heat oven to 500 degrees.

SHAPING BAGUETTES

1. Make indentation along length of dough with side of your outstretched hand.

2. Working along length of dough, press your thumb against dough while folding and rolling upper edge down with other hand. Repeat 5 times until upper edge meets lower edge.

3. Using your fingertips, press seam to seal. At this point, dough will have formed cylinder about 12 inches long.

4. Roll dough cylinder seam side down; gently and evenly roll and stretch dough until it measures 15 inches long by 2½ inches wide.

A proofed loaf of bread should be slashed across the top to allow some of the trapped air to escape, but the knife used for this purpose often snags and drags the loaf out of shape. For clean, neat slashes, spray the knife blade lightly with vegetable oil spray before slashing the loaf.

8. FOR THE GLAZE: Score top of breads with razor blade or sharp knife, cutting four ½-inch-deep slashes along width of each baguette. Brush breads with egg-water mixture, then spray lightly with water. Carefully slide loaves and parchment onto hot baking stone. Immediately reduce oven temperature to 425 degrees and bake until crust is deep golden brown and center of bread registers 210 degrees, about 25 minutes, rotating loaves halfway through baking.

9. Transfer loaves to wire rack, discard parchment, and let cool for about 30 minutes before slicing and serving.

SLOW-RISE BAGUETTES

While it is convenient to be able to make a baguette in one day, if you have time, a long, slow overnight rising produces a more impressive loaf, richer in color with dramatic blistering and complex nutty flavors. Make sure that the plastic wrap covers the loaves completely but is loose enough to allow the baguettes to rise upward.

In step 6, do not let baguettes rise, but refrigerate them overnight or up to 12 hours. Let baguettes sit at room temperature, covered, for 30 minutes to 1 hour while heating baking stone, then bake as directed.

Deli-Style Rye Bread

✔ WHY THIS RECIPE WORKS

Genuine rye bread should be slightly moist and chewy but not too dense, and it should have a notably tangy rye flavor. Perhaps most important, it should be able to stand up to a pile of pastrami.

ENSURE DEEP FLAVOR WITH A SPONGE Many rustic breads employ a sponge (a mix of water, flour, and yeast that is allowed to ferment) to take the place of some of the unfermented commercial yeast. We follow suit.

USE RYE FLOUR AND BREAD FLOUR We prefer bread made with light or medium rye flour. Dark rye is simply too overpowering. And because rye flour alone doesn't contain enough gluten-forming proteins to make bread rise enough, we also include bread flour. For additional flavor, we add caraway seeds to the dough.

GIVE YOUR DOUGH A REST We knead bread dough to develop gluten, but with rye bread, which has less gluten-forming protein, kneading isn't enough. We let the dough rest for a short period so the flour becomes hydrated, before turning to kneading.

SLASH AND GLAZE FOR A SHINY CRUST We slash the top of the dough before baking to make it easier for the dough to rise quickly in the oven. We like the shiny, brittle crust of traditional deli rye and found a simple mix of beaten egg white and water brushed over the scored loaf before baking was the best method for achieving this. We also mist the loaf with water to encourage a crisp crust.

DELI-STYLE RYE BREAD
MAKES I LARGE LOAF

If you don't have a stand mixer, you can mix the dough by hand following the instructions on page 115. Don't forget to reduce the oven temperature immediately after putting the loaf in the oven. We prefer to use light or medium rye flour in this bread; tasters found dark rye flour overpowering. This loaf takes two days to make, but for a faster version, see the same-day variation on page 125; it will be slightly less flavorful but still very good. If you don't have a baking stone, bake the bread on an overturned and preheated rimmed baking sheet set on the lower-middle oven rack.

SPONGE

¾ cup warm water (110 degrees)

¾ cup (4⅛ ounces) light or medium
    rye flour

¼ cup (1⅓ ounces) bread flour

½ teaspoon instant or rapid-rise yeast

DOUGH

3–3½ cups (16½ to 19¼ ounces) bread flour

1 cup (5½ ounces) light or medium
   rye flour

1 tablespoon caraway seeds

1 tablespoon vegetable oil

1 tablespoon honey

1½ teaspoons instant or rapid-rise yeast

1½ cups warm water (110 degrees)

2 teaspoons salt
   Vegetable oil spray

GLAZE

1 large egg beaten with 2 tablespoons
   water

1. FOR THE SPONGE: Stir all ingredients together in medium bowl until combined. Cover with plastic wrap and let sit at room temperature until sponge has risen and fallen, at least 6 hours or up to 24 hours.

2. FOR THE DOUGH: Using stand mixer fitted with dough hook, combine 3 cups bread flour, rye flour, caraway seeds, oil, honey, and yeast. With mixer on low speed, add water and mix until dough comes together, about 2 minutes. Stop mixer, cover bowl with plastic (no need to remove bowl from mixer), and let sit at room temperature for 20 minutes.

3. Remove plastic, add sponge and salt, and knead dough on medium-low speed until it is smooth and elastic, about 8 minutes. If after 4 minutes more flour is needed, add remaining ½ cup bread flour, 2 tablespoons at a time, until dough clears sides of bowl, but sticks to bottom.

4. Turn dough out onto lightly floured counter and knead by hand to form smooth, round ball. Place dough in large, lightly oiled bowl and cover tightly with greased plastic. Let rise in warm place until doubled in size, 1 to 1½ hours.

5. Top pizza peel with parchment paper. Turn dough out onto lightly floured counter, press it into 10-inch square without tearing it, and gently dimple it with your fingertips. Fold top corners into middle of dough, then gently roll and pinch dough into torpedo shape. Transfer to prepared peel, seam side down, and gently tuck dough into taut loaf. Mist loaf with vegetable oil spray, cover loosely with plastic, and let rise in warm place until nearly doubled in size and dough barely springs back when poked with knuckle, 1 to 1½ hours.

6. FOR THE GLAZE: One hour before baking, adjust oven rack to lower-middle position, place baking stone on rack, and heat oven to 500 degrees. Score top of loaf with razor blade or sharp knife. Brush loaf with egg-water mixture, then spray lightly with water. Carefully slide loaf and parchment onto hot baking stone. Immediately reduce oven temperature to 425 degrees and bake until center of loaf registers 210 degrees and crust is deep golden brown, 35 to 40 minutes, rotating loaf halfway through baking.

7. Transfer loaf to wire rack, discard parchment, and let cool to room temperature, about 2 hours, before slicing and serving.

SAME-DAY DELI-STYLE RYE BREAD

If you don't have time for a sponge, this loaf can be made the same day, but the flavor won't be as complex, and the crumb will be finer and more uniform (like sandwich bread).

Omit sponge. When assembling dough in step 2, increase amount of bread flour to 3¼ cups, increase rye flour to 1¾ cups, increase yeast to 2¼ teaspoons, and increase water to 2¼ cups.

CAN WAXED PAPER BE SUBSTITUTED FOR PARCHMENT PAPER?

In most cases, waxed paper should not be substituted for parchment. This is because parchment can withstand oven temperatures up to about 425 degrees without burning, while waxed paper will smoke when subjected directly to oven heat. So waxed paper will do just fine for lining a cake pan bottom, but not as a lining on a cookie sheet or when used on a baking stone.

Rustic Italian Bread

WHY THIS RECIPE WORKS

We set out to turn four basic ingredients—flour, water, yeast, and salt—into a chewy, crusty bread that would put supermarket loaves to shame.

START WITH A SPONGE As with most rustic breads, we've found a sponge (a mix of flour, water, and yeast that is allowed to ferment) to be invaluable in giving the bread a deep, complex flavor that commercial yeast alone cannot provide.

CHOOSE BREAD FLOUR Bread flour produces a hearty loaf with good height and a thick crust.

REST THE DOUGH Resting the dough for 20 minutes before the sponge is added (a technique called autolyse) allows the flour to hydrate, giving us taller, better-shaped loaves with a cleaner flavor.

FOLD THE DOUGH We noticed with this dough that the more the dough is handled, the more dense the loaf turns out. Minimal handling is key so as not to disrupt any air pockets that have developed. To minimize handling, we include a process called "folding," in which the dough is delicately folded onto itself right in the bowl. Folding the dough stretches it gently, building strength as wayward sheets of gluten—the protein that gives bread structure once flour and water have been combined—are brought into alignment. By including this step, we can produce a loaf with a consistently chewy, yet light crumb.

START AT A HIGH TEMP THEN REDUCE HEAT In early testing, we were baffled when the crust of this bread turned soft within minutes of emerging from the oven. The solution? We bake the loaf at 500 degrees for the first 10 minutes to maximize its height and then turn the oven down to 400 degrees to get a fantastically crisp crust.

RUSTIC ITALIAN BREAD
MAKES 1 LOAF

If you don't have a stand mixer, you can mix the dough by hand following the instructions on page 115. If you own two stand mixer bowls, in step 1 you can refrigerate the sponge in the bowl in which it was made. Use the second bowl to make the dough in step 2. If you don't have a baking stone, bake the bread on an overturned and preheated rimmed baking sheet set on the lower-middle oven rack. This recipe requires a bit of patience—the sponge, which gives the bread flavor, must be made 11 to 27 hours before the dough is made. We find it makes the most sense to prepare the sponge (which requires just 5 minutes of hands-on work) the day before you want to bake the bread. On the second day, remove the sponge from the refrigerator and begin step 2 at least 7 hours before you want to serve the bread.

SPONGE
- 2 cups (11 ounces) bread flour
- ¼ teaspoon instant or rapid-rise yeast
- 1 cup water, room temperature

DOUGH
- 3 cups (16½ ounces) bread flour
- 1 teaspoon instant or rapid-rise yeast
- 1¼ cups water, room temperature
- 2 teaspoons salt
- Vegetable oil spray

1. FOR THE SPONGE: Using stand mixer fitted with dough hook, mix flour, yeast, and water together on low speed until mixture forms shaggy dough, 2 to 3 minutes. Transfer sponge to medium bowl, cover tightly with plastic wrap, and let stand at room temperature until beginning to bubble and rise, about 3 hours. Refrigerate sponge for at least 8 hours or up to 24 hours.

SLICING RUSTIC BREAD

With their heavy crusts, artisan breads can pose a challenge when it comes to slicing neatly. Often, the bread knife fails to cut all the way through the thick bottom crust, leaving you to literally yank the slice free from the loaf, often tearing it in the process. To get around this problem and cut perfect slices, turn the loaf on its side and cut it. This way, you'll be able to cut through both crusts simultaneously.

1. After delicately pushing dough into 10-inch square, fold top right corner diagonally to middle.

2. Repeat step 1 with top left corner.

3. Begin to gently roll dough from top to bottom.

4. Continue rolling until dough forms rough log. Roll dough onto its seam and, sliding your hands under each end, transfer dough to sheet of parchment paper.

5. Gently shape dough into 16-inch football shape by tucking bottom edges underneath.

2. FOR THE DOUGH: Remove sponge from refrigerator and let stand at room temperature while making dough. Using stand mixer fitted with dough hook, mix flour, yeast, and water together on low speed until rough dough is formed, about 3 minutes; cover bowl loosely with plastic and let dough rest for 20 minutes.

3. Add sponge and salt to dough and knead on low speed until ingredients are incorporated and dough is formed (dough should clear sides of bowl but stick to very bottom), about 4 minutes. Increase mixer speed to medium-low and continue to knead until dough is smooth and elastic, about 1 minute. Transfer dough to large, lightly greased bowl; cover tightly with plastic and let rise at room temperature until doubled in size, about 1 hour.

4. Spray rubber spatula or bowl scraper with vegetable oil spray. Fold partially risen dough over itself by gently lifting and folding edge of dough toward middle. Turn bowl 180 degrees; fold again. Finally, fold dough in half, perpendicular to first folds. (Dough shape should be rough square.) Cover with plastic and let dough rise for 1 hour. Repeat folding, replace plastic, and let dough rise 1 hour longer.

5. Top pizza peel with parchment paper. Turn dough out onto well-floured counter (side of dough that was against bowl should now be facing up). Dust dough and hands liberally with flour and gently press dough into rough 10-inch square. Fold top corners of dough square into middle of dough, then gently roll and pinch dough into torpedo shape. Transfer loaf to prepared pizza peel, seam side down, and gently tuck dough into taut loaf. Spray loaf with oil spray, cover loosely with plastic, and let rise at room temperature until nearly doubled in size, 1 to 1½ hours. (Dough should barely spring back when poked with knuckle.)

6. One hour before baking, adjust oven rack to lower-middle position, place baking stone on rack, and heat oven to 500 degrees. Using sharp serrated knife or single-edge razor blade, make one ½-inch-deep slash lengthwise along top of loaf, starting and stopping about 1½ inches from ends. Spray loaf with water and slide loaf and parchment onto baking stone. Bake for 10 minutes, then reduce oven temperature to 400 degrees and quickly rotate loaf using edges of parchment; continue to bake until crust is deep golden brown and loaf registers 210 degrees, about 35 minutes longer. Transfer loaf to wire rack, discard parchment, and let cool to room temperature, about 2 hours, before slicing and serving. (Bread can be wrapped in double layer of plastic wrap and stored at room temperature for up to 3 days. Wrapped with additional layer of aluminum foil, bread can be frozen for up to 1 month.)

WHOLE-WHEAT RUSTIC ITALIAN BREAD

Replace 1¼ cups bread flour with 1¼ cups whole-wheat flour.

24-Hour Sourdough Bread

✔ WHY THIS RECIPE WORKS

Most recipes for sourdough require weeks of preparation just to make the starter, plus several days to make the bread. We challenged ourselves to develop a faster sourdough bread that would still deliver the taste and chew of real sourdough.

BUY READY-MADE STARTER We eliminate the weeks of intense babysitting that cultivating a home starter requires while still producing a flavorful loaf by using a ready-made starter (easily available by mail-order).

CONDENSE SPONGE DEVELOPMENT AND FERMENTATION We found that we could fold these time-consuming steps into one day instead of two, without sacrificing flavor.

PROOF OVERNIGHT For best flavor, the shaped loaves do require an overnight rest in the refrigerator (so that the loaves don't overproof and collapse). The only tricky part is determining when just the right amount of proofing time has passed. We figured out a couple of reliable indicators: the size of the shaped dough (it should double) and the elasticity of the shaped dough (when given a gentle knuckle poke, the dough should sluggishly recover).

BAKE AT HIGH HEAT We bake the bread in a hot (450-degree) oven, as high heat promotes crust development and a good rise; the bread is done when it has reached an internal temperature of 210 to 212 degrees.

24-HOUR SOURDOUGH BREAD
MAKES 2 LOAVES

If you don't have a stand mixer, you can mix the dough by hand following the instructions on page 115. If you don't have a baking stone, bake the bread on an overturned and preheated rimmed baking sheet set on the lower-middle oven rack. Once you have a healthy, refreshed starter (see page 130 for Sourdough Starter Refreshment), the bread will

take about 24 hours (over the course of two days) before it is ready for baking. It is best to start the recipe in the morning, no more than 12 hours after the last feeding of the starter. For the sponge, use the lower amount of water if you live in a humid climate, the higher amount in an arid climate. During kneading, this dough should not exceed a temperature of 80 degrees. If your kitchen is very warm or very cold, use water a few degrees cooler or warmer, respectively.

SPONGE

½	cup (4½ ounces) refreshed starter (recipe follows)
⅜–½	cup warm water (80 degrees)
1	cup (5 ounces) all-purpose flour

DOUGH

1½	cups warm water (70 degrees)
4¾	cups (23¾ ounces) all-purpose flour
2½	teaspoons salt
	Vegetable oil spray

1. FOR THE SPONGE: Stir starter and water together in large bowl until fully combined. Stir in flour until combined (mixture should resemble thick pancake batter). Cover bowl tightly with plastic wrap and let rise at room temperature until doubled in size, 2 to 3 hours.

2. FOR THE DOUGH: Add water and sponge to bowl of stand mixer fitted with dough hook. With mixer on low speed, add flour, ½ cup at a time. Once all flour has been added, continue kneading until dough forms ball, about 1 minute longer; cover bowl tightly with plastic and let dough rest for 20 minutes.

3. Using your fingers, create pocket in rested dough, then add salt to pocket. Knead dough on low speed until soft, smooth, and moist (dough should not be sticky), about 5 minutes. Transfer dough to clean counter and knead by hand to form firm ball, about

SLICING ROUND LOAVES

Slicing a boule of bread straight across like a sandwich loaf delivers smaller slices at the ends and bigger slices toward the middle. To create more even-size pieces, cut circular loaves in a unique pattern.

1. Slice away one end of the bread.

2. Rotate the bread one-quarter turn to the right and cut a slice.

3. Rotate the bread one-quarter turn to the left and slice again. Continue to rotate the bread after each cut.

Most recipes for bread dough
or batter call for combining
the dry ingredients separately
from the liquid ingredients
and then stirring the wet
stuff into the dry, rather than
the other way around. But
does the order really matter?
We mixed different types of
dough and batter both ways
to find out.

With thick pancake batter,
we got perfectly acceptable
results either way. But for
baked goods made from drier
doughs, like yeast breads,
biscuits, scones, quick breads,
and muffins, the order was
crucial. When we added
the wet ingredients to the
dry ones, we got pockets of
flour and a messy, crusted
mixing bowl. Mixing the dry
ingredients into the wet was
far more successful. Following this order made for a
more supple dough that was
easier to combine thoroughly
without overmixing (which
can overdevelop gluten), so
it turned out more delicate,
finely textured results. It also
made cleanup easier.

30 seconds. Place dough in large, lightly greased bowl, and spray surface of dough lightly with vegetable oil spray. Take internal temperature of dough; then cover tightly with plastic. If temperature is below 78 degrees, set container at room temperature (about 70 degrees) in draft-free spot; if warmer than 78 degrees, set container at cool room temperature (about 65 degrees) in draft-free spot. Let rise until dough doubles in size, 3 to 5 hours.

4. Line 2 rimmed baking sheets with parchment paper. Transfer dough to clean counter. Gently stretch dough (to redistribute and refresh yeast) as far as possible without tearing, then fold it into thirds like business letter. Divide dough in half crosswise, then loosely shape each piece into ball, cover loosely with plastic, and let rest for 15 minutes. Cup hands stiffly around 1 piece of dough (keep other piece covered), and drag in short half-circular motions toward edge of counter, forming dough into round loaf with smooth, taut surface. Pinch bottom seam closed and set loaf seam side down on prepared sheet. Repeat with second piece of dough. Spray loaves lightly with oil spray, cover loosely with plastic, and refrigerate for at least 8 hours or up to 24 hours.

5. Slide parchment and covered loaves onto clean counter, spaced at least 6 inches apart. Loosen plastic to allow loaves to rise; let rise until nearly doubled in size, 3 to 4 hours. (Dough should barely spring back when poked with knuckle.)

6. One hour before baking, adjust oven rack to lower-middle position, place baking stone on rack, and heat oven to 500 degrees. Carefully slide parchment and rounds onto pizza peel. Using sharp serrated knife or single-edge razor blade, held at 45-degree angle to work surface, slash surface of loaves ½ to ¾ inch deep. Working quickly, spray loaves with water, slide loaves and parchment onto baking stone, and immediately reduce oven temperature to 450 degrees. Bake, spraying loaves with water twice more during first 5 minutes of baking, until crust is deep golden brown and loaves register 210 degrees, about

30 minutes. Transfer loaves to wire rack, discard parchment, and let cool to room temperature, about 2 hours, before slicing and serving. (Bread can be wrapped in double layer of plastic wrap and stored at room temperature for up to 3 days. Wrapped with additional layer of aluminum foil, bread can be frozen for up to 1 month.)

SOURDOUGH STARTER REFRESHMENT

If you do not already have a starter, dried starter packets (sold by mail and in some natural foods stores) or fresh mail-order starters work well. Follow the package directions to get the starter going, then follow our directions for feeding once the starter is going strong. No matter where you get your starter and how carefully you maintain it, you should refresh it according to the instructions below before using it.

Sourdough starter
3   cups warm water (80 degrees)
4½ cups (22½ ounces) all-purpose flour

1. Beginning in evening, 2 days before you intend to use starter, stir starter well to recombine. Measure out and reserve 1 cup (9 ounces) of starter; discard remaining starter (or give it to a friend). Stir reserved starter and 1 cup water together in large bowl until combined, then stir in 1½ cups flour until evenly moistened (mixture will be lumpy). Cover with plastic wrap and let mixture stand at room temperature for 8 hours to 12 hours.

2. In morning of following day, pour off all but 1 cup starter, stir in 1 cup water, then stir in 1½ cups flour. Repeat with pouring off starter, stirring in remaining 1 cup water and remaining 1½ cups flour, letting it stand at room temperature for entire time. Starter will be fully refreshed and ready to use next morning, 8 to 12 hours after last feeding. (Starter can be kept alive over long period of nonuse in refrigerator. It's best to feed it weekly, according to instructions in step 1; let it stand at room temperature for 4 to 6 hours after feeding, then return it to refrigerator.)

Olive-Rosemary Bread

✔ WHY THIS RECIPE WORKS

Olive-rosemary bread is a basic Italian rustic loaf flavored with olives and the subtle perfume of rosemary. It should have a coarse crumb, a chewy interior, and a thick, burnished crust. But this hearty loaf is about as elusive as it is perfect. At home, it's too easy to bake loaves that are more like sandwich bread than rustic breads, with a soft crumb and thin crust. And the olives are either forced into the dough early on and mixed to the point of disintegration or added at the very end as a sparse afterthought. To perfect our home version, we first turn to the bread recipe, and then work on the olive distribution plan.

ADD A LITTLE HONEY We add a bit of honey to our bread dough to add sweetness and help bring out the savory flavor of the olives. Replacing some bread flour with whole-wheat flour gives a nuttier flavor, too. Because we add these flavors, this means that the dough doesn't need to ferment overnight like many other simple rustic breads.

PRESS THE OLIVES Pitting the olives against the stand mixer isn't a fair match. The olives and dough are like oil and water—resisting each other and leaving the olives to smear against the outside of the dough and the bottom of the bowl. We found success in rolling the olives into the dough before the first rise, pressing them into the rolled-out dough as if making cinnamon rolls. This gives us a nicely textured loaf with evenly dispersed olives. As for what kind of olives to use, any variety will do. Olive preference is highly subjective. We tend to prefer a mix.

USE MORE ROSEMARY Rosemary is often perceived as being brutish; if used excessively, it can easily overpower a dish with its piney harshness. But we soon realized that this herb behaves differently when baked into bread—its flavor is as fleeting as the little specks are invisible. We use a whopping 2 tablespoons in order to get a demure background flavor to complement the bright, fruity olives.

LET IT REST The autolyse (allowing the mixture of flours, water, and yeast to rest so that the flour has more time to absorb the water) is instrumental for more efficient kneading in this recipe. It takes 20 minutes, but this is 20 minutes we don't mind adding. Folding the dough during the first rise also drastically improves its elasticity and strength, which results in larger holes in the bread and a heartier chew.

SLASH AND SPRAY Slashing the risen loaf with a sharp paring knife or razor allows the crust to expand, preventing the bread from splitting in the oven. Misting the loaf right before it goes into the oven delays the formation of a crust, allowing the bread to fully expand without tearing or splitting. The steam also promotes the formation of a crispy, glossy crust.

OLIVE-ROSEMARY BREAD
MAKES 2 LOAVES

If you don't have a stand mixer, you can mix the dough by hand following the instructions on page 115. If you don't have a baking stone, bake the bread on an overturned and preheated rimmed baking sheet set on the lower-middle oven rack. Almost any variety of brined or oil-cured olives works in this recipe, although we prefer a mix of both green and black olives.

1¾	cups water, room temperature
2	tablespoons honey
2	teaspoons instant or rapid-rise yeast
3½	cups (19¼ ounces) bread flour, plus extra as needed
½	cup (2¾ ounces) whole-wheat flour

1. After patting dough into 12 by 6–inch rectangle, press olives evenly into dough. With long side facing you, roll rectangle into a tight log.

2. With seam side facing up, roll log into coil. Place dough, spiral side up, in oiled bowl.

3. Cover bowl with plastic wrap and let dough rise until doubled in size. Follow recipe for further rising and shaping.

Professional bread ovens
boast pressurized valves for
injecting steam into the oven
at the beginning of baking
for three important reasons.
First, a moist environment
transfers heat more rapidly
than dry heat does, allowing
the gases inside the loaf to
rapidly expand in the first few
minutes of baking, ensuring
maximum volume. At the
same time, steam prevents
the bread's exterior from
drying out too quickly, which
can limit rise. Finally, moisture
converts the exterior starches
into a thin coating that even
results in a crackly crust.

Our usual approach to
creating steam in a home
oven is to pour boiling water
into a preheated loaf pan
placed on the oven's bottom
rack, but the water doesn't
continue to boil for very long.
Inspired by the superheated
stones used in Swedish
saunas, we've come up with
a more effective approach:
using lava rocks. These
irregularly shaped rocks
(available at many hardware
stores for use in gas grills)
have a lot of surface area for
absorbing and retaining heat,
maximizing the amount of
steam produced when boiling
water is introduced. See our
steps on the facing page for
instructions.

2 teaspoons salt

2 tablespoons minced fresh rosemary

1½ cups pitted olives, rinsed, and chopped coarse

1. Whisk water, honey, and yeast together in bowl of stand mixer fitted with dough hook. Add bread flour and whole-wheat flour to bowl and mix on low speed until cohesive dough is formed, about 3 minutes; cover bowl tightly with plastic wrap and let sit at room temperature for 20 minutes.

2. Make well in center of dough and add salt and rosemary. Knead dough on low speed for 5 minutes, scraping down bowl and dough hook as needed. Increase speed to medium and continue to knead until dough is smooth and slightly tacky, about 1 minute. If dough is very sticky, add 1 to 2 tablespoons bread flour and continue mixing for 1 minute. Transfer dough to lightly floured counter and press into 12 by 6-inch rectangle, with long side facing you. Press olives evenly into dough, then roll dough toward you into firm cylinder, keeping roll taut by tucking it under itself as you go. Turn loaf seam side up and roll cylinder into coil. Transfer dough, spiral side up, to large, lightly greased bowl, cover tightly with plastic wrap, and let rise at room temperature until it increases in size by 50 percent, about 1 hour.

3. Spray rubber spatula or bowl scraper with vegetable oil spray. Fold partially risen dough over itself by gently lifting and folding edge of dough toward middle. Turn bowl 90 degrees; fold again. Turn bowl again; fold once more. Cover with plastic and let rise for 30 minutes. Repeat folding, replace plastic, and let rise until doubled in size, about 30 minutes.

4. Transfer dough to lightly floured counter, being careful not to deflate. Divide dough in half, loosely shape each piece into ball, and let rest for 15 minutes. Flip each ball over and, starting from top, roll dough toward you into firm oval shape. Using your palms, roll each

oval (seam side down) from center outward until 12-inch loaf is formed. Poke any olives that fall off into bottom seam, then pinch seam closed. Transfer each loaf, seam side down, to 12 by 6-inch piece of parchment and cover with plastic. Let rise until doubled in size, 1 to 1½ hours. (Dough should barely spring back when poked with knuckle.)

5. One hour before baking, adjust oven rack to lower-middle position, place baking stone on rack, and heat oven to 450 degrees. Slide parchment with loaves onto pizza peel. Using sharp serrated knife or single-edge razor blade, make one 3½-inch-deep slash on diagonal along top of each fully risen loaf, starting and stopping about 1 inch from ends. Spray loaves with water and slide loaves and parchment onto baking stone. Bake for 15 minutes, spraying loaves with water twice more during first 5 minutes of baking time. Reduce oven temperature to 375 degrees and continue to bake until crust is deep golden brown and loaves register 210 degrees, 25 to 30 minutes. Transfer loaves to wire rack, discard parchment, and let cool to room temperature, about 2 hours, before slicing and serving. (Bread can be wrapped in double layer of plastic wrap and stored at room temperature for up to 3 days. Wrapped with additional layer of aluminum foil, bread can be frozen for up to 1 month. To recrisp crust, thaw bread at room temperature, if frozen, and place unwrapped bread in 450-degree oven for 5 to 10 minutes.)

OLIVE-ROSEMARY ROLLS
MAKES 16 ROLLS

1. After final rise in step 3, transfer dough to lightly floured counter and gently stretch into 12 by 6-inch rectangle. Divide dough in half widthwise, then divide each half into 8 pieces (you should have 16 pieces). Loosely shape each piece into ball, cover with plastic wrap and let rest for 15 minutes. Loosely cup hand around each piece of dough (not

directly over it) and, without applying pressure, move hand in small circular motions to form smooth, taut round. Arrange shaped rolls on 2 parchment paper–lined rimmed baking sheets and cover with plastic. Let rise until doubled in size, about 1 hour. (Dough should barely spring back when poked with knuckle.)

2. Thirty minutes before baking, adjust oven racks to upper-middle and lower-middle positions and heat oven to 500 degrees.

Spray rolls lightly with water and place sheets in oven. Bake for 5 minutes, spraying rolls with water twice more. Reduce oven temperature to 400 degrees and continue to bake until rolls are deep golden brown, 15 to 20 minutes, switching and rotating sheets halfway through baking. Transfer rolls to wire rack and let cool to room temperature, about 1 hour, before serving.

Cinnamon Babka

✔ WHY THIS RECIPE WORKS

By its very definition, babka is a rich, tender dough. But go too far in that direction and the dough will collapse under the weight of the cinnamon-sugar filling, leaving large holes in the bread. We wanted a rich loaf that would support lots of layers of sweet filling.

TWEAK A BRIOCHE-STYLE DOUGH A brioche-style dough (a yeasted dough made with butter, eggs, sugar, and milk) makes a good starting point for this recipe but all that liquid and fat weakens the dough; weighed down with a heavy filling, the loaf will collapse in the oven. To strengthen the loaf, we back off on the butter by a couple of tablespoons. For added richness without too much liquid, we substitute two egg yolks for the whole egg and inject just a splash more milk. This mimics the tenderness of the lost butter without compromising the structure of the dough.

THICKEN THE FILLING To thicken our filling so that it stays put among the layers, we turn to a combination of flour and egg white. Flour binds the filling nicely but too much can leave an unpleasantly pasty aftertaste. (In tests, we could get away with ¼ cup without tasters noticing, but that amount wasn't enough to thicken the filling on its own.) Egg whites,

which are used in chocolate babka filling to help the chopped chocolate stick to the layers, add extra binding power here. Easy to spread, this filling stays evenly distributed throughout the babka.

PLUG THE LEAKS We found that the simple jelly roll–style shaping method that most recipes employ didn't integrate the filling very well. Instead, we turned to the professionals at Green's, a Brooklyn bakery famous for its babka, who recommended rolling out the dough super-thin—so thin that after rolling it forms a rectangle twice the size of other recipes. Next, the rectangle gets rolled up, creating a much longer and skinnier jelly roll, which is then folded in half lengthwise, given a couple of twists, and deposited in the loaf pan. To make working with the tender dough and slippery filling easier, we chill the dough before rolling. Once baked, this babka boasts almost quadruple the number of layers in other homemade versions, ensuring cinnamony goodness in every bite.

GLAZE, BAKE, AND COOL A beaten egg brushed over the shaped loaf gives it a shiny, nut-brown crust. After baking, allow the loaf to cool before slicing; the loaf will taste doughy if sliced hot.

MIMICKING A PROFESSIONAL BREAD OVEN

1. Place wide pan filled with lava rocks on bottom oven rack beneath baking stone (which is used to heat bread's interior as quickly as possible) and preheat. If you bake bread regularly, consider designating a pan for this purpose, since it will eventually get scratched.

2. Pour about ¼ cup of boiling water onto preheated rocks. Keep oven door closed for 1 minute to create steam. Place bread on stone, pour another ¼ cup of water over rocks, and bake bread as usual.

SHAPING BABKA

1. Roll out chilled dough into 20 by 14-inch rectangle and spread all but 1 tablespoon of filling over dough, leaving ½-inch border around edges.

2. Starting at short edge, roll filled dough into a tight cylinder and pinch to seal the seam. Stretch log to 18 inches by gently rolling it back and forth with seam side up.

3. Spread remaining 1 tablespoon of filling over top of cylinder and fold cylinder on top of itself, pinching ends together to seal.

4. Gently twist folded cylinder twice to form double figure eight and place it seam side down in parchment-lined loaf pan.

CINNAMON BABKA
SERVES 8

Once you've added the butter in step 3, if the dough is still sticking to the sides of the bowl after 5 minutes of mixing, add 2 to 4 tablespoons of extra flour. The test kitchen's preferred loaf pan measures 8½ by 4½ inches; if you use a 9 by 5-inch loaf pan, start checking for doneness 5 minutes earlier than specified in recipe.

FILLING

1	cup packed (7 ounces) light brown sugar
¼	cup (1¼ ounces) all-purpose flour
2	tablespoons unsalted butter, melted and cooled
1	large egg white
2	teaspoons ground cinnamon
⅛	teaspoon salt

DOUGH

½	cup warm whole milk (110 degrees)
2	large egg yolks plus 1 large egg
1	teaspoon vanilla extract
2	cups (10 ounces) all-purpose flour
¼	cup (1¾ ounces) sugar
1½	teaspoons instant or rapid-rise yeast
½	teaspoon salt
8	tablespoons unsalted butter, cut into 8 pieces and softened

1. FOR THE FILLING: Combine all ingredients in medium bowl. Set aside 1 tablespoon filling.

2. FOR THE DOUGH: Adjust oven rack to middle position and heat oven to 200 degrees. When oven reaches 200 degrees, turn it off. Grease large bowl. Whisk milk, egg yolks, and vanilla together in 1-cup liquid measuring cup.

3. Using stand mixer fitted with dough hook, mix flour, sugar, yeast, and salt on low speed until combined. Slowly add milk mixture and mix until dough comes together, about 3 minutes. Increase speed to medium-low and add butter, 1 piece at a time, until incorporated, about 1 minute. Continue to mix until dough is smooth and comes away from sides of bowl, 10 to 12 minutes. Transfer dough to prepared bowl, cover with plastic wrap, and place in turned-off oven until dough has risen slightly, about 1 hour. Place in refrigerator until dough is firm and has doubled in size, at least 1 hour.

4. Line 8½ by 4½-inch loaf pan with parchment paper, allowing excess to hang over edges. Punch down dough on lightly floured counter. Roll out dough to 20 by 14-inch rectangle. Spread all but 1 tablespoon reserved filling over dough, leaving ½-inch border around edges. Working from short side, roll dough into cylinder and pinch along seam to seal. Position cylinder seam side up and roll back and forth until stretched to 18-inch length. Spread reserved filling over top of cylinder. Fold cylinder on top of itself and pinch ends to seal. Gently twist double cylinder twice to form double figure eight. Place shaped dough seam side down in prepared pan, cover loosely with plastic, and let rise in turned-off oven until doubled in size, about 1 hour.

5. Lightly beat whole egg in bowl. Remove loaf from oven and discard plastic. Heat oven to 350 degrees. Brush loaf with beaten egg. Bake until deep golden brown and loaf registers 190 degrees, about 45 minutes. Let cool in pan on wire rack for 20 minutes. Remove loaf from pan and cool completely, about 2 hours. Serve.

TO MAKE AHEAD: Instead of letting dough rise in step 4, cover shaped loaf with plastic wrap and refrigerate for up to 24 hours. Let dough sit at room temperature for 1 hour before baking.

Cinnamon Swirl Bread

✔ WHY THIS RECIPE WORKS

Our ideal cinnamon swirl bread sports a fluffy, delicate crumb studded with plump raisins and laced with a substantial swirl of gooey cinnamon sugar. But most versions are either austere white sandwich loaves rolled up with a bare sprinkle of cinnamon and sugar or overly sweet breads ruined by gobs of filling oozing from the cracks.

TAKE A TIP FROM THE JAPANESE The Japanese bake a white sandwich bread, called *shokupan*, that is just perfect for the base of our cinnamon bread. Its hallmark lift and airy texture come from considerable gluten, the network of proteins that builds structure. To achieve this, Japanese bakers use high-gluten flour. We follow suit and use high-gluten bread flour in our recipe.

INCORPORATE AIR To mimic the light crumb of this bread we incorporate more air into the bread. Oxygen is the driving force behind gluten development; the more oxygen the dough gets the stronger the gluten network becomes. To this end, we increased the kneading time and introduced two sets of folds (or turns) into the process. We also waited until we were almost done kneading to add our recipe's butter, an ingredient that inhibits gluten formation. These measures gave us a gorgeously lofty loaf that serves as the perfect counterpoint for our gooey cinnamon swirl.

THICKEN THE SWIRL We thought that perfecting a thick cinnamon swirl would be the easy part of making the bread—until each test with it turned out leaky loaves that spewed molten cinnamon sugar from its crevices. To encourage binding between the swirl and the dough, we swapped granulated sugar for confectioners' and upped the amount of cinnamon. When powdery confectioners' sugar absorbs water from the dough, it forms a sticky paste. This paste is then thickened by the cornstarch in the sugar and the cinnamon.

PLUG THE LEAKS Although we'd developed a nicely thickened filling, we still needed to remember that steam inside the dough could cause blowouts. Our solution? We form our loaf into a two-pronged Russian braid, which completely eliminated gapping and leaking because it allowed trapped gas to escape.

CINNAMON SWIRL BREAD
MAKES 2 LOAVES

To achieve the proper dough consistency, make sure to weigh your ingredients. The dough will appear very wet and sticky until the final few minutes of kneading; do not be tempted to add supplemental flour. The test kitchen's preferred loaf pan measures 8½ by 4½ inches; if you use a 9 by 5-inch loaf pan, start checking for doneness 5 minutes earlier than specified in recipe.

DOUGH

8	tablespoons unsalted butter
3¾	cups (20⅔ ounces) bread flour
¾	cup (2¾ ounces) nonfat dry milk powder
⅓	cup (2⅓ ounces) granulated sugar
1	tablespoon instant or rapid-rise yeast
1½	cups warm water (110 degrees)
1	large egg, lightly beaten
1½	teaspoons salt
1½	cups (7½ ounces) golden raisins

FILLING

1	cup (4 ounces) confectioners' sugar
3	tablespoons ground cinnamon
1	teaspoon vanilla extract
½	teaspoon salt
1	large egg, lightly beaten with pinch salt

1. FOR THE DOUGH: Cut butter into 32 pieces and toss with 1 tablespoon flour; set aside to soften while mixing dough. Whisk remaining flour, milk powder, sugar, and yeast together in bowl of stand mixer fitted with dough hook. Add water and egg and mix on medium-low speed until cohesive mass forms, about 2 minutes, scraping down bowl as needed. Cover mixing bowl with plastic wrap and let stand for 20 minutes.

2. Adjust oven rack to middle position and place loaf or cake pan on bottom of oven. Grease large bowl. Remove plastic from mixer bowl, add salt, and mix on medium-low speed until dough is smooth and elastic and clears sides of bowl, 7 to 15 minutes. With mixer running, add butter few pieces at a time and continue to knead until butter is fully incorporated and dough is smooth and elastic and clears sides of bowl, 3 to 5 minutes longer. Add raisins and mix until incorporated, 30 to 60 seconds. Transfer dough to prepared bowl and, using bowl scraper or rubber spatula, fold dough over itself by gently lifting and folding edge of dough toward middle. Turn bowl 90 degrees; fold again. Turn bowl and fold dough 6 more times (total of 8 folds). Cover tightly with plastic and transfer to middle rack of oven. Pour 3 cups boiling water into loaf pan in oven, close oven door, and allow dough to rise for 45 minutes.

3. Remove bowl from oven and gently press down on center of dough to deflate. Repeat folding (making total of 8 folds), recover, and return to oven until doubled in volume, about 45 minutes.

4. FOR THE FILLING: Whisk all ingredients together in bowl until well combined; set aside.

5. Grease two 8½ by 4½-inch loaf pans. Transfer dough to lightly floured counter and divide into 2 pieces. Working with 1 piece of dough, pat into rough 11 by 6-inch rectangle. With short side facing you, fold long sides in like a business letter to form 11 by 3-inch rectangle. Roll dough away from you into ball. Dust ball with flour and flatten with rolling pin into 18 by 7-inch rectangle with even ¼-inch thickness. Using spray bottle, spray dough lightly with water. Sprinkle half of filling mixture evenly over dough, leaving ¼-inch border on sides and ¾-inch border on top and bottom; spray filling lightly with water. (Filling should be speckled with water over entire surface.) With short side facing you, roll dough away from you into firm cylinder. Turn loaf seam side up and pinch closed; pinch ends closed. Dust loaf lightly on all sides with flour and let rest for 10 minutes. Repeat with second ball of dough and remaining filling.

6. Working with 1 loaf at a time, use bench scraper to cut loaf in half lengthwise; turn halves so cut sides are facing up. Gently stretch each half into 14-inch length. Line up pieces of dough and pinch 2 ends of strips together. Take piece on left and lay over piece on right. Repeat, keeping cut side up, until pieces of dough are tightly twisted. Pinch ends together. Transfer loaf, cut side up, to prepared loaf pan; push any exposed raisins into seams of braid. Repeat with second loaf. Cover loaves loosely with plastic, return to oven, and allow to rise for 45 minutes. Remove loaves and water pan from oven; heat oven to 350 degrees. Allow loaves to rise at room temperature until almost doubled in size, about 45 minutes (tops of loaves should rise about 1 inch over lip of pans).

7. Brush loaves with egg mixture. Bake until crust is well browned, about 25 minutes. Reduce oven temperature to 325 degrees, tent loaves with aluminum foil, and continue to bake until internal temperature registers 200 degrees, 15 to 25 minutes longer.

8. Transfer pans to wire rack and let cool for 5 minutes. Remove loaves from pans, return to rack, and let cool to room temperature before slicing, about 2 hours.

WEAVING A TIGHT CINNAMON SWIRL BREAD, RUSSIAN-STYLE

1. Using bench scraper or sharp chef's knife, cut filled dough in half lengthwise. Turn halves so cut sides are facing up.

2. With cut sides up, stretch each half into 14-inch length.

3. Pinch 2 ends of strips together. To braid, take left strip of dough and lay it over right strip of dough.

4. Repeat braiding, keeping cut sides facing up, until pieces are tightly twisted. Pinch ends together.

Almost No-Knead Bread

✓ WHY THIS RECIPE WORKS

*In 2006, New York Times writer Mark Bittman
published a recipe developed by Jim Lahey of the
Sullivan Street Bakery in Manhattan that promised
to shake up the world of home baking: It allowed the
average cook to bake bread that looked like it had
been produced in a professional bakery and involved
no kneading at all. However, as we baked loaf after
loaf, we found two big problems: The dough deflated
when carried to the pot, causing misshapen loaves,
and it lacked flavor. In our rendition, we lower the
hydration and add the bare minimum of kneading
time to compensate.*

DON'T KNEAD—MUCH The origi-
nal no-knead bread has a hydration level of
85 percent, while most rustic breads max out
at around 80 percent hydration, and standard sandwich breads hover between 60 percent and 75 percent hydration. This high level
of water, along with the long rest, helps to
form the gluten strands and, in effect, takes
the place of kneading. Here, we cut back on
the water in order to make the dough easier
to handle. But with a lower level of hydration
the gluten strands are not rearranged to the
same degree as they are in the original recipe
and need some help. This is why we knead
our "no-knead" dough. Fifteen seconds is all
it takes.

ADD VINEGAR AND BEER Two ingredients proved key to help boost the loaf's flavor:
vinegar and beer. Bottled vinegars are generally 5 percent solutions of acetic acid—the
same acid produced by bacteria during dough
fermentation. The inclusion of 1 tablespoon
of distilled white vinegar adds tang. Bread's
unique flavor comes during fermentation,
when yeast produces alcohol, carbon dioxide,
and sulfur compounds. These three elements
are present together in another location—a
bottle of beer. We choose lager over other
types of beer because most nonlager beers
undergo a process called "top fermentation,"
whereby yeast floats on top of the wort (grain
mashed in hot water), which is exposed to
oxygen and kept warm. Oxygen and warmth
persuade yeast to produce spicy, astringent
flavor compounds called phenols and fruity,
floral compounds called esters that are desirable in beer but not in bread. Lagers, on the
other hand, undergo "bottom fermentation,"
where the yeast is kept submerged in the low-
oxygen environment at the bottom of the
wort at colder temperatures, which causes the
yeast to produce fewer phenols and esters, but
more sulfur compounds, so that the breadier
yeast and sulfur flavors come forward.

BAKE IN A DUTCH OVEN Baking
the bread in a Dutch oven acts like a minia-
ture version of the steam-injected ovens used
by professional bakers: The lid traps steam
released by the loaf for maximum rise. But
be careful of the knob on your Dutch oven.
The manufacturers of our favorite Dutch oven
(the 7¼-Quart Round French Oven by Le
Creuset) and our Best Buy Dutch oven (the
6.5-Quart Cast Iron Dutch Oven by Tramon-
tina) recommend against heating the pots to
this temperature due to the phenolic (black)
knobs used on the lids. But there is a simple
solution. The knobs on both lids are secured
with a single screw that is easily removed.
Once the knob is removed, you can replace it
with an inexpensive all-metal drawer handle
purchased from a hardware store.

ALMOST NO-KNEAD BREAD

MAKES 1 LOAF

We prefer to use a mild American lager, such as Budweiser here; strongly flavored beers will make this bread taste bitter. You will need at least a 6-quart Dutch oven for this recipe. An enameled cast-iron Dutch oven with a tight-fitting lid yields the best results, but the recipe also works in a regular cast-iron Dutch oven or heavy stockpot. Check the knob on your Dutch oven lid, as not all are ovensafe to 425 degrees; look for inexpensive replacement knobs from the manufacturer of your Dutch oven (or try using a metal drawer handle from a hardware store). This dough rises best in a warm kitchen that is at least 68 degrees.

3	cups (15 ounces) all-purpose flour
1½	teaspoons salt
¼	teaspoon instant or rapid-rise yeast
¾	cup (6 ounces) water, room temperature
½	cup (4 ounces) mild lager, room temperature
1	tablespoon distilled white vinegar

1. Whisk flour, salt, and yeast together in large bowl. Whisk water, beer, and vinegar together in 4-cup liquid measuring cup. Using rubber spatula, gently fold water mixture into flour mixture, scraping up dry flour from bottom of bowl, until dough starts to form and no dry flour remains. Cover bowl tightly with plastic wrap and let sit at room temperature for at least 8 hours or up to 18 hours.

2. Lay 18 by 12-inch sheet of parchment paper inside 10-inch skillet and spray with vegetable oil spray. Transfer dough to lightly floured counter and knead by hand until smooth and elsastic, about 1 minute. Shape dough into ball by pulling edges into middle, then transfer seam side down to prepared skillet and spray surface of dough with oil spray. Cover loosely with plastic wrap and let rise until doubled in size and dough springs back minimally when poked gently with your knuckle, 1½ to 2 hours.

3. Adjust oven rack to middle position. Using sharp paring knife or single-edge razor blade, make two 5-inch-long, ½-inch-deep slashes along top of loaf to form cross. Pick up loaf by lifting parchment overhang and lower into pot (let any excess parchment hang over pot edge). Cover pot and place in oven. Turn oven to 425 degrees and bake loaf for 30 minutes while oven heats. Remove lid and continue to bake until loaf is deep golden brown and registers 205 to 201 degrees, 25 to 30 minutes. Using parchment sling, remove loaf from pot and transfer to wire rack, discard parchment. Let cool completely, about 3 hours, before slicing and serving. (Bread is best eaten on day it is baked but will keep wrapped in double layer of plastic and stored at room temperature for up to 2 days. To recrisp crust, place unwrapped bread in 450-degree oven for 6 to 8 minutes.)

ALMOST NO-KNEAD BREAD WITH OLIVES, ROSEMARY, AND PARMESAN

If you prefer black olives, substitute them for the green olives, or try a mix of green and black olives.

Add 2 cups finely grated Parmesan cheese and 1 tablespoon minced fresh rosemary to flour mixture in step 1. Add 1 cup pitted green olives, chopped, with water.

ALMOST NO-KNEAD SEEDED RYE BREAD

Replace 1⅜ cups all-purpose flour with 1⅛ cups rye flour. Add 2 tablespoons caraway seeds to flour mixture in step 1.

ALMOST NO-KNEAD WHOLE-WHEAT BREAD

Replace 1 cup all-purpose flour with 1 cup whole-wheat flour. Stir 2 tablespoons honey into water before adding it to dry ingredients in step 1.

ALMOST NO-KNEAD CRANBERRY-PECAN BREAD

Add ½ cup dried cranberries and ½ cup toasted pecans to flour mixture in step 1.

MAKING ALMOST NO-KNEAD BREAD

1. Stir the wet ingredients into the dry ingredients with a spatula. Leave the dough to rest for eight to 18 hours.

2. Knead the dough for about 1 minute and shape it into a ball.

3. Allow the dough to rise for 1½ to 2 hours in a parchment-lined skillet.

4. Put the dough in a Dutch oven, cover pot, and place it in a cold oven. Set the oven dial to 425 degrees and let bake as oven heats up, first covered, then uncovered.

Challah

✔ WHY THIS RECIPE WORKS

Challah is a braided bread that is traditionally made for the Jewish Sabbath. The best challah is rich with eggs and lightly sweetened, with a dark, shiny crust and a firm but light and tender texture. The mass-produced challah found in grocery stores can be dry, disappointingly bland, and disconcertingly fluffy. We wanted ours to be at once tender but substantial, with a rich, eggy flavor.

USE READILY AVAILABLE ALL-PURPOSE FLOUR We began by pitting all-purpose flour against bread flour. There was no significant difference, so we decided to stick with the more readily available all-purpose flour. We use 2¼ teaspoons (one envelope) of instant yeast to give the challah the right amount of lift.

ADD JUST A FEW EGGS Some challah can be overly eggy. We found that combination of two whole eggs and one yolk is the best, making a loaf with good egg flavor and a tender texture. Most recipes call for water, although a few use milk. We tried both. The challah made with milk was slightly more dense and heavy. We preferred the lighter texture of the challah made with water, which also makes the bread dairy-free, as is tradition. Keeping in line with tradition, we stuck with vegetable oil over butter, which had no adverse affect on flavor or texture.

SWEETEN WITH GRANULATED SUGAR We tried granulated sugar, brown sugar, and honey in our working recipe. Differences were minimal, but we found that granulated sugar made challah with the cleanest flavor.

MAKE TWO BRAIDS—AND STACK The recommended shape for challah is a simple braid, but we found this to be a problem because the loaf rose out but not up. Some recipes call for braiding six strands for a higher loaf but this can get complicated. Our solution is to make two braids, one large and one small, and place the smaller braid on top of the other.

BRUSH WITH RESERVED EGG WHITE FOR A SHINY CRUST We reserve the egg white from the extra yolk used in the dough, mix it with water, and brush it over the loaf before putting it into the oven.

CHALLAH

MAKES 1 LOAF

Remember to save the leftover egg white from the dough for the glaze. If you don't have a stand mixer, you can mix the dough by hand following the instructions on page 115. Leftover challah makes sensational French toast (see page 93).

DOUGH

½	cup warm water (110 degrees)
¼	cup vegetable oil
2	large eggs, plus 1 large yolk
3–3½	cups (15 to 17½ ounces) all-purpose flour
¼	cup (1¾ ounces) sugar
2¼	teaspoons instant or rapid-rise yeast
1¼	teaspoons salt

GLAZE

1	large egg white
2	tablespoons water
1	teaspoon poppy or sesame seeds (optional)

1. FOR THE DOUGH: Whisk water, oil, and eggs and yolk together in large liquid measuring cup. Using stand mixer fitted with dough hook, combine 3 cups flour, sugar, yeast, and salt. With mixer on low speed, add water mixture and mix until dough comes together, about 2 minutes.

2. Increase mixer speed to medium-low and knead until dough is smooth and elastic, about 8 minutes. If after 4 minutes more flour is needed, add remaining ½ cup flour, 2 tablespoons at a time, until dough clears sides of bowl but sticks to bottom.

1. Divide dough into 2 pieces—one weighing 18 ounces, the other weighing 9 ounces. Shape large piece of dough into 3 ropes, each 16 inches long and 1 inch thick. Line up ropes side by side and pinch top ends together. Take dough rope on right and lay it over center rope. Take dough rope on left and lay it over center rope.

2. Repeat this process until ropes of dough are entirely braided. Pinch ends together, tuck both ends under braid, and transfer braid to lightly greased baking sheet. Divide smaller piece of dough into 3 equal ropes about 16 inches long and ½ inch thick and repeat braiding process.

3. Brush larger braid with some of egg wash and place smaller braid on top. Cover loosely with plastic wrap. Once dough has become puffy (this will take 30 to 45 minutes), brush top of loaf with remaining egg wash and bake.

3. Turn dough out onto lightly floured counter and knead by hand to form smooth, round ball. Place dough in large, lightly oiled bowl and cover with greased plastic wrap. Let rise in warm place until doubled in size, 1 to 1½ hours.

4. Line baking sheet with parchment paper. Turn dough out onto lightly floured counter and divide dough into 2 pieces, one twice as large as the other. Divide each piece into 3 pieces and roll each piece out into 16-inch-long rope (3 ropes will be much thicker).

5. FOR THE GLAZE: Beat egg white and water together in small bowl. Braid 2 loaves, one large and one small. Transfer larger braid to prepared sheet, brush with some egg white–water mixture, and secure smaller braid on top. Tuck both ends under loaf.

Cover with greased plastic and let rise in warm place until nearly doubled in size and dough barely springs back when poked with knuckle, 45 minutes to 1¼ hours.

6. Adjust oven rack to lower-middle position and heat oven to 375 degrees. Brush loaf with remaining egg white–water mixture, sprinkle with seeds, if using, then spray lightly with water. Bake until golden and center of loaf registers 200 degrees, 30 to 40 minutes, rotating loaf halfway through baking. Let bread cool on sheet for 15 minutes, then transfer to wire rack and let cool to room temperature, about 2 hours, before slicing and serving.

TO MAKE AHEAD: In step 3, do not let dough rise, but refrigerate it overnight or up to 16 hours; let dough sit at room temperature for 30 minutes, then continue with step 4.

No-Knead Brioche

✓ WHY THIS RECIPE WORKS

Most butter-enriched doughs contain between 10 and 20 percent butter. The average brioche recipe brings the ratio up to 50 percent (or 5 parts butter to 10 parts flour). Because fat lubricates the wheat proteins in the flour, any amount at all will inhibit their ability to form gluten, the network of cross-linked proteins that gives bread its structure. The more fat the greater the interference. This can make brioche incredibly tender—or it can cause the dough to separate into a greasy mess. We wanted to make tender, plush brioche with butter-rich flavor but no butter-induced headache.

MELT YOUR BUTTER Typically, softened butter is added to the dough in increments. Only after one portion is fully incorporated into the dough is the next added to ensure that the butter is completely and evenly combined without causing the dough to separate. But guess what? We found that

simply melting the butter is just fine—and we add it all at once.

SKIP KNEADING We apply the same technique here as we do for our Almost No-Knead Bread (page 139). Basically, you combine all your ingredients and let the mixture sit for hours. During this long rest, enzymes naturally present in wheat help untangle the wheat proteins that eventually come together to form an organized gluten network. This allows the dough to stitch itself together into a loaf containing plenty of structure with only a bit of stirring and a couple of folds, or turns. The key to this technique is a very wet dough (the more water the more efficient the enzymes).

CHOOSE HIGH-PROTEIN BREAD FLOUR Brioche made with flour containing the highest amount of protein—bread flour—stands head and shoulders above loaves made with lower-protein flours.

EMPLOY A COLD FERMENT Allowing dough to rest allows not just for gluten development but also adds more flavor, since it gives the starches in the dough more time to ferment (a role normally played by a sponge). Gluten development and fermentation are slowed but not halted by cold temperatures, so we extend the dough's second rest in the fridge (where it doesn't run the risk of overproofing and collapsing), giving it even more strength.

ADD MORE STRENGTH THROUGH SHAPING Instead of shaping the dough into a single long loaf we found that we could add even more strength and structure to the dough by dividing it in two and shaping each half into a tight, round ball. Placed side by side in the pan, the two balls merge during rising and baking to form a single loaf. Even this little bit of extra manipulation makes the crumb a bit finer and more uniform. But while shaping them once is good, shaping twice is even better. After letting the dough rounds rest, we pat them flat once more and then reshape them into tight balls. As a result, our brioche boasts a finely textured, resilient crumb with complex flavor.

NO-KNEAD BRIOCHE
MAKES 2 LOAVES

High-protein King Arthur Bread Flour works best with this recipe, though other bread flours will suffice. The test kitchen's preferred loaf pans measure 8½ by 4½ inches; if you use 9 by 5-inch loaf pans, start checking for doneness 5 minutes earlier than advised in recipe. If you don't have a baking stone, bake the bread on an overturned and preheated rimmed baking sheet set on the lowest oven rack.

3¼ cups (17¾ ounces) bread flour
2¼ teaspoons instant or rapid-rise yeast
1½ teaspoons salt
7 large eggs, 1 lightly beaten with pinch salt

½ cup water, room temperature
⅓ cup (2⅓ ounces) sugar
16 tablespoons unsalted butter, melted and cooled slightly

1. Whisk flour, yeast, and salt together in large bowl. Whisk 6 eggs, water, and sugar together in medium bowl until sugar has dissolved. Whisk in melted butter until smooth. Add egg mixture to flour mixture and stir with wooden spoon until uniform mass forms and no dry flour remains, about 1 minute. Cover bowl with plastic wrap and let stand for 10 minutes.

2. Holding edge of dough with your fingertips, fold dough over itself by gently lifting and folding edge of dough toward middle. Turn bowl 45 degrees; fold again. Turn bowl and fold dough 6 more times (total of 8 folds). Cover with plastic and let rise for 30 minutes. Repeat folding and rising every 30 minutes, 3 more times. After fourth set of folds, cover bowl tightly with plastic and refrigerate for at least 16 hours or up to 48 hours.

3. Transfer dough to well-floured counter and divide into 4 pieces. Working with 1 piece of dough at a time, pat dough into 4-inch disk. Working around circumference of dough, fold edges of dough toward center until ball forms. Flip dough over and, without applying pressure, move your hands in small circular motions to form dough into smooth, taut round. (If dough sticks to your hands, lightly dust top of dough with flour.) Repeat with remaining dough. Cover dough rounds loosely with plastic and let rest for 5 minutes.

4. Grease two 8½ by 4½-inch loaf pans. After 5 minutes, flip each dough ball so seam side is facing up, pat into 4-inch disk, and repeat rounding step. Place 2 rounds, seam side down, side by side into prepared pans and press gently into corners. Cover loaves loosely with plastic and let rise at room temperature until almost doubled in size (dough should rise to about ½ inch below top edge

CLEANING UP AFTER BREAD MAKING

Cleaning up hands, workbowl, and kneading surface after bread making can be a pain. A scrubbing pad is most effective for removing the dough, but the dough tends to stick to the pad so it has to be discarded. Instead, tackle dough cleanup with a square of the plastic mesh used to package shallots, onions, potatoes, and so forth, which can then simply be thrown away.

Folding the dough as it proofs is an important step—and the only active work you'll have to do for our No-Knead Brioche. Gently lift an edge of the dough and fold it over itself, turning the bowl 45 degrees and repeating until you've made a full circle (total of eight folds).

BRIOCHE MOLD

For our No-Knead Brioche à Tête, we tested four models, each 8 to 8½ inches in diameter. Only our favorite, the **Gobel 8-Inch Tinned Steel Brioche Mold, 6-Cup,** produced loaves that were perfect, with golden crusts, airy crumbs, and flawless shapes.

of pan), 1½ to 2 hours. Thirty minutes before baking, adjust oven rack to middle position, place baking stone on rack, and heat oven to 350 degrees.

5. Remove plastic and brush loaves gently with remaining 1 egg beaten with salt. Set loaf pans on stone and bake until golden brown and internal temperature registers 190 degrees, 35 to 45 minutes, rotating pans halfway through baking. Transfer pans to wire rack and let cool for 5 minutes. Remove loaves from pans, return to wire rack, and let cool completely before slicing and serving, about 2 hours.

NO-KNEAD BRIOCHE BUNS
MAKES 10 BUNS

1. Line 2 rimmed baking sheets with parchment paper. Transfer dough to well-floured counter and divide into 10 equal pieces. Working with 1 piece of dough at a time, pat dough into disk. Working around circumference of dough, fold edges of dough toward center until ball forms. Flip dough over and, without applying pressure, move your hands in small circular motions to form dough into smooth, taut round. (Tackiness of dough against counter and circular motion should work dough into smooth, even ball, but if dough sticks to your hands, lightly dust top of dough with flour.) Repeat with remaining dough.

2. Arrange buns on prepared sheets, 5 per sheet. Cover loosely with plastic and let rise at room temperature until almost doubled in size, 1 to 1½ hours. Thirty minutes before baking, adjust oven racks to upper-middle and lower-middle positions and heat oven to 350 degrees.

3. Remove plastic and brush rolls gently with remaining 1 egg beaten with salt. Bake until golden brown and internal temperature registers 190 degrees, 15 to 20 minutes, rotating and switching sheets halfway through baking. Transfer sheets to wire rack and let cool for 5 minutes. Transfer buns to wire rack. Serve warm or at room temperature.

NO-KNEAD BRIOCHE À TÊTE
MAKES 2 LOAVES

Traditional loaves of brioche à tête achieve their fluted sides and conical shape from a brioche mold.

1. Transfer dough to well-floured counter and divide into 2 pieces. Remove golf ball–size piece of dough from each. Pat 2 large pieces of dough into 4-inch disks and 2 small pieces of dough into ½-inch disks. Working with 1 piece of dough at a time, work around circumference of dough; fold edges of dough toward center until ball forms. Flip dough over and, without applying pressure, move your hands in small circular motions to form dough into smooth, taut round. (Tackiness of dough against counter and circular motion should work dough into smooth, even ball, but if dough sticks to your hands, lightly dust top of dough with flour.) Repeat with remaining dough. Cover dough rounds loosely with plastic and let rest for 5 minutes.

2. Grease two 8- to 8½-inch fluted brioche pans. After 5 minutes, flip each dough ball so seam side is facing up, pat into 4-inch and ½-inch disks, and repeat rounding step. Place larger rounds, seam side down, into prepared pans and press gently into corners. Place smaller rounds, seam side down, in center of larger rounds, pushing down gently so only top halves of smaller rounds are showing. Cover loaves loosely with plastic and let rise at room temperature until almost doubled in size (dough should rise to about ½ inch below top edge of pan), 1½ to 2 hours. Thirty minutes before baking, adjust oven rack to middle position, place baking stone on rack, and heat oven to 350 degrees.

3. Remove plastic and brush loaves gently with remaining 1 egg beaten with salt. Set pans on stone and bake until golden brown and internal temperature registers 190 degrees, 35 to 45 minutes, rotating pans halfway through baking. Transfer pans to wire rack and let cool for 5 minutes. Remove loaves from pans, return to wire rack, and let cool completely before slicing and serving, about 2 hours.

Ciabatta

✔ **WHY THIS RECIPE WORKS**

Unless your source is an artisanal bakery, most of loaves of ciabatta just aren't any good. We wanted homemade ciabatta with airy texture, full and tangy flavor, and perfect lift.

START WITH A BIGA Ciabatta, like many rustic breads, starts with a sponge, known in Italian as a *biga*. Like stock in soup, the biga provides a strong flavor foundation. The biga is made with a little flour and water along with a scant amount of yeast. As it ferments, the yeast in the biga produces a byproduct of lactic and acetic acids, which give the bread its characteristic sourness. We settled on 30 percent sponge and 70 percent dough as the ideal proportion for nonalcoholic tang.

USE LOTS OF WATER Like many rustic bread doughs, ciabatta dough is extremely wet. So much water makes the dough unwieldy, but it's essential for the final texture. Not only does water reinforce gluten development, it also creates the bread's signature holes. As the water turns to steam during baking, the moisture rushes out, filling the existing bubbles created by the carbon dioxide and then enlarging them.

CHOOSE ALL-PURPOSE FLOUR All-purpose, which is made from both hard and soft wheat and has less protein than bread flour, produces loaves with a more open, springy texture.

KNEAD, THEN FOLD The dough is simply too wet to knead by hand, so use a stand mixer. But kneading alone in this recipe doesn't deliver a well-risen loaf. After kneading, it's necessary to fold (or turn) the dough using a rubber spatula or bowl scraper to fold the dough, as if you were folding egg whites into a batter. Ten minutes of kneading augmented by a few folds is the perfect pick-me-up.

INCLUDE A SECRET INGREDIENT Some recipes for ciabatta include milk. We initially thought the milk was added solely for flavor, but when we tried it, the results surprised us. Cutting into this ciabatta revealed a uniform crumb pockmarked with medium-size bubbles. Curious about why this addition worked, we learned that milk contains a protein fragment called glutathione, which acts to slightly weaken the gluten strands. A small amount of milk was enough to moderately reduce the size of the bubbles.

SHAPE, SPRITZ, AND BAKE Shaping the dough is easy. Shape the dough into a rough rectangle, then fold the shorter ends over each other to form a stubby rectangle. To avoid extra handling of the dough, form the loaves on parchment paper so you can slide them straight onto a baking stone. Spray the loaves with water in the first minutes of baking. This produces a crispier crust and loaves that rose a bit higher (steam delays crust formation and promotes a higher spring in the oven).

CIABATTA

MAKES 2 LOAVES

As you make this bread, keep in mind that the dough is wet and very sticky. The key to manipulating it is working quickly and gently; rough handling will result in flat, tough loaves. When possible, use a large rubber spatula or bowl scraper to move the dough. If you have to use your hands, make sure they are well floured. Because the dough is so sticky, it must be prepared in a stand mixer. If you don't have a baking stone, bake the bread on an overturned and preheated rimmed baking sheet set on the lowest oven rack.

STORING BREAD

Without preservatives to keep it tasting fresh, artisanal loaves can quickly stale. We've found that storing the bread cut side down on a cutting board works better than wrapping the loaf in paper or plastic. The crust will stay dry, while contact with the board will keep moisture inside the crumb. After two days, slice and wrap bread tightly wrapped in aluminum foil, place in a freezer bag, and freeze. Thaw the slices at room temperature, or in the microwave or oven. (For a frozen full- or half-loaf, we recommend heating the bread, still wrapped in foil, in a 450-degree oven for 10 to 15 minutes, then crisping it by removing the foil and returning it to the oven for a minute or two.) If you find yourself with stale bread, wrap it in plastic wrap and reheat briefly in a microwave, but be prepared to use it almost immediately as retrogradation will set in again fairly quickly. Finally, only refrigerate bread that you're intending to reheat (e.g., toast or grill) later on.

SHAPING CIABATTA

After pressing dough into rough 12 by 6-inch shape, grasp 1 end of dough with 1 hand and other end with bench scraper. Fold shorter sides of dough toward center, overlapping them like business letter to form 7 by 4-inch loaf.

SPONGE

1	cup (5 ounces) all-purpose flour
⅛	teaspoon instant or rapid-rise yeast
½	cup water, room temperature

DOUGH

2	cups (10 ounces) all-purpose flour
1½	teaspoons salt
½	teaspoon instant or rapid-rise yeast
¾	cup water, room temperature
¼	cup milk, room temperature

1. FOR THE SPONGE: Combine flour, yeast, and water in medium bowl and stir with wooden spoon until uniform mass forms, about 1 minute. Cover bowl tightly with plastic wrap and let stand at room temperature for at least 8 hours or up to 24 hours.

2. FOR THE DOUGH: Place sponge and dough ingredients in bowl of stand mixer fitted with paddle attachment. Mix on low speed until roughly combined and shaggy dough forms, about 1 minute, scraping down bowl and paddle as needed. Increase speed to medium-low and continue mixing until dough becomes uniform mass that collects on paddle and pulls away from sides of bowl, 4 to 6 minutes. Change to dough hook and knead bread on medium speed until smooth and shiny (dough will be very sticky), about 10 minutes, scraping down bowl and dough hook as needed. Transfer dough to large bowl, cover tightly with plastic, and let rise at room temperature until doubled in size, about 1 hour. (Dough should barely spring back when poked with knuckle.)

3. Spray rubber spatula or bowl scraper with vegetable oil spray. Fold partially risen dough over itself by gently lifting and folding edge of dough toward middle. Turn bowl 90 degrees; fold again. Turn bowl and fold dough 6 more times (for total of 8 turns).

Cover with plastic and let rise for 30 minutes. Repeat folding, replace plastic, and let rise until doubled in size, about 30 minutes longer.

4. One hour before baking, adjust oven rack to lower-middle position, place baking stone on rack, and heat oven to 450 degrees. Cut two 12 by 6-inch pieces of parchment paper and dust liberally with flour. Transfer dough to floured counter, being careful not to deflate it completely. Liberally flour top of dough and divide in half with bench scraper. Turn 1 piece of dough cut side up and dust with flour. With well-floured hands, press dough into rough 12 by 6-inch rectangle. Fold shorter sides of dough toward center, overlapping them like business letter to form 7 by 4-inch loaf. Repeat with second piece of dough. Gently transfer each loaf, seam side down, to parchment sheets, dust with flour, and cover with plastic. Let loaves sit at room temperature for 30 minutes (surface of loaves will develop small bubbles).

5. Slide parchment with loaves onto pizza peel. Using floured fingertips, evenly poke entire surface of each loaf to form 10 by 6-inch rectangle; spray loaves lightly with water. Slide loaves and parchment onto baking stone. Bake, spraying loaves with water twice more during first 5 minutes of baking time, until crust is deep golden brown and loaves register 210 degrees, 22 to 27 minutes. Transfer loaves to wire rack, discard parchment, and let cool to room temperature, about 1 hour, before slicing and serving. (Bread can be wrapped in double layer of plastic and stored at room temperature for up to 3 days. Wrapped with additional layer of aluminum foil, bread can be frozen for up to 1 month. To recrisp crust, thaw bread at room temperature, if frozen, and place unwrapped bread in 450-degree oven for 6 to 8 minutes.)

Indian Flatbread (Naan)

✓ **WHY THIS RECIPE WORKS**

Even in India, naan is considered "restaurant" bread. This may be because it calls for a traditional tandoor oven, which few home cooks own. We set out to reproduce the charred exterior and tender interior of naan baked in a tandoor—but without the 1,000-degree heat.

WORK IN EXTRA FAT Don't cut corners with fat in this bread. Working in some extra fat, by way of whole-milk yogurt, vegetable oil, and an egg yolk, kept the dough from drying out even after being cooked.

CHILL THE DOUGH Refrigerating the dough for several hours kept it from snapping back during stretching. This cold fermentation encourages the relaxation of gluten strands so that the dough is more flexible. And there was an added bonus: Preparing the dough the day before freed up time the following day for cooking the rest of the meal.

COOK IN CAST-IRON We wanted naan with good color and char but grilling and baking our naan were failures. Instead we use a preheated cast-iron skillet and cooked the bread on the stovetop.

POKE, MIST, AND COVER Before cooking, we poke the dough with a fork to keep it from puffing and we mist it with water to help the bread retain moistness. Lastly, we cover the pan to trap steam around the bread as it bakes, which keeps it tender.

INDIAN FLATBREAD (NAAN)
MAKES 4 PIECES

This recipe worked best with a high-protein all-purpose flour such as King Arthur brand. Do not use nonfat yogurt in this recipe. A 12-inch nonstick skillet may be used in place of the cast-iron skillet. For efficiency, stretch the next ball of dough while each naan is cooking.

½ cup ice water
⅓ cup plain whole-milk yogurt
3 tablespoons plus 1 teaspoon vegetable oil
1 large egg yolk
2 cups (10 ounces) all-purpose flour
1¼ teaspoons sugar
½ teaspoon instant or rapid-rise yeast
1¼ teaspoons salt
1½ tablespoons unsalted butter, melted

1. In measuring cup or small bowl, combine water, yogurt, 3 tablespoons oil, and egg yolk. Process flour, sugar, and yeast in food processor until combined, about 2 seconds. With processor running, slowly add water mixture; process until dough is just combined and no dry flour remains, about 10 seconds. Let dough stand for 10 minutes.

2. Add salt to dough and process until dough forms satiny, sticky ball that clears sides of workbowl, 30 to 60 seconds. Transfer dough to lightly floured work surface and knead until smooth, about 1 minute. Shape dough into tight ball and place in large, lightly oiled bowl. Cover tightly with plastic wrap and refrigerate for 16 to 24 hours.

3. Adjust oven rack to middle position and heat oven to 200 degrees. Place heatproof plate on rack. Transfer dough to lightly floured work surface and divide into 4 equal pieces. Shape each piece into smooth, tight ball. Place dough balls on lightly oiled baking sheet, at least 2 inches apart; cover loosely with plastic coated with vegetable oil spray. Let stand for 15 to 20 minutes.

4. Transfer 1 ball to lightly floured work surface and sprinkle with flour. Using your hands and a rolling pin, press and roll piece of dough into 9-inch round of even thickness, sprinkling dough and work surface with flour as needed to prevent sticking. Using fork, poke entire surface of round 20 to 25 times. Heat remaining 1 teaspoon oil in 12-inch cast-iron skillet over medium heat until shimmering. Wipe oil out of skillet completely with paper towels. Mist top of dough lightly with water. Place dough in pan, moistened side down; mist top surface of dough with water; and cover. Cook until bottom is browned in spots across surface, 2 to 4 minutes. Flip naan, cover, and continue to cook on second side until lightly browned, 2 to 3 minutes. (If naan puffs up, gently poke with fork to deflate.) Flip naan, brush top with about 1 teaspoon melted butter, transfer to plate in oven, and cover plate tightly with aluminum foil. Repeat rolling and cooking remaining 3 dough balls. Once last naan is baked, serve immediately.

QUICKER INDIAN FLATBREAD (NAAN)

This variation, which can be prepared in about two hours, forgoes the overnight rest, but the dough may be a little harder to roll out.

After shaping dough in step 2, let dough rise at room temperature for 30 minutes. After 30 minutes, fold partially risen dough over itself 8 times by gently lifting and folding edge of dough toward middle, turning bowl 90 degrees after each fold. Cover with plastic wrap and let rise for 30 minutes. Repeat folding, turning, and rising one more time, for total of three 30-minute rises. After last rise, proceed with recipe from step 3.

A SAFER WAY TO CUT BAGELS

1. Lay bagel flat on counter and cut through center to make two pieces.

2. Place each piece, cut side down, on counter to safely slice in half.

Bagels

✔ WHY THIS RECIPE WORKS

If you live in New York or another large city (although some bagel fans would argue that good bagels don't exist outside of New York), you can get great bagels. But what about everyone who lives in the rest of the country? We decided there was a need for a simple way to bake delicious, attractive, authentic bagels at home.

CHOOSE HIGH-GLUTEN FLOUR Among commonly used flours, bread flour is the highest in gluten, about 13 percent protein. But even bread flour doesn't have enough gluten to make chewy, plump bagels. Instead, we turn specifically to high gluten flour which is about 14 percent protein and is the flour of choice at most professional bagel bakeries. Another specialty ingredient we include is barley malt syrup, which gives the bagels an authentic malty flavor.

MIX UNTIL SMOOTH AND ELASTIC After the dough has come together in the first 5 minutes of mixing, it should not stick to your fingers when pressed. And when you have completely kneaded the dough, a piece about the size of a golf ball should hold its shape and should not sag.

INCLUDE A COLD RISE Traditionally, bagels are placed in a specially designed refrigerator, called a retarder, for several hours or overnight after being formed. This practice allows for a slower, more natural fermentation. It is during this retarding process that bagels develop most of their flavor. We wanted to test the impact of retarding, so after mixing and forming a batch of bagels, we placed them in a refrigerator overnight. The results were both dramatic and surprising. The long, slow fermentation process the

SHAPING BAGELS

1. Form each dough ball into rope 11 inches long by rolling it under your outstretched palms. Do not taper ends of rope. Overlap ends of rope about 1½ inches and pinch entire overlapped area firmly together. If ends of rope do not stick together, dampen them slightly with water.

2. Place loop of dough around base of your fingers and, with overlap under your palm, roll rope several times, applying firm pressure to seal seam. The bagel should be roughly same thickness all around.

bagels had undergone yielded the complex flavor and aroma we were seeking. We were even more surprised by the other effects of retarding: The crust of these bagels had taken on a dark, reddish sheen, and the surface was covered in crispy bubbles.

USE LESS YEAST In subsequent tests, because our initial bagels had overrisen during the long cold rise, we lowered the yeast level in our recipe by half. We also lowered the temperature of the water we used in the dough, to control the activity of the yeast. Initially, we had been proofing the yeast in 110-degree water as recommended on the envelope. We ultimately decided against dissolving the yeast before adding it to the flour in favor of using 80-degree water.

BOIL BRIEFLY AND BAKE Boiling a bagel before baking it serves three purposes. Most important, it sets the shape of the bagel by cooking the surface and killing off some of the yeast in the outer layer of dough. This helps to limit the expansion of the bagel when it is baked. A bagel that is not boiled, we discovered, will expand into a round ball in the heat of the oven. The second function of the boiling process is to give the bagel its characteristic shine. When you boil the bagel, starches on the surface become gelatinized. These starches then cook to a crispy, shiny coating in the oven. The third purpose of boiling is to activate the yeast in the inner layers of dough, which has been made sluggish by the retarding process. All of the home recipes we reviewed recommend boiling the bagels for a period of 1 to 4 minutes. We find that a shorter boil of only 30 seconds yields the best results. All that is left to do is drain and bake the bagels on a parchment-lined baking sheet.

PLAIN BAGELS
MAKES 8

Because bagel dough is much drier and stiffer than bread dough, it takes longer for the ingredients to cohere during mixing. For this reason, we recommend that you neither double this recipe nor try to knead the dough by hand. Most natural foods stores carry barley malt syrup. High-gluten flour might be more difficult to find. You can order both the syrup and the flour from The Baker's Catalogue at King Arthur Flour: KingArthurFlour.com.

- 4 cups (22 ounces) high-gluten flour
- 2 teaspoons salt
- 1 tablespoon barley malt syrup
- 1½ teaspoons instant or rapid-rise yeast
- 1¼ cups warm water (80 degrees)
- 3 tablespoons cornmeal

1. Using stand mixer fitted with dough hook, combine flour, salt, and barley malt. Add yeast and water; mix at lowest speed until dough looks scrappy, like shreds just beginning to come together, about 4 minutes. Increase speed to medium-low; continue mixing until dough is cohesive, smooth, and stiff, 8 to 10 minutes.

2. Turn dough onto counter; divide into 8 portions, about 4 ounces each. Roll pieces into smooth balls and cover with plastic wrap to rest for 5 minutes.

3. Form each dough ball into rope 11 inches long by rolling it under your outstretched palms. Do not taper ends of rope. Shape rope into circle, overlapping ends of rope about 1½ inches. Pinch overlapped area firmly together, dampening it slightly with water if ends won't stick. Place ring of dough around your hand at base of your fingers and, with overlap under your palm, roll dough ring several times, applying firm pressure to seal seam. Dough ring should be roughly same thickness all around. Dust rimmed baking sheet with cornmeal, place dough rings on sheet, cover tightly with plastic, and refrigerate overnight (12 to 18 hours).

4. About 1 hour before baking, remove dough rings from refrigerator. Adjust oven rack to middle position and heat oven to 450 degrees. Pour water into large pot to depth of 3 inches and bring water to boil.

5. Working four at a time, drop dough rings into boiling water, stirring and submerging them with metal skimmer or slotted spoon, until very slightly puffed, 30 to 35 seconds. Remove dough rings from water and transfer them to wire rack, bottom side down, to drain.

6. Transfer oiled rings, rough side down, to parchment-lined baking sheet. Bake until deep golden brown and crisp, about 14 minutes, rotating sheet halfway through baking. Use tongs to transfer to wire rack to cool. Serve warm or at room temperature. (Bagels can be wrapped in double layer of plastic and stored at room temperature for up to 3 days. Wrapped with additional layer of aluminum foil, bagels can be frozen for up to 1 month. To recrisp, thaw bagels at room temperature, if frozen, and place unwrapped bagels in 450-degree oven for 6 to 8 minutes.)

TOPPED BAGELS

Dunk dough rings into one of following: ½ cup raw sesame seeds, poppy or caraway seeds, dehydrated onion or garlic flakes, or sea or kosher salt while they are still wet and sticky (at end of step 5, after draining).

EVERYTHING BAGELS

Dunk dough rings into mixture of 2 tablespoons each sesame and poppy seeds and 1 tablespoon each caraway seeds, sea or kosher salt, dehydrated onion flakes, and dehydrated garlic flakes.

CINNAMON-RAISIN BAGELS

Mix 1 teaspoon vanilla extract, 1 tablespoon ground cinnamon, and ½ cup raisins into flour, salt, and barley malt in step 1.

SMOKED SALMON SPREAD
MAKES ABOUT 1 CUP

Here we mix the classic bagel toppings into a spread.

1	(8-ounce) package cream cheese
4	ounces sliced smoked salmon, chopped fine
2	tablespoons minced red onion
2	tablespoons capers, rinsed
1	tablespoon minced fresh dill
2	tablespoons milk

Microwave cream cheese on high power until very soft, 20 to 30 seconds. Stir smoked salmon, onion, capers, dill, and milk into softened cheese. Allow spread to chill for 1 hour before serving. The prepared spread will keep, covered and refrigerated, for up to 1 week.

SWEET NUT SPREAD
MAKES ABOUT 1 CUP

In addition to bagels, this spread is great on quick breads such as Zucchini Bread (page 26) or Boston Brown Bread (page 35). For information on toasting nuts, see page 9.

1	(8-ounce) package cream cheese
¼	cup walnuts or pecans, toasted and chopped fine
2	tablespoons honey or dark brown sugar
2	tablespoons milk

Microwave cream cheese on high power until very soft, 20 to 30 seconds. Stir walnuts, honey, and milk into softened cheese. Allow spread to chill for 1 hour before serving. The prepared spread will keep, covered and refrigerated, for up to 1 week.

CREAM CHEESE

Supermarket shelves aren't exactly overflowing with cream cheese options. Whenever we needed cream cheese in the test kitchen, we instinctively reached for Philadelphia brand. But was Philadelphia the best, or just the most familiar and widely available?

To find out, we gathered all the types of cream cheese we could find: a paltry five. We tasted them plain and in our New York–Style Cheesecake (page 336). Tasters judged the cream cheeses on richness, tanginess, creaminess, and overall quality, and one product swept both the plain and cheesecake tastings in all categories—you guessed it, **Philadelphia Brand Cream Cheese.**

PIZZA BIANCA

CHAPTER 5

Pizza and Focaccia

Pizza Bianca

✔ WHY THIS RECIPE WORKS

With no cheese or sauce—just a gloss of olive oil and flakes of salt—Pizza Bianca looks more like focaccia than pizza. But its crisp exterior and chewy, bubbly middle make us forget all about nomenclature. In some ways, this is the simplest bread imaginable because it does not involve shaping the dough into a loaf, just stretching it into a pan.

ADD WATER To achieve its chewy, bubbly texture, our recipe calls for 9 parts water to 10 parts flour—an almost 30 percent higher level of hydration than in most other pizza dough. Water aids the development of gluten, the network of cross-linked proteins that gives bread its internal structure and chew. Up to a point, the more water in the dough, the stronger and more elastic the gluten strands and the chewier the bread. These strands, in turn, help to support the gas bubbles formed as the dough bakes, preventing them from bursting and creating an open, airy crust.

MIX, REST, AND KNEAD We let the dough rest for 20 minutes before kneading. This rest time, called autolyse, allows gluten to develop and therefore cuts down drastically on the kneading time. Instead of a half-hour of kneading in the mixer, now we need less than 10 minutes.

PRESS THE DOUGH Because this recipe is traditionally baked in a pan, it is easy to avoid handling the wet dough; simply pour it onto a well-oiled baking sheet. Shaping is easy: Press the dough from its middle toward the edges of the pan. It's important, however, to stop pressing the dough if it is resisting. Give it a little rest: Resting allows the large gluten molecules to relax and stretch more easily.

USE A BAKING STONE Most pizza kitchens are equipped with stone- or tile-lined ovens that supply the steady, dry, intense heat necessary to make pizzas with crisp, cracker-like crusts. Baking stones (also called pizza stones) were created to simulate these conditions in the home oven.

PIZZA BIANCA
SERVES 6 TO 8

This dough must be prepared in a stand mixer. Place a damp dish towel under the mixer and watch it at all times during kneading to prevent it from wobbling off the counter. Handle the dough with lightly oiled hands to prevent sticking. Resist flouring your fingers or the dough might stick further.

3	cups (15 ounces) all-purpose flour
1⅔	cups water, room temperature
1¼	teaspoons salt
1½	teaspoons instant or rapid-rise yeast
1¼	teaspoons sugar
5	tablespoons extra-virgin olive oil
1	teaspoon kosher salt
2	tablespoons fresh rosemary leaves

1. Using stand mixer fitted with dough hook, mix flour, water, and salt together on low speed until no areas of dry flour remain, 3 to 4 minutes, scraping down bowl as needed. Turn off mixer and let dough rest for 20 minutes.

2. Sprinkle yeast and sugar over dough. Knead on low speed until fully combined, 1 to 2 minutes. Increase mixer speed to high and knead until dough is glossy and smooth and pulls away from sides of bowl, 6 to 10 minutes. (Dough will pull away from sides only while mixer is on. When mixer is off, dough will fall back to sides.)

3. Using your fingers, coat large bowl with 1 tablespoon oil, rubbing excess oil from fingers onto blade of rubber spatula. Using oiled spatula, transfer dough to prepared bowl and pour 1 tablespoon oil over top. Flip dough over once so that it is well coated with oil; cover bowl tightly with plastic wrap and let dough rise at room temperature until nearly tripled in volume and large bubbles have formed, 2 to 2½ hours. (Dough can be refrigerated for up to 24 hours. Bring dough to room temperature, 2 to 2½ hours, before proceeding with step 4.)

4. One hour before baking, adjust oven rack to middle position, place baking stone on rack, and heat oven to 450 degrees. Coat rimmed baking sheet with 2 tablespoons oil. Using rubber spatula, turn dough out onto prepared baking sheet along with any oil in bowl. Using your fingertips, press dough out toward edges of baking sheet, taking care not to tear it. (Dough will not fit snugly into corners. If dough resists stretching, let it relax for 5 to 10 minutes before trying to stretch it again.) Let dough rest until slightly bubbly, 5 to 10 minutes. Using dinner fork, poke surface of dough 30 to 40 times and sprinkle with kosher salt.

5. Bake until golden brown, 20 to 30 minutes, sprinkling rosemary over top and rotating baking sheet halfway through baking. Using metal spatula, transfer pizza to cutting board. Brush dough lightly with remaining 1 tablespoon oil. Slice and serve immediately.

PIZZA BIANCA WITH CARAMELIZED ONIONS AND GRUYÈRE

Heat 1 tablespoon butter and 1 tablespoon vegetable oil in 12-inch nonstick skillet over high heat until butter is melted. Stir in 1 teaspoon light brown sugar and ½ teaspoon salt, then add 2 pounds onions, halved and sliced ¼ inch thick, and stir to coat; cook, stirring occasionally, until onions begin to soften and release some moisture, about 5 minutes. Reduce heat to medium and cook, stirring often, until onions are deeply browned and slightly sticky, about 40 minutes longer. (If onions are sizzling or scorching, reduce heat. If onions are not browning after 15 to 20 minutes, raise heat.) Off heat, stir in 1 tablespoon water; season with pepper to taste. Transfer to large plate and let cool to room temperature. In step 5, bake pizza until spotty brown, 15 to 17 minutes. Remove pizza from oven, spread onions evenly over surface, and sprinkle with 2 cups shredded Gruyère and 2 teaspoons minced fresh thyme

(do not brush pizza with remaining 1 tablespoon oil). Return pizza to oven and continue to bake until cheese begins to brown in spots, 5 to 10 minutes longer.

PIZZA BIANCA WITH TOMATOES AND MOZZARELLA

Place one 28-ounce can crushed tomatoes in fine-mesh strainer set over medium bowl. Let sit for 30 minutes, stirring 3 times to allow juices to drain. Combine ¾ cup tomato solids, 1 tablespoon olive oil, and ⅛ teaspoon salt. (Save remaining solids and juice for another use). Omit kosher salt and rosemary. In step 5, bake pizza until spotty brown, 15 to 17 minutes. Remove pizza from oven, spread tomato mixture evenly over surface, and sprinkle with 1½ cups shredded mozzarella (do not brush pizza with remaining 1 tablespoon oil). Return pizza to oven and continue to bake until cheese begins to brown in spots, 5 to 10 minutes longer.

PIZZA BIANCA WITH TOMATOES, SAUSAGE, AND FONTINA

Cook 12 ounces sweet Italian sausage, casings removed, in 12-inch nonstick skillet over medium heat, breaking it into small pieces with wooden spoon, until no longer pink, about 5 minutes. Remove sausage with slotted spoon and transfer to paper towel–lined plate. Place one 28-ounce can crushed tomatoes in fine-mesh strainer set over medium bowl. Let sit for 30 minutes, stirring 3 times to allow juices to drain. Combine ¾ cup tomato solids, 1 tablespoon olive oil, and ⅛ teaspoon salt. (Save remaining solids and juice for another use). Omit kosher salt and rosemary. In step 5, bake pizza until spotty brown, 15 to 17 minutes. Remove pizza from oven, spread tomato mixture evenly over surface, and sprinkle with 2 cups shredded fontina cheese and sausage (do not brush pizza with remaining 1 tablespoon oil). Return pizza to oven and continue to bake until cheese begins to brown in spots, 5 to 10 minutes longer.

Rosemary Focaccia

✔ WHY THIS RECIPE WORKS

Focaccia can easily disappoint when it turns out heavy and thick. We wanted a light, airy loaf, crisp-crusted and topped with just a smattering of herbs. To start, a sponge (a mixture of flour, water, and yeast that rests for at least 8 hours) gives us the flavor benefits of a long fermentation with minimal effort.

BEGIN WITH THE BIGA A brush of fruity olive oil and heady seasonings give focaccia an addictive savory edge, but that doesn't mean a thing if the dough itself lacks flavor. The biggest key here is fermentation—the process by which long chains of carbohydrates with little taste convert to sugars, alcohol, acids, and carbon dioxide. And like many other organic processes, it's most effective over a long period of time. To get the benefits of long fermentation with minimal effort, we use a "pre-ferment" (also known as a sponge, or *biga* in Italian): a mixture of flour, water, and a small amount of yeast that rests overnight before being incorporated into a dough either in place of or along with more yeast. With a biga, our focaccia dough holds plenty of flavor—with or without toppings added.

USE A LOT OF WATER As we've learned, a dough with a higher level of hydration is more capable of expanding without tearing, promoting the formation of larger bubbles. A high proportion of water to flour and a long resting process let the natural enzymes in the wheat replicate the effect of kneading. We use a higher level of hydration here in our focaccia—84 percent—to help open up the crumb structure.

REST AND FOLD As for our Almost No-Knead Bread (page 139), we don't knead our focaccia, per se. But we do fold it. To prevent squat loaves of bread, we fold the dough while it rises. A standard no-knead dough develops structure gradually because the individual gluten clusters are relatively slow to combine into larger units. But gently turning the dough over itself at regular intervals accomplishes three things: It brings the wheat proteins into closer proximity with one another, keeping the process going at maximum clip; it aerates the dough, replenishing the oxygen that the yeasts consume during fermentation; and it elongates and redistributes the bubbles. After turning our dough three times in the process, we end up with a well-risen focaccia with a tender, moist crumb.

KEEP THE OIL IN THE PAN Olive oil is a key ingredient in focaccia, but we find that if added straight to the dough, it can turn the bread dense and cakelike. (Just as with shortbread, fat "shortens" the dough by blocking gluten's ability to form continuous networks.) Instead, we bake the bread in round cake pans, where a few tablespoons of oil coating the exterior can be contained. After swirling the dough in the oil and some coarse salt, we flip it over, gently stretch it into the pan's edges, and let it rest for just a few extra minutes before sliding the pan onto the hot pizza stone. This focaccia has a crackly, crisp bottom, a deeply browned top, and an interior that is open and airy.

POKE AND SPRINKLE With a dinner fork, we poke the dough surface 25 to 30 times. This will pop large bubbles of air and allow any extra gas to escape. Then we sprinkle the dough with a healthy dose of minced fresh rosemary.

ROSEMARY FOCACCIA

MAKES TWO 9-INCH ROUND LOAVES

Fresh, not dried, rosemary is a must with this bread.

SPONGE

½ cup (2½ ounces) all-purpose flour
⅓ cup warm water (110 degrees)
¼ teaspoon instant or rapid-rise yeast

DOUGH

2½ cups (12½ ounces) all-purpose flour
1¼ cups warm water (110 degrees)
1 teaspoon instant or rapid-rise yeast
Kosher salt
¼ cup extra-virgin olive oil
2 tablespoons minced fresh rosemary

1. FOR THE SPONGE: Combine flour, water, and yeast in large bowl and stir with wooden spoon until uniform mass forms and no dry flour remains, about 1 minute. Cover bowl tightly with plastic wrap and let stand at room temperature for at least 8 hours or up to 24 hours. Use immediately or store in refrigerator for up to 3 days (allow to stand at room temperature for 30 minutes before proceeding with recipe).

2. FOR THE DOUGH: Stir flour, water, and yeast into sponge with wooden spoon until uniform mass forms and no dry flour remains, about 1 minute. Cover with plastic and let rise at room temperature for 15 minutes.

3. Sprinkle 2 teaspoons salt over dough; stir into dough until thoroughly incorporated, about 1 minute. Cover with plastic and let rise at room temperature for 30 minutes. Spray rubber spatula or bowl scraper with vegetable oil spray. Fold partially risen dough over itself by gently lifting and folding edge of dough toward middle. Turn bowl 90 degrees; fold again. Turn bowl and fold dough 6 more times (for total of 8 folds). Cover with plastic and let rise for 30 minutes. Repeat folding, turning, and rising 2 more times, for total of three 30-minute rises.

4. One hour before baking, adjust oven rack to upper-middle position, place baking stone on rack, and heat oven to 500 degrees. Gently transfer dough to lightly floured counter. Lightly dust top of dough with flour and divide it in half. Shape each piece of dough into 5-inch round by gently tucking under edges. Coat two 9-inch round cake pans with 2 tablespoons oil each. Sprinkle each pan with ½ teaspoon salt. Place round of dough in 1 pan, top side down; slide dough around pan to coat bottom and sides with oil, then flip dough over. Repeat with second piece of dough. Cover pans with plastic and let rest for 5 minutes.

5. Using your fingertips, press dough out toward edges of pan, taking care not to tear it. (If dough resists stretching, let it relax for 5 to 10 minutes before trying to stretch it again.) Using dinner fork, poke entire surface of dough 25 to 30 times, popping any large bubbles. Sprinkle rosemary evenly over top of dough. Let dough rest in pans until slightly bubbly, 5 to 10 minutes.

6. Place pans on baking stone and lower oven temperature to 450 degrees. Bake until tops are golden brown, 25 to 28 minutes, rotating pans halfway through baking. Transfer pans to wire rack and let cool for 5 minutes. Remove loaves from pans and return to rack. Brush tops with any oil remaining in pans. Let cool for 30 minutes before serving. (Leftover bread can be wrapped in double layer of plastic and stored at room temperature for 2 days. Wrapped with additional layer of aluminum foil, bread can be frozen for up to 1 month.)

All About Baking Stones

ABOUT BAKING STONES

An oven's heat does not run at one steady temperature, no matter what your oven dial reads. Both electric and gas home ovens are furnished with thermostats that switch on and off to maintain the oven's internal temperature. This change, coupled with the opening and closing of the oven door, causes the temperature to fluctuate, which can be damaging to baked goods that require extremely high heat, like pizza or crusty artisanal bread. A baking stone reduces the fluctuation by absorbing and storing heat, thereby maintaining a constant temperature. Stones also wick the moisture away from pizza dough to guarantee a crisp crust. For the best results, they should be preheated for one hour to ensure that they are at the ideal temperature.

When purchasing a baking stone, be sure to look for the thickest and biggest possible stone (ensuring that it fits into your oven), which is indicative of a stone's ability to retain heat. Thick stones are also less likely to crack than thinner, lighter stones.

Test Kitchen Favorite: **Old Stone**

Oven Pizza Baking Stone is rectangular, roomy, and boasts ridged "feet" that lift the edge, allowing for a comfortable grip. Pizza and calzones emerged evenly golden brown and crisp when baked on this clay stone.

THE IMPORTANCE OF PREHEATING

Generally, the hotter the baking stone, the better the browning and expansion of the dough. Since a baking stone can match an oven's highest temperature and store that heat, a stone preheated for an hour should make a better crust than one preheated for less time, or not at all.

To demonstrate the point, we cooked thin-crust pizzas on stones that had been preheated for 60 and 30 minutes and compared them to pizza prepared on an unheated stone. The 60-minute stone produced the best pizza by far, with a tender, airy, well-browned crust. The 30-minute stone produced decent but not stellar results. As we expected, the pizza baked on the unheated stone emerged with a blond, dense crust, even after spending twice as long in the oven.

In short, to achieve the best possible thin-crust pizza, preheat your stone for a full hour.

CLEANING

A stone can accumulate unsightly black stains where cheese, sauce, and flour burn onto the stone's surface. While it's tempting to scrub the blemishes away with a sponge and hot soapy water, the porous stone can absorb the smell—and taste—of detergent.

Here's a better way: Remove the oven racks, place the stone directly on the oven's floor, and run the oven's self-cleaning cycle. The super-hot temperatures (often in excess of 800 degrees) will burn off any surface stains, returning your stone to near-new condition.

STORAGE

Although baking stones can be stored in the oven, it's important to note that the stone lengthens the oven's preheating time to about 1 hour. You may not use a stone enough to deal with the hassle of a long preheating time, but storing a stone elsewhere can have its challenges too. The rough edges and long, heavy profile can scrape cabinet linings, but there is a solution that starts with a simple trip to a hardware store.

1. Cut piece of rubber hose (standard irrigation hose will work) to length of baking stone's short edge.

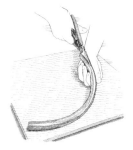

2. Slit tube open along 1 side.

3. Insert stone into slit, creating cover for rough edge.

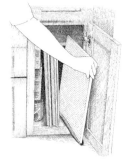

4. To store, slide stone into cabinet with covered edge on bottom. Remove hose before using stone.

Two Ways to Shape Pizza Dough

Pizza dough is very easy to prepare, but shaping that dough into a perfect circle can intimidate even the most experienced cook. Many cooks resort to the rolling pin and roll the dough like a pie crust, but that forces out the air bubbles trapped in the dough and makes for a flat, tough-crusted pizza. Others yank the dough to and fro, yielding pizza that can be thick on one end and paper-thin and ripped open on the other. The experts fling the dough skyward and use centrifugal force for their perfect rounds, but this technique takes lots of practice and steely nerves. Here are two simple methods to easily shape your dough. Try both and see which one you prefer.

PRESS AND STRETCH

1. For 12- to 14-inch pizza, flatten dough ball into 8-inch round using palms of your hands.

2. Starting at center of disk and working outward, use your fingertips to press dough until it is about ½ inch thick.

3. Holding center in place, stretch dough outward. Rotate the dough one-quarter turn and stretch again. Repeat until dough reaches desired diameter.

4. Use your palm to press down and flatten thick edge of dough.

PRESS, DRAPE, AND STRETCH

1. For 12- to 14-inch pizza, press dough into 8-inch round on well-floured counter.

2. Drape half of dough over counter. Lift top half of dough off counter, with your hands at approximately 10 and 2 o'clock.

3. Rotate dough clockwise, using your left hand to feed dough to your right hand, meeting at 12 o'clock. Continue until gravity has pulled it to desired diameter.

4. Return fully stretched dough to counter or transfer it to pizza peel for topping.

Four Steps to Pizza Success

1. Carefully lift dough round and transfer it to peel dusted with semolina flour or cornmeal. Alternatively, you can place dough round on parchment paper and slide onto peel.

2. If dough loses its round shape, adjust it on peel to return it to original shape.

3. Add toppings. Leave a ½-inch border of dough uncovered.

4. Use quick jerking action to slide pizza off peel and onto stone. Make sure that pizza lands far enough back so that front edge does not hang off stone.

Classic Homemade Pizza

ALTERNATIVE TO A BAKING STONE OR PEEL

A baking stone (see page 158) is a terrific investment if you enjoy making bread and pizza and a peel makes the process easier. But, you can also make do with a rimless or inverted baking sheet for both the stone and peel. To improvise a baking stone, preheat a baking sheet for 30 minutes (ample time for the baking sheet's lesser mass). As for an improvised peel, simply cover a rimless or inverted baking sheet with parchment paper, shape and top the pizza on the parchment, and slide it directly onto the hot, preheated stone.

✓ WHY THIS RECIPE WORKS

While we all settle for convenience over quality on occasion, the difference between a takeout or frozen pizza and homemade is extreme. Homemade pizza really is superb, but the tomato sauce and dough are time-consuming. We set out to shortcut those steps for homemade pizza that could practically be made in the time it takes to heat the oven.

USE A BAKING STONE   Using a stone is the only way to get a seriously crisp crust. If you don't have one, use an overturned preheated baking sheet.

MAKE THE DOUGH IN A FOOD PROCESSOR   Mixing and kneading the dough (made with protein-rich bread flour for great chew) takes just a couple of minutes.

KEEP THE SAUCE SIMPLE   We find that a quick tomato sauce, enlivened with olive oil and garlic tastes just as good as a long-cooked tomato sauce.

USE TOPPINGS JUDICIOUSLY   Loading down your pizza with toppings will weigh down the dough and result in a soggy crust. Instead, scatter a modest amount of toppings over your dough. And hold off on the cheese. Adding it from the outset will result in burnt cheese. We wait until the pizza has baked halfway through before adding the cheese.

TOP THE PIZZA ON PARCHMENT FOR EASY TRANSFER   After you shape the pizza, transfer it to parchment paper add the toppings, then slide it right onto a peel, and finally onto the preheated baking stone. You can also use a semolina flour- or cornmeal-dusted peel in place of parchment paper

CLASSIC PIZZA DOUGH

MAKES 2 POUNDS DOUGH, ENOUGH FOR TWO 14-INCH PIZZAS

All-purpose flour can be substituted for the bread flour, but the resulting crust will be a little less chewy.

4–4¼	cups (22 to 23⅓ ounces) bread flour
2¼	teaspoons instant or rapid-rise yeast
1½	teaspoons salt
2	tablespoons olive oil
1½	cups warm water (110 degrees)

1. Pulse 4 cups flour, yeast, and salt together in food processor (fitted with dough blade if possible) until combined, about 5 pulses. With processor running, slowly add oil, then water; process until rough ball forms, 30 to 40 seconds. Let dough rest for 2 minutes, then process for 30 seconds longer. (If after 30 seconds dough is sticky and clings to blade, add remaining ¼ cup flour 1 tablespoon at a time as needed.)

2. Transfer dough to lightly floured counter and knead by hand into smooth, round ball. Place dough in a large, lightly greased bowl; cover bowl tightly with greased plastic wrap and let rise at room temperature until doubled in size, 1 to 1½ hours, before using.

QUICK TOMATO SAUCE FOR PIZZA

MAKES ABOUT 3 CUPS

If you don't have time to cook this sauce, drain the tomatoes slightly, then mix the ingredients together and let them stand while you stretch the dough.

2	large garlic cloves, minced
2	tablespoons olive oil
1	(28-ounce) can crushed tomatoes
	Salt and pepper

Heat garlic with oil in saucepan over medium heat. When garlic starts to sizzle, add tomatoes, bring to simmer, and cook until sauce is thick enough to mound on spoon, about 15 minutes. Season with salt and pepper to taste. (Sauce can be stored in refrigerator for up to 1 week or frozen for up to 1 month.)

SAUSAGE AND BELL PEPPER PIZZA WITH BASIL AND MOZZARELLA

MAKES TWO 14-INCH PIZZAS, SERVING 4 TO 6

If bulk sausage is not available, just buy cased sausage, remove the casing, and break the meat into bite-size chunks. You can shape the second dough round while the first pizza bakes, but don't add the toppings until just before baking. For more information on shaping the pizza dough, see page 159.

1	tablespoon olive oil, plus extra as needed
4	ounces pork sausage, broken into bite-size pieces
1	red or yellow bell pepper, stemmed, seeded, and cut into thin strips
	Salt and pepper
1	recipe Classic Pizza Dough (page 160)
1½	cups Quick Tomato Sauce for Pizza (page 160)
¼	cup shredded fresh basil
4	ounces whole-milk mozzarella cheese, shredded (1 cup)

1. One hour before baking, adjust oven rack to lowest position, set baking stone on rack, and heat oven to 500 degrees.

2. Meanwhile, heat oil in 12-inch skillet over medium-high heat until shimmering. Add sausage and cook until browned, about 5 minutes. Remove sausage with slotted spoon and transfer to paper towel–lined plate. Pour off all but 1 tablespoon fat from skillet, add bell pepper, and cook over medium heat until softened, about 5 minutes. Season with salt and pepper to taste; set aside.

3. Transfer dough to lightly floured counter, divide in half, and cover with greased plastic wrap. Use your fingertips to gently flatten 1 piece of dough into 8-inch disk (keep other piece covered). Using your hands, gently stretch disk into 14-inch round, working along outer edge and giving disk quarter turns. Transfer dough to piece of parchment paper and reshape as needed.

4. Using back of spoon or ladle, spread ¾ cup tomato sauce over dough, leaving ½-inch border around edge. Sprinkle 2 tablespoons basil, half of sausage, and half of pepper over sauce. Slide parchment with pizza onto pizza peel, then slide onto baking stone. Bake until crust begins to brown, 7 to 8 minutes.

5. Remove pizza from oven by sliding parchment back onto pizza peel, close oven door, and top pizza evenly with ½ cup mozzarella. Return pizza to baking stone and continue baking until cheese is just melted, about 3 minutes longer. Transfer to cutting board and discard parchment; slice and serve immediately. Repeat steps 3 and 4 to shape, top, and bake second pizza.

CLASSIC PEPPERONI PIZZA

MAKES TWO 14-INCH PIZZAS, SERVING 4 TO 6

This pizzeria favorite is especially easy to prepare. You can shape the second dough round while the first pizza bakes, but don't add the toppings until just before baking. For more information on shaping the pizza dough, see page 159.

1	recipe Classic Pizza Dough (page 160)
1½	cups Quick Tomato Sauce for Pizza (page 160)
8	ounces pepperoni, peeled and sliced thin
4	ounces whole-milk mozzarella cheese, shredded (1 cup)
¼	cup grated Parmesan cheese

1. One hour before baking, adjust oven rack to lowest position, set baking stone on rack, and heat oven to 500 degrees.

2. Transfer dough to lightly floured counter, divide in half, and cover with greased plastic wrap. Use your fingertips to gently

KEEPING PIZZA TOPPING ON HAND

Homemade pizza is like a blank canvas for the creative use of myriad toppings. The problem is that you don't always have that many topping options on hand. Try this simple solution. Whenever cooking something such as roasted red peppers, caramelized onions, or sausage, reserve some in a plastic container, label it, and freeze it. The next time you're making pizza, simply defrost and top away.

DEGREASING PEPPERONI

If your pepperoni happens to be very greasy, try this tip, which will render the fat for a meaty, not greasy, pizza topping.

Put 2 ounces of pepperoni at a time in a single layer on a plate lined with 2 paper towels. Cover with 2 more paper towels and microwave on high for 30 seconds. Discard the towels and set pepperoni aside; repeat with new paper towels and remaining pepperoni.

REHEATING PIZZA

Reheated leftover pizza always pales in comparison with a freshly baked pie. The microwave turns it soggy, while throwing it into a hot oven can dry it out. We recently discovered a reheating method that really works: Place the cold slices on a rimmed baking sheet, cover the sheet tightly with aluminum foil, and place it on the lowest rack of a cold oven. Then set the oven temperature to 275 degrees and let the pizza warm for 25 to 30 minutes. This approach leaves the interior of the crust soft, the cheese melty, and the toppings and bottom hot and crisp but not dehydrated.

Why does this method work? Like other breads stored for a day, pizza crust initially hardens not through moisture loss but because its starches undergo a process called retrogradation, whereby the starch molecules crystallize and absorb moisture, making the pizza crust appear stiff and dry. As long as the pizza has been stored well wrapped, however, retrogradation can be temporarily reversed by reheating the pizza to at least 140 degrees—the temperature at which the starch crystals break down and release the trapped moisture, softening the crust. Placing the slices in a cold oven lets them warm up gradually, with ample time to release moisture and soften, while sealing the pan helps keep them from drying out as they reheat. Finally, placing the pan as low as possible in the oven means the slices are heated from the bottom up, so the underside of the crust crisps but the toppings don't shrivel.

flatten 1 piece of dough into 8-inch disk (keep other piece covered). Using your hands, gently stretch disk into 14-inch round, working along outer edge and giving disk quarter turns. Transfer dough to piece of parchment paper and reshape as needed.

3. Using back of spoon or ladle, spread ¾ cup tomato sauce over dough, leaving ½-inch border around edge. Scatter half of pepperoni slices over sauce. Slide parchment with pizza onto pizza peel, then slide onto baking stone. Bake until crust begins to brown, 7 to 8 minutes.

4. Remove pizza from oven by sliding parchment back onto pizza peel, close oven door, and top pizza evenly with ½ cup mozzarella and 2 tablespoons Parmesan. Return pizza to baking stone and continue baking until cheese is just melted, about 3 minutes longer. Transfer to cutting board and discard parchment; slice and serve immediately. Repeat steps 3 and 4 to shape, top, and bake second pizza.

MUSHROOM PIZZA WITH SAGE, FONTINA, AND PARMESAN

MAKES TWO 14-INCH PIZZAS, SERVING 4 TO 6

You can shape the second dough round while the first pizza bakes, but don't add the toppings until just before baking. For more information on shaping the pizza dough, see page 159.

- 2   tablespoons olive oil
- 2   large garlic cloves, minced
- 1   pound cremini or white mushrooms, trimmed and sliced thin
- 1   teaspoon minced fresh sage
      Salt and pepper
- 1   recipe Classic Pizza Dough (page 160)
- 1   cup Quick Tomato Sauce for Pizza (page 160)
- 4   ounces fontina cheese, shredded (1 cup)
- ¼   cup grated Parmesan cheese

1. One hour before baking, adjust oven rack to lowest position, set baking stone on rack, and heat oven to 500 degrees.

2. Meanwhile, heat oil and garlic in 12-inch skillet. When garlic begins to sizzle, add mushrooms and cook, stirring often, until mushrooms release their liquid and begin to brown, about 5 minutes. Stir in sage and season with salt and pepper to taste; set aside.

3. Transfer dough to lightly floured counter, divide in half, and cover with greased plastic wrap. Use your fingertips to gently flatten 1 piece of dough into 8-inch disk (keep other piece covered). Using your hands, gently stretch disk into 14-inch round, working along outer edge and giving disk quarter turns. Transfer dough to piece of parchment paper and reshape as needed.

4. Using back of spoon or ladle, spread ½ cup tomato sauce over dough, leaving ½-inch border around edge. Sprinkle half of mushrooms over sauce. Slide parchment with pizza onto pizza peel, then slide onto baking stone. Bake until crust begins to brown, 7 to 8 minutes.

5. Remove pizza from oven by sliding parchment back onto pizza peel, close oven door, and top pizza evenly with ½ cup fontina and 2 tablespoons Parmesan. Return pizza to baking stone and continue baking until cheese is just melted, about 3 minutes longer. Transfer to cutting board and discard parchment; slice and serve immediately. Repeat steps 3 and 4 to shape, top, and bake second pizza.

FRESH TOMATO PIZZA WITH ARUGULA AND PROSCIUTTO

MAKES TWO 14-INCH PIZZAS, SERVING 4 TO 6

You can shape the second dough round while the first pizza bakes, but don't add the toppings until just before baking. When tossing the arugula with oil, you may also sprinkle on a teaspoon or so of balsamic vinegar, if you like. For more information on shaping the pizza dough, see page 159.

1 recipe Classic Pizza Dough (page 160)
1 pound tomatoes, cored and sliced thin
   Salt and pepper
2 tablespoons olive oil
4 ounces thinly sliced prosciutto
4 ounces whole-milk mozzarella cheese, shredded (1 cup)
2 ounces (2 cups) baby arugula

1. One hour before baking, adjust oven rack to lowest position, set baking stone on rack, and heat oven to 500 degrees.

2. Transfer dough to lightly floured counter, divide in half, and cover with greased plastic wrap. Use your fingertips to gently flatten 1 piece of dough into 8-inch disk (keep other piece covered). Using your hands, gently stretch disk into 14-inch round, working along outer edge and giving disk quarter turns.

Transfer dough to piece of parchment paper and reshape as needed.

3. Arrange half of tomatoes in concentric circles over dough and season with salt and pepper. Drizzle with 2 teaspoons oil. Slide parchment with pizza onto pizza peel, then slide onto baking stone. Bake until crust begins to brown, 7 to 8 minutes.

4. Remove pizza from oven by sliding parchment back onto pizza peel, close oven door, and top pizza evenly with half of prosciutto and ½ cup mozzarella. Return pizza to baking stone and continue baking until cheese is just melted, about 3 minutes longer. Meanwhile, toss arugula with remaining 2 teaspoons oil. Transfer pizza to cutting board and discard parchment. Sprinkle with half of arugula, slice, and serve immediately. Repeat steps 2 and 3 to shape, top, and bake second pizza.

New York–Style Thin-Crust Pizza

✓ **WHY THIS RECIPE WORKS**

With home ovens that reach only 500 degrees and dough that's impossible to stretch thin, even the savviest cooks can struggle to produce New York–style parlor-quality pizza. We were in pursuit of a New York–style pizza with a perfect crust—thin, crisp, and spottily charred on the exterior, tender yet chewy within.

USE HIGH-PROTEIN FLOUR We opt for high-protein bread flour in our pizza dough. The dough is a little sticky, but we add some extra flour to the exterior as we shape and stretch the dough. We use a food processor to mix the dough. A more conventional stand-mixer method might take 15 to 20 minutes to produce a shiny, elastic dough, but the food processor turns out comparably kneaded dough in less than 2 minutes. (Though for many bread recipes, we would caution against the rough treatment of a food processor, which can tear apart the strands of gluten that give bread structure and the ability to rise, here the amount of flour used is relatively small. Also, because this is a pizza, we do not need to develop the structure of a dough destined to be a flatbread.)

CHILL THE DOUGH Cool fermentation of the dough not only helps keep the bubbles in the dough smaller and tighter, it creates more flavor via the production of sugar, alcohol, and acids.

ADD SUGAR AND OIL Adding oil and sugar to the dough helps to encourage more crunch and color in the crust. (We often sprinkle a spoonful of sugar over poultry skin to help it darken and crisp up in the oven, and

there's no reason the same trick can't be used here.) The sugar undergoes both caramelization and the Maillard reaction to produce aromas and brown pigments.

STRETCH BY HAND   Flatten and stretch the dough by hand. On a well-floured surface and using your fingertips, gently flatten half of the dough into an 8-inch disk, leaving the outer edge slightly thicker than the center to create a fatter "handle." With your hands, stretch the dough into a 12-inch round, working along the edges and giving the dough quarter turns. Transfer to a well-floured peel and stretch to a 13-inch round. (You can also "drape" the dough; see page 159.)

SHRINK YOUR HEADROOM   For an authentic New York–style charred crust, we move the oven rack to a higher position to mimic the shallow chamber of a commercial pizza oven. The best position for the stone is really as close to the top of the oven as possible—about 4 inches or so from the ceiling, which leaves just enough headroom to comfortably house the pie.

MAKE AN EASY SAUCE   We use a no-cook sauce here—canned tomatoes, garlic, olive oil, and spices pureed in a food processor. Red wine vinegar enhances the tomatoes' bright acidity. We supplement the creamy, stretchy mozzarella with a fistful of sharp, salty, finely grated Parmesan.

TOP WELL   We like our thin-crust pizza simply dressed with tomato sauce and shredded mozzarella and Parmesan, but additional toppings are always an option—provided they're prepared correctly and added judiciously. (An overloaded pie will become soggy.) If you're using hearty vegetables, aim for a maximum of 6 ounces per pie, precooked to remove excess moisture. Leafy green vegetables and herbs like spinach and basil are best placed beneath the cheese to protect them or added raw to the fully cooked pie. Meats (no more than 4 ounces per pie) should be precooked and drained to remove excess fat.

NEW YORK–STYLE THIN-CRUST PIZZA

MAKES TWO 13-INCH PIZZAS, SERVING 4 TO 6

You can shape the second dough round while the first pizza bakes, but don't add the toppings until just before baking. You will need a pizza peel for this recipe. It is important to use ice water in the dough to prevent the dough from overheating while in the food processor. Semolina flour is ideal for dusting the peel; use it in place of bread flour if you have it. The sauce will yield more than needed in the recipe; extra sauce can be refrigerated for up to one week or frozen for up to one month.

DOUGH

3	cups (16½ ounces) bread flour
2	teaspoons sugar
½	teaspoon instant or rapid-rise yeast
1⅓	cups ice water
1	tablespoon vegetable oil
1½	teaspoons salt

SAUCE

1	(28-ounce) can whole tomatoes, drained
1	tablespoon extra-virgin olive oil
1	teaspoon red wine vinegar
2	garlic cloves, minced
1	teaspoon salt
1	teaspoon dried oregano
¼	teaspoon pepper

CHEESE

1	ounce Parmesan cheese, grated fine (½ cup)
8	ounces whole-milk mozzarella, shredded (2 cups)

1. FOR THE DOUGH: Pulse flour, sugar, and yeast in processor (fitted with dough blade if possible) until combined, about 5 pulses. With food processor running, slowly add water; process until dough is just combined and no dry flour remains, about 10 seconds. Let dough sit for 10 minutes.

NEATER CHEESE GRATING

Use a clean plastic bag (a large zipper-lock bag works best) to hold the grater and the cheese. By placing the bag around both, you can grate without getting your hands dirty, and you don't have to worry about rogue pieces flying off into your kitchen. The best part? Leftover grated cheese is ready for storage, no transfer needed.

2. Add oil and salt to dough and process until dough forms satiny, sticky ball that clears sides of bowl, 30 to 60 seconds. Transfer dough to lightly oiled counter and knead briefly by hand until smooth, about 1 minute. Shape dough into tight ball and place in large, lightly oiled bowl; cover bowl tightly with plastic wrap and refrigerate for at least 24 hours or up to 3 days.

3. FOR THE SAUCE: Process all ingredients in clean bowl of food processor until smooth, about 30 seconds. Transfer to bowl and refrigerate until ready to use.

4. FOR THE CHEESE: One hour before baking, adjust oven rack to upper-middle position (rack should be 4 to 5 inches from broiler), set baking stone on rack, and heat oven to 500 degrees. Transfer dough to clean counter and divide in half. With cupped palms, form each half into smooth, tight ball. Place balls of dough on lightly greased baking sheet, spacing them at least 3 inches apart; cover loosely with greased plastic and let sit for 1 hour.

5. Coat 1 ball of dough generously with flour and place on well-floured counter (keep other ball covered). Use your fingertips to gently flatten dough into 8-inch disk, leaving 1 inch of outer edge slightly thicker than center. Using your hands, gently stretch disk into 12-inch round, working along outer edge and giving disk quarter turns. Transfer dough to well-floured pizza peel and stretch into 13-inch round. Using back of spoon or ladle, spread ½ cup tomato sauce in thin layer over surface of dough, leaving ¼-inch border around edge. Sprinkle ¼ cup Parmesan evenly over sauce, followed by 1 cup mozzarella. Slide pizza carefully onto baking stone and bake until crust is well browned and cheese is bubbly and beginning to brown, 10 to 12 minutes, rotating pizza halfway through baking. Transfer pizza to wire rack and let cool for 5 minutes before slicing and serving. Repeat step 5 to shape, top, and bake second pizza.

FREEZING PIZZA DOUGH

It can be convenient to keep a stash of homemade pizza dough in your freezer but at what point in the dough-making process do you freeze it? To answer this question, we made our basic pizza dough recipe—which makes enough for two pizza crusts—and froze it at two stages: immediately after mixing the dough and after allowing the dough to fully rise. After we shaped the dough into balls, we wrapped them in plastic wrap coated with vegetable oil spray, placed them in zipper-lock bags, and froze them. A few days later, we thawed both doughs on the counter, letting the unrisen dough rise for the 2 hours specified in the recipe. Next, we shaped both batches of dough—along with a freshly made batch and refrigerated dough from the supermarket—topped them with tomato sauce and mozzarella cheese, and baked them at 500 degrees for 10 minutes.

Tasted side by side, one of the frozen versions was nearly as good as the freshly made dough: The dough that had been frozen after rising was easy to shape (the gluten strands had had ample time to relax), crisp on the outside, chewy in the middle, and fresh-tasting. The dough that had been frozen before rising, on the other hand, was flatter and slightly tough. The freezing step had killed many of the yeast cells, resulting in a partially arrested rise and lackluster crust. Finally, the store-bought pizza dough received surprisingly good ratings from tasters.

If you have extra dough you'd like to keep around for later, be sure to let it rise fully before freezing. The best way to defrost dough is to let it sit on the counter for a couple of hours or overnight in the refrigerator. (Thawing pizza dough in a microwave or low oven isn't recommended as it will dry the dough out.) And for last-minute pizza cravings, store-bought refrigerated dough is an entirely acceptable option.

NEW YORK–STYLE THIN-CRUST WHITE PIZZA

MAKES TWO 13-INCH PIZZAS, SERVING 4 TO 6

You can shape the second dough round while the first pizza bakes, but don't add the toppings until just before baking. You will need a pizza peel for this recipe. It is important to use ice water in the dough to prevent the dough from overheating while in the food processor. Semolina flour is ideal for dusting the peel; use it in place of bread flour if you have it.

Substitute white sauce for red sauce: Whisk together 1 cup whole-milk ricotta cheese, ¼ cup extra-virgin olive oil, ¼ cup heavy cream, 1 large egg yolk, 4 minced garlic cloves, 2 teaspoons minced fresh oregano, 1 teaspoon minced fresh thyme, ½ teaspoon salt, ¼ teaspoon pepper, ⅛ teaspoon cayenne, and thinly sliced whites of 2 scallions (reserve green tops for garnish); refrigerate until ready to use.

Substitute Pecorino Romano for Parmesan. After sprinkling pizza with Pecorino and mozzarella, dollop ¼ cup whole-milk ricotta cheese in teaspoon amounts evenly over pizza. Proceed as directed.

Thin-Crust Whole-Wheat Pizza

WHY THIS RECIPE WORKS

Most whole-wheat pizza crust is as dry and dense as cardboard. We wanted to find a way to make it as crisp and chewy as traditional pizza crust—and highlight its nutty, wheaty flavor. We also wanted to find toppings that complemented, not clashed, with our whole-wheat crust.

ADD BREAD FLOUR Using both whole-wheat flour and white bread flour (which has more structure-building proteins than all-purpose flour) increases chewiness.

USE LOTS OF (ICE) WATER Our highly hydrated dough helps strengthen the gluten network; ice water keeps the dough from overheating as it is kneaded in the food processor.

REST AT LEAST A FULL DAY A long rest gives enzymes in the dough time to slightly weaken gluten strands, increasing extensibility; it also allows for more flavor-boosting fermentation.

USE THE BROILER Because our dough is so wet, preheating the pizza stone under the broiler's high heat is key for a nicely browned crust.

DITCH THE TOMATOES The sweet-tart flavors of tomato sauce clash with earthy whole wheat. Instead, we top our pizza with three cheeses, garlicky oil, and basil.

THIN-CRUST WHOLE-WHEAT PIZZA WITH GARLIC OIL, THREE CHEESES, AND BASIL

MAKES TWO 13-INCH PIZZAS, SERVING 4 TO 6

We recommend King Arthur brand bread flour for this recipe. Some baking stones, especially thinner ones, can crack under the intense heat of the broiler. Our recommended stone, by Old Stone Oven (see page 158), is fine if you're using this technique. If you use another stone, you might want to check the manufacturer's website.

DOUGH

1½	cups (8¼ ounces) whole-wheat flour
1	cup (5½ ounces) bread flour
2	teaspoons honey
¾	teaspoon instant or rapid-rise yeast
1¼	cups ice water
2	tablespoons extra-virgin olive oil
1¾	teaspoons salt

GARLIC OIL

¼	cup extra-virgin olive oil
2	garlic cloves, minced
2	anchovy fillets, rinsed, patted dry, and minced (optional)
½	teaspoon pepper
½	teaspoon dried oregano
⅛	teaspoon red pepper flakes
⅛	teaspoon salt

1	cup fresh basil leaves
1	ounce Pecorino Romano cheese, grated (½ cup)
8	ounces whole-milk mozzarella cheese, shredded (2 cups)
6	ounces (¾ cup) whole-milk ricotta cheese

1. FOR THE DOUGH: Process whole-wheat flour, bread flour, honey, and yeast in food processor until combined, about 2 seconds. With processor running, add water and process until dough is just combined and no dry flour remains, about 10 seconds. Let dough stand for 10 minutes.

2. Add oil and salt to dough and process until it forms satiny, sticky ball that clears sides of workbowl, 45 to 60 seconds. Remove from bowl and knead on oiled counter until smooth, about 1 minute. Shape dough into tight ball and place in large, lightly oiled bowl. Cover tightly with plastic wrap and

If you use a knife to cut pizza, you risk pulling cheese in every direction. A pizza wheel negates this risk (or should), and we wanted one large and sharp enough to glide through thick and thin crusts without dislodging toppings. We tested five types: three with stainless steel blades, one with polycarbonate plastic, and one dual wheel. For overall comfort, extreme sharpness, and heft, one pizza wheel was named the test kitchen's favorite.

The **OXO Good Grips 4-Inch Pizza Wheel** won points for its well-designed wheel, which was easy to clean, its thumb guard, and the large, soft handle that absorbed extra pressure.

refrigerate for at least 18 hours or up to 2 days.

3. FOR THE GARLIC OIL: Heat oil in 8-inch skillet over medium-low heat until shimmering. Add garlic, anchovies, if using, pepper; oregano, pepper flakes, and salt. Cook, stirring constantly, until fragrant, about 30 seconds. Transfer to bowl and let cool completely before using.

4. One hour before baking pizza, adjust oven rack 4½ inches from broiler element, set pizza stone on rack, and heat oven to 500 degrees. Remove dough from refrigerator and divide in half. Shape each half into smooth, tight ball. Place balls on lightly oiled baking sheet, spacing them at least 3 inches apart. Cover loosely with plastic coated with vegetable oil spray; let stand for 1 hour.

5. Heat broiler for 10 minutes. Meanwhile, coat 1 ball of dough generously with flour and place on well-floured counter. Using your fingertips, gently flatten into 8-inch disk, leaving 1 inch of outer edge slightly thicker than center. Lift edge of dough and, using back of your hands and knuckles, gently stretch disk into 12-inch round, working along edges and giving disk quarter turns as you stretch. Transfer dough to well-floured pizza peel and stretch into 13-inch round. Using back of spoon, spread half of garlic oil over surface of dough, leaving ¼-inch border around edge. Layer ½ cup basil leaves over pizza. Sprinkle with ¼ cup Pecorino, followed by 1 cup mozzarella. Slide pizza carefully onto stone and return oven to 500 degrees. Bake until crust is well browned and cheese is bubbly and partially browned, 8 to 10 minutes, rotating pizza halfway through baking. Remove pizza and place on wire rack. Dollop half of ricotta over surface of pizza. Let pizza rest for 5 minutes, slice, and serve.

6. Heat broiler for 10 minutes. Repeat process of stretching, topping, and baking with remaining dough and toppings, returning oven to 500 degrees when pizza is placed on stone.

THIN-CRUST WHOLE-WHEAT PIZZA WITH PESTO AND GOAT CHEESE

Some baking stones, especially thinner ones, can crack under the intense heat of the broiler. Our recommended stone, by Old Stone Oven, is fine if you're using this technique. If you use another stone, you might want to check the manufacturer's website.

Process 2 cups basil leaves, 7 tablespoons extra-virgin olive oil, ¼ cup pine nuts, 3 minced garlic cloves, and ½ teaspoon salt in food processor until smooth, scraping down sides of bowl as needed, about 1 minute. Stir in ¼ cup finely grated Parmesan or Pecorino Romano and season with salt and pepper to taste. Substitute pesto for garlic oil. In step 5, omit basil leaves, Pecorino Romano, mozzarella, and ricotta. Top each pizza with ½ cup crumbled goat cheese before baking.

THIN-CRUST WHOLE-WHEAT PIZZA WITH ONION AND BLUE CHEESE

Some baking stones, especially thinner ones, can crack under the intense heat of the broiler. Our recommended stone, by Old Stone Oven, is fine if you're using this technique. If you use another stone, you might want to check the manufacturer's website.

Bring 1 onion, sliced 1 inch thick, 1½ cups water, ¾ cup red wine, 3 tablespoons sugar, and ¼ teaspoon salt to simmer over medium-high heat in 10-inch skillet. Reduce heat to medium and simmer, stirring often, until liquid evaporates and onion is crisp-tender, about 30 minutes. Stir in 2 teaspoons red wine vinegar, transfer to bowl, and let cool completely before using. (Onion mixture can be refrigerated, covered, for up to 2 days.) Substitute onion mixture for garlic oil. In step 5, omit Pecorino Romano, mozzarella, ricotta, and basil. Using back of spoon, spread ⅓ cup crème fraîche over surface of dough, leaving ¼-inch border around edge. Sprinkle half of onion mixture evenly over each pizza, followed by ½ cup walnuts and ½ cup crumbled blue cheese, before baking. Let each pizza rest for 5 minutes, top each with 2 tablespoons shredded basil, slice, and serve.

Chicago-Style Deep-Dish Pizza

✓ WHY THIS RECIPE WORKS

We wanted a recipe to rival the best deep-dish pizza Chicago has to offer, with a thick, crisp crust; an airy, flaky interior; and a rich taste that could hold its own under any kind of topping. A pastry-making technique turned out to be one trick to achieving our goals.

INCLUDE BUTTER AND CORNMEAL Traditional recipes for Chicago deep-dish pizza crust include more fat for a richer crust. Some recipes rely on oil while just a handful call for butter. We found the rich flavor of butter unbeatable in this crust. Cornmeal was found in just about every ingredient list we reviewed and we could see why—it adds good earthy flavor and crunch.

LAMINATE THE DOUGH After mixing the dough and letting it rise, we laminate it to increase its flakiness. Laminating is a technique that involves layering butter and dough through a sequence of rolling and folding to create ultraflaky pastries. Adding melted butter to the dough and spreading the rolled-out dough with softened butter before folding did the trick.

REFRIGERATE AND RISE AGAIN During laminating, the dough warms so much that the softened butter melts, leading to a crust that was more tender and breadlike than flaky. The solution? Moving the dough into the refrigerator for its second rise so that any butter that had melted or gotten overly soft could firm up again.

OIL THE PAN WELL Deep-dish pizza is made in a round cake pan. We add plenty of olive oil to ensure an easy release and a crisp and flavorful crust. Shaping the pizza is as easy as pressing the disk of dough into the oiled pan so the dough is spread into the corners and up the sides for a tall crust to cradle the layers of cheese and sauce.

TOP WITH CHEESE Following Chicago tradition, we cover the dough with freshly shredded mozzarella and then top the cheese with our thick, quick-to-make tomato sauce. The cheese forms a barrier between the crust and sauce, which prevents our thick, flavorful crust from turning soggy. A sprinkle of nutty Parmesan over the sauce provides a second layer of cheesy flavor.

CHICAGO-STYLE DEEP-DISH PIZZA
MAKES TWO 9-INCH PIZZAS, SERVING 6 TO 8

This dough must be prepared in a stand mixer. Place a damp dish towel under the mixer and watch it at all times during kneading to prevent it from wobbling off the counter. Handle the dough with slightly oiled hands to prevent sticking. Grate the onion on the large holes of a box grater.

DOUGH

3¼	cups (16¼ ounces) all-purpose flour
½	cup (2¾ ounces) cornmeal
2¼	teaspoons instant or rapid-rise yeast
2	teaspoons sugar
1½	teaspoons salt
1¼	cups water, room temperature
3	tablespoons unsalted butter, melted, plus 4 tablespoons, softened
1	teaspoon plus 4 tablespoons olive oil

SAUCE

2	tablespoons unsalted butter
¼	cup grated onion
¼	teaspoon dried oregano
	Salt and pepper
2	garlic cloves, minced
1	(28-ounce) can crushed tomatoes
¼	teaspoon sugar
2	tablespoons chopped fresh basil
1	tablespoon extra-virgin olive oil

PRESSING PAN PIZZA DOUGH

Press dough into corners and up sides of 9-inch round cake pan.

DETERMINING WHEN PAN PIZZA IS DONE

Use a spatula to lift up the pizza slightly. If the bottom crust is nicely browned, the pizza is done.

MAKING FLAKY CHICAGO-STYLE PIZZA CRUST

1. On dry counter, roll dough into 15 by 12-inch rectangle. Spread softened butter over dough, leaving ½-inch border along edges.

2. Starting at short end closest to you, roll dough into tight cylinder.

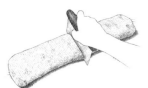

3. Flatten cylinder into 18 by 4-inch rectangle. Halve crosswise.

4. Fold each piece of dough into thirds; pinch seams to form balls. Let dough balls rise in refrigerator 40 to 50 minutes to chill butter.

TOPPINGS

1 pound mozzarella cheese, shredded (4 cups)

¼ cup grated Parmesan cheese

1. FOR THE DOUGH: Using stand mixer fitted with dough hook, mix together flour, cornmeal, yeast, sugar, and salt on low speed until combined, about 1 minute. Add water and melted butter and mix until fully combined, 1 to 2 minutes, scraping down bowl as needed. Increase speed to medium and knead until dough is glossy and smooth and pulls away from sides of bowl, 4 to 5 minutes. (Dough will only pull away from sides while mixer is on. When mixer is off, dough will fall back to sides.)

2. Using your fingers, coat large bowl with 1 teaspoon olive oil, rubbing excess oil from fingers onto blade of rubber spatula. Using oiled spatula, transfer dough to prepared bowl, turning once to oil top. Cover bowl tightly with plastic wrap. Let dough rise at room temperature until nearly doubled in size, 45 minutes to 1 hour.

3. FOR THE SAUCE: While dough rises, melt butter in medium saucepan over medium heat. Add onion, oregano, and ½ teaspoon salt and cook, stirring occasionally, until onion is softened and lightly browned, about 5 minutes. Stir in garlic and cook until fragrant, about 30 seconds. Stir in tomatoes and sugar, bring to simmer, and cook until sauce has reduced to 2½ cups, 25 to 30 minutes. Off heat, stir in basil and oil, then season with salt and pepper to taste.

4. Adjust oven rack to lowest position and heat oven to 425 degrees. Using rubber spatula, turn dough out onto dry, clean counter and roll into 15 by 12-inch rectangle with short side facing you. Spread softened butter over surface of dough using offset spatula, leaving ½-inch border along edges. Starting at short end, roll dough into tight cylinder. With seam side down, flatten cylinder into 18 by 4-inch rectangle. Cut rectangle in half crosswise. Working with 1 half at a time, fold dough into thirds like business letter, then pinch seams together to form ball. Return dough balls to oiled bowl, cover tightly with plastic, and let rise in refrigerator until nearly doubled in size, 40 to 50 minutes.

5. Coat two 9-inch round cake pans with 2 tablespoons olive oil each. Transfer 1 dough ball to clean counter and roll into 13-inch disk about ¼ inch thick. Transfer dough round to cake pan by rolling dough loosely around rolling pin, then unrolling dough into pan. Lightly press dough into pan, working it into corners and 1 inch up sides. If dough resists stretching, let it relax 5 minutes before trying again. Repeat with remaining dough ball.

6. For each pizza, sprinkle 2 cups mozzarella evenly over surface of dough. Spread 1¼ cups tomato sauce over cheese and sprinkle 2 tablespoons Parmesan over sauce for each pizza. Bake until crust is golden brown, 20 to 30 minutes. Remove pizzas from oven and let rest for 10 minutes before slicing and serving.

CHICAGO-STYLE DEEP-DISH PIZZA WITH SAUSAGE

Cook 1 pound hot Italian sausage, casings removed, in 12-inch nonstick skillet over medium-high heat, breaking it into ½-inch pieces with wooden spoon, until browned, about 5 minutes. Remove sausage with slotted spoon and transfer to paper towel–lined plate. Sprinkle half of cooked sausage over mozzarella in each pizza before continuing with additional toppings in step 6.

CHICAGO-STYLE DEEP-DISH PIZZA WITH OLIVES, RICOTTA, AND ARUGULA

Sprinkle each pizza with 2 tablespoons chopped pitted kalamata olives along with Parmesan in step 6. Using 2 tablespoons ricotta cheese per pizza, dot surface with teaspoons of cheese. Bake as directed. Remove pizzas from oven and sprinkle ¼ cup chopped arugula over surface of each pizza.

Classic Pan Pizza

✔ WHY THIS RECIPE WORKS

Unlike its thin-crust cousin, pan pizza has a soft, chewy, thick crust that can stand up to substantial toppings. We wanted to try our hand at making this pizza without a lot of fuss. Most of the allure of deep-dish pizza is in the crust, so it was important to get it right.

ADD A POTATO We found that mixing potato into our dough—a trick we picked up from some recipes for focaccia—contributes moisture and richness to the crust. The potato also makes the dough easier to handle.

OIL THE PAN GENEROUSLY Covering the pan with oil before loading it with dough makes for a deeply caramelized crust that looks and tastes delicious.

PRECOOK DOUGH, THEN ADD TOPPINGS To keep the toppings from weighing down the crust and making it soggy, we precook the dough for 15 minutes, giving it a chance to rise and firm up a bit. This practice benefits the toppings as well, giving them just enough time to heat through and melt or brown.

CLASSIC PAN PIZZA WITH TOMATOES, MOZZARELLA, AND BASIL

MAKES ONE 14-INCH PIZZA, SERVING 4 TO 6

If you don't have a stand mixer, you can mix the dough by hand following the instructions on page 115. Prepare the topping while the dough is rising so it will be ready at the same time the dough is ready. The amount of oil used to grease the pan may seem excessive, but in addition to preventing sticking, the oil helps the crust brown nicely.

DOUGH

9	ounces russet potatoes, peeled and quartered
3½	cups (17½ ounces) all-purpose flour
1	cup warm water(110 degrees)
1½	teaspoons instant or rapid-rise yeast
6	tablespoons extra-virgin olive oil
1¾	teaspoons salt

TOPPING

4	tomatoes, cored, seeded, and cut into 1-inch pieces
2	garlic cloves, minced
	Salt and pepper
6	ounces mozzarella cheese, shredded (1½ cups)
1	ounce Parmesan cheese, grated (½ cup)
3	tablespoons shredded fresh basil

1. FOR THE DOUGH: Bring 1 quart water and potato to boil in medium saucepan and cook until tender, 10 to 15 minutes. Drain potato and process through ricer or food mill onto plate. Measure out and reserve 1⅓ cups potato; discard remaining potato.

2. Adjust oven racks to upper-middle and lowest positions and heat oven to 200 degrees. Once oven temperature reaches 200 degrees, maintain heat for 10 minutes, then turn off oven.

3. Using stand mixer fitted with dough hook, mix ½ cup flour, ½ cup water, and yeast together on low speed until combined; cover bowl tightly with plastic wrap and let sit until bubbly, about 20 minutes.

4. Add 2 tablespoons oil, remaining 3 cups flour, remaining ½ cup water, salt, and potato to flour mixture and mix on low speed until dough comes together. Increase speed to medium and knead until dough comes together and is slightly tacky, about 5 minutes. Transfer dough to large, lightly greased bowl; cover tightly with plastic and let rise on lower rack in warm oven until doubled in size, 30 to 35 minutes.

5. Grease bottom of 14-inch cake pan with remaining 4 tablespoons oil. Remove dough from oven; transfer to clean counter and press into 12-inch round. Transfer round to pan, cover with plastic, and let rest until dough no longer resists shaping, about 10 minutes. Uncover dough and pull up into edges and up sides of pan to form 1-inch-high lip. Cover with plastic; let rise at room temperature until doubled in size, about 30 minutes.

6. FOR THE TOPPING: Mix tomatoes and garlic together in bowl and season with salt and pepper to taste; set aside.

7. One hour before baking, set baking stone on lower rack and heat oven to 425 degrees. Uncover dough and prick generously with fork. Bake on baking stone until dry and lightly browned, about 15 minutes.

8. Remove pizza from oven. Spread partially baked crust with tomato mixture; sprinkle with mozzarella, then Parmesan. Return pizza to baking stone and continue baking until cheese melts, 10 to 15 minutes. Move pizza to upper rack and continue to bake

until cheese is spotty brown, about 5 minutes longer. Remove pizza from oven, sprinkle with basil, and let rest for 10 minutes before slicing and serving.

CLASSIC FOUR-CHEESE PAN PIZZA WITH PESTO

Omit tomatoes, garlic, salt, pepper, and basil from topping. Process 2 cups basil leaves, 7 tablespoons extra-virgin olive oil, ¼ cup pine nuts, 3 minced garlic cloves, and ½ teaspoon salt in food processor until smooth, scraping down sides of bowl as needed, about 1 minute. Stir in ¼ cup finely grated Parmesan or Pecorino Romano and season with salt and pepper to taste. Spread ½ cup pesto onto partially baked crust in step 8, then sprinkle with mozzarella, followed by 1 cup shredded provolone cheese, ¼ cup crumbled blue cheese, and Parmesan. Continue baking as directed.

10-INCH CLASSIC PAN PIZZA

If you don't own a 14-inch deep-dish pizza pan, divide dough between two 10-inch cake pans. Grease bottom of each cake pan with 2 tablespoons olive oil. Turn dough onto clean, dry counter and divide in half. Pat each half into 9-inch round; continue with recipe, reducing initial baking time on lowest rack to 5 to 10 minutes and dividing topping evenly between pizzas.

SHREDDING SEMISOFT CHEESE IN A FOOD PROCESSOR

It's easy to shred semisoft cheeses such as mozzarella or cheddar in the food processor—until, of course, a big chunk sticks in the feed tube or gums up the shredding disk. Avoid problem stickiness with this trick.

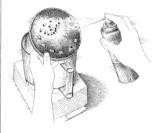

Spray feed tube, disk, and workbowl of food processor with light coating of vegetable oil spray before you begin shredding.

PEANUT BUTTER SANDWICH COOKIES

CHAPTER 6

Cookies

Chewy Sugar Cookies

1. Take 2 tablespoons of dough and roll it between your palms into ball. Roll ball of dough in sugar and then place it on prepared baking sheet.

2. Use bottom of greased drinking glass with flat bottom or measuring cup to flatten balls of dough until 2 inches in diameter. Sprinkle tops of cookies evenly with sugar, using 2 teaspoons for each baking sheet. (Discard remaining sugar.)

✓ WHY THIS RECIPE WORKS

Traditional recipes for sugar cookies require obsessive attention to detail. The butter must be at precisely the right temperature and it must be creamed to the proper degree of airiness. Slight variations in measures can result in cookies that spread or become brittle and hard upon cooling. We didn't want a cookie that depended on such a finicky process; we wanted an approachable recipe for great sugar cookies that anyone could make anytime.

MELT THE BUTTER Because we use less butter, we melt it rather than cream it. This accomplishes three things. First, it eliminates one of the trickier aspects of baking sugar cookies: ensuring that the solid butter is just the right temperature. Second, melted butter aids in our quest for chewiness. When liquefied, the small amount of water in butter mixes with the flour to form gluten, which makes for chewier cookies. Finally, with creaming out of the equation, we no longer need to pull out our stand mixer. We can make these cookies completely by hand.

USE CREAM CHEESE Cream cheese enriches the dough's flavor without adding moisture like other tangy dairy products. Cream cheese contains less than one-third the amount of overall fat of vegetable oil. We use a modest 2 ounces of cream cheese, which doesn't detract from the chewy texture of the cookies.

ADD BAKING SODA Cream cheese doesn't just add flavor, it adds acidity. And this allows us to use baking soda. As long as there's an acidic ingredient present, baking soda has all sorts of special powers, including the ability to solve the cookies' other two pesky problems: a slightly humped shape and not enough crackle. Just ½ teaspoon produces cookies that look as good as they taste.

CHEWY SUGAR COOKIES

MAKES ABOUT 24 COOKIES

The final dough will be slightly softer than most cookie dough. For the best results, handle the dough as briefly and gently as possible when shaping the cookies. Overworking the dough will result in flatter cookies.

2¼	cups (11¼ ounces) all-purpose flour
1	teaspoon baking powder
½	teaspoon baking soda
½	teaspoon salt
1½	cups (10½ ounces) sugar, plus ⅓ cup for rolling
2	ounces cream cheese, cut into 8 pieces
6	tablespoons unsalted butter, melted and still warm
⅓	cup vegetable oil
1	large egg
1	tablespoon whole milk
2	teaspoons vanilla extract

1. Adjust oven rack to middle position and heat oven to 350 degrees. Line 2 baking sheets with parchment paper. Whisk flour, baking powder, baking soda, and salt together in medium bowl. Set aside.

2. Place 1½ cups sugar and cream cheese in large bowl. Place remaining ⅓ cup sugar in shallow dish and set aside. Pour warm butter over sugar and cream cheese and whisk to combine (some small lumps of cream cheese will remain but will smooth out later). Whisk in oil until incorporated. Add egg, milk, and vanilla; continue to whisk until smooth. Add flour mixture and mix with rubber spatula until soft, homogeneous dough forms.

3. Working with 2 tablespoons of dough at a time, roll into balls. Working in batches, roll half of dough balls in sugar to coat and set on

DYNAMIC DUO: BAKING POWDER + BAKING SODA

Many cookie recipes, including our Chewy Sugar Cookies, contain both baking soda and baking powder. Since each is a leavening agent, why do you need both? The answer is that the two work in tandem to create cookies that not only rise but also spread to the right degree. Plus in our recipe, baking soda has one more purely aesthetic effect: It creates cookies with an appealingly crackly top.

Baking powder is responsible for lift, since it is engineered to produce most of its gas after the cookies go into the oven, where the dough sets before these bubbles can burst.

But too much lift can mean cookies that turn out humped. Here's where baking soda comes in: As long as there's an acidic ingredient in the dough for it to react with, a small amount of baking soda can even things out. Baking soda raises the pH of dough (baking powder does too, but not as high), weakening gluten. Weaker gluten means less structure and cookies that spread. Goodbye, humped shapes.

As for crackly tops, baking soda reacts immediately in the wet dough to produce large bubbles of carbon dioxide that can't all be contained by the weakened dough. Before the cookies can set in the oven, the bubbles rise to the top and burst, leaving fissures in their wake.

The bottom line: For a baker who likes cookies just so, the use of both baking powder and baking soda can be a potent combo.

prepared sheet; repeat with remaining dough balls. Using bottom of greased drinking glass or measuring cup, flatten dough balls until 2 inches in diameter. Sprinkle tops of cookies evenly with sugar remaining in shallow dish for rolling, using 2 teaspoons for each sheet. (Discard remaining sugar.)

4. Bake 1 sheet at a time until edges of cookies are set and beginning to brown, 11 to 13 minutes, rotating sheet halfway through baking. Let cookies cool on sheet for 5 minutes; transfer cookies to wire rack and let cool to room temperature before serving.

CHEWY HAZELNUT–BROWNED BUTTER SUGAR COOKIES

Nutty browned butter gives these cookies a toffee-like flavor. For information on toasting nuts see page 9. And for information on removing skins from hazelnuts, see page 99.

Add ¼ cup finely chopped toasted hazelnuts to sugar and cream cheese mixture. Instead of melting butter, heat it in 10-inch skillet over medium-high heat until melted, about 2 minutes. Continue to cook, swirling pan constantly until butter is dark golden brown and has nutty aroma, 1 to 3 minutes. Immediately pour butter over sugar and cream cheese mixture and proceed with recipe as directed, increasing milk to 2 tablespoons and omitting vanilla.

CHEWY CHAI-SPICE SUGAR COOKIES

Add ¼ teaspoon ground cinnamon, ¼ teaspoon ground ginger, ¼ teaspoon ground cardamom, ¼ teaspoon ground cloves, and pinch pepper to sugar and cream cheese mixture and reduce vanilla to 1 teaspoon.

CHEWY COCONUT-LIME SUGAR COOKIES

Whisk ½ cup sweetened shredded coconut, chopped fine, into flour mixture in step 1. Add 1 teaspoon finely grated lime zest to sugar and cream cheese mixture and substitute 1 tablespoon lime juice for vanilla.

Snickerdoodles

✔ WHY THIS RECIPE WORKS
With their crinkly tops and liberal dusting of cinnamon sugar, chewy snickerdoodles are a favorite in New England. The name is a corruption of a German word that translates as "crinkly noodles." Often, snickerdoodles are just sugar cookies in disguise, flavored too generously with vanilla and without the satisfying chewiness that defines a proper snickerdoodle. We wanted an old-fashioned snickerdoodle, one that met the following criteria: a texture we could sink our teeth into, a slightly tangy flavor, and a crinkly cinnamon-coated surface.

USE TWO LEAVENERS We tested both baking powder and baking soda as well as the traditional combination of baking soda and cream of tartar. As we expected, the latter is essential to this cookie. Double-acting baking powder caused the cookies to rise too much in the oven. The leavening power of baking soda and cream of tartar is short-lived by comparison, so the cookies rise and then fall rather quickly for the characteristic crinkly appearance and the cream of tartar provides the subtle tang in the cookies.

AVOID VANILLA To make the cookies especially tangy, we found it helpful not to add vanilla. The vanilla can distract from the trademark tartness.

ADD PLENTY OF SUGAR We noticed that most of the recipes we tested were not nearly chewy enough. We found that increasing the sugar helped, because sugar doesn't just add sweetness, it affects texture as well.

INCLUDE BUTTER AND SHORTENING We wondered why some traditional snickerdoodle recipes contained vegetable shortening. Although we generally don't recommend using shortening in cookies (it does not taste as good as butter), we thought it might be worth trying in this case. Unlike butter, which contains about 18 percent water, shortening is 100 percent fat. The water in butter evaporates in the oven and helps the cookies to spread. Since shortening does not contain water, in theory it should help reduce spread in the oven and keep cookies thick and chewy. Our tests revealed that this bit of common culinary wisdom is in fact true. After several attempts, we discovered that a 1:1 ratio of shortening to butter keeps the cookies both chewy and buttery tasting.

ROLL IN CINNAMON SUGAR Rolling the balls of dough in cinnamon sugar—we like a full tablespoon for warm spice flavor—imparts a spicy sweet crunch to the cookies.

DON'T OVERBAKE These cookies will look underdone, but once they are just beginning to brown and soft and puffy in the middle, pull them from the oven. They will continue to cook as they cool briefly on the baking sheet.

SNICKERDOODLES
MAKES ABOUT 24 COOKIES

Cream of tartar is essential to the flavor of these cookies and it works in combination with the baking soda to give the cookies lift; do not substitute baking powder. For the best results, bake only one sheet of cookies at a time.

1½ cups (10½ ounces) sugar, plus ¼ cup for rolling
1 tablespoon ground cinnamon
2½ cups (12½ ounces) all-purpose flour
2 teaspoons cream of tartar
1 teaspoon baking soda
½ teaspoon salt
8 tablespoons unsalted butter, softened
8 tablespoons vegetable shortening
2 large eggs

1. Adjust oven rack to middle position and heat oven to 375 degrees. Line 2 baking sheets with parchment paper. Combine ¼ cup sugar and cinnamon in shallow dish. Whisk flour, cream of tartar, baking soda, and salt together in medium bowl.

2. Using stand mixer, beat butter, shortening, and remaining 1½ cups sugar together on medium speed until light and fluffy, 3 to 6 minutes. Beat in eggs, one at a time, until incorporated, about 30 seconds, scraping down bowl as needed.

3. Reduce speed to low and slowly add flour mixture until combined, about 30 seconds. Give dough final stir to ensure that no flour pockets remain.

4. Working with 2 tablespoons of dough at a time, roll into balls. Working in batches, roll half of dough balls in cinnamon sugar to coat and set on prepared sheet spaced 2 inches apart; repeat with remaining dough balls.

5. Bake 1 sheet at a time until edges of cookies are set and just beginning to brown but centers are still soft and puffy, 10 to 12 minutes, rotating sheet halfway through baking. (Cookies will look raw between cracks and seem underdone.)

6. Let cookies cool on sheet for 10 minutes; transfer cookies to wire rack and let cool to room temperature before serving.

BUSTING UP SUGAR CLUMPS

Even when stored in an airtight container, granulated sugar can form large, solid lumps. A few strokes with a potato masher will return it to a pourable state.

Brown Sugar Cookies

BROWNED BUTTER

Browned butter, or *beurre noisette*, as it is called in French, gives our Brown Sugar Cookies and Ultimate Chocolate Chip Cookies (page 183) a deep, rich flavor. Beurre noisette translates literally as "hazelnut butter"; as the butter browns, it takes on the flavor and aroma of toasted nuts. Browned butter is used in both baked goods and savory preparations; brightened with lemon juice, it makes a classic, simple "sauce" for fish *meunière* as well as for vegetables such as asparagus and green beans.

When making browned butter, use a saucepan or skillet with a light-colored interior; the dark color of nonstick or anodized aluminum cookware makes it difficult to judge the color of the butter as it browns. Use medium to medium-high heat, and stir or swirl the butter occasionally so that the milk solids brown evenly; depending on the heat setting and the amount of butter, the process may take as few as 3 minutes if browning just a couple of tablespoons or as long as 10 minutes if browning a full cup. Finally, if not using the browned butter immediately, transfer it to a bowl; if left in the saucepan or skillet, residual heat can cause it to continue cooking—and then it becomes *beurre noir*.

✔ WHY THIS RECIPE WORKS

We wanted to turn up the volume on the sugar cookie by switching out the granulated sugar in favor of brown sugar. We had a clear vision of this cookie. It would be oversized, with a crackling crisp exterior and a chewy interior. And its flavor would scream "brown sugar."

BROWN THE BUTTER Melting the butter is a good start if you want a chewy cookie, but if you brown that butter you develop a range of butterscotch and toffee flavors, too. We add a full tablespoon of vanilla to help boost the nutty flavors in our cookies without using more brown sugar (which would have made them overly sweet). Make sure to use the full ½ teaspoon of salt—you need it to balance the sweetness of these cookies.

LOSE A WHITE Egg whites tend to make cookies cakey—they cause the cookies to puff and dry out. We use a whole egg plus a yolk for richness, leaving out the second white.

USE TWO LEAVENERS Many baked goods with brown sugar call for baking soda. This is because while granulated sugar is neutral, dark brown sugar can be slightly acidic. But when we used baking soda by itself, the cookies had an open, coarse crumb and craggy top. Tasters loved the craggy top, not the coarse crumb. When we used baking powder by itself, the cookies had a finer, tighter crumb but the craggy top disappeared. After a dozen rounds of testing, we settled on using a combination of both leaveners to moderate the coarseness of the crumb without compromising the craggy tops.

ROLL IN BROWN SUGAR Dark brown sugar is the obvious choice for the dough itself—more butterscotch, brown sugar flavor, and more chewiness because it has more moisture and a little more invert sugar than light brown sugar. Rolling balls of dough in more brown sugar helps boost their flavor further

and adding some granulated sugar keeps the brown sugar from clumping.

BAKE ONE SHEET AT A TIME We had hoped to be able to bake two sheets of cookies at a time, but even with rotating and changing tray positions at different times during baking, we could not get two-tray baking to work. Some of the cookies had the right texture, but others were inexplicably dry. Baking one tray at a time allows for even heat distribution and ensures that every cookie has the same texture. It's important not to overbake these cookies. To check cookies for doneness, gently press halfway between the edge and center of the cookie. When the cookie is done, your finger will form an indentation with slight resistance.

BROWN SUGAR COOKIES
MAKES ABOUT 24 COOKIES

Avoid using a nonstick skillet to brown the butter; the dark color of the nonstick coating makes it difficult to gauge when the butter is sufficiently browned. Use fresh, moist brown sugar, as hardened brown sugar will make the cookies too dry. Achieving the proper texture—crisp at the edges and chewy in the middle—is critical to this recipe. Because the cookies are so dark, it's hard to judge doneness by color. Instead, gently press halfway between the edge and center of the cookie. When it's done, it will form an indentation with slight resistance. Check early and err on the side of underdone.

14	tablespoons unsalted butter
1¾	cups packed (12¼ ounces) dark brown sugar, plus ¼ cup for rolling
¼	cup granulated sugar
2	cups plus 2 tablespoons (10⅔ ounces) all-purpose flour
½	teaspoon baking soda
¼	teaspoon baking powder
½	teaspoon salt
1	large egg plus 1 large yolk
1	tablespoon vanilla extract

1. Melt 10 tablespoons butter in 10-inch skillet over medium-high heat. Continue cooking, swirling pan constantly, until butter is dark golden brown and has nutty aroma, 1 to 3 minutes. Transfer browned butter to large heatproof bowl. Add remaining 4 tablespoons butter and stir until completely melted; set aside for 15 minutes.

2. Meanwhile, adjust oven rack to middle position and heat oven to 350 degrees. Line 2 baking sheets with parchment paper. In shallow dish, mix ¼ cup brown sugar and granulated sugar until well combined; set aside. Whisk flour, baking soda, and baking powder together in medium bowl; set aside.

3. Add remaining 1¾ cups brown sugar and salt to bowl with cooled butter; mix until no sugar lumps remain, about 30 seconds. Scrape down bowl; add egg and yolk, and vanilla and mix until fully incorporated, about 30 seconds. Scrape down bowl. Add flour mixture and mix until just combined, about 1 minute. Give dough final stir to ensure that no flour pockets remain.

4. Working with 2 tablespoons of dough at a time, roll into balls. Roll half of dough balls in sugar mixture to coat. Space dough balls 2 inches apart on prepared sheet; repeat with remaining dough balls.

5. Bake 1 sheet at a time until cookies are browned and still puffy and edges have begun to set but centers are still soft (cookies will look raw between cracks and seem underdone), 12 to 14 minutes, rotating sheet halfway through baking. Let cookies cool on baking sheet for 5 minutes; transfer cookies to wire rack and let cool to room temperature before serving.

PREVENTING CURLING PARCHMENT PAPER

To prevent parchment paper from curling toward the center as you're portioning out cookie or biscuit dough, place a small magnet at each corner of the sheet to hold down the paper. After you're done portioning, remove the magnets and place the baking sheet in the oven.

Ultimate Chocolate Chip Cookies

✔ WHY THIS RECIPE WORKS

Since Nestlé first began printing the recipe for Toll House cookies on the back of chocolate chip bags in 1939, generations of bakers have packed chocolate chip cookies into lunches and taken them to potlucks. But after a few samples, we wondered if this was really the best that a chocolate chip cookie could be. We wanted to refine this recipe to create a moist and chewy chocolate chip cookie with crisp edges and deep notes of toffee and butterscotch to balance its sweetness.

CHANGE THE SUGAR RATIO Traditionally, Toll House cookies have a 1:1 ratio of brown sugar to white sugar. White sugar granules lend crispness, while brown sugar, which is more hygroscopic (meaning it attracts and retains water, mainly from the air) than white sugar, enhances chewiness. All that moisture sounds like a good thing—but it's too good, in fact. Cookies made with all brown sugar are beyond chewy. They are so moist they're nearly floppy. We got the best results when we used a 3:2 ratio of dark brown sugar to white. This recipe works with light brown sugar, but the cookies will be less full-flavored.

BROWN THE BUTTER, LOSE ONE WHITE As with our Brown Sugar Cookies (page 180), we brown the butter here for flavor. (Melting the butter increases chewiness as well.) Losing an egg white (which makes cookies more cakey) also improves chewiness.

WHISK AND WAIT After stirring together the butter, sugar, and eggs, wait.

After 10 minutes, the sugar will have dissolved and the mixture will turn thick and shiny, like frosting. All that's left is to stir in a mix of flour and baking soda and of course, chocolate chips. The finished cookies will emerge from the oven with a slight glossy sheen and an alluring surface of cracks and crags, with a deep, toffeelike flavor. This is because by allowing the sugar to rest in the liquids, more of it dissolves in the small amount of moisture before baking. The dissolved sugar caramelizes more easily and helps to create a cookie with crisp edges and a chewy center.

BAKE IN A MODERATE OVEN With caramelization in mind, we bake our cookies in a 375-degree oven—the same as for Toll House cookies. Baking two trays a time may be convenient, but it leads to uneven cooking with our recipe. The cookies on the top tray are often browner around the edges than those on the bottom, even when rotated halfway through baking. These cookies will finish crisp and chewy, gooey with chocolate, with a complex medley of sweet, buttery, caramel, and toffee flavors. In other words? Perfect.

ULTIMATE CHOCOLATE CHIP COOKIES

MAKES ABOUT 16 LARGE COOKIES

Avoid using a nonstick skillet to brown the butter; the dark color of the nonstick coating makes it difficult to gauge when the butter is sufficiently browned. Use fresh, moist brown sugar, as hardened brown sugar will make the cookies too dry. This recipe works with light brown sugar, but the cookies will be less full-flavored. See page 9 for information on toasting nuts.

1¾   cups (8¾ ounces) all-purpose flour
½   teaspoon baking soda
14   tablespoons unsalted butter
¾   cup packed (5¼ ounces) dark brown sugar

½   cup (3½ ounces) granulated sugar
1   teaspoon salt
2   teaspoons vanilla extract
1   large egg plus 1 large yolk
1¼   cups (7½ ounces) semisweet or bittersweet chocolate chips or chunks
¾   cup pecans or walnuts, toasted and chopped (optional)

1. Adjust oven rack to middle position and heat oven to 375 degrees. Line 2 baking sheets with parchment paper. Whisk flour and baking soda together in medium bowl; set aside.

2. Melt 10 tablespoons butter in 10-inch skillet over medium-high heat. Continue cooking, swirling pan constantly, until butter is dark golden brown and has nutty aroma, 1 to 3 minutes. Transfer browned butter to large heatproof bowl. Add remaining 4 tablespoons butter and stir until completely melted.

3. Add brown sugar, granulated sugar, salt, and vanilla to melted butter; whisk until fully incorporated. Add egg and yolk; whisk until mixture is smooth with no sugar lumps remaining, about 30 seconds. Let mixture stand for 3 minutes, then whisk for 30 seconds. Repeat process of resting and whisking 2 more times until mixture is thick, smooth, and shiny. Using rubber spatula, stir in flour mixture until just combined, about 1 minute. Stir in chocolate chips and nuts, if using. Give dough final stir to ensure that no flour pockets remain and ingredients are evenly distributed.

4. Working with 3 tablespoons of dough at a time, roll into balls and space 2 inches apart on prepared sheets.

5. Bake 1 sheet at a time until cookies are golden brown and still puffy and edges have begun to set but centers are still soft, 10 to 14 minutes, rotating sheet halfway through baking. Transfer sheet to wire rack; let cookies cool to room temperature.

FREEZING COOKIE DOUGH

Keeping some frozen dough on hand means that you can bake just as many, or as few, cookies as you like whenever the feeling strikes. To freeze the dough, form it into balls, arrange the balls on a rimmed baking sheet or cookie sheet, and place the sheet in the freezer. Once the individual balls of dough are frozen, place them in a zipper-lock freezer bag and stow the bag in the freezer. To bake, arrange the frozen cookies (do not thaw) on a parchment-lined baking sheet and bake as directed, increasing the baking time by 2 to 5 minutes.

Troubleshooting Cookies

Cookies are simple to make, yet sometimes there can be issues—from batches that don't add up to a correct yield to cookies that burn on their undersides. Here are common cookie-making problems and their solutions.

PROBLEM: The last cookies always seem short on chips
SOLUTION: Reserve some morsels to add later

When chocolate chips, nuts, or raisins are in the mix, the last few cookies from a batch never seem to have as many of these goodies as the first few. To get around this, reserve some of the mix-ins and stir them into the dough after about half of it has been scooped out.

PROBLEM: Cookies don't add up to the correct yield
SOLUTION: Use a portion scoop

When cookies are portioned out larger or smaller than the recipe directs, they may not produce the intended texture. To ensure consistent size and the proper yield, we use a portion scoop. (We keep many different sizes on hand for just this purpose.)

PROBLEM: Cookies keep burning on bottom
SOLUTION: Use a light-colored baking sheet and line with parchment paper

We typically don't like light-colored bakeware since it doesn't absorb heat as well as darker finishes, leading to spotty browning. But the cookie sheet is the exception. All of the dark nonstick cookie sheets we've tested consistently overbrown the bottoms of cookies. Light-colored sheets, on the other hand, prevent over-browning but are prone to sticking. We get around this by baking cookies on parchment paper.

PROBLEM: Cookies run together
SOLUTION: Bake in staggered rows

When scoops of dough are placed too close together on the sheet, the cookies can fuse together. To ensure enough space between cookies, alternate the rows. For example, place three cookies in the first row, two in the second, three in the third, and so on.

PROBLEM: Chewy cookies that aren't chewy
SOLUTION: Underbake

To ensure a chewy texture, take cookies out of the oven when they are still slightly underdone, which often means they will droop over the end of a spatula. Crevices should appear moist and edges on smooth cookies should be lightly browned.

PROBLEM: Unevenly baked batches
SOLUTION: Rotate during baking

The temperature in most ovens varies from front to back, top to bottom—even side to side. To prevent uneven baking, rotate the cookie sheet partway through baking so that the back side faces front.

PROBLEM: It's hard to tell when dark chocolate cookies are done
SOLUTION: Press the middle

Most cookies, irrespective of texture, are done when pressing them lightly with your finger leaves just a slight indentation.

PROBLEM: Overly crisp edges
SOLUTION: Briefly chill dough and don't use a hot sheet

If your kitchen is particularly hot, the butter in the dough can start to melt, softening the dough and leading to overcooked edges. If the dough seems too soft, chill it for 10 to 15 minutes before portioning.

Putting raw dough on cookie sheets still warm from the oven can cause them to begin spreading, leading to burnt edges. Always allow baking sheets to cool completely before adding more batches. To expedite cooling, rinse warm—but not hot— sheets under cold tap water.

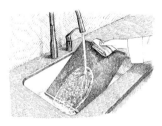

Thin, Crisp Chocolate Chip Cookies

✓ WHY THIS RECIPE WORKS

While our Ultimate Chocolate Chip Cookies (page 183) are rich and buttery, with soft, tender cores and crisp edges, we sometimes get a hankering for a thin, crisp version. We could see the thin, crisp cookies clearly. They would be very flat, almost praline in appearance, and would pack a big crunch. They'd have the simple, gratifying flavors of deeply caramelized sugar and rich butter. The chips, tender and super-chocolaty, would not overwhelm but leave plenty of room for enjoyment of the surrounding cookie.

USE LESS BROWN SUGAR Aside from contributing sweetness, sugar also affects the texture, flavor, and color of the cookies. Doughs high in granulated sugar yield crisp cookies. As the cookies cool, the sugar crystallizes and the cookies harden. Brown sugar, by contrast, contains 35 percent more moisture and is also more hygroscopic (that is, it more readily absorbs moisture). Consequently, cookies made with brown sugar come out of the oven tender and pliable and often soften further as they stand. Nevertheless, we knew the recipe had to include some brown sugar, because it helps impart the irresistible butterscotch flavor we associate with chocolate chip cookies. After some tinkering, we settled on ⅓ cup light brown sugar and ½ cup granulated sugar, yielding cookies with a notable butterscotch flavor and sufficient crunch.

AVOID CREAMING AND ADD MILK FOR THIN COOKIES A cookie's spread is determined largely by the type, treatment, and melting properties of the fat in the dough. When butter and sugar are creamed, rigid sugar crystals cut into the butterfat and create air cells. As the remaining ingredients are incorporated into the airy mixture, the air cells get locked up in the dough and capture moisture from the butter (and other ingredients) as it vaporizes in the oven. The cells expand and the cookies rise. Our other option, melting the butter, was much more successful. Because melted butter, unlike creamed butter, does not accommodate air cells, the moisture from various ingredients has nowhere to go except out. To get the cookies thinner still, we add a couple tablespoons of milk. Adding a small amount of liquid to a low-moisture dough thins the dough and enhances its spread.

ADD BAKING SODA FOR BROWNING Having spent all of our time thus far perfecting the cookies' texture and spread, we were surprised to notice that they were looking slightly pallid and dull. Knowing that corn syrup browns at a lower temperature than sugar, we tried adding a few tablespoons. As it happened, the corn syrup made the surface of the cookies shiny and crackly. Despite their new spiffy, dressed-up look, though, they remained a little on the pale side. We rectified the situation by adding a bit of baking soda, which enhances browning reactions in doughs. The cookies went from washed-out to a beautiful deep golden brown.

BAKE ONE SHEET AT A TIME After a few batches, we found that these cookies need to be baked one sheet at a time. In 12 minutes at 375 degrees, they spread, flatten, and caramelize, and when cooled they are thin, crisp, and delicious.

BAKING COOKIES IN A CONVECTION OVEN?

Most ovens heat from the bottom when set to "Bake." Cookies bake according to their orientation to the heat source, so if you are baking two sheets of cookies at a time (which is standard), they will brown unevenly. To prevent that, recipes often suggest switching and rotating the sheets halfway through. That's unnecessary when you bake on a convection setting; a fan (or fans) in the back of the oven circulates the hot air, and this air distribution promotes even cooking in all parts of the oven.

But while many modern ovens are equipped with a convection feature, most recipes have been developed for the standard baking cycle. We tried baking ordinary recipes in a convection oven. We baked shortbread rounds at 400 degrees and sugar cookies at 375 degrees. Even with two trays in the oven at once, all the cookies browned evenly, but they overbrowned long before the recipes' suggested baking times. We found that if we reduced the time slightly and the temperature by 25 degrees, the convection oven produced two sheets of evenly baked cookies without our needing to rotate the sheets.

Is it possible to refrigerate cookie dough and then bake the cookies a few at a time over several days? We found that the presence and type of leavener in the dough is the key to the answer. To sort through holding times for doughs with different (or no) leaveners, we made four batches of sugar cookies: one with baking powder, one with baking soda, one with both, and the last (an icebox cookie) with neither. We baked six cookies from each batch. We found that the dough with baking soda held well for two days, but was a little flatter on the third. Cookies with both baking powder and soda began to lose lift after four days. Baking powder–leavened cookie dough maintained good lift all week. The unleavened cookies held well all week.

The cookies with baking soda were the losers in the holding test because soda is a single-acting leavener, meaning that it begins to make lift-giving air bubbles as soon as it gets wet and comes in contact with an acid. Once started, this action continues until all the leavening power is spent—so there's a time limit. Baking powder is double acting, so it releases gas twice: once when it gets wet, and again when it heats up. So even if the first batch of air bubbles is spent, the second action will allow cookies to rise in the oven. The bottom line? Cookie dough made with baking soda is best used within two days. Recipes with both powder and soda can be made four days ahead. Recipes with baking powder or no leavener can be made up to seven days ahead.

THIN AND CRISPY CHOCOLATE CHIP COOKIES

MAKES ABOUT 40 COOKIES

Whole or low-fat milk can be used here.

- 1½ cups (7½ ounces) all-purpose flour
- ¾ teaspoon baking soda
- ¼ teaspoon salt
- 8 tablespoons unsalted butter, melted and cooled
- ½ cup (3½ ounces) granulated sugar
- ⅓ cup packed (2⅓ ounces) light brown sugar
- 2 tablespoons light corn syrup
- 1 large egg yolk
- 2 tablespoons milk
- 1 tablespoon vanilla extract
- ¾ cup (4½ ounces) semisweet chocolate chips

1. Adjust oven rack to middle position and heat oven to 375 degrees. Line 2 baking sheets with parchment paper.

2. Whisk flour, baking soda, and salt together in medium bowl; set aside.

3. Using stand mixer fitted with paddle, beat melted butter, granulated sugar, brown sugar, and corn syrup at low speed until thoroughly blended, about 1 minute. Add egg yolk, milk, and vanilla; mix until fully incorporated and smooth, about 1 minute, scraping down bowl as needed. With mixer still running on low, slowly add dry ingredients and mix until just combined. Stir in chocolate chips. Give dough final stir to ensure that no flour pockets remain and ingredients are evenly distributed.

4. Working with 1 tablespoon of dough at a time, roll into balls and space 2 inches apart on prepared sheets. Bake 1 sheet at a time until cookies are deep golden brown and flat, about 12 minutes, rotating sheet halfway through baking.

5. Let cookies cool on sheet for 3 minutes; transfer cookies to wire rack and let cool to room temperature before serving.

Chewy Chocolate Cookies

✓ WHY THIS RECIPE WORKS

Cookie recipes that trumpet their extreme chocolate flavor always leave us a bit suspicious. While they provide plenty of intensity, these over-the-top confections also tend to be delicate and crumbly, more like cakey brownies than cookies. We set out to make an exceptionally rich chocolate cookie that we could sink our teeth into—without having it fall apart.

DELIVER DEEP CHOCOLATE FLAVOR WITH COCOA POWDER Our first batch, which used modest amounts of cocoa powder and melted chocolate, baked up too cakey and tender—just what we didn't want. The chocolate was the culprit—its fat was softening the dough. We scaled back the chocolate until we eliminated it entirely, which made the cookies less cakey and tender, and thus, more cookielike. To restore chocolate flavor without adding too much fat, we increased the cocoa powder and reduced the flour.

ADD BITTERSWEET CHOCOLATE FOR RICHNESS We fold chopped bittersweet chocolate into our dough; the chunks stay intact and add intense flavor.

DITCH THE YOLK Using an egg white rather than a whole egg (or yolk) gives us the structure we want and adding dark corn syrup gives the cookies a nice chewiness and lends a hint of caramel flavor.

TAKE A PAGE FROM MOLASSES COOKIES Molasses cookies are the ultimate in chewiness so we tried augmenting some of our sugar (both white and brown) with molasses for cookies with great chew. However, the flavor was less than perfect. We found a better match to chocolate with dark corn syrup. It lends a hint of caramel flavor that enhances the chocolate flavor and helps develop, a moist, chewy crumb.

CHILL DOUGH BEFORE SHAPING Chilling the dough before shaping helps firm up the dough so it doesn't spread too much once it hits a hot oven.

ROLL IN SUGAR FOR A SWEET CRUNCH After rolling the dough into balls, we dip them in granulated sugar before baking. When they come out of the oven, the cookies have a sweet crunch and an attractive crackled appearance.

CHEWY CHOCOLATE COOKIES
MAKES ABOUT 16 COOKIES

Use a high-quality bittersweet or semisweet chocolate here. See our top-rated brands on page 496. Light brown sugar can be substituted for the dark, as can light corn syrup for the dark, but with some sacrifice in flavor.

⅓	cup (2⅓ ounces) granulated sugar, plus ½ cup for rolling
1½	cups (7½ ounces) all-purpose flour
¾	cup (2¼ ounces) Dutch-processed cocoa powder
½	teaspoon baking soda
¼	teaspoon plus ⅛ teaspoon salt
½	cup dark corn syrup
1	large egg white
1	teaspoon vanilla extract
12	tablespoons unsalted butter, softened
⅓	cup packed (2⅓ ounces) dark brown sugar
4	ounces bittersweet or semisweet chocolate, chopped into ½-inch pieces

1. Adjust oven racks to upper-middle and lower-middle positions and heat oven to 375 degrees. Line 2 baking sheets with parchment paper. Place ½ cup granulated sugar in shallow dish. Whisk flour, cocoa, baking soda, and salt together in medium bowl. Whisk corn syrup, egg white, and vanilla together in small bowl.

2. Using stand mixer fitted with paddle, beat butter, brown sugar, and remaining ⅓ cup granulated sugar at medium-high speed until light and fluffy, about 2 minutes. Reduce speed to medium-low, add corn syrup mixture, and beat until fully incorporated, about 20 seconds, scraping down bowl as needed with rubber spatula. Reduce speed to low, add flour mixture and chopped chocolate, and mix until just incorporated, about 30 seconds, scraping down bowl as needed. Give dough final stir to ensure that no flour pockets remain and ingredients are evenly distributed. Refrigerate dough for 30 minutes to firm slightly.

3. Working with 2 tablespoons of dough at a time, roll into balls. Roll half of dough balls in sugar to coat. Space dough balls 2 inches apart on prepared sheet; repeat with remaining dough balls. Bake until cookies are puffed and cracked and edges have begun to set but centers are still soft (cookies will look raw between cracks and seem underdone), 10 to 11 minutes, switching and rotating sheets halfway through baking. Do not overbake.

4. Let cookies cool on sheets for 5 minutes; transfer cookies to wire rack and let cool to room temperature before serving.

EASY COOKIE STORAGE

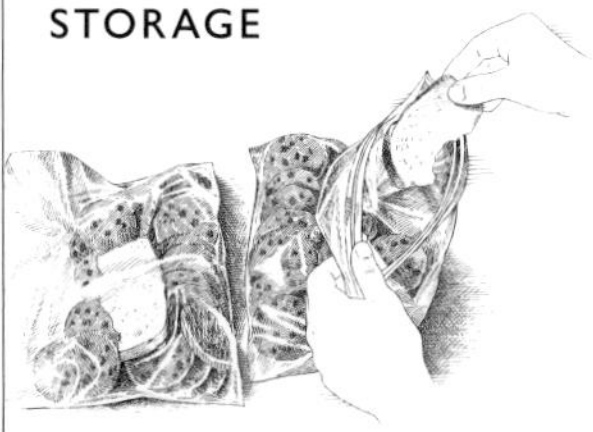

A. To keep chewy cookies from turning dry and brittle, store them in a zipper-lock bag at room temperature with a small piece of bread (no more than half of a slice) placed inside.

B. Zipper-lock bags also come in handy with decorative cookie jars. These cookie jars, like those made from ceramic, are convenient and attractive, but not always airtight. Simply line the inside of the jar with a zipper-lock bag for airtight storage.

Double-Chocolate Cookies

REVIVING STALE COOKIES

To restore cookies to just-baked freshness, recrisp them in a 425-degree oven for 4 to 5 minutes. Let the cookies cool on the baking sheet for a couple of minutes before removing them and serve them while they're warm.

✔ WHY THIS RECIPE WORKS

One of our greatest obsessions in baking has been the first transcendent bite of the perfect chocolate cookie, still warm out of the oven. We wanted a cookie with all the allure of a moist and fudgy brownie with a deep, complex chocolate flavor.

CREAM THE BUTTER AND SUGAR—DIFFERENTLY When we started creaming the butter and beating the eggs into it after creaming, we noticed an immediate improvement—the cookies were thicker and chewier. However, we finally settled on a modified creaming method with minimal beating to produce moist cookies that were chewy, but not cakey.

ADD COCOA POWDER AND MELTED CHOCOLATE Cocoa powder gives our cookies deep chocolate flavor and melted semisweet chocolate reinforces the chocolate flavor and adds deep richness.

ACCENT THE CHOCOLATE Espresso powder heightens the chocolate flavor in our cookies and vanilla extract rounds it out.

USE A MIX OF WHITE AND BROWN SUGAR Rather than relying on all granulated sugar, we combine it with brown sugar, which improves the flavor and adds just a bit more moisture for truly chewy brownielike cookies.

DON'T OVERBAKE Avoiding overbaking may be a given but it's especially important for these cookies; they will appear underbaked when removed from the oven, but will firm up as they cool.

DOUBLE-CHOCOLATE COOKIES
MAKES ABOUT 42 COOKIES

Use a high-quality bittersweet or semisweet chocolate here.

- 2 cups (10 ounces) all-purpose flour
- ½ cup (1½ ounces) Dutch-processed cocoa powder
- 2 teaspoons baking powder
- ½ teaspoon salt
- 1 pound semisweet chocolate, chopped
- 4 large eggs
- 2 teaspoons vanilla extract
- 2 teaspoons instant espresso or coffee powder
- 10 tablespoons unsalted butter, softened
- 1½ cups packed (10½ ounces) light brown sugar
- ½ cup (3½ ounces) granulated sugar

1. Adjust oven racks to upper-middle and lower-middle positions and heat oven to 350 degrees. Line 2 baking sheets with parchment paper. Whisk flour, cocoa, baking powder, and salt together in medium bowl; set aside.

2. Microwave chocolate at 50 percent power for 2 minutes. Stir chocolate and continue heating until melted, stirring once every additional minute; set aside to cool slightly. Whisk eggs and vanilla together in medium bowl, sprinkle espresso powder over top to dissolve, and set aside.

3. Using stand mixer fitted with paddle, beat butter, brown sugar, and granulated

sugar at medium speed until combined, about 45 seconds; mixture will look granular. Reduce speed to low, gradually add egg mixture, and mix until incorporated, about 45 seconds. Add melted chocolate in steady stream and mix until combined, about 40 seconds, scraping down bowl as needed. With mixer still running on low, add dry ingredients and mix until just combined. Do not overbeat. Cover bowl of dough with plastic wrap and let stand at room temperature until consistency is scoopable and fudgelike, about 30 minutes.

4. Working with 2 tablespoons of dough at a time, roll into balls and space 1½ inches apart on prepared sheets.

5. Bake until edges of cookies have just begun to set but centers are still very soft, about 10 minutes, switching and rotating sheets halfway through baking. Let cookies cool on sheets for 10 minutes; transfer cookies to wire rack and let cool to room temperature before serving.

TRIPLE-CHOCOLATE COOKIES

The addition of chocolate chips will slightly increase the yield of the cookies.

Add 2 cups semisweet chocolate chips to batter after dry ingredients are incorporated in step 3.

Chewy Oatmeal Cookies

✔ WHY THIS RECIPE WORKS

When developing this recipe, we wanted an oversized cookie that was chewy and moist. Most oatmeal cookies seem dry to us, and the flavor of the oats seems too weak. Many recipes don't call for enough oats, and spices often overwhelm the flavor of the oats that are there.

INCREASE THE OATS In our testing, we found that we needed 2 cups of oats for every cup of flour—far more oats than in most recipes. We prefer old-fashioned rolled oats to quick oats; the old-fashioned have better texture and flavor.

INCLUDE BOTH WHITE AND BROWN SUGARS We thought that using all white sugar would give us a clean-tasting sweet cookie that wouldn't overpower the oats. Instead, our cookies baked up dull-tasting.

Adding brown sugar gives us especially moist, rich-tasting cookies.

LIMIT THE SPICES We decided to eliminate cinnamon, a common ingredient in these cookies, because it was overpowering the oats. We wanted some spice, however, and chose nutmeg, which has a cleaner, subtler flavor that works well with the oats.

BE GENEROUS WHEN PORTIONING We found that shaping the dough into 2-inch balls (rather than dropping the meager rounded tablespoon called for in most recipes) helped keep the cookies more moist and chewy, especially in the center, which remains a bit underbaked in an oversized cookie. Smaller cookies are considerably drier and more cakelike, something we did not want in an oatmeal cookie.

MAKING THE MOST OF WHOLE NUTMEG

When you have grated a whole nutmeg seed to the point where you are risking your fingertips, don't throw the little nub away. Eliminate waste by grinding the leftover nutmeg with a mortar and pestle. It is actually fairly soft and pulverizes quite easily.

BAKING SHEET LINERS VERSUS PARCHMENT

With so many brands of reusable baking-pan liners available, we wondered if any could replace the countless rolls of parchment paper the test kitchen goes through every week. Like parchment, these liners offer nonstick release and easy cleanup. But they also offer multiple usage—"thousands of times," according to package claims.

We pitted five liners against plain old parchment by baking cookies on our favorite baking sheets. Sticking was never an issue and the cookies browned fine as long as the liner lay flat. But if the liner edges curved upward, some of the cookies came out pale and unevenly browned. This was a problem on about half of the baking sheets we tested. Lightweight liners can be cut to fit any size baking sheet, but these liners were less durable in our tests, creasing slightly after just a few washes. The heavy-duty, fiberglass-weave liners are designed to fit only standard half-sheet pans (about 18 by 13 inches), so cutting to fit isn't an option.

So where did we come out? If your baking sheet is exactly the right size, the heavy-duty baking mats we tested work fine, and they're not that hard to clean. Frankly, though, we're not sold on any of them. In the long run, parchment paper may be the most expensive option, but its versatility and disposability make it worth the dough.

BIG AND CHEWY OATMEAL-RAISIN COOKIES

MAKES ABOUT 18 LARGE COOKIES

If you prefer a less sweet cookie, you can reduce the granulated sugar to ¾ cup, but you will lose some crispness. Do not use instant or quick oats. Do not overbake these cookies. The edges should be brown, but the rest of the cookie should be very light in color.

- 1½ cups (7½ ounces) all-purpose flour
- ½ teaspoon salt
- ½ teaspoon baking powder
- ¼ teaspoon ground nutmeg
- 16 tablespoons unsalted butter, softened
- 1 cup packed (7 ounces) light brown sugar
- 1 cup (7 ounces) granulated sugar
- 2 large eggs
- 3 cups (9 ounces) old-fashioned rolled oats
- 1½ cups (7½ ounces) raisins (optional)

1. Adjust oven racks to upper-middle and lower-middle positions and heat oven to 350 degrees. Line 2 baking sheets with parchment paper. Whisk flour, salt, baking powder, and nutmeg together in medium bowl; set aside.

2. Using stand mixer fitted with paddle, beat butter, brown sugar, and granulated sugar at medium speed until light and fluffy, about 2 minutes. Add eggs, one at a time, and mix until combined, about 30 seconds.

3. Reduce speed to low and slowly add dry ingredients until combined, about 30 seconds. Mix in oats and raisins, if using, until just incorporated. Give dough final stir to ensure that no flour pockets remain and ingredients are evenly distributed.

4. Working with 2 tablespoons of dough at a time, roll into balls and space 2 inches apart on prepared sheets.

5. Bake until cookies turn golden brown around edges, 22 to 25 minutes, switching and rotating sheets halfway through baking. Let cookies cool on sheets for 2 minutes; transfer cookies to wire rack and let cool to room temperature before serving.

BIG AND CHEWY OATMEAL-DATE COOKIES

Substitute 1½ cups chopped dates for raisins.

BIG AND CHEWY OATMEAL-GINGER COOKIES

Omit raisins and add ¾ teaspoon ground ginger.

BIG AND CHEWY OATMEAL–CHOCOLATE CHIP COOKIES

Substitute 1½ cups semisweet chocolate chips for raisins.

BIG AND CHEWY OATMEAL-NUT COOKIES

The almonds can be ground in a food processor or blender.

Omit raisins, decrease flour to 1⅓ cups, and add ¼ cup ground almonds and 1 cup chopped walnuts along with oats.

BIG AND CHEWY ORANGE AND ALMOND OATMEAL COOKIES

Omit raisins and add 2 tablespoons grated orange zest and 1 cup chopped toasted almonds along with oats.

Chocolate-Chunk Oatmeal Cookies

✔ WHY THIS RECIPE WORKS

It's easy to get carried away and overload cookie dough with a crazy jumble of ingredients, resulting in a poorly textured cookie monster. Our ultimate oatmeal cookie would have just the right amount of added ingredients and an ideal texture—crisp around the edges and chewy in the middle.

MAKING LOADED OATMEAL COOKIES Sure, we like plain oatmeal cookies but here we wanted something special, loaded with flavorful ingredients. Many recipes add too many goodies to the batter. We found that a careful balance of bittersweet chocolate chunks (semisweet is too sweet), pecans (toasting is essential to bring out their flavor), and dried sour cherries (you need something tart) is the way to make a truly great oatmeal cookie. No spices. No coconut. No raisins or dried tropical fruits.

START WITH THE RIGHT OATS When baking we find that old-fashioned oats are far superior to the other choices. Steel-cut oats are great for breakfast but make dry, pebbly cookies. Instant oats will create dense, mealy cookies lacking in good oat flavor. Quick oats are OK, but they taste somewhat bland, and the cookies won't be quite as chewy.

USE ALL BROWN SUGAR We use brown sugar to help add moisture (it is more moist than white sugar). After testing a half-dozen combinations, we found that using all dark brown sugar is best. All light brown sugar is the second best option. In addition to being more moist, the cookies made with brown sugar are chewier than cookies made with granulated, and the brown sugar also gives the cookies a rich, dark color and deep caramel flavor.

PICK TWO LEAVENERS We began making these cookies with baking soda, which made the cookies crisp from the inside out—a problem, since we want a chewy interior and a crisp exterior. When we switched to baking powder, the cookies puffed in the oven and then collapsed, losing their shape and yielding not a hint of crispy exterior. Because we want a combination of crisp edges and chewy centers, we use a combination of baking powder and soda. This pairing produces cookies that are light and crisp on the outside but chewy, dense, and soft in the center.

CHOCOLATE-CHUNK OATMEAL COOKIES WITH PECANS AND DRIED CHERRIES

MAKES ABOUT 16 LARGE COOKIES

We like these cookies made with pecans and dried sour cherries, but walnuts or skinned hazelnuts can be substituted for the pecans and dried cranberries for the cherries. Quick oats used in place of the old-fashioned oats will yield a cookie with slightly less chewiness.

1¼	cups (6¼ ounces) all-purpose flour
¾	teaspoon baking powder
½	teaspoon baking soda
½	teaspoon salt
1¼	cups (3¾ ounces) old-fashioned rolled oats
1	cup pecans, toasted and chopped
1	cup (4 ounces) dried sour cherries, chopped coarse
4	ounces bittersweet chocolate, chopped into chocolate chip–size chunks
12	tablespoons unsalted butter, softened
1½	cups packed (10½ ounces) dark brown sugar
1	large egg
1	teaspoon vanilla extract

1. Adjust oven racks to upper-middle and lower-middle positions and heat oven to 350 degrees. Line 2 baking sheets with parchment paper.

2. Whisk flour, baking powder, baking soda, and salt together in medium bowl. In second medium bowl, stir oats, pecans, cherries, and chocolate together.

3. Using stand mixer fitted with paddle, beat butter and sugar at medium speed until no sugar lumps remain, about 1 minute, scraping down bowl as needed. Add egg and vanilla and beat on medium-low until fully incorporated, about 30 seconds, scraping down bowl as needed. Reduce speed to low, add flour mixture, and mix until just combined, about 30 seconds. Gradually add oat-nut mixture;

mix until just incorporated. Give dough final stir to ensure that no flour pockets remain and ingredients are evenly distributed.

4. Working with ¼ cup of dough at a time, roll into balls and space 2½ inches apart on prepared sheets. Press dough to 1-inch thickness using bottom of greased measuring cup. Bake until cookies are medium brown and edges have begun to set but centers are still soft (cookies will seem underdone and will appear raw, wet, and shiny in cracks) 20 to 22 minutes, switching and rotating sheets halfway through baking.

5. Let cookies cool on sheets for 5 minutes; transfer cookies to wire rack and let cool to room temperature before serving.

SMART COOKIE SHAPING

Don't let the lack of a portion scoop stand in the way of swiftly portioning cookie dough. Fill a ¼-cup measure (equal to 4 tablespoons) with dough and then divide it according to the desired size (e.g., halved for 2 tablespoons).

Thin and Crispy Oatmeal Cookies

✓ WHY THIS RECIPE WORKS

Thin and crispy oatmeal cookies can be irresistible—crunchy and delicate, these cookies really let the flavor of the oats take center stage. But the usual ingredients that give thick, chewy oatmeal cookies great texture—generous amounts of sugar and butter, a high ratio of oats to flour, a modest amount of leavener, eggs, raisins, and nuts—won't all fit in a thin, crispy cookie. We wanted to adjust the standard ingredients to create a crisp, delicate cookie in which the simple flavor of buttery oats really stands out.

GO WITH OLD-FASHIONED The toasty flavor and not-too-hearty chew of old-fashioned rolled oats make the best cookies

CREAM THE BUTTER Creaming the butter, rather than melting it, tends to make a crispier cookie. When solid butter is mixed with sugar, air is incorporated into the

mixture and held there by the crystals of solid fat. This is especially true when they're mixed on medium speed until light and fluffy. This extra air allows the cookies to dry faster in the oven, producing crispier cookies. Limiting the sugar also helps with crispness (the greater the amount of sugar, the chewier the cookie). Using all granulated sugar makes the cookies hard and crunchy, with a one-dimensional, overly sweet flavor. Using light brown sugar in place of some of the granulated aids in the flavor—with subtle caramel notes—without compromising texture.

SPREAD EVEN If the cookies don't spread evenly, the edges end up thinner and crispier than the center, which is thicker and chewier. We wanted to create a dough that would spread evenly, but a liquid-y dough baked up too thin, like lace cookies. We found that using two leaveners, and plenty of each, helped. During baking, large carbon dioxide bubbles created by the baking soda and baking powder (upped from our traditional recipe) caused the cookies to puff up, collapse, and spread out, producing the thin, flat cookies we were looking for.

PRESS, THEN BAKE   Pressing the dough balls flat encourages an even spread. Baking the cookies all the way through until they are fully set and evenly browned from center to edge makes them crisp throughout but not tough.

THIN AND CRISPY OATMEAL COOKIES
MAKES ABOUT 24 COOKIES

Do not use instant or quick oats.

I	cup (5 ounces) all-purpose flour
¾	teaspoon baking powder
½	teaspoon baking soda
½	teaspoon salt
14	tablespoons unsalted butter, softened but still cool
I	cup (7 ounces) granulated sugar
¼	cup packed (1 ¾ ounces) light brown sugar
I	large egg
I	teaspoon vanilla extract
2½	cups (7½ ounces) old-fashioned rolled oats

1. Adjust oven rack to middle position and heat oven to 350 degrees. Line 3 baking sheets with parchment paper. Whisk flour, baking powder, baking soda, and salt in medium bowl; set aside.

2. Using stand mixer fitted with paddle, beat butter, granulated sugar, and brown sugar at medium-low speed until just combined, about 20 seconds. Increase speed to medium and continue to beat until light and fluffy, about 1 minute longer, scraping down bowl as needed. Add egg and vanilla and beat on medium-low until fully incorporated, about

30 seconds, scraping down bowl as needed. Reduce speed to low, add flour mixture, and mix until just incorporated and smooth, about 10 seconds. With mixer still running, gradually add oats and mix until well incorporated, about 20 seconds. Give dough final stir to ensure that no flour pockets remain and ingredients are evenly distributed.

3. Working with 2 tablespoons of dough at a time, roll into balls and space 2½ inches apart on prepared sheets. Using fingertips, gently press each dough ball to ¾-inch thickness.

4. Bake 1 sheet at a time until cookies are deep golden brown, edges are crisp, and centers yield to slight pressure when pressed, 13 to 16 minutes, rotating sheet halfway through baking. Transfer sheet to wire rack; let cookies cool completely before serving.

THIN AND CRISPY COCONUT-OATMEAL COOKIES

Decrease oats to 2 cups and add 1½ cups sweetened flaked coconut to batter with oats in step 2.

THIN AND CRISPY ORANGE-ALMOND OATMEAL COOKIES

Beat 2 teaspoons grated orange zest with butter and sugars in step 2. Decrease oats to 2 cups and add 1 cup coarsely chopped toasted almonds to batter with oats in step 2.

SALTY THIN AND CRISPY OATMEAL COOKIES

We prefer the texture and flavor of a coarse-grained sea salt, like Maldon or fleur de sel, but kosher salt can be used. If using kosher salt, reduce the amount sprinkled over the cookies to ¼ teaspoon.

Reduce amount of salt in dough to ¼ teaspoon. Lightly sprinkle ½ teaspoon coarse sea salt evenly over flattened dough balls before baking.

Classic Peanut Butter Cookies

✓ WHY THIS RECIPE WORKS

Recipes for peanut butter cookies tend to fall into one of two categories: sweet and chewy with a mild peanut flavor, or sandy and crumbly with a strong peanut flavor. What we wanted, of course, was the best of both worlds—that is, cookies that were crisp on the edges and chewy in the center, with lots of peanut flavor.

INCLUDE BOTH WHITE AND BROWN SUGAR Sugar delivers sweetness and enhances texture. We found that we needed granulated sugar for cookies with crisp edges and chewy centers and dark brown sugar to enrich the peanut flavor.

USE TWO LEAVENERS Baking soda doesn't just leaven baked goods, it contributes to browning and amplifies the peanut flavor. Baking powder provides further lift.

GO NUTTY Extra-crunchy peanut butter helps the cookies rise and achieve a crispier edge and a softer center. But the best way to get true peanut flavor is to use peanuts and salt. Adding some roasted salted peanuts, ground in a food processor, and then adding still more salt (directly to the batter as well as in the form of salted rather than unsalted butter) produces a strong roasted nut flavor without sacrificing anything in terms of texture.

PEANUT BUTTER COOKIES
MAKES ABOUT 36 COOKIES

These cookies have a strong peanut flavor that comes from extra-crunchy peanut butter as well as from roasted salted peanuts that are ground in a food processor and worked into the dough. In our testing, we found that salted butter brings out the flavor of the nuts. If using unsalted butter, increase the salt to 1 teaspoon.

2½ cups (12½ ounces) all-purpose flour
½   teaspoon baking soda
½   teaspoon baking powder
½   teaspoon salt
16 tablespoons salted butter, softened
1   cup packed (7 ounces) dark brown sugar
1   cup (7 ounces) granulated sugar
1   cup extra-crunchy peanut butter, room temperature
2   large eggs
2   teaspoons vanilla extract
1   cup salted dry-roasted peanuts, pulsed in food processor to resemble bread crumbs, about 14 pulses

1. Adjust oven racks to upper-middle and lower-middle positions and heat oven to 350 degrees. Line 2 baking sheets with parchment paper.

2. Whisk flour, baking soda, baking powder, and salt together in medium bowl; set aside.

3. Using stand mixer fitted with paddle, beat butter, brown sugar, and granulated sugar at medium speed until light and fluffy, about 2 minutes, scraping down bowl as needed. Add peanut butter and mix until fully incorporated, about 30 seconds; add eggs, one at a time, and vanilla and mix until combined, about 30 seconds. Reduce speed to low and add dry ingredients; mix until combined, about 30 seconds. Mix in ground peanuts until just incorporated. Give dough final stir to ensure that no flour pockets remain and ingredients are evenly distributed.

CAN OTHER NUT BUTTER REPLACE PEANUT BUTTER?

Peanut allergies have become so commonplace, we looked into swapping other nut butters for peanut butter in our peanut butter cookies. We substituted almond butter and cashew butter, the two most commonly available "alternative" nut butters, for peanut butter. Since we could only find them unsalted, we bumped up the salt in our recipe to compensate.

The cashew butter cookies were very similar in texture and appearance to those made with peanut butter, but the cashew flavor was so subtle that it was easy to miss, making this nut a poor stand-in for peanuts. The almond butter cookies fared worse: The almond skins made the cookies taste noticeably bitter, and the cookies also spread more than their peanut and cashew counterparts, looking comparatively flat and unattractive. It turns out that almonds contain not only slightly more fat than peanuts and cashews (which share a similar fat percentage) but also a much higher proportion of unsaturated fat. Because unsaturated fat has a lower melting point than the saturated kind, cookies made with almond butter are more fluid, allowing the batter to spread before their structure is set.

In a nutshell: If you're concerned about peanut allergies, look for cookie recipes specifically designed for other nut butters. A direct substitution with cashew or almond butter won't produce the same results.

If you don't want to use a
fork to make a crosshatch
pattern in peanut but-
ter cookies, try this novel
method that relies on a
potato masher. Just one press
does the job.

MEASURING STICKY
INGREDIENTS

Tenaciously sticky ingredients
like peanut butter, molasses,
honey, and shortening can
be difficult to measure and
scrape out of liquid measuring
cups. But there is an easier
way: the adjustable-bottom
liquid measuring cup. This
style of measuring cup has a
plunger-like bottom that you
set to the correct measurement and then push up to
extract the ingredient. Our
favorite is the **KitchenArt
Adjust-A-Cup,** which is
also dishwasher-safe—its
measurement delineations will
stay intact through numerous
cycles.

4. Working with 2 tablespoons of dough at a time, roll into balls and space 2½ inches apart on prepared sheets. Press each dough ball twice, at right angles, with dinner fork dipped in cold water to make crisscross design.

5. Bake until cookies are puffy and slightly brown around edges but not on top, 10 to 12 minutes (cookies will not look fully baked), switching and rotating sheets halfway through baking. Let cookies cool on sheets for 5 minutes; transfer cookies to wire rack and let cool to room temperature before serving.

PEANUT BUTTER CHOCOLATE CHIP COOKIES

Add 1½ cups semisweet chocolate chips with the ground nuts.

Peanut Butter Sandwich Cookies

✔ WHY THIS RECIPE WORKS

We wanted a simple recipe that gave us thin, crunchy cookies and a smooth filling, both packed with peanut butter flavor.

BUILD A SIMPLE FILLING Most recipes call for blending peanut butter and confectioners' sugar with a creamy element, such as butter, cream cheese, heavy cream, or even marshmallow crème. We settled on butter, which provided the silkiest consistency and allowed for the purest peanut butter flavor.

CUT THE FLOUR WITH NUTS For a super-nutty tasting cookie we tried replacing all the flour with ground peanuts—there are lots of flourless peanut butter cookies if you check the Internet. While these cookies tasted great, they were far too crumbly. Instead we cut a portion of the flour with ground peanuts for an undeniably nutty cookie.

DEVELOP A THIN, CRUNCHY COOKIE SANDWICH Cookies are typically thin to accommodate a layer of filling. To achieve thin crunchy cookies, we found that cutting

an egg from our cookie dough helped by making the cookies less cakey. We replaced some of the moisture lost from the egg with milk. The moisture also helps the dough spread for a thin cookie. But baking soda turned out to be the real star of the show when it came to spread. Adding extra soda causes the bubbles within the dough to inflate so rapidly that they burst before the cookies set, leaving the cookies flatter than they would be with less baking soda.

TIME THE ASSEMBLY When we first tried spreading the filling on the cooled cookies, the cookies shattered into pieces. Adding more butter to soften the filling only makes it greasy and dilutes the peanut flavor. Instead, we warm the filling in the microwave just before assembling, which is as easy as scooping a portion of the softened filling onto each cookie. Once covered with a second cookie and gently pressed, the filling perfectly sandwiches between the two—no fussy spreading necessary.

PEANUT BUTTER SANDWICH COOKIES

MAKES 24 COOKIES

Do not use unsalted peanut butter for this recipe. Take care when chopping the peanuts in the food processor—you want to chop them, not turn them into a paste. See page 9 for information on toasting nuts.

COOKIES

1¼	cups (6¼ ounces) unsalted raw or dry-roasted peanuts, toasted and cooled
¾	cup (3¾ ounces) all-purpose flour
1	teaspoon baking soda
½	teaspoon salt
3	tablespoons unsalted butter, melted
½	cup creamy peanut butter
½	cup (3½ ounces) granulated sugar
½	cup (3½ ounces) light brown sugar
3	tablespoons whole milk
1	large egg

FILLING

¾	cup creamy peanut butter
3	tablespoons unsalted butter
1	cup (4 ounces) confectioners' sugar

1. FOR THE COOKIES: Adjust oven racks to upper-middle and lower-middle positions and heat oven to 350 degrees. Line 2 baking sheets with parchment paper. Pulse peanuts in food processor until finely chopped, about 8 pulses. Whisk flour, baking soda, and salt together in bowl. Whisk butter, peanut butter, granulated sugar, brown sugar, milk, and egg together in second bowl. Stir flour mixture into peanut butter mixture with rubber spatula until combined. Stir in chopped peanuts until evenly distributed.

2. Using #60 scoop or tablespoon measure, place 12 mounds, evenly spaced, on each prepared sheet. Using your damp hand, flatten mounds until 2 inches in diameter.

3. Bake until deep golden brown and firm to touch, 15 to 18 minutes, switching and rotating sheets halfway through baking. Let cookies cool on sheets for 5 minutes; transfer cookies to wire rack and let cool completely, about 30 minutes. Repeat portioning and baking with remaining dough.

4. FOR THE FILLING: Microwave peanut butter and butter until butter is melted and warm, about 40 seconds. Using rubber spatula, stir in sugar until combined.

5. TO ASSEMBLE: Place 24 cookies upside down on work surface. Place 1 level tablespoon (or #60 scoop) warm filling in center of each cookie. Place second cookie on top of filling, right side up, pressing gently until filling spreads to edges. Allow filling to set for 1 hour before serving. Assembled cookies can be stored at room temperature in airtight container for up to 3 days.

PEANUT BUTTER SANDWICH COOKIES WITH HONEY-CINNAMON FILLING

Omit butter from filling. Stir 5 tablespoons honey and ½ teaspoon ground cinnamon into warm peanut butter before adding confectioners' sugar.

PEANUT BUTTER SANDWICH COOKIES WITH MILK CHOCOLATE FILLING

For information on our top-rated brand of milk chocolate, see page 496.

Reduce peanut butter to ½ cup and omit butter from filling. Stir 6 ounces finely chopped milk chocolate into warm peanut butter until melted, microwaving for 10 seconds at a time if necessary, before adding confectioners' sugar.

FLOURLESS PEANUT BUTTER COOKIES?

In the testing for our Peanut Butter Sandwich Cookies, we discovered that the starch granules in flour mute the flavor of peanut butter, so we briefly turned our attention to an Internet sensation: flourless peanut butter cookies, made with just peanut butter, sugar, egg, and sometimes a bit of baking soda. Indeed, when we tried a sample batch of our cookies sans flour, they tasted super-peanutty and baked up looking much like traditional peanut butter cookies. Why didn't these flourless cookies melt right off of the cookie sheet? Because peanut butter contains approximately 20 percent carbohydrates and 25 percent protein, components that absorb moisture and harden into a stable network in the heat of the oven. But without the sturdier structure that only starch from wheat flour can provide, these cookies fell apart in our hands before we could even take a bite.

Pecan Sandies

SLICING PECAN SANDIES DOUGH

Using a sharp chef's knife, slice the log of dough into thin rounds. To prevent one side from flattening, roll the dough an eighth of a turn after every slice.

✔ WHY THIS RECIPE WORKS

Pecan sandies run the gamut from greasy and bland to dry and crumbly. We wanted a pecan sandy with a tender but crisp texture and sandy melt-in-the-mouth character.

SWEETEN AND TENDERIZE We tried both light and dark brown sugars, settling on light, which gave the cookies a gentle caramel flavor that complemented, not overwhelmed, the nuttiness of the pecans and richness of the butter, which was preferred over the more traditional oil. To tenderize our cookies, we also include a small portion of confectioners' sugar.

GRIND THE NUTS Finely ground nuts make for rich, fine-textured sandy cookies. To prevent the nuts from clumping in the food processor and turning greasy, we grind them along with the sugars.

DITCH THE WHITE A whole egg made for a too-sticky dough, so we settled on just a yolk for our rich cookies.

CHILL, SLICE, AND BAKE After briefly kneading the dough together out of the food processor, we shape it into logs and chill it, so that we can slice and bake the dough for pecan sandies with clean, crisp edges.

PECAN SANDIES
MAKES ABOUT 32 COOKIES

Don't substitute another type of sugar for the confectioners' sugar—it is important for a tender, sandy texture.

- 2 cups (8 ounces) pecans
- ½ cup packed (3½ ounces) light brown sugar
- ¼ cup (1 ounce) confectioners' sugar
- 1½ cups (7½ ounces) all-purpose flour
- ¼ teaspoon salt
- 12 tablespoons unsalted butter, cut into ½-inch pieces and chilled
- 1 large egg yolk

1. Reserve 32 prettiest pecan halves for garnishing. Process remaining pecans with brown sugar and confectioners' sugar in food processor until nuts are finely ground, about 20 seconds. Add flour and salt and process to combine, about 10 seconds.

2. Add butter pieces and process until mixture resembles damp sand and rides up sides of bowl, about 20 seconds. With processor running, add egg yolk and process until dough comes together into rough ball, about 20 seconds.

3. Transfer dough to clean counter, knead briefly, and divide into 2 equal pieces. Roll each piece of dough into a 6-inch log, about 2 inches thick. Wrap dough tightly in plastic wrap and refrigerate until firm, about 2 hours.

4. Adjust oven racks to upper-middle and lower-middle positions and heat oven to 325 degrees. Line 2 baking sheets with parchment paper.

5. Working with 1 dough log at a time, remove dough log from plastic and, using chef's knife, slice into ⅜-inch-thick rounds, rotating dough so that it won't become misshapen from weight of knife. Space rounds 1 inch apart on prepared sheets. Gently press pecan half in center of each cookie. Bake until edges of cookies are golden brown, 20 to 25 minutes, switching and rotating sheets halfway through baking. Let cookies cool on sheets for 3 minutes; transfer cookies to wire rack and let cool completely before serving.

ALMOND SANDIES

Replace pecans with equal amount of whole blanched almonds that have been toasted in 350-degree oven for 8 minutes, cooled, and then chopped. Add ¼ teaspoon almond extract with egg yolk.

Gingersnaps

✔ WHY THIS RECIPE WORKS

Most gingersnap recipes don't live up to their name. Once you get past their brittle edges, the cookies turn soft and chewy. And they always fall short on flavor, lacking sufficiently bold notes of ginger and spice. We wanted freshly baked gingersnaps with a crackly top and a texture to rival the store-bought kind, but with all-natural ginger flavor and lingering heat.

REDUCE MOISTURE The biggest obstacle to achieving our gingersnaps' signature snap was too much moisture. To scale it down, we tweaked two of our recipe's star ingredients: brown sugar and butter. Cutting back on the brown sugar resulted in noticeably drier and crunchier cookies and also allowed the ginger flavor to move to the fore.

BROWN THE BUTTER Browning the butter eliminated some of its water while keeping its fat (and introduced rich, nutty flavor) to further ensure our cookies were crisp.

DOUBLE UP ON GINGER For flavor we double the normal amount of dried ginger but also add fresh ginger, black pepper, and cayenne to ensure our cookies have real "snap."

USE PLENTY OF BAKING SODA For our cookies' crackly tops, we use enough baking soda to cause the cookies to rise dramatically but then collapse, leaving attractive fissures on their surface. This excess of leavener also has other positive effects: better browning (and therefore an even richer taste) and cookies that are crispier, since the cracks in the dough allow more moisture to escape.

BAKE LONGER AND COOL IMMEDIATELY We also extend the overall baking time, which allows the cookies to gradually (and fully) dry out without burning. And we transfer them to a wire rack immediately after baking, which allows air to circulate and steam to escape from their undersides.

GINGERSNAPS
MAKES 80 COOKIES

For the best results, use fresh spices. For efficiency, form the second batch of cookies while the first batch bakes. And no, the 2 teaspoons of baking soda is not a mistake; it's essential to getting the right texture.

2½	cups (12½ ounces) all-purpose flour
2	teaspoons baking soda
½	teaspoon salt
12	tablespoons unsalted butter
2	tablespoons ground ginger
1	teaspoon ground cinnamon
¼	teaspoon ground cloves
¼	teaspoon pepper
	Pinch cayenne
1¼	cups packed (8¾ ounces) dark brown sugar
¼	cup molasses
2	tablespoons finely grated fresh ginger
1	large egg plus 1 large yolk
½	cup granulated sugar

1. Whisk flour, baking soda, and salt together in bowl. Heat butter in 10-inch skillet over medium heat until melted. Lower heat to medium-low and continue to cook, swirling pan frequently, until foaming subsides and butter is just beginning to brown, 2 to 4 minutes. Transfer butter to large bowl and whisk in ground ginger, cinnamon, cloves, pepper, and cayenne. Let cool slightly, about 2 minutes. Add brown sugar, molasses, and fresh ginger to butter mixture and whisk to combine. Add egg and yolk and whisk to combine. Add flour mixture and stir until just combined. Cover dough tightly with plastic wrap and refrigerate until firm, about 1 hour.

2. Adjust oven racks to upper-middle and lower-middle positions and heat oven

GRATING GINGER

When grating ginger on a rasp-style grater, a brief stint in the freezer helps firm it up and keeps it from disintegrating.

1. Place peeled ginger in zipper-lock bag and freeze for 30 minutes.

2. Ginger can then be neatly grated.

to 300 degrees. Line 2 baking sheets with parchment paper. Place granulated sugar in shallow dish. Divide dough into heaping teaspoon portions; roll dough into 1-inch balls. Working in batches of 10, roll balls in sugar to coat. Evenly space dough balls on prepared sheets, 20 dough balls per sheet.

3. Place 1 sheet on upper rack and bake for 15 minutes. After 15 minutes, transfer partially baked top sheet to lower rack, rotating 180 degrees, and place second sheet of dough balls on upper rack. Continue to bake until cookies on lower tray just begin to darken around edges, 10 to 12 minutes longer. Remove lower sheet of cookies and shift upper sheet to lower rack and continue to bake until cookies begin to darken around edges, 15 to 17 minutes. Slide baked cookies, still on parchment, to wire rack and let cool completely before serving. Let baking sheets cool and repeat step 2 with remaining dough balls.

Hermit Cookies

✔ WHY THIS RECIPE WORKS
Old-fashioned recipes for hermits often produce rock-hard cookies peppered with bland, tough raisins. We wanted a moist, chewy cookie, gently redolent of molasses and warm spices.

MELT, DON'T CREAM, THE BUTTER Traditional recipes for hermits call for creaming the butter, but this produces a dry, biscuit-like cookie. Melting the butter and then cooking it until it browns delivers a chewier, moister cookie, with a nutty flavor.

PAIR LIGHT MOLASSES WITH DARK BROWN SUGAR Light, or mild, molasses provides a gentle molasses flavor, which is further underscored by the caramelized notes of dark brown sugar.

BLOOM THE SPICES Adding cinnamon, allspice, and ginger to the browned butter blooms their natural flavor, which allows us to use a smaller quantity of each for gently spiced cookies that aren't dusty-tasting like so many old-fashioned versions.

MAKE A RAISIN PUREE Hermits are typically studded with raisins, but those raisins can often bake up hard and chewy. For rich raisin flavor in every bite, we puree them with chopped crystallized ginger and then combine the mixture with the melted butter to soften the raisins. This helps distribute raisin flavor throughout the cookies, while the pureed ginger lends pungent sweetness and chew.

HERMITS
MAKES ABOUT 18 COOKIES

For this recipe, we prefer using mild (or light) molasses instead of the robust or blackstrap varieties.

1	cup raisins
2	tablespoons finely chopped crystallized ginger
8	tablespoons unsalted butter
1	teaspoon ground cinnamon
¼	teaspoon ground allspice
2	cups (10 ounces) all-purpose flour
½	teaspoon baking soda
½	teaspoon salt
¾	cup packed (5¼ ounces) dark brown sugar
½	cup molasses
2	large eggs
1½	tablespoons orange juice
¾	cup (3 ounces) confectioners' sugar

Here's a novel way to keep
cookies moist when storing
them in a tin. Slip layers of
flour tortillas and parchment
between the layers of cookies. The tortillas fit tidily into
the tin, where their moisture
keeps cookies soft for days.

1. Trace bottom of cookie tin
on sheet of parchment paper.
Cut out circle and repeat as
needed.

2. Layer parchment, tortilla,
parchment, and then layer of
completely cooled cookies.

3. Repeat until tin is full, ending with layer of cookies.

1. Adjust oven racks to upper-middle and lower-middle positions and heat oven to 350 degrees. Line 2 baking sheets with parchment paper. Process raisins and ginger in food processor until mixture sticks together and only small pieces remain, about 10 seconds. Transfer mixture to large bowl.

2. Heat butter in small saucepan over medium-low heat, swirling pan occasionally, until nutty brown in color, about 10 minutes. Stir in cinnamon and allspice and cook until fragrant, about 15 seconds. Stir butter mixture into raisin mixture until well combined; let cool to room temperature.

3. Combine flour, baking soda, and salt in bowl. Stir brown sugar, molasses, and eggs into cooled butter-raisin mixture until incorporated. Fold in flour mixture (dough will be very sticky) and refrigerate, covered, until firm, at least 1½ hours or up to 24 hours.

4. Divide dough into quarters. Transfer 1 piece of dough to lightly floured surface and roll into 10-inch log. Transfer to prepared sheet and use ruler to neatly square off sides. (Each sheet will contain 2 logs.) Repeat with remaining dough. Bake until only shallow indentation remains on edges when touched (center will appear slightly soft), 15 to 20 minutes, switching and rotating sheets halfway through baking. Let logs cool on baking sheets for 5 minutes; transfer parchment to wire racks and let cool completely.

5. Whisk orange juice and confectioners' sugar in small bowl until smooth. Drizzle glaze onto cooled logs and let sit until glaze hardens, about 15 minutes. Cut logs into 2-inch bars and serve.

Molasses Spice Cookies

✓ WHY THIS RECIPE WORKS

On the outside, a molasses cookie's cracks and crinkles gives it a humble, charming countenance. Inside, an uncommonly moist, soft yet chewy, tooth-sinking texture is half the appeal; the other is a warm, tingling spiciness an with the dark, bitter-sweet flavor of molasses. We wanted to create the ultimate molasses spice cookie—chewy and gently spiced with deep, dark molasses flavor.

CHOOSE BUTTER Many older recipes use shortening for these cookies but we found butter yields cookies with superior flavor and richness.

DETERMINE MOLASSES TYPE We found that to keep the cookies mild, using a light or mild molasses is imperative; but if it's a stronger flavor you want, dark molasses is in order. Avoid blackstrap molasses, which yields cookies with an unappealing bitter flavor. These cookies benefit from sugar as well. We like the strong caramel notes and moistness of dark brown sugar. Rolling the balls of dough in white sugar gives the finished cookies a sweet, crunchy coating.

GET YOUR SPICES IN ORDER The assertive flavor of molasses calls for strong flavor accents. The combination of vanilla, ginger, cinnamon, cloves, black pepper, and allspice gives these spiced cookies the warm bite we prefer in a gingersnap.

FINISH BAKING OUT OF THE OVEN Make sure to pull the cookies from the oven when they still look a bit underdone; residual heat will finish the baking and keep the cookies chewy and moist.

MOLASSES SPICE COOKIES
MAKES ABOUT 22 COOKIES

For the best results, use fresh spices. Light or mild molasses gives the cookies a milder flavor; for a stronger flavor, use dark molasses.

- ⅓ cup (2⅓ ounces) granulated sugar, plus ½ cup for rolling
- 2¼ cups (11¼ ounces) all-purpose flour
- 1 teaspoon baking soda
- 1½ teaspoons ground cinnamon
- 1½ teaspoons ground ginger
- ½ teaspoon ground cloves
- ¼ teaspoon ground allspice
- ¼ teaspoon pepper
- ¼ teaspoon salt
- 12 tablespoons unsalted butter, softened
- ⅓ cup packed (2⅓ ounces) dark brown sugar
- 1 large egg yolk
- 1 teaspoon vanilla extract
- ½ cup light or dark molasses

1. Adjust oven rack to middle position and heat oven to 375 degrees. Line 2 baking sheets with parchment paper. Place ½ cup granulated sugar in shallow dish; set aside.

2. Whisk flour, baking soda, cinnamon, ginger, cloves, allspice, pepper, and salt together in medium bowl; set aside.

3. Using stand mixer fitted with paddle, beat butter, brown sugar, and remaining ⅓ cup granulated sugar on medium-high speed until light and fluffy, about 3 minutes. Reduce speed to medium-low and add egg yolk and vanilla; increase speed to medium and beat until incorporated, about 20 seconds. Reduce speed to medium-low and add molasses; beat until fully incorporated, about 20 seconds, scraping down bowl as needed. Reduce speed to low and add flour mixture; beat until just incorporated, about 30 seconds, scraping down bowl as needed. Give dough final stir to ensure that no flour pockets remain. Dough will be soft.

4. Working with 1 tablespoon of dough at a time, roll into balls. Roll half of dough balls in sugar and toss to coat. Space dough balls 2 inches apart on prepared sheet. Repeat with remaining dough.

5. Bake 1 sheet at a time until cookies are browned, still puffy, and edges have begun to set but centers are still soft (cookies will look raw between cracks and seem underdone), about 11 minutes, rotating sheet halfway through baking. Do not overbake.

6. Let cookies cool on sheet for 5 minutes; transfer cookies to wire rack and let cool to room temperature before serving.

MOLASSES SPICE COOKIES WITH DARK RUM GLAZE

If the glaze is too thick to drizzle, whisk in up to an additional ½ tablespoon rum.

Whisk 1 cup confectioners' sugar and 2½ tablespoons dark rum together in medium bowl until smooth. Drizzle or spread glaze using back of spoon on cooled cookies. Allow glazed cookies to dry at least 15 minutes.

MOLASSES SPICE COOKIES WITH ORANGE ESSENCE

The orange zest in the sugar coating causes the sugar to become sticky and take on a light orange hue, giving the baked cookies a unique frosty look.

Process ⅔ cup granulated sugar and 2 teaspoons grated orange zest until pale orange, about 10 seconds; transfer sugar to shallow dish and set aside. Add 1 teaspoon grated orange zest to dough along with molasses and substitute orange sugar for granulated sugar when coating dough balls in step 4.

GLAZING MOLASSES SPICE COOKIES

To speed cleanup, line a baking sheet with parchment paper. Dip a spoon into the glaze and drizzle over the cookies.

SHAPING THE COOKIES

1. Roll dough into cylinder approximately 10 inches long and 2 inches in diameter. Center dough on piece of parchment. Fold paper over dough.

2. Grasp 1 end of parchment. With your other hand, use bench scraper to firmly press parchment against dough to form uniform cylinder.

3. Roll parchment and twist ends together to form tight seal.

KEEPING COOKIE DOUGH ROUND

Protect your rolls of cookie dough by sliding them into a paper towel roll before refrigeration.

Glazed Lemon Cookies

✔ WHY THIS RECIPE WORKS

Store-bought lemon cookies are often saccharine-sweet and artificial tasting, with a thin veneer of frosting and a barely detectable lemon flavor. We wanted a lemon cookie recipe with the perfect balance of lemony zing and rich, buttery sweetness.

BUILD A TENDER COOKIE We start with all-purpose flour, which makes our cookies tender. Using just an egg yolk instead of a whole egg adds even more tenderness, and a touch of baking powder gives our cookies just the right amount of airy crispness. Butter provides rich flavor.

USE A TRIPLE WHAMMY OF LEMON Grinding some lemon zest with the sugar before adding it to the dough contributes bold lemon flavor without harshness. A simple glaze of cream cheese, lemon juice, and confectioners' sugar perfects these lemony treats.

CHILL, SLICE, AND BAKE Many recipes for glazed lemon cookies are rolled and cut out for thin, crisp cookies. But that can make the cookies turn out tough, a result of the dough being overworked by rolling and then rerolling scraps. To preserve the delicate texture of the cookies, we went refrigerator-style by rolling the dough into a cylinder before chilling it. This allows us to slice thin, even slices for a batch full of tender, buttery cookies.

GLAZED LEMON COOKIES
MAKES ABOUT 30 COOKIES

The cookies are best eaten the day they are glazed.

COOKIES

¾   cup (5¼ ounces) granulated sugar
2   tablespoons grated lemon zest plus 2 tablespoons juice (2 lemons)
1¾   cup (8¾ ounces) all-purpose flour
¼   teaspoon salt
¼   teaspoon baking powder

12   tablespoons unsalted butter, cut into ½-inch cubes and chilled
1   large egg yolk
½   teaspoon vanilla extract

GLAZE

1   tablespoon cream cheese, softened
2   tablespoons lemon juice
1½   cups (6 ounces) confectioners' sugar

1. FOR THE COOKIES: Adjust oven racks to upper-middle and lower-middle positions and heat oven to 375 degrees.

2. Process granulated sugar and lemon zest in food processor until sugar looks damp and zest is thoroughly incorporated, about 30 seconds. Add flour, salt, and baking powder; pulse to combine, about 10 pulses. Scatter butter over flour mixture; pulse until mixture resembles fine cornmeal, about 15 pulses. In measuring cup, beat lemon juice, egg yolk, and vanilla with fork to combine. With processor running, add juice mixture in slow, steady stream (process should take about 10 seconds); continue processing until dough begins to form ball, 10 to 15 seconds longer.

3. Turn dough and any dry bits onto counter; working quickly, gently knead together to ensure that no dry bits remain and dough is homogeneous. Shape dough into log about 10 inches long and 2 inches in diameter. Wrap log in parchment paper and twist ends tightly to seal. Chill dough until firm, about 45 minutes in freezer or 2 hours in refrigerator.

4. Line 2 baking sheets with parchment. Remove dough log from parchment and, using chef's knife, slice dough into ⅜-inch-thick rounds, rotating dough so that it won't become misshapen from weight of knife. Space rounds 1 inch apart on prepared sheets. Bake until centers of cookies just begin to color and edges are golden brown, 14 to 16 minutes, switching and rotating sheets halfway

through baking. Let cookies cool on sheets for 5 minutes; transfer cookies to wire rack and let cool to room temperature before glazing.

5. FOR THE GLAZE: Whisk cream cheese and lemon juice in medium bowl until no lumps remain. Add confectioners' sugar and whisk until smooth.

6. When cookies have cooled, working with one at a time, spread glaze evenly over each cookie with back of spoon. Let cookies stand on wire rack until glaze is set and dry, about 1 hour, before serving.

GLAZED LEMON-ORANGE CORNMEAL COOKIES

Substitute 1 tablespoon grated orange zest for equal amount of lemon zest and ¼ cup cornmeal for equal amount of flour.

GLAZED LEMON AND CRYSTALLIZED GINGER COOKIES

Process 3 tablespoons finely chopped crystallized ginger along with sugar and lemon zest.

Holiday Cookies

✔ WHY THIS RECIPE WORKS

Baking holiday cookies should be a fun endeavor, but so often it's an exercise in frustration. The dough clings to the rolling pin, it rips and tears as it's rolled out, and moving the dough in and out of the fridge to make it easier to work with turns a simple 1-hour process into a half-day project. We wanted a simple recipe that would yield a forgiving, workable dough, producing cookies that would be sturdy enough to decorate yet tender enough to be worth eating.

USE SUPERFINE SUGAR Regular granulated sugar makes cookies with a flaky texture and some large holes. In contrast, superfine sugar yields crisp, compact cookies with a fine, even crumb that is preferable for a cookie that will be glazed. There's no leavener in these cookies (you want them flat) and no eggs (which would make them moist and chewy).

ADD CREAM CHEESE We use just enough butter for rich flavor and tenderness. More butter just makes the dough sticky and hard to handle. However, we found that we could supplement the butter with cream cheese. Because it's softer than butter when chilled it makes the dough easier to roll out. And it adds a nice tang.

PICK ALL-PURPOSE FLOUR While holiday glazed cookies should be delicate, cake flour makes overly fragile cookies. All-purpose flour develops enough gluten for cookies to be glazed and decorated without too much worry that they will crumble.

ROLL, THEN CHILL To prevent the dough from sticking to the counter—and to the rolling pin—roll it between two large pieces of parchment. Cold, stiff dough will cut more cleanly than soft dough, so make sure to chill the dough after rolling. Slide the bottom piece of parchment onto a baking sheet to keep the dough flat and then refrigerate it until firm, about 10 minutes.

MINIMIZE SCRAPS Cut shapes close together, starting from the outside and working your way to the middle. When making large and small cookies, alternate cutters as you stamp to use as much dough as possible. While you can reroll this dough once, you want to reduce scraps; if you overwork the dough, too much gluten will develop and the cookies will bake up tough. Make sure to chill the dough scraps again before rolling them out a second time.

GETTING A CLEAN CUT THROUGH FROZEN COOKIE DOUGH

Slicing through logs of frozen cookie dough can be a real chore, as the knife often drags, making sloppy cuts and producing misshapen cookies. We minimize the sticky knife problem by dipping the blade in flour after each couple of cuts.

EASIER ZESTING

When zesting citrus fruit over a Microplane grater onto a cutting board, it is difficult to see how much zest is accumulating. Hold the fruit in your hand and run the zester over the fruit instead. This method allows the zest to collect in the grater's chute, neatly and in full view.

PEEL AWAY SCRAPS FIRST   Use a small spatula to strip away the dough scraps from around the cookies. With excess dough out of the way, it's easier to lift the cookies and transfer them to a baking sheet without marring the shape of the cookies, or stretching the dough.

BAKE ONE SHEET AT A TIME   Baking one sheet of cookies at a time ensures even baking.

GLAZED BUTTER COOKIES
MAKES ABOUT 38 COOKIES

If you cannot find superfine sugar, process granulated sugar in a food processor for 30 seconds. If desired, the cookies can be finished with sprinkles or other decorations immediately after glazing.

COOKIES

2½	cups (12½ ounces) all-purpose flour
¾	cup (5⅔ ounces) superfine sugar
¼	teaspoon salt
16	tablespoons unsalted butter, cut into 16 pieces and softened
2	tablespoons cream cheese, room temperature
2	teaspoons vanilla extract

GLAZE

1	tablespoon cream cheese, room temperature
3	tablespoons milk
1½	cups (6 ounces) confectioners' sugar

1. FOR THE COOKIES: Using stand mixer fitted with paddle, mix flour, sugar, and salt at low speed until combined, about 5 seconds. With mixer running on low, add butter 1 piece at a time; continue to mix until mixture looks crumbly and slightly wet, about 1 to 2 minutes longer. Beat in cream cheese and vanilla until dough just begins to form large clumps, about 30 seconds.

2. Knead dough by hand in bowl, 2 to 3 turns, until it forms large, cohesive mass. Transfer dough to counter and divide it into 2 even pieces. Press each piece into 4-inch

disk, wrap disks in plastic, and refrigerate until dough is firm but malleable, about 30 minutes. (Dough can be refrigerated for up to 3 days or frozen up to 2 weeks; defrost in refrigerator before using.)

3. Adjust oven rack to middle position and heat oven to 375 degrees. Line 2 baking sheets with parchment paper. Working with 1 piece of dough at a time, roll ⅛ inch thick between 2 large sheets of parchment paper; slide rolled dough, still on parchment, onto baking sheet and refrigerate until firm, about 10 minutes.

4. Working with 1 sheet of dough at a time, peel parchment from 1 side of dough and cut into desired shapes using cookie cutters; space cookies 1½ inches apart on prepared sheets. Bake 1 sheet at a time until cookies are light golden brown, about 10 minutes, rotating sheet halfway through baking. (Dough scraps can be patted together, chilled, and rerolled once.) Let cookies cool on sheet for 3 minutes; transfer cookies to wire rack and let cool to room temperature.

5. FOR THE GLAZE: Whisk cream cheese and 2 tablespoons milk together in medium bowl until combined and no lumps remain. Add confectioners' sugar and whisk until smooth, adding remaining 1 tablespoon milk as needed until glaze is thin enough to spread easily. Using back of spoon, drizzle or spread scant teaspoon of glaze onto each cooled cookie. Allow glazed cookies to dry at least 30 minutes before serving.

LIME-GLAZED COCONUT SNOWBALLS
MAKES ABOUT 40 COOKIES

1	recipe dough for Glazed Butter Cookies, with 1 teaspoon grated lime zest added with dry ingredients, prepared through step 2
1	recipe Glaze, with 3 tablespoons lime juice (2 limes) substituted for milk
1½	cups (4½ ounces) sweetened shredded coconut, pulsed in food processor until finely chopped, about 15 pulses

1. Adjust oven racks to upper-middle and lower-middle positions and heat oven to 375 degrees. Line 2 baking sheets with parchment paper. Roll dough between your hands into 1-inch balls. Place dough balls on prepared sheets, spacing them 1½ inches apart. Bake 1 sheet at a time until cookies are lightly browned, about 12 minutes, rotating sheet halfway through baking. Let cookies cool on sheet for 3 minutes; transfer cookies to wire rack and let cool to room temperature.

2. Dip tops of cookies into glaze and scrape off excess, then dip them into coconut. Place cookies on wire rack and let stand until glaze sets, about 20 minutes, before serving.

JAM SANDWICHES
MAKES ABOUT 30 COOKIES

Turbinado sugar is commonly sold as Sugar in the Raw. Demerara sugar, sanding sugar, or another coarse sugar can be substituted.

- 1   recipe dough for Glazed Butter Cookies (page 206), prepared through step 3
- 2   tablespoons turbinado sugar
- 1¼ cups raspberry jam, simmered until reduced to 1 cup, strained, and cooled to room temperature

1. Adjust oven rack to middle position and heat oven to 375 degrees. Line 2 baking sheets with parchment paper. Using 2-inch fluted round cookie cutter, cut rounds from 1 piece of rolled dough and place on 1 prepared sheet, spacing them 1 inch apart. Bake until cookies are light golden brown, 8 to 10 minutes, rotating sheet halfway through baking. Let cookies cool on sheet for 3 minutes; transfer cookies to wire rack and let cool to room temperature.

2. Sprinkle second piece of rolled dough evenly with sugar. Using 2-inch fluted round cookie cutter, cut rounds of sugar-sprinkled dough. Using ¾-inch round cookie cutter, cut out centers of sugared rounds. Bake and cool cookies as directed in step 1, using second prepared sheet.

3. Spread 1 teaspoon jam on top of each solid cookie, then cover with cut-out cookie. Let filled cookies stand until set, about 30 minutes, before serving.

CHOCOLATE-CHERRY BAR COOKIES WITH HAZELNUTS
MAKES ABOUT 50 COOKIES

- 1   recipe dough for Glazed Butter Cookies (page 206), with 1 cup chopped dried cherries added with dry ingredients, prepared through step 2
- 1½ cups (9 ounces) semisweet chocolate chips
- 1½ cups (6 ounces) hazelnuts, toasted, skinned, and chopped

1. Adjust oven rack to lower-middle position and heat oven to 375 degrees. Line rimmed baking sheet with parchment paper. Press dough evenly onto prepared sheet and bake until golden brown, about 20 minutes, rotating sheet halfway through baking.

2. Immediately after removing baking sheet from oven, sprinkle evenly with chocolate chips; let stand to melt, about 3 minutes.

3. Spread chocolate into even layer, then sprinkle chopped hazelnuts evenly over chocolate. Let cool on wire rack until just warm, 15 to 20 minutes.

4. Using pizza wheel, cut cookies on diagonal into 1½-inch diamonds. Transfer cookies to wire rack and let cool completely.

Decorating Glazed Butter Cookies

With the right technique, decorating cookies with colored glazes in different patterns is an easy way to create festive, professional-looking results.

THREE WAYS TO GLAZE

SPREAD For a simple, smooth coat, drizzle a little glaze in the center of the cookie and then spread it out in an even layer using the back of a spoon or a small offset spatula.

PIPE To apply more intricate detail work, such as dots or lines, pipe the glaze directly onto the cookie. Fill a homemade parchment piping bag or a small pastry bag fitted with a small 1/16-inch round tip with glaze.

PAINT Use a small paintbrush to apply different colored glazes to a cookie without overlapping or to fill in an outline.

GUSSYING UP GLAZED COOKIES

DRAGGING By applying dots of a contrasting colored glaze on top of another glaze and dragging a toothpick or thin skewer carefully through the center, you can create a variety of patterns and designs.

EMBELLISHING Place decorations in the glaze while it is still soft; once the glaze dries, it will act like glue. In addition to the usual decorating options, consider cinnamon candies, jelly beans, crushed peppermint candies, gum drops, and chocolate morsels.

SUGARING Once a glaze has been applied to a cookie, sprinkle it with colored sugar. For the most even distribution, hold your hand about 12 inches above the work surface. Excess sugar can be brushed or gently shaken off when the glaze is dry.

DECORATORS' TIPS

GLITTER STICKING POINTS
Unglazed cookies require a little surface preparation to ensure that embellishments will stick. We recommend lightly misting or brushing the surface of the dough with water before applying decorations.

TACKLE BOX FOR TRIMMINGS
Decorating cookies usually means juggling a collection of tiny trimmings. To keep the items close at hand and neatly organized, we corral each one in the individual cups of a muffin tin.

COLOR YOUR SUGAR
Colored sugar is easy to make at home and offers many more color options than the grocery store does.

1. Place 1/2 cup of granulated sugar in bowl. Add about 5 drops of food coloring and mix thoroughly.

2. To ensure even color, push sugar through fine-mesh strainer. Spread sugar in pie plate and let it dry completely.

MAKE A PARCHMENT PIPING BAG

We find that the stiff opening of a homemade parchment bag works just as well as a small piping bag at drawing thin lines (and better than the usual alternative to a pastry bag, a zipper-lock bag, which is best reserved for less delicate piping). You can also make several to hold different colored glazes—with no need for washing out between uses.

1. Fold 12-inch square of parchment paper in half on diagonal. Using knife, cut it in half on fold into 2 triangles.

2. With long side of triangle facing you, fold bottom right-hand point up and under, giving it half twist until it meets triangle's top point.

3. Holding those points together, wrap left-hand point around outside of cone until all 3 points are perfectly aligned. Tape or staple points together.

4. Use scissors to snip very small hole in point of cone.

One Dough, Many Cookies

Our butter cookie dough is not only foolproof but is also the perfect vehicle for a number of different flavorings, shapes, and sizes. Here are our three favorite cookies made with this dough.

MAKING JAM SANDWICHES

1. Using 2-inch fluted round cookie cutter, cut rounds from 1 piece of dough and bake on parchment-lined baking sheet.

2. Sprinkle second piece of rolled dough evenly with sugar.

3. Using 2-inch fluted round cookie cutter, cut out rounds of sugar-sprinkled dough and place on parchment-lined baking sheet. Using ¾-inch round cookie cutter, cut out centers of rounds and bake.

4. When cookies have cooled, spread 1 teaspoon jam on solid cookies, then place cut-out cookies on top. Let filled cookies stand until set, about 30 minutes.

MAKING CHOCOLATE-CHERRY BAR COOKIES WITH HAZELNUTS

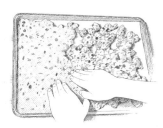 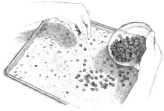  

1. Press dough in even layer onto baking sheet.

2. Immediately after removing baking sheet from oven, sprinkle evenly with chocolate chips; let stand to melt.

3. Use offset spatula to spread chocolate into even layer, then sprinkle evenly with chopped hazelnuts. Let cool on wire rack until just warm.

4. Use pizza wheel to cut cookies into 1¼-inch diamonds before serving.

MAKING LIME-GLAZED COCONUT SNOWBALLS

1. Roll dough into 1-inch balls, place on parchment-lined baking sheets, and bake.

2. When cookies have cooled dip tops of cookies into glaze and scrape away excess. Dip into coconut. Set cookies on parchment-lined baking sheet and let stand until glaze dries and sets, about 20 minutes.

Best Shortbread

WHY THIS RECIPE WORKS

In Scottish tradition, shortbread cookies are crumbly, perfectly browned, and faintly sweet. In American tradition, shortbread is often bland, chalky, and lackluster. We wanted superlative shortbread with an alluring tawny brown crumb and pure, buttery richness.

MIX WELL At its simplest, shortbread contains just four ingredients—flour, sugar, salt, and butter. But unlike crisp butter cookies, shortbread should have an ultrafine, sandy texture. It needs to hold together while still being tender and delicate. In traditional recipes, the cold butter is cut into the dry ingredients as if making pie dough. However, we found that beating the cold butter into the dry ingredients (a method called reverse creaming) works best.

USE CONFECTIONERS' SUGAR Granulated sugar won't fully dissolve in this cookie dough—there's not enough liquid, not even an egg. Fine-textured confectioners' sugar gives shortbread a much more delicate crumb.

PICK OATS AND CORNSTARCH The small amount of water in the butter activates the gluten in the flour, which can make shortbread tough. Some recipes use gluten-free rice flour but we found that flavor is sacrificed. Oats contain very few of the proteins necessary for gluten development, plus they have a nice flavor. We grind the oats to a fine meal in a spice grinder or blender and then use them (along with some cornstarch) to replace some of the flour.

GET THE RIGHT SHAPE When baking our shortbread, we had a problem with spreading. As buttery shortbread bakes, it expands, losing its shape as the edges flatten out. We tried baking the dough in a traditional shortbread mold with ½-inch-high sides, but it still widened into an amorphous mass. Needing a substantial barrier to keep its edges corralled, we use a springform pan collar. First, we set the closed collar on a parchment-lined baking sheet. We pat the dough into it, cut a hole in the center of the dough with a 2-inch biscuit cutter, and then open the collar to give the cookie about half an inch to spread out.

BAKE HIGH, THEN LOW, THEN OFF We bake our shortbread in an oven that is off for far longer than it is on. After all, early shortbread was made by leaving the dough in a still-warm oven heated only by dying embers. After removing the springform collar, we return our shortbread to a turned-off oven for an hour to let it dry out and finish.

BEST SHORTBREAD
MAKES 16 WEDGES

Use the collar of a springform pan to form the shortbread into an even round. Mold the shortbread with the collar in the closed position, then open the collar, but leave it in place. This allows the shortbread to expand slightly but keeps it from spreading too far. The extracted round of dough in step 2 is baked alongside the rest of the shortbread. The shortbread will keep for up to one week in an airtight container or cookie tin stored at room temperature.

½	cup (1 ½ ounces) old-fashioned rolled oats
1 ½	cups (7 ½ ounces) all-purpose flour
¼	cup cornstarch
⅔	cup (2 ⅔ ounces) confectioners' sugar
½	teaspoon salt
14	tablespoons unsalted butter, chilled and cut into ⅛-inch-thick slices

I. Adjust oven rack to middle position and heat oven to 450 degrees. Pulse oats in spice grinder or blender until reduced to fine powder, about 10 pulses (you should have ¼ to ⅓ cup oat flour). Using stand mixer fitted with paddle, mix oat flour, all-purpose flour, cornstarch, sugar, and salt on low speed until combined, about 5 seconds. Add butter to dry ingredients and continue to mix until dough just forms and pulls away from sides of bowl, 5 to 10 minutes.

2. Place upside-down (grooved edge should be at top) collar of 9- or 9½-inch springform pan on parchment paper–lined baking sheet (do not use springform pan bottom). Press dough into collar in even ½-inch-thick layer, smoothing top of dough with back of spoon. Place 2-inch biscuit cutter in center of dough and cut out center. Place extracted round alongside springform collar on baking sheet and replace cutter in center of dough. Open springform collar, but leave it in place.

3. Bake shortbread for 5 minutes, then reduce oven temperature to 250 degrees. Continue to bake until edges turn pale golden, 10 to 15 minutes longer. Remove baking sheet from oven; turn oven off. Remove springform pan collar; use chef's knife to score surface of shortbread into 16 even wedges, cutting halfway through shortbread. Using wooden skewer, poke about 10 holes in each wedge. Return shortbread to oven and prop door open with handle of wooden spoon, leaving 1-inch gap at top. Allow shortbread to dry in turned-off oven until pale golden in center (shortbread should be firm but giving to touch), about 1 hour.

4. Transfer sheet to wire rack; let shortbread cool to room temperature. Cut shortbread at scored marks to separate before serving.

CHOCOLATE-DIPPED PISTACHIO SHORTBREAD

Add ½ cup finely chopped toasted pistachios to dry ingredients in step 1. Bake and cool shortbread as directed. Once shortbread is cool, melt 8 ounces finely chopped bittersweet chocolate in microwave at 50 percent power for 2 minutes. Stir chocolate and continue heating until melted, stirring once every additional minute. Stir in additional 2 ounces finely chopped bittersweet chocolate until smooth. Carefully dip base of each wedge in chocolate, allowing chocolate to come halfway up cookie. Scrape off excess with your finger and place on parchment paper–lined rimmed baking sheet. Refrigerate until chocolate sets, about 15 minutes.

GINGER SHORTBREAD

Turbinado sugar is commonly sold as Sugar in the Raw. Demerara sugar, sanding sugar, or another coarse sugar can be substituted.

Add ½ cup chopped crystallized ginger to dry ingredients in step 1. Sprinkle shortbread with 1 tablespoon turbinado sugar after poking holes in shortbread in step 3.

TOASTED OAT SHORTBREAD

To toast the oats, heat them in an 8-inch skillet over medium-high heat until light golden brown, 5 to 8 minutes. We prefer the texture and flavor of a coarse-grained sea salt like Maldon or fleur de sel, but kosher salt can be used.

Add ½ cup toasted oats to dry ingredients in step 1. Sprinkle ½ teaspoon sea salt evenly over surface of dough before baking.

FORMING AND BAKING SHORTBREAD

I. Press dough into closed upside-down springform pan collar; smooth with back of spoon. Cut hole in center of dough with 2-inch biscuit cutter; replace cutter in hole.

2. Open collar. Bake 5 minutes at 450 degrees, then 10 to 15 minutes at 250 degrees.

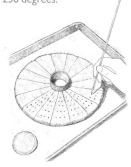

3. Score partially baked shortbread into wedges, then poke about 10 holes in each wedge.

4. Return shortbread to turned-off oven to dry; prop door open with wooden spoon or stick.

Sablé Cookies

BAKING WITH HARD-COOKED EGG YOLKS?

When we came across *sablé* recipes that called for a hard-cooked egg yolk, we were tempted to ignore this unlikely ingredient. What could it possibly do—aside from fleck our cookies with unwelcome bits of yolk? But when we actually gave the cooked yolk a try, we were surprised by the results.

We prepared one batch of sablé cookies with a raw yolk and compared it with another batch made with a hard-cooked yolk that had been pressed through a fine-mesh strainer.

The cookies prepared with the hard-cooked egg yolk were markedly sandier than those prepared with the raw yolk. Even better, we could detect no bits of cooked yolk, just rich flavor.

How does this work? An egg yolk consists of about 50 percent water by weight. When boiled, the proteins in the yolk form a solid matrix that locks in that water, making it unavailable. The sandiness in sablé cookies comes from undissolved sugar crystals. By reducing the amount of water available to dissolve the sugar, the cooked yolk promotes a crystalline texture in the finished cookies. By contrast, the liquid in the raw egg yolk dissolved the sugar, making the texture of the cookies smoother.

✓ WHY THIS RECIPE WORKS

During the holidays, these French butter cookies offer sophistication and style. That is, if you can capture their elusive sandy texture (sablé is French for sandy), which separates them from sturdy American butter cookies.

CUT BACK ON MOISTURE We started with a basic recipe using the typical method of creaming butter and sugar in a stand mixer, then adding egg and flour. We then rolled the dough into a log, chilled it, and sliced and baked—but these cookies were missing the delicate crumbliness that defines sablés. We needed to decrease the liquid in the dough so there would be less moisture to dissolve the sugar particles. Cutting back on butter helped, but that still didn't capture the elusive crumbliness.

USE A YOLK-ONLY DOUGH AND MAKE IT HARD-COOKED Switching from whole eggs to yolks was a giant step in the right direction, but we wanted to push the recipe even further to produce supremely sandy, crystalline sablés. When we came across sablé recipes that called for a hard-cooked egg yolk in the dough, we were tempted to ignore this unlikely ingredient. These recipes claimed that the hard-cooked yolk would deliver a sandy cookie. Skeptical, but intrigued, we cooked and cooled an egg and added the mashed yolk to the butter and sugar during creaming. *Voilà!* We found that this unusual step eliminated moisture and perfected the texture of the cookies.

BRUSH AND SPRINKLE Brushing the cookies with a beaten egg white and sprinkling them with coarse turbinado sugar before baking adds a delicate crunch and an attractive sparkle.

SABLÉS (FRENCH BUTTER COOKIES)
MAKES ABOUT 40 COOKIES

Turbinado sugar is commonly sold as Sugar in the Raw. Demerara sugar, sanding sugar, or another coarse sugar can be substituted. Make sure the cookie dough is well chilled and firm so that it can be uniformly sliced.

1	large egg, plus 1 large egg white, lightly beaten with 1 teaspoon water
10	tablespoons unsalted butter, softened
⅓	cup plus 1 tablespoon (2¾ ounces) granulated sugar
¼	teaspoon salt
1	teaspoon vanilla extract
1½	cups (7½ ounces) all-purpose flour
4	teaspoons turbinado sugar

1. Place egg in small saucepan, cover with water by 1 inch, and bring to boil over high heat. Remove pan from heat, cover, and let sit for 10 minutes. Meanwhile, fill small bowl with ice water. Using slotted spoon, transfer egg to ice water and let stand for 5 minutes. Crack egg and peel shell. Separate yolk from white; discard white. Press yolk through fine-mesh strainer into small bowl.

2. Using stand mixer fitted with paddle, beat butter, granulated sugar, salt, and cooked egg yolk on medium speed until light and fluffy, about 4 minutes, scraping down bowl as needed. Reduce speed to low, add vanilla, and mix until incorporated. Stop mixer; add flour and mix on low speed until just combined, about 30 seconds. Using rubber spatula, press dough into cohesive mass.

3. Divide dough in half. Shape each piece into log about 6 inches long and 1¾ inches in

Shaping Sablés

Our simple sablés just need to be sliced, sprinkled with sugar, and baked. But fancier shapes aren't much more difficult. Here's how we do it:

FORMING SANDWICH COOKIES

1. Slice 1 dough log into ⅛-inch-thick rounds.

2. Bake 10 to 13 minutes. Repeat with second log.

3. When cookies are cool, spread melted chocolate on bottom of 1 cookie.

4. Place second cookie on top, slightly off-center, so some chocolate shows.

FORMING PRETZEL SABLÉS

1. Slice slightly chilled dough into ¼-inch-thick rounds and roll into balls.

2. Roll each ball into 6-inch rope, tapering ends.

3. Pick up 1 end of rope and cross it over to form half of pretzel shape.

4. Bring second end over to complete shape.

FORMING SPIRAL SABLÉS

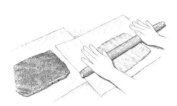

1. Halve each batch of dough. Roll out each portion on parchment paper into 8 by 6-inch rectangle, ¼ inch thick. Briefly chill dough until firm enough to handle.

2. Using bench scraper, place 1 plain cookie dough rectangle on top of 1 chocolate dough rectangle. Repeat to make 2 double rectangles.

3. Roll out each double rectangle on parchment into 9 by 6-inch rectangle (if too firm, let rest until malleable). Starting at long end, roll each into tight log.

4. Twist ends of parchment to seal and chill logs 1 hour. Slice logs into ¼-inch rounds.

diameter. Wrap each log in parchment paper and twist ends tightly to seal. Chill dough until firm, about 45 minutes in freezer or 2 hours in refrigerator.

4. Adjust oven racks to upper-middle and lower-middle positions and heat oven to 350 degrees. Line 2 baking sheets with parchment. Using chef's knife, slice dough into ¼-inch-thick rounds, rotating dough so that it won't become misshapen from weight of knife. Place cookies 1 inch apart on prepared sheets. Using pastry brush, gently brush cookies with egg white mixture and sprinkle evenly with turbinado sugar.

5. Bake until centers of cookies are pale golden brown with edges slightly darker than centers, about 15 minutes, switching and rotating sheets halfway through baking. Let cookies cool on sheets for 5 minutes; transfer cookies to wire rack and let cool to room temperature before serving.

CHOCOLATE SABLÉS

Reduce flour to 1⅓ cups and add ¼ cup Dutch-processed cocoa with flour in step 2.

LEMON SABLÉS

Add 4 teaspoons grated lemon zest with vanilla in step 2. Omit egg white mixture and turbinado sugar. Once cookies have cooled, dust with confectioners' sugar.

TOASTED COCONUT SABLÉS

Add ⅓ cup finely chopped toasted sweetened coconut to dough with flour in step 2. Omit turbinado sugar. After brushing cookies with egg white mixture, sprinkle with ⅓ cup finely chopped untoasted sweetened coconut.

ALMOND SABLÉS

Substitute 1½ teaspoons almond extract for vanilla extract and add ⅓ cup finely ground sliced almonds to dough with flour in step 2. Omit turbinado sugar. After brushing cookies with egg white mixture, gently press 3 almond slices in petal shape in center of each cookie.

CHOCOLATE SANDWICH COOKIES

See the illustrations on page 214 for shaping sandwich cookies

In step 4, slice 1 dough log into ⅛-inch-thick rounds, omitting egg white mixture and turbinado sugar. Bake cookies as directed in step 5, reducing baking time to 10 to 13 minutes. Repeat with second dough log. When all cookies are completely cool, microwave 3½ ounces chopped dark or milk chocolate at 50 percent power for 1 to 2 minutes and let cool slightly. Spread melted chocolate on bottom of 1 cookie. Place second cookie on top, slightly off-center, so some chocolate shows. Repeat with remaining melted chocolate and cookies.

VANILLA PRETZEL SABLÉS

See the illustrations on page 214 for shaping pretzel sablés.

Increase vanilla extract to 1 tablespoon and reduce chilling time in step 3 to 30 minutes (dough will not be fully hardened). Slice dough into ¼-inch-thick rounds and roll into balls. Roll each ball into 6-inch rope, tapering ends. Form ropes into pretzel shapes. Proceed with recipe, brushing with egg white mixture, sprinkling with turbinado sugar, and baking as directed.

BLACK AND WHITE SPIRAL SABLÉS

MAKES ABOUT 80 COOKIES

See the illustrations on page 214 for shaping spiral sablés.

VANILLA SABLÉS

2	large eggs
10	tablespoons unsalted butter, softened
⅓	cup plus 1 tablespoon (2¾ ounces) sugar
¼	teaspoon salt
1	teaspoon vanilla extract
1½	cups (7½ ounces) all-purpose flour

CHOCOLATE SABLÉS

10	tablespoons unsalted butter, softened
⅓	cup plus 1 tablespoon (2¾ ounces) sugar
¼	teaspoon salt
1	teaspoon vanilla extract
1⅓	cups (6⅔ ounces) all-purpose flour
¼	cup (¾ ounce) Dutch-processed cocoa powder

1. FOR THE VANILLA SABLÉS: Place 2 eggs in small saucepan, cover with water by 1 inch, and bring to boil over high heat. Remove pan from heat, cover, and let sit for 10 minutes. Meanwhile, fill small bowl with ice water. Using slotted spoon, transfer eggs to ice water and let stand 5 minutes. Crack eggs and peel shells. Separate yolks from whites; discard whites. Press yolks, 1 at a time, through fine-mesh strainer into small bowl, reserving 1 strained yolk for chocolate sables.

2. Using stand mixer fitted with paddle, beat butter, sugar, salt, and cooked egg yolk on medium until light and fluffy, about 4 minutes, scraping down bowl as needed. Reduce speed to low, add vanilla, and mix until incorporated. Stop mixer; add flour and mix on low speed until just combined, about 30 seconds. Using rubber spatula, press dough into cohesive mass.

3. FOR CHOCOLATE SABLÉS: Using stand mixer fitted with paddle, beat butter, sugar, salt, and reserved cooked egg yolk on medium speed until light and fluffy, about 4 minutes, scraping down bowl as needed. Reduce speed to low, add vanilla, and mix until incorporated. Stop mixer; add flour and cocoa and mix on low speed until just combined, about 30 seconds. Using rubber spatula, press dough into cohesive mass.

4. TO FORM SPIRAL COOKIES: Halve each batch of dough. Roll out each portion on parchment paper into 8 by 6-inch rectangle, ¼ inch thick. Briefly chill dough until firm enough to handle. Using bench scraper, place 1 plain cookie dough rectangle on top of 1 chocolate dough rectangle. Repeat to make 2 double rectangles. Roll out each double rectangle on parchment into 9 by 6-inch rectangle (if too firm, let rest until malleable). Starting at long end, roll each into tight log. Twist ends of parchment tightly to seal and chill logs 1 hour.

5. Adjust oven racks to upper-middle and lower-middle positions and heat oven to 350 degrees. Line 2 baking sheets with parchment paper. Using chef's knife, slice dough into ¼-inch-thick rounds, rotating dough so that it won't become misshapen from weight of knife. Place cookies 1 inch apart on prepared sheets.

6. Bake until centers of cookies are pale golden brown with edges slightly darker than centers, about 15 minutes, switching and rotating sheets halfway through baking. Let cookies cool on sheets for 5 minutes; transfer cookies to wire rack and let cool to room temperature before serving.

Holiday Spritz Cookies

✓ WHY THIS RECIPE WORKS

Spritz cookies, those golden-swirled holiday cookies, often end up bland, gummy, and tasteless. Unfortunately, this Scandinavian treat has fallen victim to many recipe modifications, such as the use of vegetable shortening instead of butter, an overload of eggs, and an excess of starchy confectioners' sugar. We set out to spruce up spritz cookies and make them light, crisp, buttery treats—the life of any holiday party.

LOAD UP ON BUTTER For rich flavor, we found that spritz must be made with butter (not shortening), and lots of it. We prefer creaming the butter with granulated sugar over other mixing methods for a light, tender texture.

INCLUDE A LITTLE HEAVY CREAM To make a smooth, workable dough, we needed more moisture: Butter alone doesn't provide enough. A little heavy cream softens the dough perfectly.

CHOOSE A YOLK Recipes for spritz cookies vary in whether they call for whole eggs or yolks alone, or even no eggs at all. Cookies made without eggs resemble shortbread—buttery and rich but too tender and crumbly with an ill-defined shape. A whole egg makes for chewy, tough cookies. Using just one yolk makes spritz that are tender, crispy, and sturdy.

PRESS OR PIPE Our dough is soft enough to press or pipe and still hold its shape in the oven, so whether you press or pipe is up to you.

SPRITZ COOKIES
MAKES ABOUT 72 SMALL COOKIES

If using a pastry bag, use a star tip to create the various shapes. For stars, a ½- to ⅝-inch tip (measure the diameter of the tip at the smallest point) works best, but for rosettes and S shapes, use a ⅜-inch tip.

To create stars, hold the bag at a 90-degree angle to the baking sheet and pipe the dough straight down, about 1 inch in diameter. To create rosettes, pipe the dough while moving the bag in a circular motion, ending at the center of the rosette; rosettes should be about 1¼ inches in diameter. To create S shapes, pipe the dough into compact Ss; they should be about 2 inches long and 1 inch wide. If you make an error while piping, the dough can be scraped off the baking sheet and repiped.

1	large egg yolk
1	tablespoon heavy cream
1	teaspoon vanilla extract
16	tablespoons unsalted butter, softened but still cool
⅔	cup (4⅔ ounces) granulated sugar
¼	teaspoon salt
2	cups (10 ounces) all-purpose flour

1. Adjust oven rack to middle position and heat oven to 375 degrees. Line 2 baking sheets with parchment paper. Whisk egg yolk, cream, and vanilla in small bowl until combined; set aside.

2. Using stand mixer fitted with paddle, beat butter, sugar, and salt at medium-high speed until light and fluffy, about 3 minutes, scraping down bowl and beater as needed. With mixer running at medium speed, add yolk mixture and beat until incorporated, about 30 seconds. With mixer running at low speed, gradually beat in flour until combined, scraping down bowl and beater as needed. Give dough final stir to ensure that no flour pockets remain. (Dough can be wrapped in plastic wrap and refrigerated for up to 4 days; before using, let it stand at room temperature until softened, about 45 minutes.)

3. If using cookie press to form cookies, follow manufacturer's instructions to fill press. If using pastry bag, fit it with star tip and fill

1. Make C-shape with 1 hand and hold piping bag. Fold bag over that hand about halfway down, insert tip, and scrape dough into bag.

2. When bag is about half full, pull up sides, push down dough, and twist tightly while again pushing down on dough to squeeze out air.

3. Grab bag at base of twist. Using your other hand as guide, hold tip at 90-degree angle about ½ inch above baking sheet and squeeze to form shape.

A BETTER WAY TO ROLL

With roll-and-cut cookies, there's always a danger of working too much flour into the dough during rolling and producing dry cookies. We like to roll out the dough between two sheets of parchment paper instead of on a floured counter. Chill the rolled-out dough in the fridge for 10 minutes to make cutting easier.

bag with half of dough. Press or pipe cookies onto prepared sheet, spacing them about 1½ inches apart, refilling cookie press or pastry bag as needed. Bake 1 sheet at a time until cookies are light golden brown, 10 to 12 minutes, rotating sheet halfway through baking. Let cookies cool on sheet for 10 to 15 minutes; transfer cookies to wire rack and let cool to room temperature before serving.

SPRITZ COOKIES WITH LEMON ESSENCE

Add 1 teaspoon lemon juice to yolk-cream mixture in step 1 and add 1 teaspoon finely grated lemon zest to butter along with sugar and salt in step 2.

ALMOND SPRITZ COOKIES

Pulse ½ cup sliced almonds and 2 tablespoons of flour in food processor until powdery and evenly fine, about 12 pulses; combine almond mixture with remaining flour. Substitute ¾ teaspoon almond extract for vanilla.

Chocolate Butter Cookies

✓ WHY THIS RECIPE WORKS

Chocolate butter cookies usually taste bland or surrender their crisp, delicate appeal to a chewy, brownielike texture. We wanted to cram big chocolate flavor into a tender, crisp cookie.

BLOOM THE COCOA Cocoa powder, which has a much higher percentage of cocoa solids than other forms of chocolate, is our choice for maximum chocolate flavor. Blooming the cocoa powder in melted butter (along with a teaspoon of instant espresso) before adding it to the dough yields a cookie with intense chocolate flavor.

REDUCE THE FLOUR AND ADD YOLKS The downside of using a generous amount of cocoa is a dry texture. To restore the moisture, we cut back on the flour. Adding rich egg yolks further reinforces the structure.

ADD VANILLA EXTRACT (AND MORE OF IT) Vanilla enhances the aromatics in the chocolate for even more chocolate flavor, so we use a full tablespoon in our cookies.

PULL THE COOKIES AT JUST THE RIGHT TIME Overbaking robs the cookies of chocolate flavor, so check on them at the lower end of the recommended baking time range and lightly press the cookies to gauge doneness. The cookies should show a slight resistance to touch.

CHOCOLATE BUTTER COOKIES
MAKES ABOUT 48 COOKIES

Natural cocoa powder will work in this recipe, but we found that Dutch-processed yields the best chocolate flavor. Espresso powder provides complexity, but instant coffee can be substituted in a pinch. The cookies are refined enough to serve plain, although a dusting of sifted confectioners' sugar or the chocolate glaze is a nice touch.

COOKIES
- 20 tablespoons (2½ sticks) unsalted butter, softened
- ½ cup (1½ ounces) Dutch-processed cocoa powder
- 1 teaspoon instant espresso powder
- 1 cup (7 ounces) sugar
- ¼ teaspoon salt
- 2 large egg yolks
- 1 tablespoon vanilla extract
- 2¼ cups (11¼ ounces) all-purpose flour

BITTERSWEET CHOCOLATE GLAZE
(OPTIONAL)

4 ounces bittersweet chocolate, chopped
4 tablespoons unsalted butter
2 tablespoons corn syrup
I teaspoon vanilla extract

I. FOR THE COOKIES: Melt 4 tablespoons butter in medium saucepan over medium heat. Add cocoa and espresso powder; stir until mixture forms smooth paste. Set aside to cool, 15 to 20 minutes.

2. Using stand mixer fitted with paddle, mix remaining 16 tablespoons butter, sugar, salt, and cooled cocoa mixture on high speed until well combined and fluffy, about 1 minute, scraping down bowl once or twice with rubber spatula. Add egg yolks and vanilla and mix on medium speed until thoroughly combined, about 30 seconds. Scrape down bowl. With mixer on low, add flour in 3 additions, waiting until each addition is incorporated before adding next and scraping down bowl after each addition. Continue to mix until dough forms cohesive ball, about 5 seconds. Turn dough onto counter; divide into three 4-inch disks. Wrap each disk in plastic wrap and refrigerate until dough is firm yet malleable, 45 minutes to 1 hour. (Alternatively, shape dough into log, about 12 inches long and 2 inches in diameter; use parchment paper to roll into neat cylinder and twist ends tightly to seal. Chill until very firm and cold, at least 1 hour.)

3. Adjust oven rack to middle position and heat oven to 375 degrees. Line 2 baking sheets with parchment paper. Working with 1 piece of dough at a time, roll 3/16 inch thick between 2 large sheets parchment paper. If dough becomes soft and sticky, slide rolled dough on parchment onto baking sheet and refrigerate until firm, about 10 minutes.

4. Peel parchment from 1 side of dough and cut into desired shapes using cookie cutters; place shapes 1 inch apart on prepared sheets.

(For cylinder-shaped dough, simply slice cookies ¼ inch thick and place on prepared baking sheets.) Bake 1 sheet at a time until cookies show slight resistance to touch, 10 to 12 minutes, rotating sheet halfway through baking; if cookies begin to darken on edges, they have overbaked. (Dough scraps can be patted together, chilled, and rerolled once.) Let cookies cool on sheet for 5 minutes; transfer cookies to wire rack and let cool to room temperature. Decorate as desired.

5. FOR THE GLAZE (OPTIONAL): Melt bittersweet chocolate with butter in heatproof bowl set over saucepan of barely simmering water; whisk until smooth. Add corn syrup and vanilla and mix until smooth and shiny. Use back of spoon to spread scant 1 teaspoon glaze almost to edge of each cookie. (If necessary, reheat to prolong fluidity of glaze.) Allow glazed cookies to dry at least 20 minutes before serving.

GLAZED CHOCOLATE-MINT COOKIES

Replace vanilla extract with 2 teaspoons mint extract. Glaze cookies with Bittersweet Chocolate Glaze and dry as directed. Melt 1 cup white chocolate chips by microwaving them at 50 percent power for 1 to 2 minutes, stirring occasionally. Drizzle over glazed cookies. Let dry at least 20 minutes before serving.

MEXICAN CHOCOLATE BUTTER COOKIES

In medium skillet over medium heat, toast ½ cup sliced almonds, 1 teaspoon ground cinnamon, and ⅛ teaspoon cayenne pepper until fragrant, about 3 minutes; set aside to cool. Process cooled mixture in food processor until very fine, about 15 seconds. Whisk nut-spice mixture into flour before adding flour to dough in step 2. Proceed with recipe, rolling dough into log. Roll chilled log in ½ cup turbinado or sanding sugar before slicing.

GLAZED CHOCOLATE-MINT COOKIES

Melt white chocolate chips in the microwave on low power or in a bowl set over a saucepan of simmering water. Transfer to a plastic sandwich bag. Snip off one corner of the bag, then drizzle over the cooled, glazed cookies.

PREPARING MEXICAN CHOCOLATE BUTTER COOKIES

Roll the chilled cylinder of dough in ½ cup turbinado or sanding sugar just before slicing into rounds and baking.

Rugelach

1. Place each dough disk
between 2 pieces of plastic
wrap and roll into 4½-inch
round.

2. Cover each dough round
with 2½ tablespoons pre-
serves, ¼ cup raisins, 2 tablespoons cinnamon sugar, and
½ cup walnuts.

3. Cut dough into 8 pie-
shaped wedges. Starting with
wide side opposite point, roll
up wedges to form crescents.
Brush each crescent with glaze
and sprinkle with remain-
ing cinnamon sugar. Bake as
directed.

✔ WHY THIS RECIPE WORKS

*Rugelach should be made out of a meltingly ten-
der, delicate dough with a slightly acidic tang. The
filling should be a bounteous combination of preserves, fruit, and nuts plus a spice-spiked sugar. But
the dough can be sticky, soft, and hard to work with,
and often the filling is either overwhelming or almost
negligible. We wanted a cookie with a tender pastry
and generous filling.*

INCREASE THE FLOUR We found traditional rugelach doughs (made from flour,
sugar, butter, and cream cheese) too sticky
to roll properly. Chilling the dough helps but
incorporating more flour into the dough further ensures a workable dough.

ADD SOUR CREAM FOR TANG Cream
cheese is a traditional ingredient in rugelach
but we wanted a cookie with more tang. Just a
few spoonfuls of sour cream makes for tender
and flaky cookies.

DON'T SKIP THE SUGAR We wondered
if our dough needed sugar since the filling
would be sweet. Indeed it does—the sugar
not only improves the flavor of the dough but
it also encourages browning.

REFINE THE FILLING The filling in
rugelach tends to leak. We may not be able to
entirely prevent this occurrence (which, after
all, adds to the rustic charm of these cookies),
but we take two steps to abate it. First, we
finely chop the nuts—this helps prevent tears
in the dough. We also process the preserves
in a food processor to get rid of large chunks.

**BAKE ON PARCHMENT-LINED BAKING
SHEETS** We always recommend baking
cookies on parchment-lined baking sheets.
With rugelach, it is especially important
because there will be some leakage. The
parchment doesn't just prevent sticking—
it will help protect your pans.

CRESCENT-SHAPED RUGELACH WITH RAISIN-WALNUT FILLING

MAKES 32 COOKIES

*Be sure to stop processing the dough when the mix-
ture resembles moist crumbs. If the dough gathers
into a cohesive mass around the blade of the food
processor, you have overprocessed it. If at any point
during the cutting and rolling of the crescents the
sheet of dough softens and becomes impossible to
roll, slide it onto a baking sheet and freeze it until
it is firm enough to handle. Feel free to substitute
chopped pitted prunes, chopped dried apricots, or
dried cranberries for the raisins in the filling.*

DOUGH

2¼	cups (11¼ ounces) all-purpose flour
1½	tablespoons sugar
¼	teaspoon salt
16	tablespoons unsalted butter, cut into ¼-inch pieces and chilled
8	ounces cream cheese, cut into ½-inch pieces and chilled
2	tablespoons sour cream

FILLING

⅔	cup apricot preserves
1	cup (7 ounces) sugar
1	tablespoon ground cinnamon
1	cup raisins, preferably golden
2¼	cups (9 ounces) walnuts, chopped fine

GLAZE

2	large egg yolks
2	tablespoons milk

1. FOR THE DOUGH: Pulse flour, sugar,
and salt in food processor to combine, about
3 pulses. Add butter, cream cheese, and sour
cream; process until dough comes together
in small, uneven pebbles the size of cottage

cheese curds, about 16 pulses. Turn mixture onto counter, press into 9 by 6-inch log, divide log into 4 equal sized pieces. Press each piece into 4½-inch round disk. Place each disk between 2 sheets of plastic wrap and roll out to form 8½-inch circle. Stack dough circles on plate; freeze for 30 minutes.

2. FOR THE FILLING: Meanwhile, process apricot preserves in food processor until smooth, about 10 seconds. Mix sugar and cinnamon in small bowl; set aside. Line 2 rimmed baking sheets with parchment paper. Working with 1 circle at a time, remove dough from freezer and spread 2½ tablespoons preserves, ¼ cup raisins, 2 tablespoons cinnamon sugar, and ½ cup walnuts over dough; pat down gently with your fingers. Cut dough round into 8 wedges. Roll each wedge into crescent shape and space crescents 2 inches apart on prepared sheets. Freeze crescents for 15 minutes.

3. FOR THE GLAZE: Adjust oven racks to upper-middle and lower-middle positions and heat oven to 375 degrees. Whisk egg yolks and milk in small bowl until smooth. Brush tops and sides of frozen crescents with egg and milk mixture. Bake crescents until pale gold and slightly puffy, 21 to 23 minutes, switching and rotating sheets halfway through baking. Immediately sprinkle each cookie with scant teaspoon cinnamon sugar; carefully transfer cookies to wire rack using wide metal spatula, and let cool for 30 minutes before serving.

CHOCOLATE-RASPBERRY RUGELACH

Substitute seedless raspberry preserves for apricot preserves and substitute 1 cup semisweet chocolate mini-chips for raisins in step 2.

Biscotti

✓ WHY THIS RECIPE WORKS

Italians like these cookies dry and hard, while American versions are buttery and more tender. We wanted something in between—that is, crisp but not tooth shattering.

USE A MODEST AMOUNT OF BUTTER A cookies' crunch or lack thereof corresponds, in part, with the amount of butter in the recipe. With this in mind, we settled on a judicious amount that would give us a dough that was neither too hard nor too lean.

AERATE THE DOUGH With a small amount of butter, we couldn't cream the butter and sugar, which aerates the dough. Instead, we needed to find other elements of the dough that could be aerated. The answer was eggs. Whipping the eggs until they are light in color and then adding the sugar does the trick. Next, we fold in the butter and the dry ingredients.

ADJUST TEXTURE WITH NUTS— DIFFERENTLY The whipped eggs give the dough lightness and lift, but make the finished cookies too crunchy. To rectify this, we swap out some of the flour for nuts (ground to a fine powder in a food processor), which gives us a more tender, flavorful cookie.

BE GENEROUS WITH ALMOND EXTRACT Using the traditional amount of almond extract produces biscotti with too-faint almond flavor because the extract's flavor dissipates after the biscotti's second stint in the oven. The solution? Compensate by increasing the amount of extract.

BAKE, THEN BAKE AGAIN ON WIRE RACK For biscotti with even crunch, bake the slices on a wire rack inside a baking sheet, flipping them halfway through baking. The wire rack allows for even air circulation around the cookies.

SHAPING AND BAKING BISCOTTI

1. Using your floured hands divide each dough half into 8 by 3-inch rectangle. Spray each loaf lightly with vegetable oil spray. Using rubber spatula lightly coated with oil spray, smooth tops and sides. Gently brush with egg white wash and bake.

2. Let cool 30 minutes, then use serrated knife to slice each loaf on slight bias into ½-inch-thick slices. Place biscotti on wire rack set in rimmed baking sheet and bake.

To get a glossy chocolate coating on your biscotti, many recipes have you temper the chocolate—a painstaking process that involves repeatedly taking the chocolate's temperature. Our way calls for barely melting the chocolate (so it doesn't overheat) and then rapidly cooling it by adding more chopped chocolate.

Melt 8 ounces bittersweet chocolate in bowl set over pan of almost-simmering water, stirring once or twice, until barely melted (about 89 degrees). Remove from heat.

To cool chocolate quickly, stir additional 2 ounces finely chopped bittersweet chocolate into melted chocolate until smooth. To coat cookies, dip into chocolate, scrape off excess with your finger, and place chocolate side up on parchment paper–lined baking sheet. Refrigerate until set.

ALMOND BISCOTTI

MAKES 30 COOKIES

The almonds will continue to toast while the biscotti bake, so toast the nuts only until they are just fragrant.

1¼	cups (6¼ ounces) whole almonds, lightly toasted
1¾	cups (8¾ ounces) all-purpose flour
2	teaspoons baking powder
¼	teaspoon salt
2	large eggs, plus 1 large white beaten with pinch salt
1	cup (7 ounces) sugar
4	tablespoons unsalted butter, melted and cooled
1½	teaspoons almond extract
½	teaspoon vanilla extract
	Vegetable oil spray

1. Adjust oven rack to middle position and heat oven to 325 degrees. Using ruler and pencil, draw two 8 by 3-inch rectangles, spaced 4 inches apart, on piece of parchment paper. Grease baking sheet and place parchment on it, pencil side down.

2. Pulse 1 cup almonds in food processor until coarsely chopped, 8 to 10 pulses; transfer to bowl and set aside. Process remaining ¼ cup almonds in food processor until finely ground, about 45 seconds. Add flour, baking powder, and salt; process to combine, about 15 seconds. Transfer flour mixture to second bowl. Process 2 eggs in now-empty food processor until lightened in color and almost doubled in volume, about 3 minutes. With processor running, slowly add sugar until thoroughly combined, about 15 seconds. Add melted butter, almond extract, and vanilla and process until combined, about 10 seconds. Transfer egg mixture to medium bowl. Sprinkle half of flour mixture over egg mixture and, using spatula, gently fold until just combined. Add remaining flour mixture and chopped almonds and gently fold until just combined.

3. Divide batter in half. Using your floured hands, form each half into 8 by 3-inch

rectangle, using lines on parchment as guide. Spray each loaf lightly with vegetable oil spray. Using rubber spatula lightly coated with oil spray, smooth tops and sides of rectangles. Gently brush tops of loaves with egg white wash. Bake until loaves are golden and just beginning to crack on top, 25 to 30 minutes, rotating sheet halfway through baking.

4. Let loaves cool on sheet for 30 minutes. Transfer loaves to cutting board. Using serrated knife, slice each loaf on slight bias into ½-inch-thick slices. Space slices, cut side down, about ¼ inch apart on wire rack set in rimmed baking sheet. Bake until crisp and golden brown on both sides, about 35 minutes, flipping slices halfway through baking. Let cool completely before serving. (Biscotti can be stored in airtight container for up to 1 month.)

PISTACHIO-SPICE BISCOTTI

Substitute shelled pistachios for almonds. Add 1 teaspoon ground cardamom, ½ teaspoon ground cloves, ½ teaspoon pepper, ¼ teaspoon ground cinnamon, and ¼ teaspoon ground ginger to flour mixture in step 2. Substitute 1 teaspoon water for almond extract and increase vanilla extract to 1 teaspoon.

HAZELNUT-ORANGE BISCOTTI

Substitute lightly toasted and skinned hazelnuts for almonds. Add 2 tablespoons minced fresh rosemary to flour mixture in step 2. Substitute orange-flavored liqueur for almond extract and add 1 tablespoon grated orange zest to egg mixture with butter.

HAZELNUT-LAVENDER BISCOTTI

Substitute lightly toasted and skinned hazelnuts for almonds. Add 2 teaspoons dried lavender flowers to flour mixture in step 2. Substitute 1½ teaspoons water for almond extract and add 2 tablespoons grated lemon zest to egg mixture with butter.

Macaroons

FORMING COCONUT MACAROONS

1. Using your fingers, form cookies into loose haystacks. Moisten fingers with water if needed to prevent sticking.

2. If desired, dip bottom ½ inch of baked cookies into melted chocolate, tapping off excess chocolate with your finger.

✓ WHY THIS RECIPE WORKS

Macaroons have deteriorated into lackluster mounds of beaten egg whites and coconut shreds or, at their worst, nothing more than a baked mixture of condensed milk and sweetened coconut. We set out to create a great coconut macaroon, with a pleasing texture and real, honest coconut flavor.

USE TWO TYPES OF COCONUT Unsweetened coconut results in a less sticky, more appealing texture. But sweetened shredded coconut packs more flavor than the unsweetened coconut, so we use both.

INCLUDE CREAM OF COCONUT To add one more layer of coconut flavor, we tried cream of coconut and hit the jackpot, with macaroons with deep coconut flavor.

BIND WITH WHITES AND CORN SYRUP As for the structure of our cookie, a few egg whites and some corn syrup ensure that the macaroons hold together well and bake up moist and pleasantly chewy.

TRIPLE-COCONUT MACAROONS
MAKES 48 COOKIES

Be sure to use cream of coconut (such as Coco López) and not coconut milk here. Unsweetened desiccated coconut is commonly sold in natural foods stores and Asian markets. If you are unable to find any, use all sweetened flaked or shredded coconut, but reduce the amount of cream of coconut to ½ cup, omit the corn syrup, and toss 2 tablespoons cake flour with the coconut before adding the liquid ingredients. For larger macaroons, shape haystacks from a generous ¼ cup of batter and increase the baking time to 20 minutes.

- 1 cup cream of coconut
- 2 tablespoons light corn syrup
- 4 large egg whites
- 2 teaspoons vanilla extract
- ½ teaspoon salt

- 3 cups (9 ounces) unsweetened shredded coconut
- 3 cups (9 ounces) sweetened shredded coconut

1. Adjust oven racks to upper-middle and lower-middle positions and heat oven to 375 degrees. Line 2 baking sheets with parchment paper.

2. Whisk cream of coconut, corn syrup, egg whites, vanilla, and salt together in small bowl; set aside. Combine unsweetened and sweetened coconuts in large bowl; toss together, breaking up clumps with fingertips. Pour liquid ingredients over coconut and mix until evenly moistened. Refrigerate for 15 minutes.

3. Working with 1 tablespoon of dough at a time, drop dough onto prepared sheets, spacing them 1 inch apart. Using your moistened fingertips, form dough into loose haystacks. Bake until cookies are light golden brown, about 15 minutes, switching and rotating sheets halfway through baking.

4. Let cookies cool on sheets until slightly set, about 2 minutes; transfer cookies to wire rack and let cool to room temperature before serving.

CHOCOLATE-DIPPED TRIPLE-COCONUT MACAROONS

Let baked macaroons cool to room temperature; line 2 baking sheets with parchment paper. Chop 10 ounces semisweet chocolate; microwave 8 ounces chocolate at 50 percent power for 2 minutes. Stir chocolate and continue heating until melted, stirring once every additional minute. Stir in remaining 2 ounces of chocolate until smooth. Holding macaroon by its pointed top, dip bottom ½ inch up sides in chocolate, scrape off excess, and place macaroon on prepared baking sheet. Repeat with remaining macaroons. Refrigerate until chocolate sets, about 15 minutes.

Meringue Cookies

WHY THIS RECIPE WORKS

A classic meringue cookie may have only two basic ingredients—egg whites and sugar—but it requires precise timing. Otherwise, you'll end up with a meringue that's as dense as Styrofoam or weepy, gritty, and cloyingly sweet. A great meringue cookie should emerge from the oven glossy and white, with a shatteringly crisp texture that dissolves instantly in your mouth.

PICK FRANCE There are three types of meringue: Italian, in which a hot sugar syrup is poured into the egg whites as they are beaten; Swiss, which heats the whites with the sugar; and French, in which egg whites are whipped with sugar alone without any heating. For this recipe, French is best. We find that it's the simplest of the meringues, and we prefer the results in comparison, for example, to the dense and candylike cookies made by the Italian method.

ADD SUGAR Pay attention to your egg whites as you beat them. You don't want to add the sugar too early, when it will interfere with the cross-linking proteins, or too late, when there isn't enough water in which the sugar can dissolve, resulting in a gritty, weeping meringue. Add the sugar just before the soft peak stage, when the whites have gained some volume but still have enough water for the sugar to dissolve. Adding the sugar in a slow stream down the side of the bowl of a running stand mixer helps distribute the sugar more evenly, which creates a smoother meringue.

USE CORNSTARCH When tasting traditional recipes, we found the majority of them to be too sweet. But when we cut back on the amount of sugar, it produced disastrous results. The meringues with less sugar started collapsing and shrinking in the oven. Why? Turns out sugar stabilizes in both the mixing bowl and the oven. Without sufficient sugar, the meringues lose moisture too rapidly as they bake, causing them to collapse. We solve this problem with a bit of cornstarch.

PIPE THE COOKIES To guarantee uniform shape and proper even cooking, it's essential to pipe the cookies rather than use a spoon. A pastry bag produces perfectly shaped meringues; a zipper-lock bag with a corner cut off works nearly as well.

TURN OFF YOUR OVEN Traditionally, meringues are baked at a low temperature and then left in the turned-off oven, sometimes for as long as overnight. The idea is to completely dry out the cookies while allowing them to remain snow white. We tried baking ours at 175 degrees, but our ovens had trouble maintaining this temperature. An hour in a 225-degree oven followed by another hour in the turned-off oven produces perfectly cooked meringues every time.

MERINGUE COOKIES
MAKES ABOUT 48 SMALL COOKIES

Meringues may be a little soft immediately after being removed from the oven but will stiffen as they cool. To minimize stickiness on humid or rainy days, allow the meringues to cool in a turned-off oven for an additional hour (for a total of 2 hours) without opening the door, then transfer them immediately to airtight containers and seal.

¾	cup (5¼ ounces) sugar
2	teaspoons cornstarch
4	large egg whites
¾	teaspoon vanilla extract
⅛	teaspoon salt

1. Adjust oven racks to upper-middle and lower-middle positions and heat oven to 225 degrees. Line 2 baking sheets with parchment paper. Combine sugar and cornstarch in small bowl.

2. Using stand mixer fitted with whisk, beat egg whites, vanilla, and salt together on high speed until very soft peaks start to form (peaks should slowly lose their shape when whisk is removed), 30 to 45 seconds. Reduce speed to medium and slowly add sugar mixture in steady stream down side of mixer bowl (process should take about 30 seconds). Stop mixer and scrape down bowl. Increase speed to high and beat until glossy and stiff peaks have formed, 30 to 45 seconds.

3. Working quickly, place meringue in pastry bag fitted with ½-inch plain tip or large zipper-lock bag with ½ inch of corner cut off. Pipe meringues into 1¼-inch-wide mounds about 1 inch high on prepared sheets, 6 rows of 4 meringues on each sheet. Bake for 1 hour, switching and rotating sheets halfway through baking. Turn off oven and let meringues cool in oven for at least 1 hour. Remove meringues from oven, immediately transfer from sheet to wire rack, and let cool to room temperature before serving. (Meringues can be stored in airtight container for up to 2 weeks.)

CHOCOLATE MERINGUE COOKIES

Gently fold 2 ounces finely chopped bittersweet chocolate into meringue mixture at end of step 2.

ORANGE MERINGUE COOKIES

Stir 1 teaspoon grated orange zest into sugar mixture in step 1.

ESPRESSO MERINGUE COOKIES

Stir 2 teaspoons instant espresso powder into sugar mixture in step 1.

TOASTED ALMOND MERINGUE COOKIES

MAKES ABOUT 48 SMALL COOKIES

See page 9 for information on toasting nuts.

¾	cup (5¼ ounces) sugar
2	teaspoons cornstarch
4	large egg whites
½	teaspoon almond extract
⅛	teaspoon salt
⅓	cup chopped toasted almonds
1	teaspoon coarse sea salt (optional)

1. Adjust oven racks to upper-middle and lower-middle positions and heat oven to 225 degrees. Line 2 baking sheets with parchment paper. Combine sugar and cornstarch in small bowl.

2. Using stand mixer fitted with whisk, beat egg whites, almond extract, and salt together on high speed until very soft peaks start to form (peaks should slowly lose their shape when whisk is removed), 30 to 45 seconds. Reduce speed to medium and slowly add sugar mixture in steady stream down side of mixer bowl (process should take about 30 seconds). Stop mixer and scrape down bowl. Increase speed to high and beat until glossy and stiff peaks have formed, 30 to 45 seconds.

3. Working quickly, place meringue in pastry bag fitted with ½-inch plain tip or large zipper-lock bag with ½ inch of corner cut off. Pipe meringues into 1¼-inch-wide mounds about 1 inch high on prepared sheets, 6 rows of 4 meringues on each sheet. Sprinkle meringues with chopped almonds and sea salt, if using. Bake for 1 hour, switching and rotating sheets halfway through baking. Turn off oven and let meringues cool in oven for at least 1 hour. Remove meringues from oven, immediately transfer from baking sheet to wire rack, and let cool to room temperature before serving. (Meringues can be stored in airtight container for up to 2 weeks.)

PIPING MERINGUE COOKIES

If you don't have a pastry bag, there's no need to rush out and buy one to make our Meringue Cookies. A zipper-lock bag will do just as well for piping the cookies.

1. Steady open zipper-lock bag inside measuring cup and fold top edge over your fingertips. Load bag using large rubber spatula or spoon.

2. Squeeze out excess air and seal bag. Use scissors to cut off bottom corner of bag.

3. Hold bag from back (behind filling) and squeeze gently, guiding tip with your free hand.

CHEWY BROWNIES

CHAPTER 7

Brownies and Bars

Classic Brownies

✓ WHY THIS RECIPE WORKS

Chewy and chocolaty, brownies should be a simple and utterly satisfying affair. But too often, brownies are heavy, dense, and remarkably low on chocolate flavor. We wanted old-fashioned brownies that had serious chocolate flavor.

USE UNSWEETENED CHOCOLATE Ounce for ounce, unsweetened chocolate has more chocolate flavor than bittersweet or semisweet chocolate (which are one-third to one-half sugar). Using a hefty amount of unsweetened chocolate gives us brownies that aren't too sweet but have profound chocolate notes. A big dose of vanilla (a full tablespoon) helps reinforce the chocolate flavor.

ADD CAKE FLOUR Chocolate contains starch, and if you're using a lot of chocolate (which we do here) it can negatively impact the texture of brownies. Switching from the usual all-purpose flour to cake flour (which has a lower protein content) makes the brownies fine-textured (not gritty) and tender. A little baking powder also lightens the texture a bit so they are not overly dense and fudgy.

TOAST THE NUTS If you mix nuts into the batter before baking the brownies, they steam and become soft. Sprinkling the nuts on top just before baking keeps them dry and crunchy; toasting them first makes them even crunchier while also enhancing their flavor.

DON'T OVERBAKE Chocolate flavor really suffers when baked goods are overbaked. Using a 325-degree oven ensures even baking (the edges don't dry out, which can be a problem when making a large pan of brownies, as we are here). Also, don't overbake brownies—you want a toothpick to come out of the brownies with a few moist crumbs still attached.

CLASSIC BROWNIES
MAKES 24 BROWNIES

Be sure to test for doneness before removing the brownies from the oven. If underbaked (the toothpick has batter, not just crumbs, clinging to it), the texture of the brownies will be dense and gummy; if overbaked (the toothpick comes out completely clean), the brownies will be dry and cakey. To melt the chocolate in a microwave, heat it at 50 percent power for 2 minutes. Stir the chocolate, add the butter, and continue heating until melted, stirring once every additional minute.

- 1¼ cups (5 ounces) cake flour
- ¾ teaspoon baking powder
- ½ teaspoon salt
- 6 ounces unsweetened chocolate, chopped fine
- 12 tablespoons unsalted butter, cut into 6 pieces
- 2¼ cups (15¾ ounces) sugar
- 4 large eggs
- 1 tablespoon vanilla extract
- 1 cup pecans or walnuts, toasted and chopped coarse (optional)

1. Adjust oven rack to middle position and heat oven to 325 degrees. Make foil sling for 13 by 9-inch baking pan by folding 2 long sheets of aluminum foil; first sheet should be 13 inches wide and second sheet should be 9 inches wide. Lay sheets of foil in pan perpendicular to one another, with extra foil hanging over edges of pan. Push foil into corners and up sides of pan, smoothing foil flush to pan. Grease foil and set pan aside.

2. Whisk flour, baking powder, and salt in medium bowl until combined; set aside.

3. Melt chocolate and butter in medium heatproof bowl set over saucepan of barely simmering water, stirring occasionally, until smooth. Off heat, gradually whisk in sugar.

Add eggs, one at a time, whisking after each addition, until thoroughly combined. Whisk in vanilla. Add flour mixture in 3 additions, folding with rubber spatula until batter is completely smooth and homogeneous.

4. Transfer batter to prepared pan; spread batter into corners of pan and smooth surface. Sprinkle toasted nuts, if using, evenly over batter. Bake until toothpick inserted in center of brownies comes out with few moist crumbs attached, 30 to 35 minutes, rotating pan halfway through baking. Let brownies cool in pan on wire rack to room temperature, about 2 hours. Remove brownies from pan using foil. Cut brownies into 2-inch squares and serve. (Brownies can be stored at room temperature for up to 3 days.)

CHOCOLATE-GLAZED MINT-FROSTED BROWNIES

MINT FROSTING

8	tablespoons unsalted butter, softened
2	cups (8 ounces) confectioners' sugar
1–2	tablespoons milk
1	teaspoon mint extract
1	recipe Classic Brownies (page 230), cooled and still in pan

CHOCOLATE GLAZE

4	ounces bittersweet or semisweet chocolate, chopped
4	tablespoons unsalted butter

1. FOR THE MINT FROSTING: Using stand mixer fitted with paddle, beat butter and sugar at low speed until just incorporated, about 30 seconds, then increase speed to medium and beat until smooth and fluffy, about 1½ minutes. Add 1 tablespoon milk and mint extract and continue to beat until combined, about 30 seconds, adding up to 1 tablespoon additional milk if necessary to achieve soft spreadable consistency. Using offset spatula, spread mint frosting evenly onto cooled brownies, cover with aluminum foil, and refrigerate until firm, about 1 hour.

2. FOR THE CHOCOLATE GLAZE: Microwave chocolate in bowl at 50 percent power for 1 to 2 minutes; stir, add butter, and continue heating until melted, stirring once every additional minute. Set aside to cool slightly, about 10 minutes.

3. Pour chocolate glaze on frosted brownies; using offset spatula, spread glaze into even layer. Cover with foil and refrigerate until firm, about 1 hour. Remove brownies from pan using foil, cut into 2-inch squares, and serve. (Brownies can be stored in refrigerator for up to 3 days.)

CLASSIC BROWNIES WITH COCONUT-PECAN TOPPING

2	large egg yolks
½	cup (3½ ounces) sugar
⅛	teaspoon salt
4	tablespoons unsalted butter, softened
½	cup heavy cream
½	teaspoon vanilla extract
1	cup (3 ounces) sweetened shredded coconut
¾	cup pecans, chopped
1	recipe Classic Brownies (page 230), cooled and still in pan

Whisk egg yolks, sugar, and salt in small saucepan until combined. Whisk in butter, then gradually whisk in heavy cream and vanilla. Cook over low heat, stirring constantly, until mixture is fluffy, begins to thicken, and registers about 180 degrees, 8 to 12 minutes. Off heat, stir in coconut and pecans. Spread topping evenly onto cooled brownies, cover with aluminum foil, and refrigerate until set, about 2 hours. Remove brownies from pan using foil, cut into 2-inch squares, and serve. (Brownies can be stored in refrigerator for up to 3 days.)

NO SUGAR SHAKER? NO PROBLEM.

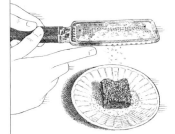

If you want to apply a light dusting of powdered sugar to brownies, cakes, or French toast and don't have a sugar shaker or fine-mesh strainer, improvise with a wide-plane rasp-style grater. A tablespoon of powdered sugar and a few quick taps create the same effect as a sifter or shaker, and the cleanup is a quick rinse under the faucet.

KNOWING WHEN BROWNIES ARE DONE

Overbaked brownies are dry and chalky and the chocolate flavor is diminished. Use the skewer test to determine doneness, but look for moist, sticky crumbs.

Ultimate Turtle Brownies

✔ WHY THIS RECIPE WORKS

Dark chocolate brownies, rich and chewy caramel, and sweet pecans—it's hard to go wrong with turtle brownies. But recipes that call for box brownie mixes and jarred caramel sauce yield lackluster results. We wanted a brownie reminiscent of a candy turtle: rich, chewy, and chocolaty, with bittersweet, gooey caramel and an abundance of pecans.

CHOOSE THE CHOCOLATE CAREFULLY
After testing a variety of chocolates, we landed on a combination of bittersweet (for complexity), unsweetened (for assertiveness), and chocolate chips, stirred into the batter (for bites of chocolate throughout).

BUILD A TENDER, YET STURDY BASE
Whole eggs, a modest amount of all-purpose flour, and baking powder give us a brownie with a structure that is partway between cakey and chewy—perfect for supporting a blanket of caramel.

INCLUDE NUTS Chopped pecans add further dimension to our brownies and whole pecans placed on top of caramel layer echo authentic "turtles."

DON'T SHORTCUT THE CARAMEL We wanted optimal flavor for our caramel topping so we made the real deal—no melted caramel candies here. Caramel made with cream, butter and sugar was pleasantly chewy and gooey. We add corn syrup to keep the caramel from crystallizing or turning gritty. Vanilla adds depth. Swirled into the batter and poured over the top, the caramel infuses every bite of these brownies with flavor.

ULTIMATE TURTLE BROWNIES
MAKES 25 BROWNIES

To drizzle the caramel in step 4, use a ¼-cup dry measuring cup that has been sprayed with vegetable oil spray. If the caramel is too cool to be fluid, reheat it in the microwave.

CARAMEL
¼	cup plus 2 tablespoons heavy cream
¼	teaspoon salt
¼	cup water
2	tablespoons light corn syrup
1¼	cups (8¾ ounces) sugar
2	tablespoons unsalted butter
1	teaspoon vanilla extract

BROWNIES
8	tablespoons unsalted butter, cut into 8 pieces
4	ounces bittersweet chocolate, chopped
2	ounces unsweetened chocolate, chopped
¾	cup (3¾ ounces) all-purpose flour
½	teaspoon baking powder
2	large eggs, room temperature
1	cup (7 ounces) sugar
¼	teaspoon salt
2	teaspoons vanilla extract
⅔	cup pecans, chopped
⅓	cup semisweet chocolate chips (optional)

GARNISH
25	pecan halves, toasted

POWDER-FREE CHOPPED CHOCOLATE

When chopped into chunks for cookies or bars, chocolate often shatters, leaving behind shavings and powder. The microwave solves the problem.

1. Place chocolate bar on microwave-safe plate and microwave on lowest setting for about 1 minute, turning chocolate halfway through microwaving. When chocolate softens and begins to melt at corners, remove it from microwave. (If chocolate bar is very thick, it may take longer to soften.)

2. Place warm chocolate on cutting board and chop it into chunks.

1. FOR THE CARAMEL: Combine cream and salt in small bowl; stir well to dissolve salt. Combine water and corn syrup in heavy-bottomed 2- to 3-quart saucepan; pour sugar into center of saucepan, taking care not to let sugar granules touch sides of pan. Gently stir with clean spatula to moisten sugar thoroughly. Cover and bring to boil over medium-high heat; cook, covered and without stirring, until sugar is completely dissolved and liquid is clear, 3 to 5 minutes. Uncover and continue to cook, without stirring, until bubbles show faint golden color, 3 to 5 minutes more. Reduce heat to medium-low. Continue to cook (swirling occasionally) until caramel is light amber and registers about 360 degrees, 1 to 3 minutes longer. Remove saucepan from heat and carefully add cream mixture to center of pan; stir with whisk or spatula (mixture will bubble and steam vigorously) until cream is fully incorporated and bubbling subsides. Stir in butter and vanilla until combined; transfer caramel to microwave-safe measuring cup or bowl and set aside.

2. FOR THE BROWNIES: Adjust oven rack to lower-middle position and heat oven to 325 degrees. Make foil sling for 9-inch square baking pan by folding 2 long sheets of aluminum foil so each is 9 inches wide. Lay sheets of foil in pan perpendicular to one another, with extra foil hanging over edges of pan. Push foil into corners and up sides of pan, smoothing foil flush to pan. Grease foil and set pan aside.

3. Melt butter, bittersweet chocolate, and unsweetened chocolate in medium heatproof bowl set over saucepan of barely simmering water, stirring occasionally, until smooth; set aside to cool slightly. Meanwhile, whisk flour and baking powder together in small bowl; set aside. When chocolate has cooled slightly, whisk eggs in large bowl to combine; add sugar, salt, and vanilla and whisk until incorporated. Add melted chocolate mixture to egg mixture; whisk until combined. Add flour mixture; stir with rubber spatula until almost combined. Add chopped pecans and chocolate chips, if using; mix until incorporated and no flour streaks remain.

4. Transfer half of brownie batter to prepared baking pan, spreading in even layer. Drizzle ¼ cup caramel over batter. Drop remaining batter in large mounds over caramel layer; spread evenly and into corners of pan with rubber spatula. Drizzle ¼ cup caramel over top. Using tip of butter knife, swirl caramel and batter. Bake until toothpick inserted in center of brownies comes out with few moist crumbs attached, 35 to 40 minutes, rotating pan halfway through baking. Let brownies cool in pan on wire rack to room temperature, about 1½ hours.

5. Heat remaining caramel (you should have about ¾ cup) in microwave until warm and pourable but still thick (do not boil), 45 to 60 seconds, stirring once or twice; pour caramel over brownies. Spread caramel to cover surface. Refrigerate brownies, uncovered, at least 2 hours.

6. Remove brownies from pan using foil, loosening sides with paring knife, if needed. Using chef's knife, cut brownies into 25 evenly sized squares. Press pecan half onto surface of each brownie. Serve chilled or at room temperature. (Brownies can be wrapped in plastic wrap and refrigerated for up to 3 days.)

Cream Cheese Brownies

✔ WHY THIS RECIPE WORKS

We set out to combine cheesecake and brownies in one perfect bar. The ideal cream cheese brownie would still be distinctly a brownie, but would have a swirl of tangy cream cheese filling in every bite. The brownie would have a rich, soft texture that would complement the lush cream cheese filling and a thin, crisp (but not overbaked) crust.

TWEAK OUR CLASSIC BROWNIES We increase the amount of ingredients of our Classic Brownies to add height, replace the cake flour with all-purpose for more structure, and use a combination of sweetened and unsweetened chocolate for more intense chocolate flavor.

ENRICH AND SWEETEN THE CREAM CHEESE An egg yolk, sugar, and vanilla add richness and flavor to the filling, and make it more fluid and easier to swirl in the batter.

LAYER AND SWIRL THE FILLING For sweet cream cheese flavor in every bite, we distribute the filling both within and on top of the brownies.

UNDERBAKE SLIGHTLY For the perfect texture, we underbake these brownies slightly, pulling them from the oven when a few crumbs still stick to a toothpick.

CREAM CHEESE BROWNIES
MAKES 16 BROWNIES

If a toothpick inserted in the middle of the pan comes out with fudgy crumbs, remove the pan immediately. If you wait until an inserted toothpick comes out clean, the brownies are overcooked. If you like nuts, you can stir 1 cup toasted walnuts or pecans into the brownie batter. To melt the chocolates in a microwave, heat them at 50 percent power for 1 to 2 minutes. Stir the chocolate, add the butter, and continue heating until melted, stirring once every additional minute.

BROWNIE BASE

- ⅔ cup (3½ ounces) all-purpose flour
- ½ teaspoon baking powder
- ¼ teaspoon salt
- 4 ounces bittersweet chocolate or semisweet chocolate
- 2 ounces unsweetened chocolate
- 8 tablespoons unsalted butter
- 1 cup (7 ounces) sugar
- 2 teaspoons vanilla extract
- 3 large eggs

CREAM CHEESE FILLING

- 8 ounces cream cheese, softened
- ¼ cup (1¾ ounces) sugar
- 1 large egg yolk
- ½ teaspoon vanilla extract

1. FOR THE BROWNIE BASE: Adjust oven rack to lower-middle position and heat oven to 325 degrees. Make foil sling for 8-inch square baking pan by folding 2 long sheets of aluminum foil so each is 8 inches wide. Lay sheets of foil in pan perpendicular to one another, with extra foil hanging over edges of pan. Push foil into corners and up sides of pan, smoothing foil flush to pan. Grease foil and set pan aside. Whisk flour, baking powder, and salt in small bowl until combined; set aside.

2. Melt bittersweet chocolate, unsweetened chocolate, and butter in medium heatproof bowl set over saucepan of barely simmering water, stirring occasionally, until smooth. Remove melted chocolate mixture from heat; whisk in sugar and vanilla; then whisk in eggs, one at time, fully incorporating each. Continue whisking until mixture is completely smooth. Add dry ingredients; whisk until just incorporated.

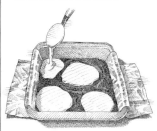

1. Pour half of brownie batter into prepared pan; then drop half of cream cheese mixture, by spoonfuls, over batter.

2. Repeat with remaining batter and cream cheese mixture. Use knife or spoon handle to gently swirl batter and cream cheese filling.

A. Neatly cutting brownies can be tricky because half the crumbs end up sticking to the knife, especially if the brownies are really fudgy. Here's a neat remedy. Instead of using a serrated or chef's knife, use a sturdy plastic knife. It glides easily through even the stickiest brownies, picking up no crumbs.

Alternately, try using a bench scraper for a clean cut:

B1. Spray both sides of bench scraper with vegetable oil spray.

B2. Push blade into brownies, spacing cuts evenly.

3. FOR THE CREAM CHEESE FILLING: Beat cream cheese in small bowl with sugar, egg yolk, and vanilla until combined.

4. Transfer half of brownie batter to prepared pan. Drop half of cream cheese mixture, by spoonfuls, over batter. Repeat layering with remaining brownie batter and cream cheese filling. Using tip of butter knife, gently swirl batter and cream cheese filling.

5. Bake until edges of brownies have puffed slightly, center feels not quite firm when touched lightly, and toothpick inserted in center comes out with several moist crumbs attached, 50 minutes to 1 hour, rotating pan halfway through baking.

6. Let brownies cool in pan on wire rack for 5 minutes. Remove brownies from pan using foil. Let brownies cool on wire rack to room temperature, about 1½ hours. Refrigerate until chilled, at least 3 hours. (To hasten chilling, place brownies in freezer for about 1½ hours.) Cut brownies into 2-inch squares and serve. (Don't cut brownies until ready to serve. Brownies can be wrapped in plastic wrap and refrigerated for up to 3 days.)

Chewy Brownies

✓ WHY THIS RECIPE WORKS

Brownies are a tricky business; homemade recipes have better flavor, while box mixes claim best texture. Our goal was clear: a homemade brownie with chewiness (and a shiny, crisp, crackly top) to rival the box-mix standard, but flush with a rich, deep, all-natural chocolate flavor.

GO FOR CHEW Most homemade brownies are either super-rich and fudgy or more cakelike and less rich. The difference between the two styles is simply the ratio of chocolate to flour. Chewy brownies, like the kind you get from a box mix, are very hard to make from scratch. We tried all kinds of tricks—everything from using condensed milk and biscuit mix instead of flour to cooking the sugar and butter into a caramel—but nothing worked. We even replaced the granulated sugar with brown sugar, but that only caused us to lose the shiny, crackly top that we expect from good brownies.

LOOK TO THE BOX It turns out that the whole key to the texture of a box brownie resides in the specific types and amounts of fat it includes. To get box-mix brownie chew in homemade, we discovered the perfect proportion of liquid to solid fat, without the aid of high-tech fats used by brownie mix makers. The magic ratio of saturated to unsaturated fat turns out to be 1:3 (as opposed to the 2:1 ratio found in homemade brownies made with butter). We balance the saturated fat of butter with unsaturated vegetable oil. To simplify the calculations in our version we eliminate melted chocolate and use cocoa powder, which contains very little fat by comparison.

ADD EXTRA YOLKS To reduce greasiness, we first tried reducing the overall fat content but found that left the brownies dry. We remembered that emulsifiers can help prevent fats from separating and leaking out during baking. We tried using mayonnaise, which worked surprisingly well, producing brownies with a rich, luxurious texture. But when we dove deeper, we identified the active emulsifier in the mayonnaise as lecithin, a phospholipid that occurs naturally in egg yolks. Rather than using mayonnaise, the simple addition of two extra yolks in exchange for a little oil makes greasiness a thing of the past.

BLOOM THE COCOA At this point, our recipe relied on just cocoa. We realized we could replace some of the butter in our recipe with unsweetened chocolate without changing the ratio of fats. Pouring boiling water over the cocoa blooms its flavor and adding a little instant espresso brings out the intensity of the cocoa. Whisking in unsweetened chocolate until melted adds another layer of full chocolate flavor.

END WITH CHUNKS OF CHOCOLATE For even more chocolate flavor, we incorporate chocolate chunks into the mixed batter. Because they don't melt until the batter starts baking, they have no effect on texture. The final results are as close to a box-mix texture as any home cook could produce without the benefits of industrial processing: chewy, fudgy bars with gooey pockets of melted chocolate that evoke images of bake sales past, but with complex flavor and just enough adult flourish to lift them out of the realm of child's fare.

CHEWY BROWNIES
MAKES 24 BROWNIES

For an accurate measurement of boiling water, bring a full kettle of water to a boil, then measure out the desired amount. For the chewiest texture, it is important to let the brownies cool thoroughly before cutting. If your baking dish is glass, cool the brownies 10 minutes, then remove them promptly from the pan (otherwise, the superior heat retention of glass can lead to overbaking). Use high-quality chocolate in this recipe.

⅓ cup (1 ounce) Dutch-processed cocoa powder

1½ teaspoons instant espresso powder (optional)

½ cup plus 2 tablespoons boiling water

2 ounces unsweetened chocolate, chopped fine

½ cup plus 2 tablespoons vegetable oil

4 tablespoons unsalted butter, melted

2 large eggs plus 2 large yolks

2 teaspoons vanilla extract

2½ cups (17½ ounces) sugar

1¾ cups (8¾ ounces) all-purpose flour

¾ teaspoon salt

6 ounces bittersweet chocolate, cut into ½-inch pieces

1. Adjust oven rack to lowest position and heat oven to 350 degrees. Make foil sling for 13 by 9-inch baking pan by folding 2 long sheets of aluminum foil; first sheet should be 13 inches wide and second sheet should be 9 inches wide. Lay sheets of foil in pan perpendicular to one another, with extra foil hanging over edges of pan. Push foil into corners and up sides of pan, smoothing foil flush to pan. Grease foil and set pan aside.

2. Whisk cocoa, espresso powder, if using, and boiling water together in large bowl until smooth. Add unsweetened chocolate and whisk until chocolate is melted. Whisk in oil and melted butter. (Mixture may look curdled.) Add eggs and yolks and vanilla and continue to whisk until smooth and homogeneous. Whisk in sugar until fully incorporated. Whisk together flour and salt in small bowl and then mix into batter with rubber spatula until combined. Fold in bittersweet chocolate pieces.

3. Transfer batter to prepared pan; spread batter into corners of pan and smooth surface. Bake until toothpick inserted in center of brownies comes out with few moist crumbs attached, 30 to 35 minutes, rotating pan halfway through baking. Transfer pan to wire rack and let cool for 1½ hours.

4. Remove brownies from pan using foil. Return brownies to wire rack and let cool completely, about 1 hour. Cut brownies into 2-inch squares and serve. (Brownies can be stored in airtight container at room temperature for up to 3 days.)

1. Place slightly stale brownies (or cookies) in food processor and pulse until they form coarse crumbs. Store in zipper-lock bag in freezer.

2. Sprinkle frozen crumbs onto ice cream or other desserts.

Fudgy Chocolate Brownies

✔ WHY THIS RECIPE WORKS

*We wanted a brownie that was distinctly fudgy—
a moist, dark, luscious brownie with a firm, smooth,
velvety texture. It must pack an intense chocolate
punch and have deep, resonant chocolate flavor.*

USE THREE KINDS OF CHOCOLATE

To develop a rich, deep chocolate flavor, we
found it necessary to give our brownies a triple
whammy of chocolate. Unsweetened chocolate lays a solid, intense foundation; semisweet
chocolate provides a mellow, even somewhat
sweet, flavor; and cocoa powder smooths out
any rough edges introduced by the unsweetened chocolate (which can contribute a sour,
acrid flavor) and adds complexity.

BUILD A MOIST, CHEWY TEXTURE

Flour, a generous three eggs, and a full stick
of butter make for a chewy, rich brownie base.
We melt the butter instead of creaming it with
the sugar and eggs; as with our Classic Brownies, the melted butter produces a more dense
and fudgy texture.

CUT SMALL PORTIONS These brown-

ies are particularly dense and rich and should
be cut into petite 1-inch squares.

FUDGY TRIPLE-CHOCOLATE
BROWNIES

MAKES 64 SMALL BROWNIES

---

*To melt the chocolates in a microwave, heat them
at 50 percent power for 2 minutes. Stir the chocolate, add the butter, and continue heating until
melted, stirring once every additional minute. Either
Dutch-processed or natural cocoa powder works well
in this recipe.*

5   ounces semisweet or bittersweet
    chocolate, chopped
2   ounces unsweetened chocolate, chopped
8   tablespoons unsalted butter, cut into
    4 pieces
3   tablespoons unsweetened cocoa
    powder

3   large eggs
1¼ cups (8¾ ounces) sugar
2   teaspoons vanilla extract
½   teaspoon salt
1   cup (5 ounces) all-purpose flour

1. Adjust oven rack to lower-middle position and heat oven to 350 degrees. Make foil
sling for 8-inch square baking pan by folding 2 long sheets of aluminum foil so each is
8 inches wide. Lay sheets of foil in pan perpendicular to one another, with extra foil hanging
over edges of pan. Push foil into corners and
up sides of pan, smoothing foil flush to pan.
Grease foil and set pan aside.

2. Melt semisweet chocolate, unsweetened
chocolate, and butter in medium heatproof
bowl set over saucepan of barely simmering
water, stirring occasionally, until smooth. Whisk
in cocoa until smooth. Set aside to cool slightly.

3. Whisk eggs, sugar, vanilla, and salt
together in medium bowl until combined,
about 15 seconds. Whisk warm chocolate mixture into egg mixture. Using rubber spatula,
stir in flour until just combined. Transfer batter to prepared pan; spread batter into corners of pan and smooth surface. Bake until
slightly puffed and toothpick inserted in center of brownies comes out with few moist
crumbs attached, 35 to 40 minutes, rotating
pan halfway through baking. Let brownies
cool in pan on wire rack to room temperature,
about 2 hours. Remove brownies from pan
using foil, loosening sides with paring knife,
if needed. Cut brownies into 1-inch squares
and serve. (Do not cut brownies until ready to
serve. Brownies can be wrapped in plastic wrap
and refrigerated for up to 3 days.)

TRIPLE-CHOCOLATE ESPRESSO BROWNIES

Whisk in 1½ tablespoons instant espresso powder or instant coffee powder along with cocoa
in step 2.

Blondies

✔ WHY THIS RECIPE WORKS

Blondies are first cousins to both brownies and chocolate chip cookies. Although blondies are baked in a pan like brownies, the flavorings are similar to those in chocolate chip cookies—vanilla, butter, and brown sugar. They're sometimes laced with nuts and chocolate chips or butterscotch chips. But even with these extras, blondies can be pretty bland, floury, and dry. We set out to fix the blondie so it would be chewy but not dense, sweet but not cloying, and loaded with nuts and chocolate.

MELT, DON'T CREAM, THE BUTTER We found that the key to chewy blondies is using melted, not creamed, butter because the creaming process incorporates too much air into the batter and makes a cakey, not chewy brownie.

GO LIGHT We prefer light brown sugar over dark. Combined with a substantial amount of vanilla extract and salt (to sharpen the sweetness), the light brown sugar develops a rich butterscotch flavor.

USE TWO KINDS OF CHOCOLATE CHIPS Semisweet chocolate chips are a given in our blondies, but adding white chocolate chips makes them even richer.

DON'T FORGET THE PECANS Pecans, toasted to intensify their flavor, cut through the sweetness of our blondies and add subtle crunch.

BLONDIES
MAKES 36 BARS

Walnuts can be substituted for the pecans. See page 9 for information on toasting nuts.

- 1½ cups (7½ ounces) all-purpose flour
- 1 teaspoon baking powder
- ½ teaspoon salt
- 1½ cups packed (10½ ounces) light brown sugar
- 12 tablespoons unsalted butter, melted and cooled
- 2 large eggs
- 1½ teaspoons vanilla extract
- 1 cup pecans, toasted and chopped coarse
- ½ cup (3 ounces) semisweet chocolate chips
- ½ cup (3 ounces) white chocolate chips

1. Adjust oven rack to middle position and heat oven to 350 degrees. Make foil sling for 13 by 9-inch baking pan by folding 2 long sheets of aluminum foil; first sheet should be 13 inches wide and second sheet should be 9 inches wide. Lay sheets of foil in pan perpendicular to one another, with extra foil hanging over edges of pan. Push foil into corners and up sides of pan, smoothing foil flush to pan. Grease foil and set pan aside.

2. Whisk flour, baking powder, and salt together in medium bowl; set aside.

3. Whisk brown sugar and melted butter together in medium bowl until combined. Add eggs and vanilla and mix well. Using rubber spatula, fold dry ingredients into egg mixture until just combined. Do not overmix. Fold in nuts and semisweet and white chocolate chips and transfer batter to prepared pan, smoothing top with rubber spatula.

4. Bake until top is shiny and cracked and feels firm to touch, 22 to 25 minutes. Transfer pan to wire rack and let cool completely. Remove bars from pan using foil. Cut into 2 by 1½-inch bars and serve.

CONGO BARS

Adjust oven rack to middle position and heat oven to 350 degrees. Toast 1½ cups unsweetened shredded coconut on rimmed baking sheet, stirring 2 or 3 times, until light golden, 4 to 5 minutes. Let cool. Add toasted coconut with chocolate chips and nuts in step 3.

Raspberry Streusel Bars

✓ WHY THIS RECIPE WORKS

Bad raspberry bars are more like crumb sandwiches than bar cookies, with a meager layer of raspberry jam that often ends up so overcooked that it turns leathery and loses every last trace of fruit flavor. We wanted just the right balance of bright, tangy fruit filling and a rich, buttery shortbread crust.

MAKE ONE DOUGH FOR TOP AND BOTTOM We realized early in developing our raspberry streusel bar recipe that the bottom crust needs to be firm and sturdy, while the topping should be light as well as sandy and dry so it can adhere to the filling. Since we didn't want to make two separate mixtures for each component, we used a butter-rich shortbread for the bottom crust and then rubbed even more butter into the same dough to produce a great streusel topping.

FILL'ER UP WITH FRUIT For full fruit flavor we use a combination of berry preserves and fresh fruit. Raspberry preserves make the filling sweet and viscous, while fresh raspberries—lightly mashed for easier spreading—produce a bright, well-rounded flavor and perfectly moist consistency.

RASPBERRY STREUSEL BARS
MAKES 20 BARS

This recipe can be made in a stand mixer or a food processor. Frozen raspberries can be substituted for fresh; be sure to defrost them before combining with the raspberry preserves. If your fresh raspberries are very tart, add only 1 or 2 teaspoons of lemon juice to the filling.

2½	cups (12½ ounces) all-purpose flour
⅔	cup (4⅔ ounces) granulated sugar
½	teaspoon salt
18	tablespoons (2¼ sticks) unsalted butter, cut into ½-inch pieces and softened
¼	cup packed (1¾ ounces) brown sugar
½	cup (1½ ounces) old-fashioned rolled oats
½	cup pecans, chopped fine
¾	cup (8½ ounces) raspberry preserves or jam
3½	ounces (¾ cup) fresh raspberries
1	tablespoon lemon juice

1. Adjust oven rack to middle position and heat oven to 375 degrees. Make foil sling for 13 by 9-inch baking pan by folding 2 long sheets of aluminum foil; first sheet should be 13 inches wide and second sheet should be 9 inches wide. Lay sheets of foil in pan perpendicular to one another, with extra foil hanging over edges of pan. Push foil into corners and up sides of pan, smoothing foil flush to pan. Grease foil and set pan aside.

2. Using stand mixer fitted with paddle, mix flour, granulated sugar, and salt at low speed until combined, about 10 seconds. Add 16 tablespoons butter, 1 piece at a time, then continue mixing until mixture resembles damp sand, 1 to 1½ minutes. (If using food processor, process flour, granulated sugar, and salt until combined, about 5 seconds. Scatter 16 tablespoons butter pieces over flour mixture and pulse until mixture resembles damp sand, about 20 pulses.)

3. Measure 1¼ cups flour mixture into medium bowl and set aside; distribute remaining flour mixture evenly in bottom of prepared baking pan. Using flat-bottomed measuring cup, firmly press mixture into even layer to form bottom crust. Bake until edges begin to brown, 14 to 18 minutes.

4. While crust is baking, add brown sugar, oats, and pecans to reserved flour mixture; toss to combine. Work in remaining 2 tablespoons butter by rubbing mixture between fingers until butter is fully incorporated. Pinch mixture with fingers to create hazelnut-size clumps; set streusel aside.

5. Combine preserves, raspberries, and lemon juice in small bowl; mash with fork until combined but some berry pieces remain.

RASPBERRY PRESERVES

In determining our top-rated brand of raspberry preserves, we first needed to define the difference between jellies, jams, preserves, and fruit spreads. A jelly is a clear, bright mixture made from fruit juice, sugar, and often pectin or acid. A jam is a thick mixture of fruit and sugar that is cooked until the pieces of fruit are very soft and almost formless. Preserves are almost identical to jams, but preserves may contain large chunks of fruit or whole fruit.

In most markets, jellies have been almost completely replaced by fruit spreads (made with juice concentrates, usually pear and white grape). Fruit spreads do not fall under the labeling standards applied to jellies and jams—hence the generic name, "fruit spreads." These products are usually made with concentrated grape and/or pear juice or low-calorie sweeteners, which replace all or part of the sugar. In our raspberry tasting, tasters felt that the concentrated fruit juices in fruit spreads obscured the flavor of the raspberries.

Based on our tasting, only a jam or preserve will do; tasters liked the bits of fruit. The difference between the two is minor; the term "preserve" implies the presence of large pieces of fruit, while a jam should have a smooth and uniform consistency. Most importantly, their flavor should speak loudly of raspberry, without too much tartness or cloying sweetness. Our top-rated brand, **Smucker's Red Raspberry Preserves**, boasted a "classic, clean" flavor, and an appropriate amount of seeds.

6. Spread filling evenly over hot crust; sprinkle streusel topping evenly over filling (do not press streusel into filling). Return pan to oven and bake until topping is deep golden brown and filling is bubbling, 22 to 25 minutes, rotating pan halfway through baking. Let cool to room temperature on wire rack, 1 to 2 hours. Loosen sides with paring knife and remove bars from pan using foil. Cut into squares and serve. (Bars are best eaten the day they are baked but can stored at room temperature for up to 3 days; crust and streusel will soften slightly.)

Is Karo corn syrup the same thing as the high-fructose corn syrup ubiquitous in soft drinks and other processed foods? In a word, no. Corn syrup (the most popular brand being Karo, introduced in 1902) is made by adding enzymes to a mixture of cornstarch and water to break the long starch strands into glucose molecules. It's valuable in candy making because it discourages crystallization; it also helps baked goods retain moisture. And because it is less sweet than granulated sugar, corn syrup makes an excellent addition to savory glazes, contributing body and sticking power.

High-fructose corn syrup (HFCS) is a newer product, coming on the market in the 1960s. It is made by putting regular corn syrup through an additional enzymatic process that converts a portion of the glucose molecules into fructose, boosting its sweetness to a level even higher than that of cane sugar. Because HFCS is considerably less expensive than cane sugar, it is widely used in processed foods, but it is not sold directly to consumers.

Pecan Bars

✓ WHY THIS RECIPE WORKS
We wanted all the best attributes of pecan pie— buttery crust, gooey filling, and nutty topping— packed into individual, bite-size bar cookies.

CHOOSE A SHORTBREAD CRUST Starting from the bottom up, we decided on a shortbread-like crust that would be substantial enough to support the filling, yet still be buttery and tender. We had the best results making the dough in a food processor, which quickly cuts the butter into the flour without overheating it. Adding nuts prevents the crust from becoming too tough.

CONCENTRATE THE FILLING'S FLAVOR Since there is less filling in a pecan bar than in a pie, the flavors must be more intense. Working with our favorite pecan pie filling recipe, we cut back on both wet and dry ingredients until we hit the delicate balance of sweetness and gooeyness we desired. To boost the flavor further, we add a substantial amount of vanilla extract, along with bourbon or rum—both common to many Southern-style pecan pie recipes. The liquor cuts through the sweetness and intensifies the flavor of the nuts. And adding salt sharpens the sweetness and also intensifies the pecan flavor.

COARSELY CHOP THE PECANS While it may sound like a minor issue, the size of the pecans is important. Whole pecans are attractive, floating on top of the bars, but they don't cut easily and make the bars hard to eat out of hand. Coarsely chopped pecans might not be as visually appealing but they are easier to eat.

PECAN BARS
MAKES 24

Assemble the pecan filling while the crust bakes. Once the crust is lightly browned, spread the filling on top and continue baking. Because of their high sugar content, pecan bars store well and taste great up to five days after baking. For efficiency, toast all the pecans at once, then measure out the nuts for the crust and the nuts for the filling. While we liked bourbon the best, dark rum is quite good. For a very boozy tasting bar cookie, add another tablespoon of liquor.

CRUST
- 1 cup (5 ounces) all-purpose flour
- ¼ teaspoon baking powder
- 1 teaspoon salt
- ⅓ cup packed (2⅓ ounces) light brown sugar
- ¼ cup pecans, toasted and chopped coarse
- 6 tablespoons unsalted butter, cut into small pieces and chilled

FILLING
- 4 tablespoons unsalted butter, melted
- ½ cup packed (3½ ounces) light brown sugar
- ⅓ cup light corn syrup

2 teaspoons vanilla extract
1 tablespoon bourbon or dark rum
½ teaspoon salt
1 large egg, lightly beaten
1¾ cups pecans, toasted and chopped
coarse

1. FOR THE CRUST: Adjust oven rack to middle position and heat oven to 350 degrees. Make foil sling for 9-inch square baking pan by folding 2 long sheets of aluminum foil so each is 9 inches wide. Lay sheets of foil in pan perpendicular to one another, with extra foil hanging over edges of pan. Push foil into corners and up sides of pan, smoothing foil flush to pan. Grease foil and set pan aside.

2. Pulse flour, baking powder, salt, brown sugar, and pecans in food processor until the mixture resembles coarse cornmeal, about 5 pulses. Add butter and pulse until the mixture resembles sand, about 8 pulses. Pat mixture evenly in the prepared pan and bake until crust is light brown and springs back when touched, about 20 minutes.

3. FOR THE FILLING: While crust is baking, whisk together melted butter, brown sugar, corn syrup, vanilla, bourbon, and salt in medium bowl until just combined. Add egg and whisk until incorporated.

4. Pour filling over hot crust and sprinkle pecans evenly over top. Bake until top is brown and cracks start to form across surface, 22 to 25 minutes. Let cool on wire rack for 1 hour. Remove brownies from pan using foil, loosening sides with paring knife, if needed. Cut into 2¼ by 1½-inch bars and serve

Lemon Bars

✓ WHY THIS RECIPE WORKS

Most lemon bars are too sweet and have a thick, soggy crust. We wanted a recipe that delivers a fresh, lemony filling paired with a thin, crisp crust.

BUILD A COOKIE CRUST Flour, butter, and sugar were the obvious go-to ingredients for this crust and it turned out okay, but swapping in confectioners' sugar for granulated made for a more tender texture. A little cornstarch added to the dough gives our crust a melt-in-the-mouth texture. To prevent the crust from turning soggy from the filling we prebake it before adding the filling.

USE BOTH JUICE AND ZEST Juice alone doesn't deliver enough bright, citrus flavor—but using both juice and zest does the trick.

THICKEN THE FILLING Eggs are a given in the lemon filling—they thicken it and provide richness. We also use a little flour to help thicken the filling further for sliceable bars.

BALANCE THE CITRUS FLAVOR To prevent the filling from tasting too puckery we found that a somewhat unexpected ingredient, whole milk, softened the citrus for a more balanced and flavorful filling.

PERFECT LEMON BARS
MAKES ABOUT 24 BARS

The lemon filling must be added to a warm crust, so be sure to prepare the filling while the crust chills and bakes. Alternatively, you can prepare the filling ahead of time and stir to blend just before pouring it into the crust.

CRUST
1¾ cups (8¾ ounces) all-purpose flour
⅔ cup (2⅔ ounces) confectioners' sugar, plus extra for dusting
¼ cup cornstarch
¾ teaspoon salt
12 tablespoons unsalted butter, chilled and cut into 1-inch pieces

LEMON FILLING

- 4 large eggs, lightly beaten
- 1⅓ cups (9⅓ ounces) granulated sugar
- 3 tablespoons all-purpose flour
- 2 teaspoons grated lemon zest plus ⅔ cup juice (4 lemons)
- ⅓ cup whole milk
- ⅛ teaspoon salt

1. FOR THE CRUST: Adjust oven rack to middle position and heat oven to 350 degrees. Make foil sling for 13 by 9-inch baking pan by folding 2 long sheets of aluminum foil; first sheet should be 13 inches wide and second sheet should be 9 inches wide. Lay sheets of foil in pan perpendicular to one another, with extra foil hanging over edges of pan. Push foil into corners and up sides of pan, smoothing foil flush to pan. Grease foil and set pan aside.

2. Process flour, sugar, cornstarch, and salt in food processor until combined, 15 seconds. Add butter and process to blend, 8 to 10 seconds, then pulse until mixture is pale yellow and resembles coarse meal, about 3 pulses.

(To do this by hand, mix flour, confectioners' sugar, cornstarch, and salt in medium bowl. Freeze butter and grate it on large holes of box grater into flour mixture. Toss butter pieces to coat. Rub pieces between fingers until flour turns pale yellow and coarse, about 1 minute.) Sprinkle mixture into prepared pan and press firmly with your fingers into even ¼-inch layer over entire pan bottom and about ½ inch up sides. Refrigerate for 30 minutes, then bake until golden brown, about 20 minutes.

3. FOR THE FILLING: Whisk eggs, sugar, and flour in medium bowl, then stir in lemon zest and juice, milk, and salt to blend well.

4. Reduce oven temperature to 325 degrees. Stir filling mixture to reblend; pour into warm crust. Bake until filling feels firm when touched lightly, about 20 minutes. Transfer pan to wire rack; let cool to near room temperature, at least 30 minutes. Remove bars from pan using foil, loosening sides with paring knife, if needed. Cut into squares and dust confectioners' sugar over squares, if desired, and serve. (Bars can be refrigerated for up to 2 days; crust will soften slightly.)

JUICING LEMONS

We've tried countless methods and gizmos for juicing lemons and dismissed most of them. However, we do endorse rolling lemons vigorously on a hard surface before slicing them open to be juiced. Why? Rolling a lemon on a hard surface is effective because it bruises, breaks up, and softens the rind's tissues while it tears the membranes of the juice vesicles (tear-shaped juice sacs), thereby filling the inside of the lemon with juice even before it is squeezed. Once a lemon is rolled, we recommend using either a wooden reamer, which effectively digs into and tears the lemon to extract as much juice as possible, or our recommended citrus juicer (see page 493), which we found was especially easy and fast and equally as effective.

However you squeeze them, we strongly recommend that you squeeze lemon juice at the last minute; testing has proven that their flavor mellows quickly and will taste bland in a short time.

Key Lime Bars

✔ WHY THIS RECIPE WORKS

We wanted to bring the essence of Key lime pie to an easy-to-eat bar, creating a cookie that balanced tart and creamy flavors and soft and crispy textures.

BUILD A STURDY, YET TENDER CRUST To support the bars so they can be picked up and eaten of hand, a thicker, sturdier crust is called for, which requires more crumbs and butter than a traditional crumb pie crust. The usual graham cracker flavor is too assertive with the lime filling; animal crackers, with their more neutral flavor, work better. Brown sugar gives the crust a mild caramel flavor.

MAKE A THICK, RICH FILLING For a thick filling that slices neatly and holds together, we supplement the usual sweetened condensed milk, lime juice, and lime zest with cream cheese and an egg yolk. These two ingredients help create a firm, rich filling that won't fall apart when the bars are picked up.

REGULAR LIME JUICE IS FINE Regular lime juice is just as good as Key lime juice, especially considering that you need to squeeze far fewer regular limes (four) than Key limes (20) to get the same amount of juice. Grated lime zest adds more citrusy lime flavor to our filling.

BAKE, COOL, AND CHILL Like cheesecake, these bars should be served fully chilled for best flavor—and so that they slice cleanly.

KEY LIME BARS
MAKES 16 BARS

The recipe can be doubled and baked in a 13 by 9-inch baking pan; increase the baking times by a minute or two.

CRUST

5   ounces animal crackers
3   tablespoons packed brown sugar
    Pinch salt
4   tablespoons unsalted butter, melted and cooled slightly

FILLING

2   ounces cream cheese, room temperature
1   tablespoon grated lime zest plus ½ cup juice (4 limes)
    Pinch salt
1   (14-ounce) can sweetened condensed milk
1   large egg yolk

GARNISH (OPTIONAL)

¾   cup (2¼ ounces) sweetened shredded coconut, toasted until golden and crisp

1. Adjust oven rack to middle position and heat oven to 325 degrees. Make foil sling for 8-inch baking pan by folding 2 long sheets of aluminum foil so each is 8 inches wide. Lay sheets of foil in pan perpendicular to each other, with extra foil hanging over edges of pan. Push foil into corners and up sides of pan, smoothing foil flush to pan. Grease foil and set pan aside.

2. FOR THE CRUST: Pulse animal crackers in food processor until broken down, about 10 pulses; process crumbs until evenly fine, about 10 seconds (you should have about 1¼ cups crumbs). Add brown sugar and salt; process to combine, 10 to 12 pulses (if large sugar lumps remain, break apart with your fingers). Drizzle melted butter over crumbs and pulse until crumbs are evenly moistened with butter, about 10 pulses. Press crumbs evenly and firmly into bottom of prepared pan. Bake until deep golden brown, 18 to 20 minutes. Let cool on wire rack while making filling. Do not turn off oven.

3. FOR THE FILLING: In medium bowl, stir cream cheese, lime zest, and salt with rubber spatula until softened, creamy, and thoroughly combined. Add sweetened condensed milk and whisk vigorously until incorporated and no lumps of cream cheese remain; whisk in egg yolk. Add lime juice and whisk gently until incorporated (mixture will thicken slightly).

4. Pour filling into crust; spread to corners and smooth surface with rubber spatula. Bake until set and edges begin to pull away slightly from sides, 15 to 20 minutes. Let cool on wire rack to room temperature, 1 to 1½ hours. Cover with foil and refrigerate until thoroughly chilled, at least 2 hours.

5. Loosen sides with paring knife and remove bars from pan using foil; cut bars into 16 squares. Sprinkle with toasted coconut, if using, and serve. (Bars can be refrigerated for up to 2 days; crust will soften slightly.)

TRIPLE-CITRUS BARS

Substitute 1½ teaspoons each grated lime zest, lemon zest, and orange zest for lime zest, and use 6 tablespoons lime juice, 1 tablespoon lemon juice, and 1 tablespoon orange juice in place of all lime juice.

TOASTING COCONUT

You can toast coconut in the oven on a baking sheet, but if you don't closely monitor it, it can burn. The microwave makes the job easier. Spread the coconut in an even layer on a large microwave-safe plate and cook it on high power until it's golden brown. It takes a couple of minutes and you need to stir it a few times (at about 30-second intervals), but there's no more worrying about leaving coconut in the oven to burn.

RUSTIC PLUM CAKE

CHAPTER 8

Snack Cakes and Fruit Cakes

Easy Chocolate Cake

Hold a fine-mesh strainer in one hand and gently tap its side with a finger from the opposite hand. (Do not shake the strainer itself; this will produce heavy spots.) Move the strainer over the next area to be covered and repeat.

✔ WHY THIS RECIPE WORKS

This easy wartime cake made with just a few ingredients (flour, sugar, cocoa powder, baking soda, vanilla, and mayonnaise, a stand-in for butter and eggs) had a lot of good things going for it, but chocolate flavor wasn't one of them. We changed that.

DEEPEN THE CHOCOLATE FLAVOR More than a half-cup of cocoa would turn the cake dry and chalky so we supplement the cocoa powder with a little melted chocolate. "Blooming" the cocoa powder in hot water intensifies its flavor, and using hot coffee instead of water enriches the flavor even more. Chopping the dark chocolate fine means we can melt it in the hot coffee as well—no need for an extra pan.

ACCENT THE CHOCOLATE WITH COFFEE A full cup of coffee adds moisture and heightens the chocolate flavor in this cake. Vanilla also serves to give the chocolate a deeper flavor.

DON'T DITCH THE MAYO As for the oddball ingredient—mayonnaise—we wondered if we could make the cake richer by replacing it with eggs and butter or eggs and oil. These cakes weren't as moist and velvety as the mayonnaise version. Why? We learned that mayonnaise contains lecithin, an emulsifier that helps keep the oil suspended in micro-droplets. These small droplets greatly aid the oil's ability to coat the flour's protein particles, leading to a supremely tender cake. Yet, while butter and oil were out, the egg was a keeper, as it helps create richer flavor and a springier texture.

AVOID OVERBAKING This cake will dry out if overbaked. Insert a toothpick into the center of the cake to gauge doneness—it should come out with a few crumbs attached.

GARNISH SIMPLY This moist and chocolaty cake needs little, if any, embellishment. A dusting of confectioners' sugar or a spoonful of whipped cream make the perfect accompaniment.

EASY CHOCOLATE CAKE
SERVES 8

Choose a high-quality chocolate for this cake. Instead of confectioners' sugar, the cake can be served with Whipped Cream (page 348).

1½	cups (7½ ounces) all-purpose flour
1	cup (7 ounces) sugar
½	teaspoon baking soda
¼	teaspoon salt
½	cup (1½ ounces) Dutch-processed cocoa powder
2	ounces bittersweet chocolate, chopped fine
1	cup brewed coffee, hot
⅔	cup mayonnaise
1	large egg, room temperature
2	teaspoons vanilla extract
	Confectioners' sugar (optional)

1. Adjust oven rack to middle position and heat oven to 350 degrees. Grease 8-inch square baking pan, line with parchment paper, grease parchment, and flour pan.

2. Whisk flour, sugar, baking soda, and salt together in large bowl. In separate bowl, combine cocoa and chocolate. Pour hot coffee over cocoa mixture and let sit, covered, for 5 minutes. Gently whisk mixture until smooth, let cool slightly, then whisk in mayonnaise, egg, and vanilla. Stir mayonnaise mixture into flour mixture until combined.

3. Scrape batter into prepared pan and smooth top with rubber spatula. Bake cake until toothpick inserted in center comes out with few crumbs attached, 30 to 35 minutes, rotating pan halfway through baking.

4. Let cake cool in pan on wire rack, 1 to 2 hours. Dust with confectioners' sugar, if using, cut into squares, and serve straight from pan; alternatively, turn cake out onto serving platter, dust with confectioners' sugar, if using, and serve.

Applesauce Cake

✔ WHY THIS RECIPE WORKS

Applesauce cake has an identity crisis. We found recipes for moist and tender spice cakes and recipes designed to be low-fat, healthy options, but what we didn't find was a lot of apple flavor. We wanted a moist and tender cake that actually tasted like its namesake.

FOLLOW THE QUICK-BREAD METHOD OF MIXING The easy challenge was to achieve the looser, more casual crumb that is best suited to a rustic snack cake. Since this texture is similar to that of quick breads and muffins, we use the same techniques, i.e. mixing the wet ingredients separately and then gently adding the dry ingredients by hand.

ADD THREE-WAY APPLE FLAVOR Most apple snack cakes are made with applesauce. But applesauce alone doesn't impart enough apple flavor in our opinion. Adding more applesauce makes for a gummy cake and fresh apples add too much moisture. But two other sources work well. Apple cider, reduced to a syrup, contributes a pleasing sweetness and a slight tang without excess moisture. And plumping dried apples in the cider while it reduces adds even more apple taste without making the cake chunky.

INCLUDE A SWEET TOPPING We like the textural contrast provided by a sweet, gently spiced streusel, made with sugar, cinnamon, nutmeg, and cloves.

APPLESAUCE SNACK CAKE

SERVES 8

The cake is very moist, so it is best to err on the side of overdone when testing its doneness. The test kitchen prefers the rich flavor of cider, but apple juice can be substituted.

- 1   cup apple cider
- ¾   cup dried apples, cut into ½-inch pieces
- 1½ cups (7½ ounces) all-purpose flour
- 1   teaspoon baking soda
- ⅔   cup (4¾ ounces) sugar
- ½   teaspoon ground cinnamon
- ¼   teaspoon ground nutmeg
- ⅛   teaspoon ground cloves
- 1   cup unsweetened applesauce, room temperature
- 1   large egg, room temperature, lightly beaten
- ½   teaspoon salt
- 8   tablespoons unsalted butter, melted and cooled
- 1   teaspoon vanilla extract

1. Adjust oven rack to middle position and heat oven to 325 degrees. Make foil sling for 8-inch square baking pan by folding 2 long sheets of aluminum foil so each is 8 inches wide. Lay sheets of foil in pan perpendicular to one another, with extra foil hanging over edges of pan. Push foil into corners and up sides of pan, smoothing foil flush to pan. Spray foil with vegetable oil spray and set pan aside.

2. Bring cider and dried apples to simmer in small saucepan over medium heat and cook until liquid evaporates and mixture appears dry, about 15 minutes. Let cool to room temperature.

3. Whisk flour and baking soda in medium bowl to combine. In second medium bowl, whisk sugar, cinnamon, nutmeg, and cloves. Measure 2 tablespoons sugar mixture into small bowl and reserve for topping.

4. Process cooled apple mixture and applesauce in food processor until smooth, 20 to 30 seconds, scraping down sides of bowl as needed, and set aside. Whisk egg and salt in large bowl to combine. Add sugar mixture and whisk until well combined and light colored, about 20 seconds. Add melted butter in 3 additions, whisking after each addition. Add applesauce mixture and vanilla and whisk to combine. Add flour mixture to wet ingredients and fold gently using rubber spatula until just combined and evenly moistened.

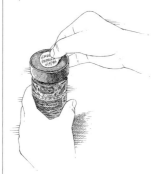

5. Scrape batter into prepared pan and smooth top with rubber spatula. Sprinkle reserved sugar mixture evenly over batter. Bake cake until toothpick inserted in center comes out clean, 35 to 40 minutes, rotating pan halfway through baking. Let cake cool completely on wire rack, about 2 hours. Remove cake from pan using foil and transfer to serving platter. Gently push side of cake with knife and remove foil, 1 piece at a time. Serve. (Cake can be stored at room temperature for up to 2 days.)

GINGER-CARDAMOM APPLESAUCE
SNACK CAKE

Omit cinnamon, nutmeg, and cloves. Whisk ½ teaspoon ground ginger and ¼ teaspoon ground cardamom into sugar in step 3. Reserve 2 tablespoons sugar mixture and add 1 tablespoon finely chopped crystallized ginger to topping.

APPLESAUCE SNACK CAKE WITH
OAT-NUT STREUSEL

In step 3, measure 2 tablespoons sugar mixture into medium bowl. Add 2 tablespoons brown sugar, ⅓ cup chopped pecans or walnuts, and ⅓ cup old-fashioned or quick oats. Work in 2 tablespoons softened unsalted butter until fully incorporated by rubbing mixture between fingers. Pinch mixture into hazelnut-size clumps and sprinkle evenly over batter before baking.

Summer Peach Cake

✓ WHY THIS RECIPE WORKS

This dessert, which marries cake with fresh summer peaches, is a bakery favorite, but most versions are plagued by soggy cake and barely noticeable peach flavor. We wanted a buttery cake that was moist yet not at all soggy, with a golden-brown exterior and plenty of peach flavor.

PRECOOK THE PEACHES Roasting chunks of peaches, tossed in sugar, peach schnapps, and a little lemon juice, helps concentrate their flavor and expel moisture before we combine them with our cake batter. However, during roasting, the peach chunks become swathed in a flavorful but unpleasantly gooey film. Our solution is to coat our roasted peaches in panko bread crumbs before combining them with the batter; the crumbs absorb the film and then dissolve into the cake during baking. To prevent the batter from pulling the crumbs off of the peaches as we fold them in, we spoon half of the batter into the pan, and arrange the panko-coated peaches on top of it. As the cake bakes, the panko disappears into the crumb, taking any trace of sticky, gloppy peach syrup with it.

BUILD A LIGHT AND TENDER CAKE BASE A simple, buttery cake, made with brown sugar for its mild caramel flavor and a little sour cream for tang, perfectly complements the sweet peaches. In addition, almond extract lends a subtle complementary note to the cake.

TOP WITH MORE PEACHES For more peach flavor and a beautiful presentation, we macerate peach slices with a little schnapps, then fan them out over the top of the cake. A sprinkling of almond extract–enhanced sugar just before baking adds sparkle and crunch.

STORING PEACHES

Keeping peaches in the fridge might seem like a good way to prolong their shelf life, but unless the fruit is ripe, the cold temperatures can turn their flesh mealy. Storing the fruit at or below 40 degrees deactivates an enzyme that breaks down its pectin during ripening. If this happens before the flesh is ripe, the pectin will remain intact and the flesh texture will be mealy. The lesson: Store peaches on the counter.

SUMMER PEACH CAKE

SERVES 8

To crush the panko bread crumbs, place them in a zipper-lock bag and smash them with a rolling pin. If you can't find panko, ¼ cup of plain, unseasoned bread crumbs can be substituted. Orange liqueur can be substituted for the peach schnapps. If using peak-of-season, farm-fresh peaches, omit the peach schnapps.

2½	pounds peaches, halved, pitted, and cut into ½-inch wedges
5	tablespoons peach schnapps
4	teaspoons lemon juice
6	tablespoons plus ⅓ cup (5 ounces) granulated sugar
1	cup (5 ounces) all-purpose flour
1¼	teaspoons baking powder
¾	teaspoon salt
½	cup packed (3½ ounces) light brown sugar
2	large eggs, room temperature
8	tablespoons unsalted butter, melted and cooled
¼	cup sour cream
1½	teaspoons vanilla extract
¼	teaspoon plus ⅛ teaspoon almond extract
⅓	cup panko bread crumbs, crushed fine

1. Adjust oven rack to middle position and heat oven to 425 degrees. Line rimmed baking sheet with aluminum foil and spray with vegetable oil spray. Grease and flour 9-inch springform pan. Gently toss 24 peach wedges with 2 tablespoons schnapps, 2 teaspoons lemon juice, and 1 tablespoon granulated sugar in bowl; set aside.

2. Cut remaining peach wedges crosswise into 3 chunks. In large bowl, gently toss chunks with remaining 3 tablespoons schnapps, remaining 2 teaspoons lemon juice, and 2 tablespoons granulated sugar. Spread peach chunks in single layer on prepared baking sheet and bake until exuded juices begin to thicken and caramelize at edges of pan, 20 to 25 minutes. Transfer pan to wire rack and let peaches cool to room temperature, about 30 minutes. Reduce oven temperature to 350 degrees.

3. Whisk flour, baking powder, and salt together in bowl. Whisk ⅓ cup granulated sugar, brown sugar, and eggs together in bowl until thick and thoroughly combined, about 45 seconds. Slowly whisk in melted butter until combined. Add sour cream, vanilla, and ¼ teaspoon almond extract; whisk until combined. Add flour mixture and whisk until just combined.

4. Pour half of batter into prepared pan. Using offset spatula, spread batter evenly to pan edges and smooth top. Sprinkle crushed panko evenly over cooled peach chunks and gently toss to coat. Arrange peach chunks on batter in pan in even layer, gently pressing peaches into batter. Gently spread remaining batter over peach chunks and smooth top. Arrange reserved peach wedges, slightly overlapped, in ring over surface of batter, placing smaller wedges in center. Stir remaining 3 tablespoons granulated sugar and remaining ⅛ teaspoon almond extract together in small bowl until sugar is moistened. Sprinkle sugar mixture evenly over top of cake.

5. Bake cake until center is set and toothpick inserted in center comes out clean, 50 minutes to 1 hour, rotating pan halfway through baking. Transfer pan to wire rack and let cool for 5 minutes. Run thin knife between cake and sides of pan; remove sides of pan. Let cake cool completely, 2 to 3 hours, before serving.

Marbled Blueberry Bundt Cake

✓ WHY THIS RECIPE WORKS

Blueberries often sink to the bottom of cake or, if they stay suspended, they burst into soggy pockets and turn the cake gummy. We wanted a tender yellow cake dotted with sweet bursts of fresh blueberries.

CREAM THE BUTTER AND SUGAR To achieve a structure that will support the berries, we cream the butter with the sugar. Buttermilk adds tang to our batter and lemon zest, brightness.

BLEND YOUR BERRIES We tried tossing the berries in flour to keep them suspended in the cake but it didn't work. And the berries burst into soggy pockets that didn't taste very good. We were stuck, until we decided to burst the berries ourselves—in a blender.

MAKE A JAM To bump up the berry flavor and add brightness we add sugar and lemon zest and juice to the puree. To ensure that the puree stays suspended throughout the cake for a marbled effect, we add pectin to the puree and let it set for several minutes.

SPOON AND SWIRL TWICE Our jam-like puree is so thick that to ensure even distribution we need to add it to the batter in two stages. We spoon in half of the batter and form a shallow channel in the middle of it. We then add half of the filling to this depression and thoroughly swirl and fold it in with a butter knife, ensuring that no large pockets of filling remain. We repeat these steps with a second layer of cake and puree. Once the cake emerges from the oven, it is lightly bronzed and smooth, with pleasing streaks of blueberry in every bite.

MARBLED BLUEBERRY BUNDT CAKE
SERVES 12

Spray the pan well in step 1 to prevent sticking. If you don't have baking spray with flour, mix 1 tablespoon melted butter and 1 tablespoon flour into a paste and brush inside the pan (see "A Truly Nonstick Bundt Pan," page 277). For fruit pectin we recommend both Sure-Jell for Less or No Sugar Needed Recipes and Ball RealFruit Low or No-Sugar Needed Pectin. If using frozen berries, thaw them before blending in step 3. This cake can be served plain or with Cinnamon Whipped Cream or Lemon Glaze (recipes follow).

CAKE

3	cups (15 ounces) all-purpose flour
1½	teaspoons baking powder
¾	teaspoon baking soda
1	teaspoon salt
½	teaspoon ground cinnamon
¾	cup buttermilk
2	teaspoons grated lemon zest plus 3 tablespoons juice
2	teaspoons vanilla extract
3	large eggs plus 1 large yolk, room temperature
18	tablespoons (2¼ sticks) unsalted butter, softened
2	cups (14 ounces) sugar

FILLING

¾	cup (5¼ ounces) sugar
3	tablespoons low- or no-sugar-needed fruit pectin
	Pinch salt
10	ounces (2 cups) fresh or thawed frozen blueberries
1	teaspoon grated lemon zest plus 1 tablespoon juice

Properly swirling the thickened blueberry puree is key to producing an elegantly marbled cake.

1. After spooning half of batter into Bundt pan, make channel with back of spoon.

2. Using spoon, fill channel with half of blueberry filling in even layer.

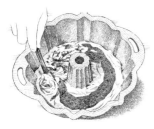

3. Using butter knife, swirl filling through batter. Repeat these steps with remaining batter and filling.

1. FOR THE CAKE: Adjust oven rack to lower-middle position and heat oven to 325 degrees. Heavily spray 12-cup nonstick Bundt pan with baking spray with flour. Whisk flour, baking powder, baking soda, salt, and cinnamon together in large bowl. Whisk buttermilk, lemon zest and juice, and vanilla together in medium bowl. Gently whisk eggs and yolk to combine in third bowl.

2. Using stand mixer fitted with paddle, beat butter and sugar on medium-high speed until pale and fluffy, about 3 minutes, scraping down bowl as needed. Reduce speed to medium and beat in half of eggs until incorporated, about 15 seconds. Repeat with remaining eggs, scraping down bowl after incorporating. Reduce speed to low and add flour mixture in 3 additions alternating with buttermilk mixture in 2 additions, scraping down bowl as needed and mixing until just incorporated after each addition, about 5 seconds. Give batter final stir to make sure batter is thoroughly combined. Remove bowl from mixer and fold batter once or twice with rubber spatula to incorporate any remaining flour. Cover bowl with plastic wrap and set aside while preparing filling (batter will inflate a bit).

3. FOR THE FILLING: Whisk sugar, pectin, and salt together in small saucepan. Process blueberries in blender until mostly smooth, about 1 minute. Transfer ¼ cup puree and lemon zest to saucepan with sugar mixture and stir to thoroughly combine. Heat sugar-blueberry mixture over medium heat until just simmering, about 3 minutes, stirring frequently to dissolve sugar and pectin. Transfer mixture to medium bowl and let cool for 5 minutes. Add remaining puree and lemon juice to cooled mixture and whisk to combine. Let sit until slightly set, about 8 minutes.

4. Spoon half of batter into prepared pan and smooth top. Using back of spoon, create ½-inch-deep channel in center of batter. Spoon half of filling into channel. Using butter knife or small offset spatula, thoroughly swirl filling into batter (there should be no large pockets of filling remaining). Repeat swirling step with remaining batter and filling.

5. Bake until top is golden brown and skewer inserted in center comes out with no crumbs attached, 1 hour to 1 hour 10 minutes, rotating pan halfway through baking. Let cake cool in pan on wire rack for 10 minutes, then invert cake directly onto wire rack. Let cake cool for at least 3 hours before serving.

CINNAMON WHIPPED CREAM
MAKES ABOUT 2 CUPS

For the best texture, whip the cream until soft peaks just form. Do not overwhip.

- 1 cup heavy cream
- 2 tablespoons confectioners' sugar
- ¼ teaspoon ground cinnamon
  Pinch salt

Using stand mixer fitted with whisk, whip all ingredients on medium-low speed until foamy, about 1 minute. Increase speed to high and whip until soft peaks form, 1 to 3 minutes.

LEMON GLAZE
MAKES ABOUT 2 CUPS

- 2 cups (8 ounces) confectioners' sugar
- 3–4 tablespoons lemon juice (2 lemons)

1. While cake is baking, whisk together sugar and 3 tablespoons lemon juice until smooth, gradually adding more lemon juice as needed until glaze is thick but still pourable (mixture should leave faint trail across bottom of mixing bowl when drizzled from whisk).

2. After cake has been removed from pan and inverted onto wire rack set in baking sheet, pour half of glaze over warm cake and let cool for 1 hour. Pour remaining glaze evenly over cake and continue to let cool to room temperature, at least 2 hours.

Rustic Plum Cake

✔ WHY THIS RECIPE WORKS

Plum cake can be anything from an Alsatian tart to a German yeasted bread. In most recipes, the plums either sink into the cake and create a sodden center or they are sliced too thin to contribute a lot of flavor. We wanted an easy-to-make cake with a sturdy yet moist crumb that had good flavor and a hefty plum presence.

CUT THE FLOUR WITH GROUND ALMONDS To create a rich, moist cake that is strong enough to hold the plums aloft, we replace some of the flour with ground almonds. Many European cakes include nut flour or ground almonds in their cakes. The ground nuts provide strength and additional flavor, and because the batter is so sturdy, it doesn't need to be mixed via the creaming method: We just mix it right in the food processor used to grind the nuts.

COAX MAXIMUM FLAVOR FROM THE PLUMS While we like the Italian plums that are especially well suited for baking, their season is very short, so we wanted a recipe that would work with common supermarket plums as well. Poaching the plums (whether Italian plums or conventional plums) in a few tablespoons of jam and brandy, as well as their own juice, sufficiently heightens their flavor and keeps them moist, even after baking.

BAKE IN A SPRINGFORM PAN Baking the cake in a springform pan ensures maximum height and makes it easy to remove this moist, rich cake from the pan.

RUSTIC PLUM CAKE
SERVES 8

This recipe works best with Italian plums, which are also called prune plums. If substituting regular red or black plums, use an equal weight of plums, cut them into eighths, and stir them a few times while cooking. Arrange the slices, slightly overlapped, in two rings over the surface of the cake. Do not use canned Italian plums. Do not add the leftover plum cooking liquid to the cake before baking; reserve it and serve with the finished cake (or reserve for serving over ice cream). The cake can be served with Whipped Cream (page 348).

3	tablespoons brandy
2	tablespoons red currant jelly or seedless raspberry jam
1	pound Italian prune plums, halved and pitted
¾	cup (5¼ ounces) sugar
⅓	cup slivered almonds
¾	cup (3¾ ounces) all-purpose flour
½	teaspoon baking powder
¼	teaspoon salt
6	tablespoons unsalted butter, cut into 6 pieces and softened
1	large egg plus 1 large yolk, room temperature
1	teaspoon vanilla extract
¼	teaspoon almond extract (optional) Confectioners' sugar

1. Cook brandy and jelly in 10-inch non-stick skillet over medium heat until thick and syrupy, 2 to 3 minutes. Remove skillet from heat and place plums cut side down in syrup. Return skillet to medium heat and cook, shaking pan to prevent plums from sticking, until plums release their juices and liquid reduces to thick syrup, about 5 minutes. Let plums cool in skillet, about 20 minutes.

2. Adjust oven rack to middle position and heat oven to 350 degrees. Grease and flour 9-inch springform pan. Process sugar and almonds in food processor until nuts are finely ground, about 1 minute. Add flour, baking powder, and salt and pulse to combine, about 5 pulses. Add butter and pulse until mixture resembles coarse sand, about 10 pulses. Add egg and yolk, vanilla, and almond extract, if using, and process until smooth, about

REMOVING FRUIT STICKERS

Fruit and vegetable stickers can be difficult to remove, especially from soft produce, such as plums and tomatoes. Try this easy solution:

I. Dip corner of paper towel in vegetable oil. Rub oiled towel over sticker and let sit for about 5 minutes.

2. Peel off offending sticker without damaging fruit.

5 seconds, scraping down bowl if needed (batter will be very thick and heavy).

3. Pour batter into prepared pan and smooth top with rubber spatula. Stir plums to coat with syrup. Arrange plum halves, skin side down, evenly over surface of batter. Bake until cake is golden brown and toothpick inserted in center comes out with few crumbs attached, 40 to 50 minutes, rotating pan halfway through baking. Run thin knife around sides of cake to loosen. Let cool in pan on wire rack until just warm or to room temperature, at least 30 minutes. Run thin knife between cake and sides of pan; remove sides of pan. Dust with confectioners' sugar and serve.

Pineapple Upside-Down Cake

JUDGING PINEAPPLE RIPENESS

Because pineapples do not continue to ripen once they're picked, we use this trick to choose ripe pineapples when we're at the grocery store. With one hand, gently tug at a leaf in the center of the fruit. If the leaf releases with little effort, the pineapple is ripe. If the leaf holds fast, choose a different pineapple. (Conversely, avoid pineapples with dried-out leaves and a fermented aroma—the fruit may be overripe.)

✓ WHY THIS RECIPE WORKS

This simple skillet dessert deserves better than bland flavors and soggy cake. We wanted a moist, rich cake with fresh pineapple flavor.

USE FRESH FRUIT AND CARAMELIZE IT The classic pineapple upside-down cake recipe relies on the simple technique of cooking the fruit (canned pineapple) in sugar and butter in a heavy skillet (usually cast iron), topping it with cake batter, and then baking it. Swapping in fresh pineapple for the canned improves its flavor but also turns the cake soggy. But we found that we could control the moisture level of the fruit by caramelizing the pineapple in the skillet with brown sugar (which we prefer over white for its mild molasses-like flavor).

REDUCE THE JUICES To further concentrate the flavor of the pineapple, we remove the fruit from the pan as soon as it turns golden brown, then add butter and reduce the syrup until it is just the right consistency. Vanilla adds depth to the pineapple flavor.

BUILD A BUTTERY BASE For a cake batter that stands up to its topping without becoming a gummy mess, we start with a classic butter cake, then cut back on the milk to alleviate gumminess and add an egg white, which lightens the texture without compromising the structure.

BALANCE THE SWEETNESS Our brown sugar–sweetened pineapple topping is plenty sweet, so we cut back on the sugar in our cake for a fruity dessert without the saccharine overload.

PINEAPPLE UPSIDE-DOWN CAKE
SERVES 8

For this recipe, we prefer to use a 9-inch nonstick cake pan with sides that are at least 2 inches high. Alternatively, a 10-inch ovensafe skillet (cast iron or stainless steel) can be used to both cook the pineapple and bake the cake. If using a skillet instead of a cake pan, cool the juices directly in the skillet while making the batter; it's fine if the skillet is warm when the batter is added.

TOPPING

1 pineapple, peeled, cored, and cut into ½-inch pieces (4 cups)
1 cup packed (7 ounces) light brown sugar
3 tablespoons unsalted butter
½ teaspoon vanilla extract

CAKE

1½ cups (7½ ounces) all-purpose flour
1½ teaspoons baking powder
½ teaspoon salt
8 tablespoons unsalted butter, softened
¾ cup (5¼ ounces) granulated sugar
1 teaspoon vanilla extract
2 large eggs plus 1 large white, room temperature
⅓ cup whole milk, room temperature

1. Adjust oven rack to lower-middle position and heat oven to 350 degrees. Grease 9-inch round nonstick cake pan, line with parchment paper, grease parchment, and flour pan.

2. FOR THE TOPPING: Cook pineapple and brown sugar in 10-inch skillet over medium heat until pineapple is translucent and has light brown hue, 15 to 18 minutes, stirring occasionally during first 5 minutes. Transfer fruit and juices to fine-mesh strainer set over bowl (you should have about 2 cups cooked fruit). Return juices to skillet and simmer over medium heat until thickened, beginning to darken, and mixture forms large bubbles, 6 to 8 minutes, adding any more juices released by fruit to skillet after about 4 minutes. Off heat, whisk in butter and vanilla. Pour caramel mixture into prepared cake pan and set aside while preparing cake. (Pineapple will continue to release liquid as it sits; do not add this liquid to already-reduced juice mixture.)

3. FOR THE CAKE: Whisk flour, baking powder, and salt in medium bowl. Using stand mixer fitted with paddle, beat butter and sugar on medium-high speed until pale and fluffy, about 3 minutes. Reduce speed to medium, add vanilla, and beat to combine. Increase speed to medium-high, add eggs and white, one at a time, and beat until combined. Reduce speed to low and add flour mixture in 3 additions, alternating with milk in 2 additions, scraping down bowl as needed (batter will be thick). Give batter final stir by hand.

4. Working quickly, distribute drained pineapple in cake pan in even layer, gently pressing fruit into caramel. Using rubber spatula, drop mounds of batter over fruit, then spread batter over fruit and to sides of pan in even layer. Gently tap pan on counter to release air bubbles. Bake cake until golden brown and toothpick inserted in center comes out clean, 45 to 50 minutes, rotating pan halfway through baking. Let cool for 10 minutes on wire rack, then place inverted serving platter over cake pan. Invert cake pan and platter together, then remove pan. Let cool to room temperature, about 2 hours, and serve.

ORANGE-CARDAMOM PINEAPPLE UPSIDE-DOWN CAKE

Add 1 tablespoon grated orange zest to skillet with pineapple in step 2 and add ¼ cup orange juice to skillet in step 2 after draining pineapple and returning juices to skillet. Whisk ¾ teaspoon ground cardamom into flour mixture in step 3.

COCONUT-GINGER PINEAPPLE UPSIDE-DOWN CAKE

Add 2 teaspoons grated fresh ginger to skillet with pineapple in step 2. Beat ¾ cup sweetened shredded coconut with butter and sugar in step 3. Substitute ½ cup room-temperature coconut milk for whole milk.

SUPERMARKET PINEAPPLE

It may not be a pressing matter for most people, but here in the test kitchen we wanted to know if all supermarket pineapples are created equal. After all, we've fallen victim to the sweet smell of these tropical beauties only to find our palates puckering from the sour fruit.

A survey of local supermarkets produced pineapple of two origins: Hawaii and Costa Rica (easily identified by their attached tags). The chosen pineapples (four from each growing region) were similar in ripeness. All yielded slightly when touched, were golden in color (green pineapples are underripe), and carried that familiar heady pineapple aroma. We tasted the fruit both straight up and in a smoothie.

The fruit from Hawaii was astoundingly astringent. Tasters could only un-pucker their mouths long enough to exclaim "bitter" and "sour." Smoothies made with this fruit were rather flavorless. The Costa Rican pineapple (sometimes labeled "extra-sweet" or "gold") triumphed in the tasting. Both straight up and in a smoothie, this fruit was packed with an ultra-sweet, honeylike flavor that one taster called "pumped-up pineapple." There are no doubt some bad Costa Rican pineapples for sale as well as some better Hawaiian fruit, but in our experience, it pays to check a pineapple's origins.

Apple Upside-Down Cake

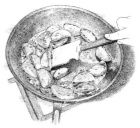

1. Precook half of apples in butter to deepen their flavor and reduce their volume, allowing more to be added. Add raw apples, brown sugar, and lemon juice to pan, then cook briefly to preserve fresh flavor.

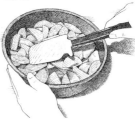

2. Transfer apple topping to cake pan and gently press into even layer.

3. Spread batter over apple topping and bake.

4. Let cake cool in pan for 20 minutes to help set apple topping, then transfer to wire rack to keep cake bottom dry.

✔ WHY THIS RECIPE WORKS

Most apple cakes we tried are plagued with weak apple flavor. We wanted a rich, buttery cake topped with tightly packed, burnished, sweet apples.

CHOOSE THE RIGHT APPLES AND USE LOTS OF THEM Most apples turned mushy and watery and were simply too sweet, but crisp, tart Granny Smiths made the cut (Golden Delicious work well, too).

PRECOOK THE APPLES We had shingled the apples in the pan and poured the cake batter over the top. But once baked and inverted, our apple layer was shrunken and dry. The solution turned out to be increasing the number of apples for a hefty layer of fruit. To prevent the extra fruit from creating a soggy cake, we sauté half the apples to draw out their moisture.

MIX A NOT-TOO-SWEET CAKE We prefer a butter cake for our base, but we wanted to offset the sweetness against the apples. We tested buttermilk, yogurt, and sour cream. Sour cream won hands down—its subtle tang balances the sweetness of the cake and complements the caramelized apples. Cornmeal gives the cake a hint of earthy flavor and a pleasantly coarse texture.

APPLE UPSIDE-DOWN CAKE

SERVES 8

You will need a 9-inch nonstick cake pan with sides that are at least 2 inches tall. Alternatively, use a 10-inch ovensafe skillet (don't use cast iron) to both cook the apples and bake the cake, with the following modifications: Cook the apples in the skillet and set them aside while mixing the batter (it's fine if the skillet is still warm when the batter is added) and increase the baking time by 7 to 9 minutes. If you don't have either a 2-inch-high cake pan or an ovensafe skillet, use an 8-inch square pan.

TOPPING

2   pounds Granny Smith or Golden Delicious apples, peeled and cored

4   tablespoons unsalted butter, cut into 4 pieces

⅔   cup packed (4⅔ ounces) light brown sugar

2   teaspoons lemon juice

CAKE

1   cup (5 ounces) all-purpose flour

1   tablespoon cornmeal (optional)

1   teaspoon baking powder

½   teaspoon salt

¾   cup (5¼ ounces) granulated sugar

¼   cup packed (1¾ ounces) light brown sugar

2   large eggs, room temperature

6   tablespoons unsalted butter, melted and cooled

½   cup sour cream

1   teaspoon vanilla extract

1. FOR THE TOPPING: Grease 9-inch round nonstick cake pan, line with parchment paper, grease parchment, and flour pan. Adjust oven rack to lowest position and heat oven to 350 degrees.

2. Halve apples from stem to blossom end. Cut 2 apples into ¼-inch-thick slices; set aside. Cut remaining 2 apples into ½-inch-thick slices. Melt butter in 12-inch skillet over medium-high heat. Add ½-inch-thick apple slices and cook, stirring 2 or 3 times, until apples begin to caramelize, 4 to 6 minutes (do not fully cook apples). Add ¼-inch-thick apple slices, brown sugar, and lemon juice and continue cooking, stirring constantly, until sugar dissolves and apples are coated, about 1 minute longer. Transfer apple mixture to prepared pan and lightly press into even layer.

ENSURING TENDER APPLES

Why do apples that go straight into the cake batter bake up too firm, while those same raw apples come out soft and tender if microwaved a bit before heading into the oven? Common sense might suggest that precooking simply hastens the fruit's breakdown. But there's more to the answer than that. As so often happens in cooking, an enzyme is involved, in this case a temperature-sensitive enzyme called pectin methylesterase (PME). As the batter's temperature climbs and lingers between 120 and 160 degrees, the PME sets the pectin in the fruit, so the slices will remain relatively firm no matter how long they are cooked. The catch, though, is that the PME is deactivated at temperatures above 160 degrees. Enter the microwave. A 3-minute zap quickly brings the apples to 180 degrees—high enough to permanently kill any activity of the PME—so the precooked fruit emerges fully soft in the finished cake.

We even double-checked the science with a side test: heating vacuum-sealed batches of both raw and microwaved apples in a *sous vide* machine to the final temperature of the cake (208 degrees) for the same amount of time it bakes (1¼ hours). The microwaved apples were predictably tender, while the slices that we didn't microwave remained firm. Furthermore, these slices never fully softened, even after we continued to cook them for another 40 minutes.

3. FOR THE CAKE: Whisk flour, cornmeal, if using, baking powder, and salt together in medium bowl. Whisk granulated sugar, brown sugar, and eggs together in large bowl until thick and thoroughly combined, about 45 seconds. Slowly whisk in butter until combined. Add sour cream and vanilla and whisk until combined. Add flour mixture and whisk until just combined. Pour batter into pan and spread evenly over fruit. Bake cake until golden brown and toothpick inserted in center comes out clean, 35 to 40 minutes, rotating pan halfway through baking.

4. Let cake cool in pan on wire rack for 20 minutes. Run thin knife around sides of cake to loosen. Place wire rack over pan and, holding rack tightly, invert cake pan and wire rack together. Lift off pan. Place wire rack with cake over baking sheet or large plate to catch any drips. If any fruit sticks to pan bottom, remove and reposition it on top of cake. Let cake cool completely, about 20 minutes, then transfer to serving platter and serve.

APPLE UPSIDE-DOWN CAKE WITH ALMONDS

You will need ¼ cup whole almonds to make ⅓ cup ground almonds. To grind the almonds, process them in a food processor for about 45 seconds.

Whisk ⅓ cup finely ground toasted almonds with flour, baking powder, and salt and add 1 teaspoon almond extract to batter with sour cream and vanilla in step 3.

APPLE UPSIDE-DOWN CAKE WITH LEMON AND THYME

Add 1 teaspoon grated lemon zest and 1 teaspoon finely chopped fresh thyme to batter with sour cream and vanilla in step 3.

French Apple Cake

✔ WHY THIS RECIPE WORKS

After tasting the ideal version of this cake in a French bistro, we were disappointed that we couldn't replicate it back home, where all the recipes produced inconsistent, unattractive cakes. We wanted a cake with the same distinct layers—a custardy, apple-rich base beneath a light, cakelike topping.

CHOOSE THE RIGHT APPLES We opted for Granny Smiths, which hold their shape well and whose tartness stands out clearly against the sweet, dense background of the cake. We toss the apples with some Calvados (a French apple brandy) and some lemon juice to add complexity.

PRECOOK THE APPLES We found that precooking the apples in the microwave for a few minutes ensures that they cook up tender in the cake and retain their structure.

LAYER TWO BATTERS To create distinct cake and custard layers, we make a basic cake batter and divide it in two. To one half we add two extra egg yolks and to the other, a bit more flour. After folding the cooked apples into the egg-rich batter, we spread it into the pan and top it with the remaining batter.

BAKE IN A SPRINGFORM PAN This ultramoist cake would be difficult to remove from a conventional cake pan in one piece, thus we use a springform pan for an easy release.

FRENCH APPLE CAKE
SERVES 8 TO 10

The microwaved apples should be pliable but not completely soft when cooked. To test for doneness, take one apple slice and try to bend it. If it snaps in half, it's too firm; microwave it for an additional 30 seconds and test again. If Calvados is unavailable, 1 tablespoon of apple brandy or white rum can be substituted.

1½ pounds Granny Smith apples, peeled, cored, cut into 8 wedges, and sliced ⅛ inch thick crosswise
1 tablespoon Calvados
1 teaspoon lemon juice
1 cup (5 ounces) plus 2 tablespoons all-purpose flour
1 cup (7 ounces) plus 1 tablespoon granulated sugar
2 teaspoons baking powder
½ teaspoon salt
1 large egg plus 2 large yolks
1 cup vegetable oil
1 cup whole milk
1 teaspoon vanilla extract
Confectioners' sugar

1. Adjust oven rack to lower-middle position and heat oven to 325 degrees. Spray 9-inch springform pan with vegetable oil spray. Place prepared pan on rimmed baking sheet lined with aluminum foil. Place apple slices in glass pie plate, cover, and microwave until apples are pliable and slightly translucent, about 3 minutes. Toss apple slices with Calvados and lemon juice and let cool for 15 minutes.

2. Whisk 1 cup flour, 1 cup granulated sugar, baking powder, and salt together in bowl. Whisk egg, oil, milk, and vanilla together in second bowl until smooth. Add dry ingredients to wet ingredients and whisk until just combined. Transfer 1 cup batter to separate bowl and set aside.

3. Add egg yolks to remaining batter and whisk to combine. Using rubber spatula, gently fold in cooled apples. Transfer batter to prepared pan; using offset spatula, spread batter evenly to pan edges, gently pressing on apples to create even, compact layer, and smooth surface.

4. Whisk remaining 2 tablespoons flour into reserved batter. Pour over batter in pan and spread batter evenly to pan edges and smooth surface. Sprinkle remaining 1 tablespoon granulated sugar evenly over cake.

5. Bake until center of cake is set, toothpick inserted in center comes out clean, and top is golden brown, about 1¼ hours, rotating pan halfway through baking. Transfer pan to wire rack; let cool for 5 minutes. Run thin knife around sides of pan and let cool completely, 2 to 3 hours. Dust lightly with confectioners' sugar, cut into wedges, and serve.

Gingerbread

✔ WHY THIS RECIPE WORKS

Most gingerbread cake recipes that are moist also suffer from a dense, sunken center, and flavors range from barely gingery to addled with enough spices to make a curry fan cry for mercy. Our ideal gingerbread is moist through and through and utterly simple—a snack cake that is baked in a square pan.

DOUBLE UP ON GINGER For a cake that tastes unabashedly of ginger, we use a hefty dose of ground ginger as well as grated fresh ginger.

CHOOSE SUPPORTING SPICES CAREFULLY We wanted to avoid the muddied spice flavors of so many gingerbreads that take the spotlight off the ginger. After testing a variety of spices, we found that just two—cinnamon and fresh-ground pepper—help produce a warm, complex, lingering heat without taking away from the ginger.

INCLUDE THREE SWEETENERS A combination of white sugar, brown sugar, and molasses works best in this cake. When we tried to cut back to one or two sweeteners, either the flavor or the texture of the cake suffered.

MAKE YOUR LIQUIDS COUNT Some recipes use water or milk as the liquid component, which in the flavor department seemed

DIY INSULATED CAKE STRIPS

Cake strips promote more even baking, preventing doming and cracking as well as keeping the edges of a cake from overbaking. This extra insulation is particularly important if the walls of your pan are thin. Here's how to make them yourself.

1. Soak 2 by 32-inch piece of cheesecloth or folded newspaper with water. Gently wring out excess water.

2. Place damp strip at bottom of 36-inch length of foil. Repeatedly fold foil over dampened strip to cover to make 2 by 36-inch strip.

3. Mold insulating strip around pan and pinch ends together to seal.

4. To ensure insulating strip stays in place around pan, secure with twine.

like a missed opportunity to us. We tried buttermilk but its tanginess dulled the ginger. Ginger beer, ginger ale, and hard apple cider seemed likely contenders but their flavors were barely detectable after baking. By contrast, dark stout, gently heated to minimize its booziness, has a bittersweet flavor that brings out the caramel undertones of the molasses.

LEAVEN WITH BAKING SODA AND STIR VIGOROUSLY To prevent a sunken center, we looked at our leaveners first. Baking powder isn't as effective at leavening if too many other acidic ingredients are present in the batter. In this cake, there are three: molasses, brown sugar, and stout. Bucking the usual protocol for cakes and incorporating the baking soda with the wet ingredients instead of the other dry ones helps to neutralize those acidic ingredients before they get incorporated into the batter and allows the baking powder to do a better job. And while stirring develops flour's gluten, which is typically the enemy of tenderness, our batter is so loose that vigorous stirring actually gives the cake the structure it needs so that its center doesn't collapse.

GINGERBREAD CAKE
SERVES 8

This cake packs potent, yet well-balanced, fragrant, spicy heat. If you are particularly sensitive to spice, you can decrease the amount of dried ginger to 1 tablespoon. Avoid opening the oven door until the minimum baking time has elapsed. Serve the gingerbread plain or with Whipped Cream (page 348).

- ¾ cup stout, such as Guinness
- ½ teaspoon baking soda
- ⅔ cup molasses
- ¾ cup packed (5¼ ounces) light brown sugar
- ¼ cup (1¾ ounces) granulated sugar
- 1½ cups (7½ ounces) all-purpose flour
- 2 tablespoons ground ginger
- ½ teaspoon baking powder
- ½ teaspoon salt
- ¼ teaspoon ground cinnamon
- ¼ teaspoon pepper
- 2 large eggs, room temperature
- ⅓ cup vegetable oil
- 1 tablespoon grated fresh ginger

1. Adjust oven rack to middle position and heat oven to 350 degrees. Grease 8-inch square baking pan, line with parchment paper, grease parchment, and flour pan.

2. Bring stout to boil in medium saucepan over medium heat, stirring occasionally. Remove from heat and stir in baking soda (mixture will foam vigorously). When foaming subsides, stir in molasses, brown sugar, and granulated sugar until dissolved; set aside. Whisk flour, ground ginger, baking powder, salt, cinnamon, and pepper together in large bowl.

3. Transfer stout mixture to second large bowl. Whisk in eggs, oil, and grated ginger until combined. Whisk wet mixture into flour mixture in thirds, stirring vigorously until completely smooth after each addition.

4. Scrape batter into prepared pan, smooth top with rubber spatula, and gently tap pan on counter to release air bubbles. Bake cake until top is just firm to touch and toothpick inserted in center comes out clean, 35 to 45 minutes. Let cake cool in pan on wire rack, about 1½ hours. Serve warm or at room temperature. (Cake can be stored at room temperature for up to 2 days.)

CHOCOLATE POUND CAKE

CHAPTER 9

Chiffon Cakes, Angel Food Cakes, Pound Cakes, and Bundt Cakes

LINING THE BOTTOM OF A TUBE PAN

If your tube pan doesn't have a removable bottom, we recommend lining it with parchment for easy cake removal. The center tube can make it tricky to cut out that perfect "circle within a circle." Here's a foolproof technique for doing so.

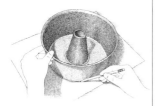

1. Place pan right side up and trace outside perimeter.

2. Turn pan upside down, place parchment on top of pan, and then place measuring cup that fits opening of center hole right in middle of traced circle, where hole is. Use it as guide to trace center hole.

3. Fold parchment into quarters and cut out hole. Finally, cut out circle.

Chiffon Cake

✔ WHY THIS RECIPE WORKS

Like the Hollywood stars of the 1920s who were the first to taste Harry Baker's secret-recipe cakes at the Brown Derby, we were delighted by the uniquely light yet full richness and deep flavor of this American invention, which came to be known as the chiffon cake. With the airy height of angel food cake (from using whipped egg whites) and the richness of pound cake (from incorporating egg yolks and oil), we sought to make our own best version.

KNOW THE HISTORY Chiffon cake was invented in 1927 by Harry Baker, a Los Angeles insurance salesman turned caterer who had been wholesaling fudge from the kitchen of the apartment that he shared with his aging mother. When the cake became a featured attraction at the Brown Derby, then the restaurant of the stars, Baker converted a spare room into his top-secret bakery, with 12 tin hotplate ovens, and personally baked 42 cakes a day. The cakes sold for a remarkable two dollars each to prestigious hostesses and the MGM and RKO studio commissaries.

Baker kept his recipe a secret for 20 years. Finally, having been evicted from his apartment, and fearing memory loss, Baker sold the recipe to General Mills. There ensued considerable testing, but with only a couple of minor changes to the technique and a new name—"chiffon cake"—the cake appeared before the American public in a 1948 pamphlet called "Betty Crocker Chiffon." It was an instant hit and became one of the most popular cakes of the time.

TINKER WITH A CLASSIC We tried the original 1920s recipe and found it too dry and cottony. Using cake flour, with its lower amount of protein and therefore less gluten, is key, but this recipe also simply needs less flour. We reduce the amount of flour used and add an extra egg yolk to help make up for the reduction in the structure of the cake. We also whip only some of the egg whites, adding the rest as is, to keep the structure without causing the cake to spill over the top of the pan.

BEAT THOSE WHITES In the original recipe the directions for beating the egg whites read, "Whip until whites form very stiff peaks. They should be much stiffer than for angel food or meringue. DO NOT UNDERBEAT." These instructions, with their anxiety-inducing capitalized words, are well taken. If the whites are not very stiff, the cake will not rise properly and the bottom will be heavy, dense, wet, and custardlike. Better to overbeat than underbeat. In fact, if you overwhip the egg whites and they end up dry and "blocky," you can simply smudge and smear any stubborn clumps with the flat side of the spatula to break them up without worrying about deflating the beaten whites, as you would when making an angel food cake. The cream of tartar helps create an especially stable egg foam.

CHIFFON CAKE

SERVES 12

If your tube pan has a removable bottom, you do not need to line it with parchment. Serve this cake as is or dust with confectioners' sugar.

- 1½ cups (10½ ounces) sugar
- 1⅓ cups (5⅓ ounces) cake flour
- 2 teaspoons baking powder
- ½ teaspoon salt
- 7 large eggs (2 whole, 5 separated), room temperature
- ¾ cup water
- ½ cup vegetable oil
- 1 tablespoon vanilla extract
- ½ teaspoon almond extract
- ½ teaspoon cream of tartar

1. Adjust oven rack to lower-middle position and heat oven to 325 degrees.

Line bottom of 16-cup tube pan with parchment paper but do not grease. Whisk sugar, flour, baking powder, and salt together in large bowl. Whisk in eggs and yolks, water, oil, vanilla, and almond extract until batter is just smooth.

2. Using stand mixer fitted with whisk, whip egg whites and cream of tartar on medium-low speed until foamy, about 1 minute. Increase speed to medium-high and whip until stiff peaks form, 3 to 4 minutes. Using large rubber spatula, fold whites into batter, smearing any stubborn pockets of egg white against side of bowl.

3. Pour batter into prepared pan, smooth top with rubber spatula, and gently tap pan on counter to release air bubbles.

4. Bake cake until skewer inserted in center comes out clean, 55 minutes to 1 hour 5 minutes, rotating pan halfway through baking. If cake has prongs around rim for elevating cake, invert pan on them. If not, invert pan over neck of bottle or funnel so that air can circulate all around it. Let cake cool completely, about 2 hours.

5. Run thin knife around edge of cake to loosen, then gently tap pan upside down on counter to release cake. Peel off parchment, turn cake right side up onto serving platter, and serve. (Cake can be stored at room temperature for up to 2 days or refrigerated for up to 4 days.)

MOCHA-NUT CHIFFON CAKE

Substitute ¾ cup brewed espresso or strong coffee for water and omit almond extract. Add ½ cup finely chopped toasted walnuts and 1 ounce unsweetened grated chocolate to batter before folding in whites.

LEMON OR LEMON-COCONUT CHIFFON CAKE

Substitute ½ teaspoon baking soda for baking powder, decrease water to ⅔ cup and vanilla to 1 teaspoon, and omit almond extract. Add 3 tablespoons grated lemon zest plus 2 tablespoons juice (3 lemons) along with vanilla in step 1. (For Lemon-Coconut Chiffon Cake, also add ¾ cup sweetened shredded coconut, coarsely chopped, to batter before folding in whites.)

ORANGE OR CRANBERRY-ORANGE CHIFFON CAKE

Substitute 2 tablespoons grated orange zest plus ¾ cup orange juice (2 oranges) for water. Decrease vanilla to 1 teaspoon and omit almond extract. (For Cranberry-Orange Chiffon Cake, also add 1 cup minced cranberries and ½ cup finely chopped toasted walnuts to batter before folding in whites.)

CHOCOLATE MARBLE CHIFFON CAKE

Combine ¼ cup unsweetened cocoa powder and 2 tablespoons packed dark brown sugar in small bowl, then stir in 3 tablespoons boiling water and mix until smooth. Follow recipe as directed, dividing batter equally into 2 separate bowls at end of step 2. Mix scant ½ cup batter from 1 bowl into cocoa mixture, then partially fold mixture back into same bowl (so that you have 1 bowl of white batter and one of chocolate batter). Sift 3 tablespoons flour over chocolate batter and continue to fold until just mixed. Pour half the white and then half the chocolate batter into the pan; repeat. Do not tap pan on counter before baking. Bake as directed.

GLAZE FOR CHIFFON CAKE
MAKES ENOUGH FOR 1 CAKE

- **4** tablespoons unsalted butter, melted
- **4–5** tablespoons milk, coffee, lemon juice, or orange juice
- **2** cups (8 ounces) confectioners' sugar

Beat butter, 4 tablespoons milk, coffee, or juice and sugar in medium bowl until smooth, thinning with more juice, milk, or coffee if necessary. Use immediately.

FILLING TUBE PANS WITH BATTER

Many bakers know the frustration of spilling batter down the hole in the center of a tube pan. Here's how to keep the batter from running inside the tube, where it can burn and cause a mess.

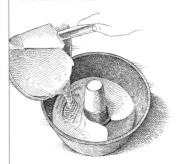

After the pan has been prepared, set a small paper cup over the center tube. You can then scrape the batter into the pan without worrying that some may end up in the tube.

GLAZING CHIFFON CAKE

Spread glaze a little at a time over cake and spread dribbles before they have a chance to harden, to make thin smooth coat. If cake starts to tear, thin glaze with up to 1 tablespoon more liquid.

Angel Food Cake

DON'T BE AFRAID TO ROTATE CAKES

In the test kitchen, we often recommend rotating cakes, pastries, and breads in the oven halfway through baking to promote even browning. (This is especially important because most ovens do not heat evenly.) But we don't generally recommended rotating delicate, airy cakes for fear that they will collapse. Without any conclusive evidence that this was the case, however, we decided to put it to the test.

We made two pairs of the most delicate cakes we could think of: fluffy yellow layer cake and angel food cake, both containing whipped egg whites, which we figured would make them prone to collapse if disturbed during baking. One set of cakes we rotated at the halfway point, jostling them clumsily in order to drive the point home. The other we left alone.

The result? Neither of the rotated cakes was worse for wear, and both were more evenly browned than the undisturbed cakes. It seems that even delicate cakes are fully set early on during baking, so there's little risk of collapse halfway through.

From now on, we will call for rotating all baked goods—even delicate cakes—halfway through baking. If you are baking on upper and lower racks, we recommend switching rack positions and rotating the cakes at the same time. It will only improve your results.

✔ WHY THIS RECIPE WORKS

Unlike other cakes, angel food cake uses no oil or butter—you don't even grease the cake pan. It doesn't call for baking soda or baking powder, either, relying solely on beaten egg whites for its dramatic height. At its heavenly best, an angel food cake should be tall and perfectly shaped, have a snowy-white, tender crumb, and be encased in a thin, delicate, golden crust. We wanted a foolproof recipe.

GRIND SUGAR EXTRA-FINE Granulated or confectioners' sugar will make acceptable but somewhat heavy cakes. For an extraordinary angel food cake, process granulated sugar in the food processor until powdery. It will dissolve much faster, so it won't deflate the egg whites.

KEEP YOLKS AT BAY We stirred ½ teaspoon of egg yolk into a dozen whites, just to see what would happen. The eggs turned white and frothy with whipping, but even after 25 minutes, they failed to form peaks. Lesson learned: Separate eggs with care.

FLUFF WITH FLOUR Some recipes call for sifting the flour and/or sugar as many as eight times. What a pain! We tried skipping sifting altogether, but the resulting cake was squat. Ultimately, we figured out that by processing the flour (with half the sugar) in the food processor to aerate it, we could get away with sifting just once.

FOLD GENTLY Use a rubber spatula to gently turn or "fold" the flour and egg whites over one another until they are thoroughly combined. Add the flour in three batches so you don't deflate the whites.

COOL UPSIDE DOWN Invert the cooked cake until it is completely cool, about 3 hours. If you don't have a pan with feet, invert it over the neck of a bottle. Angel food cakes cooled right side up can be crushed by their own weight.

ANGEL FOOD CAKE
SERVES 10 TO 12

Do not use all-purpose flour. Our tasters unflatteringly compared a cake made with it to Wonder Bread. If your angel food cake pan does not have a removable bottom, line the bottom of the pan with parchment paper (see page 268). In either case, do not grease the pan (or the paper).

1	cup plus 2 tablespoons (4½ ounces) cake flour
¼	teaspoon salt
1¾	cups (12¼ ounces) sugar
12	large egg whites
1½	teaspoons cream of tartar
1	teaspoon vanilla extract

1. Adjust oven rack to lower-middle position and heat oven to 325 degrees. Whisk flour and salt together in bowl. Process sugar in food processor until fine and powdery, about 1 minute. Reserve half of sugar in small bowl. Add flour mixture to food processor with remaining sugar and process until aerated, about 1 minute.

2. Using stand mixer fitted with whisk, whip egg whites and cream of tartar on medium-low speed until foamy, about 1 minute. Increase speed to medium-high, slowly add reserved sugar, and whip until soft peaks form, about 6 minutes. Add vanilla and mix until incorporated.

3. Sift flour mixture over egg whites in 3 additions, folding gently with rubber spatula after each addition until incorporated. Scrape mixture into ungreased 12-cup tube pan.

4. Bake until skewer inserted in center comes out clean and cracks in cake appear dry, 40 to 45 minutes, rotating pan halfway through baking. Let cake cool completely in

pan, upside down, about 3 hours. Run thin knife around edge of cake to loosen, then gently tap pan upside down on counter to release cake. Turn cake right side up onto serving platter and serve.

LEMON–POPPY SEED ANGEL FOOD CAKE

Add 2 tablespoons grated lemon zest and 2 tablespoons juice (2 lemons) along with vanilla extract in step 2. Fold 1 tablespoon poppy seeds into batter along with flour in step 3.

CHOCOLATE-ALMOND ANGEL FOOD CAKE

Replace ½ teaspoon vanilla extract with ½ teaspoon almond extract in step 2. Fold 2 ounces finely grated bittersweet chocolate into batter following flour in step 3.

CAFÉ AU LAIT ANGEL FOOD CAKE

Add 1 tablespoon instant coffee or espresso powder to food processor along with flour in step 1. Replace ½ teaspoon vanilla with 1 tablespoon coffee liqueur in step 2.

Classic Pound Cake

✓ WHY THIS RECIPE WORKS

A perfect recipe for pound cake is hard to find. Good-looking pound cakes tend to resemble yellow layer cakes: fluffy, bouncy, and open-textured. Those that taste good often bake up as flat and firm as bricks. We wanted to retool this classic recipe to make it great-tasting and ultraplush, every time.

CREAM PROPERLY Good pound cake should have a fine, even crumb and suedelike texture. To get a good rise, you have to cream the butter properly. That's because traditional recipes contain no leavener—all the rise is provided by air incorporated into the butter and the eggs. Modern recipes often cheat and add baking powder. Sure, the pound cake rises, but now the texture is too light—more like yellow layer cake than pound cake.

START WITH COLD BUTTER Many recipes that call for creaming butter start with softened butter (65 to 67 degrees). Because the butter in this recipe needs to be beaten quite a long time (to work in as much air as possible) you need to start with the butter at a lower temperature—60 degrees is best. For best results, check the temperature of the butter with an instant-read thermometer.

USE CHILLY EGGS Even when the butter is properly creamed, this doesn't mean success is guaranteed. The temperature of the eggs plays a role as well. Too-warm eggs can deflate the batter. And if the eggs are too cold or added too quickly, they are difficult to incorporate and the air is knocked out of the butter by the time you have a smooth batter. After trial and error, we've found that 60 degrees is also the perfect temperature for the eggs in this recipe.

ADD EGGS SLOWLY Most cake recipes say to add eggs one at a time, mixing well and scraping the bowl after each addition. Frankly, the pound cake never worked well using this method. The delicate batter just couldn't absorb a whole egg at once yet retain its aeration. Some pound cake recipes require a more extreme method—the eggs are beaten together in a measuring cup then slowly dribbled into the creamed butter and sugar, a process that takes up to 5 minutes. We discovered that if the beaten eggs are added very gradually, they can be incorporated in 60 to 90 seconds, as long as the mixture is beaten a few additional minutes once the last egg is added. This technique results in batter that is more stable and produces a much better pound cake that rises higher and has a lighter texture.

SIFT THE CAKE FLOUR   Lower-protein cake flour helps create a pound cake that is tender. Sifting the flour over the batter makes it easier to incorporate the flour.

CLASSIC POUND CAKE
SERVES 8

The butter and eggs should be the first ingredients prepared so they have a chance to stand at room temperature and lose their chill while the oven heats, the loaf pan is greased and floured, and the other ingredients are measured. The test kitchen's preferred loaf pan measures 8½ by 4½ inches; if you use a 9 by 5-inch loaf pan, start checking for doneness 5 minutes earlier than advised in the recipe.

16	tablespoons unsalted butter, chilled
3	large eggs plus 3 large yolks
2	teaspoons vanilla extract
½	teaspoon salt
1¼	cups (8¾ ounces) sugar
1¾	cups (7 ounces) cake flour

1. Cut butter into 16 pieces and place in bowl of stand mixer; let stand at room temperature for 20 to 30 minutes to soften slightly (butter should reach no more than 60 degrees). Using dinner fork, beat eggs and yolks and vanilla in 4-cup liquid measuring cup until combined. Let egg mixture stand at room temperature until ready to use.

2. Adjust oven rack to middle position and heat oven to 325 degrees. Grease and flour 8½ by 4½-inch loaf pan.

3. Fit stand mixer with paddle and beat butter and salt at medium-high speed until shiny, smooth, and creamy, 2 to 3 minutes, scraping down bowl once. Reduce speed to medium and gradually pour in sugar (this should take about 1 minute). Once all sugar is added, increase speed to medium-high and beat until mixture is light and fluffy, 5 to 8 minutes, scraping down bowl once. Reduce speed to medium and gradually add egg mixture in slow, steady stream (this should take

1 to 1½ minutes). Scrape down bowl, then beat mixture at medium-high speed until light and fluffy, 3 to 4 minutes (batter may look slightly curdled). Remove bowl from mixer and scrape down bowl.

4. Sift flour over butter-egg mixture in 3 additions, folding gently with rubber spatula until combined after each addition. Scrape along bottom of bowl to ensure batter is homogeneous.

5. Pour batter into prepared pan and smooth top with rubber spatula. Bake cake until golden brown and toothpick inserted in center comes out clean, 1 hour 10 minutes to 1 hour 20 minutes, rotating pan halfway through baking. Let cake cool in pan on wire rack for 15 minutes, then invert cake onto wire rack and turn cake right side up. Let cake cool completely on rack, about 2 hours, before serving. (Cake can be stored at room temperature for up to 3 days.)

ALMOND POUND CAKE

Reduce vanilla to 1 teaspoon and add 1½ teaspoons almond extract to eggs along with vanilla. Sprinkle 2 tablespoons sliced almonds over surface of batter just before baking.

POUND CAKE WITH ORANGE ESSENCE

Reduce vanilla to 1 teaspoon and add 1 tablespoon grated then minced orange zest to mixer bowl just after adding eggs in step 3.

CLASSIC POUND CAKE IN A TUBE PAN

Double all ingredients and substitute greased and floured 16-cup tube pan for loaf pan. Bake cake at 350 degrees for 15 minutes, then reduce oven temperature to 325 degrees and continue to bake until cake is golden brown and skewer inserted in center of cake comes out clean, 40 to 45 minutes. Let cake cool in pan on wire rack for 30 minutes, then invert cake onto wire rack and turn cake right side up. Let cake cool completely on rack, about 3 hours, before serving.

MAKING POUND CAKE

In addition to properly creaming the butter and sugar for pound cake, you must also take care with the flour and eggs. Pound cake batter is so delicate that it will deflate if you add the flour too quickly or add the eggs one at a time, as most recipes suggest.

FOR THE EGGS: With mixer running, pour in beaten egg mixture in slow, steady stream.

FOR THE FLOUR: Sift flour over batter in 3 additions, folding in each addition with rubber spatula.

Cake recipes often call for room-temperature eggs, which incorporate into the batter more readily than cold eggs. We wondered, though, if the difference between room-temperature and cold eggs was so great that it could actually ruin a basic cake recipe. To find out, we conducted a blind tasting of two yellow cakes: one made with room-temperature eggs, the other with chilled eggs. The cake prepared with cold eggs produced a slightly thicker batter and took 5 minutes longer to bake. The cake made with room-temperature eggs had a slightly finer, more even crumb, but the cold-egg cake was entirely acceptable. Overall, tasters strained to detect differences between the two cakes, so it's fine to use cold eggs in most basic cake recipes.

However, cold eggs can cause problems in finicky cakes, such as pound, angel food, and chiffon, that rely on air incorporated into the beaten eggs as a primary means of leavening. In these cases, we found that cold eggs didn't whip nearly as well as room-temperature eggs and the cakes didn't rise properly. To quickly warm whole eggs, place them in a bowl and cover them with hot—but not boiling—tap water for 5 minutes. Since it is easier to separate eggs when they are cold, eggs can be separated first and allowed to warm up while the remaining ingredients are assembled. If necessary, the whites or yolks can be placed in a bowl nestled within another bowl filled with warm water to speed up the process.

Easy Lemon Pound Cake

✔ **WHY THIS RECIPE WORKS**

Lemon pound cakes often lack true lemon flavor. We wanted to produce a superior lemon pound cake while making the process as simple and foolproof as possible.

PICK CAKE FLOUR Cake flour produces a tender crumb and the addition of baking powder increases lift and creates a fine, consistent texture.

EXTRACT LEMON OILS THE EASY WAY We pulse a generous amount of lemon zest in a food processor with sugar to break down the zest so that it incorporates smoothly into the batter. This method also extracts oils from the lemon zest so that they fully coat the sugar, and it more evenly distributes lemon flavor throughout the batter.

MIX THE BATTER IN A FOOD PROCESSOR Since we had our food processor out to mince the lemon zest and mix it with the sugar, we found that we could use it to mix the batter as well. A food processor ensures a perfect emulsification of the eggs, sugar, and melted butter (a blender works, too).

POKE AND GLAZE For a final layer of sweet lemon flavor, we glaze the finished cake with lemon sugar syrup—but first we poke holes all over the cake to ensure that the tangy, sweet glaze infuses the cake with citrus and just doesn't pool across the top.

EASY LEMON POUND CAKE
SERVES 8

You can use a blender instead of a food processor to mix the batter. To add the butter, remove the center cap of the lid so the butter can be drizzled into the whirling blender with minimal splattering. This batter looks almost like a thick pancake batter and is very fluid. The test kitchen's preferred loaf pan measures 8½ by 4½ inches; if you use a 9 by 5-inch loaf pan, start checking for doneness 5 minutes earlier than advised in the recipe. You will need a total of 2 lemons for this recipe.

CAKE

1½	cups (6 ounces) cake flour
1	teaspoon baking powder
½	teaspoon salt
16	tablespoons unsalted butter
1¼	cups (8¾ ounces) sugar
2	tablespoons grated lemon zest plus 2 teaspoons juice (2 lemons)
4	large eggs, room temperature
1½	teaspoons vanilla extract

LEMON GLAZE

½	cup (3½ ounces) sugar
¼	cup lemon juice (2 lemons)

1. FOR THE CAKE: Adjust oven rack to middle position and heat oven to 350 degrees. Grease and flour 8½ by 4½-inch loaf pan. In medium bowl, whisk together flour, baking powder, and salt; set aside.

2. Melt butter in small saucepan over medium heat. Whisk melted butter thoroughly to reincorporate any separated milk solids.

3. Pulse sugar and lemon zest in food processor until combined, about 5 pulses. Add lemon juice, eggs, and vanilla and process until combined, about 5 seconds. With processor running, add melted butter in steady stream (this should take about 20 seconds). Transfer mixture to large bowl. Sift flour mixture over eggs in 3 additions, whisking gently after each addition until just combined.

4. Pour batter into prepared pan and smooth top with rubber spatula. Bake for 15 minutes, then reduce oven temperature to 325 degrees and continue baking cake until deep golden brown and toothpick inserted in center comes out clean, about 35 minutes, rotating pan halfway through baking. Let cake cool in pan for 10 minutes, then turn onto wire rack. Poke cake's top and sides with toothpick. Let cool to room temperature, at least 1 hour. (Cooled cake can be stored at room temperature for up to 5 days.)

5. FOR THE GLAZE: While cake is cooling, bring sugar and lemon juice to boil in small saucepan, stirring occasionally to dissolve sugar. Reduce heat to low and simmer until thickened slightly, about 2 minutes. Brush top and sides of cake with glaze and let cool to room temperature before serving.

LEMON–POPPY SEED POUND CAKE

After whisking flour mixture in step 1, toss 1 tablespoon flour mixture with ⅓ cup poppy seeds in small bowl; set aside. Fold poppy seed mixture into batter after incorporating flour in step 3.

Lemon Bundt Cake

✓ WHY THIS RECIPE WORKS

Lemons are tart, brash, and aromatic. Why, then, is it so hard to capture their assertive flavor in a straightforward Bundt cake? The flavor of lemon juice is drastically muted when exposed to the heat of an oven, and its acidity can wreak havoc on the delicate nature of baked goods. We wanted to develop a Bundt cake with potent lemon flavor without ruining its texture.

START WITH 1-2-3-4 Many baking recipes are based on simple formulas, mnemonic tools used to pass down recipes through the generations. Bundt cakes commonly fall into the 1-2-3-4 cake category: 1 cup butter, 2 cups sugar, 3 cups flour, and 4 eggs (plus 1 cup of milk, a liquid component that sets both layer and Bundt cakes apart from pound cake). We follow this formula—almost. We increase the butter by 2 tablespoons and replace the milk with buttermilk for a lighter, more tender crumb and a nice, mild tang.

CREAM THE BUTTER We tried to create a recipe that eliminated the step of creaming the butter, but that didn't work and gave us rubbery, dense cakes. Creaming is indeed necessary to achieve a light and even crumb. The whipping action aerates the batter, contributing lightness to the final cake. After all, the Bundt cake must be tall, almost statuesque, and chemical leaveners need all the help they can get from properly creamed butter.

USE LEMON JUICE SPARINGLY Desperate to get some good lemon flavor into our

cake, we were quickly reminded that playing with acid (as in lemon juice) is no casual affair. (Lemon juice has a pH of about 2.2 to 2.4, even lower than vinegar.) Acids interfere with the formation of gluten, the protein that's so vital to a cake's structure. The more acidic the batter, the less structure in the cake, making the cake literally fall-apart tender. But fragile is not what we're going for here. Instead, we harness the acid's gluten-weakening tendency to produce a slightly more delicate crumb. A modest 3 tablespoons does the trick.

ADD ZEST FOR BIG LEMON FLAVOR To really get the lemon flavor into our cake, we use zest (just the yellow part of the peel; the white pith beneath is very bitter and unpleasant). Three lemons' worth of zest gives us a floral, perfumed lemon flavor. We mince the grated zest and then steep it in the lemon juice so that its long-stranded texture is not distracting in the baked cake.

PREPARE THE PAN Baking spray with flour works well in our Bundt cake pan. The uniformly blended flour-oil mixture makes it easy to achieve an even coating, and the more solid texture of baking sprays keeps grease from pooling in crevices, which can dull the ridges of a Bundt cake. If you don't have baking spray, a mixture of 1 tablespoon of flour and 1 tablespoon of melted butter can replace it. This does a better job of evenly coating the pan than the usual method of coating the pan with softened butter, then dusting with flour.

GRATING LEMON ZEST

The next time a recipe calls for the zest of one lemon, take care when choosing your zesting tool. We grated the zest of three lemons of equal girth on three different types of grater—a hand-held zester (the tool that removes the zest in long strips), a box grater (using the fine teeth), and a rasp-style grater. Then we packed the zest into a measuring spoon to see the difference.

The zester yielded 1½ tablespoons zest, the box grater gave us 1½ teaspoons, and the rasp grater netted 1 tablespoon. The differences could be explained by the thickness of the zest that was removed. The zester removed a pretty thick strip of zest, the box grater removed only the thin surface of the peel, while the rasp grater fell in between.

To see what impact all of this might have on flavor, we made "lemonade" with each batch of zest. We steeped the zest in ½ cup of warm water for 10 minutes, then tasted (with no sugar!). The drink made with the zesting-tool zest was bitter, while the drink made with zest from the box grater was bland and lemon-less. Evidently, the zester had removed too much white pith and the box grater hadn't removed enough of the colored peel. The rasp-style grater provided the best flavor, with a drink that provided a full lemon punch and little bitterness.

You need perfectly even coverage in order to ensure that the cake releases from the Bundt pan and no bits get stuck in the pan's crevices.

FINISH WITH A DOUBLE GLAZE For the glaze, we first tried mixing just lemon juice and confectioners' sugar but found that it was too sour and overwhelmed the delicate flavor of the cake. Adding zest made it too floral, butter only muted the flavor, but buttermilk did the trick. Supplementing some of the sour juice with the more mild yet tangy buttermilk smooths out the flavor without dulling the brightness. We apply the first round of glaze while the cake is still warm so it will melt into the cake and then dry into a thin, mottled shellac. We reserve half of the glaze for use once the cake has cooled.

LEMON BUNDT CAKE

SERVES 12

It is important to pour the glaze over the cake after it has cooled for just 10 minutes and is still warm. Serve this cake as is or dress it up with lightly sweetened berries. The cake has a light, fluffy texture when eaten the day it is baked, but if well wrapped and held at room temperature overnight its texture becomes more dense—like that of pound cake—the following day.

CAKE

- 3 tablespoons grated lemon zest plus 3 tablespoons juice (3 lemons)
- 3 cups (15 ounces) all-purpose flour
- 1 teaspoon baking powder
- ½ teaspoon baking soda
- 1 teaspoon salt
- ¾ cup buttermilk
- 1 teaspoon vanilla extract
- 3 large eggs plus 1 large yolk, room temperature
- 18 tablespoons unsalted butter (2¼ sticks), softened but still cool
- 2 cups (14 ounces) granulated sugar

GLAZE

- 2–3 tablespoons lemon juice
- 1 tablespoon buttermilk
- 2 cups (8 ounces) confectioners' sugar

1. FOR THE CAKE: Adjust oven rack to lower-middle position; heat oven to 350 degrees. Spray 12-cup Bundt pan with baking spray with flour. Mince lemon zest to fine paste (you should have about 2 tablespoons). Combine zest and lemon juice in small bowl; set aside to soften, 10 to 15 minutes.

2. Whisk flour, baking powder, baking soda, and salt in large bowl. Combine lemon juice mixture, buttermilk, and vanilla in medium bowl. In small bowl, gently whisk eggs and yolk to combine. Using stand mixer fitted with paddle, beat butter and sugar on medium-high speed until pale and fluffy, about 3 minutes. Reduce speed to medium and add half of eggs, mixing until incorporated, about 15 seconds. Repeat with remaining eggs and scrape down bowl. Reduce speed to low and add flour mixture in 3 additions, alternating with buttermilk mixture in 2 additions, scraping down bowl as needed. Give batter final stir by hand.

3. Scrape batter into prepared pan and smooth top with rubber spatula. Bake cake until top is golden brown and skewer inserted in center comes out with no crumbs attached, 45 to 50 minutes, rotating pan halfway through baking. Let cake cool in pan on wire rack set over baking sheet for 10 minutes, then invert cake onto rack.

4. FOR THE GLAZE: While cake is baking, whisk 2 tablespoons lemon juice, buttermilk, and sugar together until smooth, adding remaining lemon juice gradually as needed until glaze is thick but still pourable. Pour half of glaze over warm cake and let cool for 1 hour; pour remaining glaze evenly over top of cake and continue to cool to room temperature, at least 2 hours, before serving.

1. Make paste with 1 tablespoon flour and 1 tablespoon melted butter.

2. Use pastry brush to apply to pan.

Chocolate Pound Cake

STORING POUND CAKE

What's the best way to store pound cake? We have had much better luck storing both whole and leftover pound cake in the freezer, wrapped in a double layer of plastic wrap and aluminum foil, than in the refrigerator, where it quickly stales. The cake usually defrosted nicely on the counter, but sometimes the top became soft and sticky. After some head scratching, we realized the problem only occurred when we unwrapped the frozen cake before defrosting it. Keeping the cake wrapped as it thawed (which takes about 4 hours) ensured a nice, firm crust.

Because it contradicts the test kitchen's method for defrosting most baked goods, it took us a while to uncover this solution. For instance, we've had better luck when we unwrapped cupcakes before defrosting. Why the discrepancy? Pound cakes have much less internal moisture than cupcakes or other baked goods that contain a liquid ingredient such as milk, cream, or yogurt. When unwrapped, liquid-free pound cake has a propensity to draw moisture from the air, causing the crust to become wet; cupcakes, on the other hand, let off moisture, which gets trapped when the wrapping is left on but evaporates when the wrapping is removed.

✔ WHY THIS RECIPE WORKS

Most versions of chocolate pound cake fail to capture the best of either: the buttery, mild, dense, and velvety nature of pound cake or the deep, rich chocolate flavor of chocolate cake. In a sampling of recipes, we found that textures ranged from coarse to crumbly to fudgy; none evinced the tight, compact crumb that should characterize pound cake. We were determined to develop a recipe that walked the line between pound and chocolate cake.

START WITH BASIC POUND CAKE RECIPE We tweak the usual amounts of butter, eggs, flour, and sugar to account for the addition of chocolate. In addition, we follow the usual pound cake method of creaming the butter and sugar, then whipping in the eggs to create volume—no chemical leaveners needed.

INCORPORATE COCOA Adding cocoa powder is the simplest way to add chocolate flavor to cake. However, simply introducing this additional dry ingredient into the batter turns a formerly moist pound cake dry. We looked into adding milk or buttermilk but then came up with a better idea: "blooming" the cocoa. The test kitchen uses this technique—stirring cocoa into hot water (in this case ⅓ cup of water)—because it frees the cocoa's flavor particles, amping up chocolate taste. In one stroke, we get a cake that is both more moist and more flavorful.

DEEPEN THE CHOCOLATE FLAVOR FURTHER Bloomed cocoa lends our cake chocolate flavor, but on its own it is a bit harsh and sharp. To soften and deepen the cake's flavor, we looked beyond cocoa and decided to add a little chopped milk chocolate. Melted into the hot water used to bloom the cocoa, the chocolate gives our cake a lush,

moist chocolate flavor. In addition, for more moisture, we swapped out some of the white sugar for brown sugar. The caramel notes of brown sugar also help underscore chocolate flavor.

ADD LOTS OF VANILLA It sounds counterintuitive but vanilla actually enhances chocolate flavor. From the start of our testing to the end, we found we had quadrupled the amount of vanilla in our cake. The final result: a pound cake that is moist, buttery, and mildly sweet, with a tight crumb and deep, rounded chocolate flavor.

CHOCOLATE POUND CAKE
SERVES 8

The test kitchen's preferred loaf pan measures 8½ by 4½ inches; if you use a 9 by 5-inch loaf pan, start checking for doneness 5 minutes earlier than advised in the recipe. For an accurate measurement of boiling water, bring a full kettle of water to a boil, then measure out the desired amount.

1	cup (5 ounces) all-purpose flour
1	teaspoon salt
⅓	cup boiling water
¾	cup (2¼ ounces) Dutch-processed cocoa powder
2	ounces milk chocolate, chopped fine
16	tablespoons unsalted butter, softened
1	cup (7 ounces) granulated sugar
¼	cup packed (1¾ ounces) light brown sugar
2	teaspoons vanilla extract
5	large eggs, room temperature

1. Adjust oven rack to lower-middle position and heat oven to 325 degrees. Grease and

flour 8½ by 4½-inch loaf pan. Combine flour and salt in bowl. Pour water over cocoa and chocolate in second bowl and stir until chocolate is melted and no dry streaks of cocoa remain. Let mixture cool for 5 minutes.

2. Using stand mixer fitted with paddle, beat butter, cocoa mixture, granulated sugar, brown sugar, and vanilla on medium-high speed until fluffy, 2 to 3 minutes. Add eggs, one at a time, and beat until combined. Reduce speed to low and add flour mixture in 3 additions, scraping down bowl as needed, until just combined. Give batter final stir by hand (it may look curdled).

3. Scrape batter into prepared pan and gently tap pan on counter to release air bubbles. Bake until toothpick inserted in center comes out clean, 1 hour to 1 hour 10 minutes, rotating pan halfway through baking. Let cake cool in pan on wire rack for 10 minutes. Remove cake from pan and let cool for 2 hours. Serve.

Chocolate Bundt Cake

✔ WHY THIS RECIPE WORKS

With its decorative shape, a Bundt cake doesn't require frosting or fussy finishing techniques, especially if it's chocolate. We wanted a cake that would deliver that moment of pure chocolate ecstasy with the first bite—a chocolate Bundt cake that tastes every bit as good as it looks, with a fine crumb, moist texture, and rich chocolate flavor.

DOUBLE UP ON CHOCOLATE We use both bittersweet chocolate and natural cocoa and dissolve them in boiling water, which "blooms," or intensifies, their flavor.

SWAP WHITE SUGAR FOR BROWN SUGAR The caramel notes of brown sugar complement the chocolate flavor and lends moisture to the cake. Sour cream also adds moist richness and a subtle tang.

INCLUDE CHOCOLATE FLAVOR ENHANCERS A small amount of espresso powder heightens the chocolate flavor and vanilla extract also complements the floral nuances of the chocolate.

CHOCOLATE SOUR CREAM BUNDT CAKE

SERVES 12

We prefer natural (or regular) cocoa here since Dutch-processed cocoa will result in a compromised rise. Because coating the Bundt pan with baking spray with flour will leave a whitish film on the baked cake, we prefer to coat the pan with a paste made from cocoa and melted butter, which ensures a clean release (see page 277). For an accurate measurement of boiling water, bring a full kettle of water to a boil, then measure out the desired amount. The cake can be served with just a dusting of confectioners' sugar but is easily made more impressive with Lightly Sweetened Raspberries and Tangy Whipped Cream (recipes follow).

¾ cup (2¼ ounces) natural unsweetened cocoa powder, plus 1 tablespoon for pan

12 tablespoons unsalted butter, softened, plus 1 tablespoon, melted, for pan

6 ounces bittersweet chocolate, chopped
1 teaspoon instant espresso powder (optional)
¾ cup boiling water
1 cup sour cream, room temperature
1¾ cups (8¾ ounces) all-purpose flour
1 teaspoon salt
1 teaspoon baking soda
2 cups packed (14 ounces) light brown sugar
1 tablespoon vanilla extract
5 large eggs, room temperature
Confectioners' sugar

1. FOR THE PAN: Mix 1 tablespoon cocoa and melted butter into paste. Using pastry brush, thoroughly coat interior of 12-cup Bundt pan. Adjust oven rack to lower-middle position and heat oven to 350 degrees.

2. FOR THE CAKE: Combine remaining ¾ cup cocoa, chocolate, and espresso, if using, in medium heatproof bowl, pour boiling water over mixture, and let sit, covered, for 5 minutes. Whisk mixture gently until smooth. Let cool to room temperature, then whisk in sour cream. Whisk flour, salt, and baking soda in second bowl to combine.

3. Using stand mixer fitted with paddle, beat 12 tablespoons butter, sugar, and vanilla on medium-high speed until pale and fluffy, about 3 minutes. Add eggs, one at a time, and beat until combined. Reduce speed to low and add flour mixture in 3 additions, alternating with chocolate–sour cream mixture in 2 additions, scraping down bowl as needed. Give batter final stir by hand.

4. Scrape batter into prepared pan and smooth top with rubber spatula. Bake cake until skewer inserted in center comes out with few crumbs attached, 45 to 50 minutes, rotating pan halfway through baking. Let cake cool in pan for 10 minutes, then invert cake onto wire rack; let cool to room temperature, about 3 hours. Dust with confectioners' sugar, transfer to serving platter, and serve.

LIGHTLY SWEETENED RASPBERRIES
MAKES 3 CUPS

The amount of sugar you use will depend on the sweetness of your raspberries.

15 ounces (3 cups) raspberries
1–2 tablespoons sugar

Gently toss raspberries with sugar, then let stand until berries have released some juices and sugar has dissolved, about 15 minutes.

TANGY WHIPPED CREAM
MAKES 1½ CUPS

Sour cream adds a pleasing tang to this whipped cream.

1 cup heavy cream, chilled
¼ cup sour cream
¼ cup packed (1¾ ounces) light brown sugar
⅛ teaspoon vanilla extract

Using stand mixer fitted with whisk, whip all ingredients on medium-low speed until foamy, about 1 minute. Increase speed to high and whip until soft peaks form, 1 to 3 minutes.

STRAWBERRY CREAM CAKE

CHAPTER 10

Layer Cakes, Sheet Cakes, and Special Occasion Cakes

Fluffy Yellow Layer Cake

LINING CAKE PANS WITH PARCHMENT PAPER

To ensure an easy release, cake pans should be greased, floured, and fit with a piece of parchment paper. The paper prevents the formation of a tough outer crust and helps the cake hold together when it is removed from the pan.

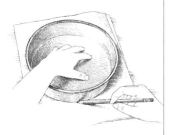

1. Trace bottom of your cake pan roughly in center of sheet of parchment paper (use double sheet if using 2 pans).

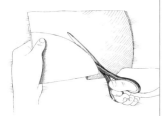

2. Fold traced circle in half and then in half again, then cut just inside outline of quarter-circle formed in this way. Resulting round of parchment will exactly fit your pan.

✔ WHY THIS RECIPE WORKS

Box mixes are famous for producing cakes with ultra-light texture. We set out to make an even fluffier cake—one without chemicals and additives. We also wanted a luscious chocolate frosting—one that was almost as easy as popping open a can of frosting but with fresh ingredients and deep chocolate flavor.

MAKE AN EGG FOAM For a tender yet tall cake, we adapted a technique used in cakes such as angel food and chiffon, which rely on egg foams for their height. We use the standard butter-cake ingredients but combine them by the method used to make chiffon cake—combine the dry ingredients, combine the wet ingredients, mix the dry and wet together, then fold in whipped egg whites. (This is basically the quick-bread method, with the added step of whipping the egg whites and folding them into the batter at the end.) This method gives us a light, delicate cake with just enough heft to stand up to a slathering of frosting.

BAKE WITH BUTTERMILK We began testing this cake with milk but found that switching milk for buttermilk produced a crumb that was slightly porous and so fine it was almost downy. The buttermilk's tang also brings a new flavor dimension to our cake. (Using acidic buttermilk means we need to replace some of the baking powder with baking soda to ensure an even rise.)

USE TWO FATS A cake made with all butter is fluffy, but it doesn't have the moisture we want in this cake. We know that oil, even more than butter, can be a key factor in improving the moisture level of a cake. (Butter contains between 16 and 18 percent water, which can evaporate in the oven and leave a cake dry.) After testing a combination of both types of fat, we found that 10 tablespoons of butter plus 3 tablespoons of oil keeps the butter flavor intact and improves the moistness of the cake.

ADD SUGAR While vegetable oil adds moisture to our cake, we turn to a different ingredient to make it tender. Sugar is well known for increasing tenderness in cakes by attracting and bonding with water, thus preventing the water from hydrating the proteins in the flour. With less liquid available to them, fewer proteins are able to link together, resulting in weaker gluten. Adding an additional ½ cup of sugar does the trick.

DON'T FORGET COCOA POWDER We top the cake with a simple frosting made with butter, confectioners' sugar, melted chocolate, and cocoa powder for more chocolate oomph.

CORN SYRUP IS KEY Even though confectioners' sugar dissolves more easily than granulated sugar, it can give frosting a slightly gritty texture, so we replace some of the confectioners' sugar with corn syrup to help dissolve the sugar and make for a smooth frosting.

FLUFFY YELLOW LAYER CAKE WITH CHOCOLATE FROSTING

SERVES 10 TO 12

Bring all the ingredients to room temperature before beginning this recipe. Be sure to use cake pans with at least 2-inch-tall sides. This frosting may be made with milk, semisweet, or bittersweet chocolate; we prefer a frosting made with milk chocolate for this recipe. Let the chocolate cool to between 85 and 100 degrees before adding it to the butter mixture. For more information on frosting a layer cake, see page 288.

CAKE

2½ cups (10 ounces) cake flour
1¼ teaspoons baking powder
¼ teaspoon baking soda
¾ teaspoon salt
1¾ cups (12¼ ounces) granulated sugar
1 cup buttermilk, room temperature

10 tablespoons unsalted butter, melted and cooled

3 tablespoons vegetable oil

2 teaspoons vanilla extract

3 large eggs, separated, plus 3 large yolks, room temperature
  Pinch cream of tartar

FROSTING

20 tablespoons (2½ sticks) unsalted butter, softened (68 degrees)

1 cup (4 ounces) confectioners' sugar

¾ cup (2¼ ounces) Dutch-processed cocoa powder
  Pinch salt

¾ cup light corn syrup

1 teaspoon vanilla extract

8 ounces milk, bittersweet, or semisweet chocolate, melted and cooled

1. FOR THE CAKE: Adjust oven rack to middle position and heat oven to 350 degrees. Grease two 9-inch round cake pans, line with parchment paper, grease parchment, and flour pans. Whisk flour, baking powder, baking soda, salt, and 1½ cups sugar together in large bowl. In medium bowl, whisk together buttermilk, melted butter, oil, vanilla, and egg yolks.

2. Using stand mixer fitted with whisk, whip egg whites and cream of tartar on medium-low speed until foamy, about 1 minute. Increase speed to medium-high and whip whites to soft billowy mounds, about 1 minute. Gradually add remaining ¼ cup sugar and whip until glossy, stiff peaks form, 2 to 3 minutes. Transfer to bowl and set aside.

3. Add flour mixture to now-empty mixer bowl. With mixer on low speed, gradually pour in butter mixture and mix until almost incorporated (a few streaks of dry flour will remain), about 15 seconds. Scrape down bowl, then beat on medium-low speed until smooth and fully incorporated, 10 to 15 seconds.

4. Using rubber spatula, stir one-third of whites into batter, then add remaining two-thirds of whites and gently fold into batter until no white streaks remain. Divide batter evenly between prepared pans, smooth tops with rubber spatula, and gently tap pans on counter to release air bubbles.

5. Bake until toothpick inserted in center of cake comes out clean, 20 to 22 minutes, rotating pans halfway through baking. Let cakes cool in pans on wire rack for 10 minutes. Remove cakes from pans, discard parchment, and let cool completely, about 2 hours, before frosting. (Cooled cakes can be wrapped tightly in plastic wrap and kept at room temperature for up to 1 day. Wrapped tightly in plastic, then aluminum foil, cakes can be frozen for up to 1 month. Defrost cakes at room temperature before unwrapping and frosting.)

6. FOR THE FROSTING: Process butter, sugar, cocoa, and salt in food processor until smooth, about 30 seconds, scraping down bowl as needed. Add corn syrup and vanilla and process until just combined, 5 to 10 seconds. Scrape down bowl, then add chocolate and process until smooth and creamy, 10 to 15 seconds. (Frosting can be kept at room temperature for up to 3 hours before frosting cake or refrigerated for up to 3 days. If refrigerated, let stand at room temperature for 1 hour before using.)

7. Line edges of cake platter with 4 strips of parchment paper to keep platter clean. Place 1 cake layer on prepared platter. Place about 1½ cups frosting in center of cake layer and, using large spatula, spread in even layer right to edge of cake. Place second cake layer on top, making sure layers are aligned, then frost top in same manner as first layer, this time spreading frosting until slightly over edge. Gather more frosting on tip of spatula and gently spread icing onto side of cake. Smooth frosting by gently running edge of spatula around cake and leveling ridge that forms around top edge, or create billows by pressing back of spoon into frosting and twirling spoon as you lift away. Carefully pull out pieces of parchment from beneath cake before serving. (Assembled cake can be refrigerated for up to 1 day. Bring to room temperature before serving.)

PUTTING THE YELLOW IN YOLKS

As we developed the recipe for our Fluffy Yellow Layer Cake, we were surprised by the lack of any real yellow color in the cake. A closer look at the standard supermarket eggs we were using provided a clue: The yolks were all relatively pale. When we compared them with yolks from free-range eggs bought fresh at the farmers' market, the contrast was striking: The yolks were much darker. What accounts for the difference in color? It all boils down to the hens' diet. Bright golden-yellow yolks show that the hens are well supplied with carotenoids. These substances are found in a wide range of plants that a true free-range hen could find merely by pecking around the farmyard.

Cakes made with light and dark yolks actually tasted the same; the difference was merely aesthetic.

Genoise Layer Cake

✓ **WHY THIS RECIPE WORKS**

Less rich than the more buttery American layer cake, the lean, light crumb of genoise is often brushed with a flavorful soaking syrup and coated in an extra-rich buttercream frosting. Genoise is an occasion cake that has a reputation for being fickle. Poorly done genoise is squat, dry, and flavorless. We wanted a foolproof recipe for this classic cake.

WARM THE EGG MIXTURE AND RIBBON The standard method for making genoise calls for warming a mixture of whole eggs and sugar over simmering water and beating the mixture until it is voluminous and billowy. The best way to tell when your egg mixture is ready is when it turns pale and slightly shiny and, when the beaters are lifted, it falls in thick ribbons that rest on top of the batter.

TEMPER THE BUTTER We pour the melted butter into a portion of the whipped egg mixture and fold it in until just barely incorporated. Tempering the butter with some of the batter first helps it incorporate more easily into the remaining batter without deflating it.

SIFT THE FLOUR We sift half the flour over the batter, then gently fold it in. Sifting the flour makes it easier to incorporate evenly into the batter and helps to prevent clumping in this delicate cake.

BAKE IN A SPRINGFORM PAN We tried baking our genoise in two standard round cake pans but the exterior crust was thicker than we liked and the tops domed slightly. In order to get the soaking syrup to penetrate the cake and to make even layers, we had to cut away the top crusts. It seemed a shame to discard so much cake, so we turned to a springform pan. Because the pan is deeper than a standard cake pan, we're able to bake all the batter in one pan. And better yet, the crust bakes up thin and even.

SLICE INTO THREE LAYERS For this ultra-elegant cake, we prefer three thin layers of cake alternating with paper-thin layers of buttercream and raspberry jam, rather than one thick layer of filling between the two cake layers. To make sure our layered cake is tall and even, we assemble the cake layers in the same order as the cake was cut—bottom layer on bottom, middle layer in middle, and top layer on top. For an elegant finish, we make sure to leave a ¼-inch border at the edges when spreading the jam, so no leaks mar the frosting.

CHILL THE CAKE After we frost the cake, we refrigerate it for at least 2 hours so that the cake absorbs the soaking syrup. And before serving, we bring the cake back to room temperature and press toasted sliced almonds on the sides for an elegant finish.

GENOISE LAYER CAKE WITH ALMOND AND RASPBERRY FILLING

SERVES 8 TO 10

Do not grease and flour the sides of the cake pan, but simply line the bottom with parchment paper. This batter is very delicate, so be very gentle when transferring it to the pan to avoid deflating it. To ensure an even, level cake, be sure to cool it completely in the pan. For more information on frosting a layer cake, see page 288.

GENOISE
- 1¼ cups (5 ounces) cake flour
- ½ teaspoon salt
- 5 large eggs, room temperature
- ¾ cup (5¼ ounces) sugar
- 1 teaspoon vanilla extract
- 5 tablespoons unsalted butter, melted and cooled

AMARETTO SOAKING SYRUP
- ¼ cup (1¾ ounces) sugar
- ⅓ cup water, plus extra as needed
- ¼ cup amaretto

BUTTERCREAM AND FILLING

- 4 large egg whites, room temperature
- 1 cup (7 ounces) sugar
  Pinch salt
- 4 sticks (1 pound) unsalted butter, cut into chunks and softened
- ¼ cup amaretto
- ½ cup seedless raspberry jam
- 1 cup (3½ ounces) sliced almonds, toasted

1. FOR THE GENOISE: Adjust oven rack to middle position and heat oven to 350 degrees. Line bottom of 9-inch springform pan with parchment paper (do not grease). Whisk flour and salt together in medium bowl.

2. Whisk eggs and sugar in bowl of stand mixer until combined. Set bowl over large saucepan of barely simmering water, making sure that water does not touch bottom of bowl. Heat egg mixture, whisking constantly, until warm but not hot (about 100 degrees), 1 to 2 minutes.

3. Remove from heat, fit stand mixer with whisk attachment, and whip mixture on medium-high speed until very thick and voluminous, 4 to 6 minutes. Whip in vanilla.

4. Transfer 1 cup of whipped egg mixture to medium bowl and set aside. Sift half of flour mixture over remaining egg mixture and fold very gently with large rubber spatula to incorporate, 12 to 15 folds. Sift remaining flour mixture over batter and very gently fold together until just combined, 8 to 10 folds.

5. Stir melted butter into reserved egg mixture and then fold it gently into cake batter until just barely incorporated, being careful not to deflate batter, 4 to 6 folds.

6. Immediately scrape batter into prepared springform pan. Bake cake until deep golden brown and toothpick inserted in center of cake comes out with few crumbs attached, 18 to 22 minutes, rotating pan halfway through baking.

7. Let cake cool completely in pan, about 2 hours. Run thin knife around edge of cake, then remove sides of pan. Flip cake out onto parchment-lined plate (to protect delicate top). Peel off parchment, flip cake right side up onto wire rack, and discard parchment.

8. FOR THE AMARETTO SOAKING SYRUP: Bring sugar and water to boil in small saucepan over high heat until sugar dissolves, then set mixture aside to cool. Transfer cooled syrup to liquid measuring cup, add amaretto, then add extra water as needed to measure ⅔ cup.

9. FOR THE BUTTERCREAM AND FILLING: Whisk egg whites, sugar, and salt in bowl of stand mixer until combined. Set bowl over saucepan filled with 1 inch of barely simmering water, making sure that water does not touch bottom of bowl. Heat egg mixture, whisking constantly, until opaque and warm but not hot (about 120 degrees), about 2 minutes. Remove from heat, fit stand mixer with whisk, and whip mixture on medium-high speed until glossy, sticky, and barely warm (about 80 degrees), about 7 minutes. Reduce mixer speed to medium and add butter, 1 chunk at a time, until incorporated, 1 to 2 minutes. Add amaretto until combined. Cover frosting with plastic wrap until needed, or refrigerate for up to 3 days.

10. Cut 2 horizontal lines around sides of cake; then, following scored lines, cut cake into 3 even layers using long serrated knife. Brush cut side of each layer (including both sides of middle layer) evenly with soaking syrup.

11. Line edges of cake platter with 4 strips of parchment paper to keep platter clean. Place bottom cake layer on prepared platter. Spread ¼ cup jam over cake, leaving ¼-inch border at edge. Spread ½ cup buttercream evenly over jam, right to edge of cake. Repeat with middle cake layer, remaining ¼ cup jam, and ½ cup buttercream. Place remaining cake layer on top and press lightly to adhere. Frost cake with remaining buttercream.

12. Refrigerate cake until it absorbs soaking syrup, at least 2 hours or up to 24 hours. Before serving, let cake sit at room temperature, 30 minutes to 1 hour, press almonds into sides of cake, and carefully pull out pieces of parchment from beneath cake before serving.

LEVELING AND SPLITTING A CAKE

1. If cake has mounded in center, it should be leveled before being split. Gently press hand on its surface and, holding serrated knife parallel to counter, use steady sawing motion to slice off mound.

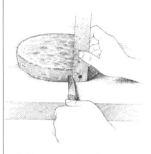

2. To cut into 2 or 3 even layers, measure height of cake with ruler. Then, using small knife, mark thickness of layers at several points around cake.

3. Using marks as guide, score entire edge of cake with long serrated knife and, following scored lines, run knife around cake several more times, cutting inward, to slice layers apart.

How to Frost a Layer Cake

Most cooks think a bakery-smooth frosted cake is well beyond their ability and make do with a decidedly "homemade" looking cake. The common problems include uneven frosting, including holes and thick patches; weak transitions from the sides to the top; and crumbs caught in the frosting. With the directions that follow, these problems are easily avoided. A professional rotating cake stand makes icing a cake easy. You can use cardboard rounds as shown here or set the cake on a platter and place the platter on the stand. Remember to line the edges of your platter with strips of parchment paper to keep it clean. Slide the pieces of parchment out from under the cake once you're done frosting.

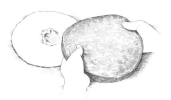

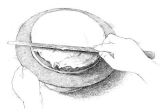

1. To anchor cake, spread dab of frosting in center of cardboard round. Center first cake layer on round. If using split layer, place it crust side up; if using whole layer, place it bottom side down. Set cake on stand.

2. Dollop portion of frosting in center of cake and spread it to edges with icing spatula. Imagine that you are pushing filling into place rather than scraping it on as if it were peanut butter on toast.

3. To level frosting, hold spatula at 45-degree angle to cake and, starting at edge farthest away from you, gently drag spatula toward you. Turn cake slightly and repeat. It will take a few sweeps to level frosting.

4. Using second cardboard round, slide next cake layer, crust side up, on top of frosted bottom layer, making sure that layers are aligned. Press cake firmly into place.

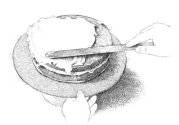

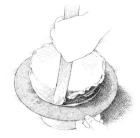

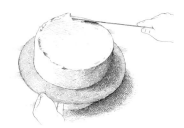

5. A thin base coat of frosting helps seal in crumbs. To coat top, dollop portion of frosting in center of cake and spread it out to edges, letting any excess hang over edge. Don't worry if it is imperfect.

6. Scoop a few tablespoons of frosting on spatula's tip, then gently smear onto side of cake. Repeat until entire side is covered with thin coat. Refrigerate cake to set frosting, about 10 minutes.

7. Apply thick final coat of frosting to top and sides, following steps 5 and 6, making sure that coat is even and smooth. Dipping spatula in hot water will help create smooth coat.

8. After you've finished icing, gently run edge of spatula around sides to smooth out any bumps and tidy area where frosting from top and sides merge.

PUTTING A PATTERN IN FROSTING

A frosted cake can be easily styled in three ways. All of these designs are best accomplished when the frosting has just been applied and is still soft.

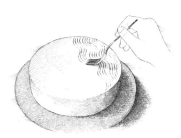

A. Use tines of dinner fork to make wave designs in frosting. Wipe fork clean intermittently.

B. Use tip of thin metal icing spatula to stipple top and sides of cake.

C. Use back of large dinner spoon to make swirls on top of cake.

Simple Ideas for Cake Decorating

You don't need to be a practiced pastry chef to decorate a cake. Here are several easy-to-follow ideas for giving your cake a professional finish.

WRITING ON A CAKE

When writing a message on top of a frosted cake, it's easiest to use chocolate on a light-colored frosting.

1. Put chopped semisweet or bittersweet chocolate in zipper-lock plastic bag and immerse bag in hot water until chocolate melts. Dry bag, then snip off small piece from 1 corner.

2. Holding bag in 1 hand, gently squeeze chocolate from hole as you write.

REMOVING STENCILS

Store-bought stencils are an easy way to decorate an unfrosted cake with confectioners' sugar or cocoa powder. Removing the stencil without marring the design can be tricky. Here's how we do it.

1. Create 2 handles for stencil by folding 2 short lengths of masking tape back onto themselves, pinching middle sections together. Stick ends of tape to top and bottom of stencil, placing handle on either side.

2. Place stencil on top of cake and dust with confectioners' sugar or cocoa powder. When you are done, use tape handles to grasp and lift stencil straight up and off cake.

DECORATING WITH CHOCOLATE SHAVINGS

If the block of chocolate is too hard, it can be difficult to pull off thick shavings. Even if you do cut off nice shavings, warmth from your fingers can cause the pieces to melt as you try to place them on the cake. Here's how to avoid both problems.

1. Warm block of bittersweet or semisweet chocolate by sweeping hair dryer over it, taking care not to melt chocolate. Holding paring knife at 45-degree angle against chocolate, scrape toward you, anchoring block with your other hand.

2. Pick up shavings with toothpick and place them as desired on frosted cake.

DECORATING WITH ALMONDS

The shape and color of sliced almonds lend them to simple, elegant designs. Use these tips separately or in combination.

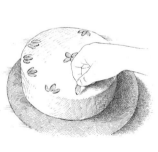 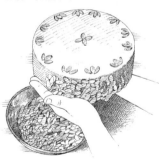

1. Arrange sliced almonds in fleur-de-lis design around perimeter of frosted cake. Use 4 slices to make flower design in center of cake.

2. Hold cake with 1 hand by cardboard round on its underside. Use other hand to press nuts into frosting, letting excess fall back into bowl of nuts. You will need about 1 cup of nuts to coat sides of 9-inch cake. Sliced almonds (pictured here) or chopped pecans or walnuts work well.

Lemon Layer Cake

EASIER CAKE REMOVAL

If you allow a cake to cool completely in its pan, you may run into trouble trying to remove it cleanly. (Genoise Layer Cake on page 286 is an exception.) This tip can help:

Carefully run the cake pan over low heat on the stovetop. This melts the grease that was initially spread on the pan bottom. The cake should pop out easily when the pan is flipped over. This technique also works well for loosening stubborn flans and crème caramels.

✔ WHY THIS RECIPE WORKS

Most versions of lemon layer cake are concoctions of heavy cake stacked with filling and frosting that taste more like butter than lemon. We wanted an old-fashioned cake in which tangy, creamy lemon filling divides layers of tender, delicate cake draped in sweet frosting—an ideal contrast of sweet and tart.

START WITH A WHITE CAKE   For the cake, we suspected that the light, fresh flavor of lemon would be best served by something ethereal. We found that a white butter cake is the perfect choice, as it is nicely flavored by butter yet light enough for the lemon flavor.

USE THE REVERSE CREAMING METHOD   We use the reverse creaming method to mix the batter, which calls for cutting the butter into the dry ingredients as is done with biscuit dough. This results in a soft, moist, and tender cake. The reason? The traditional creaming method, which relies on aerating the butter with the sugar, creates large air pockets that result in a coarser crumb. In reverse creaming, the butter coats the flour before the batter is aerated, keeping the cake tender and fine-crumbed.

CHOOSE LEMON CURD   Lemon layer cake is often filled with lemon-scented buttercream, but this mutes the lemon flavor and makes the cake far too rich. We prefer the brightness of lemon curd, reinforced with a little gelatin for neater slicing.

TWEAK 7-MINUTE ICING   The traditional icing for this cake, 7-minute icing, was a little too sweet and thick, and required holding a hand-held mixer for longer than was comfortable. We cut back on the sugar and added a squeeze of lemon juice to solve the first two problems. Heating the mixture to at least 160 degrees and then transferring it to a stand mixer for whipping (rather than holding a hand mixer for 7 minutes) gives us a frosting as billowy and shiny as the old-fashioned version.

LEMON LAYER CAKE WITH FLUFFY ICING

SERVES 10 TO 12

Be sure to use cake pans with at least 2-inch-tall sides. After filling the cake in step 6, cover it with plastic wrap and refrigerate while making the icing. For more information on frosting a layer cake, see page 288. For neater slices, dip a knife into hot water before cutting the cake.

FILLING
- 1   teaspoon unflavored gelatin
- 1   cup lemon juice (5 or 6 lemons)
- 1½   cups (10½ ounces) sugar
- ⅛   teaspoon salt
- 4   large eggs plus 6 large yolks, room temperature (reserve whites for cake)
- 8   tablespoons unsalted butter, cut into ½-inch pieces and frozen

CAKE
- 1   cup whole milk, room temperature
- 6   large egg whites, room temperature
- 2   teaspoons vanilla extract
- 2¼   cups (9 ounces) cake flour
- 1¾   cups (12¼ ounces) sugar
- 4   teaspoons baking powder
- 1   teaspoon salt
- 12   tablespoons unsalted butter, cut into 12 pieces and softened

- 1   recipe fluffy icing (recipes follow)

1. FOR THE FILLING: Sprinkle gelatin over 1 tablespoon lemon juice in small bowl; set aside. Heat remaining lemon juice, sugar, and salt in medium saucepan over medium-high heat, stirring occasionally, until sugar dissolves and mixture is hot but not boiling. Whisk eggs and yolks in large bowl. Whisking constantly, slowly pour hot lemon-sugar mixture into eggs, then return mixture to saucepan.

Cook over medium-low heat, stirring constantly with heatproof spatula, until mixture registers 170 degrees and is thick enough to leave trail when spatula is scraped along pan bottom, 4 to 6 minutes. Immediately remove pan from heat and stir in gelatin mixture until dissolved. Stir in frozen butter until incorporated. Pour filling through fine-mesh strainer into bowl (you should have 3 cups). Place plastic wrap directly on surface of filling; refrigerate until firm enough to spread, at least 4 hours. (Filling can be made up to 1 day in advance and refrigerated; fold with rubber spatula to loosen before spreading onto cake.)

2. FOR THE CAKE: Adjust oven rack to middle position and heat oven to 350 degrees. Grease two 9-inch round cake pans, line with parchment paper, grease parchment, and flour pans. Whisk milk, egg whites, and vanilla together in 2-cup liquid measuring cup.

3. Using stand mixer fitted with paddle, mix flour, sugar, baking powder, and salt on low speed until combined. Add butter, 1 piece at a time, and mix until only pea-size pieces remain, about 1 minute. Add all but ½ cup milk mixture, increase speed to medium-high, and beat until light and fluffy, about 1 minute. Reduce speed to medium-low, add remaining ½ cup milk mixture, and beat until incorporated, about 30 seconds. Give batter final stir by hand.

4. Divide batter evenly between prepared pans and smooth tops with rubber spatula. Bake until toothpick inserted in center of cake comes out clean, 23 to 25 minutes, rotating pans halfway through baking. Let cakes cool in pans on wire rack for 10 minutes. Remove cakes from pans, discard parchment, and let cool completely, about 2 hours, before frosting. (Cooled cakes can be wrapped tightly in plastic and kept at room temperature for up to 1 day. Wrapped tightly in plastic, then aluminum foil, cakes can be frozen for up to 1 month. Defrost cakes at room temperature before unwrapping and frosting.)

5. Cut 1 horizontal line around sides of each layer; then, following scored lines, cut each layer into 2 even layers using long serrated knife.

6. Line edges of cake platter with 4 strips of parchment paper to keep platter clean. Place 1 cake layer on prepared platter. Spread 1 cup lemon filling evenly over top of cake, leaving ½-inch border around edge. Carefully place second cake layer on top of filling, aligning cuts so that layers are even. Spread 1 cup filling on top; repeat using remaining cake layers and filling. Smooth out any filling that has leaked from sides of cake.

7. Using spatula, spread icing over top of cake, spreading icing until slightly over edge. Gather more frosting on tip of spatula and gently spread icing onto side of cake. Smooth icing by gently running edge of spatula around cake and leveling ridge that forms around top edge, or create billows by pressing back of spoon into icing and twirling spoon as you lift away. Carefully pull out pieces of parchment from beneath cake before serving. (Assembled cake can be refrigerated for up to 1 day. Bring to room temperature before serving.)

FLUFFY WHITE ICING
MAKES 3 CUPS

2	large egg whites
1	cup (7 ounces) sugar
¼	cup water
1	tablespoon lemon juice
1	tablespoon corn syrup

Combine all ingredients in bowl of stand mixer and set bowl over medium saucepan filled with 1 inch of barely simmering water (do not let bottom of bowl touch water). Cook, stirring constantly, until sugar is dissolved and mixture registers 160 degrees, 5 to 10 minutes. Remove bowl from heat. Fit stand mixer with whisk and whip egg white mixture on medium speed until soft peaks form, about 5 minutes. Increase speed to medium-high and continue to whip until mixture has cooled to room temperature and stiff peaks form, about 5 minutes longer.

FLUFFY VANILLA ICING
MAKES 3 CUPS

2   large egg whites
1   cup (7 ounces) sugar
5   tablespoons water
1   tablespoon corn syrup
1   teaspoon vanilla extract

Combine all ingredients in bowl of stand mixer and set bowl over medium saucepan filled with 1 inch of barely simmering water (do not let bottom of bowl touch water). Cook, stirring constantly, until sugar is dissolved and mixture registers 160 degrees, 5 to 10 minutes. Remove bowl from heat. Fit stand mixer with whisk and whip egg white mixture on medium speed until soft peaks form, about 5 minutes. Increase speed to medium-high and continue to whip until mixture has cooled to room temperature and stiff peaks form, about 5 minutes longer.

FLUFFY TOASTED ALMOND ICING
MAKES 3 CUPS

See page 9 for information on toasting nuts.

2   large egg whites
1   cup (7 ounces) sugar
5   tablespoons water
1   tablespoon corn syrup
½   teaspoon almond extract
¾   cup almonds, toasted and chopped

Combine egg whites, sugar, water, corn syrup, and almond extract in bowl of stand mixer and set bowl over medium saucepan filled with 1 inch of barely simmering water (do not let bottom of bowl touch water). Cook, stirring constantly, until sugar is dissolved and mixture registers 160 degrees, 5 to 10 minutes. Remove bowl from heat. Fit stand mixer with whisk and whip egg white mixture on medium speed until soft peaks form, about 5 minutes. Increase speed to medium-high and continue to whip until mixture has cooled to room temperature and stiff peaks form, about 5 minutes longer. Using rubber spatula, gently fold in almonds.

FLUFFY COCONUT ICING
MAKES 3 CUPS

To toast the coconut, place it in a small skillet over medium heat and cook, stirring often, for 3 to 5 minutes. It burns quite easily, so keep a close eye on it. To toast the coconut using a microwave, see page 247.

2   large egg whites
1   cup (7 ounces) sugar
5   tablespoons water
1   tablespoon corn syrup
½   teaspoon vanilla extract
¾   cup (2¼ ounces) unsweetened shredded coconut, toasted and cooled

Combine egg whites, sugar, water, corn syrup, and vanilla in bowl of stand mixer and set over medium saucepan filled with 1 inch of barely simmering water (do not let bottom of bowl touch water). Cook, stirring constantly, until sugar is dissolved and mixture registers 160 degrees, 5 to 10 minutes. Remove bowl from heat. Fit stand mixer with whisk and whip egg white mixture on medium speed until soft peaks form, about 5 minutes. Increase speed to medium-high and continue to whip until mixture has cooled to room temperature and stiff peaks form, about 5 minutes longer. Using rubber spatula, gently fold in coconut.

Boston Cream Pie

✓ WHY THIS RECIPE WORKS

When a Boston cream pie hits all the marks, it's a superstar dessert. But from the base to the glaze, there's the opportunity for failure in every component. The sponge cake can turn out dry and crumbly, the pastry cream can curdle or fail to thicken and leak out the sides of the cake, and the chocolate glaze can seize or fail to taste truly chocolaty. We wanted to lead the dessert's revival with a fail-safe recipe.

MAKE A HOT-MILK SPONGE CAKE Traditionally, Boston cream pie was made with a genoise-style cake (page 286), but we wanted a simpler more tender cake, so we turned to the hot-milk sponge cake. The mixing method involves whipping eggs with sugar, then simply stirring in the remaining ingredients (including warm milk)—no finicky folding or separating of eggs required. Not only is this cake easy to prepare, but its light texture and subtle flavor are the perfect platform for a creamy filling.

FIRM UP THE PASTRY CREAM Getting the pastry cream to have the proper consistency can be tricky. Pastry cream is typically made by bringing dairy (we prefer half-and-half) to a simmer and then using it to temper—or slowly raise the temperature of—a mixture of egg yolks, sugar, and cornstarch or flour. The mixture is then returned to the heat and whisked until it has thickened and the eggs are lightly cooked. But if insufficiently heated or overwhisked, the pastry cream will be too loose to be sandwiched between cake layers. In addition to using flour (which we prefer over cornstarch there) to thicken our pastry cream, we tried gelatin, but it gave the cream a rubbery texture. In the end, we landed on butter. Butter not only reinforces the richness of the pastry cream and firms it up just enough, but it also enhances its luxurious flavor. Once it is spread on the cake and refrigerated, our cake slices cleanly.

ENRICH THE GLAZE WITH CORN SYRUP For the crowning touch to our cake, we wanted a rich chocolate glaze that would retain its softness and shine after refrigeration. Adding corn syrup to the typical ganache mixture of heavy cream and melted chocolate did the trick, producing a glaze with a soft, smooth, glossy consistency that clings to the top of the cake and drips attractively down its sides, even after being chilled.

WICKED GOOD BOSTON CREAM PIE
SERVES 10 TO 12

Chill the assembled cake for at least 3 hours to make it easy to cut and serve.

PASTRY CREAM
- 2 cups half-and-half
- 6 large egg yolks, room temperature
- ½ cup (3½ ounces) sugar
- Pinch salt
- ¼ cup (1¼ ounces) all-purpose flour
- 4 tablespoons unsalted butter, cut into 4 pieces and chilled
- 1½ teaspoons vanilla extract

CAKE
- 1½ cups (7½ ounces) all-purpose flour
- 1½ teaspoons baking powder
- ¾ teaspoon salt
- ¾ cup whole milk
- 6 tablespoons unsalted butter
- 1½ teaspoons vanilla extract
- 3 large eggs, room temperature
- 1½ cups (10½ ounces) sugar

GLAZE

½   cup heavy cream

2   tablespoons corn syrup

4   ounces bittersweet chocolate,
    chopped fine

I. FOR THE PASTRY CREAM: Heat half-and-half in medium saucepan over medium heat until just simmering. Meanwhile, whisk egg yolks, sugar, and salt in medium bowl until smooth. Add flour to yolk mixture and whisk until incorporated. Remove half-and-half from heat and, whisking constantly, slowly add ½ cup to yolk mixture to temper. Whisking constantly, return tempered yolk mixture to half-and-half in saucepan.

2. Return saucepan to medium heat and cook, whisking constantly, until mixture thickens slightly, about 1 minute. Reduce heat to medium-low and continue to simmer, whisking constantly, 8 minutes.

3. Increase heat to medium and cook, whisking vigorously, until bubbles burst on surface, 1 to 2 minutes. Remove saucepan from heat; whisk in butter and vanilla until butter is melted and incorporated. Strain pastry cream through fine-mesh strainer set over medium bowl. Press lightly greased parchment paper directly on surface and refrigerate until set, at least 2 hours or up to 24 hours.

4. FOR THE CAKE: Adjust oven rack to middle position and heat oven to 325 degrees. Grease two 9-inch round cake pans, line with parchment paper, grease parchment, and flour pans. Whisk flour, baking powder, and salt together in medium bowl. Heat milk and butter in small saucepan over low heat until butter is melted. Remove from heat, add vanilla, and cover to keep warm.

5. Using stand mixer fitted with whisk, whip eggs and sugar on high speed until light and airy, about 5 minutes. Remove mixer bowl from stand, add hot milk mixture, and whisk by hand until incorporated. Add dry ingredients and whisk until incorporated.

6. Working quickly, divide batter evenly between prepared pans and smooth tops with rubber spatula. Bake cakes until tops are light brown and toothpick inserted in center comes out clean, 20 to 22 minutes, rotating pans halfway through baking.

7. Transfer cakes to wire rack and let cool completely in pan, about 2 hours. Run thin knife around edge of pans, then invert cakes onto wire rack. Carefully remove parchment, then turn cakes right side up. (Cooled cakes can be wrapped tightly in plastic wrap and kept at room temperature for up to 1 day. Wrapped tightly in plastic, then aluminum foil, cakes can be frozen for up to 1 month. Defrost cakes at room temperature before unwrapping and frosting.)

8. Line edges of cake platter with 4 strips of parchment paper to keep platter clean. Place 1 cake layer on prepared platter. Whisk pastry cream briefly, then spoon onto center of cake. Using rubber spatula, spread evenly to cake edge. Place second layer on top of pastry cream, bottom side up, making sure layers line up. Press lightly on top of cake to level. Refrigerate cake while preparing glaze.

9. FOR THE GLAZE: Bring cream and corn syrup to simmer in small saucepan over medium heat. Remove from heat, add chocolate, and let sit, covered, for 5 minutes. Whisk mixture gently until smooth.

10. Pour glaze onto center of cake. Use rubber spatula to spread glaze to edge of cake, letting excess drip decoratively down sides. Chill for at least 3 hours. Carefully pull out pieces of parchment from beneath cake before serving. (Assembled cake can be refrigerated for up to 1 day. Bring to room temperature before serving.)

Coconut Layer Cake

FIXING BROKEN CAKE

If you find yourself with broken cake halves, you can repair the fracture by letting the cakes cool, then spreading a thin layer of soft buttercream frosting over the broken surfaces and reattaching the pieces. Chill the repaired cake for about an hour before continuing to assemble and frost it.

✔ WHY THIS RECIPE WORKS

Too often, a coconut cake is just plain white cake with plain white frosting sprinkled with shredded coconut, lacking any real coconut flavor. Coconut cake should be perfumed inside and out with the cool, subtle, mysterious essence of coconut. Its layers of snowy white cake should be moist and tender, with a delicate, yielding crumb, and the icing a silky, gently sweetened coat covered with a deep drift of downy coconut.

START WITH A BUTTER CAKE BASE For this moist and tender cake, we prefer a rich and moist butter cake made with low-protein cake flour.

FLAVOR TWO WAYS To infuse this cake with maximum coconut flavor, we rely on coconut extract and cream of coconut. We tried coconut milk but found that the fat content among brands varies too much, and cream of coconut simply delivers fuller coconut flavor in our cake.

CREATE A FLUFFY BUTTERCREAM In lieu of 7-minute icing, which is too sweet with this cake, we turn to a related frosting—an egg white buttercream. We flavor it with coconut extract and cream of coconut, just as we had done to flavor our cake. We also give our cake a woolly coating of shredded coconut for more coconut flavor and textural interest.

COCONUT LAYER CAKE
SERVES 10 TO 12

Be sure to use cream of coconut (such as Coco López) and not coconut milk here. One 15-ounce can is enough for both the cake and the icing; make sure to stir it well before using because it separates upon standing. For more information on splitting cake layers evenly, see page 287. For more information on frosting a layer cake, see page 288.

CAKE

1	large egg plus 5 large whites
¾	cup cream of coconut
¼	cup water
1	teaspoon vanilla extract
1	teaspoon coconut extract
2¼	cups (9 ounces) cake flour
1	cup (7 ounces) sugar
1	tablespoon baking powder
¾	teaspoon salt
12	tablespoons unsalted butter, cut into 12 pieces and softened
2	cups (6 ounces) sweetened shredded coconut

ICING

4	large egg whites
1	cup (7 ounces) sugar
	Pinch salt
1	pound unsalted butter (4 sticks), each stick cut into 6 pieces and softened
¼	cup cream of coconut
1	teaspoon coconut extract
1	teaspoon vanilla extract

1. FOR THE CAKE: Adjust oven rack to lower-middle position and heat oven to 325 degrees. Grease two 9-inch round cake pans, line with parchment paper, grease parchment, and flour pans.

2. Whisk egg and whites together in 2-cup liquid measuring cup. Add cream of coconut, water, vanilla, and coconut extract and whisk until thoroughly combined.

3. Using stand mixer fitted with paddle, mix flour, sugar, baking powder, and salt on low speed until combined. Add butter, 1 piece at a time, and mix until only pea-size pieces remain, about 1 minute. Add half of egg mixture, increase speed to medium-high, and beat until light and fluffy, about 1 minute. Reduce speed to medium-low, add remaining milk mixture, and beat until incorporated, about 30 seconds. Give batter final stir by hand.

4. Divide batter evenly between prepared pans and smooth tops with rubber spatula. Bake until toothpick inserted in center of cake comes out clean, about 30 minutes. Do not turn off oven. Let cakes cool in pans on wire rack for 10 minutes. Remove cakes from pans, discard parchment, and let cool completely, about 2 hours, before frosting. (Cooled cakes can be wrapped tightly in plastic wrap and kept at room temperature for up to 1 day. Wrapped tightly in plastic, then aluminum foil, cakes can be frozen for up to 1 month. Defrost cakes at room temperature before unwrapping and frosting.)

5. While cakes are cooling, spread shredded coconut on rimmed baking sheet; toast in oven until shreds are a mix of golden brown and white, about 15 to 20 minutes, stirring 2 or 3 times. Let cool to room temperature.

6. FOR THE ICING: Combine egg whites, sugar, and salt in bowl of stand mixer and set bowl over medium saucepan filled with 1 inch of barely simmering water (do not let bottom of bowl touch water). Whisk constantly until mixture is opaque and warm to the touch and registers 120 degrees, about 2 minutes.

7. Remove bowl from heat. Fit stand mixer with whisk and whip egg white mixture on high speed until barely warm (about 80 degrees), glossy, and sticky, about 7 minutes. Reduce speed to medium-high and whip in butter, 1 piece at a time, followed by cream

of coconut, coconut extract, and vanilla, scraping down bowl as needed. Continue to whip at medium-high speed until combined, about 1 minute.

8. Cut 1 horizontal line around sides of each layer; then, following scored lines, cut each layer into 2 even layers with long serrated knife.

9. Line edges of cake platter with 4 strips of parchment paper to keep platter clean. Place 1 cake layer on prepared platter. Place about ¾ cup icing in center of cake layer and, using large spatula, spread in even layer right to edge of cake. Carefully place other cake layer on top of icing, aligning cuts so that layers are even. Repeat using remaining cake layers and more icing, spreading icing until slightly over edge of top layer. Gather more frosting on tip of spatula and gently spread icing onto side of cake. Smooth icing by gently running edge of spatula around cake and leveling ridge that forms around top edge. Sprinkle top of cake evenly with toasted coconut. Then press remaining toasted coconut into sides of cake. Carefully pull out pieces of parchment from beneath cake before serving. (Assembled cake can be refrigerated for up to 1 day. Bring to room temperature before serving.)

MOISTENING DRY CAKE

If you find yourself with a dry, overbaked cake, we recommend brushing the cake with a flavored simple syrup to restore moistness. The technique works with yellow, white, and chocolate cakes.

1. Bring ½ cup each of water and sugar to simmer in small saucepan. Cook, stirring occasionally, until sugar dissolves. Remove from heat and add 2 tablespoons of liqueur, such as framboise, Frangelico, Chambord, or Kahlúa.

2. Brush each cake layer with a few tablespoons of flavored syrup before frosting cake.

Strawberry Cream Cake

✔ WHY THIS RECIPE WORKS

What could possibly ruin the heavenly trio of cake, cream, and ripe strawberries? How about soggy cake, bland berries, and squishy cream? We wanted a sturdy cake, a firm filling, and strawberry flavor fit for a starring role—a cake that would serve a formal occasion better than a simple strawberry shortcake.

CHOOSE CHIFFON CAKE After testing, we learned that butter cakes couldn't support a substantial strawberry filling, so we use a chiffon-style cake (page 268) that combines

the rich flavor of a butter cake with the light-yet-sturdy texture of a sponge cake.

MAKE A JAMMY FRUIT FILLING We make a flavorful berry "mash" with half of the berries and then reduce the macerated juice in a saucepan (with a little kirsch, a cherry-flavored liqueur) to help concentrate and round out the flavor. We slice the rest of the berries and place them around the edges of the cake for bites of fresh berry and visual appeal.

BUILDING STRAWBERRY CREAM CAKE

1. Cut 2 horizontal lines around sides of cake; then, following scored lines, cut cake into 3 even layers.

2. Place sliced berries evenly around edges of first layer, then completely cover center of cake with half of pureed strawberries.

3. Spread one-third of whipped cream over berries, leaving ½-inch border. Repeat layering with second layer of cake.

4. Press last layer into place, spread with remaining whipped cream, and decorate with remaining berries.

REINFORCE THE CREAM To prevent the cream filling from squirting out the sides, we fortify the whipped-cream filling with cream cheese, whose tang also offsets the cake's sweet elements.

STRAWBERRY CREAM CAKE

SERVES 10 TO 12

If using a cake pan, be sure to use one with at least 2-inch-tall sides. For more information on splitting cake layers evenly, see page 287.

CAKE

- 1 cup (7 ounces) sugar
- 1¼ cups (5 ounces) cake flour
- 1½ teaspoons baking powder
- ¼ teaspoon salt
- 5 large eggs (2 whole and 3 separated), room temperature
- 6 tablespoons unsalted butter, melted and cooled
- 2 tablespoons water
- 2 teaspoons vanilla extract
  Pinch cream of tartar

FILLING

- 2 pounds strawberries, hulled (6 cups)
- 4–6 tablespoons sugar
- 2 tablespoons kirsch
  Pinch salt

WHIPPED CREAM

- 8 ounces cream cheese, room temperature
- ½ cup (3½ ounces) sugar
- 1 teaspoon vanilla extract
- ⅛ teaspoon salt
- 2 cups heavy cream, chilled

1. FOR THE CAKE: Adjust oven rack to lower-middle position and heat oven to 325 degrees. Grease 9-inch round cake pan or 9-inch springform pan, line with parchment paper, grease parchment, and flour pan. Reserve 3 tablespoons sugar in small bowl. Whisk flour, baking powder, salt, and remaining sugar in medium bowl. Whisk in 2 whole eggs and 3 yolks, melted butter, water, and vanilla until smooth.

2. Using stand mixer fitted with whisk, whip egg whites and cream of tartar on medium-low speed until foamy, about 1 minute. Increase speed to medium-high and whip whites to soft billowy mounds, about 1 minute. Gradually add reserved 3 tablespoons sugar and whip until glossy, soft peaks form, 1 to 2 minutes. Stir one-third of whites into batter to lighten; add remaining whites and gently fold into batter until no white streaks remain.

3. Pour batter into prepared pan and smooth top with rubber spatula. Bake until toothpick inserted in center of cake comes out clean, 30 to 40 minutes, rotating pan halfway through baking. Let cake cool in pan on wire rack for 10 minutes. Remove cake from pan, discard parchment, and let cool completely, about 2 hours, before assembling. (Cooled cake can be wrapped tightly in plastic wrap and kept at room temperature for up to 1 day. Wrapped tightly in plastic, then aluminum foil, cake can be frozen for up to 1 month. Defrost cake at room temperature before unwrapping and frosting.)

4. FOR THE FILLING: Halve 24 of best-looking berries and reserve. Quarter remaining berries, toss with 4 to 6 tablespoons sugar (depending on sweetness of berries) in medium bowl, and let sit for 1 hour, stirring occasionally. Strain juices from berries and reserve (you should have about ½ cup). Pulse macerated berries in food processor until coarsely chopped, about 5 pulses (you should have about 1½ cups). In small saucepan, simmer reserved juices and kirsch over medium-high heat until syrupy and reduced to about 3 tablespoons, 3 to 5 minutes. Pour reduced syrup over macerated berries, add salt, and toss to combine. Set aside until cake is cooled.

5. FOR THE WHIPPED CREAM: When cake has cooled, whip cream cheese, sugar, vanilla, and salt using stand mixer fitted with whisk on medium-high speed until light and fluffy, 1 to 2 minutes, scraping down bowl as needed. Reduce speed to low and add heavy cream in

slow, steady stream; when almost fully combined, increase speed to medium-high and whip until stiff peaks form, 2 to 2½ minutes more, scraping down bowl as needed (you should have about 4½ cups).

6. Cut 2 horizontal lines around sides of cake; then, following scored lines, cut cake into 3 even layers using long serrated knife.

7. Line edges of cake platter with 4 strips of parchment paper to keep platter clean. Place 1 cake layer on prepared platter. Arrange ring of 20 strawberry halves, cut sides down and stem ends facing out, around perimeter of cake layer. Pour half of pureed berry mixture (about ¾ cup) in center, then spread to cover any exposed cake. Gently spread about one-third of whipped cream (about 1½ cups) over berry layer, leaving ½-inch border around edge. Place next cake layer on top and press down gently (whipped cream layer should become flush with cake edge). Repeat with 20 strawberry halves, remaining berry mixture, and half of remaining whipped cream; gently press last cake layer on top. Spread remaining whipped cream over top and decorate with remaining 8 strawberry halves. Carefully pull out pieces of parchment from beneath cake before serving. (Assembled cake can be refrigerated for up to 4 hours.)

Chocolate Layer Cake

✔ WHY THIS RECIPE WORKS

Over the years, chocolate cakes have become denser, richer, and squatter. We wanted an old-style, mile-high chocolate layer cake with a tender, airy, open crumb and a soft, billowy frosting.

INCLUDE A PUDDING To achieve a moist cake with rich chocolate flavor, we found the answer in historical sources, which suggest using buttermilk and making a "pudding" with a mixture of chocolate, water, and sugar. We simply melt unsweetened chocolate and cocoa powder in hot water over a double boiler, then stir in sugar until it dissolves.

RIBBON THE BATTER The mixing method is key to getting the right texture in this cake. After trying a variety of techniques, we turned to a popular old-fashioned method, ribboning. Ribboning involves whipping eggs with sugar until they double in volume, then adding the butter, dry ingredients, and milk. The egg foam aerates the cake, giving it both structure and tenderness.

MAKE A GANACHE FROSTING—BACKWARD We wanted the intense chocolate flavor of a ganache and the volume of a meringue or buttercream. The solution turned out to be a simple reversal of the conventional ganache procedure: We pour cold (rather than heated) cream into warm (rather than room-temperature) chocolate, wait for it to cool to room temperature, then whip it until thick and fluffy.

OLD-FASHIONED CHOCOLATE LAYER CAKE

SERVES 10 TO 12

Be sure to use cake pans with at least 2-inch-tall sides. For a smooth, spreadable frosting, use chopped semisweet chocolate, not chocolate chips—chocolate chips contain less cocoa butter than bar chocolate and will not melt as readily. As for other bar chocolate, bittersweet chocolate that is 60 percent cacao can be substituted but it will produce a stiffer, although still spreadable, frosting. Bittersweet chocolate with 70 percent cacao, however, should be avoided—it will produce a frosting that is crumbly and will not spread. For best results, do not make the frosting until the cakes are cooled, and use the frosting as soon as it is ready. If the frosting gets too cold and stiff to spread

CAN LAYER CAKES EASILY CONVERT INTO SHEET CAKES?

To answer this question, we followed our recipes for Fluffy Yellow Layer Cake (page 284) and Old-Fashioned Chocolate Layer Cake without altering a thing in either batter. But instead of pouring each batter into two 9-inch round cake pans, we baked each cake in a 13 by 9-inch baking dish lined with parchment paper, following the baking times and oven temperatures in the recipes.

Each sheet cake required about 5 extra minutes of baking until a toothpick inserted in its center revealed a few moist crumbs: perfectly done. So the next time you want to prepare a recipe for two 9-inch layer cakes in a 13 by 9-inch baking dish, bake the cake as usual and add about 5 minutes of baking time to the original recipe (checking for doneness a few minutes early to prevent overbaking). Let the cake cool completely before frosting it in the pan or turning it out to be frosted.

easily, wrap the mixer bowl with a dish towel soaked in hot water and mix on low speed until the frosting appears creamy and smooth. For more information on splitting cake layers evenly, see page 287. For more information on frosting a layer cake, see page 288.

CAN BROWN RICE SYRUP BE SUBSTITUTED FOR CORN SYRUP?

Like corn syrup, brown rice syrup is made by treating the cooked grain with enzymes that convert starches into sugar; the resulting liquid is reduced until thick. To see if it makes a suitable substitute, we tasted Lundberg Organic Sweet Dreams Brown Rice Syrup plain and used it in two recipes in which we normally use corn syrup: chocolate frosting and glazed chicken.

Corn syrup is approximately 45 percent as sweet as sugar; Lundberg claims that its rice syrup is about 50 percent as sweet as sugar, and we found the sweetness levels comparable when we sampled the products plain. But the rice syrup's viscosity and pronounced cereal aroma made us skeptical about its feasibility as a stand-in for clear, neutral-tasting corn syrup.

To our surprise, tasters found the frosting and chicken samples very similar in taste, texture, and appearance—the complex flavors of the other ingredients masked the brown rice syrup's toasty notes. But since Karo corn syrup costs $3.50 per 16-ounce bottle while a 21-ounce jar of Lundberg rice syrup set us back $6, we'll stick with corn syrup.

CAKE

- 4 ounces unsweetened chocolate, chopped coarse
- ¼ cup (¾ ounce) Dutch-processed cocoa powder
- ½ cup hot water
- 1¾ cups (12¼ ounces) sugar
- 1¾ cups (8¾ ounces) all-purpose flour
- 1½ teaspoons baking soda
- 1 teaspoon salt
- 1 cup buttermilk
- 2 teaspoons vanilla extract
- 4 large eggs plus 2 large yolks, room temperature
- 12 tablespoons unsalted butter, cut into 12 pieces and softened

FROSTING

- 1 pound semisweet chocolate, chopped fine
- 8 tablespoons unsalted butter
- ⅓ cup (2⅓ ounces) sugar
- 2 tablespoons corn syrup
- 2 teaspoons vanilla extract
- ¼ teaspoon salt
- 1¼ cups heavy cream, chilled

1. FOR THE CAKE: Adjust oven rack to middle position and heat oven to 350 degrees. Grease two 9-inch round cake pans, line with parchment paper, grease parchment, and flour pans. Combine chocolate, cocoa, and hot water in medium heatproof bowl set over saucepan filled with 1 inch of barely simmering water and stir with heatproof rubber spatula until chocolate is melted, about 2 minutes. Add ½ cup sugar to chocolate mixture and stir until thick and glossy, 1 to 2 minutes. Remove bowl from heat; set aside to cool.

2. Whisk flour, baking soda, and salt together in medium bowl. Combine buttermilk and vanilla in small bowl. Using stand mixer fitted with whisk, whip eggs and yolks on medium-low speed until combined, about 10 seconds. Add remaining 1¼ cups sugar, increase speed to high, and whip until light and fluffy, 2 to 3 minutes. Replace whisk with paddle. Add cooled chocolate mixture to egg mixture and mix on medium speed until thoroughly combined, 30 to 45 seconds, scraping down bowl as needed. Add softened butter 1 piece at a time, mixing about 10 seconds after each addition. Add flour in 3 additions, alternating with buttermilk mixture in 2 additions, mixing until incorporated after each addition (about 15 seconds), scraping down bowl as needed (batter may appear curdled). Mix at medium-low speed until batter is thoroughly combined, about 15 seconds. Remove bowl from mixer and give batter final stir by hand.

3. Divide batter evenly between prepared pans and smooth tops with rubber spatula. Bake until toothpick inserted in center of cake comes out with few crumbs attached, 25 to 30 minutes, rotating pans halfway through baking. Let cakes cool in pans on wire rack for 10 minutes. Remove cakes from pans, discard parchment, and let cool completely, about 2 hours, before frosting. (Cooled cakes can be wrapped tightly in plastic wrap and kept at room temperature for up to 1 day. Wrapped tightly in plastic, then aluminum foil, cakes can be frozen for up to 1 month. Defrost cakes at room temperature before unwrapping and frosting.)

4. FOR THE FROSTING: Melt chocolate in heatproof bowl set over saucepan containing 1 inch of barely simmering water, stirring occasionally until smooth. Remove from heat and set aside. Meanwhile, melt butter in small saucepan over medium-low heat. Increase heat to medium, add sugar, corn syrup, vanilla, and salt and stir with heatproof rubber spatula until sugar is dissolved, 4 to 5 minutes. In bowl of stand mixer, combine melted chocolate, butter mixture, and cream and stir until thoroughly combined.

5. Fill large bowl halfway with ice and water, place mixer bowl over ice bath, and stir mixture constantly with rubber spatula until frosting is thick and just beginning to harden against sides of bowl, 1 to 2 minutes (frosting should be 70 degrees). Fit stand mixer with paddle and beat frosting on medium-high speed until frosting is light and fluffy, 1 to 2 minutes. Using rubber spatula, stir until completely smooth.

6. Line edges of cake platter with 4 strips of parchment paper to keep platter clean. Place 1 cake layer on prepared platter. Place about 1½ cups frosting in center of cake layer and, using large spatula, spread in even layer right to edge of cake. Place second cake layer on top, making sure layers are aligned, then frost top in same manner as first layer, this time spreading frosting until slightly over edge. Gather more frosting on tip of spatula and gently spread icing onto side of cake. Smooth frosting by gently running edge of spatula around cake and leveling ridge that forms around top edge, or create billows by pressing back of spoon into frosting and twirling spoon as you lift away. Carefully pull out pieces of parchment from beneath cake before serving. (Assembled cake can be refrigerated for up to 1 day. Bring to room temperature before serving.)

German Chocolate Cake

✔ WHY THIS RECIPE WORKS

Most German chocolate cake recipes are similar, if not identical, to the one on the German's Sweet Chocolate box. Our tasters found several shortcomings in this recipe. It produced a cake that was too sweet, with chocolate flavor that was too mild, and with a texture so listless that the filling and cake together formed a soggy, sweet mush. We wanted a cake that was less sweet and more chocolaty than the original, but we didn't want to sacrifice the overall blend of flavors and textures that makes German chocolate cake so appealing in the first place.

CREATE A FOUR-LAYER CAKE The first order of business was to scale back the recipe by one quarter, which allowed us to fit the batter into two cake pans, thereby producing a cake with four thinner layers rather than three thicker layers. This would make the cake, with its thick coconut filling, easier to slice.

AMP UP CHOCOLATE FLAVOR German chocolate cake typically calls for German's Sweet Chocolate, but its flavor is too sweet. A combination of cocoa powder and semisweet or bittersweet chocolate mixed with boiling water intensifies their flavor for a cake with full, not faint, chocolate flavor.

USE A MIX OF SUGARS Both brown and white sugars give this cake the right level of caramel-like sweetness and tender texture. The tang of sour cream offsets some of the sweetness and contributes moistness.

TOAST THE PECANS—BUT NOT THE COCONUT We tried toasting the coconut, but it made for a brittle filling. But toasting the pecans intensifies their flavor and has no adverse effect on structure.

BOIL, THEN COOL THE FILLING The filling base, made with egg yolks, evaporated milk sugar (both brown and white), and butter needs to be boiled—when we followed traditional recipes where the filling was just simmered, it came out too loose. After we cook the filling, we refrigerate it to allow it to chill and firm up further. Sweetened shredded coconut is stirred into the filling just before chilling and the toasted pecans are stirred into the filling just before the cake is assembled to preserve their crunch.

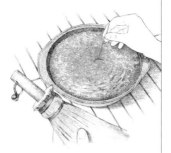
GERMAN CHOCOLATE CAKE WITH COCONUT-PECAN FILLING

SERVES 10 TO 12

For an accurate measurement of boiling water, bring a full kettle of water to a boil, then measure out the desired amount. When you assemble the cake, the filling should be cool or cold (or room temperature, at the very warmest). Be sure to use cake pans with at least 2-inch-tall sides. To be time-efficient, first make the filling, then use the refrigeration time to prepare, bake, and cool the cakes. The toasted pecans are stirred into the filling just before assembly to keep them from becoming soft and soggy. For more information on splitting cake layers evenly, see page 287. For more information on frosting a layer cake, see page 288.

FILLING

4	large egg yolks, room temperature
1	(12-ounce) can evaporated milk
1	cup (7 ounces) granulated sugar
¼	cup packed (1¾ ounces) light brown sugar
6	tablespoons unsalted butter, cut into 6 pieces
⅛	teaspoon salt
2	teaspoons vanilla extract
2⅓	cups (7 ounces) sweetened shredded coconut
1½	cups (6 ounces) pecans, toasted and chopped fine

CAKE

4	ounces semisweet or bittersweet chocolate, chopped fine
¼	cup (¾ ounce) Dutch-processed cocoa powder
½	cup boiling water
2	cups (10 ounces) all-purpose flour
¾	teaspoon baking soda
12	tablespoons unsalted butter, softened
1	cup (7 ounces) granulated sugar
⅔	cup packed (4⅔ ounces) light brown sugar
¾	teaspoon salt
4	large eggs, room temperature
1	teaspoon vanilla extract
¾	cup sour cream, room temperature

1. FOR THE FILLING: Whisk egg yolks in medium saucepan, then gradually whisk in evaporated milk. Add granulated sugar, brown sugar, butter, and salt and cook over medium-high heat, whisking constantly, until mixture is boiling, frothy, and slightly thickened, about 6 minutes. Transfer mixture to bowl, whisk in vanilla, then stir in coconut. Cool until just warm, cover with plastic wrap, and refrigerate until cool or cold, at least 2 hours or up to 3 days. (Do not stir in pecans until just before cake assembly.)

2. FOR THE CAKE: Adjust oven rack to lower-middle position and heat oven to 350 degrees. Grease two 9-inch round cake pans, line with parchment paper, grease parchment, and flour pans. Combine chocolate and cocoa in small heatproof bowl, pour boiling water over mixture, and let sit, covered, for 5 minutes. Whisk mixture gently until smooth, then let cool to room temperature. Whisk flour and baking soda together in medium bowl and set aside.

3. Using stand mixer fitted with paddle, beat butter, granulated sugar, brown sugar, and salt on medium-high speed until light and fluffy, about 3 minutes. Add eggs, one at a time, and beat until combined. Beat in vanilla, increase speed to medium-high and beat until light and fluffy, about 45 seconds. Reduce speed to low, add chocolate, then increase speed to medium and beat until combined, about 30 seconds, scraping down bowl once (batter may appear curdled). Reduce speed to low, add flour mixture in 3 additions, alternating with sour cream in 2 additions, scraping down bowl as needed. Give batter final stir by hand (batter will be thick).

4. Divide batter evenly between prepared pans and smooth tops with rubber spatula. Bake until toothpick inserted in center of cake comes out clean, about 30 minutes, rotating pans halfway through baking. Let cakes cool in pans on wire rack for 10 minutes. Remove cakes from pans, discard parchment, and let cool completely, about 2 hours, before filling. (Cooled cakes can be wrapped tightly in plastic wrap and kept at room temperature for

Line the bottom of a cake carrier, box, or other container with a small piece of nonskid shelf liner to keep the cake from sliding into the walls of the carrier while in transit.

HARD HAT FOR CAKES

Frosted cakes make lousy travel companions because even the most minor mishap can ruin their appearance. If you don't have a cake keeper, improvise with a common kitchen tool: the clean, dry bowl from a salad spinner, inverted over the cake. It may not be beautiful, but the bowl is spacious, lightweight, and rigid, and it provides the cake with a much-needed measure of protection. This is also a great way to cover leftover cake that's staying home, not hitting the road.

up to 1 day. Wrapped tightly in plastic, then aluminum foil, cakes can be frozen for up to 1 month. Defrost cakes at room temperature before unwrapping and frosting.)

5. Cut 1 horizontal line around sides of each layer; then, following scored lines, cut each layer into 2 even layers using long serrated knife.

6. Line edges of cake platter with 4 strips of parchment paper to keep platter clean. Place 1 cake layer on prepared platter. Stir toasted pecans into chilled filling. Spread 1 cup filling evenly across top of cake layer, spreading filling to very edge. Carefully place next cake layer on top of filling, aligning cuts so that layers are even. Repeat using remaining filling and cake layers. Carefully pull out pieces of parchment from beneath cake before serving. (Assembled cake can be refrigerated for up to 1 day. Bring to room temperature before serving.)

GERMAN CHOCOLATE CAKE WITH COFFEE, CASHEW, AND COCONUT FILLING

Add 2 teaspoons ground coffee to filling mixture with sugars in step 1. Substitute roasted unsalted cashews for pecans.

GERMAN CHOCOLATE CAKE WITH BANANA, MACADAMIA, AND COCONUT FILLING

If you cannot find roasted unsalted macadamia nuts, substitute salted ones, but first remove excess salt by spreading them on a clean dish towel and giving them a good rub.

Reduce vanilla in filling to 1 teaspoon and add 2 teaspoons dark rum with vanilla in step 1. Substitute unsalted macadamia nuts for pecans. Just before assembling cake, peel and cut 4 bananas into ⅜-inch-thick slices. Arrange one quarter of banana slices on first

cake layer, then spread filling evenly over; repeat with remaining cake layers, bananas, and filling.

GERMAN CHOCOLATE SHEET CAKE
SERVES 15

The towering layers of chocolate cake separated by coconut-pecan filling look impressive in our German Chocolate Cake, but splitting the cake layers and assembling the cake is a fair amount of work, so we developed this simplified sheet cake variation, which slathers the entire cake with a thick layer of the coconut-pecan filling. In addition to being easier to assemble, the cake is also a cinch to serve to a crowd. When you frost the cake, the frosting should be cool or cold (or room temperature, at the very warmest). To be time-efficient, first make the frosting, then use the refrigeration time to prepare, bake, and cool the cake. The toasted pecans are stirred into the frosting just before the cake is frosted to keep them from becoming soft and soggy.

Grease 13 by 9-inch baking pan, line with parchment paper, grease parchment, and flour pan. Follow recipe as directed through step 3, preparing filling to use as frosting. In step 4, pour batter into prepared pan, smooth top with rubber spatula, and gently tap pan on counter to release air bubbles. Bake cake until toothpick inserted in center comes out clean, 30 to 35 minutes. Let cake cool in pan on wire rack for 10 minutes. Remove cake from pan, discard parchment, and let cool completely, about 2 hours, before frosting. Frost top of cake and serve. (Refrigerate cake if not serving immediately; if refrigerated longer than 2 hours, let cake sit at room temperature 15 to 20 minutes before serving. Cooled, unfrosted cake can be stored at room temperature for up to 1 day. Frosted cake can be refrigerated for up to 3 days.)

Moist and Tender Devil's Food Cake

✔ WHY THIS RECIPE WORKS

The problem with defining the devil's food cake is that over time the recipe has been changed and embellished to the point where different recipes have little in common. After reviewing a number of recipes, we came to the conclusion that the essence of devil's food cake is a very moist, velvety texture combined with an intense chocolate experience.

CREAM THE BUTTER AND SUGAR Creaming the butter and sugar and then adding the eggs one at a time helps build structure in this cake. Baking powder and baking soda also help give the cake lift.

INCLUDE SOUR CREAM Sour cream deepens the rich flavor of the cake and provides moistness.

USE TWO CHOCOLATES Using a combination of unsweetened chocolate and Dutch-processed cocoa gives our the cake great chocolaty flavor, and using hot water rather than milk ensures that its flavor is deep and full (think of dark versus milk chocolate). The heat of the water also helps bloom, or heighten, the chocolate flavor in the cocoa.

CHOOSE ALL-PURPOSE FLOUR We like the structure all-purpose flour provides to this cake—cake flour is simply too delicate.

FROST WITH BUTTERCREAM This moist, rich cake is best matched by a rich vanilla buttercream or chocolate frosting.

MOIST AND TENDER DEVIL'S FOOD CAKE

SERVES 10 TO 12

If using 9-inch cake pans, note that the layers will be quite thin. For an accurate measurement of boiling water, bring a full kettle of water to a boil, then measure out the desired amount. For more information on frosting a layer cake, see page 288.

½ cup (1½ ounces) Dutch-processed cocoa powder, plus extra as needed
1½ cups (7½ ounces) all-purpose flour
1 teaspoon baking soda
½ teaspoon baking powder
¼ teaspoon salt
1¼ cups boiling water
4 ounces unsweetened chocolate, chopped
1 teaspoon instant espresso powder or instant coffee powder
10 tablespoons unsalted butter, softened
1½ cups packed (10½ ounces) light brown sugar
3 large eggs, room temperature
½ cup sour cream, room temperature
1 teaspoon vanilla extract
1 recipe buttercream frosting (recipes follow)

1. Adjust oven racks to upper-middle and lower-middle positions and heat oven to 350 degrees. Grease three 8- or 9-inch round cake pans, line with parchment paper, grease parchment, then dust with cocoa. Whisk flour, baking soda, baking powder, and salt together in large bowl. In medium bowl, whisk boiling water, chocolate, ½ cup cocoa, and espresso powder together until smooth.

2. Using stand mixer fitted with paddle, beat butter and sugar together on medium speed until light and fluffy, 3 to 6 minutes. Beat in eggs, one at a time, until combined, about 30 seconds. Beat in sour cream and vanilla until incorporated.

3. Reduce speed to low and add flour in 3 additions, alternating with chocolate mixture in 2 additions, scraping down bowl as needed (do not overbeat). Give batter final stir by hand.

4. Divide batter evenly among prepared pans, smooth tops with rubber spatula, and

SUBSTITUTING FOR INSTANT ESPRESSO POWDER

Instant espresso powder is often used to boost the intensity of chocolate flavor. Because instant espresso isn't always available, we often call for instant coffee as a substitute. To test just how much instant coffee should be used in place of instant espresso, we prepared *pots de crème*, triple-chocolate espresso brownies, and devil's food cake—each with the amount of espresso called for in the recipe, an equal amount of instant coffee, and twice the amount of instant coffee.

The pots de crème made with espresso had a rich, dark chocolate flavor. When the espresso was replaced with an equal amount of a popular brand of instant coffee, the chocolate flavor was weak and lacked depth. Doubling the amount of instant coffee, however, made the flavor comparable to the original recipe. The opposite was true with the espresso brownies, which exhibited a bitter, overwhelming coffee flavor when twice the amount of instant coffee was used. Tasters preferred the brownies made with a one-to-one conversion, which had a strong, but not undesirable, coffee flavor. As for the cake, tasters couldn't detect much of a difference among the three batches.

In short, if you can't find instant espresso powder, we recommend replacing it with the same amount of instant coffee in baked goods and with double the amount in creamy applications like puddings, frostings, and mousses, which contain proportionally more chocolate as a percentage of the total ingredients.

Trying to ice a cake with stiff frosting can yield unappealing flecks of torn-off cake. To keep things spreadable, heat up a spatula or spoon in hot water before slathering on the frosting.

1. Dip metal spatula (or spoon) into hot water for 5 seconds.

2. Remove and dry completely.

3. Spread frosting on cake, repeating process as necessary.

gently tap pans on the counter to release air bubbles. Bake until toothpick inserted in center of cake comes out with few crumbs attached, 15 to 20 minutes, rotating pans halfway through baking.

5. Let cakes cool in pans on wire rack for 10 minutes. Remove cakes from pans, discard parchment, and let cool completely, about 2 hours, before frosting. (Cooled cakes can be wrapped tightly in plastic wrap and kept at room temperature for up to 1 day. Wrapped tightly in plastic, then aluminum foil, cakes can be frozen for up to 1 month. Defrost cakes at room temperature before unwrapping and frosting.)

6. Line edges of cake platter with 4 strips of parchment paper to keep platter clean. Place 1 cake layer on prepared platter. Place about 1 cup frosting in center of cake layer and, using large spatula, spread in even layer right to edge of cake. Repeat with second and third layer, spreading frosting on top layer until slightly over edge. Gather more frosting on tip of spatula and gently spread icing onto side of cake. Smooth frosting by gently running edge of spatula around cake and leveling ridge that forms around top edge, or create billows by pressing back of spoon into frosting and twirling spoon as you lift away. Carefully pull out pieces of parchment from beneath cake before serving. (Assembled cake can be refrigerated for up to 1 day. Bring to room temperature before serving.)

VANILLA BUTTERCREAM FROSTING
MAKES ABOUT 4 CUPS

The whole eggs, whipped until airy, give this buttercream a light, satiny-smooth texture that melts on the tongue.

4	large eggs, room temperature
1	cup (7 ounces) sugar
2	teaspoons vanilla extract
	Pinch salt
1	pound unsalted butter (4 sticks), each stick cut into quarters and softened

1. Combine eggs, sugar, vanilla, and salt in bowl of stand mixer and set bowl over saucepan containing 1 inch of barely simmering water. Whisking gently but constantly, heat mixture until thin and foamy and registers 160 degrees.

2. Fit stand mixer with whisk and whip egg mixture on medium-high speed until light, airy, and cooled to room temperature, about 5 minutes. Reduce speed to medium and add butter, 1 piece at a time. (After adding half of butter, buttercream may look curdled; it will smooth with additional butter.) Once all butter is added, increase speed to high and whip until light, fluffy, and thoroughly combined, about 1 minute. (Frosting can be refrigerated for up to 5 days. Let frosting sit at room temperature until softened, about 2 hours, then, using stand mixer fitted with whisk, whip on medium speed until smooth, 2 to 5 minutes.)

RICH COFFEE BUTTERCREAM FROSTING

Omit vanilla. Dissolve 3 tablespoons instant espresso powder in 3 tablespoons warm water and beat mixture into buttercream after butter has been added.

RICH CHOCOLATE CREAM FROSTING
MAKES ABOUT 3 CUPS

16	ounces semisweet chocolate, chopped fine
1½	cups heavy cream
⅓	cup corn syrup
1	teaspoon vanilla extract

Place chocolate in heatproof bowl. Bring heavy cream to boil in small saucepan over medium-high heat, then pour over chocolate. Add corn syrup and let sit, covered, for 5 minutes. Whisk mixture gently until smooth, then stir in vanilla. Refrigerate 1 to 1½ hours, stirring every 15 minutes, until mixture reaches spreadable consistency.

Jelly Roll Cake

✔ WHY THIS RECIPE WORKS

Though just a basic sponge cake that is filled, rolled, and dusted with powdered sugar, a jelly roll cake becomes complicated when it resists assuming its characteristic shape or cracks. But when done right, a jelly roll cake is an impressive-looking crowd pleaser. We wanted a simple version that was reliably uncomplicated to make.

START WITH A SPONGE CAKE For our jelly roll we turned to a classic American sponge cake, which adds no fat in the form of butter or milk and calls for beaten egg whites folded into beaten egg yolks to create a foamy batter which bakes into a springy, tender cake that's a perfect match for a layer of jam.

SPREAD THE BATTER EVENLY Once we pour the batter into the sheet pan, we spread it evenly with an offset spatula. The cake bakes and sets up quickly so it's critical to make the batter as level as possible in the pan before it goes into the oven.

ROLL THE CAKE WHILE WARM For the neatest-looking spiral—without any cracks—we remove the cake from the pan straight out of the oven and roll it up in a clean dish towel into a log. Rolling the warm cake helps "train" it so that it will roll easily after it's cooled and spread with jam.

SPREAD THE FILLING AND REROLL After unrolling the cooled cake, we spread it with a thin layer of jam using an offset spatula, making sure to leave a ½-inch border at the sides so that the jam doesn't leak out, then we reroll it. Cut into thick slices and dusted with powdered sugar, our cake looks picture perfect and tastes every bit as good as it looks.

FOOLPROOF JELLY ROLL CAKE
SERVES 8 TO 10

Any flavor of seedless jam will work here; for an added treat, sprinkle 2 cups fresh blueberries, raspberries, blackberries, or sliced strawberries over the jam before rolling up the cake.

¾	cup (3¾ ounces) all-purpose flour
1	teaspoon baking powder
¼	teaspoon salt
5	large eggs, room temperature
¾	cup (5¼ ounces) granulated sugar
½	teaspoon vanilla extract
1¼	cups (12 ounces) seedless jam
	Confectioners' sugar

1. Adjust oven rack to lower-middle position and heat oven to 350 degrees. Grease 18 by 13-inch rimmed baking sheet, line with parchment paper, grease parchment, then flour sheet. Grease second large sheet of parchment and set aside. Whisk flour, baking powder, and salt together in medium bowl; set aside.

2. Using stand mixer fitted with whisk, whip eggs at medium-high speed and gradually add granulated sugar and then vanilla, about 1 minute. Continue to whip mixture until very thick and voluminous, 4 to 8 minutes. Sift flour mixture over egg mixture and fold in with rubber spatula until just incorporated.

3. Scrape batter into prepared baking sheet and spread out to even layer. Bake cake until it feels firm and springs back when touched, 12 to 17 minutes, rotating baking sheet halfway through baking. Lay clean dish towel on counter.

4. Immediately run knife around edge of cake, then flip hot cake out onto towel. Peel off and discard parchment baked on bottom of cake. Starting from 1 short end of cake, roll cake and towel snugly into log and let cool, seam side down, for 15 minutes.

5. Gently unroll cake. Spread jam over cake, leaving ½-inch border at sides of cake. Reroll cake gently but snugly around jam, leaving towel behind as you roll. Trim ends of cake, transfer cake to serving platter, and let cake cool completely, about 30 minutes. Dust with confectioners' sugar before serving.

1. Starting from short side, roll cake—towel and all—into jelly roll shape. Cool for 15 minutes.

2. Unroll cooled cake. Using offset spatula, spread jam over the surface of cake, leaving ½-inch border around sides of cake.

3. Reroll cake gently but snugly around filling, carefully peeling off towel as you roll. Dust top of cake with confectioners' sugar.

4. Trim thin slices from both ends and then cut cake into individual slices, using electric or serrated knife, and garnish with fresh berries if desired.

Simple Chocolate Sheet Cake

✔ **WHY THIS RECIPE WORKS**

Sheet cakes, for all their simplicity, can still turn out dry, sticky, or flavorless and, on occasion, can even sink in the middle. We wanted a simple, dependable recipe, one that was moist yet also light and chocolaty.

TWEAK A BASIC CHOCOLATE CAKE Adding buttermilk and baking soda to our basic mixture of butter, eggs, flour, sugar, and cocoa helps lighten the batter. Mixing the batter is simple—no creaming or beating required.

INCREASE CHOCOLATE FLAVOR To further deepen the chocolate taste, we use semisweet chocolate in addition to the cocoa.

BAKE LOW AND SLOW We bake the cake at a low temperature for a long time—40 minutes—to produce a perfectly baked cake with a lovely flat top.

FROST WITH A SIMPLE BUTTERCREAM Though this cake can be frosted with almost anything, we like a classic American milk chocolate frosting, which pairs well with the darker flavor of the cake.

SIMPLE CHOCOLATE SHEET CAKE
SERVES 15

We prefer Dutch-processed cocoa for the deeper chocolate flavor it gives the cake. The baked and cooled cake can also be served with lightly sweetened whipped cream or topped with any frosting you like in lieu of the milk chocolate frosting. This frosting needs about an hour to cool before it can be used, so begin making it when the cake comes out of the oven.

CAKE

1¼	cups (6¼ ounces) all-purpose flour
¾	cup (2¼ ounces) Dutch-processed cocoa powder
¼	teaspoon salt
8	ounces semisweet chocolate, chopped
12	tablespoons unsalted butter
4	large eggs, room temperature
1½	cups (10½ ounces) granulated sugar
1	teaspoon vanilla extract
1	cup buttermilk
½	teaspoon baking soda

FROSTING

½	cup heavy cream
1	tablespoon corn syrup
	Pinch salt
10	ounces milk chocolate, chopped
½	cup (2 ounces) confectioners' sugar
8	tablespoons unsalted butter, cut into 8 pieces and chilled

1. FOR THE CAKE: Adjust oven rack to middle position and heat oven to 325 degrees. Grease 13 by 9-inch baking pan, line with parchment paper, grease parchment, and flour pan.

2. Sift flour, cocoa, and salt together into medium bowl; set aside. Microwave chocolate at 50 percent power for 2 minutes; stir, add butter, and continue heating until melted, stirring once every additional minute. Whisk eggs, sugar, and vanilla together in medium bowl.

3. Whisk chocolate into egg mixture until combined. Combine buttermilk and baking soda; whisk into chocolate mixture, then whisk in dry ingredients until batter is smooth and glossy. Pour batter into prepared pan and smooth top with rubber spatula. Bake until firm in center when lightly pressed and toothpick inserted in center of cake comes out

When frosting a cake, the act of spreading can dislodge some of the crumbs, which then get incorporated into the frosting, muddying its smoothness. Here's how to minimize the problem.

1. Place large, evenly spaced dollops of frosting over top of cake.

2. Using offset spatula, spread 1 dollop to another until frosting is smooth and evenly distributed.

clean, about 40 minutes, rotating pan halfway through baking. Let cool on wire rack until room temperature, at least 1 hour.

4. FOR THE FROSTING: Microwave cream, corn syrup, and salt in bowl until simmering, about 1 minute, or bring to simmer in small saucepan over medium heat. Place chocolate in food processor. With processor running, gradually add hot cream mixture, then process for 1 minute. Stop processor, add sugar, and process to combine, about 30 seconds. With processor running, add butter, 1 piece at a time, then process until incorporated and smooth, about 20 seconds longer. Transfer frosting to medium bowl and let cool to room temperature, stirring frequently, until thick and spreadable, about 1 hour. Spread frosting over cake and serve.

Ultimate Carrot Layer Cake

✓ WHY THIS RECIPE WORKS

Building a showstopping carrot cake comes with plenty of obstacles. The carrots make the cake sticky and prone to breaking. No more than two layers of the moist, heavy cake can be stacked without risk of toppling. And the frosting often gets compromised in the process. We wanted to reengineer humble carrot cake as a four-tier, nut-crusted confection that could claim its place among the most glamorous desserts.

BAKE IN A SHEET PAN Removing, slicing, and stacking carrot cake from traditional cake rounds was almost impossible. Instead, we decided to bake our cake in a rimmed baking sheet and then divide it into four equal pieces and stack them into a tall, rectangular cake. This concept has a lot going for it: The cake bakes quickly and takes only 30 minutes to cool. And because the middle sets almost as quickly as the edges, the cake doesn't dome.

SOFTEN THE CARROTS We ran into one issue with our baking sheet method. Thanks to the drastically reduced baking time, the coarse shreds of carrot don't have time to soften and they bake up coarse and crunchy. We remedy this by adding some extra alkaline baking soda to the batter. This raises the pH of the cake and breaks down the carrot shreds' cell walls for softer carrots.

FINESSE THE FROSTING Cream cheese frosting makes the perfect partner to carrot cake, but we needed it to be thick enough to stay sandwiched between the cake layers. Confectioners' sugar provides structure, but it can also overshadow the cream cheese's tanginess. A secret ingredient enabled us to get the best of both worlds: Buttermilk powder lends the frosting a pleasant, cheesy tang and also allows us to add as much confectioners' sugar as we needed without sacrificing flavor.

FINISH WITH NUTS To make our cake special occasion–ready, we needed to hide the delicate cut sides, which looked messy compared with the pristine top layer. That's where nuts come in. We had omitted them from the batter because they caught on our knife during slicing. To camouflage the imperfections— and to satisfy tasters who missed the crunch of the pecans in the cake—we press toasted nuts on the crumb-speckled sides.

ULTIMATE CARROT LAYER CAKE

SERVES 10 TO 12

Shred the carrots on the large holes of a box grater or in a food processor fitted with the shredding disk. Do not substitute liquid buttermilk for the buttermilk powder. To ensure the proper spreading consistency for the frosting, use cold cream cheese. If your baked cake is of an uneven thickness, adjust the orientation of the layers as they are stacked to produce a level cake. Assembling this cake on a cardboard cake round trimmed to a 6 by 8-inch rectangle makes it easy to press the pecans onto the sides of the frosted cake.

CAKE

1¾	cups (8¾ ounces) all-purpose flour
2	teaspoons baking powder
1	teaspoon baking soda
1½	teaspoons ground cinnamon
¾	teaspoon ground nutmeg
½	teaspoon salt
¼	teaspoon ground cloves
1¼	cups packed (8¾ ounces) light brown sugar
¾	cup vegetable oil
3	large eggs
1	teaspoon vanilla extract
2⅔	cups shredded carrots (4 carrots)
⅔	cup dried currants

FROSTING

3	cups (12 ounces) confectioners' sugar
16	tablespoons unsalted butter, softened
⅓	cup buttermilk powder
2	teaspoons vanilla extract
¼	teaspoon salt
12	ounces cream cheese, chilled and cut into 12 equal pieces
2	cups (8 ounces) pecans, toasted and chopped coarse

1. FOR THE CAKE: Adjust oven rack to middle position and heat oven to 350 degrees. Grease 18 by 13-inch rimmed baking sheet, line with parchment paper, and grease parchment. Whisk flour, baking powder, baking soda, cinnamon, nutmeg, salt, and cloves together in large bowl.

2. Whisk sugar, oil, eggs, and vanilla together in second bowl until mixture is smooth. Stir in carrots and currants. Add flour mixture and fold with rubber spatula until mixture is just combined.

3. Transfer batter to prepared sheet and smooth surface with offset spatula. Bake until center of cake is firm to touch, 15 to 18 minutes, rotating pan halfway through baking. Cool in pan on wire rack for 5 minutes. Invert cake onto wire rack (do not remove parchment), then reinvert onto second wire rack. Cool cake completely, about 30 minutes.

4. FOR THE FROSTING: Using stand mixer fitted with paddle, beat sugar, butter, buttermilk powder, vanilla, and salt together on low speed until smooth, about 2 minutes, scraping down bowl as needed. Increase speed to medium-low; add cream cheese, 1 piece at a time, and mix until smooth, about 2 minutes.

5. Transfer cooled cake to cutting board, parchment side down. Using sharp chef's knife, cut cake and parchment in half crosswise, then lengthwise, to make 4 equal rectangles, about 6 by 8 inches each.

6. Place 6 by 8-inch cardboard rectangle on cake platter. Place 1 cake layer, parchment side up, on cardboard and carefully remove parchment. Using offset spatula, spread ⅔ cup frosting evenly over top, right to edge of cake. Repeat with 2 more layers of cake, pressing lightly to adhere and frosting each layer with ⅔ cup frosting. Top with last cake layer and spread 1 cup frosting evenly over top. Spread remaining frosting evenly over sides of cake. (It's fine if some crumbs show through frosting on sides, but if you go back to smooth top of cake, be sure that spatula is free of crumbs.)

7. Hold cake with 1 hand and gently press chopped pecans onto sides with other hand. Chill for at least 1 hour before serving. (The frosted cake can be refrigerated for up to 24 hours before serving.)

BUILDING THE ULTIMATE CARROT LAYER CAKE

1. Bake batter on baking sheet to create thin, level cake that doesn't need to be split horizontally.

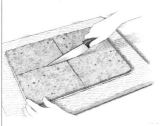

2. Slice cooled sheet cake into 4 equal rectangles.

3. Spread frosting over rectangular layer placed on cardboard; repeat with remaining layers.

4. Press chopped pecans onto sides of cake to hide any imperfections and add crunch.

To test whether peeling carrots has a noticeable effect on their flavor or texture, we compared batches of scrubbed unpeeled carrots with peeled carrots. We tasted the samples raw, cut into coins and glazed, and roasted in a 425-degree oven.

Although a few tasters found the unpeeled raw carrots to be earthier-tasting than their stripped siblings, most were distracted by their "dusty exterior" and "bitter finish." The results were even more clear-cut when the carrots were cooked. Tasters unanimously preferred the peel-free carrots in the glazed and roasted samples. In both cases, the skins on the unpeeled carrots became wrinkled, tough, and gritty. Their flavor was "again earthier, but not in a good way" and they weren't particularly appealing looking. On the other hand, the peeled versions remained bright orange, tender, and sweet.

In sum: It takes only an extra minute or two to peel carrots. We think it's time well spent.

Classic Carrot Cake with Cream Cheese Frosting

✔ WHY THIS RECIPE WORKS

Once heralded for its use of vegetable oil in place of butter and carrots as a natural sweetener, classic carrot cake slathered with cream cheese frosting boasts loads of homey appeal. Sure, the carrots add some sweetness, but they also add a lot of moisture, which means soggy cake. And oil? It. can make this cake awfully dense. We wanted a moist, not soggy, cake that was rich with balanced spice flavor.

BUILD A STURDY, BUT TENDER CAKE
We start with all-purpose flour—cake flour is too delicate to support the grated carrots that get mixed in. For lift, we like a combination of baking soda and baking powder.

KEEP THE SPICES IN CHECK   Some carrot cakes use a heavy hand with the spices; we take a conservative approach and use modest amounts of cinnamon, nutmeg, and cloves.

GRATE AND MIX IN THE FOOD PROCESSOR   We found that the simplest mixing method was actually the food processor. We use the processor fitted with the shredding disk to shred the carrots, then swap out the blade to make the batter (but if you don't own a food processor a box grater and mixer will suffice). After trying varying amounts of grated carrots, we settled on 1 pound for a pleasantly moist texture. For a rich, but not greasy, cake, 1½ cups vegetable oil does the trick.

MAKE A RICH FROSTING   Cream cheese frosting is the perfect partner to carrot cake—we enrich our version with sour cream for extra tang and vanilla for depth of flavor. Once again, it was easy enough to prepare the frosting in the food processor so that start to finish, we only had to dirty one piece of equipment.

CLASSIC CARROT SHEET CAKE WITH CREAM CHEESE FROSTING

SERVES 15

If you like nuts in your cake, stir 1½ cups toasted chopped pecans or walnuts into the batter along with the carrots. Raisins are also a good addition; 1 cup can be added along with the carrots. If you add both nuts and raisins, the cake will need an additional 10 to 12 minutes in the oven.

2½	cups (12½ ounces) all-purpose flour
1¼	teaspoons baking powder
1	teaspoon baking soda
1¼	teaspoons ground cinnamon
½	teaspoon ground nutmeg
⅛	teaspoon ground cloves
½	teaspoon salt
1	pound carrots, peeled
1½	cups (10½ ounces) granulated sugar
½	cup packed (3½ ounces) light brown sugar
4	large eggs, room temperature
1½	cups vegetable oil
1	recipe Cream Cheese Frosting (recipe follows)

1. Adjust oven rack to middle position and heat oven to 350 degrees. Grease 13 by 9-inch baking pan, line with parchment paper, grease parchment, and flour pan.

2. Whisk flour, baking powder, baking soda, cinnamon, nutmeg, cloves, and salt together in large bowl and set aside.

3A. FOOD PROCESSOR METHOD: Using food processor fitted with large shredding disk, shred carrots (you should have about 3 cups); transfer to bowl. Wipe out workbowl and fit processor with metal blade. Process granulated sugar, brown sugar, and eggs in food processor until frothy and thoroughly combined, about 20 seconds. With processor running, add oil in steady stream and process until mixture is light in color and well emulsified, about 20 seconds. Transfer mixture to medium bowl and stir in carrots and flour mixture until incorporated and no streaks of flour remain.

3B. STAND MIXER METHOD: Shred carrots on large holes of box grater (you should have about 3 cups); transfer carrots to bowl and set aside. Using stand mixer fitted with paddle, beat granulated sugar, brown sugar, and eggs on medium-high speed until thoroughly combined, about 45 seconds. Reduce speed to medium; with mixer running, add oil in slow, steady stream, being careful to pour oil against inside of bowl (if oil begins to splatter, reduce speed to low until oil is incorporated, then resume adding oil). Increase speed to high and mix until mixture is light in color and well emulsified, about 45 seconds to 1 minute longer. Turn off mixer and stir in carrots and dry ingredients by hand until incorporated and no streaks of flour remain.

4. Scrape batter into prepared pan, smooth top with rubber spatula, and gently tap pan on counter to release air bubbles. Bake until toothpick inserted in center of cake comes out clean, 35 to 40 minutes, rotating pan halfway through baking. Let cake cool completely in pan on wire rack, about 2 hours.

5. Run thin knife around edge of cake to loosen from pan. Invert cake onto wire rack, discard parchment, then turn cake right side up onto serving platter. Spread frosting evenly over cake and serve. (Cake can be refrigerated for up to 3 days.)

CREAM CHEESE FROSTING
MAKES 3 CUPS

Do not use low-fat or nonfat cream cheese or the frosting will turn out too soupy to work with.

12	ounces cream cheese, softened
6	tablespoons unsalted butter, softened
4	teaspoons sour cream
1	teaspoon vanilla extract
¼	teaspoon salt
1¾	cups (7 ounces) confectioners' sugar

1A. FOOD PROCESSOR METHOD: Process cream cheese, butter, sour cream, vanilla, and salt in food processor until combined, about 5 seconds, scraping down bowl as needed. Add confectioners' sugar and process until smooth, about 10 seconds.

1B. STAND MIXER METHOD: Using stand mixer fitted with whisk, mix cream cheese, butter, sour cream, vanilla, and salt at medium-high speed until well combined, about 30 seconds, scraping down bowl as needed. Add confectioners' sugar and mix until very fluffy, about 1 minute.

SPICED CARROT SHEET CAKE WITH VANILLA BEAN– CREAM CHEESE FROSTING
SERVES 15

The Indian tea called chai inspired this variation.

For the cake, substitute ½ teaspoon pepper for nutmeg, increase cloves to ¼ teaspoon, and add 1 tablespoon ground cardamom along with spices. For the frosting, halve and scrape seeds from 2 vanilla beans and add seeds to food processor along with vanilla extract.

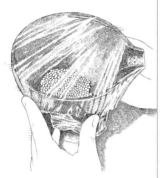

1. Put spices in mortar and cover it tightly with plastic wrap.

2. Make tiny slit in plastic and poke pestle through. Even though slit will end up stretching as you grind, as long as plastic seals edges, spices will stay put.

Spice Cake with Cream Cheese Frosting

✔ WHY THIS RECIPE WORKS

The problem with spice cakes? Spice. Some variations suffer spice overload, which makes them gritty and dusty. Others are so lacking in spice flavor that it seems as if a cinnamon stick has only been waved in their general direction. We wanted an old-fashioned, moist, and substantial spice cake with spices that were warm and bold without being overpowering, and a rich, but complementary cream cheese frosting. We needed a less-than-tender cake, one with a substantial and open crumb that could stand up to the spices.

BUILD A CAKE WITH THE RIGHT HEFT All-purpose flour, rather than cake flour, adds structure to our cake, while butter and eggs add richness.

BLOOM THE SPICES Adding spices raw to the cake batter isn't enough for warm spice flavor. We bloom the spices in butter to intensify their aromas and give the cake a heightened spice impact throughout. We use the classic mixture of cinnamon, cloves, cardamom, allspice, and nutmeg, but add a tablespoon of grated fresh ginger and a couple of tablespoons of molasses to give the cake an extra zing.

ENRICH THE FROSTING WITH SPICES TOO Reserving a little of the spice mixture to add to the cream cheese frosting adds extra spice flavor and unites the frosting and the cake.

SPICE CAKE WITH CREAM CHEESE FROSTING

SERVES 15

To save time, let the eggs, buttermilk, and butter come up to temperature while the browned butter and spice mixture cools. For information on toasting nuts, see page 9.

1	tablespoon ground cinnamon
¾	teaspoon ground cardamom
½	teaspoon ground allspice
½	teaspoon ground cloves
¼	teaspoon ground nutmeg
16	tablespoons unsalted butter, softened
2¼	cups (11¼ ounces) all-purpose flour
½	teaspoon baking powder
½	teaspoon baking soda
½	teaspoon salt
2	large eggs plus 3 large yolks, room temperature
1	teaspoon vanilla extract
1¾	cups (12¼ ounces) granulated sugar
2	tablespoons molasses
1	tablespoon grated fresh ginger
1	cup buttermilk, room temperature
1	recipe Cream Cheese Frosting (page 313)
¾	cup walnuts, toasted and chopped coarse (optional)

1. Adjust oven rack to middle position and heat oven to 350 degrees. Grease 13 by 9-inch baking pan, line with parchment paper, grease parchment, and flour pan. Combine cinnamon, cardamom, allspice, cloves, and nutmeg in small bowl; reserve ½ teaspoon of spice mixture for frosting.

2. Melt 4 tablespoons butter in 8-inch skillet over medium heat, 1 to 2 minutes. Cook, swirling pan constantly, until butter is light brown and has faint nutty aroma, 2 to 4 minutes. Add spice mixture and continue to cook, stirring constantly, 15 seconds. Remove from heat and let cool to room temperature, about 30 minutes.

3. Whisk flour, baking powder, baking soda, and salt together in medium bowl. In small bowl, gently whisk eggs and yolks and

vanilla to combine. Using stand mixer fitted with paddle, beat remaining 12 tablespoons butter with sugar and molasses on medium-high speed until pale and fluffy, about 3 minutes, scraping down bowl as needed. Reduce speed to medium and add cooled butter-spice mixture, ginger, and half of egg mixture; mix until incorporated, about 15 seconds. Repeat with remaining egg mixture; scrape down bowl. Reduce speed to low and add flour mixture in 3 additions, alternating with buttermilk in 2 additions, scraping down bowl as needed. Mix at medium speed until batter is thoroughly combined, about 15 seconds. Give batter final stir by hand.

4. Scrape batter into prepared pan, smooth top with rubber spatula, and gently tap pan on counter to release air bubbles. Bake until toothpick inserted in center of cake comes out clean, 32 to 37 minutes, rotating pan halfway through baking. Let cake cool completely in pan on wire rack, about 2 hours. Run thin knife around edge of cake to loosen from pan. Invert cake onto wire rack, discard parchment, then turn cake right side up onto serving platter.

5. Stir reserved spice mixture into frosting. Spread frosting evenly over cake, sprinkle with walnuts, if using, and serve. (Cake can be refrigerated for up to 2 days. Bring cake to room temperature before serving.)

SPICE CAKE WITH ORANGE–CREAM CHEESE FROSTING

Add 1½ teaspoons grated orange zest to frosting with vanilla. Substitute slivered almonds or toasted, skinned, and coarsely chopped hazelnuts for walnuts.

Ultimate Chocolate Cupcakes

✓ WHY THIS RECIPE WORKS

A chocolate cupcake Catch-22 befalls bakery and homemade confections alike: If the cupcakes have decent chocolate flavor, their structure is too crumbly for out-of-hand consumption. Conversely, if the cakes balance moisture and tenderness without crumbling, the cake and frosting are barely palatable, with the chocolate flavor hardly registering at all. We wanted moist, tender (but not crumbly) cupcakes capped with just enough creamy, not-too-sweet frosting.

DON'T MAKE CRUMBLY CUPCAKES Our regular chocolate cake batter, made with cocoa powder, bittersweet chocolate, buttermilk, and brewed coffee, bakes up into cupcakes that taste great but are too delicate. Reducing the amount of cocoa powder helps with the structure because cocoa powder contains no gluten-forming proteins and dilutes the strength of the flour. To cut back on fat (which produces an overly tender texture), we use less chocolate.

MAXIMIZE CHOCOLATE FLAVOR To make the most of the reduced amount of chocolate in our recipe, we got rid of the dairy, which can dull chocolate flavor, and used more brewed coffee, which helps amp up the chocolate. We bloomed the cocoa by pouring the hot coffee over the cocoa powder and chopped chocolate. At this point, our cupcakes were very chocolaty but dry.

CHANGE TO OIL We added moisture by replacing the butter with oil. Oil, after all, is 100 percent fat, while butter contains

COCONUT OIL

Once demonized, coconut oil is experiencing a come-back. As long as the oil isn't hydrogenated (which creates the dreaded trans fats that clog arteries), some scientists say that it isn't as bad as once thought. In fact, coconut oil may even have health benefits, such as boosting metabolism and strengthening the immune system. It's also gaining popularity with vegans as a nondairy butter substitute. Coconut oil is sold in two forms, both solid at room temperature: refined, which has virtually no taste or aroma, and virgin, which retains a strong coconut flavor. Since we have limited use for an oil that makes food smell and taste like a piña colada, we tested only the refined product.

We tried the melted oil in chocolate chip cookies and found that it performed just as well as melted butter, though we missed butter's sweet dairy flavor. Ditto when we creamed the oil for cake and used it to sauté carrots. (Because of its steep price—about $8 for 16 ounces—coconut oil is impractical for deep frying.) In an all-butter pie crust, subbing coconut oil for butter required an adjustment. Most pie dough needs to be chilled before rolling, but coconut oil becomes hard and brittle when refrigerated, leading to dough that is too firm to roll out without cracking. The simple fix: Rest the dough on the counter instead of in the fridge.

In short: If you're avoiding dairy, refined coconut oil makes a perfectly good substitute for butter (or oil, for that matter) in baking and sautéing.

around 16 to 18 percent water, which can evaporate in the oven, leaving the cupcakes dry. Oil likewise improved the chocolate flavor a bit more, because the milk solids in butter can mute chocolate flavors.

PICK BREAD FLOUR We began our testing with all-purpose flour but wondered if bread flour, with more gluten, might allow us to use more cocoa and chocolate. It did, giving us a less crumble-prone but not tough cupcake with big chocolate flavor.

MAKE A GANACHE CENTER Topping each cupcake with a teaspoon of cooled ganache before baking is the ticket for even bigger chocolate flavor. The ganache sinks in the batter during baking, providing a rich, trufflelike center to the cupcakes, otherwise known as chocolate nirvana.

RECONSIDER THE FROSTING We decided to abandon the super-sweet, grainy classic frosting made by whipping together softened butter and confectioners' sugar. Instead, we use a cooked buttercream—the Swiss meringue variety, where egg whites and granulated sugar are heated over a double boiler, then whipped with knobs of softened butter. The result is utterly silky and decadent, without the weight and greasiness of other rich frostings.

ULTIMATE CHOCOLATE CUPCAKES WITH GANACHE FILLING

MAKES 12 CUPCAKES

Use a high-quality bittersweet or semisweet chocolate for this recipe. Though we highly recommend the ganache filling, you can omit it for a more traditional cupcake.

FILLING

2   ounces bittersweet chocolate, chopped fine
¼   cup heavy cream
1   tablespoon confectioners' sugar

CUPCAKES

3   ounces bittersweet chocolate, chopped fine
⅓   cup (1 ounce) Dutch-processed cocoa powder
¾   cup brewed coffee, hot
¾   cup (4⅛ ounces) bread flour
¾   cup (5¼ ounces) sugar
½   teaspoon salt
½   teaspoon baking soda
6   tablespoons vegetable oil
2   large eggs
2   teaspoons distilled white vinegar
1   teaspoon vanilla extract

1   recipe Creamy Chocolate Frosting (recipe follows)

1. FOR THE FILLING: Microwave chocolate, cream, and sugar in medium bowl until mixture is warm to touch, about 30 seconds. Whisk until smooth, then transfer bowl to refrigerator and let sit until just chilled, no longer than 30 minutes.

2. FOR THE CUPCAKES: Adjust oven rack to middle position and heat oven to 350 degrees. Line 12-cup muffin tin with paper or foil liners. Place chocolate and cocoa in medium heatproof bowl. Pour hot coffee over mixture and let sit, covered, for 5 minutes. Whisk mixture gently until smooth, then transfer to refrigerator to cool completely, about 20 minutes.

3. Whisk flour, sugar, salt, and baking soda together in medium bowl. Whisk oil, eggs, vinegar, and vanilla into cooled chocolate mixture until smooth. Add flour mixture and whisk until smooth.

4. Using ice cream scoop or large spoon, divide batter evenly among prepared muffin cups. Place 1 slightly rounded teaspoon ganache filling on top of each portion of batter. Bake cupcakes until set and just firm to touch, 17 to 19 minutes, rotating muffin tin

BAKING OUTSIDE THE TIN

If you don't own a muffin tin, we found that foil liners are sturdy enough to hold our cupcake batter. Simply arrange the liners on a rimmed baking sheet and then fill them with batter. Note that cupcakes baked in a muffin tin brown on both the bottom and sides. If the cupcakes are baked without a muffin tin, only the bottoms (and not the sides) will brown.

halfway through baking. Let cupcakes cool in muffin tin on wire rack until cool enough to handle, about 10 minutes. Lift each cupcake from tin, set on wire rack, and let cool completely, about 1 hour, before frosting. (Unfrosted cupcakes can be stored at room temperature for up to 1 day.)

5. Spread 2 to 3 tablespoons frosting over each cooled cupcake and serve.

CREAMY CHOCOLATE FROSTING
MAKES ABOUT 2¼ CUPS

The melted chocolate should be cooled to between 85 and 100 degrees before being added to the frosting. If the frosting seems too soft after adding the chocolate, chill it briefly in the refrigerator and then rewhip it until creamy.

- ⅓ cup (2⅓ ounces) sugar
- 2 large egg whites
  Pinch salt
- 12 tablespoons unsalted butter, cut into 12 pieces and softened (68 degrees)
- 6 ounces bittersweet chocolate, melted and cooled
- ½ teaspoon vanilla extract

1. Combine sugar, egg whites, and salt in bowl of stand mixer and set bowl over saucepan filled with 1 inch of barely simmering water. Whisking gently but constantly, heat mixture until slightly thickened, foamy, and registers 150 degrees, 2 to 3 minutes.

2. Fit stand mixer with whisk and beat mixture on medium speed until consistency of shaving cream and slightly cooled, 1 to 2 minutes. Add butter, 1 piece at a time, until

smooth and creamy. (Frosting may look curdled after half of butter has been added; it will smooth with additional butter.) Once all butter is added, add cooled melted chocolate and vanilla; mix until combined. Increase speed to medium-high and beat until light, fluffy, and thoroughly combined, about 30 seconds, scraping down beater and sides of bowl with rubber spatula as necessary.

TO MAKE AHEAD: Frosting can be made up to 1 day in advance and refrigerated in airtight container. When ready to frost, warm frosting briefly in microwave until just slightly softened, 5 to 10 seconds. Once warmed, stir until creamy.

CREAMY MALTED MILK FROSTING

Reduce sugar to ¼ cup, substitute milk chocolate for bittersweet chocolate, and add ¼ cup malted milk powder with vanilla extract in step 2.

CREAMY VANILLA FROSTING

Omit bittersweet chocolate and increase sugar to ½ cup. (If final frosting seems too thick, warm mixer bowl briefly over saucepan filled with 1 inch of barely simmering water and beat a second time until creamy).

CREAMY PEANUT BUTTER FROSTING

Omit bittersweet chocolate, increase sugar to ½ cup, and increase salt to ⅛ teaspoon. Add ⅔ cup creamy peanut butter with vanilla extract in step 2. Garnish cupcakes with ½ cup chopped peanuts.

Yellow Cupcakes with Chocolate Ganache Frosting

✓ WHY THIS RECIPE WORKS

Many cupcakes are tasteless, dry, and crumbly, while others are greasy and eggy. Still others are cloyingly sweet or rubbery and leaden. We wanted a yellow cupcake so delicious that the cake itself would be savored as much as its rich icing, a grown-up cupcake good enough to satisfy the parents at a kid's birthday party.

PICK ALL-PURPOSE FLOUR We rejected cake flour and pastry flour for netting too fine a texture. And pastry flour is difficult to obtain. All-purpose flour gives us cupcakes with a tender crumb and good structure.

DITCH A FEW WHITES We started our recipe with three whole eggs but we found that our cupcakes were richer when we omitted two of the whites.

ADD RICHNESS AND TANG White sugar and butter were a given with these cupcakes but we ran tests with various dairy ingredients such as whole milk, buttermilk, yogurt, sour cream, and heavy cream. None of these were flops, but the cupcakes made with sour cream held a slightly tangy edge.

MIX THE EASY WAY Forget creaming, which calls for beating together the butter and sugar until fluffy, then adding the eggs, and finally adding the alternating wet and dry ingredients. What works best? Simply whisking the dry ingredients and sugar together, followed by beating in the butter, eggs, sour cream, and vanilla. Once portioned into muffin tins and baked, these cupcakes emerge from the oven lightly golden and tender.

FROST WITH GANACHE You can frost these cupcakes with almost any frosting, but we prefer a simple whipped ganache, made of just heavy cream and semisweet chocolate.

YELLOW CUPCAKES WITH CHOCOLATE GANACHE FROSTING

MAKES 12 CUPCAKES

These cupcakes are best eaten the day they are made, but unfrosted extras can be kept in an airtight container at room temperature for up to three days. To double the recipe, use three whole eggs and two yolks, and double the remaining ingredients. See more frostings on page 318.

CUPCAKES

- 1½ cups (7½ ounces) all-purpose flour
- 1 cup (7 ounces) sugar
- 1½ teaspoons baking powder
- ½ teaspoon salt
- 8 tablespoons unsalted butter, softened
- ½ cup sour cream
- 1 large egg plus 2 large yolks, room temperature
- 1½ teaspoons vanilla extract

FROSTING

- 1 cup heavy cream
- 8 ounces semisweet chocolate, chopped

1. FOR THE CUPCAKES: Adjust oven rack to middle position and heat oven to 350 degrees. Line 12-cup muffin tin with paper or foil liners.

2. Whisk flour, sugar, baking powder, and salt together in bowl of stand mixer. Fit stand mixer with paddle, add butter, sour cream, egg and yolks, and vanilla and beat on medium speed until smooth and satiny, about 30 seconds. Scrape down bowl, then mix by hand using rubber spatula until smooth and no flour pockets remain.

Colored sugar or sprinkles can add a special touch to freshly frosted cakes or cupcakes. To apply the colored sugar in neat shapes, use a cookie cutter outline as a guide. Once you've covered the area outlined by the cookie cutter with colored sugar, carefully remove the cutter to reveal a fanciful decoration.

3. Using ice cream scoop or large spoon, divide batter evenly among prepared muffin cups. Bake cupcakes until tops are pale gold and toothpick inserted in center comes out clean, 20 to 24 minutes, rotating muffin tin halfway through baking. Lift each cupcake from tin, set on wire rack, and let cool completely, about 45 minutes, before frosting.

4. FOR THE FROSTING: Place chocolate in medium heatproof bowl. Bring cream to boil in small saucepan. Pour boiling cream over chocolate, and let sit, covered, for 5 minutes. Whisk mixture until smooth, then cover with plastic wrap and refrigerate until cool and slightly firm, 45 minutes to 1 hour.

5. Using stand mixer fitted with whisk, whip cooled chocolate mixture on medium speed until fluffy and mousselike and soft peaks form, about 2 minutes.

6. Spread 2 to 3 generous tablespoons frosting over each cooled cupcake and serve.

Chocolate Raspberry Torte

✔ WHY THIS RECIPE WORKS

Sachertorte, the classic Viennese dessert with layers of chocolate cake sandwiching apricot jam and enrobed in a creamy-rich chocolate glaze, always sounds more promising than it typically is in reality— dry, flavorless cake and sweet jam with little fruity complexity, all covered in a glaze that is nothing more than a thin, overly sugary coating. We set out to create a rich, deeply chocolaty dessert using Sachertorte as the inspiration, giving it our own spin by pairing the chocolate with raspberries.

ADD GROUND NUTS TO FLOURLESS CHOCOLATE CAKE We baked our Ultimate Flourless Chocolate Cake (page 325) in two 9-inch pans, so we could sandwich the two cakes together rather than deal with halving a single delicate cake. But the dense cake tore and fell apart when stacked.

Adding ground nuts (almonds were preferred over other nuts) gave it the structure it needed, plus a good boost of flavor. Since we were using the food processor to grind the nuts, we tweaked our cake recipe so that it could be prepared using the same appliance.

MIX A JUICY, FRESH-FLAVORED FILLING We combine jam with lightly mashed fresh berries for a tangy-sweet mixture that clings to the cake.

TOP WITH A GANACHE For the glaze, we keep things simple, melting bittersweet chocolate with heavy cream to create a rich-tasting, glossy ganache that pours smoothly over the cake. And to up the glamour quotient, we dot fresh raspberries around the top perimeter of the torte and press sliced, toasted almonds along its sides.

CHOCOLATE RASPBERRY TORTE
SERVES 12 TO 16

Be sure to use cake pans with at least 2-inch-tall sides.

CAKE
- 8 ounces bittersweet chocolate, chopped fine
- 12 tablespoons unsalted butter, cut into ½-inch pieces
- 2 teaspoons vanilla extract
- ¼ teaspoon instant espresso powder
- 1¾ cups (6⅛ ounces) sliced almonds, toasted
- ¼ cup (1¼ ounces) all-purpose flour
- ½ teaspoon salt
- 5 large eggs, room temperature
- ¾ cup (5¼ ounces) sugar

FILLING

2½ ounces (½ cup) raspberries, plus 16 individual raspberries

¼ cup seedless raspberry jam

GLAZE

5 ounces bittersweet chocolate, chopped fine

½ cup plus 1 tablespoon heavy cream

1. FOR THE CAKE: Adjust oven rack to middle position and heat oven to 325 degrees. Grease two 9-inch round cake pans, line with parchment paper, grease parchment, and flour pans. Melt chocolate and butter in large heatproof bowl set over saucepan filled with 1 inch of barely simmering water, stirring occasionally until smooth. Remove from heat and let cool to room temperature, about 30 minutes. Stir in vanilla and espresso powder.

2. Pulse ¾ cup almonds in food processor until coarsely chopped, 6 to 8 pulses, and set aside. Process remaining 1 cup almonds until very finely ground, about 45 seconds. Add flour and salt and continue to process until combined, about 15 seconds. Transfer almond-flour mixture to medium bowl. Process eggs until lightened in color and almost doubled in volume, about 3 minutes. With processor running, slowly add sugar and process until thoroughly combined, about 15 seconds. Using whisk, gently fold egg mixture into chocolate mixture until some streaks of egg remain. Sprinkle half of almond-flour mixture over chocolate mixture and gently whisk until just combined. Sprinkle with remaining almond-flour mixture and gently whisk until just combined.

3. Divide batter evenly between prepared pans and smooth tops with rubber spatula. Bake cakes until center is firm and toothpick inserted in center comes out with few moist crumbs attached, 14 to 16 minutes, rotating pans halfway through baking. Transfer cakes to wire rack and let cool completely in pans, about 30 minutes.

4. Cut 2 cardboard rounds to same diameter as cakes. Run thin knife around edges of cakes to loosen, then invert cakes onto cardboard rounds; discard parchment. Using wire rack, turn 1 cake right side up, then slide from rack back onto cardboard round.

5. FOR THE FILLING: Place ½ cup raspberries in medium bowl and coarsely mash with fork. Stir in raspberry jam until just combined.

6. Spread raspberry mixture onto cake layer that is right side up. Top with second cake layer, leaving it upside down. Transfer assembled cake, still on cardboard round, to wire rack set in rimmed baking sheet.

7. FOR THE GLAZE: Melt chocolate and cream in medium heatproof bowl set over saucepan filled with 1 inch of barely simmering water, stirring occasionally until smooth. Remove from heat and gently whisk until very smooth. Pour glaze onto center of assembled cake. Using offset spatula, spread glaze evenly over top of cake, letting it drip down sides. Spread glaze along sides of cake to coat evenly.

8. Using fine-mesh strainer, sift reserved almonds to remove any fine bits. Holding bottom of cake on cardboard round with 1 hand, gently press sifted almonds onto cake sides with other hand. Arrange remaining 16 raspberries around circumference. Refrigerate cake on rack until glaze is set, at least 1 hour or up to 24 hours (if refrigerating cake for more than 1 hour, let sit at room temperature for about 30 minutes before serving). Transfer cake to serving platter and serve.

ASSEMBLING CHOCOLATE-RASPBERRY TORTE

1. Run paring knife around sides of cake and invert layers onto cardboard rounds.

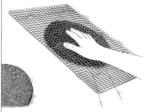

2. Using wire rack, reinvert 1 cake so top faces up; slide back onto cardboard round.

3. Spread raspberry filling over cake layer with its top side facing up.

4. Top with second cake, leaving bottom facing up.

5. Use offset spatula to evenly spread glaze over top and sides.

To create perfectly smooth slices of soft desserts such as our Triple-Chocolate Mousse Cake and cheesecakes, the best tool is not a knife. It's a cheese wire—the minimal surface area produces less drag for cleaner, neater slices. If you don't have a cheese wire, dental floss will work almost as well.

1. Hold handles; pull wire taut. Using your thumbs to apply even pressure, slice down through cake. Wipe wire clean with dry dish towel.

2. Make second cut, perpendicular to first. Continue to make cuts around circumference.

Triple-Chocolate Mousse Cake

✓ WHY THIS RECIPE WORKS

With overpowering rich flavor and a homogeneous texture, layered mousse cake can be more a spectacle than a tasty treat. By finessing one layer at a time, we aimed to create a tri-layered cake that was incrementally lighter in texture—and richness—with each layer.

START WITH A FLOURLESS CHOCOLATE CAKE For simplicity's sake, we decided to build the whole dessert, layer by layer, in the same springform pan. For a base layer that had the heft to support the upper two tiers, we chose flourless chocolate cake instead of the typical mousse. Our own flourless chocolate cake recipe was a bit too rich and dense to support two layers of mousse, so we lightened it up. Folding egg whites into the batter helps lighten the cake without affecting its structural integrity. We make sure to cool the cake completely before adding the mousse layer; otherwise, the mousse will turn fluid and deflate.

GIVE CHOCOLATE MOUSSE A TWEAK For the middle layer, we started with a traditional chocolate mousse, but the texture seemed too heavy when combined with the cake, so we removed the eggs and cut back on the chocolate a bit, resulting in a lighter, creamier layer. A combination of cocoa powder bloomed in hot water to intensify its flavor and bittersweet chocolate deliver a mousse with deep chocolate flavor.

TOP WITH WHITE CHOCOLATE MOUSSE And for the crowning layer, we make an easy white chocolate mousse by folding whipped cream into melted white chocolate. To prevent the soft mousse from oozing during slicing, we add a little gelatin to the mix.

TRIPLE-CHOCOLATE MOUSSE CAKE

SERVES 12 TO 16

This recipe requires a springform pan with sides that are at least 3 inches high. It is imperative that each layer is made in sequential order. Cool the base completely before topping it with the middle layer. For best results, chill the mixer bowl before whipping the heavy cream. For neater slices, use a cheese wire or dip your knife in hot water before cutting each slice.

BOTTOM LAYER

- 6 tablespoons unsalted butter, cut into 6 pieces
- 7 ounces bittersweet chocolate, chopped fine
- ¾ teaspoon instant espresso powder
- 4 large eggs, separated
- 1½ teaspoons vanilla extract
  Pinch cream of tartar
  Pinch salt
- ⅓ cup packed (2⅓ ounces) light brown sugar

MIDDLE LAYER

- 5 tablespoons hot water
- 2 tablespoons Dutch-processed cocoa powder
- 7 ounces bittersweet chocolate, chopped fine
- 1½ cups heavy cream, chilled
- 1 tablespoon granulated sugar
- ⅛ teaspoon salt

TOP LAYER

- ¾ teaspoon unflavored gelatin
- 1 tablespoon water
- 6 ounces white chocolate chips
- 1½ cups heavy cream, chilled
  Shaved chocolate (optional)
  Unsweetened cocoa powder (optional)

1. FOR THE BOTTOM LAYER: Adjust oven rack to middle position and heat oven to 325 degrees. Grease 9½-inch springform pan. Melt butter, chocolate, and espresso powder in large heatproof bowl set over saucepan filled with 1 inch of barely simmering water, stirring occasionally until smooth. Remove from heat and let mixture cool slightly, about 5 minutes. Whisk in egg yolks and vanilla; set aside.

2. Using stand mixer fitted with whisk, whip egg whites, cream of tartar, and salt on medium-low speed until foamy, about 1 minute. Add half of sugar and whip until combined, about 15 seconds. Add remaining sugar, increase speed to high, and whip until soft peaks form, about 1 minute longer, scraping down bowl halfway through. Using whisk, fold one-third of beaten egg whites into chocolate mixture by hand to lighten. Using rubber spatula, fold in remaining egg whites until no white streaks remain. Carefully transfer batter to prepared springform pan and smooth top with rubber spatula.

3. Bake cake until risen, firm around edges, and center has just set but is still soft (center of cake will spring back after pressing gently with your finger), 13 to 18 minutes, rotating pan halfway through baking. Transfer cake to wire rack and let cool completely, about 1 hour. (Cake will collapse as it cools.) Do not remove cake from pan.

4. FOR THE MIDDLE LAYER: Combine hot water and cocoa in small bowl; set aside. Melt chocolate in large heatproof bowl set over saucepan filled with 1 inch of barely simmering water, stirring occasionally until smooth. Remove from heat and let cool slightly, 2 to 5 minutes.

5. Using stand mixer fitted with whisk, whip cream, sugar, and salt on medium-low speed until foamy, about 1 minute. Increase speed to high and whip until soft peaks form, 1 to 3 minutes.

6. Whisk cocoa mixture into melted chocolate until smooth. Using whisk, fold one-third of whipped cream into chocolate mixture to lighten. Using rubber spatula, fold in remaining whipped cream until no white streaks remain. Spoon mousse into springform pan over cooled cake, smooth top with rubber spatula, and gently tap pan on counter to release air bubbles. Wipe inside edge of pan with damp cloth to remove any drips. Refrigerate cake for at least 15 minutes while preparing top layer.

7. FOR THE TOP LAYER: In small bowl, sprinkle gelatin over water and let sit for at least 5 minutes. Place white chocolate in medium heatproof bowl. Bring ½ cup cream to simmer in small saucepan over medium-high heat. Remove from heat, add gelatin mixture, and stir until fully dissolved. Pour cream mixture over white chocolate and let sit, covered, for 5 minutes. Whisk mixture gently until smooth. Let cool to room temperature, stirring occasionally (mixture will thicken slightly).

8. Using stand mixer fitted with whisk, whip remaining 1 cup cream on medium-low speed until foamy, about 1 minute. Increase speed to high and whip until soft peaks form, 1 to 3 minutes. Using whisk, fold one-third of whipped cream into white chocolate mixture to lighten. Using rubber spatula, fold remaining whipped cream into white chocolate mixture until no white streaks remain. Spoon white chocolate mousse into pan over middle layer. Smooth top with rubber spatula. Return cake to refrigerator and chill until set, at least 2½ hours. (Cake can be refrigerated for up to 1 day; leave at room temperature for up to 45 minutes before removing from pan.)

9. Garnish top of cake with shaved chocolate and/or dust with cocoa, if using. Run thin knife between cake and sides of pan; remove sides of pan. Run cleaned knife along outside of cake to smooth. Hold handles of cheese wire and pull wire taut. Using your thumbs to apply even pressure, slice down through the cake. Wipe wire clean with dry dish towel. Make second cut, perpendicular to first. Continue to make cuts around circumference. Serve.

Ultimate Flourless Chocolate Cake

WHY THIS RECIPE WORKS

While all flourless chocolate cake recipes share common ingredients (chocolate, butter, and eggs), the techniques used to make them vary, as do the results. You can end up with anything from a fudge brownie to a chocolate soufflé. We wanted something dense, moist, and ultrachocolaty, but with some textural finesse.

GO BITTER- OR SEMI-SWEET A cake made with unsweetened chocolate was neither smooth nor silky enough. Bittersweet and semisweet chocolate were each well liked, delivering deep chocolate flavor and a smooth texture. Including coffee heightens the chocolate flavor and adds complexity.

USE CHILLED EGGS AND PLENTY OF BUTTER We beat the eggs into a foam, then we fold the egg foam, a little at a time, into the melted chocolate and butter—a half pound of butter. Beating chilled, rather than room-temperature, eggs results in a denser foam that bakes into a velvety cake.

BAKE IN A WATER BATH Like rich, creamy cheesecake, this type of cake requires long, gentle cooking at a low temperature. A water bath keeps the cooking slow, even, and gentle, so the exterior of the cake doesn't overcook by the time the interior is done.

DON'T OVERBAKE You won't be able to tell when this cake is baked just by looking at it. Temping the cake is essential. The cake should be pulled from the oven at 140 degrees—it will still be jiggly in the center but will firm up into a lush, confection-like cake as it cools.

CHILL BEFORE SERVING As is done with cheesecake, flourless chocolate cake needs to be thoroughly cooled so it sets before serving. We refrigerate our cake overnight so it sets into a densely fudgy layer.

ULTIMATE FLOURLESS CHOCOLATE CAKE

SERVES 12 TO 16

Even though the cake may not look done, pull it from the oven when it registers 140 degrees. It will continue to firm up as it cools. If you use a 9-inch springform pan instead of the preferred 8-inch, reduce the baking time to 18 to 20 minutes.

8	large eggs, chilled
1	pound bittersweet or semisweet chocolate, chopped coarse
16	tablespoons unsalted butter, cut into ½-inch pieces
¼	cup strong brewed coffee, room temperature
	Confectioners' sugar or unsweetened cocoa powder (optional)

1. Adjust oven rack to lower-middle position and heat oven to 325 degrees. Grease 8-inch springform pan, line with parchment paper, then grease sides. Wrap outside of pan with two 18-inch-square pieces of aluminum foil; set in roasting pan. Bring kettle of water to boil.

2. Using stand mixer fitted with whisk, whip eggs on medium speed until doubled in volume, about 5 minutes.

3. Meanwhile, melt chocolate with butter and coffee in large heatproof bowl set over saucepan filled with 1 inch of barely simmering water, stirring once or twice until smooth and very warm (should register about 115 degrees). Using large rubber spatula, fold one-third of egg foam into chocolate mixture until few streaks of egg are visible. Fold in remaining foam in 2 additions until mixture is totally homogeneous.

DUSTING WITH CONFECTIONERS' SUGAR

Simple single-layer cakes, such as a flourless chocolate cake, are rarely frosted, but they can be dressed up with some confectioners' sugar. This trick adds a bit of flair to an otherwise plain sugar dusting.

1. Lay strips of paper about ¾ inch wide across top of cake, then sift confectioners' sugar over cake.

2. Carefully lift away paper strips to reveal attractive striped pattern.

4. Scrape batter into prepared pan and smooth top with rubber spatula. Set roasting pan on oven rack and pour enough boiling water into roasting pan to come about halfway up sides of springform pan. Bake until cake has risen slightly, edges are just beginning to set, thin glazed crust (like a brownie crust) has formed on surface, and cake registers 140 degrees, 22 to 25 minutes. Remove cake pan from water bath and set on wire rack; let cool to room temperature. Cover and refrigerate overnight. (Cake can be refrigerated for up to 4 days).

5. About 30 minutes before serving, run thin knife between cake and sides of pan; remove sides of pan. Invert cake onto sheet of waxed paper, discard parchment, and turn cake right side up onto serving platter. Dust with confectioners' sugar, if using, and serve.

Chocolate Espresso Dacquoise

✔ WHY THIS RECIPE WORKS

You rarely see dacquoise, a multilayered show-piece of nut meringue and buttercream, anywhere but fancy patisseries or high-end restaurants—and with good reason: Making one is a project to rival all projects. We wanted a chocolate dacquoise that was manageable at home and eliminated some of the more bothersome features. And we didn't want our dessert to just satisfy our guests; we wanted it to render them speechless.

BUILD LIGHT AND CRISP MERINGUE LAYERS Crisp layers of meringue enriched with ground nuts (almonds and hazelnuts) stand in for cake in this layered confection. We chose a modified version of the traditional method of making meringue. Instead of slowly adding all of the sugar after the egg whites reached soft peaks, we add just half of the sugar between the soft- and stiff-peak stages and then fold in the remainder at the end with the ground nuts. Once baked, the meringue boasts a crisp-delicate texture that is easy to slice.

PICK RECTANGLE OVER ROUND A round dacquoise can be a nightmare to slice into wedges, so we chose to make ours in an easier-to-slice rectangular loaf shape.

Rather than baking multiple layers, which can be hard to spread into even rectangles, we spread the meringue into one big rectangular piece, spritz the top with water to prevent it from cooking faster than the bottom, and bake it. Once it's cool, we cut it into four even pieces using a serrated bread knife, a gentle scoring motion, and a ruler.

GO GERMAN For the buttercream, we settled on German-style, which is whipped together from butter and pastry cream, a simple custard made with egg yolks that doesn't need to be tempered with a thermometer. To boost its flavor, we include espresso powder and almond liqueur, which complements the nutty meringue.

SPREAD GANACHE INSIDE AND OUT To make sure our dacquoise bursts with chocolate flavor, we spread some ganache on each layer of meringue. The assembled dacquoise has crisp, nutty meringue; rich buttercream; and silky ganache in every bite. Toasted sliced almonds pressed along the sides of the dacquoise and whole hazelnuts dotted across the top are the final touches on this spectacular dessert.

CHOCOLATE ESPRESSO DACQUOISE

SERVES 10 TO 12

The components of this recipe can easily be prepared in advance. Use a rimless baking sheet or an overturned rimmed baking sheet to bake the meringue. Instant coffee powder may be substituted for the espresso powder. To skin the hazelnuts, simply place the warm toasted nuts in a clean dish towel and rub gently. Use a high-quality chocolate in this recipe. See information on our recommended brand on page 496.

MERINGUE

- ¾ cup blanched sliced almonds, toasted
- ½ cup hazelnuts, toasted and skinned
- 1 tablespoon cornstarch
- ⅛ teaspoon salt
- 1 cup (7 ounces) sugar
- 4 large egg whites, room temperature
- ¼ teaspoon cream of tartar

BUTTERCREAM

- ¾ cup whole milk
- 4 large egg yolks
- ⅓ cup (2⅓ ounces) sugar
- 1½ teaspoons cornstarch
- ¼ teaspoon salt
- 2 tablespoons amaretto or water
- 1½ tablespoons instant espresso powder
- 16 tablespoons unsalted butter, softened

GANACHE

- 6 ounces bittersweet chocolate, chopped fine
- ¾ cup heavy cream
- 2 teaspoons corn syrup

- 12 whole hazelnuts, toasted and skinned
- 1 cup blanched sliced almonds, toasted

1. FOR THE MERINGUE: Adjust oven rack to middle position and heat oven to 250 degrees. Using ruler and permanent marker, draw 13 by 10½-inch rectangle on piece of parchment paper. Grease baking sheet and place parchment on it, ink side down.

2. Process almonds, hazelnuts, cornstarch, and salt together in food processor until nuts are finely ground, 15 to 20 seconds. Add ½ cup sugar and pulse to combine, 1 to 2 pulses.

3. Using stand mixer fitted with whisk, whip egg whites and cream of tartar together on medium-low speed until foamy, about 1 minute. Increase speed to medium-high and whip whites to soft, billowy mounds, about 1 minute. With mixer running at medium-high speed, slowly add remaining ½ cup sugar and continue to whip until glossy, stiff peaks form, 2 to 3 minutes. Fold nut mixture into egg whites in 2 batches. With offset spatula, spread meringue evenly into 13 by 10½-inch rectangle on parchment, using lines on parchment as guide. Using spray bottle, evenly mist surface of meringue with water until glistening. Bake for 1½ hours. Turn off oven and allow meringue to cool in oven for 1½ hours. (Do not open oven during baking and cooling.) Remove from oven and let cool to room temperature, about 10 minutes. (Cooled meringue can be kept at room temperature, tightly wrapped, for up to 2 days.)

4. FOR THE BUTTERCREAM: Heat milk in small saucepan over medium heat until just simmering. Meanwhile, whisk egg yolks, sugar, cornstarch, and salt together in bowl until smooth. Remove milk from heat and, whisking constantly, add half of milk to yolk mixture to temper. Whisking constantly, return tempered yolk mixture to milk in saucepan. Return saucepan to medium heat and cook, whisking constantly, until mixture is bubbling and thickens to consistency of warm pudding, 3 to 5 minutes. Transfer pastry cream to bowl. Cover and refrigerate until set, at least 2 hours or up to 24 hours. Before using, warm gently to room temperature in microwave at 50 percent power, stirring every 10 seconds.

5. Stir together amaretto and espresso powder; set aside. Using stand mixer fitted with paddle, beat butter at medium speed until smooth and light, 3 to 4 minutes. Add pastry cream in 3 batches, beating for 30 seconds after each addition. Add amaretto mixture and continue to beat until light and fluffy, about 5 minutes longer, scraping down bowl thoroughly halfway though mixing.

6. FOR THE GANACHE: Place chocolate in heatproof bowl. Bring cream and corn syrup to simmer in small saucepan over medium heat. Pour cream mixture over chocolate and let stand for 1 minute. Stir mixture until smooth. Set aside to cool until chocolate mounds slightly when dripped from spoon.

7. Carefully invert meringue and peel off parchment. Reinvert meringue and place on cutting board. Using serrated knife and gentle, repeated scoring motion, trim edges of meringue to form 12 by 10-inch rectangle. Discard trimmings. With long side of rectangle parallel to counter, use ruler to mark top and bottom edges of meringue at 3-inch intervals. Using serrated knife, score surface of meringue by drawing knife toward you from mark on top edge to corresponding mark on bottom edge. Repeat scoring until meringue is fully cut through. Repeat until you have four 10 by 3-inch rectangles. (If any meringue breaks during cutting, use as middle layers.)

8. Place 3 rectangles on wire rack set in rimmed baking sheet. Using offset spatula, spread ¼ cup ganache evenly over surface of each meringue. Refrigerate until ganache is firm, about 15 minutes. Set aside remaining ganache.

9. Using offset spatula, spread top surface of remaining meringue rectangle with ½ cup buttercream; place on wire rack with ganache-coated meringues. Invert one ganache-coated meringue, place on top of buttercream, and press gently to level. Repeat 2 more times, spreading meringue with ½ cup buttercream and topping with inverted ganache-coated meringue. When last ganache-coated meringue is in place, spread half of remaining buttercream to lightly coat sides of cake, then use remaining buttercream to coat top of cake. Smooth sides and top until cake resembles box. Refrigerate until buttercream is firm, about 2 hours. (Once buttercream is firm,

DACQUOISE MADE DOABLE

Here's how to assemble the three different components of dacquoise—cooled, baked meringue; buttercream; and ganache—into a dessert that looks as though it was made in a professional bakery.

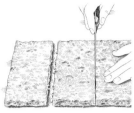

1. TRIM MERINGUE EDGES: Using serrated knife and gentle, repeated scoring motion, trim edges of cooled meringue to form 12 by 10-inch rectangle.

2. MEASURE AND MARK: With long side of rectangle parallel to counter, mark both long edges at 3-inch intervals.

3. CUT INTO 4 STRIPS: Repeatedly score surface by gently drawing knife from top mark to bottom mark until cut through. Repeat to make 4 strips.

4. TOP 3 STRIPS WITH GANACHE: Place 3 strips on wire rack and spread ¼ cup ganache evenly over each. Refrigerate for 15 minutes.

5. TOP 1 STRIP WITH BUTTERCREAM: Spread remaining strip with ½ cup buttercream.

6. STACK STRIPS: Invert 1 ganache-coated strip on top of buttercream-coated strip. Spread with buttercream. Repeat. Invert final ganache-coated strip on top.

7. COAT WITH BUTTERCREAM: Coat sides of cake with half of remaining buttercream; coat top with remainder. Smooth and refrigerate until firm.

8. TOP WITH GANACHE: Pour warm ganache over cake and spread in thin, even layer, letting excess flow down sides. Spread thinly across sides.

9. GARNISH WITH NUTS: Use spatula to lift cake off rack. Arrange whole hazelnuts on top of cake and, holding cake with 1 hand, gently press almonds onto sides.

assembled cake may be wrapped tightly in plastic wrap and refrigerated for up to 2 days.)

10. Warm remaining ganache in heatproof bowl set over saucepan filled with 1 inch of barely simmering water, stirring occasionally, until mixture is very fluid but not hot. Keeping assembled cake on wire rack, pour ganache over top of cake. Using offset spatula, spread ganache in thin, even layer over top of cake, letting excess flow down sides. Spread ganache over sides in thin layer (top must be completely covered, but some small gaps on sides are OK).

11. Garnish top of cake with toasted whole hazelnuts. Holding cake with 1 hand, gently press sliced almonds onto sides with other hand. Chill for at least 3 hours or up to 12 hours. Transfer to platter. Cut into slices and serve. For best results, slice with sharp knife that has been dipped in hot water and wiped dry before each slice.

Hot Fudge Pudding Cake

✔ WHY THIS RECIPE WORKS

Instead of providing enough spoon-coating sauce to accompany the cake, some hot fudge pudding cakes are dry, with a disproportionate amount of cake, while others are soupy, with a wet, sticky, underdone cake. We wanted the hot fudge pudding cake of our dreams.

AMP UP FLAVOR WITH CHOCOLATE AND COCOA Pudding cake is made by sprinkling brownie batter with a mixture of sugar and cocoa, then pouring hot water on top and baking. For fuller chocolate flavor, we make our batter with a combination of Dutch-processed cocoa and semisweet chocolate. Just one egg yolk is enough egg to give us a fudgy consistency. Whole eggs make a cake that is too dry.

SWEETEN WITH BROWN AND WHITE SUGAR A combination of brown and white sugars gives our cake caramel-like sweetness. Including instant coffee with the hot water (which we bumped up to make plenty of "sauce") heightens the chocolate flavor and keeps the sweetness in check.

BAKE LOW AND SLOW We bake the cake at a low oven temperature for 45 minutes to promote a good top crust and a silky sauce and rest the cake for 20 to 30 minutes before serving for fudgy cake with thick sauce.

HOT FUDGE PUDDING CAKE

SERVES 8

If you have cold, brewed coffee on hand, it can be used in place of the instant coffee and water, but to make sure it isn't too strong, use 1 cup of cold coffee mixed with ½ cup of water. Serve the cake warm with vanilla or coffee ice cream.

2	teaspoons instant coffee powder
1½	cups water
⅔	cup (2 ounces) Dutch-processed cocoa powder
⅓	cup packed (2⅓ ounces) brown sugar
1	cup (7 ounces) granulated sugar
6	tablespoons unsalted butter
2	ounces semisweet or bittersweet chocolate, chopped
¾	cup (3¾ ounces) all-purpose flour
2	teaspoons baking powder
⅓	cup whole milk
1	tablespoon vanilla extract
¼	teaspoon salt
1	large egg yolk

1. Adjust oven rack to lower-middle position and heat oven to 325 degrees. Grease 8-inch square baking dish. Stir coffee powder into water and set aside to dissolve. Combine ⅓ cup cocoa, brown sugar, and ⅓ cup granulated sugar in small bowl, breaking up large clumps with fingers; set aside.

2. Melt butter, remaining ⅓ cup cocoa, and chocolate in small heatproof bowl set over saucepan filled with 1 inch of barely simmering water; whisk until smooth and set aside to cool slightly. Whisk flour and baking powder in small bowl to combine; set aside. Whisk remaining ⅔ cup granulated sugar, milk, vanilla, and salt in medium bowl until combined; whisk in egg yolk. Add chocolate mixture and whisk to combine. Add flour mixture and whisk until batter is evenly moistened.

3. Pour batter into prepared baking dish and spread to sides and corners. Sprinkle cocoa-sugar mixture evenly over batter (cocoa mixture should cover entire surface of batter); pour coffee mixture gently over cocoa mixture.

Bake cake until puffed and bubbling and just beginning to pull away from sides of baking dish, about 45 minutes. (Do not overbake.) Let cake cool in dish on wire rack for about 25 minutes before serving. (Cake can be reheated, covered with plastic wrap, in microwave oven.)

INDIVIDUAL HOT FUDGE PUDDING CAKES

Adjust oven rack to lower-middle position and heat oven to 400 degrees. Grease eight 6- to 8-ounce ramekins with vegetable oil spray and set on rimmed baking sheet. Prepare batter as directed, then divide batter evenly among ramekins (about ¼ cup per ramekin) and level with back of spoon. Sprinkle about 2 tablespoons cocoa-sugar mixture over batter in each ramekin, then pour 3 tablespoons coffee mixture over cocoa-sugar mixture in each ramekin. Bake cakes until puffed and bubbling, about 20 minutes. (Do not overbake.) Let cakes cool for about 15 minutes before serving (cakes will fall).

MAKING HOT FUDGE PUDDING CAKE

1. Pour batter into prepared baking dish and spread evenly into sides and corners with rubber spatula.

2. Sprinkle cocoa-sugar mixture over batter. Mixture should cover entire surface of batter.

3. Pour coffee mixture gently over cocoa mixture, and put baking dish in oven.

Individual Sticky Toffee Pudding Cakes

✔ WHY THIS RECIPE WORKS

Studded with dates and coated in a sweet toffee sauce, this moist, rich cake is a British favorite that we hoped to translate for the American kitchen. We wanted a cake packed full of date flavor, with a tolerable sweetness level and a moist, tender crumb.

REDUCE THE BUTTER We cut down the conventional amount of butter in the cakes and sauce but keep the sauce rich and flavorful—splashes of rum and lemon juice cut through the sticky richness of the sauce. Eggs and all-purpose flour give our cakes structure and stability.

MAXIMIZE THE FRUIT FLAVOR We increase the fruit flavor by first soaking the dates, then processing a portion of them with sugar while leaving the remainder coarsely chopped. Brown sugar stands in for traditional, but hard-to-find, treacle.

BAKE IN A WATER BATH To keep the cakes moist, we use a water bath. After placing the batter-filled ramekins in a roasting pan, we add boiling water and then cover the pan with foil before baking. Poking the cakes with a toothpick allows the sauce to be thoroughly absorbed.

INDIVIDUAL STICKY TOFFEE PUDDING CAKES

SERVES 8

We place a dish towel on the bottom of the roasting pan to stabilize the ramekins. It is important to form a tight seal with the foil to trap the steam inside the roasting pan before baking the cakes.

CAKES

8	ounces pitted dates, cut crosswise into ¼-inch slices (1⅓ cups)
¾	cup warm water
½	teaspoon baking soda
1¼	cups (6¼ ounces) all-purpose flour
½	teaspoon baking powder
½	teaspoon salt
¾	cup packed (5¼ ounces) brown sugar
2	large eggs
4	tablespoons unsalted butter, melted
1½	teaspoons vanilla extract

SAUCE

4	tablespoons unsalted butter
1	cup packed (7 ounces) brown sugar
¼	teaspoon salt
1	cup heavy cream
1	tablespoon rum
½	teaspoon lemon juice

1. FOR THE CAKES: Adjust oven rack to middle position and heat oven to 350 degrees. Grease and flour eight 4-ounce ramekins. Lay folded dish towel in bottom of roasting pan and set ramekins inside. Bring kettle of water to boil.

2. Combine half of dates, water, and baking soda in 2-cup liquid measuring cup (dates should be submerged beneath water) and soak dates for 5 minutes. Meanwhile, whisk flour, baking powder, and salt together in medium bowl.

3. Process remaining dates and sugar in food processor until no large date chunks remain and mixture has texture of damp, coarse sand, about 45 seconds, scraping down bowl as needed. Drain soaked dates and add soaking liquid to processor. Add eggs, melted butter, and vanilla and process until smooth, about 15 seconds. Transfer mixture to bowl with dry ingredients and sprinkle drained soaked dates on top.

4. With rubber spatula or wooden spoon, gently fold wet mixture into dry mixture until just combined and date pieces are evenly dispersed. Divide batter evenly among prepared ramekins (ramekins should be two-thirds full). Quickly pour enough boiling water into roasting pan to come ¼ inch up sides of molds. Cover pan tightly with aluminum foil, crimping edges to seal. Bake cakes until puffed and surfaces are spongy, firm, and moist to touch, about 40 minutes. Immediately transfer ramekins from water bath to wire rack and let cool for 10 minutes.

5. FOR THE SAUCE: While cakes cool, melt butter in medium saucepan over medium-high heat. Whisk in sugar and salt until smooth. Continue to cook, stirring occasionally, until sugar is dissolved and slightly darkened, 3 to 4 minutes. Add ⅓ cup cream and stir until smooth, about 30 seconds. Slowly pour in remaining ⅔ cup cream and rum, whisking constantly until smooth. Reduce heat to low and simmer until frothy, about 3 minutes. Remove from heat and stir in lemon juice.

6. Using toothpick, poke 25 holes in top of each cake and spoon 1 tablespoon toffee sauce over each cake. Let cakes sit until sauce is absorbed, about 5 minutes. Invert each ramekin onto plate or shallow bowl and remove ramekin. Divide remaining toffee sauce evenly among cakes and serve immediately.

TO MAKE AHEAD: Prepare batter and divide among individual ramekins as directed, then cover and refrigerate, unbaked, for up to 1 day. Bake as directed in step 4. Sauce can be made up to 2 days in advance; microwave on 50 percent power, stirring often, until hot, about 3 minutes.

Individual Fallen Chocolate Cakes

✓ WHY THIS RECIPE WORKS

Fallen chocolate cake, or molten chocolate cake, is an undercooked-in-the-center mound of intense, buttery chocolate cake. We wanted to turn this restaurant staple, typically baked in individual ramekins, into a practical recipe for home cooks. We were after individual portions of intensely flavored chocolate cake that had a light texture and an irresistibly runny center.

MAKE A FOAM We tried beating the egg whites and yolks separately and then folding them together as some recipes instruct, but we found that beating the eggs with sugar (and vanilla) to a foam, then folding in melted chocolate (we like semisweet), delivers cakes with a rich, moist texture.

ADD JUST A LITTLE FLOUR These cakes need flour for body but not too much or the cake will turn out dry instead of fudgy. A mere 2 tablespoons does the job.

MAKE AHEAD IF YOU LIKE These cakes are perfect for entertaining. We discovered that the batter could be made and poured into the ramekins ahead of time and refrigerated, then baked during dinner, which meant they could arrive at the table piping hot at the right time.

INDIVIDUAL FALLEN CHOCOLATE CAKES

SERVES 8

You can substitute 5 ounces unsweetened chocolate for the semisweet; if you opt to do so, increase the sugar to ¾ cup plus 2 tablespoons.

- 8 tablespoons unsalted butter
- 8 ounces semisweet chocolate, chopped coarse
- 4 large eggs plus 1 large yolk, room temperature
- ½ cup granulated sugar
- 1 teaspoon vanilla extract
- ¼ teaspoon salt
- 2 tablespoons all-purpose flour
  Confectioners' sugar or unsweetened cocoa powder (optional)
  Whipped Cream (page 348) (optional)

1. Adjust oven rack to middle position and heat oven to 400 degrees. Grease eight 6-ounce ramekins and dust with flour or cocoa. Arrange ramekins on rimmed baking sheet. Melt butter and chocolate in medium heatproof bowl set over saucepan filled with 1 inch of barely simmering water, stirring once or twice, until smooth. Remove from heat.

2. Using stand mixer fitted with whisk, whip eggs and yolk, sugar, vanilla, and salt on high speed until volume nearly triples, color is very light, and mixture drops from beaters in smooth, thick stream, about 5 minutes.

3. Scrape egg mixture over chocolate mixture, then sprinkle flour on top. Gently fold egg mixture and flour into chocolate until mixture is uniformly colored. Ladle or pour batter into prepared ramekins. (Unbaked cakes can be refrigerated for up to 8 hours. Return to room temperature for 30 minutes before baking.)

4. Bake until cakes have puffed about ½ inch above rims of ramekins, have thin crust on top, and jiggle slightly at center when ramekins are shaken very gently, 12 to 13 minutes. Run thin knife around inside edges of ramekins to loosen cakes, invert onto individual serving plates, and let sit until cakes release themselves from ramekins, about 1 minute. Lift off ramekins, dust with confectioners' sugar, if using, and/or dollop with whipped cream, if using, and serve.

Fold 1 tablespoon grated orange zest and 2 tablespoons orange liqueur into beaten egg and melted chocolate mixture with flour in step 3.

FALLEN CHOCOLATE CAKE

One large fallen chocolate cake can be prepared in a springform pan. Do not use a regular cake pan, as the cake will be impossible to remove once baked. Though the cake is best when served warm (within about 30 minutes of being unmolded), it can be held in the pan for up to 2 hours before serving.

Substitute greased 8- or 9-inch springform pan for ramekins. Reduce oven temperature to 375 degrees and bake until cake looks puffed, thin top crust has formed, and center jiggles slightly when pan is shaken gently, 22 to 25 minutes for 9-inch pan or 27 to 30 minutes for 8-inch pan. Let cake cool for 15 minutes, then run thin knife between cake and sides of pan and remove sides of pan. Sprinkle with confectioners' sugar, if using, and/or dollop with whipped cream, if using, and serve.

New York–Style Cheesecake

✓ WHY THIS RECIPE WORKS

A rejection of the Ben and Jerry school of everything-but-the-kitchen-sink concoctions, the ideal New York cheesecake is timeless in its adherence to simplicity. It is a tall, toasty-skinned, dense affair, a classic cheesecake with bronzed top and lush interior. We wanted to find the secret to perfect New York cheesecake.

MAKE A HOMEMADE CRUST Though some New York–style cheesecakes have pastry crusts, we find they become soggy beneath the filling. Our preference? Graham crackers. We enrich graham crackers ground to crumbs in a food processor with butter and sugar and press them into place in a springform pan. Prebaking keeps this crust from becoming soggy.

USE ROOM-TEMPERATURE CHEESE A New York cheesecake should be one of great stature. When we made one with 2 pounds (four bars) of cream cheese, it was not tall enough. Therefore, we fill the springform pan to the very top with an added half-pound. It's important that the cream cheese is at least moderately soft so that it can fully incorporate into the batter and you aren't left with a piece of cake containing small nodules of unmixed cream cheese amid an otherwise smooth bite.

CHOOSE THE RIGHT DAIRY Cream cheese alone as the filling of a cheesecake makes for a pasty cake—much like a bar of cream cheese straight from its wrapper. Additional dairy loosens up the texture of the cream cheese, giving the cake a smoother, more luxurious texture. Although some recipes call for large amounts of sour cream, we use only ⅓ cup so that the cake has a nice tang but doesn't end up tasting sour and acidic.

MIX WHOLE EGGS AND YOLKS In this cheesecake, eggs do a lot of work. They help to bind, making the cake cohesive and giving it structure. Whole eggs alone are often called for in softer, airier cheesecakes. But recipes for

GAUGING DONENESS OF CHEESECAKE

A cheesecake is done when the center just barely jiggles. Since this can be difficult to judge, try this tip.

Cheesecake is ready to come out of the oven when the internal temperature reaches 150 degrees. (At higher temperatures, the texture will suffer.) if possible, insert the thermometer into the side of the cheesecake where it rises above the pan (otherwise, insert it into the center of the cake).

We wondered if it would be
possible to freeze a just-
baked cheesecake or simply
leftovers. To find out, we
made our New York-Style
Cheesecake. We suspected
that the cake, with its dense
texture, would hold up well
to freezing and thawing but
that the crust, made with
graham crackers, would lose
some crispness. We were
right. Soggy crust notwith-
standing, a cheesecake that
had spent three to four weeks
in the freezer was almost as
good as fresh baked.

Here's how to freeze
leftover cheesecake: Return
the remaining cake to the
springform pan it was baked
in, with the sides in place for
protection. Wrap the pan
twice in plastic wrap and then
once in aluminum foil.

To serve, pull the cake
from the freezer and let it
defrost in the refrigerator 8 to
12 hours or overnight. About
an hour before serving, let
the cake sit out at room
temperature to shake off the
last of the deep-freeze chill.
To freeze a whole cheese-
cake, wrap the cooled cake,
still in its springform pan, then
freeze and thaw as described.

New York cheesecakes tend to include additional yolks, which add fat and emulsifiers,
and less water than whole eggs, to help produce a velvety, lush texture. We use six eggs
plus two yolks, a combination that produces a
dense but not heavy, firm but not rigid, perfectly rich cake.

FLAVOR, PLEASE   We keep the flavor of
this cake simple. Lemon juice is a great addition, perking things up without adding a dis-
tinctively lemon flavor (no zest!). Just a bit
of salt and a couple of teaspoons of vanilla
extract round out the flavors well.

GO HIGH TO LOW   There are many
ways to bake a cheesecake—in a moderate oven, in a low oven, in a water bath, or
in the New York fashion, in which the cake
bakes at 500 degrees for about 10 minutes
and then at 200 degrees for about an hour
and a half. This super-simple, no-water-bath,
dual-temperature baking method produces
a lovely graded texture—soft and creamy at
the center and firm and dry at the periphery.
It also yields the attractive nut-brown surface
we prize.

PREVENT CRACKS   Some cooks use the
crack to gauge when a cheesecake is done. But
we say if there's a crack it's already overdone.
The best way to prevent a cheesecake from
cracking is to use an instant-read thermometer to test its doneness. Take the cake out of
the oven when it reaches 150 degrees to avoid
overbaking. Higher temperatures cause the
cheesecake to rise so much that the delicate
network of egg proteins tears apart as the center shrinks and falls during cool-down.

SEPARATE AND COOL   During baking is not the only time a cheesecake can
crack. There is a second opportunity outside
the oven. A perfectly good-looking cake can
crack as it sits on the cooling rack. The cake
shrinks during cooling and will cling to the
sides of the springform pan. If the cake clings

tenaciously enough, the delicate egg structure
splits at its weakest point, the center. To avoid
this type of late cracking, cool the cheesecake
for only a few minutes, then free it from the
sides of the pan with a paring knife before
allowing it to cool fully.

NEW YORK–STYLE CHEESECAKE
SERVES 12 TO 16

---

*For the crust, chocolate wafers can be substituted
for graham crackers; you will need about 14 wafers.
The flavor and texture of the cheesecake is best if
the cake is allowed to sit at room temperature for
30 minutes before serving. When cutting the cake,
have a pitcher of hot tap water nearby; dipping the
blade of the knife into the water and wiping it clean
with a dish towel after each cut helps make neat
slices. Serve with Fresh Strawberry Topping (recipe
follows) if desired.*

CRUST

8	whole graham crackers, broken into rough pieces
1	tablespoon sugar
5	tablespoons unsalted butter, melted

FILLING

2½	pounds cream cheese, cut into 1-inch chunks and softened
1½	cups (10½ ounces) sugar
⅛	teaspoon salt
⅓	cup sour cream
2	teaspoons lemon juice
2	teaspoons vanilla extract
6	large eggs plus 2 large yolks
1	tablespoon unsalted butter, melted

1. FOR THE CRUST: Adjust oven rack
to lower-middle position and heat oven to
325 degrees. Process graham cracker pieces in
food processor to fine crumbs, about 30 seconds. Combine graham cracker crumbs and

sugar in medium bowl, add melted butter, and toss with fork until evenly moistened. Empty crumbs into 9-inch springform pan and, using bottom of ramekin or dry measuring cup, press crumbs firmly and evenly into pan bottom, keeping sides as clean as possible. Bake crust until fragrant and beginning to brown around edges, about 13 minutes. Let crust cool in pan on wire rack while making filling.

2. FOR THE FILLING: Increase oven temperature to 500 degrees. Using stand mixer fitted with paddle, beat cream cheese on medium-low speed, about 1 minute. Scrape down bowl. Add ¾ cup sugar and salt and beat on medium-low speed until combined, about 1 minute. Scrape down bowl, then beat in remaining ¾ cup sugar until combined, about 1 minute. Scrape down bowl, add sour cream, lemon juice, and vanilla, and beat on low speed until combined, about 1 minute. Scrape down bowl, add egg yolks, and beat on medium-low speed until thoroughly combined, about 1 minute. Scrape down bowl, add whole eggs, two at a time, beating until thoroughly combined, about 1 minute, and scraping down bowl between additions.

3. Being careful not to disturb baked crust, brush inside of pan with melted butter and set pan on rimmed baking sheet to catch any spills in case pan leaks. Pour filling into cooled crust and bake 10 minutes; without opening oven door, reduce temperature to 200 degrees and continue to bake until cheesecake registers about 150 degrees, about 1½ hours. Let cake cool on wire rack for 5 minutes, then run thin knife around cake to loosen from pan. Let cake continue to cool until barely warm, 2½ to 3 hours. Wrap tightly in plastic wrap and refrigerate until cold, at least 3 hours. (Cake can be refrigerated for up to 4 days.)

4. To unmold cheesecake, wrap hot dish towel around pan and let stand for 1 minute. Remove sides of pan. Slide thin metal spatula between crust and pan bottom to loosen, then slide cake onto serving platter. Let cheesecake sit at room temperature for about 30 minutes before serving. (Cheesecake can be made up to 3 days in advance; however, crust will begin to lose its crispness after only 1 day.)

MARBLE CHEESECAKE

Melt 5 ounces chopped semisweet chocolate and ¼ cup heavy cream together in microwave, stirring often, until melted and smooth, 1 to 3 minutes. Let mixture cool completely. Drop spoonfuls of chocolate over top of batter. Using butter knife or small offset spatula, swirl chocolate into cheesecake batter, creating attractive marbled pattern.

FRESH STRAWBERRY TOPPING
MAKES ABOUT 1½ QUARTS

This accompaniment to cheesecake is best served the same day it is made.

    2   pounds strawberries, hulled and sliced
        lengthwise ⅛ to ¼ inch thick (5 cups)
    ½   cup (3½ ounces) sugar
        Pinch salt
    1   cup strawberry jam
    2   tablespoons lemon juice

1. Toss berries, sugar, and salt in medium bowl and let sit until berries have released juices and sugar has dissolved, about 30 minutes, tossing occasionally to combine.

2. Process jam in food processor until smooth, about 8 seconds, then transfer to small saucepan. Bring jam to simmer over medium-high heat and simmer, stirring frequently, until dark and no longer frothy, about 3 minutes. Stir in lemon juice, then pour warm liquid over strawberries and stir to combine. Let cool, then cover with plastic wrap and refrigerate until cold, at least 2 hours or up to 12 hours.

Spiced Pumpkin Cheesecake

✓ WHY THIS RECIPE WORKS

Those who suffer from pumpkin pie ennui embrace pumpkin cheesecake as "a nice change," but the expectations are low. Undoubtedly, pumpkin cheesecake can be good in its own right, though it rarely is. Textures run the gamut from dry and dense to wet, soft, and mousselike. Flavors veer from far too cheesy and tangy to pungently overspiced to totally bland. We wanted a creamy, velvety smooth pumpkin cheesecake that tasted of sweet, earthy pumpkin as well as tangy cream cheese; that struck a harmonious spicy chord; and, of course, that had a crisp, buttery, cookie-crumb crust.

PREBAKE THE CRUST We use crumbled graham crackers for the crust, as we do in our New York–Style Cheesecake recipe (page 336). Here we add butter and sugar and a bit of ground cinnamon, ginger, nutmeg, and cloves to them in order to complement the spices in the filling. Also, as with our New York cheesecake, we prebake the crust. This way a sturdy, crisp, buttery crust forms. (Without prebaking, the crust becomes a pasty, soggy layer beneath the filling.)

DRY YOUR CANNED PUMPKIN Anyone who has prepared fresh pumpkin for pumpkin pie can attest to the fact that cutting, seeding, peeling, and cooking it can take hours and is not time and effort well spent. We prefer opening a can, which takes only a few seconds. But pumpkin in any form is filled with liquid. We could remove some of the moisture by cooking, as we do in our Pumpkin Pie (page 395). But that involves frequent stirring, a cooking period, and waiting for it to cool. An easier way? Paper towels. Spread the pumpkin on a baking sheet lined with paper towels and then press additional paper towels on the surface to wick away more moisture. In seconds, the pumpkin will shed enough liquid to yield a cheesecake with a lovely texture, and the paper towels will peel away almost effortlessly. Removing this moisture allows us to add heavy cream to the mix, which gives us a cheesecake that is smooth and lush.

PICK YOUR EGGS While cheesecake recipes can take various amounts of eggs in different configurations (whole eggs, egg whites, or egg yolks for a range of textures), we prefer simply using five whole eggs here. This produces a satiny, creamy, unctuous cheesecake.

FLAVOR IT UP Our Spiced Pumpkin Cheesecake is flavored with lemon juice, salt, and vanilla extract to start. But we also add sweet, warm cinnamon and sharp, spicy ground ginger alongside small amounts of cloves, nutmeg, and allspice. In unison, these spices provide a deep, resounding flavor but not an overspiced burn.

GIVE IT A BATH In a springform pan, a cheesecake can be baked either directly on the oven rack like a regular cake or in a water bath like a delicate custard. Because we bake this cheesecake at 325 degrees, a water bath is needed for even cooking on the edges and the center.

SPICED PUMPKIN CHEESECAKE
SERVES 12 TO 16

Make sure to buy unsweetened canned pumpkin, not pumpkin pie filling, which is preseasoned and sweetened. This cheesecake is good on its own, but Brown Sugar and Bourbon Whipped Cream (page 341) is a great addition. When cutting the cake, have a pitcher of hot tap water nearby; dipping the blade of the knife into the water and wiping it clean with a dish towel after each cut helps make neat slices.

Canned pumpkin contains a significant amount of moisture that can make for a very wet, dense cheesecake. We solve the problem by wicking away the excess moisture with paper towels.

1. Line baking sheet with triple layer of paper towels. Spread pumpkin on paper towels in roughly even layer.

2. Cover pumpkin with second triple layer of paper towels and press firmly until paper towels are saturated.

3. Peel back top layer of towels and discard.

CRUST

9   whole graham crackers, broken into rough pieces
3   tablespoons sugar
½   teaspoon ground ginger
½   teaspoon ground cinnamon
¼   teaspoon ground cloves
6   tablespoons unsalted butter, melted

FILLING

1⅓   cups (10⅓ ounces) sugar
1   teaspoon ground cinnamon
½   teaspoon ground ginger
¼   teaspoon ground nutmeg
¼   teaspoon ground cloves
¼   teaspoon allspice
½   teaspoon salt
1   (15-ounce) can unsweetened pumpkin puree
1½   pounds cream cheese, cut into 1-inch chunks and softened
1   tablespoon vanilla extract
1   tablespoon lemon juice
5   large eggs, room temperature
1   cup heavy cream
1   tablespoon unsalted butter, melted

1. FOR THE CRUST: Adjust oven rack to lower-middle position and heat oven to 325 degrees. Pulse crackers, sugar, ginger, cinnamon, and cloves in food processor until crackers are finely ground, about 15 pulses. Transfer crumbs to medium bowl, drizzle with melted butter, and mix with rubber spatula until evenly moistened. Empty crumbs into 9-inch springform pan and, using bottom of ramekin or dry measuring cup, press crumbs firmly and evenly into pan bottom, keeping sides as clean as possible. Bake crust until fragrant and browned around edges, about 15 minutes. Let crust cool completely on wire rack, about 30 minutes. When cool, wrap outside of pan with two 18-inch square pieces heavy-duty aluminum foil and set springform pan in roasting pan. Bring kettle of water to boil.

2. FOR THE FILLING: Whisk sugar, cinnamon, ginger, nutmeg, cloves, allspice, and salt in small bowl; set aside. Line baking sheet with triple layer of paper towels. Spread pumpkin on paper towels in roughly even layer and pat puree with several layers of paper towels to wick away moisture.

3. Using stand mixer fitted with paddle, beat cream cheese on medium speed, about 1 minute. Scrape down bowl, then beat in sugar mixture in 3 additions on medium-low speed until combined, about 1 minute, scraping down bowl after each addition. Add pumpkin, vanilla, and lemon juice and beat on medium speed until combined, about 45 seconds; scrape down bowl. Reduce speed to medium-low, add eggs, one at a time, and beat until incorporated, about 1 minute. Reduce speed to low, add heavy cream, and beat until combined, about 45 seconds. Give filling final stir by hand.

4. Being careful not to disturb baked crust, brush inside of pan with melted butter. Pour filling into prepared pan and smooth top with rubber spatula. Set roasting pan on oven rack and pour enough boiling water into roasting pan to come about halfway up sides of springform pan. Bake cake until center is slightly wobbly when pan is shaken and cake registers 150 degrees, about 1½ hours. Set roasting pan on wire rack then run paring knife around cake. Let cake cool in roasting pan until water is just warm, about 45 minutes. Remove springform pan from water bath, discard foil, and set on wire rack; continue to let cool until barely warm, about 3 hours. Wrap with plastic wrap and refrigerate until chilled, at least 4 hours.

5. To unmold cheesecake, wrap hot dish towel around pan and let stand for 1 minute. Remove sides of pan. Slide thin metal spatula between crust and pan bottom to loosen, then slide cake onto serving platter. Let cheesecake sit at room temperature for about 30 minutes before serving. (Cheesecake can be made up to 3 days in advance; however, the crust will begin to lose its crispness after only 1 day.)

PUMPKIN-BOURBON CHEESECAKE WITH GRAHAM-PECAN CRUST

Reduce graham crackers to 5 whole crackers, process ½ cup chopped pecans with crackers, and reduce butter to 4 tablespoons. In filling, omit lemon juice, reduce vanilla extract to 1 teaspoon, and add ¼ cup bourbon along with heavy cream.

BROWN SUGAR WHIPPED CREAM
MAKES ABOUT 2½ CUPS

Refrigerating the mixture in step 1 gives the brown sugar time to dissolve. This whipped cream pairs well with Spiced Pumpkin Cheesecake or with any dessert that has lots of nuts, warm spices, or molasses, like gingerbread, pecan pie, or pumpkin pie.

1   cup heavy cream, chilled
½   cup sour cream
½   cup packed (3½ ounces) light brown sugar
⅛   teaspoon salt

1. Using stand mixer fitted with whisk, whip heavy cream, sour cream, sugar, and salt until combined. Cover with plastic wrap and refrigerate until ready to serve, at least 4 hours or up to 1 day, stirring once or twice during chilling to ensure that sugar dissolves.

2. Before serving, using stand mixer fitted with whisk, whip mixture on medium-low speed until foamy, about 1 minute. Increase speed to high and whip until soft peaks form, 1 to 3 minutes.

BROWN SUGAR AND BOURBON WHIPPED CREAM

Add 2 teaspoons bourbon to cream mixture before whipping.

Lemon Cheesecake

✔ WHY THIS RECIPE WORKS
We love cheesecake it in its unadulterated form, but sometimes the fresh flavor of citrus can take it to a refreshing new level. We aimed to develop a creamy cheesecake with a bracing but not overpowering lemon flavor.

USE ANIMAL CRACKERS   Most cheesecakes have sweet and spicy graham cracker crusts that remain crunchy under the weight of the cheesy filling. But here the strong molasses taste of the graham crackers overwhelms the lemon flavor. We experimented with several kinds of more neutral-flavored crumb crusts and found that we liked the one made with animal crackers the best.

PROCESS ZEST FOR FLAVOR   Zest offers a nice balance of lemon flavor, but it comes with a hitch: The fibrous texture of the zest can mar the creamy smoothness of the filling. To solve this, we process the zest and ¼ cup of sugar together before adding them to the cream cheese. This produces a wonderfully potent lemon flavor by breaking down the zest and releasing its oils. Don't process all the sugar, though; that would wreak havoc with its crystalline structure (necessary for aerating the cream cheese) as well as meld it with the oils from the lemon zest, creating a strangely dense cake.

BAKE IN A BATH   This cheesecake is baked in a water bath in a 325-degree oven. But here we turn the oven off and leave the cake in the oven for an additional hour with the door ajar. This technique of cooking at a very slow crawl so as not to overcook the eggs gives us a foolproof creamy consistency in our cheesecake from edge to center.

LEAK-PROOFING SPRINGFORM PANS

We'd love to find a springform pan that doesn't let moisture seep in when you place it in a water bath, but so far a less-than-watertight seal seems unavoidable on pans with removable bottoms. Our solution has always been to wrap the pan with a double layer of aluminum foil. But steam from the water bath can condense inside the foil, so that the pan still sits in liquid. There is a better way to address the problem: placing the springform pan inside a slightly larger metal pan or pot—a 10 by 3-inch cake pan or deep-dish pizza pan is ideal—before lowering it into the bath. The slight gap between the pans isn't wide enough to prevent the water from insulating the springform pan, and there is zero danger of exposing the cheesecake to water, since any moisture that condenses on the sides of the pan rapidly evaporates. If you bake cheesecakes regularly, this method is worth the minimal expense.

The flavorful oil that is found
in the outer layer, or zest,
of lemon skin protects the
fruit from drying out. Once
you remove that layer, you
remove its primary defense
against dehydration.

We stripped the zest (but
not the white pith) from four
lemons and stored them in
the fridge in three different
ways: wrapped in plastic
wrap, enclosed in a zipper-
lock bag, and rubbed with a
thin layer of vegetable oil. As
a control, we refrigerated a
fourth zested lemon that we
left alone. To measure moisture loss, we weighed the
lemons before and after three
weeks of refrigeration. The
plastic-wrapped and bagged
lemons lost only 2.5 percent
and 6 percent of their weight,
respectively, yielding plenty
of juice. By contrast, the
oil-coated lemon suffered a
40 percent loss in weight and
was almost indistinguishable
from the shriveled control
sample, in both its firmness
and the miserly portion of
bitter juice it released. (Without skin or other protection,
the juice in a lemon oxidizes,
changing its flavor profile.)

The upshot? If you're not
going to be juicing a zested
lemon for a while, wrap it in
plastic before refrigerating it.

CHILL THE CAKE If the cheesecake
is not thoroughly chilled, it will not hold its
shape when sliced. After 4 hours in the refrigerator (and preferably longer), the cheesecake
has set up. Likewise, the curd will firm up only
when the cheesecake is thoroughly chilled.
Only then can the cake be sliced neatly.

TIME TO TEMPER Like other stovetop
custards, lemon curd combines eggs with hot
liquid. To heat the eggs gently, we temper
them, or slowly whisk in the hot liquid before
putting the eggs on the stove. On the stove,
we stir the mixture constantly (this motion
reduces the amount that the egg proteins will
bond so that the end product is a sauce rather
than a solid mass) until it reaches 170 degrees.
Be careful not to overcook the curd. While
you want to get the maximum thickening
power from the heat, you don't want so much
that the eggs will curdle.

LEMON CHEESECAKE
SERVES 12 TO 16

*When cutting the cake, have a pitcher of hot tap
water nearby; dipping the blade of the knife into
the water and wiping it clean with a dish towel after
each cut helps make neat slices.*

CRUST
5 ounces Nabisco Barnum's Animals
   Crackers or Social Tea Biscuits
3 tablespoons sugar
4 tablespoons unsalted butter, melted

FILLING
1¼ cups (8¾ ounces) sugar
1   tablespoon grated lemon zest plus
    ¼ cup juice (2 lemons)
1½ pounds cream cheese, cut into 1-inch
    chunks, room temperature
4   large eggs, room temperature
2   teaspoons vanilla extract
¼   teaspoon salt
½   cup heavy cream
1   tablespoon unsalted butter, melted

LEMON CURD
⅓ cup lemon juice (2 lemons)
2 large eggs plus 1 large yolk
½ cup (3½ ounces) sugar
2 tablespoons unsalted butter, cut into
   ½-inch pieces and chilled
1 tablespoon heavy cream
¼ teaspoon vanilla extract
   Pinch salt

1. FOR THE CRUST: Adjust oven rack
to lower-middle position and heat oven to
325 degrees. Process cookies in food processor
to fine crumbs, about 30 seconds (you should
have about 1 cup). Add sugar and pulse 2 or
3 times to incorporate. Add melted butter in
slow, steady stream while pulsing; pulse until
mixture is evenly moistened and resembles
wet sand, about 10 pulses. Empty crumbs into
9-inch springform pan and, using bottom of
ramekin or dry measuring cup, press crumbs
firmly and evenly into pan bottom, keeping
sides as clean as possible. Bake crust until fragrant and golden brown, 15 to 18 minutes.
Let cool on wire rack to room temperature,
about 30 minutes. When cool, wrap outside of
pan with two 18-inch square pieces heavy-duty
aluminum foil and set springform pan in roasting pan. Bring kettle of water to boil.

2. FOR THE FILLING: While crust is cooling, process ¼ cup sugar and lemon zest in
food processor until sugar is yellow and zest
is broken down, about 15 seconds, scraping
down bowl as needed. Transfer lemon-sugar
mixture to small bowl and stir in remaining
1 cup sugar.

3. Using stand mixer fitted with paddle,
beat cream cheese on low speed until broken up and slightly softened, about 5 seconds. With mixer running, add lemon-sugar
mixture in slow, steady stream; increase speed
to medium and continue to beat until mixture is creamy and smooth, about 3 minutes,
scraping down bowl as needed. Reduce speed
to medium-low and beat in eggs, two at a
time, until incorporated, about 30 seconds,

scraping down bowl well after each addition. Add lemon juice, vanilla, and salt and mix until just incorporated, about 5 seconds. Add heavy cream and mix until just incorporated, about 5 seconds longer. Give filling final stir by hand.

4. Being careful not to disturb baked crust, brush inside of pan with melted butter. Pour filling into prepared pan and smooth top with rubber spatula. Set roasting pan on oven rack and pour enough boiling water into roasting pan to come halfway up sides of pan. Bake cake until center jiggles slightly, sides just start to puff, surface is no longer shiny, and center of cake registers 150 degrees, 55 minutes to 1 hour. Turn off oven and prop open oven door with potholder or wooden spoon handle; allow cake to cool in water bath in oven for 1 hour. Transfer pan to wire rack. Remove foil, then run thin knife around cake and let cake cool completely on wire rack, about 2 hours.

5. FOR THE LEMON CURD: While cheesecake bakes, heat lemon juice in small saucepan over medium heat until hot but not boiling. Whisk eggs and yolk together in medium bowl, then gradually whisk in sugar. Whisking constantly, slowly pour hot lemon juice into eggs, then return mixture to saucepan and cook over medium heat, stirring constantly with wooden spoon, until mixture is thick enough to cling to spoon and registers 170 degrees, about 3 minutes. Immediately remove pan from heat and stir in cold butter until incorporated. Stir in cream, vanilla, and salt, then pour curd through fine-mesh strainer into small bowl. Place plastic wrap directly on surface of curd and refrigerate until needed.

6. When cheesecake is cool, scrape lemon curd onto cheesecake still in springform pan. Using offset spatula, spread curd evenly over top of cheesecake. Cover tightly with plastic and refrigerate for at least 4 hours or up to

1 day. To unmold cheesecake, wrap hot dish towel around pan and let stand for 1 minute. Remove sides of pan. Slide thin metal spatula between crust and pan bottom to loosen, then slide cake onto serving platter and serve. (Cheesecake can be made up to 3 days in advance; however, the crust will begin to lose its crispness after only 1 day.)

GOAT CHEESE AND LEMON CHEESECAKE WITH HAZELNUT CRUST

The goat cheese gives this cheesecake a distinctive tang and a slightly savory edge. Use a mild-flavored goat cheese. See page 9 for information on toasting nuts. To skin the hazelnuts, simply place the warm toasted nuts in a clean dish towel and rub gently.

For crust, process generous ⅓ cup hazelnuts, toasted, skinned, and cooled, in food processor with sugar until finely ground and mixture resembles coarse cornmeal, about 30 seconds. Add cookies and process until mixture is finely and evenly ground, about 30 seconds. Reduce melted butter to 3 tablespoons. For filling, reduce cream cheese to 1 pound and beat 8 ounces room-temperature goat cheese with cream cheese in step 3. Omit salt.

TRIPLE-CITRUS CHEESECAKE

For filling, reduce lemon zest to 1 teaspoon and lemon juice to 1 tablespoon. Process 1 teaspoon grated lime zest and 1 teaspoon grated orange zest with lemon zest in step 2. Add 1 tablespoon lime juice and 2 tablespoons orange juice to mixer with lemon juice in step 3. For curd, reduce lemon juice to 2 tablespoons and heat 2 tablespoons lime juice, 4 teaspoons orange juice, and 2 teaspoons grated orange zest with lemon juice in step 5. Omit vanilla extract.

PREVENTING SOGGY CHEESECAKE

After refrigerating a baked and cooled cheesecake, unwanted moisture can collect on the top of the cake. Try this solution: Arrange a layer of paper towels over the cheesecake before covering it with plastic wrap and refrigerating.

PEACH SHORTCAKES

Fruit Desserts and Crêpes

Blanching helps loosen the
skins for fuss-free peeling.

1. With paring knife, score
small X at base of each peach.

2. Lower peaches into pan of
simmering water with slotted
spoon. Turn peaches occa-
sionally and simmer until their
skins loosen, about 15 seconds, depending on ripeness
of peaches.

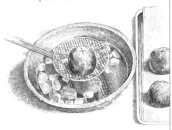

3. Transfer peaches to bowl
of ice water and let stand
about 1 minute to stop cooking process and cool.

4. Starting from scored X,
peel each peach. Use paring
knife to lift skin from flesh and
pull skin off in strips.

Peach Shortcakes

✔ WHY THIS RECIPE WORKS

*Making peach shortcake with supermarket peaches
often produces a flavorless filling over a dry, crumbly
biscuit. We wanted to develop a foolproof recipe for
peach shortcake that would work with either farm
stand or supermarket peaches.*

SLICE THE FRUIT THIN   For strawberry
shortcake, we macerate the berries in sugar
to pull out the fruit's juice, but for peaches,
this step alone isn't enough. To ensure juicy
shortcakes, we first slice the peaches very thin
to maximize the surface that will come in contact with the sugar.

SPIKE WITH SCHNAPPS   In addition to
our macerated peaches, we toss a few more
peaches with peach schnapps and microwave
them until tender. Mashing these cooked
peaches provides us with a peach jam that provides plenty of moisture and sweetness along
with our sliced fruit.

**CREATE A TENDER, BUT STURDY,
BISCUIT**   We add an egg to our shortcake
dough and mechanically develop more gluten
(by vigorous stirring) to make a cake that will
hold up under the weight of the fruit. We also
sprinkle the shaped biscuits with sugar before
baking for browning and a sweet crunch.

FINISH WITH SWEET WHIPPED CREAM
Freshly whipped cream spooned over the
fruit and over the biscuit, ensures peaches and
cream in every bite.

PEACH SHORTCAKES
SERVES 6

*If your peaches are firm, you should be able to peel
them with a vegetable peeler. If they are too soft
and ripe to withstand the pressure of a peeler, you'll
need to blanch them in a pot of simmering water
for 15 seconds and then shock them in a bowl of
ice water before peeling. This recipe works well with
any peaches, regardless of quality. You can substitute ½ cup low-fat yogurt mixed with 3 tablespoons
of milk for the buttermilk, if desired. Orange juice
or orange liqueur can be used in place of the peach
schnapps.*

FRUIT
2	pounds peaches, peeled, halved, pitted, and cut into ¼-inch wedges
6	tablespoons sugar
2	tablespoons peach schnapps

BISCUITS
2	cups (10 ounces) all-purpose flour
2	tablespoons sugar
2	teaspoons baking powder
¾	teaspoon salt
⅔	cup buttermilk, chilled
1	large egg
8	tablespoons unsalted butter, melted and cooled

WHIPPED CREAM
½	cup heavy cream, chilled
1	tablespoon sugar
½	teaspoon vanilla extract

1. **FOR THE FRUIT:** Gently toss three-
quarters of peaches with 4 tablespoons sugar
in large bowl. Let sit for 30 minutes. Toss
remaining peaches with remaining 2 tablespoons sugar and schnapps in medium bowl.
Microwave until peaches are bubbling, about
1 to 1½ minutes, stirring twice. Using potato
masher, crush peaches into coarse pulp. Let sit
for 30 minutes.

2. **FOR THE BISCUITS:** Meanwhile, adjust
oven rack to middle position and heat oven
to 475 degrees. Line baking sheet with
parchment paper. Whisk flour, 1 tablespoon
sugar, baking powder, and salt together in

large bowl. Whisk buttermilk and egg together in bowl; add melted butter and stir until butter forms small clumps.

3. Add buttermilk mixture to dry ingredients and stir with wooden spoon until dough comes together and no dry flour remains. Continue to stir vigorously for 30 seconds. Using greased ⅓-cup measure, portion dough onto prepared baking sheet to create 6 biscuits, spaced about 1½ inches apart. Sprinkle remaining 1 tablespoon sugar evenly over top of biscuits. Bake until tops are golden brown and crisp, about 15 minutes, rotating baking sheet halfway through baking. Transfer baking sheet to wire rack and let cool, about 15 minutes. (Cooled biscuits can be stored at room temperature for up to 1 day. Reheat in 350-degree oven for 3 to 5 minutes before assembling.)

4. FOR THE WHIPPED CREAM: Using stand mixer fitted with whisk, whip cream, sugar, and vanilla on medium-low speed until foamy, about 1 minute. Increase speed to high and whip until soft peaks form, 1 to 3 minutes.

5. To assemble, split each biscuit in half and place bottoms on individual plates. Spoon portion of crushed peach mixture over each bottom, followed by peach slices and juice. Dollop each shortcake with 2 tablespoons whipped cream, cap with biscuit tops, and dollop with remaining whipped cream. Serve immediately.

Strawberry Shortcakes

✔ WHY THIS RECIPE WORKS

While some folks like to spoon strawberries over pound cake, sponge cake, or even angel food cake, our idea of strawberry shortcake definitely involves biscuits. We wanted a juicy strawberry filling and mounds of freshly whipped cream sandwiched in the middle of a lightly sweetened, tender biscuit.

MACERATE YOUR BERRIES Most strawberry shortcakes are made with sliced or quartered berries, which simply slide off the biscuit when you go to eat it. We mash some of the berries and then stir in the sliced berries and sugar. The sugar dissolves after about 30 minutes and you have plenty of thickened, juicy berry puree that will anchor the sliced berries in place.

ENRICH THOSE BISCUITS Yes, you can use regular biscuits to make a shortcake, but we think a true shortcake should be sweeter (we add more sugar to the biscuits) and richer (we add an egg and use half-and-half rather than milk). Brushing the biscuits with a beaten egg white and then sprinkling them with sugar gives them a crunchy, appealingly browned top.

USE CHILLED CREAM The secret to billowy whipped cream is to start with cold cream. If the cream has been well chilled in the refrigerator, it should whip just fine. If your kitchen is warm, chill the mixer bowl and whisk, too. To sweeten the cream, we prefer granulated sugar, added at the outset.

STRAWBERRY SHORTCAKES
SERVES 6

Preparing the fruit first gives it time to release its juice.

FRUIT
2½ pounds strawberries, hulled (8 cups)
6 tablespoons (2⅔ ounces) sugar

BISCUITS

- 2 cups (10 ounces) all-purpose flour
- 5 tablespoons (2¼ ounces) sugar
- 1 tablespoon baking powder
- ½ teaspoon salt
- 8 tablespoons unsalted butter, cut into ½-inch pieces and chilled
- ½ cup plus 1 tablespoon half-and-half or milk
- 1 large egg, lightly beaten, plus 1 large white, lightly beaten

- 1 recipe Whipped Cream (recipe follows)

1. FOR THE FRUIT: Crush 3 cups strawberries in large bowl with potato masher. Slice remaining 5 cups strawberries. Stir sliced strawberries and sugar into crushed strawberries. Set aside until sugar has dissolved and strawberries are juicy, at least 30 minutes or up to 2 hours.

2. FOR THE BISCUITS: Adjust oven rack to lower-middle position and heat oven to 425 degrees. Line baking sheet with parchment paper. Pulse flour, 3 tablespoons sugar, baking powder, and salt in food processor until combined. Scatter butter pieces over top and pulse until mixture resembles coarse meal, about 15 pulses. Transfer mixture to large bowl.

3. Whisk half-and-half and whole egg together in bowl, then stir into flour mixture until large clumps form. Turn out onto lightly floured counter and knead lightly until dough comes together (do not overwork dough).

4. Pat dough into 9 by 6-inch rectangle, about ¾ inch thick. Using floured 2¾-inch biscuit cutter, cut out 6 dough rounds. Arrange biscuits on prepared sheet, spaced about 1½ inches apart. Brush tops with egg white and sprinkle evenly with remaining 2 tablespoons sugar. (Unbaked biscuits can be refrigerated, covered with plastic wrap, for up to 2 hours.)

5. Bake until biscuits are golden brown, 12 to 14 minutes, rotating baking sheet halfway through baking. Transfer baking sheet to wire rack and let cool, about 10 minutes. (Cooled biscuits can be stored at room temperature for up to 1 day. Reheat in 350-degree oven for 3 to 5 minutes before assembling.)

6. To assemble, split each biscuit in half and place bottoms on individual plates. Spoon portion of strawberries over each bottom, dollop with whipped cream, and cap with biscuit tops. Serve immediately.

WHIPPED CREAM
MAKES ABOUT 2 CUPS

For lightly sweetened whipped cream, reduce the sugar to 1½ teaspoons.

- 1 cup heavy cream, chilled
- 1 tablespoon sugar
- 1 teaspoon vanilla extract

Using stand mixer fitted with whisk, whip cream, sugar, and vanilla on medium-low speed until foamy, about 1 minute. Increase speed to high and whip until soft peaks form, 1 to 3 minutes. (Whipped cream can be refrigerated in fine-mesh strainer set over small bowl and covered with plastic wrap for up to 8 hours.)

Fresh Peach Cobbler

✓ WHY THIS RECIPE WORKS

Bad peaches, syrupy filling, and a soggy biscuit topping were just three of the problems we had to solve when developing our recipe for fresh peach cobbler. Our goal was an appealing dish of warm, tender biscuits set atop rich, juicy peaches.

SUGAR THE FRUIT, THEN THICKEN THE JUICE To guarantee that our cobblers would be consistently juicy every time, we came up with a way to even out the variation in juiciness from peach to peach. First we macerate our peaches in sugar to draw out their juice, then we measure out a portion of the drained juice to mix back in with the fruit, discarding any extra. Thickening the peach juice with a small amount of cornstarch gives the filling body without overwhelming the delicate texture of the peaches. Lemon adds brightness.

CREATE A DAIRY-RICH BISCUIT TOPPING For the topping, we created a biscuit with a little more dairy, which gives us a moister dough that bakes up with a tender interior and crunchy top. For the dairy, we opt for yogurt, for its tangy flavor.

PARCOOK THE PEACHES THEN ADD THE TOPPING Giving the fruit a head start in the oven allows for the bubbling juice to jump-start the baking process of the biscuit topping when it's dropped over the fruit. The result is an evenly baked, tender, crunchy topping that perfectly complements the juicy peach filling.

FRESH PEACH COBBLER
SERVES 6

If your peaches are firm, you should be able to peel them with a vegetable peeler. If they are too soft and ripe to withstand the pressure of a peeler, you'll need to blanch them in a pot of simmering water for 15 seconds and then shock them in a bowl of ice water before peeling. Do not prepare the biscuit dough any sooner than the recipe indicates or the biscuits may not rise properly. If desired, plain low-fat or nonfat yogurt can be substituted for the whole-milk yogurt, but the biscuits will be a little less rich. If the dough does not come together, you can add up to 1 tablespoon more yogurt. This recipe can be doubled; use a 13 by 9-inch baking dish and increase the baking times in steps 1 and 3 by about 5 minutes. Serve with vanilla ice cream or Whipped Cream (page 348).

FILLING
2½	pounds peaches, peeled, halved, pitted, and cut into ¾-inch wedges
¼	cup (1¾ ounces) sugar
1	tablespoon lemon juice
1	teaspoon cornstarch
	Pinch salt

BISCUIT TOPPING
1	cup (5 ounces) all-purpose flour
3	tablespoons plus 1 teaspoon sugar
¾	teaspoon baking powder
¼	teaspoon baking soda
¼	teaspoon salt
5	tablespoons unsalted butter, cut into ¼-inch pieces and chilled
⅓	cup plain whole-milk yogurt

1. FOR THE FILLING: Adjust oven rack to lower-middle position and heat oven to 425 degrees. Line rimmed baking sheet with aluminum foil. Gently toss peaches and sugar together in large bowl and let sit for 30 minutes, gently stirring several times. Drain peaches in colander set over large bowl and reserve ¼ cup juice (discard remaining juice). Whisk reserved juice, lemon juice, cornstarch, and salt together in small bowl. Combine peaches and juice mixture in bowl and transfer to 8-inch square baking dish; place on prepared

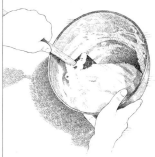

baking sheet. Bake until peaches begin to bubble around edges, about 10 minutes.

2. FOR THE BISCUIT TOPPING: Meanwhile, pulse flour, 3 tablespoons sugar, baking powder, baking soda, and salt in food processor until combined, about 5 pulses. Scatter butter pieces over top and pulse until mixture resembles coarse meal, about 10 pulses. Transfer to medium bowl, add yogurt, and toss with rubber spatula until cohesive dough is formed (don't overmix dough). Divide dough into 6 equal pieces.

3. After removing peaches from oven, place dough mounds on top, spacing them at least ½ inch apart (they should not touch). Sprinkle dough mounds evenly with remaining 1 teaspoon sugar. Bake until filling is bubbling and biscuits are golden brown, 16 to 18 minutes, rotating baking sheet halfway through baking. Transfer baking dish to wire rack and let cool until warm, about 20 minutes; serve.

BLUEBERRY-PEACH COBBLER WITH LEMON-CORNMEAL BISCUIT TOPPING

Reduce peaches to 2 pounds. Toss 1 cup fresh blueberries with peach and juice mixture before transferring to baking dish in step 1. Substitute 2 tablespoons stone-ground cornmeal for equal amount flour in biscuit topping and add ½ teaspoon grated lemon zest to food processor with dry ingredients in step 2.

PEACH COBBLER WITH FROZEN PEACHES

Start defrosting the peaches about 2 hours before assembling and baking the cobbler.

Using frozen peaches, reduce peaches to 2 pounds. Defrost peaches completely in colander, reserving 2 tablespoons juice. Proceed as directed, increasing baking time in step 1 to 15 to 20 minutes.

Blueberry Cobbler

✔ WHY THIS RECIPE WORKS

Too often, blueberry cobbler means a filling that is too sweet, overspiced, and unappealingly thick. We wanted a juicy, but not-too-thin filling where the blueberry flavor would be front and center. And over the fruit, we wanted a light, tender biscuit topping that could hold its own against the fruit filling, with an ingredient list simple enough to allow the blueberries to play a starring role.

SWEETEN MODESTLY We start by preparing a not-too-sweet filling using 6 cups of fresh berries and just half a cup of sugar. Cornstarch works well to thicken the fruit's juice.

ADD BRIGHTNESS A little lemon and cinnamon work perfectly to enhance the filling without masking the blueberry flavor.

PICK A RUSTIC BISCUIT TOPPING AND BAKE THE FILLING FIRST For an easy to prepare topping, we make light, rustic drop biscuits enriched with a little cornmeal. Adding the biscuit topping to the cobbler after the filling has baked on its own allows the biscuits to brown evenly and cook through. A sprinkling of cinnamon sugar on the dropped biscuit dough adds a sweet crunch.

BLUEBERRY COBBLER
SERVES 6 TO 8

While the blueberries are baking, prepare the ingredients for the topping, but do not stir the wet ingredients into the dry ingredients until just before the berries come out of the oven. A standard or

deep-dish 9-inch pie plate works well; an 8-inch square baking dish can also be used. Serve with vanilla ice cream or Whipped Cream (page 348).

FILLING

½ cup (3½ ounces) sugar
1 tablespoon cornstarch
   Pinch ground cinnamon
   Pinch salt
30 ounces (6 cups) blueberries
1½ teaspoons grated lemon zest plus
   1 tablespoon juice

BISCUIT TOPPING

1 cup (5 ounces) all-purpose flour
¼ cup (1¾ ounces) plus 2 teaspoons sugar
2 tablespoons stone-ground cornmeal
2 teaspoons baking powder
¼ teaspoon baking soda
¼ teaspoon salt
⅓ cup buttermilk
4 tablespoons unsalted butter, melted
½ teaspoon vanilla extract
⅛ teaspoon ground cinnamon

1. FOR THE FILLING: Adjust oven rack to lower-middle position and heat oven to 375 degrees. Line rimmed baking sheet with aluminum foil. Whisk sugar, cornstarch, cinnamon, and salt together in large bowl. Add blueberries and mix gently until evenly coated; add lemon zest and juice and mix to combine. Transfer berry mixture to 9-inch pie plate, place plate on prepared baking sheet, and bake until filling is hot and bubbling around edges, about 25 minutes.

2. FOR THE BISCUIT TOPPING: Meanwhile, whisk flour, ¼ cup sugar, cornmeal, baking powder, baking soda, and salt together in large bowl. Whisk buttermilk, melted butter, and vanilla together in small bowl. Combine remaining 2 teaspoons sugar with cinnamon in second small bowl and set aside. One minute before blueberries come out of oven, add wet ingredients to dry; stir until just combined and no dry pockets remain.

3. Remove blueberries from oven; increase oven temperature to 425 degrees. Divide dough into 8 equal pieces and place them on hot filling, spacing them at least ½ inch apart (they should not touch). Sprinkle dough mounds evenly with cinnamon sugar. Bake until filling is bubbling and biscuits are golden brown on top and cooked through, 15 to 18 minutes, rotating pie plate halfway through baking. Transfer pie plate to wire rack and let cool 20 minutes; serve warm.

BLUEBERRY COBBLER WITH GINGERED BISCUITS

Add 3 tablespoons minced crystallized ginger to flour mixture and substitute ⅛ teaspoon ground ginger for cinnamon in sugar for sprinkling on biscuits.

ALL-SEASON BLUEBERRY COBBLER

Thaw 30 ounces frozen blueberries in colander set over bowl to catch juice. Transfer juice (you should have about 1 cup) to small saucepan; simmer over medium heat until syrupy and thick enough to coat back of spoon, about 10 minutes. Mix syrup with blueberries and other filling ingredients; increase baking time for filling to 30 minutes and increase baking time in step 3 to 20 to 22 minutes.

Peach Crumble

✓ WHY THIS RECIPE WORKS

A soggy topping and watery, flavorless filling are the norm for the simple, humble peach crumble. The problem is the peaches—you never know just how juicy or how flavorful they will be until you cut them open. We wanted a peach crumble that consisted of fresh-tasting, lightly sweetened peaches topped with a buttery, crisp, and nutty-tasting crumble—no matter how sweet the peaches were (or weren't).

MACERATE AND MEASURE Many peaches shed a ton of liquid when baked, causing a soggy crumble that's not nearly crisp enough on top. Our solution is to macerate the sliced peaches for 30 minutes. We then drain the juice and discard all but ¼ cup. We add a little thickener (cornstarch) to the reserved juice, along with the flavorings (lemon juice, salt, cinnamon, and nutmeg), and toss this with the macerated fruit. This way we know just how much juice will be in the baking dish.

MAKE A CRISP TOPPING For our crumble we use softened butter rather than melted butter. Melted butter makes a crumble topping that is too sandy. We prefer to make the topping in a food processor. This way, we end up with a cohesive dough, which can be easily broken apart into large chunks that bake up nice and crisp in the oven.

BAKE THE TOPPING FIRST For an exceptionally crisp topping, we bake the topping on a separate baking sheet until lightly browned. We then add the baked topping to the fruit and put the crumble in the oven. A sprinkling of sugar over the crumble topping adds a sweet crunch on top. This method ensures that as soon as the fruit is cooked, the topping will be browned and crisp.

PEACH CRUMBLE
SERVES 6

Add the lemon juice to taste in step 2 according to the sweetness of your peaches. If ripe peaches are unavailable, you can substitute 3 pounds of frozen peaches, thawed overnight in the refrigerator. If your peaches are firm, you should be able to peel them with a vegetable peeler. If they are too soft and ripe to withstand the pressure of a peeler, you'll need to blanch them in a pot of simmering water for 15 seconds and then shock them in a bowl of ice water before peeling. Serve with vanilla ice cream.

FILLING

3½	pounds peaches, peeled, halved, pitted, and cut into ¾-inch wedges
⅓	cup (2⅓ ounces) granulated sugar
1¼	teaspoons cornstarch
3–5	teaspoons lemon juice
	Pinch salt
	Pinch ground cinnamon
	Pinch ground nutmeg

CRUMBLE TOPPING

1	cup (5 ounces) all-purpose flour
5	tablespoons (2¼ ounces) granulated sugar
¼	cup packed (1¾ ounces) brown sugar
⅛	teaspoon salt
2	teaspoons vanilla extract
6	tablespoons unsalted butter, cut into 6 pieces and softened
½	cup sliced almonds

1. Adjust oven racks to lowest and middle positions and heat oven to 350 degrees. Line rimmed baking sheet with parchment paper.

TRANSFERRING BAKED CRUMBLE TOPPING

1. After crumble topping is baked, lift short sides of parchment paper. (Crumble will break apart into uneven ½- to ¾-inch pieces.)

2. Carefully slide broken crumble pieces onto peaches or apples, then spread into even layer with spatula.

Line second rimmed baking sheet with aluminum foil.

2. FOR THE FILLING: Gently toss peaches and sugar together in large bowl and let sit for 30 minutes, gently stirring several times. Drain peaches in colander set over large bowl and reserve ¼ cup juice (discard remaining juice). Whisk reserved juice, cornstarch, lemon juice to taste, salt, cinnamon, and nutmeg together in small bowl. Combine peaches and juice mixture in bowl and transfer to 8-inch square baking dish.

3. FOR THE CRUMBLE TOPPING: While peaches are macerating, combine flour, ¼ cup granulated sugar, brown sugar, and salt in food processor and drizzle vanilla over top. Pulse to combine, about 5 pulses. Scatter butter pieces and ¼ cup almonds over top and process until mixture clumps together into large, crumbly balls, about 30 seconds, scraping down bowl halfway through processing. Sprinkle remaining ¼ cup almonds over mixture and pulse 2 times to combine. Transfer mixture to parchment-lined baking sheet and spread into even layer (mixture should break up into roughly ½-inch chunks with some smaller, loose bits). Bake on middle rack until chunks are lightly browned and firm, 18 to 22 minutes, rotating baking sheet halfway through baking. (Cooled topping can be stored in airtight container for up to 2 days.)

4 Grasp edges of parchment paper, slide topping off paper over peaches, and spread into even layer with spatula, packing down lightly and breaking up any very large pieces. Sprinkle remaining 1 tablespoon sugar evenly over top and place dish on foil-lined baking sheet; place on lower rack. Increase oven temperature to 375 degrees and bake until well browned and filling is bubbling around edges, 25 to 35 minutes, rotating baking sheet halfway through baking. Transfer baking dish to wire rack and let cool for at least 15 minutes; serve warm.

APPLE CRUMBLE

In this variation, the apples do not need to macerate with the sugar. Serve with vanilla ice cream.

½	teaspoon cornstarch
4	teaspoons lemon juice
1½	pounds Granny Smith apples, peeled, cored, and cut into ½-inch cubes
1½	pounds Golden Delicious apples, peeled, cored, and cut into ½-inch cubes
⅔	cup (4⅔ ounces) sugar
	Pinch salt
	Pinch ground cinnamon
	Pinch ground nutmeg
1	recipe Crumble Topping (page 353)

1. Adjust oven racks to lowest and middle positions and heat oven to 350 degrees. Line rimmed baking sheet with parchment paper. Line second rimmed baking sheet with aluminum foil.

2. Stir cornstarch and lemon juice together in large bowl until cornstarch is dissolved. Add apples, sugar, salt, cinnamon, and nutmeg; toss to combine. Transfer mixture to 8-inch square glass dish. Cover tightly with aluminum foil; set aside.

3. Place topping mixture on middle rack in oven and apple filling mixture on lowest rack. Bake topping until chunks are lightly browned and firm, about 20 minutes. Remove topping and apples from oven.

4. Uncover apple filling and gently stir. Grasp edges of parchment paper, slide topping off paper over apples, and spread into even layer with spatula, packing down lightly and breaking up any very large pieces. Sprinkle remaining 1 tablespoon sugar evenly over top and place dish on foil-lined baking sheet; place on lower rack. Increase oven temperature to 375 degrees and bake until well browned and filling is bubbling around edges, about 25 minutes, rotating baking sheet halfway through baking. Transfer baking dish to wire rack and let cool for 15 minutes; serve warm.

Skillet Apple Pie

✓ WHY THIS RECIPE WORKS

Apple pandowdy harks back to Colonial-era New England—the dessert takes a more rustic approach to apple pie in that it features just one pastry crust, placed on top of a lightly sweetened apple filling. During or after baking, the pastry is broken and pushed into the filling—a technique known as "dowdying." We found the idea of an easier approach to apple pie very appealing—no fussy crimping and only one piece of pastry dough to roll out—so we set out to make our own version.

CARAMELIZE THE APPLES Parcooking the apples in a skillet until caramelized before adding the other ingredients helps to deepen their flavor.

ENRICH THE FILLING WITH CIDER AND MAPLE For a juicy apple filling with bright fruit flavor, we add cider to the apples and sweeten them with maple syrup, both of which make for a pleasantly saucy filling.

SCORE THE CRUST We cut a standard pie crust into squares after rolling it over the fruit right in the skillet—this encourages a multitude of crisp edges that contrast nicely with the tender fruit and recalls (in a less dowdy way) the broken-up crusts of a traditional pandowdy.

BAKE QUICKLY Our precooked apples need less time in the oven, so we transfer our skillet pie to a hot oven and bake for just 20 minutes—less than half the time of a traditional apple pie.

SKILLET APPLE PIE
SERVES 6 TO 8

If your skillet is not ovensafe, precook the apples and stir in the cider mixture as instructed, then transfer the apples to a 13 by 9-inch baking dish. Roll out the dough to a 13 by 9-inch rectangle and cut the crust and bake as instructed. If you do not have apple cider, reduced apple juice may be used as a substitute; simmer 1 cup apple juice in a small saucepan over medium heat until reduced to ½ cup, about 10 minutes. Serve warm or at room temperature with vanilla ice cream. Use a combination of sweet, crisp apples such as Golden Delicious and firm, tart apples such as Cortland or Empire.

CRUST

1	cup (5 ounces) all-purpose flour
1	tablespoon sugar
½	teaspoon salt
2	tablespoons vegetable shortening, chilled
6	tablespoons unsalted butter, cut into ¼-inch pieces and chilled
3–4	tablespoons ice water

FILLING

½	cup apple cider
⅓	cup maple syrup
2	tablespoons lemon juice
2	teaspoons cornstarch
⅛	teaspoon ground cinnamon (optional)
2	tablespoons unsalted butter
2½	pounds apples, peeled, cored, and cut into ½-inch-thick wedges
1	large egg white, lightly beaten
2	teaspoons sugar

1. FOR THE CRUST: Pulse flour, sugar, and salt in food processor until combined, about 4 pulses. Add shortening and pulse until mixture resembles coarse sand, about 10 pulses. Sprinkle butter pieces over top and pulse until mixture is pale yellow and resembles coarse crumbs, with butter bits no larger than small peas, about 10 pulses. Transfer mixture to medium bowl.

2. Sprinkle 3 tablespoons ice water over mixture. With rubber spatula, use folding motion to mix, pressing down on dough until dough is slightly tacky and sticks together, adding up to 1 tablespoon more ice water if dough does not come together. Flatten dough

SCORING SKILLET PIE CRUST

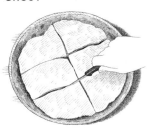

With a sharp knife, gently cut dough into 6 pieces by making 1 vertical cut followed by 2 evenly spaced horizontal cuts (perpendicular to the first cut). This encourages a crisp crust and allows the juice from the apples to bubble up and caramelize.

into 4-inch disk, wrap in plastic wrap, and refrigerate for at least 1 hour or up to 2 days. Let sit at room temperature for 15 minutes before rolling.

3. FOR THE FILLING: Adjust oven rack to upper-middle position and heat oven to 500 degrees. Whisk cider, maple syrup, lemon juice, cornstarch, and cinnamon, if using, together in bowl until smooth. Melt butter in 12-inch ovensafe skillet over medium-high heat. Add apples and cook, stirring 2 or 3 times, until apples begin to caramelize, about 5 minutes. (Do not fully cook apples.) Off heat, add cider mixture and gently stir until apples are well coated. Set aside to cool slightly.

4. Roll dough out on lightly floured counter to 11-inch round. Roll dough loosely around rolling pin and unroll over apple filling. Brush dough with egg white and sprinkle with sugar. With sharp knife, gently cut dough into 6 pieces by making 1 vertical cut followed by 2 evenly spaced horizontal cuts (perpendicular to first cut). Bake until apples are tender and crust is deep golden brown, about 20 minutes, rotating skillet halfway through baking. Let cool about 15 minutes; serve warm.

PREPPING APPLES AHEAD

Cutting damages the cells of apples, allowing enzymes and compounds stored separately within each cell to mix with one another and with the oxygen in the air, creating brown-colored pigments. To see if this brown color does anything more than mar the fresh look of the fruit, we compared an apple crisp made with just-cut fruit with crisp made with apples that we had cut and peeled (and refrigerated in zipper-lock bags) one and two days earlier. The brown apples and the fresh apples baked up equally tender and juicy and were similar in flavor, and—surprisingly—all had pretty much the same light golden color. It turns out that as the apples' cell walls rupture during baking, acids are released that partially break down the brown pigments, resulting in a lighter color. The bottom line: If you're going to cook apples, it's fine to prep them a day or two in advance.

Skillet Apple Crisp

✔ WHY THIS RECIPE WORKS

Most recipes for apple crisp yield unevenly cooked fruit and an unremarkable topping. We wanted an exemplary apple crisp—a lush (but not mushy) sweet-tart apple filling covered with truly crisp morsels of buttery, sugary topping.

SWITCH TO A SKILLET AND STIR Spread out in a baking dish in the oven, the apples tend to cook unevenly. Stirring the fruit helps solve the texture problem, but reaching into a hot oven to do so is a hassle. Instead, we soften the apples on the stovetop—in a skillet. The shallow, flared pan also encourages evaporation, browning, and better flavor overall.

SPIKE WITH CIDER To improve the flavor further, we turn to apple cider, first reducing it to a syrupy consistency. Lemon juice adds brightness and cinnamon, spicy warmth.

TOP WITH STREUSEL AND BAKE As for the topping, we supplement white sugar with brown sugar to play up the apples' caramel notes, and swap out some flour for rolled oats to give the topping character and chew.

Chopped pecans not only improve the crunch factor, but add rich flavor as well. After a few minutes in the oven, our crisp is just that.

SKILLET APPLE CRISP
SERVES 6 TO 8

If your skillet is not ovensafe, prepare the recipe through step 3 and then transfer the filling to a 13 by 9-inch baking dish; top the filling as directed and bake for an additional 5 minutes. We like Golden Delicious apples in this recipe, but Honeycrisp or Braeburn apples can be substituted; do not use Granny Smith apples. While old-fashioned rolled oats are preferable in this recipe, quick oats can be used. Serve with vanilla ice cream.

TOPPING
- ¾ cup (3¾ ounces) all-purpose flour
- ¾ cup pecans, chopped fine
- ¾ cup (2¼ ounces) old-fashioned rolled oats
- ½ cup packed (3½ ounces) light brown sugar

¼ cup (1 ¾ ounces) granulated sugar

½ teaspoon ground cinnamon

½ teaspoon salt

8 tablespoons unsalted butter, melted

FILLING

3 pounds Golden Delicious apples, peeled, cored, halved, and cut into ½-inch-thick wedges

¼ cup (1 ¾ ounces) granulated sugar

¼ teaspoon ground cinnamon (optional)

1 cup apple cider

2 teaspoons lemon juice

2 tablespoons unsalted butter

1. FOR THE TOPPING: Adjust oven rack to middle position and heat oven to 450 degrees. Line rimmed baking sheet with aluminum foil. Combine flour, pecans, oats, brown sugar, granulated sugar, cinnamon, and salt in bowl. Stir in butter until mixture is thoroughly moistened and crumbly. Set aside.

2. FOR THE FILLING: Toss apples, sugar, and cinnamon, if using, together in large bowl; set aside. Bring cider to simmer in 12-inch ovensafe skillet over medium heat; cook until reduced to ½ cup, about 5 minutes. Transfer reduced cider to bowl or liquid measuring cup; stir in lemon juice and set aside.

3. Melt butter in now-empty skillet over medium heat. Add apple mixture and cook, stirring frequently, until apples are beginning to soften and become translucent, 12 to 14 minutes. (Do not fully cook apples.) Off heat, gently stir in cider mixture until apples are coated.

4. Sprinkle topping evenly over fruit, breaking up any large chunks. Place skillet on

prepared baking sheet and bake until fruit is tender and topping is deep golden brown, 15 to 20 minutes, rotating baking sheet halfway through baking. Transfer to wire rack and let cool for 15 minutes; serve warm.

SKILLET APPLE CRISP WITH RASPBERRIES AND ALMONDS

Substitute slivered almonds for pecans. Add ⅛ teaspoon almond extract to reduced cider with lemon juice in step 2. Stir 5 ounces raspberries into apple mixture along with reduced cider in step 3.

SKILLET APPLE CRISP WITH VANILLA, CARDAMOM, AND PISTACHIOS

Substitute ½ cup shelled pistachios and ¼ cup walnuts for pecans. Substitute ½ teaspoon ground cardamom for cinnamon in filling and add seeds from 1 vanilla bean to apple, sugar, and cardamom mixture.

SKILLET APPLE CRISP WITH MAPLE AND BACON

Cook 6 slices bacon, cut into ¼-inch pieces, in 12-inch skillet over medium heat, stirring frequently, until crisp, 5 to 7 minutes. Using slotted spoon, transfer bacon to paper towel–lined plate. Pour off bacon fat from skillet and discard. (Do not wash skillet.) Stir bacon into topping mixture after adding butter. Omit sugar and cinnamon from filling. Toss apples with ⅓ cup maple syrup in step 2 and proceed as directed.

THREE STEPS TO GREAT APPLE CRISP

1. Reducing cider and adding it to filling concentrates fruity flavor, even when apples are out of season.

2. Sautéing sugared apples in butter contributes caramelized flavor and allows for stirring, so slices turn out evenly cooked.

3. Just 15 minutes at 450 degrees browns topping without overcooking apples and keeps topping from turning mushy.

Pear Crisp

✓ WHY THIS RECIPE WORKS

Simply substituting pears for apples in this classic American dessert is a recipe for disaster; pears exude so much moisture that a traditional crisp topping will sink into the filling and won't get crunchy. We wanted to create a classic crisp—one with tender fruit and a crunchy, sweet topping using pears.

BARTLETTS ARE BEST While pears and apples contain almost the same amount of moisture, they have cell walls of very different strengths. When heated, pear cell walls break down much faster, exuding a lot more juice and making baked pears mushy. We found that different pear types react differently from each other; the strongest are ripe yet firm Bartlett pears. Bosc pears are a close second.

THICKEN THE JUICE Even with Bartletts, juice is released. To compensate for this exuded liquid, we add a slurry of cornstarch mixed with lemon juice.

CREATE A CRUNCHY TOPPING A streusel-type topping, made by incorporating melted butter into the flour using a food processor, proves sturdy and keeps its crunch over the juicy fruit. Adding nuts to the topping provides additional flavor and crunch. And keeping the topping to a modest amount prevents it from sinking down into the fruit.

PEAR CRISP
SERVES 6

The test kitchen prefers a crisp made with Bartlett pears, but Bosc pears can also be used. The pears should be ripe but firm, which means the flesh at the base of the stem should give slightly when gently pressed with a finger. Bartlett pears will turn from green to greenish-yellow when ripe. Although almost any unsalted nut may be used in the topping, we prefer almonds or pecans. Serve with vanilla ice cream.

TOPPING
- ¾ cup nuts, chopped coarse
- ½ cup (2½ ounces) all-purpose flour
- ¼ cup packed (1¾ ounces) light brown sugar
- 2 tablespoons granulated sugar
- ¼ teaspoon ground cinnamon
- ⅛ teaspoon ground nutmeg
- ⅛ teaspoon salt
- 5 tablespoons unsalted butter, melted and cooled

FILLING
- 2 tablespoons granulated sugar
- 2 teaspoons lemon juice
- 1 teaspoon cornstarch
- Pinch salt
- 3 pounds pears, peeled, halved, cored, and cut into 1½-inch pieces

1. Adjust oven rack to lower-middle position and heat oven to 425 degrees. Line rimmed baking sheet with aluminum foil.

2. FOR THE TOPPING: Pulse nuts, flour, brown sugar, granulated sugar, cinnamon, nutmeg, and salt in food processor until nuts are finely chopped, about 9 pulses. Drizzle melted butter over flour mixture and pulse until mixture resembles crumbly wet sand, about 5 pulses, scraping down bowl halfway through. Set aside.

3. FOR THE FILLING: Whisk sugar, lemon juice, cornstarch, and salt together in large bowl. Gently toss pears with sugar mixture and transfer to 8-inch square baking dish.

4. Sprinkle topping evenly over fruit, breaking up any large chunks. Transfer baking dish to prepared baking sheet. Bake until fruit is bubbling around edges and topping is deep golden brown, about 30 minutes,

---

CORING AND CUTTING PEARS

For Pear Crisp, the pears are best peeled and halved, from stem to blossom end, then cored and cut into pieces.

1. Use melon baller to cut around central core of halved, peeled pear with circular motion; remove core.

2. Draw melon baller from central core to top of pear, removing interior stem. Remove blossom end.

3. Quarter each half lengthwise then cut each piece in half crosswise for 8 pieces.

rotating baking sheet halfway through baking. Transfer baking dish to wire rack and let cool until warm, about 15 minutes; serve.

PEAR CRISP WITH OAT TOPPING

Reduce nuts to ½ cup and increase butter to 6 tablespoons. After incorporating melted butter into flour mixture in step 2, add ½ cup old-fashioned rolled oats to food processor and process until evenly incorporated, about 3 pulses.

TRIPLE-GINGER PEAR CRISP

Use almonds for nuts and replace cinnamon and nutmeg with ¾ teaspoon ground ginger. Process 2 tablespoons coarsely chopped crystallized ginger with nuts and flour in step 2. Reduce lemon juice to 1 teaspoon and add 1 teaspoon grated fresh ginger to sugar-cornstarch mixture in step 3.

Blueberry Buckle

✔ WHY THIS RECIPE WORKS

The classic blueberry buckle can be regarded as a streusel-topped blueberry coffee cake, but that sells it short—the substance of blueberry buckle should be the blueberries. We wanted to keep the emphasis on the berries yet also keep the berry-to-cake ratio in balance so the moisture released from the fruit during baking wouldn't create a soggy cake.

INCREASE THE BLUEBERRIES We use an ample amount of blueberries—4 cups— to keep them as the headliner in our buckle. Fresh berries are preferred to frozen, as frozen will release too much moisture in the cake.

CREATE A STIFF BATTER To build a batter with more structure to support the blueberries, we ended up with a batter that was more like a cookie dough than the traditional cake batter. The batter is so stiff that it must be spread, rather than poured, into the cake pan.

We use all-purpose flour and add baking powder to supplement the natural leavening provided by creamed butter and sugar. Vanilla adds depth and lemon zest is a natural bright complement to the berries.

TOP WITH STREUSEL For the streusel, we like a combination of light brown and granulated sugars, softened butter, and cinnamon, which adds some warmth to the topping.

BLUEBERRY BUCKLE
SERVES 8

The batter will be extremely thick and heavy, and some effort will be required to spread it into the prepared pan. Be sure to use a cake pan with at least 2-inch-high sides. This buckle is best made with fresh blueberries, not frozen ones, which are too moist. Serve with Cream Cheese Whipped Cream (recipe follows) or vanilla ice cream.

STREUSEL
½ cup (2½ ounces) all-purpose flour
½ cup packed (3½ ounces) light brown sugar
2 tablespoons granulated sugar
¼ teaspoon ground cinnamon
   Pinch salt
4 tablespoons unsalted butter, cut into 8 pieces and softened

CAKE

1½	cups (7½ ounces) all-purpose flour
1½	teaspoons baking powder
10	tablespoons unsalted butter, softened
⅔	cup (4⅔ ounces) granulated sugar
½	teaspoon salt
½	teaspoon grated lemon zest
1½	teaspoons vanilla extract
2	large eggs, room temperature
20	ounces (4 cups) blueberries

1. FOR THE STREUSEL: Using stand mixer fitted with paddle, combine flour, brown sugar, granulated sugar, cinnamon, and salt on low speed until well combined and no large brown sugar lumps remain, about 45 seconds. Add butter; beat on low speed until mixture resembles wet sand and no large butter pieces remain, about 2½ minutes. Transfer to bowl; set aside.

2. FOR THE CAKE: Adjust oven rack to lower-middle position and heat oven to 350 degrees. Grease 9-inch round cake pan, line bottom with parchment paper, grease parchment, then flour pan.

3. Whisk flour and baking powder together in bowl; set aside. Using stand mixer fitted with paddle, beat butter, sugar, salt, and zest on medium-high speed until light and fluffy, about 3 minutes, scraping down bowl as necessary. Beat in vanilla until combined, about 30 seconds. With mixer on medium speed, add eggs one at a time; beat until partially incorporated, scrape down bowl, and continue to beat until fully incorporated (mixture will appear broken). With mixer on low speed, gradually add flour mixture; beat until flour is almost fully incorporated, about 20 seconds. Stir batter with rubber spatula, scraping down bowl, until no flour pockets remain and batter is homogeneous; batter will be very heavy and thick. Gently fold in blueberries until evenly distributed.

4. Transfer batter to prepared pan. Spread batter evenly to pan edges and smooth surface. Squeeze portion of streusel in your hand to form large cohesive clump; break up clump with your fingers and sprinkle streusel evenly over batter. Repeat with remaining streusel. Bake until cake is deep golden brown and toothpick inserted in center comes out clean, about 55 minutes, rotating pan halfway through baking. Transfer pan to wire rack and let cool, 15 to 20 minutes (cake will fall slightly as it cools).

5. Run thin knife around edges to loosen. Invert cake, then peel off and discard parchment. Invert cake onto serving platter. Let cool at least 1 hour. Cut into wedges and serve warm or at room temperature. (Buckle can be stored at room temperature, wrapped in plastic wrap, for up to 2 days.)

INDIVIDUAL BLUEBERRY BUCKLES

Line 12-cup muffin tin with paper or foil liners. In step 4, transfer batter to prepared tin; spread batter evenly to cup edges and smooth surface. (Batter will reach top of liners.) Reduce baking time to 35 minutes. Let buckles cool in pan on wire rack for 10 minutes. Remove from tin and let cool at least 30 minutes. Serve warm or at room temperature.

CREAM CHEESE WHIPPED CREAM
MAKES ABOUT 2 CUPS

4	ounces cream cheese
⅓	cup confectioners' sugar
	Pinch salt
½	teaspoon vanilla extract
1	cup heavy cream

Using stand mixer fitted with whisk, whip cream cheese, sugar, and salt at medium-high speed until light and fluffy, 1 to 2 minutes, scraping down bowl with rubber spatula as needed. Add vanilla and beat at medium speed until combined, about 30 seconds; scrape down bowl. With mixer running at low speed, add heavy cream in slow steady stream; when almost fully combined, increase speed to medium-high and beat until mixture holds soft peaks when whisk is lifted, another 1 to 2 minutes, scraping down bowl as needed.

MINIMIZING STAND MIXER MESS

When mixing dry ingredients that tend to puff out in a cloud or whipping wet ingredients that splatter, here's how to contain the mess: Drape a clean, damp dish towel over the front of the mixer and the bowl. Drawing the towel snug with one hand also helps.

Fresh Berry Gratin

BROILER-SAFE MINI GRATIN DISHES

We wanted broilerproof individual mini gratin dishes that would be shallow enough to ensure maximum surface area for a lightly browned, nicely crisp crust for a berry gratin. We tested four dishes and found that all produced evenly heated, well-browned gratin. However, one was flimsy and a few were ridiculously pricey. Our favorite, the **Le Creuset Petite Au Gratin Dish**, 6 ounces, heats evenly, offers a generous surface for good browning, and possesses protruding handles that are easy to grasp,

✔ WHY THIS RECIPE WORKS

Gratins can be very humble, where the topping is simply sweetened bread crumbs. Or they can be a bit more sophisticated, as when they are topped with the foamy Italian custard called zabaglione. Zabaglione is made with just three ingredients—egg yolks, sugar, and alcohol—but it requires constant watching so that the mixture doesn't overcook. It also needs to be whisked until it's the ideal thick, creamy texture. We were after a foolproof method for this topping for a gratin that could serve as an elegant finale to a summer meal.

MACERATE THE BERRIES We like a mix of fresh berries (raspberries, blueberries, blackberries, and strawberries), which we toss with sugar and salt to draw out their juice. Frozen berries will release too much moisture in this dessert.

TWEAK THE CUSTARD-MAKING TECHNIQUE For the zabaglione, which is essentially a custard, we make three small but significant tweaks so that it is foolproof. First, to ward off scrambled yolks, we turn down the heat slightly, keeping the water beneath the custard bowl to barely a simmer. Second, we use a thick, heatproof glass bowl instead of a metal bowl for even, gentle cooking, as metal conducts heat more quickly, making the custard more likely to overcook. Finally, to get the right texture, we don't stop whisking when soft peaks form; instead we wait until the custard becomes slightly thicker, similar to the texture of hollandaise sauce.

CHOOSE A DIFFERENT WINE Zabaglione is traditionally flavored with Marsala wine, but we found that it makes it overly sweet; crisp, dry Sauvignon Blanc provides a clean flavor that works better with the berries. To thicken the custard, we fold in whipped cream once it's cooled.

SPOON AND BAKE We spoon our zabaglione over the berries and sprinkle a mixture of brown and white sugars on top before broiling, for a crackly, caramelized crust.

INDIVIDUAL FRESH BERRY GRATINS WITH ZABAGLIONE

SERVES 4

When making the zabaglione, make sure to cook the egg mixture in a glass bowl over water that is barely simmering; glass conducts heat more evenly and gently than metal. If the heat is too high, the yolks around the edges of the bowl will start to scramble. Constant whisking is required. Do not use frozen berries for this recipe. You will need four shallow 6-inch gratin dishes, but a broiler-safe pie plate or large gratin dish can be used instead. To prevent scorching, pay close attention to the gratins when broiling.

BERRY MIXTURE

- 15 ounces (3 cups) mixed blackberries, blueberries, raspberries, and strawberries (strawberries hulled and halved lengthwise if small, quartered if large)
- 2 teaspoons granulated sugar
  Pinch salt

ZABAGLIONE

- 3 large egg yolks
- 3 tablespoons granulated sugar
- 3 tablespoons dry white wine, such as Sauvignon Blanc
- 2 teaspoons light brown sugar
- 3 tablespoons heavy cream, chilled

1. FOR THE BERRY MIXTURE: Line rimmed baking sheet with aluminum foil. Toss berries, sugar, and salt together in bowl. Divide berry mixture evenly among 4 shallow 6-ounce gratin dishes set on prepared baking sheet; set aside.

2. FOR THE ZABAGLIONE: Whisk egg yolks, 2 tablespoons plus 1 teaspoon granulated sugar, and wine together in medium bowl until sugar is dissolved, about 1 minute. Set bowl over saucepan of barely simmering water and cook, whisking constantly, until mixture is frothy. Continue to cook, whisking constantly, until mixture is slightly thickened, creamy, and glossy, 5 to 10 minutes (mixture will form loose mounds when dripped from whisk). Remove bowl from saucepan and whisk constantly for 30 seconds to cool slightly. Transfer bowl to refrigerator and chill until egg mixture is completely cool, about 10 minutes.

3. Meanwhile, adjust oven rack 6 inches from broiler element and heat broiler. Combine brown sugar and remaining 2 teaspoons granulated sugar in bowl.

4. Whisk heavy cream in large bowl until it holds soft peaks, 30 to 90 seconds. Using rubber spatula, gently fold whipped cream into cooled egg mixture. Spoon zabaglione over berries and sprinkle sugar mixture evenly on top; let stand at room temperature for 10 minutes, until sugar dissolves.

5. Broil gratins until sugar is bubbly and caramelized, 1 to 4 minutes. Serve immediately.

INDIVIDUAL FRESH BERRY GRATINS WITH HONEY-LAVENDER ZABAGLIONE

Heat 2 teaspoons dried lavender and ¼ cup dry white wine in small saucepan over medium heat until barely simmering; remove from heat and let stand for 10 minutes. Strain wine through fine-mesh strainer and discard lavender (you should have 3 tablespoons wine). Substitute lavender-infused wine for white wine and 2 teaspoons honey for 1 teaspoon granulated sugar in step 2.

INDIVIDUAL FRESH BERRY GRATINS WITH LEMON ZABAGLIONE

Replace 1 tablespoon wine with equal amount lemon juice and add 1 teaspoon grated lemon zest to egg yolk mixture in step 2.

Crêpes with Sugar and Lemon

✔ WHY THIS RECIPE WORKS

A crêpe is nothing but a thin pancake cooked quickly on each side and wrapped around a sweet or savory filling, but it has a reputation for being difficult. We wanted an easy method for crêpes that were thin and delicate yet rich and flavorfully browned in spots.

WHISK THE BATTER Using the perfect ratio of milk to flour and sugar gives us rich-tasting, lightly sweet pancakes. Mixing is easy as whisking together the dry and wet ingredients.

DON'T BUY A CRÊPE PAN There's no need to invest in a special crêpe pan; an oiled nonstick pan works just fine for this recipe.

PRACTICE MAKES PERFECT Use a dry measuring cup with a ¼-cup capacity to portion the batter. When you're ready to go, tilt the oiled and heated nonstick skillet slightly to the right and begin pouring in a scant ¼ cup of batter. Continue tilting the pan slowly, in a counterclockwise motion, until a thin, even crêpe is formed. Loosen the edge with a heat-resistant rubber spatula and, with your fingertips on the top side, grab the edge and flip. The first few may not come out perfectly (or even be usable at all). Here, practice really does make perfect.

IS THE PAN READY?

Here's a test to make sure that the pan is hot enough: Drop a teaspoon of batter into its center. If this mini crêpe is golden brown on the bottom after 20 seconds, the pan is ready. If it's blond—or burned—adjust the heat accordingly.

Most recipes for traditional American pancakes caution against overmixing the batter; doing so activates the formation of gluten and will render the results tough and dense. In theory, the same logic would apply to crêpes, but our mixing tests showed that all that worry was for naught. Why? It all comes down to the liquid-to-flour ratio. The high proportion of liquid in crêpe batter makes it so diluted that gluten development—that is, the network of proteins that give baked goods their chew—is not actually a factor. This also means that you can use anything from low-protein cake flour to high-protein bread flour and get a similarly tender crêpe.

PAIR WITH SIMPLE OR RICH FILLINGS
Fillings such as lemon and sugar, bananas and Nutella, honey and almonds, chocolate and orange, and dulce de leche and pecans turn our thin crêpes into a sweet treat.

CRÊPES WITH SUGAR AND LEMON
SERVES 4

Crêpes will give off steam as they cook, but if at any point the skillet begins to smoke, remove it from the heat immediately and turn down the heat. Stacking the crêpes on a wire rack allows excess steam to escape so they won't stick together. To allow for practice, the recipe yields 10 crêpes; only eight are needed for the filling.

½ teaspoon vegetable oil
1 cup (5 ounces) all-purpose flour
3 tablespoons sugar
¼ teaspoon salt
1½ cups whole milk
3 large eggs
2 tablespoons unsalted butter, melted and cooled
Lemon wedges

1. Heat oil in 12-inch nonstick skillet over low heat for at least 10 minutes.

2. While skillet is heating, whisk flour, 1 teaspoon sugar, and salt together in medium bowl. In separate bowl, whisk together milk and eggs. Add half of milk mixture to dry ingredients and whisk until smooth. Add melted butter and whisk until incorporated. Whisk in remaining milk mixture until smooth.

3. Wipe out skillet with paper towel, leaving thin film of oil on bottom and sides of pan. Increase heat to medium and let skillet heat for 1 minute. After 1 minute, test heat of skillet by placing 1 teaspoon batter in center and cook for 20 seconds. If mini crêpe is golden brown on bottom, skillet is properly heated; if it is too light or too dark, adjust heat accordingly and retest.

4. Pour ¼ cup batter into far side of pan and tilt and shake gently until batter evenly covers bottom of pan. Cook crêpe without moving until top surface is dry and edges are starting to brown, loosening crêpe from side of pan with heat-resistant rubber spatula, about 25 seconds. Gently slide spatula underneath edge of crêpe, grasp edge with your fingertips, and flip crêpe. Cook until second side is lightly spotted, about 20 seconds. Transfer cooked crêpe to wire rack, inverting so spotted side is facing up. Return pan to heat and heat for 10 seconds before repeating with remaining batter. As crêpes are done, stack on wire rack.

5. Transfer stack of crêpes to large plate and invert second plate over crêpes. Microwave until crêpes are warm, 30 to 45 seconds (45 to 60 seconds if crêpes have cooled completely). Remove top plate and wipe dry with paper towel. Sprinkle half of top crêpe with 1 teaspoon sugar. Fold unsugared bottom half over sugared half, then fold into quarters. Transfer sugared crêpe to second plate. Continue with remaining crêpes. Serve immediately, passing lemon wedges separately.

CRÊPES WITH DULCE DE LECHE AND TOASTED PECANS

Dulce de leche is a milk-based caramel sauce and spread. Look for it in the international foods aisle of supermarkets or in Latin markets.

Omit 8 teaspoons sprinkling sugar and lemon wedges. Drizzle 1 teaspoon dulce de leche over half of each crêpe and sprinkle with 2 teaspoons finely chopped toasted pecans and pinch salt. Fold crêpes into quarters. Serve immediately.

CRÊPES WITH CHOCOLATE AND ORANGE

Omit 8 teaspoons sprinkling sugar and lemon wedges. Using your fingertips, rub 1 teaspoon finely grated orange zest into ¼ cup sugar. Stir in 2 ounces finely grated bittersweet chocolate. Sprinkle 1½ tablespoons chocolate-orange mixture over half of each crêpe. Fold crêpes into quarters. Serve immediately.

CRÊPES WITH BANANAS AND NUTELLA

Omit 8 teaspoons sprinkling sugar and lemon wedges. Spread 2 teaspoons Nutella over half of each crêpe followed by eight to ten ¼-inch-thick banana slices. Fold crêpes into quarters. Serve immediately.

CRÊPES WITH HONEY AND TOASTED ALMONDS

Omit 8 teaspoons sprinkling sugar and lemon wedges. Drizzle 1 teaspoon honey over half of each crêpe and sprinkle with 2 teaspoons finely chopped toasted sliced almonds and pinch salt. Fold crêpes into quarters. Serve immediately.

Crêpes Suzette

✓ WHY THIS RECIPE WORKS

This classic recipe for crêpes flambéed with an orange-cognac sauce is certainly dramatic but the reality is often disappointing. The sauce can fail to ignite, which makes the dish too boozy. And even if the sauce does flambé, the crêpes are too soggy. Finally, we wanted a reliable recipe that we could make for a small crowd rather than an individual, as is the custom when this dish is made tableside in a restaurant.

BLEND AND GO To stand up to the classic sauce, these crêpes need to be sturdier than other crêpes. We maximize gluten development by simply throwing all the batter ingredients (eggs, milk, water, melted butter, flour, and sugar) into a blender. A splash of cognac and a dash of salt give our crêpes additional flavor.

FLAMBÉ FIRST For a foolproof flambé that doesn't create a frightening fireball or, conversely, doesn't burn at all, we ignite the alcohol (cognac) alone in the skillet before building the sauce. We then enrich a reduction of butter, sugar, and orange juice with additional orange juice, orange zest, and triple sec.

BROIL THE CRÊPES Before saucing, we sprinkle our crêpes with sugar and broil them, forming a crunchy, sugary barrier that provides partial protection from the sauce, so our crêpes don't turn soggy.

CRÊPES SUZETTE
SERVES 6

To allow for practice, the recipe yields about 16 crêpes; only 12 are needed for the dish. We prefer crêpes made with whole milk, but skim milk or 1 percent or 2 percent low-fat milk can also be used. Before flambéing, be sure to roll up long shirtsleeves, tie back long hair, and turn off the exhaust fan and any lit burners.

CRÊPES
- 1½ cups whole milk
- 1½ cups (7½ ounces) all-purpose flour
- 3 large eggs
- ½ cup water
- 5 tablespoons unsalted butter, melted, plus extra for pan
- 3 tablespoons sugar
- 2 tablespoons cognac
- ½ teaspoon salt

ORANGE SAUCE
- ¼ cup cognac
- 1 tablespoon finely grated orange zest plus 1¼ cups juice (3 oranges)
- 6 tablespoons unsalted butter, cut into 6 pieces
- ¼ cup sugar
- 2 tablespoons orange liqueur, such as triple sec

1. **FOR THE CRÊPES:** Process all ingredients in blender until smooth, about 10 seconds. Transfer to bowl.

2. Brush bottom and sides of 10-inch nonstick skillet lightly with melted butter and heat skillet over medium heat. Pour in scant ¼ cup batter in slow, steady stream, twirling skillet slowly until bottom is evenly covered. Cook crêpe until it starts to lose its opaqueness and turns spotty light golden brown on bottom, 30 seconds to 1 minute, loosening edge with heat-resistant rubber spatula. Gently slide spatula underneath edge of crêpe, grasp edge with your fingertips, and flip crêpe. Cook until dry on second side, about 20 seconds.

3. Transfer cooked crêpe to wire rack, inverting so spotted side is facing up. Return pan to heat, brush pan lightly with butter, and heat for 10 seconds before repeating with remaining batter. As crêpes are done, stack on wire rack. (Cooked crêpes can be refrigerated, wrapped in plastic wrap, for up to 3 days; bring them to room temperature before proceeding with recipe.)

4. **FOR THE ORANGE SAUCE:** Adjust oven rack to lower-middle position and heat broiler. Heat 3 tablespoons cognac in 12-inch broiler-safe skillet over medium heat just until warmed through, about 5 seconds. Off heat, wave lit match over pan until cognac ignites, then shake pan to distribute flames.

5. When flames subside, add 1 cup orange juice, butter, and 3 tablespoons sugar and simmer over high heat, stirring occasionally, until many large bubbles appear and mixture reduces to thick syrup, 6 to 8 minutes (you should have just over ½ cup sauce). Transfer sauce to small bowl; do not wash skillet. Stir remaining ¼ cup orange juice, orange zest, orange liqueur, and remaining 1 tablespoon cognac into sauce; cover to keep warm.

6. To assemble, fold each crêpe in half, then fold into quarters. Arrange 9 folded crêpes around edge of now-empty skillet, with rounded edges facing inward, overlapping as necessary to fit. Arrange remaining 3 crêpes in center of pan. Sprinkle crêpes evenly with remaining 1 tablespoon sugar. Broil until sugar caramelizes and crêpes turn spotty brown, about 5 minutes. (Watch crêpes constantly to prevent scorching; turn pan as necessary.) Carefully remove pan from oven and pour half of sauce over crêpes, leaving some areas uncovered. Transfer crêpes to individual plates and serve immediately, passing extra sauce separately.

TIPS TO FEARLESS FLAMBÉING

Flambéing is more than just tableside theatrics: As dramatic as it looks, igniting alcohol actually helps develop a deeper, more complex flavor in sauces, thanks to flavor-boosting chemical reactions that occur only at the high temperature reached in flambéing. But accomplishing this feat at home can be daunting. Here are some tips for successful—and safe—flambéing at home.

BE PREPARED: Turn off the exhaust fan, tie back long hair, and have a lid ready to smother dangerous flare-ups.

USE PROPER EQUIPMENT: A pan with flared sides (such as a skillet) rather than straight sides will allow more oxygen to mingle with the alcohol vapors, increasing the chance that you'll spark the desired flame. If possible, use long wooden chimney matches, and light the alcohol with your arm extended to full length.

IGNITE WARM ALCOHOL: If the alcohol becomes too hot, the vapors can rise to dangerous heights, causing large flare-ups once lit. Inversely, if the alcohol is too cold, there won't be enough vapors to light at all. We found that heating alcohol to 100 degrees Fahrenheit (best achieved by adding alcohol to a pan off the heat, then letting it heat for 5 to 10 seconds) produced the most moderate, yet long-burning flames.

LIGHT THE ALCOHOL OFF THE HEAT: If using a gas burner, be sure to turn off the flame to eliminate accidental ignitions near the side of the pan. Removing the pan from the heat also gives you more control over the alcohol's temperature.

IF A DANGEROUS FLARE-UP SHOULD OCCUR: Simply slide the lid over the top of the skillet (coming in from the side of, rather than over, the flames) to put out the fire quickly. Let the alcohol cool down and start again.

IF THE ALCOHOL WON'T LIGHT: If the pan is full of other ingredients, the potency of the alcohol can be diminished as it becomes incorporated. For a more foolproof flame, ignite the alcohol in a separate small skillet or saucepan; once the flame has burned off, add the reduced alcohol to the remaining ingredients.

Baked Apples

✔ WHY THIS RECIPE WORKS

This homey (and typically dowdy) dessert is often plagued with a mushy texture and one-dimensional, cloyingly sweet flavor. We wanted baked apples that were tender and firm with a filling that perfectly complemented their sweet, tart flavor.

GO GRANNY SMITH Granny Smith apples, with their firm flesh and tart, fruity flavor, are the best apples for the job.

LOSE THE PEEL To ensure that our fruit avoids even the occasional collapse, we peel the apples after cutting off the top; this allows steam to escape and the apples to retain their tender-firm texture.

AMP UP THE FLAVOR OF THE FILLING Our filling base of tangy dried cranberries, brown sugar, and pecans benefits from some finessing by way of cinnamon, orange zest, and butter. To punch up the flavor even more, we intensify the nuttiness with chewy rolled oats, and diced apple added substance. A melon baller helps us scoop out a spacious cavity for the filling. We then cap the filled apples with the tops we had lopped off.

BAKE AND BASTE Once they're in the oven, we baste the apples with an apple cider and maple syrup sauce, both of which add moisture and caramelized flavor.

BEST BAKED APPLES
SERVES 6

See page 9 for information on toasting nuts. If you don't have an ovensafe skillet, transfer the browned apples to a 13 by 9-inch baking dish and bake as directed. The recipe calls for seven apples; six are left whole and one is diced and added to the filling. Serve with vanilla ice cream, if desired.

7	large Granny Smith apples (8 ounces each)
6	tablespoons unsalted butter, softened
⅓	cup dried cranberries, chopped coarse
⅓	cup pecans, toasted and chopped coarse
¼	cup packed (1¾ ounces) brown sugar
3	tablespoons old-fashioned rolled oats
1	teaspoon finely grated orange zest
½	teaspoon ground cinnamon
	Pinch salt
⅓	cup maple syrup
⅓	cup plus 2 tablespoons apple cider

1. Adjust oven rack to middle position and heat oven to 375 degrees. Peel, core, and cut 1 apple into ¼-inch dice. Combine diced apple, 5 tablespoons butter, cranberries, pecans, sugar, oats, orange zest, cinnamon, and salt in bowl; set aside.

2. Shave thin slice off bottom (blossom end) of remaining 6 apples to allow them to sit flat. Cut top ½ inch off stem end of apples and reserve. Peel apples and use melon baller or small measuring spoon to remove 1½-inch-diameter core, being careful not to cut through bottom of apples.

3. Melt remaining 1 tablespoon butter in 12-inch ovensafe nonstick skillet over medium heat. Add apples, stem side down, and cook until cut surface is golden brown, about 3 minutes. Flip apples, reduce heat to low, and spoon filling inside, mounding excess filling over cavities; top with reserved apple caps. Add maple syrup and ⅓ cup cider to skillet. Transfer skillet to oven and bake until skewer inserted into apples meets little resistance, 35 to 40 minutes, basting every 10 minutes with maple syrup mixture in pan.

4. Transfer apples to serving platter. Stir up to 2 tablespoons of remaining cider into sauce in skillet to adjust consistency. Pour sauce over apples and serve.

KEY STEPS TO BETTER BAKED APPLES

1. Slicing off tops allows for generous room for filling and removing entire peel prevents blowouts and keeps flesh firm.

2. Sautéing apples in butter before baking contributes rich, caramelized flavor.

3. Capping apples with sliced-off tops shields filling from burning in oven.

CLASSIC PECAN PIE

CHAPTER 12

Pies and Tarts

When making pie pastry or any recipe requiring ice water, put ice cubes and water into a fat separator. You can then measure out the water you need through the spout, leaving the ice behind.

MAKE-AHEAD PIE DOUGH

To speed thawing and rolling, we use a 9-inch cake pan to create even rounds.

1. Line 9-inch cake pan with plastic wrap. Gently press pie dough into pan in even layer. Wrap dough in plastic and freeze until firm.

2. Once frozen, dough rounds can be removed from cake pan and stored in large zipper-lock bag until needed.

Classic Pie Dough

✔ WHY THIS RECIPE WORKS

Classic pie dough, sometimes called American pie dough, often contains vegetable shortening, which makes the dough easier to handle and yields a crust that is remarkably flaky. But vegetable shortening crusts can lack flavor. We set out to create a basic pie dough that combined the right fat and the right proportion of fat to flour to give us a supremely tender and flaky crust that was also incredibly flavorful.

ADD BUTTER When it comes to flavor, nothing beats butter. We experimented with a variety of combinations and ultimately settled on a proportion of 3 parts butter to 2 parts shortening as optimal for both flavor and texture. We also settled on a ratio of 2 parts flour to 1 part fat. We found that the 2:1 ratio produces dough that is easier to work with and a baked crust that is more tender and flavorful than any other.

MIX FAT AND FLOUR IN A FOOD PROCESSOR While this pie dough can be made by hand, the food processor is faster and easier and does the best job of cutting the fat into the flour.

FOLD IN THE WATER BY HAND You can mix the water into the dough in the food processor, but we found that it was too easy to overwork this fat-rich dough. Instead, we transfer the flour-butter mixture to a large bowl, sprinkle a portion of the water over the mixture, then fold it in by hand. The folding action exposes all of the dough to moisture without overworking it, thus minimizing the water used and reducing the likelihood that the dough will be overworked.

SHAPE THE DOUGH INTO A ROUND Many bakers struggle to roll dough into an even circle. The first mistake they make is not shaping the dough into a round disk before refrigerating it. Take a minute to shape the dough into a 4-inch disk and you will find it much easier to roll it out into a 12-inch circle.

CHILL THE DOUGH AND FLOUR THE COUNTER To prevent the dough from sticking to the counter (and to keep the butter from melting), it's best to chill the dough.

CLASSIC DOUBLE-CRUST PIE DOUGH
MAKES ENOUGH FOR ONE 9-INCH PIE

If you don't have a food processor, see "Hand-Mixing Pie Dough," on page 374.

2½	cups (12½ ounces) all-purpose flour
2	tablespoons sugar
1	teaspoon salt
8	tablespoons vegetable shortening, cut into ½-inch pieces and chilled
12	tablespoons unsalted butter, cut into ¼-inch pieces and chilled
6–8	tablespoons ice water

1. Process flour, sugar, and salt in food processor until combined, about 5 seconds. Scatter shortening over top and process until mixture resembles coarse cornmeal, about 10 seconds. Scatter butter over top and pulse until mixture resembles coarse crumbs, about 10 pulses.

2. Transfer mixture to large bowl. Sprinkle 6 tablespoons ice water over mixture. Stir and press dough together, using stiff rubber spatula, until dough sticks together. If dough does not come together, stir in remaining ice water, 1 tablespoon at a time, until it does.

3. Divide dough into 2 even pieces. Turn each piece of dough onto sheet of plastic wrap and flatten each into 4-inch disk. Wrap each piece tightly in plastic and refrigerate for 1 hour. Before rolling out dough, let it sit on counter to soften slightly, about 10 minutes. (Dough can be wrapped tightly in plastic and refrigerated for up to 2 days or frozen for up to 1 month. If frozen, let dough thaw completely on counter before rolling it out.)

CLASSIC SINGLE-CRUST PIE DOUGH

MAKES ENOUGH FOR ONE 9-INCH PIE

If you don't have a food processor, see "Hand-Mixing Pie Dough," page 374. For more information on rolling and fitting pie dough, see page 380.

1¼	cups (6¼ ounces) all-purpose flour
1	tablespoon sugar
½	teaspoon salt
4	tablespoons vegetable shortening, cut into ½-inch pieces and chilled
6	tablespoons unsalted butter, cut into ¼-inch pieces and chilled
3–4	tablespoons ice water

1. Process flour, sugar, and salt in food processor until combined, about 5 seconds. Scatter shortening over top and process until mixture resembles coarse cornmeal, about 10 seconds. Scatter butter over top and pulse until mixture resembles coarse crumbs, about 10 pulses.

2. Transfer mixture to medium bowl. Sprinkle 3 tablespoons ice water over mixture. Stir and press dough together, using stiff rubber spatula, until dough sticks together. If dough does not come together, stir in remaining ice water, 1 teaspoon at a time, until it does.

3. Turn dough onto sheet of plastic wrap and flatten into 4-inch disk. Wrap tightly in plastic and refrigerate for 1 hour. Before rolling out dough, let it sit on counter to soften slightly, about 10 minutes. (Dough can be wrapped tightly in plastic and refrigerated for up to 2 days or frozen for up to 1 month. If frozen, let dough thaw completely on counter before rolling it out.)

4. Adjust oven rack to middle position and heat oven to 375 degrees. Roll dough into 12-inch circle on lightly floured counter. Loosely roll dough around rolling pin and gently unroll it onto 9-inch pie plate, letting excess dough hang over edge. Ease dough into plate by gently lifting edge of dough with your hand while pressing into plate bottom with your other hand. Leave any dough that over-hangs plate in place.

5. Trim overhang to ½ inch beyond lip of pie plate. Tuck overhang under itself; folded edge should be flush with edge of pie plate. Crimp dough evenly around edge of pie plate using your fingers. Wrap dough-lined pie plate loosely in plastic and place in freezer until dough is fully chilled and firm, about 30 minutes, before using.

6. Line chilled pie shell with parchment paper or double layer of aluminum foil, covering edges to prevent burning, and fill with pie weights.

7A. FOR A PARTIALLY BAKED CRUST: Bake until pie dough looks dry and is light in color, 25 to 30 minutes. Transfer pie plate to wire rack and remove weights and parchment. (Crust must still be warm when filling is added.)

7B. FOR A FULLY BAKED CRUST: Bake until pie dough looks dry and is light in color, 25 to 30 minutes. Remove weights and parchment and continue to bake crust until deep golden brown, 10 to 12 minutes longer. Transfer pie plate to wire rack and let crust cool completely, about 1 hour.

CLASSIC SINGLE-CRUST PIE DOUGH FOR CUSTARD PIES

We like rolling our single-crust dough in fresh graham cracker crumbs because they add flavor and crisp textural appeal to our custard pies.

Crush 3 whole graham crackers to fine crumbs. (You should have about ½ cup crumbs.) In step 4, dust counter with graham cracker crumbs instead of flour. Continue sprinkling dough with crumbs, both underneath and on top, as it is being rolled out.

SIMPLIFIED SHORTENING MEASURING

It can be difficult to measure vegetable shortening that is sold in a tub (rather than sticks) accurately using a conventional measuring cup. An adjustable measuring cup (page 196) is ideal, but if you don't have one, try this method, which measures shortening by displacement.

1. For shortening amounts less than 1 cup, fill 2-cup liquid measuring cup with 1 cup cold water.

2. Spoon shortening into cold water.

3. Add or remove shortening until water level equals desired amount plus 1 cup (e.g., for ¼ cup shortening, water level should be at 1¼ cups).

While a food processor
makes quick work of mixing
pie dough, our all-butter pie
doughs and classic pie doughs
(pages 372–376) can be
mixed by hand. Here's how.

Freeze butter in its stick
form until very firm. Whisk
flour, sugar, and salt together
in a large bowl. Add chilled
shortening, if using, and press
it into the flour using a fork.
Grate the frozen butter on
the large holes of a box grater
into the flour mixture, then
cut the mixture together, using
two butter or dinner knives,
until the mixture resembles
coarse crumbs. Add liquid
as directed, stirring with a
rubber spatula.

All-Butter Pie Dough

✓ WHY THIS RECIPE WORKS

All-butter pie doughs possess great flavor, but they often fail to be flaky and are notoriously difficult to work with. We wanted an all-butter dough that was easier to mix, handle, and roll, producing a pie crust with all the tenderness and flavor that the description "all-butter" promises.

CHILL THE BUTTER If the butter is too warm, it will melt during mixing, cause sticking, and bake into a tough, not flaky, crust. To ensure our butter is at the right temperature for mixing, we cut the butter straight from the refrigerator into ¼-inch pieces and freeze the cut pieces for 10 minutes.

ADD MORE FAT To make the dough easier to handle, we tried reducing the amount of butter, but this resulted in bland flavor and dry texture. Instead, we experimented with other forms of fat, including heavy cream, cream cheese, and sour cream. In the end, we found that sour cream not only adds flavor to our crust but, because acid reduces gluten development, it also helps keep the dough tender and flaky. To distribute the sour cream evenly, mix it first with the water.

MIX IN A FOOD PROCESSOR A food processor brings the ingredients together quickly and evenly, which is particularly important because the butter must be cut into coarse crumbs about the size of peas. These pea-size pieces promote the formation of flaky layers.

ADD ICE WATER—AND TEST THE DOUGH We sprinkle water (mixed with the sour cream) in two stages over the flour-butter mixture. You may need to add more water, depending on your brand of flour. (Our tests have shown that, when it comes to water absorption, flour brand matters more than the weather; see "Humidity and Flour," page 375.) After you have pulsed in the water mixture, stop the food processor and pinch the dough with your fingertips. If the dough is at all floury or dry, pour more water over the dough and pulse again.

SHAPE THE DOUGH INTO A ROUND Many bakers struggle to roll dough into an even circle. The first mistake they make is not shaping the dough into a round disk before refrigerating it. Take a minute to shape the dough into a 4-inch disk and you will find it much easier to roll it out into a 12-inch circle.

CHILL THE DOUGH, FLOUR THE COUNTER To prevent the dough from sticking to the counter (and to keep the butter from melting), it's best to chill the dough for an hour before attempting to roll it out. Chilling and resting also serve to hydrate the dough. If you don't rest the dough before rolling, the moisture won't be evenly distributed throughout the dough and you'll have wet and dry pockets throughout. If you choose to refrigerate the dough for longer (it can keep in the fridge for two days or be frozen for up to one month and then defrosted on the counter) it will be too cold. Let it warm up on the counter for 10 minutes before rolling it out.

ALL-BUTTER DOUBLE-CRUST PIE DOUGH

MAKES ENOUGH FOR ONE 9-INCH PIE

Freezing the butter for 10 to 15 minutes is crucial to the flaky texture of this crust—do not skip this step. If preparing the dough in a very warm kitchen, refrigerate all of the ingredients (including the flour) before making the dough.

⅓ cup ice water, plus extra as needed
3 tablespoons sour cream
2½ cups (12½ ounces) all-purpose flour
1 tablespoon sugar
1 teaspoon salt
16 tablespoons unsalted butter, cut into ¼-inch pieces and frozen for 10 to 15 minutes

1. Mix together ice water and sour cream in bowl. Process flour, sugar, and salt in food processor until combined, about 5 seconds. Scatter butter over top and pulse mixture until butter is size of large peas, about 10 pulses.

2. Pour half of sour cream mixture over flour mixture and pulse until incorporated, about 3 pulses. Repeat with remaining sour cream mixture. Pinch dough with your fingers; if dough feels dry and does not hold together, sprinkle 1 to 2 tablespoons more ice water over mixture and pulse until dough forms large clumps and no dry flour remains, 3 to 5 pulses.

3. Divide dough into 2 even pieces. Turn each piece of dough onto sheet of plastic wrap and flatten each into 4-inch disk. Wrap each piece tightly in plastic and refrigerate for 1 hour. Before rolling dough out, let it sit on counter to soften slightly, about 10 minutes. (Dough can be wrapped tightly in plastic and refrigerated for up to 2 days or frozen for up to 1 month. If frozen, let dough thaw completely on counter before rolling it out.)

ALL-BUTTER SINGLE-CRUST PIE DOUGH

MAKES ENOUGH FOR ONE 9-INCH PIE

Freezing the butter for 10 to 15 minutes is crucial to the flaky texture of this crust—do not skip this step. If preparing the dough in a very warm kitchen, refrigerate all of the ingredients (including the flour) before making the dough. If you don't have a food processor, see "Hand-Mixing Pie Dough," on page 374. For more information on rolling and fitting pie dough, see page 380.

4	teaspoons sour cream
3–4	tablespoons ice water
1¼	cups (6¼ ounces) all-purpose flour
1½	teaspoons sugar
½	teaspoon salt
8	tablespoons unsalted butter, cut into ¼-inch pieces and frozen for 10 to 15 minutes

1. Mix together sour cream and 3 tablespoons ice water in bowl. Process flour, sugar, and salt in food processor until combined, about 5 seconds. Scatter butter over top and pulse mixture until butter is size of large peas, about 10 pulses.

2. Pour half of sour cream mixture over flour mixture and pulse until incorporated, about 3 pulses. Repeat with remaining sour cream mixture. Pinch dough with your fingers; if dough feels dry and does not hold together, sprinkle remaining 1 tablespoon ice water over mixture and pulse until dough forms large clumps and no dry flour remains, 3 to 5 pulses.

3. Turn dough onto sheet of plastic wrap and flatten into 4-inch disk. Wrap tightly in plastic and refrigerate for 1 hour. Before rolling dough out, let it sit on counter to soften slightly, about 10 minutes. (Dough can be wrapped tightly in plastic and refrigerated for up to 2 days or frozen for up to 1 month. If frozen, let dough thaw completely on counter before rolling it out.)

4. Adjust oven rack to middle position and heat oven to 375 degrees. Roll dough into 12-inch circle on lightly floured counter. Loosely roll dough around rolling pin and gently unroll it onto 9-inch pie plate, letting excess dough hang over edge. Ease dough into plate by gently lifting edge of dough with your hand while pressing into plate bottom with your other hand. Leave any dough that overhangs plate in place.

5. Trim overhang to ½ inch beyond lip of pie plate. Tuck overhang under itself; folded edge should be flush with edge of pie plate. Crimp dough evenly around edge of pie plate using your fingers. Wrap dough-lined pie plate loosely in plastic and place in freezer until dough is fully chilled and firm, about 30 minutes, before using.

6. Line chilled pie shell with parchment paper or double layer of aluminum foil, covering edges to prevent burning, and fill with pie weights.

7A. FOR A PARTIALLY BAKED CRUST: Bake until pie dough looks dry and is light in color, 25 to 30 minutes. Transfer pie plate to wire rack and remove weights and parchment. (Crust must still be warm when filling is added.)

7B. FOR A FULLY BAKED CRUST: Bake until pie dough looks dry and is light in color, 25 to 30 minutes. Remove weights and foil and continue to bake crust until deep golden brown, 10 to 12 minutes longer. Transfer pie plate to wire rack and let crust cool completely, about 1 hour.

Pie and tart recipes with loose, liquid-y fillings (like quiche or pumpkin pie) often call for "blind" baking, or prebaking, the bottom crust empty to ensure that it turns out crisp and fully cooked. To prevent the pastry from puffing up as it bakes, pie weights are placed inside the shell when it first goes into the oven. Once the dough has begun to firm, the weights are removed to allow the shell to brown completely.

To easily remove the weights, recipes variously call for lining the shell with waxed paper, foil, or parchment paper. When we checked with Reynolds, one of the biggest manufacturers of waxed paper, they said it should never be directly exposed to the heat of the oven, so that left us with just foil and parchment paper to test. We blind-baked batches of our Foolproof Single-Crust Pie Dough (page 377) with each one. The high conductivity of aluminum foil helped to efficiently transmit the oven's heat to the shell as it baked, but it also trapped steam on its underside and resulted in slightly spotty browning. Parchment paper fared best; its more permeable structure allowed the shell to breathe—and then brown—as it baked. It's our go-to choice for blind baking, with foil as a backup.

ALL-BUTTER SINGLE-CRUST PIE DOUGH
FOR CUSTARD PIES

We like rolling our single-crust dough in fresh graham cracker crumbs because they add flavor and crisp textural appeal to our custard pies.

Crush 3 whole graham crackers to fine crumbs. (You should have about ½ cup crumbs.) In step 4, dust counter with graham cracker crumbs instead of flour. Continue sprinkling dough with crumbs, both underneath and on top, as it is being rolled out.

Foolproof Pie Dough

✔ WHY THIS RECIPE WORKS
We wanted a recipe for pie dough that would roll out like a dream and produce a tender, flaky crust. In short, we wanted a pie dough that even the most novice baker could pull off their very first time.

USE TWO FATS Butter contributes rich taste—but also water, which encourages gluten development. For a crust that's both flavorful and tender, we use a 3:2 ratio of butter to shortening, a pure fat with no water.

CREATE FLAKY LAYERS Traditional recipes process all the flour and fat at once, but we add the flour in two batches. We first process the fat with part of the flour for a good 15 seconds to thoroughly coat it, we then give the mixture just a few quick pulses once the remaining flour is added, so less of it gets coated. Besides providing protection against toughness, this approach aids in flakiness by creating two distinct layers of dough—one with gluten and one without.

AUGMENT WATER WITH VODKA Yes, vodka. While gluten (the protein that makes crust tough) forms readily in water, it doesn't form in ethanol, and vodka is 60 percent water and 40 percent ethanol. Adding ¼ cup of vodka (along with ¼ cup ice water) produces a moist, easy-to-roll dough that stays tender. (The alcohol vaporizes in the oven, so you won't taste it in the baked crust.)

SHAPE THE DOUGH INTO A ROUND Many bakers struggle to roll dough into an even circle. The first mistake they make is not shaping the dough into a round disk before refrigerating it. Take a minute to shape the dough into a 4-inch disk and you will find it much easier to roll it out into a 12-inch circle.

CHILL AND ROLL ON A WELL-FLOURED COUNTER To prevent the dough from sticking to the counter (and to keep the butter from melting), it's best to chill the dough for an hour before attempting to roll it out. Chilling and resting also serve to hydrate the dough. If you don't rest the dough before rolling, the moisture won't be evenly distributed throughout the dough and you'll have wet and dry pockets throughout. If you choose to refrigerate the dough for longer (it can keep in the fridge for two days or be frozen for up to one month and then defrosted on the counter) it will be too cold. Let it warm up on the counter for 10 minutes before rolling it out. Because this dough is moister than traditional doughs, it's critical to use enough flour for rolling to prevent the dough from sticking. We use up to ¼ cup of flour.

FOOLPROOF DOUBLE-CRUST PIE DOUGH

MAKES ENOUGH FOR ONE 9-INCH PIE

Vodka is essential to the tender texture of this crust and imparts no flavor—do not substitute water. This dough is moister than most standard pie doughs and will require lots of flour to roll out (up to ¼ cup). A food processor is essential for making this dough—it cannot be made by hand.

2½ cups (12½ ounces) all-purpose flour
2   tablespoons sugar
1   teaspoon salt
12   tablespoons unsalted butter, cut into ¼-inch pieces and chilled
8   tablespoons vegetable shortening, cut into 4 pieces and chilled
¼   cup vodka, chilled
¼   cup ice water

1. Process 1½ cups flour, sugar, and salt in food processor until combined, about 5 seconds. Scatter butter and shortening over top and continue to process until incorporated and mixture begins to form uneven clumps with no remaining floury bits, about 15 seconds.

2. Scrape down bowl and redistribute dough evenly around processor blade. Sprinkle remaining 1 cup flour over dough and pulse until mixture has broken up into pieces and is evenly distributed around bowl, 4 to 6 pulses.

3. Transfer mixture to large bowl. Sprinkle vodka and ice water over mixture. Stir and press dough together, using stiff rubber spatula, until dough sticks together.

4. Divide dough into 2 even pieces. Turn each piece of dough onto sheet of plastic wrap and flatten each into 4-inch disk. Wrap each piece tightly in plastic and refrigerate for 1 hour. Before rolling out dough, let it sit on counter to soften slightly, about 10 minutes. (Dough can be wrapped tightly in plastic and refrigerated for up to 2 days or frozen for up to 1 month. If frozen, let dough thaw completely on counter before rolling it out.)

FOOLPROOF SINGLE-CRUST PIE DOUGH

MAKES ENOUGH FOR ONE 9-INCH PIE

Vodka is essential to the tender texture of this crust and imparts no flavor—do not substitute water. This dough is moister than most standard pie doughs and will require lots of flour to roll out (up to ¼ cup). A food processor is essential for making this dough—it cannot be made by hand. For more information on rolling and fitting pie dough, see page 380.

1¼ cups (6¼ ounces) all-purpose flour
1   tablespoon sugar
½   teaspoon salt
6   tablespoons unsalted butter, cut into ¼-inch pieces and chilled
4   tablespoons vegetable shortening, cut into 2 pieces and chilled
2   tablespoons vodka, chilled
2   tablespoons ice water

1. Process ¾ cup flour, sugar, and salt in food processor until combined, about 5 seconds. Scatter butter and shortening over top and continue to process until incorporated and mixture begins to form uneven clumps with no remaining floury bits, about 10 seconds.

2. Scrape down bowl and redistribute dough evenly around processor blade. Sprinkle remaining ½ cup flour over dough and pulse until mixture has broken up into pieces and is evenly distributed around bowl, 4 to 6 pulses.

3. Transfer mixture to medium bowl. Sprinkle vodka and ice water over mixture. Stir and press dough together, using stiff rubber spatula, until dough sticks together.

4. Turn dough onto sheet of plastic wrap and flatten into 4-inch disk. Wrap tightly in plastic and refrigerate for 1 hour. Before rolling out dough, let it sit on counter to soften slightly, about 10 minutes. (Dough can be wrapped tightly in plastic and refrigerated for up to 2 days or frozen for up to 1 month. If frozen, let dough thaw completely on counter before rolling it out.)

5. Adjust oven rack to middle position and heat oven to 425 degrees. Roll dough into

DOES THE ALCOHOL IN OUR PIE DOUGH EVAPORATE?

Because alcohol binds with water during cooking, trace amounts will remain in food as long as there's still moisture. This includes our foolproof pie dough, which we partially moisten with vodka since alcohol—unlike water—does not contribute to gluten development, so you can use more liquid, which in turn leads to a tender, easy-to-roll dough. When we sent a filled double-crust pie made with the dough to a lab for analysis, it found that 5 percent of the vodka's alcohol (or about ¼ teaspoon) remained—far too little for any of its flavor to be detected. In a single crust that was "blind-baked" without filling, the trace amount of alcohol left was too tiny to be measured.

In sum, the alcohol that remains in our foolproof pie dough after baking is minuscule, even if it's baked with a filling, which gets in the way of alcohol vaporizing.

PROTECTING THE RIM

The fluted edge on a pie can burn in the oven because it's so exposed. Many recipes suggest piecing together strips of aluminum foil to fashion a protective cover for the edge. Instead of trying to twist pieces of foil together, we prefer to use a single sheet to cover the pie edge.

1. Lay out square of aluminum foil slightly larger than pie. Fold square in half to form rectangle. Cut arc that is roughly half the size of pie.

2. When you unfold foil, you will have cut out a circle from middle of sheet. This open circle exposes filling, while surrounding foil covers crust.

12-inch circle on floured counter. Loosely roll dough around rolling pin and gently unroll it onto 9-inch pie plate, letting excess dough hang over edge. Ease dough into plate by gently lifting edge of dough with your hand while pressing into plate bottom with your other hand. Leave any dough that overhangs plate in place. Wrap dough-lined pie plate loosely in plastic and refrigerate until dough is firm, about 30 minutes.

6. Trim overhang to ½ inch beyond lip of pie plate. Tuck overhang under itself; folded edge should be flush with edge of pie plate. Crimp dough evenly around edge of pie plate using your fingers. Wrap dough-lined pie plate loosely in plastic and refrigerate until dough is fully chilled and firm, about 15 minutes, before using.

7. Line chilled pie shell with parchment paper or double layer of aluminum foil, covering edges to prevent burning, and fill with pie weights.

8A. FOR A PARTIALLY BAKED CRUST: Bake until pie dough looks dry and is pale in color, about 15 minutes. Remove weights and parchment and continue to bake crust until light golden brown, 4 to 7 minutes longer. Transfer pie plate to wire rack. (Crust must still be warm when filling is added.)

8B. FOR A FULLY BAKED CRUST: Bake until pie dough looks dry and is pale in color, about 15 minutes. Remove weights and foil and continue to bake crust until deep golden brown, 8 to 12 minutes longer. Transfer pie plate to wire rack and let crust cool completely, about 1 hour.

FOOLPROOF SINGLE-CRUST PIE DOUGH FOR CUSTARD PIES

We like rolling our single-crust dough in fresh graham cracker crumbs because they add flavor and crisp textural appeal to our custard pies.

Crush 3 whole graham crackers to fine crumbs. (You should have about ½ cup crumbs.) Dust counter with graham cracker crumbs instead of flour. Continue sprinkling dough with crumbs, both underneath and on top, as it is being rolled out.

Deep-Dish Apple Pie

✔ WHY THIS RECIPE WORKS

The problem with deep-dish apple pie is that the apples are often unevenly cooked and the exuded juices leave the apples swimming in liquid, producing a bottom crust that is pale and soggy. Then there is the gaping hole left between the shrunken apples and the top crust, making it impossible to slice and serve a neat piece of pie. We wanted our piece of deep-dish pie to be a towering wedge of tender, juicy apples, fully framed by a buttery, flaky crust.

PRECOOK THE APPLES For a deep-dish pie you need a lot of apples. But all those apples make the crust soggy and the filling soupy. And when the apples cook down you're left with a top crust that sits far above the filling. Precooking the apples solves all of these problems—and precooked apples require no thickener, which can dull their flavor.

COOK GENTLY Though it's tempting to cook the apples over high heat in order to quickly drive off their liquid, it's not the right choice. Precooked at high heat, the apples in the pie end up mealy and soft. Cooking apples slowly over gentle heat gets rid of excess moisture and actually strengthens the internal structure of the apples, making them better able to hold their shape when baked.

USE TWO APPLES, TWO SUGARS, AND SPICE We like tart apples, like Granny Smith

Pie Dough 101

Despite its "difficult" reputation, perfect pie dough is a whole lot easier than most bakers think. To minimize handling of the dough, which can make a tough crust, follow our recommendations for rolling and fitting perfect pie crust.

THE RIGHT WAY TO ROLL OUT

Two key pointers to keep in mind when rolling dough: First, always work with well-chilled pastry; otherwise, the dough will stick to the counter and tear. Second, never roll out dough by rolling back and forth over the same section; each time you press on the same spot, more gluten develops that can toughen the dough.

1. Place chilled dough on floured counter and sprinkle lightly with flour. Place rolling pin in center of dough with ends at 9 o'clock and 3 o'clock and roll dough outward from center to edge, applying even, gentle pressure.

2. Using dough scraper, lift and turn dough 90 degrees. Roll outward again from center, making sure to keep hands at 9 and 3 positions. Lightly flour underneath dough as necessary to prevent sticking.

3. Repeat rolling and turning steps (keeping hands at 9 and 3) until dough is wide enough to overhang pie plate by 2 inches.

4. Place rolling pin about 2 inches from top of dough round. Flip top edge of round over rolling pin and turn once to loosely roll around pin. Gently unroll dough over pie plate.

FITTING THE DOUGH AND FINISHING A SINGLE CRUST PIE

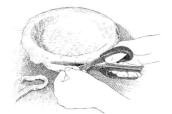

1. Lift dough around edges and gently press into corners of plate, letting excess dough hang over edge.

2. Trim dough, leaving ½-inch overhang.

3. Roll trimmed overhang under so that it is even with lip of pan.

4. Use your thumb and index fingers to create fluted ridges perpendicular to edge of pie plate.

ASSEMBLING A DOUBLE-CRUST PIE

1. Unroll untrimmed top piece of dough over filled pie, taking care not to stretch it and create thin spots.

2. Trim overhanging edges of both crusts to about ½ inch.

3. Press edges of top and bottom crusts together firmly to prevent leaking, then fold edges underneath to make flush with lip of pan.

4. Use knife to make four 2-inch slits in top crust to vent pie. (The number and size of slits may depend on the pie.)

and Empire, because of their brash flavor, but used alone their flavor can seem one-dimensional. To achieve a fuller, more balanced flavor, we find it necessary to add a sweeter variety, such as Golden Delicious or Braeburn. Another important factor in choosing the right apple is the texture. Even over the gentle heat of the stovetop, softer varieties such as McIntosh break down readily and turn to mush. We add some light brown sugar along with the granulated sugar to heighten the flavor, as well as a pinch of salt and a squeeze of lemon juice (added after stovetop cooking to retain its flavor). We're also content with just a hint of cinnamon.

START IN A HOT OVEN We begin baking our pie in a hot oven (425 degrees), on a baking sheet set on the lowest rack, in order to help brown up the bottom crust and keep it from becoming soggy. We then turn the temperature down to 375 degrees to finish it off.

DEEP-DISH APPLE PIE
SERVES 8

You can use Foolproof, All-Butter, or Classic Double-Crust Pie Dough (pages 372–377) for this pie. You can substitute Empire or Cortland apples for the Granny Smith apples and Jonagold, Fuji, or Braeburn for the Golden Delicious apples.

1	recipe double-crust pie dough
2½	pounds Granny Smith apples, peeled, cored, and sliced ¼ inch thick
2½	pounds Golden Delicious apples, peeled, cored, and sliced ¼ inch thick
½	cup (3½ ounces) plus 1 tablespoon granulated sugar
¼	cup packed (1¾ ounces) light brown sugar
½	teaspoon grated lemon zest plus 1 tablespoon juice
¼	teaspoon salt
⅛	teaspoon ground cinnamon
1	large egg white, lightly beaten

1. Roll 1 disk of dough into 12-inch circle on lightly floured counter. Loosely roll dough around rolling pin and gently unroll it onto 9-inch pie plate, letting excess dough hang over edge. Ease dough into plate by gently lifting edge of dough with your hand while pressing into plate bottom with your other hand. Leave any dough that overhangs plate in place. Wrap dough-lined pie plate loosely in plastic wrap and refrigerate until dough is firm, about 30 minutes. Roll other disk of dough into 12-inch circle on lightly floured counter, then transfer to parchment paper–lined baking sheet; cover with plastic and refrigerate for 30 minutes.

2. Toss apples, ½ cup granulated sugar, brown sugar, lemon zest, salt, and cinnamon together in Dutch oven. Cover and cook over medium heat, stirring often, until apples are tender when poked with fork but still hold their shape, 15 to 20 minutes. Transfer apples and their juices to rimmed baking sheet and let cool to room temperature, about 30 minutes.

3. Adjust oven rack to lowest position and heat oven to 425 degrees. Drain cooled apples thoroughly in colander, reserving ¼ cup of juice. Stir lemon juice into reserved juice.

4. Spread apples into dough-lined pie plate, mounding them slightly in middle, and drizzle with lemon juice mixture. Loosely roll remaining dough round around rolling pin and gently unroll it onto filling. Trim overhang to ½ inch beyond lip of pie plate. Pinch edges of top and bottom dough crusts firmly together. Tuck overhang under itself; folded edge should be flush with edge of pie plate. Crimp dough evenly around edge of pie using your fingers. Cut four 2-inch slits in top of dough. Brush surface with egg white and sprinkle evenly with remaining 1 tablespoon granulated sugar.

5. Place pie on rimmed baking sheet and bake until crust is light golden brown, about 25 minutes. Reduce oven temperature to 375 degrees, rotate sheet, and continue to bake until juices are bubbling and crust is deep golden brown, 30 to 40 minutes longer. Let pie cool on wire rack until filling has set, about 2 hours; serve slightly warm or at room temperature.

VENTING JUICY PIES

Pies with especially juicy fillings such as Blueberry Pie (page 388) or Sweet Cherry Pie (page 385), require more ventilation to encourage evaporation, which can be done by cutting more slits, or alternatively, by punching holes with a small biscuit cutter before transferring the top crust to pie a plate.

MAKING A DECORATIVE EDGE

In addition to fluting the edge of a pie crust (see opposite page) you can press the tines of a fork into the dough to flatten it against the rim of the pie plate. An attractive border is more than window dressing on a pie—it provides support to the edge to prevent leaking.

Apple-Cranberry Pie

✔ WHY THIS RECIPE WORKS

Adding cranberries to an apple pie can overwhelm the subtle perfume of the apples and shed a lot of liquid, making for a soggy bottom crust. We wanted to find a way to combine these two classic fall fruits so that the full flavor of both came through and the crust remained crisp.

PRECOOK THE CRANBERRIES Adding raw cranberries to the filling means bites of whole berries delivering a sour burst in the finished pie. Cooking the cranberries with a little sugar and orange juice in a saucepan allows the berries to break down so that their tart character is tamed.

REDUCE THE JUICE Once the cranberries break down and release their juice, we continue to cook them until the juices thicken, which prevents a soggy crust.

PRECOOK THE APPLES Microwaving the apples until they just turn translucent keeps them from turning too soft while baking. When we assemble the pie, we arrange the cooked cranberries and the apples in two distinct layers, allowing the flavor of each to come through clearly.

APPLE-CRANBERRY PIE
SERVES 8

You can use Foolproof, All-Butter, or Classic Double-Crust Pie Dough (pages 372–377) for this pie. You can substitute Jonagold, Fuji, or Braeburn apples for the Golden Delicious apples. For more information on fitting pie dough and assembling double-crust pies, see page 380.

- 8 ounces (2 cups) fresh or frozen cranberries
- ¼ cup orange juice
- 1 cup (7 ounces) plus 1 tablespoon sugar
- ½ teaspoon ground cinnamon
- ½ teaspoon salt
- ¼ cup water
- 1 tablespoon cornstarch
- 3½ pounds Golden Delicious apples, peeled, cored, and sliced ¼ inch thick
- 1 recipe double-crust pie dough
- 1 large egg white, lightly beaten

1. Bring cranberries, orange juice, ½ cup sugar, ¼ teaspoon cinnamon, and ¼ teaspoon salt to boil in medium saucepan. Cook, stirring occasionally and pressing berries against side of pot, until berries have completely broken down and juices have thickened to jam-like consistency (wooden spoon scraped across bottom should leave clear trail that doesn't fill in), 10 to 12 minutes. Off heat, stir in water and let cool to room temperature, about 30 minutes. (Cooled filling can be refrigerated for up to 2 days.)

2. Meanwhile, mix ½ cup sugar, remaining ¼ teaspoon cinnamon, remaining ¼ teaspoon salt, and cornstarch together in large bowl. Add apples and toss to combine. Cover and microwave, stirring with rubber spatula every 3 minutes, until apples are just starting to turn translucent around edges and liquid is thick and glossy, 10 to 14 minutes. Let cool to room temperature, about 30 minutes. (Cooled filling can be refrigerated for up to 2 days.)

3. While fillings cool, adjust oven rack to lowest position and heat oven to 425 degrees. Roll 1 disk of dough into 12-inch circle on lightly floured counter. Loosely roll dough around rolling pin and gently unroll it onto 9-inch pie plate, letting excess dough hang over edge. Ease dough into plate by gently lifting edge of dough with your hand while pressing into plate bottom with your other hand. Leave any dough that overhangs plate in place. Wrap dough-lined pie plate loosely in plastic wrap and refrigerate until dough is firm, about 30 minutes. Roll other disk of dough into 12-inch circle on lightly floured counter, then transfer to parchment paper–lined baking sheet; cover with plastic and refrigerate for 30 minutes.

4. Spread cooled cranberry mixture into even layer in dough-lined pie plate. Place apple mixture on top of cranberries, mounding it slightly in center. Loosely roll remaining dough round around rolling pin and gently unroll it onto filling. Trim overhang to ½ inch beyond lip of pie plate. Pinch edges of top and bottom crusts firmly together. Tuck overhang under itself; folded edge should be flush with edge of pie plate. Crimp dough evenly around edge of pie using your fingers. Cut four 2-inch slits in top of dough. Brush surface with egg white and sprinkle evenly with remaining 1 tablespoon sugar.

5. Place pie on rimmed baking sheet and bake until crust is light golden brown, about 25 minutes. Reduce oven temperature to 375 degrees, rotate sheet, and continue to bake until juices are bubbling and crust is deep golden brown, 30 to 40 minutes longer. Let pie cool on wire rack until filling has set, about 2 hours; serve slightly warm or at room temperature.

Mincemeat Pie

✔ WHY THIS RECIPE WORKS

Meatless mincemeat pies have been around for more than a century and are about as old-fashioned as pies get these days. All too often though, these pies are made with jarred mincemeat filling, or if the filling is homemade, it is murky, boozy, and overly rich. We wanted to bring mincemeat pie into the modern age with lighter, cleaner flavors.

LOSE THE BEEF Although some modern recipes include beef, we want our pie firmly in dessert territory. To that end, we build a foundation of fresh fruit flavor with two kinds of apples—McIntosh and Granny Smith. And instead of relying on suet for richness, we reach for sweet butter.

SUPPLEMENT WITH DRIED FRUIT Golden raisins and currants pair well with the apples, lending the filling a deep, earthy flavor.

SIMMER WITH CIDER SPIKED WITH CITRUS JUICES AND ZEST Adding orange and lemon juices (and zest) along with cider to the pot of simmering fruit intensifies the filling's flavors and prevents the mixture from scorching. A variety of warm spices (cinnamon, allspice, ginger, and clove) adds depth without muddying the flavors of the fruit. Keeping the booziness of the filling in check is as simple as adding ⅓ cup of rum toward the end of the cooking time and letting it cook long enough to mellow its punch.

BAKE AT TWO TEMPERATURES The baking temperature needs to be hot enough to brown the crust before the wet filling can render the bottom soggy. But if the oven is too hot, the filling won't set properly. We found that starting the pie at 400 degrees and then reducing it to 350 degrees midway through yields a crisp, well-browned crust and a thick, flavorful filling.

MODERN MINCEMEAT PIE
SERVES 10 TO 12

You can use Foolproof, All-Butter, or Classic Double-Crust Pie Dough (pages 372–378) for this pie. For more information on fitting pie dough and assembling double-crust pies, see page 380.

1½	pounds Granny Smith apples, peeled, cored, and cut into ¼-inch dice
1½	pounds McIntosh apples, peeled, cored, and cut into ¼-inch dice
1	cup golden raisins
1	cup currants
¾	cup packed (5¼ ounces) dark brown sugar

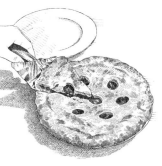

During the holidays, pie baking is in full swing and a free
pie plate can be hard to come
by. We found a seasoned
cast-iron skillet makes a great
alternative. (Make sure the
skillet is 9 or 10 inches in
diameter to keep the volume
and baking times consistent
with the recipe.)

8 tablespoons unsalted butter

¼ cup diced candied orange peel
(optional)

1½ tablespoons grated orange zest plus
½ cup juice

1 tablespoon grated lemon zest plus
3 tablespoons juice

1 teaspoon ground cinnamon

½ teaspoon ground allspice

½ teaspoon ground ginger

¼ teaspoon ground cloves

¼ teaspoon salt

1½ cups apple cider, plus more as needed

⅓ cup rum or brandy

1 recipe double-crust pie dough

1 large egg white, lightly beaten

1 tablespoon granulated sugar

1. Bring apples, raisins, currants, brown sugar, butter, orange peel, if using, orange and lemon zest and juice, cinnamon, allspice, ginger, cloves, salt, and 1 cup cider to boil in saucepan over medium-low heat. Reduce to simmer and cook gently, stirring occasionally to prevent scorching, until mixture thickens and darkens in color, about 3 hours, adding more cider as necessary to prevent scorching. Continue cooking, stirring mixture every minute or two, until it has jamlike consistency, about 20 minutes. Stir in remaining ½ cup apple cider and rum and cook until liquid in pan is thick and syrupy, about 10 minutes; let filling cool. (At this point, mincemeat can be refrigerated for 4 days.)

2. Meanwhile, roll 1 disk of dough into 12-inch circle on lightly floured counter. Loosely roll dough around rolling pin and gently unroll it onto 9-inch pie plate, letting excess dough hang over edge. Ease dough into plate by gently lifting edge of dough with your hand while pressing into plate bottom with your other hand. Leave any dough that overhangs plate in place. Wrap dough-lined pie plate loosely in plastic wrap and refrigerate until dough is firm, about 30 minutes. Roll other disk of dough into 12-inch circle on lightly floured counter, then transfer to parchment paper–lined baking sheet; cover with plastic and refrigerate for 30 minutes.

3. Adjust oven rack to lowest position and heat oven to 400 degrees. Spoon mincemeat into pie shell. Loosely roll remaining dough round around rolling pin and gently unroll it onto filling. Trim overhang to ½ inch beyond lip of pie plate. Pinch edges of top and bottom crusts firmly together. Tuck overhang under itself; folded edge should be flush with edge of pie plate. Crimp dough evenly around edge of pie using your fingers. Cut four 2-inch slits in top of dough. Brush surface with egg white and sprinkle evenly with granulated sugar.

4. Place pie on rimmed baking sheet and bake until crust is light golden brown, about 25 minutes. Reduce oven temperature to 350 degrees, rotate sheet, and continue to bake until juices are bubbling and crust is deep golden brown, 30 to 35 minutes longer. Let pie cool on wire rack to room temperature, about 4 hours. Serve.

Cherry Pie

✔ WHY THIS RECIPE WORKS

Great cherry pie is typically made with sour cherries because their soft, juicy flesh and bright, punchy flavor isn't dulled by oven heat or sugar. But cherry season is cruelly short and chances are the cherries that are available are the sweet variety. Sweet cherries have mellower flavors and meaty, firm flesh—traits that make them ideal for eating straight off the stem but don't translate well to baking. Our challenge was obvious: develop a recipe for sweet cherry pie with all the intense, jammy flavor and softened but still intact fruit texture of the best sour cherry pie.

PICK SOME PLUMS To mimic the bright, tart flavor of a sour cherry pie filling, we supplement the sweet cherries with chopped plums, which are tart and help tame the cherries' sweet flavor.

SLICE THE CHERRIES To fix the texture problem, we cut the cherries in half to expose their sturdy flesh. This step encourages the cherries to soften and give up their juices. A splash of bourbon and lemon juice also offset the sweetness and add flavorful depth. A little ground tapioca helps thicken the filling without diluting the fruit flavor.

COVER IT UP To keep the filling juicy, rather than dry, we switch out the typical lattice pie crust in favor of a traditional top crust, which prevents any moisture from evaporating.

SWEET CHERRY PIE
SERVES 8

You can use Foolproof, All-Butter, or Classic Double-Crust Pie Dough (pages 372–377) for this pie. Grind the tapioca to a powder in a spice grinder or mini food processor. You can substitute 2 pounds frozen sweet cherries for the fresh cherries. If you are using frozen fruit, measure it frozen, but let it thaw before filling the pie. If not, you run the risk of partially cooked fruit and undissolved tapioca. For more information on fitting pie dough and assembling double-crust pies, see page 380.

1	recipe double-crust pie dough
2	red plums, halved and pitted
2½	pounds fresh sweet cherries, pitted and halved
½	cup (3½ ounces) sugar
2	tablespoons instant tapioca, ground
1	tablespoon lemon juice
2	teaspoons bourbon (optional)
⅛	teaspoon salt
⅛	teaspoon ground cinnamon (optional)
2	tablespoons unsalted butter, cut into ¼-inch pieces
1	large egg, lightly beaten with 1 teaspoon water

1. Roll 1 disk of dough into 12-inch circle on lightly floured counter. Loosely roll dough around rolling pin and gently unroll it onto 9-inch pie plate, letting excess dough hang over edge. Ease dough into plate by gently lifting edge of dough with your hand while pressing into plate bottom with your other hand. Leave any dough that overhangs plate in place. Wrap dough-lined pie plate loosely in plastic wrap and refrigerate until dough is firm, about 30 minutes. Roll other disk of dough into 12-inch circle on lightly floured counter, then transfer to parchment paper–lined baking sheet; cover with plastic and refrigerate for 30 minutes.

2. Adjust oven rack to lowest position and heat oven to 400 degrees. Process plums and 1 cup halved cherries in food processor until smooth, about 1 minute, scraping down bowl as necessary. Strain puree through fine-mesh strainer into large bowl, pressing on solids to extract as much liquid as possible; discard solids. Stir in remaining halved cherries, sugar, tapioca, lemon juice, bourbon, if using, salt, and cinnamon, if using, into puree; let stand for 15 minutes.

3. Spread cherry mixture with its juices into dough-lined pie plate and scatter butter

PITTING CHERRIES

Pitting cherries for pie is a tedious but essential task if you want to use fresh fruit. If you don't own a cherry pitter, you can use one of these two methods for removing the pits.

A. Push cherry firmly down against pointed, jagged end of small pastry bag tip. Take care not to cut your fingers on points as they pierce fruit.

B. Push drinking straw through bottom of cherry, forcing pit up and out through stem end.

over top. Loosely roll remaining dough round around rolling pin and gently unroll it onto filling. Trim overhang to ½ inch beyond lip of pie plate. Pinch edges of top and bottom crusts firmly together. Tuck overhang under itself; folded edge should be flush with edge of pie plate. Crimp dough evenly around edge of pie using your fingers. Cut eight 1-inch slits in top of dough. Brush surface with egg mixture. Freeze pie for 20 minutes.

4. Place pie on rimmed baking sheet and bake until crust is light golden brown, about 30 minutes. Reduce oven temperature to 350 degrees, rotate sheet, and continue to bake until juices are bubbling and crust is deep golden brown, 35 to 50 minutes longer. Let pie cool on wire rack to allow juices to thicken, 2 to 3 hours. Serve.

Blueberry Pie

✓ WHY THIS RECIPE WORKS

If the filling in blueberry pie doesn't gel, a wedge can collapse into a soupy puddle topped by a sodden crust. But use too much thickener and the filling can be so dense that it's unpleasantly gluey to eat. We wanted a pie that had a firm, glistening filling full of fresh, bright flavor and still-plump berries.

START WITH TAPIOCA We prefer using tapioca to thicken the filling of a pie made with juicy fruit. (Flour and cornstarch yield a pasty, starchy filling no matter how much, or how little, we use.) We pulverize the tapioca in a spice grinder before adding it to the filling so that it doesn't leave any telltale "pearls" in the finished pie. The amount of tapioca needed to get the pie to set enough to slice neatly turns the filling gluey and dull, so we reduce the tapioca and turn to a second strategy.

ADD AN APPLE Blueberry jam provides inspiration for additional thickening. And the secret to the great texture of well-made jam is pectin, found in fruit. Blueberries are low in natural pectin, so commercial pectin in the form of a liquid or powder is usually added when making blueberry jam. The only downside to commercial pectin is that it needs the presence of a certain proportion of sugar and acid in order to work. Regular pectin makes for a too-sweet pie filling, while "no-sugar-needed" pectin is so acidic that the resulting filling is unappealingly sour. Our solution? Apples, which contain a lot of natural pectin. One peeled and grated Granny Smith apple along with a bit of tapioca provides enough thickening power to set the pie beautifully, plus it enhances the flavor of the berries without anyone guessing the secret ingredient.

PRECOOK HALF THE BERRIES Cooking just half of the berries is enough to adequately reduce their liquid and prevent an overly juicy pie. After cooking, we fold in the remaining berries, creating a satisfying combination of intensely flavored cooked fruit and bright-tasting fresh fruit. (This allows us to cut down on the tapioca, as well.)

ADD SUGAR, NOT SPICE We add sugar and lemon juice and zest to our filling, but nothing else. We want the filling to taste like berries, not cinnamon.

MAKE HOLES, NOT A LATTICE To vent the steam from the berries, we found a faster, easier alternative to a lattice top in a cookie (or biscuit) cutter, which we use to cut out circles in the top crust.

START HOT We begin baking our pie in a 400-degree oven on a rimmed baking sheet to help promote the browning process. After 25 minutes, we lower the heat to 350 degrees and bake the pie for another 35 to 50 minutes.

THE POWER OF PECTIN

When making our blueberry pie filling, we found that if we used more than 2 tablespoons of tapioca, the texture of the filling took on a gummy consistency we didn't like. But 2 tablespoons or less resulted in a filling that was too loose. Could we solve this problem with pectin, a gentle thickener that occurs naturally in fruit?

As a control, we thickened one pie with 2 tablespoons of tapioca. We then compared it with a second pie thickened with 2 tablespoons of tapioca and a grated apple, which is high in pectin and has a mild flavor. (We hoped that grating the apple would make it less noticeable in the baked pie.)

As expected, the pie thickened with tapioca alone was loose and soupy. But the pie thickened with tapioca plus an apple had a naturally gelled texture that was just right. The apple bits seemed to melt into the berry filling during baking, boosting fruity flavor but leaving no textural sign of their presence.

Pectin creates structure in a plant by helping to bind its cell walls together. This same substance is used to thicken jams and jellies into a set, but soft, mass. Pectin content varies from fruit to fruit and also within a plant (more pectin is found in the skin of a fruit than in its flesh, for example). Apples are a great source of pectin because they contain high levels of high-methoxyl pectin, the best natural pectin for making gels. By mashing some of the blueberries and grating the apple, we helped to release the pectin from the fruits' cell walls so that it could thicken the pie filling.

LET IT COOL If you want neat slices of pie, it must cool. The filling will continue to set as the pie cools down to room temperature—a process that will take 4 hours. If you like to serve warm pie, let it cool fully (so the filling sets), then briefly warm the pie in the oven before slicing. But don't overdo it! Leave the pie in a 350-degree oven for 10 minutes—just long enough to warm the pie without causing the filling to loosen.

BLUEBERRY PIE
SERVES 8

This recipe was developed using fresh blueberries, but unthawed frozen blueberries will work as well. In step 3, cook half the frozen berries over medium-high heat, without mashing, until reduced to 1¼ cups, 12 to 15 minutes. Use the large holes of a box grater to shred the apple. Grind the tapioca to a powder in a spice grinder or mini food processor. For more information on fitting pie dough and assembling double-crust pies, see page 380.

1	recipe Foolproof Double-Crust Pie Dough (page 377)
30	ounces (6 cups) blueberries
1	Granny Smith apple, peeled, cored, and shredded
¾	cup (5¼ ounces) sugar
2	tablespoons instant tapioca, ground
2	teaspoons grated lemon zest plus 2 teaspoons juice
	Pinch salt
2	tablespoons unsalted butter, cut into ¼-inch pieces
1	large egg white, lightly beaten

1. Roll 1 disk of dough into 12-inch circle on lightly floured counter. Loosely roll dough around rolling pin and gently unroll it onto 9-inch pie plate, letting excess dough hang over edge. Ease dough into plate by gently lifting edge of dough with your hand while pressing into plate bottom with your other hand. Leave any dough that overhangs plate in place.

Wrap dough-lined pie plate loosely in plastic wrap and refrigerate until dough is firm, about 30 minutes.

2. Roll other disk of dough into 12-inch circle on lightly floured counter. Using 1¼-inch round cookie cutter, cut round from center of dough. Cut 6 more rounds from dough, 1½ inches from edge of center hole and equally spaced around center hole. Transfer dough to parchment paper–lined baking sheet; cover with plastic and refrigerate for 30 minutes.

3. Place 3 cups berries in medium saucepan and set over medium heat. Using potato masher, mash berries several times to release juices. Continue to cook, stirring often and mashing occasionally, until about half of berries have broken down and mixture is thickened and reduced to 1½ cups, about 8 minutes; let cool slightly.

4. Adjust oven rack to lowest position and heat oven to 400 degrees.

5. Place shredded apple in clean dish towel and wring dry. Transfer apple to large bowl and stir in cooked berries, remaining 3 cups uncooked berries, sugar, tapioca, lemon zest and juice, and salt until combined. Spread mixture in dough-lined pie plate and scatter butter over top.

6. Loosely roll remaining dough round around rolling pin and gently unroll it onto filling. Trim overhang to ½ inch beyond lip of pie plate. Pinch edges of top and bottom crusts firmly together. Tuck overhang under itself; folded edge should be flush with edge of pie plate. Crimp dough evenly around edge of pie using your fingers. Brush surface with egg white.

7. Place pie on rimmed baking sheet and bake until crust is light golden brown, about 25 minutes. Reduce oven temperature to 350 degrees, rotate sheet, and continue to bake until juices are bubbling and crust is deep golden brown, 35 to 50 minutes longer. Let pie cool on wire rack to room temperature, about 4 hours. Serve.

Fresh Peach Pie

✔ WHY THIS RECIPE WORKS

In our opinion, a perfect slice of peach pie is a clean slice of pie, with fruit that's tender yet intact. In the past, we've had some success in perfecting a filling by using potato starch, but this ingredient isn't always readily available. Furthermore, it still leaves the filling a little looser than we'd like. We wanted to make a peach pie with a filling that holds the slices in place without being the least bit gluey, grainy, or cloudy or preventing any of the fresh peach flavor from shining through.

PICK THE RIGHT CRUST After experimenting with a few recipes, we learned that pies with lattice-top crusts had far better consistencies than those in pies with solid tops, since the openings allow moisture to evaporate during cooking. Moreover, the lattice serves as windows into the pie's interior, making it easy to know when the filling is bubbly at the center, a sure sign that it is fully cooked. For a lattice crust, we developed a dough that calls for a few more tablespoons of water than usual and a little less fat, both of which help create a sturdy dough that can withstand the extra handling involved in making a lattice. Just as important, this dough still manages to bake up tender and tastes rich and buttery.

REIN IN THE JUICINESS OF RIPE SUMMER PEACHES First, we keep the peach slices on the larger size to minimize moisture-shedding surface area. Second, we macerate the peaches in sugar for at least 30 minutes and add back only a portion of the juice they shed. Next, we mash a portion of the macerated peaches as a flavorful binder. Finally, we use a combination of pectin and cornstarch as thickeners to provide a glossy and smooth filling with just the right amount of body.

CREATE A FAUX LATTICE Whether you cut out strips and then weave them directly over the filling or do this handiwork on the side and then transfer the finished lattice to the pie, it takes practice to create neat, professional-looking results. We wanted a lattice that a novice baker could do perfectly. The best approach is one we use in our Linzertorte (page 426), which skips the weaving in favor of simply laying one strip over the previous one in a pattern that allows all but a few strips to appear woven.

FRESH PEACH PIE
SERVES 8

If your peaches are too soft to withstand the pressure of a peeler, blanch them in a pot of simmering water for 15 seconds and then shock them in a bowl of ice water before peeling. For fruit pectin we recommend both Sure-Jell for Less or No Sugar Needed Recipes and Ball RealFruit Low or No-Sugar Needed Pectin. For illustrations of our no-weave lattice, see page 390.

LATTICE PIE DOUGH

- 3   cups (15 ounces) all-purpose flour
- 2   tablespoons sugar
- 1   teaspoon salt
- 7   tablespoons vegetable shortening, cut into ½-inch pieces and chilled
- 10   tablespoons unsalted butter, cut into ¼-inch pieces and frozen for 30 minutes
- 10–12   tablespoons ice water

PEACH FILLING

- 3   pounds peaches, peeled, quartered, and pitted, each quarter cut into thirds
- ½   cup (3½ ounces) plus 3 tablespoons sugar
- 1   teaspoon grated lemon zest plus 1 tablespoon juice
- ⅛   teaspoon salt
- 2   tablespoons low- or no-sugar-needed fruit pectin
- ¼   teaspoon ground cinnamon
  Pinch ground nutmeg
- 1   tablespoon cornstarch

STORING FRUIT AND CREAM PIES

Because of their high dairy content, leftover custard- and cream-filled pies (including pumpkin) must be wrapped tightly in plastic wrap and stored in the refrigerator. They will generally last for a day or two stored this way. Whipped cream–topped pies do not store well, because the whipped cream breaks down and begins to weep after a short period of time. If you're planning on serving only a few slices from a whipped cream–topped pie, top each slice individually with whipped cream and save the rest of the pie for later.

Double-crust and lattice-topped fruit pies such as apple, peach, blueberry, or cherry can safely be stored at room temperature because of their high sugar content and acidity, which retard the growth of bacteria. To find out if fruit pies taste better when refrigerated or stored at room temperature, we held a baking marathon, then stored pies both ways. In all cases, refrigeration turned the crisp crusts on fruit pies gummy. This occurs as a result of retrogradation, or the process by which the structure of the starch changes and becomes stale. So when it comes to fruit pies, room temperature is the way to go. Wrapped well in aluminum foil and stored at room temperature, pies made with cooked fruit will last up to two days.

Note that pies made with fresh, uncooked fruit such as strawberries are a different story. These delicate pies often contain gelatin and should be stored in the refrigerator for up to one day.

BUILDING A "NO-WEAVE" LATTICE TOP

Making a lattice-top pie can be intimidating to many bakers. But it need not be if you use this simple no-weave method in which you freeze strips of dough and then lay each strip one at a time over the previous strip. Done in the proper order, it gives the illusion of a woven lattice, without the difficulty.

1. Roll dough into 12-inch circle, transfer to parchment paper–lined baking sheet, and cut into ten 1¼-inch-wide strips with a fluted pastry wheel, pizza wheel, or paring knife. Freeze for 30 minutes.

2. Lay 2 longest strips perpendicular to each other across center of pie to form cross. Place 4 shorter strips along edges of pie, parallel to center strips.

3. Lay 4 remaining strips between each edge strip and center strip. Trim off excess lattice ends, press edges of bottom crust and lattice strips together, and fold under.

1. FOR THE PIE DOUGH: Process flour, sugar, and salt in food processor until combined, about 5 seconds. Scatter shortening over top and process until mixture resembles coarse cornmeal, about 10 seconds. Scatter butter over top and pulse mixture until it resembles coarse crumbs, about 10 pulses. Transfer to bowl.

2. Sprinkle 5 tablespoons ice water over flour mixture. With rubber spatula, use folding motion to evenly combine water and flour mixture. Sprinkle another 5 tablespoons ice water over mixture and continue using folding motion to combine until small portion of dough holds together when squeezed in palm of hand, adding up to 2 tablespoons more ice water if necessary. (Dough should feel quite moist.) Turn out dough onto clean, dry counter and gently press together into cohesive ball. Divide dough into 2 even pieces and flatten each into 4-inch disk. Wrap disks tightly in plastic wrap and refrigerate for 1 hour or up to 2 days.

3. FOR THE PEACH FILLING: Toss peaches, ½ cup sugar, lemon zest and juice, and salt in medium bowl. Let stand at room temperature for at least 30 minutes or up to 1 hour. Combine pectin, cinnamon, nutmeg, and 2 tablespoons sugar in small bowl and set aside.

4. Remove dough from refrigerator. Before rolling out dough, let it sit on counter to soften slightly, about 10 minutes. Roll 1 disk of dough into 12-inch circle on lightly floured counter. Transfer to parchment paper–lined baking sheet. With pizza wheel, fluted pastry wheel, or paring knife, cut round into ten 1¼-inch-wide strips. Freeze strips on sheet until firm, about 30 minutes.

5. Adjust oven rack to lowest position and heat oven to 425 degrees. Roll other disk of dough into 12-inch circle on lightly floured counter. Loosely roll dough around rolling pin and gently unroll it onto 9-inch pie plate, letting excess dough hang over edge. Ease dough into plate by gently lifting edge of dough with your hand while pressing into plate bottom with your other hand. Leave any dough that overhangs plate in place. Wrap dough-lined

pie plate loosely in plastic and refrigerate until dough is firm, about 30 minutes.

6. Meanwhile, transfer 1 cup peach mixture to small bowl and mash with fork until coarse paste forms. Drain remaining peach mixture through colander set in large bowl. Transfer peach juice to liquid measuring cup (you should have about ½ cup liquid; if liquid measures more than ½ cup, discard remainder). Return peach pieces to bowl and toss with cornstarch. Transfer peach juice to 12-inch skillet, add pectin mixture, and whisk until combined. Cook over medium heat, stirring occasionally, until slightly thickened and pectin is dissolved (liquid should become less cloudy), 3 to 5 minutes. Remove skillet from heat, add peach pieces and peach paste, and toss to combine.

7. Transfer peach mixture to dough-lined pie plate. Remove dough strips from freezer; if too stiff to be workable, let stand at room temperature until malleable and softened slightly but still very cold. Lay 2 longest strips across center of pie perpendicular to each other. Using 4 shortest strips, lay 2 strips across pie parallel to 1 center strip and 2 strips parallel to other center strip, near edges of pie; you should have 6 strips in place. Using remaining 4 strips, lay each one across pie parallel and equidistant from center and edge strips. If dough becomes too soft to work with, refrigerate pie and dough strips until dough firms up.

8. Trim overhang to ½ inch beyond lip of pie plate. Press edges of bottom crust and lattice strips together and fold under. Folded edge should be flush with edge of pie plate. Crimp dough evenly around edge of pie using your fingers. Using spray bottle, evenly mist lattice with water and sprinkle with remaining 1 tablespoon sugar.

9. Place pie on rimmed baking sheet and bake until crust is set and begins to brown, about 25 minutes. Reduce oven temperature to 375 degrees, rotate sheet, and continue to bake until crust is deep golden brown and filling is bubbly at center, 30 to 40 minutes longer. Let pie cool on wire rack for 3 hours before serving.

Fresh Strawberry Pie

✔ WHY THIS RECIPE WORKS

We wanted a recipe for our ideal strawberry pie, featuring fresh berries lightly held together by a sheer, glossy glaze that made their flavor pop in the buttery shell.

DOUBLE UP ON THICKENERS We knew that the success of our strawberry pie hinged on getting the thickener just right. When none of the thickeners we tried worked on their own, we decided to use a combination of two: pectin (in the form of pureed strawberries cooked into a jam) and cornstarch. Alone, pectin produces a filling that is too firm and cornstarch one that is too loose. But together they create just the right supple, lightly clingy glaze.

TOSS STRAWBERRIES WITH GLAZE We start with a lot of strawberries—some get pureed into the glaze and the remaining are tossed with the glaze and piled high into the pie shell. Extra-large berries should be halved and all the berries should be arranged cut side down into an attractive mound.

REFRIGERATE BEFORE SERVING This pie slices cleanly, but it must be chilled for about 2 hours.

FRESH STRAWBERRY PIE
SERVES 8

You can use Foolproof, All-Butter, or Classic Single-Crust Pie Dough (pages 373–378) for this pie. To account for any imperfect strawberries, the ingredient list calls for several more ounces of berries than will be used in the pie. If possible, seek out ripe, farmers' market–quality berries. Make sure to thoroughly dry the strawberries after washing. For the fruit pectin we recommend both Sure-Jell for Less or No Sugar Needed Recipes and Ball RealFruit Low or No-Sugar Needed Pectin The pie is at its best after 2 or 3 hours of chilling; as it continues to chill, the glaze becomes softer and wetter, though the pie will taste just as good.

3 pounds strawberries, hulled (9 cups)
¾ cup (5¼ ounces) sugar
2 tablespoons cornstarch
1½ teaspoons low- or no-sugar-needed fruit pectin
    Pinch salt
1 tablespoon lemon juice
1 recipe single-crust pie dough, fully baked and cooled

1. Select 6 ounces misshapen, underripe, or otherwise unattractive berries, halving those that are large; you should have about 1½ cups. Process berries in food processor to smooth puree, 20 to 30 seconds, scraping down bowl as needed (you should have about ¾ cup puree).

2. Whisk sugar, cornstarch, pectin, and salt together in medium saucepan. Stir in berry puree, making sure to scrape corners of pan. Cook over medium-high heat, stirring constantly, and bring to boil. Boil, scraping bottom and sides of pan to prevent scorching, for 2 minutes to ensure that cornstarch is fully cooked (mixture will appear frothy when it first reaches boil, then will darken and thicken with further cooking). Transfer glaze to large bowl and stir in lemon juice; let cool to room temperature.

3. Meanwhile, pick over remaining berries and measure out 2 pounds of most attractive ones; halve only extra-large berries. Add berries to bowl with glaze and fold gently with rubber spatula until berries are evenly coated. Scoop berries into baked and cooled pie crust piling into mound. If any cut sides face up on top, turn them face down. If necessary, rearrange berries so that holes are filled and mound looks attractive. Refrigerate pie until filling is chilled and has set, about 2 hours. Serve within 5 hours of chilling.

PICKING RIPE STRAWBERRIES

Few inhabitants of the produce aisle have as uncanny an ability to look perfect yet taste disappointingly bland as strawberries. Unlike fruits such as bananas and peaches, which continue to ripen after picking (and are called climacteric), strawberries (nonclimacteric) don't get any sweeter once off the vine, so it's vital to select the sweetest ones you can find. Strawberries continue to develop a deep red pigment (called anthocyanin), but a berry that looks redder is not necessarily a berry that tastes sweeter.

What, then, is the best way to pick out a ripe pint of strawberries? Being upstanding citizens, we would never officially recommend one method: tearing open a berry or two to see if the red pigment extends all the way to the core, which can be a reliable sign. (Or, better yet, stealing a quick taste.) The third-best method? Taking a whiff. A sweet, fruity aroma is a much better indicator of what lies beneath the rosy exterior than the rosy exterior itself.

HULLING STRAWBERRIES

A grapefruit spoon is a better tool than a paring knife for removing the green crown from strawberries. It's faster, easier to maneuver, and wastes less fruit.

Graham Cracker Crust

✓ WHY THIS RECIPE WORKS

Store-bought graham cracker pie crusts are tempting but they taste stale and bland. We wanted a fresh-tasting homemade crust with a crisp texture.

CRUMBLE THEN PROCESS For fine, even crumbs we break graham crackers into 1-inch pieces and then process them in a food processor along with butter and sugar, which not only bind the crumbs, but they add flavor as well.

PACK WITH A MEASURING CUP To evenly press the crumbs into the pie plate, use the bottom of a measuring cup. The flat surface of the cup packs the crumbs into a pie plate more evenly than your fingertips and the curved edge of the cup easily presses the crumbs into the corners.

GRAHAM CRACKER CRUST
MAKES ENOUGH FOR ONE 9-INCH PIE

We don't recommend using store-bought graham cracker crumbs here as they can often be stale.

Be sure to note whether the crust needs to be warm or cool before filling (the pie recipes will specify) and plan accordingly.

9 whole graham crackers, broken into 1-inch pieces
5 tablespoons unsalted butter, melted and cooled
3 tablespoons sugar

1. Adjust oven rack to middle position and heat oven to 325 degrees. Process graham cracker pieces in food processor to fine, even crumbs, about 30 seconds. Sprinkle melted butter and sugar over crumbs and pulse to incorporate, about 5 pulses.

2. Sprinkle mixture into 9-inch pie plate. Using bottom of measuring cup, press crumbs into even layer on bottom and sides of pie plate. Bake until crust is fragrant and beginning to brown, 13 to 18 minutes; transfer to wire rack. Following particular pie recipe, use crust while it is still warm or let it cool completely.

Summer Berry Pie

✓ WHY THIS RECIPE WORKS

A fresh berry pie might seem like an easy-to-pull-off summer dessert, but most of the recipes we tried buried the berries in gluey thickeners or embedded them in bouncy gelatin. Our goal was to make a pie with great texture and flavor—and still keep it simple.

START WITH A GRAHAM CRACKER CRUST We start with the test kitchen's quick and easy homemade graham cracker crust, which is crisp and not too sweet.

PICK A MIX OF BERRIES For the filling, we use a combination of raspberries, blackberries, and blueberries. After trying

a few different methods, we found a solution (sparked by our Fresh Strawberry Pie on page 391) that both binds the berries in the graham cracker crust and intensifies their bright flavor. We process a portion of berries in a food processor until they make a smooth puree, then we thicken the puree with cornstarch.

ADD A SHEEN To finish our pie, we toss the remaining berries with warm jelly for a glossy coat and a shot of sweetness. Pressed gently into the puree, the berries stay put and taste great.

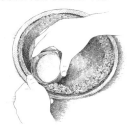

1. Press crumb mixture into pie plate. Use thumb and measuring cup to square off top of crust. Bake.

2. Drizzle melted jelly over whole berries and gently toss them together until berries are glazed.

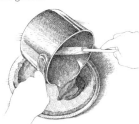

3. Pour slightly cooled berry puree into cooled crust and smooth top with rubber spatula.

4. Distribute glazed berries evenly over puree and gently press into surface.

SUMMER BERRY PIE
SERVES 8

Feel free to vary the amount of each berry as desired as long as you have 6 cups of berries total; do not substitute frozen berries here. Serve with Whipped Cream (page 348).

10	ounces (2 cups) raspberries
10	ounces (2 cups) blackberries
10	ounces (2 cups) blueberries
½	cup (3½ ounces) sugar
3	tablespoons cornstarch
⅛	teaspoon salt
1	tablespoon lemon juice
1	recipe Graham Cracker Crust (page 392), baked and cooled
2	tablespoons red currant or apple jelly

1. Gently toss berries together in large bowl. Process 2½ cups of berries in food processor until very smooth, about 1 minute (do not underprocess). Strain puree through fine-mesh strainer into small saucepan, pressing on solids to extract as much puree as possible (you should have about 1½ cups); discard solids.

2. Whisk sugar, cornstarch, and salt together in bowl, then whisk into strained puree. Bring puree mixture to boil, stirring constantly, and cook until it is as thick as pudding, about 7 minutes. Off heat, stir in lemon juice; set aside to cool slightly.

3. Pour warm berry puree into baked and cooled pie crust. Melt jelly in clean small saucepan over low heat, then pour over remaining 3½ cups berries and toss to coat. Spread berries evenly over puree and lightly press them into puree. Cover pie loosely with plastic wrap and refrigerate until filling is chilled and has set, about 3 hours; serve chilled or at room temperature.

Pumpkin Pie

✓ WHY THIS RECIPE WORKS

Too many pumpkin pie recipes result in a grainy custard in a soggy crust. We wanted to create a pumpkin pie recipe destined to be a new classic: velvety smooth, packed with pumpkin flavor, and redolent of just enough fragrant spices.

COOK THE PUMPKIN To maximize flavor, we concentrate the pumpkin's liquid rather than remove it, and we've found it best to do this on the stove. This is an added bonus for the spices that we add to the filling as well. Cooking the fresh ginger and spices along with the pumpkin puree intensifies their taste—the direct heat blooms their flavors. In addition, cooking minimizes the mealy texture in this pie where pumpkin is the star.

SUPPLEMENT WITH YAMS When we used solely pumpkin puree, we craved more flavor complexity. Therefore, we experimented with roasted sweet potatoes, which added a surprisingly deep flavor without a wholly recognizable taste. In an effort to streamline this technique, we tried adding canned sweet potatoes—commonly labeled as yams—instead. They were a hit. The yams add a complex flavor that complements the pumpkin.

ADD EXTRA YOLKS Our goal with this pie was to eliminate the grainy texture that plagues most custard in favor of a creamy, sliceable, not-too-dense pie. We start with a balance of whole milk and cream, and firm up the mixture with eggs. We don't simply add whole eggs, though—that just makes the pie too eggy. Because the whites are filled with much more water than the yolks, we exchange some whole eggs for yolks alone. Don't forget to pass the mixed filling through a fine-mesh strainer to remove any stringy bits. This will ensure the ultimate smooth texture.

ADD THE HOT FILLING TO A WARM CRUST If you're tempted to bake the pie crust way ahead of time, don't. It's imperative that the pie crust is warm when you add the hot filling. If it is not, the pie will become soggy. Using a hot filling in a warm crust allows the custard to firm up quickly in the oven, preventing it from soaking into the crust and turning it soggy. This is even true if you let the filling cool to room temperature. Keep that crust warm!

TURN THE OVEN HIGH TO LOW Most pumpkin pie recipes call for a high oven temperature to expedite cooking time. But as we've learned, baking any custard at high heat has its dangers. Once the temperature of custard rises above 185 degrees it curdles, turning the filling coarse and grainy. This is why we cannot bake the pie at 425 degrees, as most recipes suggest. Lowering the temperature to 350 only produces a pie that is curdled and overcooked at the edges and still underdone in the center. But baking at a low 300 degrees would mean leaving the pie in the oven for 2 hours. What to do? As with our New York–Style Cheesecake (page 336) we combine the two techniques, blasting the pie for 10 minutes on high heat and then baking it at 300 degrees for the rest of the baking time. This lessens the cooking time exponentially and leaves us with a creamy pie that's fully and evenly cooked from edge to center.

PUMPKIN PIE
SERVES 8

You can use Foolproof, All-Butter, or Classic Single-Crust Pie Dough (pages 373-378) for this pie. Make sure to buy unsweetened canned pumpkin; avoid pumpkin pie mix. If candied yams are unavailable, regular canned yams can be substituted. When

the pie is properly baked, the center 2 inches of the pie should look firm but jiggle slightly. The pie finishes cooking with residual heat; to ensure that the filling sets, let it cool at room temperature and not in the refrigerator. Do not cool this fully baked crust; the crust and filling must both be warm when the filling is added. Serve with Whipped Cream (page 348).

I	cup heavy cream
I	cup whole milk
3	large eggs plus 2 large yolks
I	teaspoon vanilla extract
I	(15-ounce) can unsweetened pumpkin puree
I	cup candied yams, drained
¾	cup (5¼ ounces) sugar
¼	cup maple syrup
2	teaspoons grated fresh ginger
I	teaspoon salt
½	teaspoon ground cinnamon
¼	teaspoon ground nutmeg
I	recipe single-crust pie dough, fully baked and still warm

I. Adjust oven rack to lowest position and heat oven to 400 degrees. Whisk cream, milk, eggs and yolks, and vanilla together in bowl. Bring pumpkin puree, yams, sugar, maple syrup, ginger, salt, cinnamon, and nutmeg to simmer in large saucepan and cook, stirring constantly and mashing yams against sides of pot, until thick and shiny, 15 to 20 minutes.

2. Remove saucepan from heat and whisk in cream mixture until fully incorporated. Strain mixture through fine-mesh strainer into bowl, using back of ladle or spatula to press solids through strainer. Whisk mixture, then pour into warm prebaked pie crust.

3. Place pie on rimmed baking sheet and bake for 10 minutes. Reduce oven temperature to 300 degrees and continue to bake until edges of pie are set and center registers 175 degrees, 20 to 35 minutes longer. Let pie cool on wire rack to room temperature, about 3 hours. Serve.

PATCHING CRACKED PIE SHELLS

Rather than throw away pie pastry trimmings, save the scraps for patchwork. If there are any cracks or holes after prebaking a pie shell, "spackle" them with the leftover dough, pressing it into place, and then finish baking according to the recipe.

Pecan Pie

✔ WHY THIS RECIPE WORKS

Pecan pies can be overwhelmingly sweet, with no real pecan flavor. And they too often turn out curdled and separated. What's more, the weepy filling makes the bottom crust soggy. The fact that the crust usually seems underbaked to begin with doesn't help matters. We wanted to create a recipe for a not-too-sweet pie with a smooth-textured filling and a properly baked bottom crust.

CUT BACK ON THE SUGAR To keep the pecans center stage, we cut back on the amount of dark brown sugar (and corn syrup) in the pie. To bring out the flavor of the pecans we toast them and then for easy slicing, we chop the nuts fine before adding them to the filling.

GENTLY COOK THE FILLING We simulate a double boiler when melting the butter (and making the filling) in a bowl set in a skillet of simmering water. This is an easy way to maintain gentle heat, which helps ensure that the filling, which contains eggs, doesn't curdle.

ADD THE HOT FILLING TO A WARM CRUST To keep the finished pie crust crisp, we partially bake the crust, then we add the hot filling to the warm pie crust and return it to the oven to finish cooking through.

DON'T OVERBAKE Pecan pie filling should be soft and creamy like a custard pie. The pie should be removed from the oven once it's just set, but still soft in the middle. It will continue to set as it cools.

CLASSIC PECAN PIE
SERVES 8

You can use Foolproof, All-Butter, or Classic Single-Crust Pie Dough (pages 373–378) for this pie. See page 9 for information on toasting nuts. The crust must still be warm when the filling is added. To serve the pie warm, let it cool thoroughly so that it sets completely, then warm it in a 250-degree oven for about 15 minutes and slice. Serve with vanilla ice cream or Whipped Cream (page 348).

6   tablespoons unsalted butter, cut into 1-inch pieces
1   cup packed (7 ounces) dark brown sugar
½   teaspoon salt
3   large eggs
¾   cup light corn syrup
1   tablespoon vanilla extract
2   cups (8 ounces) pecans, toasted and chopped fine
1   recipe single-crust pie dough, partially baked and still warm

1. Adjust oven rack to lower-middle position and heat oven to 275 degrees. Melt butter in heatproof bowl set in skillet of barely simmering water. Remove bowl from skillet and stir in sugar and salt until butter is absorbed. Whisk in eggs, then corn syrup and vanilla until smooth. Return bowl to hot water and stir until mixture is shiny, hot to touch, and registers 130 degrees. Off heat, stir in pecans.

2. Pour pecan mixture into warm prebaked pie crust set on rimmed baking sheet. Bake pie until filling looks set but yields like Jell-O when gently pressed with back of spoon, 50 minutes to 1 hour. Let pie cool on wire rack until filling has set, about 2 hours; serve slightly warm or at room temperature.

BUTTERMILK PECAN PIE WITH RAISINS

To make chess pie, omit the nuts and raisins.

Substitute 1½ cups granulated sugar for brown sugar and ⅔ cup buttermilk for corn syrup and vanilla. Reduce pecans to ½ cup and stir into pie filling along with ½ cup raisins, chopped fine.

MAPLE PECAN PIE

Toasted walnuts can be substituted for pecans. We prefer to use Grade B or Grade A dark amber maple syrup for this recipe.

Reduce butter to 4 tablespoons and pecans to 1½ cups. Substitute ½ cup granulated sugar for brown sugar and 1 cup maple syrup for corn syrup and vanilla.

TRIPLE-CHOCOLATE-CHUNK PECAN PIE

SERVES 8

You can use Foolproof, All-Butter, or Classic Single-Crust Pie Dough (pages 373–348) for this pie. Use either just one type of chocolate listed or a combination of two or three types. The crust must still be warm when the filling is added. To serve the pie warm, let it cool thoroughly so that it sets completely, then warm it in a 250-degree oven for about 15 minutes and slice.

- 3 tablespoons unsalted butter, cut into 3 pieces
- ¾ cup packed (5¼ ounces) dark brown sugar
- ½ teaspoon salt
- 2 large eggs
- ½ cup light corn syrup
- 1 teaspoon vanilla extract
- 1 cup pecans, toasted and chopped coarse
- 6 ounces semisweet, milk, and/or white chocolate, chopped coarse
- 1 recipe single-crust pie dough, partially baked and still warm

1. Adjust oven rack to lower-middle position and heat oven to 275 degrees. Melt butter in heatproof bowl set in skillet of barely simmering water. Remove bowl from skillet and stir in sugar and salt until butter is absorbed. Whisk in eggs, then corn syrup and vanilla until smooth. Return bowl to hot water and stir until mixture is shiny, hot to touch, and registers 130 degrees. Off heat, stir in pecans.

2. Pour pecan mixture into warm pre-baked pie crust. Scatter chocolate over top and lightly press it into filling with back of spoon. Bake pie until filling looks set but yields like Jell-O when gently pressed with back of spoon, 50 minutes to 1 hour. Let pie cool on wire rack until filling has set, about 2 hours; serve slightly warm or at room temperature.

TRANSPORTING PIES

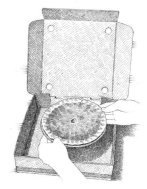

Transporting freshly baked pies from home to a holiday party can be hazardous, as the pies slide every which way in the car. But a small, unused 10-inch-square pizza box is just the right size for keeping flat-topped pies, such as pecan and pumpkin, safe. (This tip won't work for domed pies, like lemon meringue.)

Banana Cream Pie

✔ WHY THIS RECIPE WORKS

This layered concoction of pastry cream and sliced bananas topped with whipped cream is often delicious and sometimes sliceable, but very rarely both. We wanted a banana cream pie that had it all.

GIVE THE FILLING A BANANA-Y BOOST We start with a standard pastry cream for our filling made with half-and-half, egg yolks, butter, and cornstarch for a rich, sliceable, but not rubbery, texture. In looking to add banana flavor, we found banana extract simply tasted artificial. Liqueur wasn't practical. Instead, before making our pastry cream, we infuse the half-and-half with a few sautéed bananas, which we later strain out.

PREVENT BROWN BANANA SLICES We also add fresh banana slices to our pie. It helps to slice the bananas shortly before assembly since bananas turn brown when cut. To slow down the browning, we also add a splash of orange juice to the fresh banana slices.

LAYER INTO COOLED PASTRY SHELL Cookie-crumb crusts are too sweet for this pie, so we chose a simple pie dough shell, which we bake and cool before layering our banana-infused pastry cream, sliced bananas, and more pastry cream. Finally we top off our pie with a slather of sweetened whipped cream.

USING DISPOSABLE PIE PLATES

Initially, we assumed that disposable aluminum pie plates would absorb and conduct heat too quickly, leading to burnt crusts, so we did not place them on a metal baking sheet before sliding them into the oven. But after blind-baking a few pie shells, we found just the opposite to be true—the bottoms were still pale and damp long after the fluted edges had crisped and browned. Placing them on a baking sheet helped, but the sides were still undercooked and tended to slump after we removed the pie weights to let the insides of the shells brown.

It turns out that, due to their thin walls, aluminum plates can't hold or transfer a significant amount of heat from the oven to the crust. The upshot is that crusts bake more slowly in aluminum, so they need to spend more time in the oven. For prebaking empty crusts, you'll need to increase the time that the crust bakes with weights by up to 10 minutes or until you see any visual doneness cues indicated by the recipe. For filled double-crust pies, increase the baking time by up to 10 minutes and cover the top of the pie with aluminum foil if it starts to get too dark. Place aluminum pie plates on a baking sheet for a well-browned bottom crust and for added stability when moving pies in and out of the oven.

BANANA CREAM PIE
SERVES 8

You can use Foolproof, All-Butter, or Classic Single-Crust Pie Dough for Custard Pies (pages 373–378) for this pie. Peel and slice the bananas just before using to help prevent browning.

- 5 ripe bananas
- 4 tablespoons unsalted butter
- 2½ cups half-and-half
- ½ cup (3½ ounces) plus 2 tablespoons granulated sugar
- 6 large egg yolks
- ¼ teaspoon salt
- 2 tablespoons cornstarch
- 1½ teaspoons vanilla extract
- 2 tablespoons orange juice
- 1 cup heavy cream
- 2 tablespoons confectioners' sugar
- 1 recipe single-crust pie dough, fully baked and cooled

1. Peel 2 bananas and slice into ½-inch-thick pieces. Melt 1 tablespoon butter in medium saucepan over medium-high heat. Add sliced bananas and cook until they begin to soften, about 2 minutes. Add half-and-half, bring to boil, and boil for 30 seconds. Remove from heat, cover, and let sit for 40 minutes.

2. Whisk granulated sugar, egg yolks, and salt together in large bowl until smooth. Whisk in cornstarch. Strain cooled half-and-half mixture through fine-mesh strainer into egg yolk mixture—do not press on bananas—and whisk until incorporated; discard cooked bananas.

3. Transfer mixture to clean medium saucepan. Cook over medium heat, whisking constantly, until thickened to consistency of warm pudding (180 degrees), 4 to 6 minutes. Remove pan from heat; whisk in remaining 3 tablespoons butter and 1 teaspoon vanilla. Transfer pastry cream to bowl, press greased parchment paper directly against surface, and let cool for about 1 hour.

4. Peel and slice remaining 3 bananas ¼ inch thick and toss with orange juice. Whisk pastry cream briefly, then spread half over bottom of baked and cooled pie crust. Arrange sliced bananas on pastry cream. Top with remaining pastry cream.

5. Using stand mixer fitted with whisk, whip cream, confectioners' sugar, and remaining ½ teaspoon vanilla on medium-low speed until foamy, about 1 minute. Increase speed to high and whip until stiff peaks form, 1 to 3 minutes. Spread whipped cream evenly over top of pie. Refrigerate until set, at least 5 hours or up to 24 hours. Serve.

CHOCOLATE–PEANUT BUTTER BANANA CREAM PIE

Increase half-and-half to 2½ cups plus 1½ tablespoons; use 2½ cups in pastry cream as directed. In step 3, while pastry cream cools, combine 4 ounces chopped milk chocolate and remaining 1½ tablespoons half-and-half in bowl and microwave until melted, about 40 seconds, stirring halfway through microwaving. In step 4, after tossing banana slices with juice, spread melted chocolate in bottom of empty baked pie shell and sprinkle ⅓ cup chopped salted dry-roasted peanuts over chocolate. Layer with pastry cream and bananas as directed. In step 5, whisk ¼ cup heavy cream with 2 tablespoons peanut butter in bowl until smooth. Using stand mixer fitted with whisk, whip remaining ¾ cup heavy cream, confectioners' sugar, and remaining ½ teaspoon vanilla on medium-low speed until foamy, about 1 minute. Increase speed to high and whip until stiff peaks form, 1 to 3 minutes. Fold peanut butter mixture into whipped cream and spread evenly over pie. Sprinkle pie with 2 tablespoons chopped salted dry-roasted peanuts. Refrigerate until set, 5 to 24 hours. Serve.

Chocolate Cream Pie

✔ WHY THIS RECIPE WORKS

Chocolate cream pies can look superb but they're often gluey, overly sweet, and impossible to slice. We wanted a voluptuously creamy pie, with a well-balanced chocolate flavor somewhere between milkshake and melted candy bar, and a delicious, easy-to-slice crust.

MAKE A COOKIE CRUST After testing every type of cookie on the market, we settled on Oreos. We pulverize the cookies with a bit of melted butter for the tastiest, most tender, sliceable crumb crust.

TEMPER THE YOLKS We make our custard by heating the half-and-half with the sugar until simmering. Then we pour a small portion of the half-and-half mixture into the beaten egg yolks to temper, or gently warm, them, before we add them to the rest of the simmering half-and-half mixture. If we simply added the yolks straight to the pot of half-and-half, they would curdle. This method ensures a creamy, smooth custard.

COMBINE TWO TYPES OF CHOCOLATE For deeper, more complex flavor, we like a combination of semisweet or bittersweet chocolate and intensely flavored unsweetened chocolate. We chop the chocolate fine, so that it can easily be whisked into the hot custard and dissolve along with the butter, which adds richness and sheen.

COVER AND CHILL To allow the pie to set so that it slices into neat wedges, it needs to be refrigerated until cold. We cover the filling with plastic wrap, which prevents a skin from forming over the filling. Once it's chilled, we serve the pie with freshly whipped cream.

CHOCOLATE CREAM PIE
SERVES 8

Other brands of chocolate sandwich cookies may be substituted for the Oreos, but avoid any "double-filled" cookies because the proportion of cookie to filling won't be correct. Do not combine the egg yolks and sugar in advance of making the filling—the sugar will begin to break down the yolks, and the finished cream will be pitted.

CRUST
- 16 Oreo cookies, broken into rough pieces
- 4 tablespoons unsalted butter, melted and cooled

FILLING
- 2½ cups half-and-half
- ⅓ cup (2⅓ ounces) sugar
- Pinch salt
- 6 large egg yolks
- 2 tablespoons cornstarch
- 6 tablespoons unsalted butter, cut into 6 pieces
- 6 ounces semisweet or bittersweet chocolate, chopped fine
- 1 ounce unsweetened chocolate, chopped fine
- 1 teaspoon vanilla extract

TOPPING
- 1½ cups heavy cream, chilled
- 2 tablespoons sugar
- ½ teaspoon vanilla extract

1. FOR THE CRUST: Adjust oven rack to middle position and heat oven to 350 degrees. Pulse cookies in food processor until coarsely ground, about 15 pulses, then continue to

The whipped cream or meringue topping on a pie can be marred easily when covered directly with plastic wrap. We recommend tenting the plastic: Stand a few strands of uncooked spaghetti or linguini in the pie, then suspend the wrap on the pasta.

process to fine, even crumbs, about 15 seconds. Sprinkle melted butter over crumbs and pulse to incorporate, about 5 pulses.

2. Sprinkle mixture into 9-inch pie plate. Using bottom of measuring cup, press crumbs into even layer on bottom and sides of pie plate. Bake until crust is fragrant and looks set, 10 to 15 minutes. Transfer pie plate to wire rack and let crust cool completely.

3. FOR THE FILLING: Bring half-and-half, 3 tablespoons sugar, and salt to simmer in medium saucepan, stirring occasionally.

4. As half-and-half mixture begins to simmer, whisk egg yolks, cornstarch, and remaining sugar in medium bowl until smooth. Slowly whisk 1 cup of simmering half-and-half mixture into yolk mixture to temper, then slowly whisk tempered yolk mixture back into remaining half-and-half mixture. Reduce heat to medium and cook, whisking vigorously, until mixture is thickened and few bubbles burst on surface, about 30 seconds. Off heat, whisk in butter, semisweet chocolate, and unsweetened chocolate until completely smooth and melted, then stir in vanilla.

5. Pour warm filling into baked and cooled pie crust. Lay sheet of plastic wrap directly on surface of filling and refrigerate pie until filling is chilled and set, about 4 hours.

6. FOR THE TOPPING: Once pie is chilled, use stand mixer fitted with whisk to whip cream, sugar, and vanilla on medium-low speed until foamy, about 1 minute. Increase speed to high and whip until soft peaks form, 1 to 3 minutes. Spread whipped cream attractively over pie and serve immediately.

Coconut Cream Pie

✓ WHY THIS RECIPE WORKS

Most recipes for this diner dessert are nothing more than a redecorated vanilla cream pie. A handful of coconut shreds stirred into the filling or sprinkled on the whipped cream might be enough to give it a new name, but certainly not enough to give it flavor. We wanted a coconut cream pie with the exotic and elusive flavor of tropical coconut rather than a thinly disguised vanilla custard.

PICK A GRAHAM CRACKER CRUST We found that a not-too-sweet graham cracker crust provides a delicate, cookielike texture that doesn't overshadow the coconut filling.

DOUBLE UP ON COCONUT For the filling, we start with a basic custard, using a combination of unsweetened coconut milk and whole milk. And for more coconut flavor, we stir in unsweetened shredded coconut and cook it so the shreds soften slightly in the hot milk.

TOP WITH FLAVORED WHIPPED CREAM We add a little rum to our whipped cream, slather it over the top of the pie, and then dust the top with crunchy shreds of toasted coconut for one more layer of coconut flavor.

COCONUT CREAM PIE
SERVES 8

Do not use light coconut milk here because it does not have enough flavor. Also, do not confuse coconut milk with cream of coconut. The filling should be warm when poured into the cooled pie crust. To toast the coconut, place it in a small skillet over medium heat and cook, stirring often, for 3 to 5 minutes. It burns quite easily, so keep a close eye on it.

MAKING A COCONUT CREAM PIE

1. After heating coconut milk–sugar mixture, whisk egg yolks, cornstarch, and remaining sugar together. Temper yolk mixture by gradually pouring or ladling hot coconut milk mixture over yolks while whisking constantly.

2. Add remaining hot coconut milk mixture to yolk mixture, whisking constantly until combined.

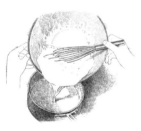

3. Pour mixture back into saucepan and cook, whisking constantly, until thickened. Off heat, whisk in butter and vanilla until butter is melted and fully incorporated.

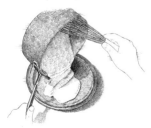

4. Pour warm filling into cooled pie shell and chill until firm.

FILLING

- 1 (14-ounce) can coconut milk
- 1 cup whole milk
- 2/3 cup (4 2/3 ounces) sugar
- 1/2 cup (1 1/4 ounces) unsweetened shredded coconut
- 1/4 teaspoon salt
- 5 large egg yolks
- 1/4 cup cornstarch
- 2 tablespoons unsalted butter, cut into 2 pieces
- 1 1/2 teaspoons vanilla extract

- 1 recipe Graham Cracker Crust (page 392), baked and cooled

TOPPING

- 1 1/2 cups heavy cream, chilled
- 1 1/2 tablespoons sugar
- 1 1/2 teaspoons dark rum (optional)
- 1/2 teaspoon vanilla extract
- 1 tablespoon unsweetened shredded coconut, toasted

1. FOR THE FILLING: Bring coconut milk, whole milk, 1/3 cup sugar, shredded coconut, and salt to simmer in medium saucepan, stirring occasionally.

2. As milk mixture begins to simmer, whisk egg yolks, cornstarch, and remaining 1/3 cup sugar in medium bowl until smooth. Slowly whisk 1 cup of simmering coconut milk mixture into yolk mixture to temper, then slowly whisk tempered yolk mixture back into remaining coconut milk mixture. Reduce heat to medium and cook, whisking vigorously, until mixture is thickened and few bubbles burst on surface, about 30 seconds. Off heat, whisk in butter and vanilla. Let mixture cool until just warm, stirring often, about 5 minutes.

3. Pour warm filling into baked and cooled pie crust. Lay sheet of plastic wrap directly on surface of filling and refrigerate pie until filling is chilled and set, about 4 hours.

4. FOR THE TOPPING: Once pie is chilled, use stand mixer fitted with whisk to whip cream, sugar, rum, if using, and vanilla on medium-low speed until frothy, about 1 minute. Increase speed to high and continue to whip until soft peaks form, 1 to 3 minutes. Spread whipped cream attractively over pie, sprinkle with toasted coconut, and serve immediately.

LIME-COCONUT CREAM PIE

Whisk 1 1/2 teaspoons grated lime zest into filling along with butter and vanilla.

BANANA-CARAMEL COCONUT CREAM PIE

This variation is a test kitchen favorite. Light coconut milk lacks rich coconut flavor, so skip it in favor of regular coconut milk. You may be left with 1/3 cup or so of filling that will not fit into the crust because of the caramel and banana.

1. Add 3 tablespoons water to small saucepan, then pour 1/2 cup sugar into center of saucepan. Gently stir sugar with clean spatula to wet thoroughly. Bring to boil and cook until sugar mixture turns dark amber, 5 to 8 minutes, swirling pan occasionally once sugar begins to color. Off heat, add 3 tablespoons heavy cream (caramel will bubble vigorously) and pinch salt; whisk to combine. Whisk in 2 tablespoons unsalted butter. Pour caramel into cooled prebaked pie crust, tilting pie plate to coat evenly; set aside to cool. When caramel is cool, peel 2 slightly under-ripe bananas and slice crosswise 1/4 inch thick. Arrange slices in single layer on top of caramel.

2. Whisk 2 teaspoons dark rum into filling along with butter and vanilla and pour filling over sliced bananas. Continue with recipe.

Key Lime Pie

✔ WHY THIS RECIPE WORKS

Key lime pie is often harsh and artificial-tasting. We wanted a recipe for classic Key lime pie with a fresh flavor and silky filling.

USE FRESH LIME JUICE (AND ZEST) We thought the artificial taste in many Key lime pies came from the sweetened condensed milk. We were wrong. It was the reconstituted lime juice. Just one simple swap—from bottled, reconstituted lime juice to juice and zest from fresh limes—gives us a pie that is pungent and refreshing, cool and yet creamy, and very satisfying.

KEY LIMES ARE NOT KEY Despite this pie's name, we found that most tasters could not tell the difference between pies made with regular supermarket limes (called Persian limes) and true Key limes. Since Persian limes are easier to find and juice, we recommend them.

BAKE THE PIE Traditional Key lime pie is usually not baked; instead, the combination of egg yolks, lime juice, and sweetened condensed milk firms up when chilled because the juice's acidity causes the proteins in the eggs and milk to bind. But we found that the pie sets much more nicely after being baked for only 15 minutes.

KEY LIME PIE
SERVES 8

The timing here is different from other pies; you need to make the filling first, then prepare the crust. We developed our recipe using regular supermarket Persian limes.

PIE

- 4 large egg yolks
- 4 teaspoons grated lime zest plus ½ cup juice (5 limes)
- 1 (14-ounce) can sweetened condensed milk
- 1 recipe Graham Cracker Crust (page 392), baked and still warm

TOPPING (OPTIONAL)

- 1 cup heavy cream, chilled
- ¼ cup (1 ounce) confectioners' sugar

1. FOR THE PIE: Whisk egg yolks and lime zest together in medium bowl until mixture has light green tint, about 2 minutes. Whisk in condensed milk until smooth, then whisk in lime juice. Cover mixture and set aside at room temperature until thickened, about 30 minutes.

2. Meanwhile, prepare and bake crust. Transfer pie plate to wire rack and leave oven at 325 degrees. (Crust must still be warm when filling is added.)

3. Pour thickened filling into warm prebaked pie crust. Bake pie until center is firm but jiggles slightly when shaken, 15 to 20 minutes. Let pie cool slightly on wire rack, about 1 hour, then cover loosely with plastic wrap and refrigerate until filling is chilled and set, about 3 hours.

4. FOR THE TOPPING, IF USING: Once pie is chilled, use stand mixer fitted with whisk to whip cream and sugar on medium-low speed until foamy, about 1 minute. Increase speed to high and whip until soft peaks form, 1 to 3 minutes. Spread whipped cream attractively over pie and serve immediately.

SHORTCUT FOR JUICING LIMES (AND LEMONS)

When you're faced with a lot of limes or lemons to juice, try this handy trick. Place two or three quartered limes in the hopper of a potato ricer and squeeze the handles together.

Lemon Chiffon Pie

✔ WHY THIS RECIPE WORKS

We wanted a lemon chiffon pie with a filling that was creamy, rich, and set but not stiff—and that packed plenty of bright lemon punch.

USE TWO THICKENERS—AND LESS OF THEM For the most part, the formulas for chiffon pie are about the same: After lemon curd is cooked until it thickens, a couple of teaspoons of unflavored gelatin (dissolved in a little water) are stirred in and the mixture is cooled. Egg whites are then whipped with sugar until they hold stiff peaks, then they are gently but thoroughly combined with the curd. The pale yellow filling is poured into a prebaked crumb crust and chilled until set. But we found pies made this way too bouncy and springy. Cutting back on the gelatin resulted in a too-soft filling and switching to cornstarch simply dulled the flavor. The answer turned out to be a reduced amount of cornstarch and a reduced amount of gelatin; together they produce a lush, perfectly thickened filling.

ENRICH THE FILLING WITH CREAM CHEESE We liked the flavor and texture of our filling, but we also thought it could be richer. Just 4 ounces of cream cheese gives our chiffon a richness and tang that complements the citrus.

ADD A SECOND LAYER OF LEMON FLAVOR We decided to make extra lemon curd so that in addition to using it in our chiffon filling, we could pour a layer of it in the bottom of our crust (a crisp graham cracker crust is traditional). It delivers precisely the extreme tanginess we crave, not to mention an eye-catching pop of color.

CHILL AND CHILL AGAIN After we pour the lemon curd into the crust, we chill it until set. Then we mound the chiffon layer on top and refrigerate the pie until the chiffon layer sets so that the pie is sliceable. Creamy but sturdy, rich but still lightweight, and full of bright citrus tang, this pie is a showstopper.

LEMON CHIFFON PIE
SERVES 8 TO 10

Before cooking the curd mixture, be sure to whisk thoroughly so that no clumps of cornstarch or streaks of egg white remain. Pasteurized egg whites can be substituted for the three raw egg whites. Serve with lightly sweetened Whipped Cream (page 348).

1	teaspoon unflavored gelatin
4	tablespoons water
5	large eggs (2 whole, 3 separated)
1¼	cups (8¾ ounces) sugar
1	tablespoon cornstarch
⅛	teaspoon salt
1	tablespoon grated lemon zest plus ¾ cup juice (4 lemons)
¼	cup heavy cream
4	ounces cream cheese, cut into ½-inch pieces, softened
1	recipe Graham Cracker Crust (page 392), baked and cooled

1. Sprinkle ½ teaspoon gelatin over 2 tablespoons water in small bowl and let sit until gelatin softens, about 5 minutes. Repeat with remaining ½ teaspoon gelatin and remaining 2 tablespoons water in second small bowl.

2. Whisk 2 eggs and 3 yolks together in medium saucepan until thoroughly combined. Whisk in 1 cup sugar, cornstarch, and salt until well combined. Whisk in lemon zest and juice and heavy cream. Cook over medium-low heat, stirring constantly, until thickened and slightly translucent, 4 to 5 minutes (mixture should register 170 degrees). Stir in 1 bowl water-gelatin mixture until dissolved. Remove pan from heat and let stand for 2 minutes.

3. Remove 1¼ cups curd from pan and pour through fine-mesh strainer set in bowl. Transfer strained curd to baked and cooled pie crust (do not wash out strainer or bowl).

Place filled pie shell in freezer. Add remaining bowl water-gelatin mixture and cream cheese to remaining curd in pan and whisk to combine. (If cream cheese does not melt, briefly return pan to low heat.) Pour through strainer into now-empty bowl.

4. Using stand mixer, whip 3 egg whites on medium-low speed until foamy, about 2 minutes. Increase speed to medium-high and slowly add remaining ¼ cup sugar. Continue whipping until whites are stiff and glossy, about 4 minutes. Add curd–cream cheese mixture and whip on medium speed until few streaks remain, about 30 seconds. Remove bowl from mixer and, using spatula, scrape sides of bowl and stir mixture until no streaks remain. Remove pie shell from freezer and carefully pour chiffon over curd, allowing chiffon to mound slightly in center. Refrigerate for at least 4 hours or up to 2 days before serving.

Lemon Meringue Pie

✓ WHY THIS RECIPE WORKS

Lemon meringue pie can be tricky to prepare. We wanted a crisp crust, brightly flavored lemon filling and a tall, fluffy meringue topping that wouldn't weep.

ADD GRAHAM CRACKERS TO THE CRUST To promote browning and really crisp the crust, we roll our single crust pie dough for custard pies (pages 373–378) in graham cracker crumbs. Not only does this help the texture of our crust, but it adds a wonderful graham flavor to complement the lemon pie without masking the character of the dough itself.

MAKE THE RIGHT FILLING The filling for our Lemon Meringue Pie is a close relative of lemon curd, but because you need so much more of it to fill a pie shell it's diluted with water (all lemon juice would be too intense) and stabilized with cornstarch (so you can slice cleanly through the thick filling). We also chill our pie before adding the meringue topping.

PICK ITALIAN For the meringue, rather than simply beating egg whites with raw sugar (the French method), here we pour hot sugar syrup into the whites as they are beaten (the Italian method). The hot syrup cooks the whites and helps transform them into a soft, smooth meringue that is stable enough to resist weeping during its short time in the oven. With a French meringue, the bottom portion often doesn't cook through and weeping is a greater risk.

BAKE, DON'T BROIL While some recipes throw the pie under the broiler to brown the meringue topping, we find the intense heat too much. Instead, we bake the pie in 400-degree oven for an evenly browned, not burned finish.

LEMON MERINGUE PIE

SERVES 8

You can use Foolproof, All-Butter, or Classic Single-Crust Pie Dough for Custard Pies (pages 373–378) for this pie. Be sure that the filling is cool when spreading the meringue onto the pie. This pie should be served the same day that it is prepared.

FILLING

1½	cups water
1	cup (7 ounces) sugar
¼	cup cornstarch
⅛	teaspoon salt
6	large egg yolks
1	tablespoon grated lemon zest plus ½ cup juice (3 lemons)
2	tablespoons unsalted butter, cut into 2 pieces

APPLYING A MERINGUE TOPPING

A meringue topping that is uneven or has shrunk back around the edges of the pie is disappointing. Here's how to get an even meringue topping that covers the entire surface of the pie.

1. Put dabs of meringue over filling.

2. Once all of meringue has been placed on pie, use rubber spatula to "anchor" meringue to edge of crust. As long as meringue touches crust, it won't pull away or shrink in oven.

1 recipe single-crust pie dough for custard pie, fully baked and cooled

MERINGUE
¾ cup (5¼ ounces) sugar
⅓ cup water
3 large egg whites
¼ teaspoon cream of tartar
 Pinch salt
¼ teaspoon vanilla extract

1. FOR THE FILLING: Bring water, sugar, cornstarch, and salt to simmer in large saucepan over medium heat, whisking constantly. When mixture starts to turn translucent, whisk in egg yolks, two at a time. Whisk in lemon zest and juice and butter. Return mixture to brief simmer, then remove from heat.

2. Pour filling into baked and cooled pie crust. Lay sheet of plastic wrap directly on surface of filling and refrigerate pie until filling is cold, about 2 hours.

3. FOR THE MERINGUE: Adjust oven rack to middle position and heat oven to 400 degrees. Bring sugar and water to vigorous boil in small saucepan over medium-high heat. Once syrup comes to rolling boil, cook for 4 minutes (mixture will become slightly thickened and syrupy). Remove from heat and set aside while beating whites.

4. Using stand mixer fitted with whisk, whip whites, cream of tartar, and salt on medium-low speed until foamy, about 1 minute. Increase speed to medium-high and whip until soft peaks form, about 2 minutes. With mixer running, slowly pour hot syrup into whites (avoid pouring syrup onto whisk or it will splash). Add vanilla and beat until meringue has cooled and becomes very thick and shiny, 3 to 6 minutes.

5. Using rubber spatula, mound meringue over filling, making sure meringue touches edges of crust. Use spatula to create peaks all over meringue. Bake until peaks turn golden brown, about 6 minutes. Transfer to wire rack and let cool to room temperature. Serve.

Tarte Tatin

✔ WHY THIS RECIPE WORKS

When this French dessert—basically an apple tart in which the apples are caramelized and the tart is served upside down—first came to this country, all sorts of different recipes for it appeared. Some were based on traditional French formulas, but others were highly Americanized. When we tried the latter, we were disappointed—we got desserts that tasted like apples coated with caramel sauce or, worse, were just an unidentifiable caramel glop. We wanted a tart that tasted like caramelized apples and looked great, too.

COOK THE CARAMEL FIRST We stir the butter and sugar together in a skillet and cook the mixture until light golden. The caramel will continue to cook after the apples are added.

CRAM THE SKILLET WITH APPLES We wanted a tart with lots of fruit, so we took a step back to see how we could fit more pieces of apples in our skillet. We started with apple halves, as some French recipes do, but found difficulty in getting the caramel to penetrate the large pieces of fruit. Instead, we cut the apples in quarters, which we arrange in concentric circles on their cut edge. And to keep them upright, we hold one in place while placing the next one by its side. To make sure the apples are fully caramelized we carefully turn the apples partway through cooking.

REINFORCE THE PASTRY WITH AN EGG The crust on a *tarte Tatin* needs extra durability and strength, so that it can cradle the apples and caramel once the tart is flipped out of the skillet. A single egg makes for a sturdier crust. We also swap in confectioners' sugar for granulated, for pastry that's less grainy and more tender.

CUT THE SWEETNESS WITH TANGY CREAM We top individual slices of our tart Tatin with an unsweetened mixture of whipped cream and sour cream. The cool and tangy cream provides a welcome counterpoint to the warm, sweet fruit and pastry.

TARTE TATIN
SERVES 8

Make sure that the caramel doesn't get too brown before adding the apples in step 5; it should be just golden. Be sure to let the tart rest for 30 minutes before serving, or it will likely break into pieces when you unmold it.

DOUGH

1⅓	cups (6⅔ ounces) all-purpose flour
¼	cup (1 ounce) confectioners' sugar
½	teaspoon salt
8	tablespoons unsalted butter, cut into ¼-inch pieces and chilled
1	large egg, lightly beaten

APPLES

8	tablespoons unsalted butter
¾	cup (5¼ ounces) granulated sugar
3	pounds Granny Smith apples, peeled, cored, and quartered

TOPPING

1	cup heavy cream, chilled
½	cup sour cream, chilled

1. FOR THE DOUGH: Process flour, sugar, and salt in food processor until combined, about 5 seconds. Scatter butter over top and pulse until mixture resembles coarse cornmeal, about 15 pulses. With processor running, add egg and continue to process until dough just comes together around processor blade, about 12 seconds.

2. Turn dough onto sheet of plastic wrap and flatten into 6-inch disk. Wrap tightly in plastic and refrigerate for 1 hour. Before rolling dough out, let it sit on counter to soften slightly, about 10 minutes. (Dough can be wrapped tightly in plastic and refrigerated for up to 2 days or frozen for up to 1 month. If frozen, let dough thaw completely on counter before rolling it out.)

3. Roll dough into 14-inch circle on lightly floured counter, then transfer to parchment paper–lined baking sheet; cover with plastic and refrigerate until needed.

4. FOR THE APPLES: Adjust oven rack to upper-middle position and heat oven to 425 degrees. Melt butter in 12-inch ovensafe nonstick skillet over medium-high heat. Stir in sugar and cook until mixture is light golden, 2 to 4 minutes.

5. Off heat, place first apple quarter cut side down, with end touching skillet wall. Continue to arrange apples, lifting each quarter on its edge and placing next apple quarter on its edge, so that apples stand straight up on cut edge. Fill skillet middle with remaining quarters, halved if necessary. Cook apples over medium heat until they are lightly golden and caramel is darkly colored, about 6 minutes, turning apples over halfway through cooking using fork or paring knife.

6. Off heat, slide chilled dough over apples in skillet. Being careful not to burn your fingers, fold back edge of dough so that it fits snugly into skillet. Transfer skillet to oven and bake tart until crust is golden brown, about 20 minutes, rotating skillet halfway through baking.

7. Using potholder (skillet handle will be very hot), remove skillet from oven. Let tart cool in skillet for 30 minutes. Run thin knife around edge, place inverted serving platter (or cutting board) over top and gently flip tart onto platter, using mitts or dish towels if skillet is still hot. Scrape out any apples that stick to skillet and put them back into place on tart.

8. FOR THE TOPPING: Using stand mixer fitted with whisk, whip heavy cream and sour cream on medium-low speed until foamy, about 1 minute. Increase speed to high and whip until soft peaks form, 1 to 3 minutes. Serve individual portions with dollop of topping.

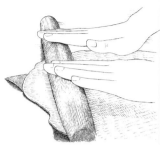

1. Roll dough out onto 16 by 12-inch piece of floured parchment paper.

2. Trim dough so that edges are even with parchment paper.

3. Roll up 1 inch of each edge to create ½-inch-thick border on all sides. Transfer dough and parchment to rimmed baking sheet.

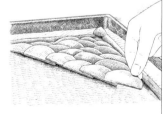

4. Starting in 1 corner, shingle sliced apples on diagonal to form even row over dough, overlapping each row by one-third.

Apple Galette

✔ WHY THIS RECIPE WORKS

The French tart known as an apple galette should have a flaky crust and a substantial layer of nicely shingled sweet caramelized apples. But it's challenging to make a crust strong enough to hold the apples and still be eaten out of hand—most recipes create a crust that is tough, crackerlike, and bland. Our ideal galette has the buttery flakiness of a croissant but is strong enough to support a generous layer of caramelized apples.

SMEAR THE DOUGH Fraisage is a French method of making pastry and involves smearing the dough with the heel of the hand. This spreads the butter pieces into long streaks between thin layers of flour and water, which bake up into thin, but sturdy layers and protects against leaking.

CUT ALL-PURPOSE FLOUR WITH INSTANT FLOUR Even when we used the mixing method, fraisage, to make our dough tender and flaky, we found that when using all-purpose flour, it just wasn't tender enough. The answer? Instant flour. Instant flour is made by slightly moistening all-purpose flour with water. After being spray-dried, the tiny flour granules look like small clusters of grapes. Since these aggregated flour granules are larger than those of finer-ground all-purpose flour, they absorb less water, making it harder for the proteins to form gluten. Replacing ½ cup of all-purpose with instant flour gives us dough that is tender but sturdy enough to cut neat slices of galette that can be eaten out of hand.

ROLL, TRIM, AND TUCK To make the rectangular pastry, first roll out the dough over a floured piece of parchment paper cut to 16 by 12 inches. Dust with more flour as needed. Trim the dough to fit and then roll up 1 inch of each edge, pinching firmly with your fingers to create a solid border.

SHINGLE AND GLAZE Although any apples will work in this recipe, we prefer Granny Smith. To arrange the apples, start in one corner and shingle to form even rows, overlapping by about one-third. The apples are sugared and dotted with butter. Although not all galette recipes call for it, many brush hot-out-of-the-oven tarts with apple jelly. This glaze provides an attractive sheen and helps to reinforce the apple flavor.

USE A FAIRLY HOT OVEN We bake the tart at 400 degrees, a temperature that strikes the right balance between intensely caramelized and simply burnt for a French-style tart that is simply spectacular.

APPLE GALETTE
SERVES 10 TO 12

The most common brand of instant flour is Wondra; it is sold in canisters in the baking aisle. The galette can be made without instant flour, using 2 cups all-purpose flour and 2 tablespoons cornstarch; however, you might have to increase the amount of ice water. Serve with vanilla ice cream, Whipped Cream (page 348) or Tangy Whipped Cream (page 280).

DOUGH
1½ cups (7½ ounces) all-purpose flour
½ cup (2½ ounces) instant flour
½ teaspoon salt
½ teaspoon sugar
12 tablespoons unsalted butter, cut into ¼-inch pieces and chilled
7–9 tablespoons ice water

TOPPING
1½ pounds Granny Smith apples, peeled, cored, halved, and sliced ⅛ inch thick
2 tablespoons unsalted butter, cut into ¼-inch pieces
¼ cup (1¾ ounces) sugar
3 tablespoons apple jelly

We also use this technique to mix the dough for our Free-Form Fruit Tart on page 413.

1. Starting at farthest end of dough pile, use heel of hand to smear small amount of dough against counter. Continue to smear dough until all crumbs have been worked.

2. Gather smeared crumbs together and repeat process.

1. FOR THE DOUGH: Process all-purpose flour, instant flour, salt, and sugar in food processor until combined, about 5 seconds. Scatter butter over top and pulse until mixture resembles coarse cornmeal, about 15 pulses. Continue to pulse, adding ice water 1 tablespoon at a time until dough begins to form small curds that hold together when pinched with your fingers (dough will be crumbly), about 10 pulses.

2. Turn dough crumbs onto lightly floured counter and gather into rectangular-shaped pile. Starting at farthest end, use heel of your hand to smear small amount of dough against counter. Continue to smear dough until all crumbs have been worked. Gather smeared crumbs together in another rectangular-shaped pile and repeat process. Press dough into 4-inch square, wrap it tightly in plastic wrap, and refrigerate for 1 hour. Before rolling dough out, let it sit on counter to soften slightly, about 10 minutes. (Dough can be wrapped tightly in plastic and refrigerated for up to 2 days or frozen for up to 1 month. If frozen, let dough thaw completely on counter before rolling it out.)

3. Adjust oven rack to middle position and heat oven to 400 degrees. Cut piece of parchment paper to measure exactly 16 by 12 inches. Roll dough out over parchment, dusting with flour as needed, until it just overhangs parchment. Trim edges of dough even with parchment. Roll outer 1 inch of dough up to create ½-inch-thick border. Slide parchment with dough onto baking sheet.

4. FOR THE TOPPING: Starting in 1 corner of tart, shingle apple slices into crust in tidy diagonal rows, overlapping them by one-third. Dot with butter and sprinkle evenly with sugar. Bake tart until bottom is deep golden brown and apples have caramelized, 45 minutes to 1 hour, rotating baking sheet halfway through baking.

5. Melt jelly in small saucepan over medium-high heat, stirring occasionally to smooth out any lumps. Brush glaze over apples and let tart cool slightly on sheet for 10 minutes. Slide tart onto large platter or cutting board and slice tart in half lengthwise, then crosswise into individual portions. Serve warm or at room temperature.

Classic Tart Dough

✔ WHY THIS RECIPE WORKS

While regular pie crust is tender and flaky, classic tart crust should be fine-textured, buttery-rich, crisp, and crumbly—it is often described as being shortbreadlike. We set out to achieve the perfect tart dough, one that we could use in a number of tart recipes.

DON'T SKIMP ON BUTTER Butter packs flavor and makes for a delicate crumb. We found that a full stick was the maximum amount we could include in our recipe—any more and then dough becomes difficult to handle.

PICK CONFECTIONERS' SUGAR AND ALL-PURPOSE FLOUR Instead of using the hard-to-find superfine sugar and pastry flour that many other recipes call for, we make our tart dough with confectioners' sugar and all-purpose flour.

INCLUDE A YOLK (AND CREAM) For a rich crumb and easier to handle dough, we incorporate an egg yolk and a little heavy cream.

CHILL BEFORE ROLLING Chilling allows the dough to hydrate to make it more manageable.

CLASSIC TART DOUGH
MAKES ENOUGH FOR ONE 9-INCH TART

- 1   large egg yolk
- 1   tablespoon heavy cream
- ½   teaspoon vanilla extract
- 1¼   cups (6¼ ounces) all-purpose flour
- ⅔   cup (2⅔ ounces) confectioners' sugar
- ¼   teaspoon salt
- 8   tablespoons unsalted butter, cut into ¼-inch pieces and chilled

1. Whisk egg yolk, cream, and vanilla together in bowl. Process flour, sugar, and salt in food processor until combined, about 5 seconds. Scatter butter over top and pulse until mixture resembles coarse cornmeal, about 15 pulses. With processor running, add egg mixture and continue to process until dough just comes together around processor blade, about 12 seconds.

2. Turn dough onto sheet of plastic wrap and flatten into 6-inch disk. Wrap tightly in plastic and refrigerate for 1 hour. Before rolling out dough, let it sit on counter to soften slightly, about 10 minutes. (Dough can be wrapped tightly in plastic wrap and refrigerated for up to 2 days or frozen for up to 1 month. If frozen, let dough thaw completely on counter before rolling it out.)

3. Roll dough into 11-inch circle on lightly floured counter (if at any point dough becomes too soft and sticky to work with, slip dough onto baking sheet and freeze or refrigerate until workable). Place dough round on baking sheet, cover with plastic, and refrigerate for about 30 minutes.

4. Remove dough from refrigerator; discard plastic but keep dough on baking sheet. Loosely roll dough around rolling pin and gently unroll it onto 9-inch tart pan with removable bottom, letting excess dough hang over edge. Ease dough into pan by gently lifting edge of dough with your hand while pressing into corners with your other hand. Leave any dough that overhangs pan in place.

5. Press dough into fluted sides of pan, forming distinct seam around pan's circumference. (If some sections of edge are too thin, reinforce them by folding excess dough back on itself.) Run rolling pin over top of tart pan to remove any excess dough. Wrap dough-lined tart pan loosely in plastic, place on large plate, and freeze until dough is fully chilled and firm, about 30 minutes, before using. (Dough-lined tart pan can be wrapped tightly in plastic and frozen for up to 1 month.)

6. Adjust oven rack to middle position and heat oven to 375 degrees. Set dough-lined tart pan on rimmed baking sheet. Press parchment paper or double layer of aluminum foil into frozen tart shell, covering edges to prevent burning, and fill with pie weights.

7A. FOR A PARTIALLY BAKED SHELL: Bake until tart shell is golden brown and set, about 30 minutes, rotating baking sheet halfway through baking. Transfer tart shell with baking sheet to wire rack and carefully remove weights and foil. Use crust while it is still warm or let it cool completely (see individual tart recipe instructions).

7B. FOR A FULLY BAKED SHELL: Bake until tart shell is golden brown and set, about 30 minutes, rotating baking sheet halfway through baking. Carefully remove weights and foil and continue to bake tart shell until it is fully baked and golden, 5 to 10 minutes longer. Transfer tart shell with baking sheet to wire rack and let tart shell cool completely, about 1 hour.

11-INCH CLASSIC TART DOUGH

Substitute 11-inch tart pan for 9-inch tart pan. Increase cream to 2 tablespoons, flour to 1½ cups, sugar to ¾ cup, and butter to 10 tablespoons. In step 3, roll dough into 15-inch circle.

FITTING TART DOUGH INTO THE PAN

1. After rolling out dough, loosely roll it around rolling pin, then gently unroll it evenly onto tart pan.

2. Lift up edges of dough and ease it down into corners of pan.

3. Press dough into fluted sides of pan.

4. Reinforce any thin areas of edge by folding dough back on itself.

5. Run rolling pin over top of tart pan to remove any excess dough. Finished edge should be ¼ inch thick. If it is not, press dough up over edge and trim excess.

Sometimes the edges of a tart
shell can burn before the bottom is cooked through and
nicely browned. Instead of
trying to fold together strips
of aluminum foil, we invert
the ring from a second, larger
tart pan over the endangered
crust. The tart can continue
to bake without further coloring of the edges.

Baked Raspberry Tart

✔ WHY THIS RECIPE WORKS

Tart raspberries, rich custard, and a buttery crust are a classic white-tablecloth combination. But we wanted something a little less labor-intensive; we were seeking a more rustic, casual approach that still provided the perfect marriage of fruit, custard, and pastry.

BLIND-BAKE CLASSIC TART DOUGH The rich, buttery crust of our Classic Tart Dough is a terrific foil to sweet raspberries and a custard filling. We blind-bake our crust, lining it with foil and pie weights to prevent the crust from puffing up. After baking, we remove the foil and weights and return it to the oven to brown slightly.

ADD BERRIES Once the tart shell is cool, we add fresh raspberries in a single layer.

BLANKET WITH CUSTARD AND BAKE The base of our custard is a mix of butter, egg, sugar, and flour. We heighten the custard's flavor by browning the butter instead of sim-ply melting it. Lemon zest and juice further brighten the flavor and the optional kirsch underscores the fruit flavor of the raspberries. Using one whole egg plus an egg white ensures the filling sets into a nicely firm yet creamy texture. And substituting instant flour for all-purpose flour gives us a smooth and silky (rather than starchy and coarse) texture.

BAKED RASPBERRY TART
SERVES 8 TO 10

The most common brand of instant flour is Wondra; it is sold in canisters in the baking aisle. To minimize waste, reserve the egg white left from making the tart pastry for use in the filling. If your raspberries are either very tart or very sweet, adjust the amount of sugar in the filling by about a tablespoon or so. This tart is best eaten the day it is made.

6	tablespoons unsalted butter
1	large egg plus 1 large white
½	cup (3½ ounces) plus 1 tablespoon sugar
¼	teaspoon salt
1	teaspoon vanilla extract
1	teaspoon kirsch or framboise (optional)
¼	teaspoon grated lemon zest plus 1½ teaspoons juice
2	tablespoons instant flour
2	tablespoons heavy cream
10	ounces (2 cups) raspberries
1	recipe Classic Tart Dough (page 411), partially baked and cooled

1. Adjust oven rack to middle position and heat oven to 375 degrees. Melt butter in small saucepan over medium heat, swirling occa-sionally, until butter is browned and releases nutty aroma, about 7 minutes. Transfer butter to small bowl and let cool slightly. Whisk egg and white in medium bowl until combined. Add sugar and salt and whisk vigorously until light colored, about 1 minute. Whisk in warm browned butter until combined, then whisk in vanilla, kirsch, if using, and lemon zest and juice. Whisk in instant flour, then whisk in cream until combined.

2. Distribute raspberries in single tightly packed layer in bottom of cooled prebaked tart shell. Pour filling mixture evenly over raspber-ries. Bake tart on baking sheet until fragrant, filling is set (it does not jiggle when shaken) and bubbling lightly around edges, and sur-face is puffed and deep golden brown, about 30 minutes, rotating baking sheet halfway through baking. Transfer tart with baking sheet to wire rack and let cool to room temper-ature, about 2 hours. To serve, remove outer metal ring of tart pan, slide thin metal spatula between tart and tart pan bottom, and carefully slide tart onto serving platter or cutting board.

Free-Form Fruit Tart

✔ WHY THIS RECIPE WORKS

We wanted a simple take on summer fruit pie, one without the rolling and fitting usually required for a traditional pie or tart.

CREATE A STRONG BUT FLAKY DOUGH Using too much butter results in a weak, leaky crust. Too little makes for a crust that is crackerlike and edging toward tough. We settled on 10 tablespoons for 1½ cups of flour. But just as important as the amount of butter is the mixing method. We tried mixing the dough in a food processor, with a stand mixer, and by hand. We found that the latter two methods mashed the butter into the flour and produced a less flaky crust. Quick pulses with the food processor, however, "cut" the butter into the flour so that it remains in distinct pieces. We mix the butter to be about the size of coarse bread crumbs—just big enough to create the steamed spaces needed for flakiness.

SMEAR THE DOUGH Fraisage is a French method of making pastry and involves smearing the dough with the heel of the hand. This spreads the butter pieces into long streaks between thin layers of flour and water, which results in a stable, yet tender, flaky crust.

DON'T ADD SUGAR OR LEMON We tried adding sugar and lemon juice to the crust dough, but lemon juice made the crust too tender, as acid weakens the gluten structure in dough. Sugar improved the flavor of the crust but was detrimental to the texture, even a small amount making it brittle. We sprinkle sugar on top of the dough before baking instead.

KEEP THE FILLING SIMPLE There is no butter needed in our simple fruit filling. We use just ripe fruit sprinkled with 3 to 5 tablespoons of sugar (depending on the type of fruit and its natural sweetness). Though we prefer a tart made with a mix of stone fruits and berries (our favorite combinations are plums and raspberries, peaches and blueberries, and apricots and blackberries), you can use only one type of fruit if you prefer. Peeling the stone fruit (even the peaches) is not necessary.

ROLL AND FOLD We roll out the dough to about the height of three stacked quarters (or ³⁄₁₆ inch). This is thick enough to contain a lot of fruit but thin enough to bake evenly and thoroughly. After mounding the fruit in the center, leaving a 2½-inch border, we lift the dough up and back over the fruit (leaving the center of the tart exposed) and loosely pleat the dough to allow for shrinkage.

USE A HOT OVEN, COOL ON A RACK When testing this recipe, we baked it on the center rack of the oven at 350, 375, 400, and 425 degrees. Baking at the lowest temperature took too long; it also dried out the fruit and failed to brown the crust. At too high a temperature, the crust darkened on the folds but remained pale and underdone in the creases, and the fruit became charred. Setting the oven to 375 degrees generates the ideal time and temperature for an evenly baked, flaky tart. The last small but significant step toward a crisp crust is to cool the tart directly on a wire rack; this keeps the crust from steaming itself as it cools.

FREE-FORM FRUIT TART
SERVES 6

See page 410 for more information on mixing the tart dough in step 2. Taste the fruit before adding sugar to it; use the lesser amount if the fruit is very sweet, more if it is tart. However much sugar you use, do not add it to the fruit until you are ready to fill and form the tart. Serve with vanilla ice cream or Whipped Cream (page 348).

DOUGH
- 1½   cups (7½ ounces) all-purpose flour
- ½   teaspoon salt
- 10   tablespoons unsalted butter, cut into ½-inch pieces and chilled
- 4–6   tablespoons ice water

WASHING BERRIES
Washing berries before you use them is always a safe practice, and we think that the best way to wash them is to place the berries in a colander and rinse them gently under running water for at least 30 seconds. As for drying them, we've tested a variety of methods and have found that a salad spinner lined with a buffering layer of paper towels is the best approach.

As for storage, berries are prone to growing mold and rotting quickly. If the berries aren't to be used immediately, we recommend cleaning the berries with a mild vinegar solution (3 cups water mixed with 1 cup white vinegar), which will destroy the bacteria, before drying them and storing them in a paper-towel lined airtight container.

1. Gently rinse berries in colander under running water.

2. Place berries in salad spinner lined with 3 layers of paper towels. Spin for 15 seconds or until berries are completely dry.

MAKING A FREE-FORM TART

1. For an even circle, roll in short motions, working from center outward and moving dough ¼ turn after each roll.

2. Pile fruit in center of dough, leaving 2½-inch border around fruit.

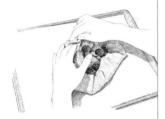

3. Working your way around dough, gently pull up sides and create fold every 2 inches.

4. Working quickly, brush top and sides of dough with water and sprinkle with 1 tablespoon sugar.

FILLING

1 pound peaches, nectarines, apricots, or plums, halved, pitted, and cut into ½-inch wedges

5 ounces (1 cup) blueberries, raspberries, or blackberries

4–6 tablespoons sugar

1. FOR THE DOUGH: Process flour and salt in food processor until combined, about 5 seconds. Scatter butter over top and pulse until mixture resembles coarse bread crumbs and butter pieces are about size of small peas, about 10 pulses. Continue to pulse, adding ice water 1 tablespoon at a time, until dough begins to form small curds that hold together when pinched with your fingers (dough will be crumbly), about 10 pulses.

2. Turn dough crumbs onto lightly floured counter and gather into rectangular-shaped pile. Starting at farthest end, use heel of your hand to smear small amount of dough against counter. Continue to smear dough until all crumbs have been worked. Gather smeared crumbs together in another rectangular-shaped pile and repeat process. Press dough into 6-inch disk, wrap it tightly in plastic wrap, and refrigerate for 1 hour. Before rolling out dough, let it sit on counter to soften slightly, about 10 minutes. (Dough can be wrapped tightly in plastic and refrigerated for up to 2 days or frozen for up to 1 month. If frozen, let dough thaw completely on counter before rolling it out.)

3. Roll dough into 12-inch circle between 2 large sheets of floured parchment paper. (If dough sticks to parchment, gently loosen and lift sticky area with bench scraper and dust parchment with additional flour.) Slide dough, still between parchment sheets, onto rimmed baking sheet and refrigerate until firm, 15 to 30 minutes. (If refrigerated longer and dough is hard and brittle, let stand at room temperature until pliant.)

4. FOR THE FILLING: Adjust oven rack to middle position and heat oven to 375 degrees. Gently toss fruit and 3 to 5 tablespoons sugar together in bowl. Remove top sheet of parchment paper from dough. Mound fruit in center of dough, leaving 2½-inch border around edge of fruit. Being careful to leave ½-inch border of dough around edge of fruit, fold outermost 2 inches of dough over fruit, pleating it every 2 to 3 inches as needed; gently pinch pleated dough to secure, but do not press dough into fruit. Working quickly, brush top and sides of dough with water and sprinkle evenly with remaining 1 tablespoon sugar.

5. Bake until crust is deep golden brown and fruit is bubbling, about 1 hour, rotating baking sheet halfway through baking. Transfer tart with baking sheet to wire rack and let cool for 10 minutes, then use parchment to gently transfer tart to wire rack. Use metal spatula to loosen tart from parchment and remove parchment. Let tart cool on rack until juices have thickened, about 25 minutes; serve slightly warm or at room temperature.

FREE-FORM SUMMER FRUIT TARTLETS
MAKES 4 TARTLETS

Divide dough into 4 equal portions before rolling out in step 3. Roll each portion into 7-inch circle on parchment paper; stack rounds and refrigerate until firm. Continue with recipe from step 4, mounding one-quarter of fruit in center of dough round, leaving 1½-inch border around edge. Being careful to leave ¼-inch border of dough around edge of fruit, fold outermost 1 to 1¼ inches of dough over fruit. Transfer parchment with tart to rimmed baking sheet. Repeat with remaining fruit and dough. Brush dough with water and sprinkle each tartlet with portion of remaining 1 tablespoon sugar. Bake until crust is deep golden brown and fruit is bubbling, 40 to 45 minutes, rotating baking sheet halfway through baking.

Fresh Fruit Tart

✓ WHY THIS RECIPE WORKS

Fresh fruit tarts usually offer little substance beyond their dazzling beauty, with rubbery or puddinglike fillings, soggy crusts, and underripe, flavorless fruit. We set out to create a buttery, crisp crust filled with rich, lightly sweetened pastry cream, topped with fresh fruit.

START WITH A STURDY, BUT TENDER CRUST We bake and cool our Classic Tart Dough (page 411) for our fruit tart. And to preserve its crisp texture, we wait to fill it with the pastry cream and fruit until just before serving.

FILL WITH PASTRY CREAM We make our pastry cream with plenty of egg yolks, half-and-half, butter, and just enough cornstarch so that the cream keeps its shape without becoming gummy. To prevent the pastry cream from curdling, we temper, or warm, the yolks with a portion of the hot half-and-half mixture before mixing it all together.

USE A MIX OF FRESH FRUIT We like a combination of sliced kiwis, raspberries, and blueberries. We find that it is important not to wash the berries, as washing causes them to bruise and bleed and makes for a less than attractive tart (buy organic if you're worried about pesticide residues).

GLAZE WITH JELLY For a glistening finishing touch reminiscent of a French patisserie, we heat red currant or apple jelly until smooth and then gently brush it over the fresh fruit.

CLASSIC FRESH FRUIT TART
SERVES 8 TO 10

Do not fill the prebaked tart shell until just before serving. Once filled, the tart should be topped with fruit, glazed, and served within 30 minutes or so. Don't wash the berries or they will lose their flavor and shape.

2	cups half-and-half
½	cup (3½ ounces) sugar
	Pinch salt
5	large egg yolks
3	tablespoons cornstarch
4	tablespoons unsalted butter, cut into 4 pieces
1½	teaspoons vanilla extract
1	recipe Classic Tart Dough (page 411), fully baked and cooled
2	large kiwis, peeled, halved lengthwise, and sliced ⅜ inch thick
10	ounces (2 cups) raspberries
5	ounces (1 cup) blueberries
½	cup red currant or apple jelly

1. Bring half-and-half, 6 tablespoons sugar, and salt to simmer in medium saucepan, stirring occasionally.

2. As half-and-half mixture begins to simmer, whisk egg yolks, cornstarch, and remaining 2 tablespoons sugar in medium bowl until smooth. Slowly whisk 1 cup of simmering half-and-half mixture into yolk mixture to temper, then slowly whisk tempered yolk mixture back into remaining half-and-half mixture. Reduce heat to medium and cook, whisking vigorously, until mixture is thickened and few bubbles burst on surface, about 30 seconds. Off heat, whisk in butter and vanilla. Transfer mixture to clean bowl, lay sheet of plastic wrap directly on surface, and refrigerate pastry cream until chilled and firm, about 3 hours. (Pastry cream can be refrigerated for up to 2 days.)

3. Spread chilled pastry cream evenly over bottom of cooled prebaked tart shell. Shingle kiwi slices around edge of tart, then arrange 3 rows of raspberries inside kiwi. Finally, arrange mound of blueberries in center.

4. Melt jelly in small saucepan over medium-high heat, stirring occasionally to smooth out any lumps. Using pastry brush,

A vegetable peeler can crush soft kiwi flesh if you attempt to remove the hairy skin with this tool. We like this method, which won't bruise the fruit.

1. Trim ends of fruit and insert small spoon between skin and flesh, with bowl of spoon facing flesh. Push spoon down and carefully move it around fruit, separating flesh from skin.

2. Gently remove spoon and pull loosened skin away from flesh.

Place the berries in a large plastic bag. Hold the bag closed with one hand and use the other to gently jostle the berries about to combine them. Empty the mixed berries into the tart.

To fill gaps between whole berries, begin at the center of the tart and place quartered berries between them, pointed side up and skin side out, leaning the quartered berries toward the center.

dab melted jelly over fruit. To serve, remove outer metal ring of tart pan, slide thin metal spatula between tart and tart pan bottom, and carefully slide tart onto serving platter or cutting board.

STRAWBERRY TART

Substitute 3 quarts strawberries, hulled, and sorted by height for kiwi, raspberries, and blueberries. Starting in center with largest of strawberries, arrange them in tight, concentric circles over tart. Quarter remaining strawberry and use to fill any gaps. Glaze and serve as directed.

MIXED BERRY TART

Omit kiwi and add 2 cups extra berries (including blackberries or hulled and quartered strawberries). Combine berries in large plastic bag and toss them gently to mix. Carefully spread berries in even layer over tart. Glaze and serve as directed.

Lemon Tart

✓ WHY THIS RECIPE WORKS
Despite its apparent simplicity, there is much that can go wrong with a lemon tart. It can slip over the edge of sweet into cloying; its tartness can grab at your throat; it can be gluey or eggy or, even worse, metallic-tasting. Its crust can be too hard, too soft, too thick, or too sweet.
PREBAKE THE TART SHELL The filling for our lemon tart only takes 10 to 15 minutes to set, so the tart shell should be fully baked.
MAKE A RICH, BRIGHT LEMON CURD For our lemon filling, we zeroed in on homemade lemon curd. For just enough sugar to offset the acid in the lemons, we use 3 parts sugar to 2 parts lemon juice, plus a whopping ¼ cup of lemon zest. To achieve a curd that is creamy and dense with a vibrant lemony yellow color, we use a combination of whole eggs and egg yolks. We cook the curd over direct heat, then whisk in butter. And for a smooth, light texture, we strain the curd, then stir in heavy cream just before baking.
DON'T OVERBAKE We pour the filling into the tart shell while it's still warm to preserve the crisp texture and we bake the tart just until the filling is set. The center should jiggle slightly when shaken. The color of the curd will have deepened and, once cool, it will be supple and creamy, yet firm enough to be sliceable.

CLASSIC LEMON TART
SERVES 8 TO 10

Once the lemon curd ingredients have been combined, cook the curd immediately; otherwise, it will have a grainy finished texture. The shell should still be warm when the filling is added. Dust with confectioners' sugar before serving, or serve with Whipped Cream (page 348).

- 2 large eggs plus 7 large yolks
- 1 cup (7 ounces) sugar
- ¼ cup grated lemon zest plus ⅔ cup juice (4 lemons)
  Pinch salt
- 4 tablespoons unsalted butter, cut into 4 pieces
- 3 tablespoons heavy cream
- 1 recipe Classic Tart Dough (page 411), fully baked and still warm

1. Adjust oven rack to middle position and heat oven to 375 degrees. Whisk eggs and

When making an acidic curd or sauce such as the lemon curd filling for our Classic Lemon Tart, it's important to use nonreactive cookware and bowls—these can be stainless steel or glass, or have nonstick or enameled surfaces. If you use reactive cookware, such as cast iron or aluminum, the acidity of the lemons will react with the metal and your curd will wind up tasting metallic.

yolks together in medium saucepan. Whisk in sugar until combined, then whisk in lemon zest and juice and salt. Add butter and cook over medium-low heat, stirring constantly, until mixture thickens slightly and registers 170 degrees, about 5 minutes. Immediately pour mixture through fine-mesh strainer into bowl and stir in cream.

2. Pour warm lemon filling into warm pre-baked tart shell. Bake tart on baking sheet until filling is shiny and opaque and center jiggles slightly when shaken, 10 to 15 minutes, rotating baking sheet halfway through baking. Transfer tart with baking sheet to wire rack and let cool to room temperature, about 2 hours. To serve, remove outer metal ring of tart pan, slide thin metal spatula between tart and tart pan bottom, and carefully slide tart onto serving platter or cutting board.

Poached Pear and Almond Tart

✓ WHY THIS RECIPE WORKS
We wanted satin-ribbon slices of tender, sweet, perfumed poached pears embedded in a custard-cake almond filling, all contained in a crisp, buttery pastry. In short, we wanted a showstopper of a fruit tart.

MAKE A FRANGIPANE FILLING For the almond filling, we make a classic frangipane (a thick, almond-flavored custard) by processing blanched slivered almonds in a food processor with sugar. Grinding the nuts with the sugar helps prevent the superfine mixture from turning greasy. An egg, egg white, vanilla and almond extracts, and butter finish the filling.

PICK BOSCS OR BARTLETTS AND POACH During our testing, we determined that ripe yet firm Bosc or Bartlett pears give the tart the best flavor. We poach pear halves in white wine spiced with a cinnamon stick, black peppercorns, whole cloves, and a vanilla bean. To ensure the flavorful poaching liquid fully penetrates the fruit, we let the pears cool in the liquid.

DRY AND SLICE THE POACHED PEAR HALVES We dry the pears before setting them on the frangipane—otherwise, they release moisture, turning the dessert sticky and wet. For an elegant presentation and easy serving, we slice the pear halves into thin crosswise slices, keeping the slices intact.

BAKE AND GLAZE Once the tart is baked, we glaze the pears with warm apple jelly for a glossy, shiny finish.

POACHED PEAR AND ALMOND TART
SERVES 10 TO 12

If you cannot find blanched slivered almonds, use whole blanched almonds, but chop them coarse before processing to make sure they form a fine, even grind. If you cannot find blanched almonds, see our method on page 9. The pears should be ripe but firm, the flesh near the stem giving slightly when gently pressed with a finger. Many tasters liked the bright, crisp flavor of pears poached in Sauvignon Blanc. Chardonnay-poached pears had deeper, oakier flavors and were also well liked.

POACHED PEARS

1	(750-ml) bottle white wine
2/3	cup (4 2/3 ounces) sugar
5	(2-inch) strips lemon zest plus 2 tablespoons juice
1	cinnamon stick
15	whole peppercorns
3	whole cloves
1/8	teaspoon salt
1/2	vanilla bean (optional)
4	Bosc or Bartlett pears (8 ounces each), peeled, halved, and cored

FILLING AND GLAZE

1	cup blanched slivered almonds
1/2	cup (3 1/2 ounces) sugar
1/8	teaspoon salt
1	large egg plus 1 large white
1/2	teaspoon almond extract
1/2	teaspoon vanilla extract
6	tablespoons unsalted butter, cut into 6 pieces and softened
1	recipe 11-Inch Classic Tart Dough (page 411), partially baked and cooled
1/4	cup apple jelly

1. FOR THE POACHED PEARS: Adjust oven rack to middle position and heat oven to 350 degrees. Combine wine, sugar, lemon zest and juice, cinnamon stick, peppercorns, cloves, and salt in large saucepan. If using, cut vanilla bean in half lengthwise, then, using tip of paring knife, scrape out seeds, and add seeds and pod to saucepan. Bring mixture to simmer, stirring occasionally to dissolve sugar. Slide pear halves into simmering wine mixture; return to simmer, then reduce heat to low, cover, and poach pears, turning them occasionally, until tender and skewer can be inserted into pear with very little resistance, about 10 minutes. Off heat, let pears cool in liquid, partially covered, until pears have turned translucent and are cool enough to handle, about 1 hour. (Pears and liquid can be transferred to bowl, cooled to room temperature, covered, and refrigerated for up to 3 days.)

2. FOR THE FILLING: Pulse almonds, sugar, and salt in food processor until finely ground, about 25 pulses. Continue to process until nut mixture is as finely ground as possible, about 10 seconds. Add egg and white, almond extract, and vanilla and process until combined, about 10 seconds. Add butter and process until no lumps remain, about 20 seconds, scraping down bowl as needed. (Filling can transferred to bowl, covered, and refrigerated for up to 3 days. Before using, let stand at room temperature about 30 minutes to soften, stirring 3 or 4 times.)

3. Spread filling evenly over bottom of cooled, partially baked tart shell. Remove pears from poaching liquid and pat dry with paper towels. Cut 1 poached pear half crosswise into 3/8-inch slices, leaving pear half intact on cutting board (do not separate slices). Pat dry again with paper towels to absorb excess moisture. Discard first 4 slices from narrow end of sliced pear half. Slide spatula under sliced pear and, steadying it with your hand, slide pear off spatula onto center of tart. Cut and dry another pear half. Slide spatula under pear and gently press pear to fan slices toward narrow end. Slide fanned pear half onto filling, narrow end toward center, almost touching center pear. Repeat slicing, fanning, and placing remaining pear halves, spacing them evenly and making flower petal pattern off center pear.

4. Bake tart on baking sheet until crust is deep golden brown and almond filling is puffed, browned, and firm to the touch, about 45 minutes, rotating baking sheet halfway through baking. Transfer tart with baking sheet to wire rack and let cool for 10 minutes.

5. FOR THE GLAZE: Melt jelly in small saucepan over medium-high heat, stirring occasionally to smooth out lumps. Using pastry brush, dab melted jelly over fruit. Let tart cool to room temperature, about 2 hours. To serve, remove outer metal ring of tart pan, slide thin metal spatula between tart and tart pan bottom, and carefully slide tart onto serving platter or cutting board.

ASSEMBLING A POACHED PEAR TART

1. Cut 1 poached pear half crosswise into 3/8-inch slices, leaving pear half intact on cutting board (do not separate slices). Pat dry with paper towels to absorb excess moisture.

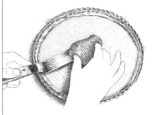

2. Discard first 4 slices from narrow end of sliced pear half. Slide icing spatula under sliced pear and, steadying it with 1 hand, slide pear off spatula onto center of frangipane-filled tart.

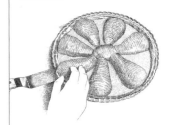

3. Cut and dry second pear half following step 1. Slide spatula under pear and gently press pear to fan slices toward narrow end. Slide fanned pear half onto frangipane, narrow end toward center, almost touching center pear. Repeat with remaining pear halves, spacing them evenly and making flower petal pattern off center pear.

A footed cake stand might
be the best plate for serving
a pretty tart, but it won't fit
in the refrigerator to protect
leftovers. For that job, we
use an inverted springform
pan. Place the tart, still on
the removable pan bottom,
on a shelf in the refrigerator
and cover with an inverted
springform pan.

Best Chocolate Tart

✔ WHY THIS RECIPE WORKS

Inflated descriptors like "irresistibly chocolaty" and "ridiculously scrumptious" are de rigueur when it comes to chocolate tarts. For us, though, the real draw of the dessert is its pure, uncomplicated nature: The best versions boast a flawlessly smooth texture, clean chocolate flavor, and a sophisticated look. We wanted to uncover the makings of a chocolate tart par excellence.

MAKE A CUSTARD-STYLE FILLING Various tart styles exist for a chocolate tart. We like a custard-style tart by melting chocolate into hot cream, then eggs are incorporated before baking. Once baked, this filling boasts an agreeable "set" consistency. Two eggs along with 1¼ cups cream provides the right ratio for a soft, but not-too-dense filling.

CHOOSE THE RIGHT CHOCOLATE We like a dark chocolate with 60 percent cocoa solids in this recipe. It has a pleasantly intense taste and supplies enough sweetness that no additional sugar is necessary.

ADD BUTTER Our filling tasted good, but was somewhat one-dimensional. We were able to fix that by taking a page from ganache-style tarts, which include butter. Just 4 tablespoons amplified the chocolate flavor and gave our custard depth.

KEEP THE FOCUS ON THE CHOCOLATE It's tempting to pair ingredients like orange zest and cognac with chocolate, but we found that these only detract from its taste. The exception was instant espresso, which adds an echo of bittersweetness that highlights the chocolate.

PICK YOUR PASTRY We test drove a number of pastry options, pitting cocoa tart dough against almond tart dough. The cocoa pastry makes for a dramatic-looking dessert (dark crust, dark filling), but chocolate-on-chocolate doesn't offer any flavor contrast.

We struck gold with the almond pastry—its deep, nutty flavor; pleasantly nubby texture; and speckled look (from flecks of almond skin) is an ideal match for the chocolate filling.

GLAZE IT We wanted this celebratory dessert to boast a slick, glistening sheen. A simple chocolate glaze does the trick: a combination of chocolate and cream, plus a measure of corn syrup for glossiness.

BAKE LOW AND SLOW Custards have a tendency to curdle under high heat. It's essential to bake this tart at a very low temperature, 250 degrees, for a smooth and silky texture.

BEST CHOCOLATE TART

SERVES 12

Toasted and skinned hazelnuts can be substituted for the almonds. Use good-quality dark chocolate containing a cacao percentage between 60 and 65 percent; our favorites are Callebaut Intense Dark Chocolate, L-60–40NV, and Ghirardelli 60% Cacao Bittersweet Chocolate. Let tart sit at room temperature before glazing in step 6. The finished tart can be garnished with chocolate curls or with a flaky coarse sea salt, such as Maldon. Serve with Whipped Cream (page 348); if you like, substitute cognac for the vanilla extract.

CRUST
- 1 large egg yolk
- 2 tablespoons heavy cream
- ½ cup sliced almonds, toasted
- ¼ cup (1¾ ounces) sugar
- 1 cup (5 ounces) all-purpose flour
- ¼ teaspoon salt
- 6 tablespoons unsalted butter, cut into ½-inch pieces

FILLING

1¼	cups heavy cream
½	teaspoon instant espresso powder
¼	teaspoon salt
9	ounces bittersweet chocolate, chopped fine
4	tablespoons unsalted butter, cut into thin slices and softened
2	large eggs, lightly beaten, room temperature

GLAZE

3	tablespoons heavy cream
1	tablespoon light corn syrup
2	ounces bittersweet chocolate, chopped fine
1	tablespoon hot water

1. FOR THE CRUST: Beat egg yolk and cream together in small bowl. Process almonds and sugar in food processor until nuts are finely ground, 15 to 20 seconds. Add flour and salt; pulse to combine, about 10 pulses. Scatter butter over flour mixture; pulse to cut butter into flour until mixture resembles coarse meal, about 15 pulses. With processor running, add egg yolk mixture and process until dough forms ball, about 10 seconds. Transfer dough to large sheet of plastic wrap and press into 6-inch disk; wrap dough in plastic and refrigerate until firm but malleable, about 30 minutes. (Dough can be refrigerated for up to 3 days; before using, let stand at room temperature until malleable but still cool.)

2. Roll out dough between 2 large sheets of plastic into 11-inch round about ⅜ inch thick. (If dough becomes too soft and sticky to work with, slip it onto baking sheet and refrigerate until workable.) Place dough round on baking sheet and refrigerate until firm but pliable, about 15 minutes.

3. Adjust oven rack to middle position and heat oven to 375 degrees. Spray 9-inch tart pan with removable bottom with vegetable oil spray. Keeping dough on sheet, remove top layer of plastic. Invert tart pan (with bottom) on top of dough round. Press on tart pan to cut dough. Using both hands, pick up sheet and tart pan and carefully invert both, setting tart pan right side up. Remove sheet and peel off plastic; reserve plastic. Roll over edges of tart pan with rolling pin to cut dough. Gently ease and press dough into bottom of pan, reserving scraps. Roll dough scraps into ¾-inch rope (various lengths are OK). Line edge of tart pan with rope(s) and gently press into fluted sides. Line tart pan with reserved plastic and, using measuring cup, gently press and smooth dough to even thickness (sides should be about ¼ inch thick). Using paring knife, trim any excess dough above rim of tart; discard scraps. Freeze dough-lined pan until dough is firm, 20 to 30 minutes.

4. Set dough-lined pan on baking sheet. Spray 12-inch square of aluminum foil with oil spray and press foil, sprayed side down, into pan; fill with 2 cups pie weights. Bake until dough is dry and light golden brown, about 25 minutes, rotating sheet halfway through baking. Carefully remove foil and weights and continue to bake until pastry is rich golden brown and fragrant, 8 to 10 minutes longer. Let cool completely on baking sheet on wire rack.

5. FOR THE FILLING: Heat oven to 250 degrees. Bring cream, espresso powder, and salt to simmer in small saucepan over medium heat, stirring once or twice to dissolve espresso powder and salt. Meanwhile, place chocolate in large heatproof bowl. Pour simmering cream mixture over chocolate, cover, and let stand for 5 minutes to allow chocolate to soften. Using whisk, stir mixture slowly and gently (so as not to incorporate air) until homogeneous. Add butter and continue to whisk gently until fully incorporated. Pour beaten eggs through fine-mesh strainer into chocolate mixture; whisk slowly until mixture is homogeneous and glossy. Pour filling into tart crust and shake gently from side to side to

FITTING THE TART DOUGH

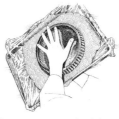

1. Invert tart pan (with bottom) on top of dough round. (The removable bottom will drop onto dough.) Press on tart pan to cut dough. Pick up baking sheet, carefully invert it, and set tart pan down. Remove sheet and peel off plastic wrap.

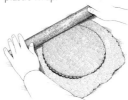

2. Roll over dough edges with rolling pin to cut, reserving scraps. Gently ease and press dough into bottom of pan.

3. Roll dough scraps into ¾-inch rope. Line edge of tart pan with rope and gently press into fluted sides.

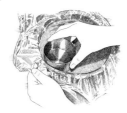

4. Line tart pan with reserved plastic. Using measuring cup, gently press dough to an even thickness. The sides should be ¼ inch thick. Use paring knife to trim excess dough above rim of tart.

distribute and smooth surface; pop any large bubbles with toothpick or skewer. Bake tart, on baking sheet, until outer edge of filling is just set and very faint cracks appear on surface, 30 to 35 minutes; filling will still be very wobbly. Let cool completely on baking sheet on wire rack. Refrigerate, uncovered, until filling is chilled and set, at least 3 hours or up to 18 hours.

6. FOR THE GLAZE: Thirty minutes before glazing, remove tart from refrigerator. Bring cream and corn syrup to simmer in small saucepan over medium heat; stir once or twice to combine. Remove pan from heat, add chocolate, and cover. Let stand for 5 minutes to allow chocolate to soften. Whisk gently (so as not to incorporate air) until mixture is smooth, then whisk in hot water until glaze is homogeneous, shiny, and pourable. Working quickly, pour glaze onto center of tart. To distribute glaze, tilt tart and allow glaze to run to edge. (Spreading glaze with spatula will leave marks on surface.) Pop any large bubbles with toothpick or skewer. Let cool completely, about 1 hour.

7. To serve: Remove outer ring from tart pan. Insert thin-bladed metal spatula between crust and pan bottom to loosen tart; slide tart onto serving platter. Cut into wedges and serve.

Chocolate Caramel Walnut Tart

✔ WHY THIS RECIPE WORKS

Considering the natural affinity of its main ingredients, a chocolate caramel walnut tart would seem a hard recipe to botch. However, this trio doesn't always live in harmony. Some recipes relegate the walnuts to a mere garnish and sprinkle them over chilled chocolate fillings with textures that run the gamut from soft pudding to cold butter. Other recipes place the nuts at the fore, but these are simply uptown knockoffs of pecan pie. We wanted a show-stopping tart boasting a layer of walnuts draped with soft caramel topped with a smooth layer of rich, dark chocolate—firm enough to slice neatly but neither dense nor overpowering.

CREATE THE RIGHT CRUST We modify our sweet tart pastry (page 411) to better match the caramel and chocolate filling. Adding ground walnuts boosts the pastry's flavor and adds a secondary layer of walnut flavor and crunch. Replacing cream with an egg makes for a cleaner-cutting, crispier tart.

DON'T TAKE SHORTCUTS WITH THE CARAMEL We wanted a soft, but sliceable caramel-walnut filling. We prepare the caramel the traditional way by pouring water into a saucepan, adding sugar to the center, which prevents the granules from getting stuck to the sides of the pot and burning. As the sugar dissolves into the water and boils, it will turn a deep amber. Off heat, we carefully add cream, then we return to heat and stir until the caramel is smooth. Butter enriches the caramel further and vanilla, lemon juice, and salt add depth.

INCORPORATE THE WALNUTS We incorporate walnuts in the filling and garnish the tart with walnuts. For the garnish, we add walnut halves to the caramel to glaze them.

For the filling, we pour chopped walnuts into the caramel. The filling is then poured into the blind-baked tart crust, and allowed to chill while we prepare the chocolate filling.

LIGHTEN GANACHE WITH EGGS Somewhat similar to our Best Chocolate Tart (page 420), our chocolate filling is a modified baked custard. For the best chocolate flavor, we prefer semisweet chocolate. Once baked we garnish the tart with the candied walnut halves and give the tart a 3-hour chill to firm the layers.

CHOCOLATE CARAMEL WALNUT TART

SERVES 8 TO 10

See page 9 for information on toasting nuts. For cutting clean slices, dip the blade of the knife in warm water and wipe with a dish towel before making each cut.

WALNUT CRUST

1	large egg
¼	teaspoon vanilla extract
½	cup walnuts, toasted
½	cup (2 ounces) confectioners' sugar
1	cup (5 ounces) all-purpose flour
⅛	teaspoon salt
5	tablespoons unsalted butter, cut into ½-inch pieces and chilled

CARAMEL-WALNUT FILLING

¼	cup water
1	cup (7 ounces) granulated sugar
⅔	cup heavy cream
3	tablespoons unsalted butter, cut into 3 pieces
½	teaspoon vanilla extract
½	teaspoon lemon juice
⅛	teaspoon salt
16–18	walnut halves, plus 1 cup walnuts, toasted and chopped coarse

CHOCOLATE FILLING

2	large egg yolks
1	tablespoon plus ⅓ cup heavy cream
⅓	cup whole milk
5	ounces semisweet chocolate, chopped fine
2	tablespoons unsalted butter, cut into 4 pieces

1. FOR THE WALNUT CRUST: Whisk egg and vanilla together in bowl. Process walnuts and sugar in food processor until finely ground, 8 to 10 seconds. Add flour and salt and pulse to combine, about 5 pulses. Scatter butter over top and pulse until mixture resembles coarse cornmeal, about 15 pulses. With processor running, add egg mixture and continue to process until dough just comes together around processor blade, about 20 seconds.

2. Turn dough onto sheet of plastic wrap and flatten into 6-inch disk. Wrap tightly in plastic and refrigerate for 1 hour. Before rolling out dough, let it sit on counter to soften slightly, about 10 minutes. (Dough can be wrapped tightly in plastic and refrigerated for up to 2 days or frozen for up to 1 month. If frozen, let dough thaw completely on counter before rolling it out.)

3. Roll dough into 11-inch circle on lightly floured counter (if at any point dough becomes too soft and sticky to work with, slip dough onto baking sheet and freeze or refrigerate until workable). Place dough round on baking sheet, cover with plastic, and refrigerate for about 30 minutes.

4. Remove dough from refrigerator; discard plastic but keep dough on baking sheet. Loosely roll dough around rolling pin and gently unroll it onto 9-inch tart pan with removable bottom, letting excess dough hang over edge. Ease dough into pan by gently lifting edge of dough with your hand while pressing into corners with your other hand. Leave any dough that overhangs pan in place.

5. Press dough into fluted sides of pan, forming distinct seam around pan's circumference. (If some sections of edge are too thin, reinforce them by folding excess dough back on itself.) Run rolling pin over top of tart pan to remove any excess dough. Wrap dough-lined tart pan loosely in plastic, place on large plate, and freeze until dough is fully chilled and firm, about 30 minutes, before using. (Dough-lined tart pan can be wrapped tightly in plastic and frozen for up to 1 month.)

6. Meanwhile, adjust oven rack to middle position and heat oven to 375 degrees. Set dough-lined tart pan on rimmed baking sheet. Spray 1 side of double layer of aluminum foil with vegetable oil spray. Press foil greased side down into frozen tart shell, covering edges to prevent burning, and fill with pie weights. Bake until tart shell is golden brown and set, about 30 minutes, rotating baking sheet halfway through baking. Transfer tart shell with baking sheet to wire rack, carefully remove weights, and let cool slightly while making filling. Reduce oven temperature to 300 degrees.

7. FOR THE CARAMEL-WALNUT FILLING: While crust is cooling, add water to medium saucepan, then pour sugar into center of saucepan (don't let it hit pan sides). Gently stir sugar with clean spatula to wet it thoroughly. Bring to boil and cook, without stirring, until sugar has dissolved completely and liquid has faint golden color (about 300 degrees), 6 to 10 minutes.

8. Reduce heat to medium-low and continue to cook, stirring occasionally, until caramel has dark amber color (about 350 degrees),

1 to 3 minutes. Off heat, slowly whisk in cream until combined (mixture will bubble and steam vigorously). Stir in butter, vanilla, lemon juice, and salt until combined. Stir in walnut halves to coat. Let caramel mixture sit until slightly thickened, about 8 minutes.

9. Set wire rack over piece of parchment paper. Using slotted spoon, transfer caramel-coated walnuts to rack, flip nuts right side up, and let cool completely. Stir chopped walnuts into caramel, then pour caramel mixture into cooled prebaked tart shell. Refrigerate tart, uncovered, until caramel is firm and does not run when pan is tilted, about 20 minutes.

10. FOR THE CHOCOLATE FILLING: While caramel sets, whisk egg yolks and 1 tablespoon cream together in bowl. Bring milk and remaining 1/3 cup cream to simmer in a small saucepan. Off heat, stir in chocolate and butter, cover saucepan, and let stand until chocolate is mostly melted, about 2 minutes. Gently stir mixture until smooth, then stir in egg yolk mixture. Pour chocolate filling evenly over chilled caramel in tart shell and smooth into even layer by tilting pan. Bake tart on baking sheet until tiny bubbles are visible on surface and chocolate layer is just set, about 25 minutes.

11. Transfer tart with baking sheet to wire rack and arrange caramel-coated walnut halves around edge of tart to garnish. Let tart cool slightly on baking sheet for 30 minutes, then refrigerate, uncovered, until chocolate is firm, about 3 hours. To serve, remove outer metal ring of tart pan, slide thin metal spatula between tart and tart pan bottom, and carefully slide tart onto serving platter or cutting board.

TART UNMOLDING MADE EASY

Lifting up the removable pan bottom with your hand causes the ring to slide down your arm like a hula hoop. To remove the ring easily, place a wide can, such as a 28-ounce tomato can, on the counter and set the cooled tart pan on top of the can. Hold the pan ring and gently pull it downward.

Linzertorte

WHY THIS RECIPE WORKS

Linzertorte has proved to be a timeless classic, with its buttery nut crust and sweet raspberry jam filling. The process of transforming these two components into a finished tart, however, can drive perfectionists (like us) over the edge. We wanted to find a way to make this tart even easier.

PREPARE A NUT-RICH DOUGH We use 2 parts hazelnuts and 1 part almonds for the base. A single egg moistens and binds the dough nicely, and cinnamon and allspice add traditional spice flavors.

PAT THE CRUST INTO THE PAN For the bottom crust, we press walnut-size pieces of dough into the pan. No rolling required.

BRIGHTEN THE FILLING For the filling, we like raspberry preserves accented with a spoonful of lemon juice.

CREATE THE LATTICE We start by rolling the dough between floured sheets of parchment paper. Then, we refrigerate the dough so that it is easier to cut into strips and arrange in a lattice pattern over the filling.

LINZERTORTE

SERVES 10 TO 12

Make sure to buy blanched almonds. If you cannot find blanched almonds, see our method on page 9. See page 9 for information on toasting nuts. Be sure to use an 11-inch tart pan here. You will have some extra dough when cutting out the lattice strips; we suggest cutting out a few extra lattice strips as backup (they can be delicate and will sometimes break). If at any time while forming the lattice the dough becomes too soft, refrigerate it for 15 minutes before continuing. The Linzertorte may be served at room temperature the day it is baked, but it is at its best after a night in the refrigerator.

TART DOUGH

1	large egg
1	teaspoon vanilla extract
1	cup hazelnuts, toasted and skinned
½	cup blanched almonds
½	cup plus 2 tablespoons (4⅓ ounces) sugar
½	teaspoon salt
1	teaspoon grated lemon zest
1½	cups (7½ ounces) all-purpose flour
½	teaspoon ground cinnamon
⅛	teaspoon ground allspice
12	tablespoons unsalted butter, cut into ½-inch pieces and chilled

FILLING AND GLAZE

1¼	cups raspberry preserves
1	tablespoon lemon juice
1	tablespoon heavy cream
1½	teaspoons turbinado or Demerara sugar (optional)

1. FOR THE TART DOUGH: Whisk egg and vanilla together in bowl. Process hazelnuts, almonds, sugar, and salt in food processor until very finely ground, 45 to 60 seconds. Add lemon zest and pulse to combine, about 5 pulses. Add flour, cinnamon, and allspice and pulse to combine, about 5 pulses. Scatter butter over top and pulse until mixture resembles coarse cornmeal, about 15 pulses. With processor running, add egg mixture and continue to process until dough just comes together around processor blade, about 12 seconds.

2. Turn dough onto counter and press together to form cohesive mound. Divide dough in half and flatten each piece into 5-inch disk; if not using immediately, wrap each piece tightly in plastic wrap and refrigerate up to 48 hours. (If refrigerated until firm, let dough sit at room temperature until soft and malleable, about 1 hour.)

3. Tear 1 piece of dough into walnut-size pieces, then pat it into 11-inch tart pan with removable bottom, pressing it ¾ inch up sides of pan. Lay plastic over dough and smooth out any bumps using bottom of measuring cup. Set tart pan on large plate and freeze until dough is fully chilled and firm, about 30 minutes.

4. Roll other piece of dough into 12-inch square between 2 large sheets of floured parchment paper. (If dough sticks to parchment, gently loosen and lift sticky area with bench scraper and dust parchment with additional flour. Slide dough, still between parchment sheets, onto rimmed baking sheet and refrigerate until firm, about 15 minutes.) Remove top layer of parchment and trim edges of dough, then cut ten ¾-inch-wide strips, cutting through underlying parchment. Cover with parchment and freeze until dough is fully chilled and firm, about 20 minutes.

5. Meanwhile, adjust oven rack to middle position and heat oven to 350 degrees. Set dough-lined tart pan on rimmed baking sheet. Spray 1 side of double layer of aluminum foil with vegetable oil spray. Press foil greased side down into frozen tart shell, covering edges to prevent burning, and fill with pie weights. Bake until tart shell is golden brown and set, about 30 minutes, rotating sheet halfway

through baking. Transfer tart shell with baking sheet to wire rack, carefully remove weights, and let cool slightly while making filling. (Leave oven on).

6. FOR THE FILLING AND GLAZE: Stir raspberry preserves and lemon juice together in bowl, then spread evenly over bottom of cooled prebaked tart shell. Pick up strip of dough by parchment ends, then flip it over onto tart, positioning it near edge of pan. Remove parchment strip and trim ends of dough strip by pressing down on top edge of pan; reserve all dough scraps. Place 2 more strips parallel to first, spacing them evenly so that one is across center and other is near opposite edge of pan. Rotate pan 90 degrees, then place 3 more strips as you did first 3. Rotate pan 90 degrees again, then place 2 strips across pan, spaced evenly between first 3. Rotate pan again and complete lattice by placing last 2 strips between second set of 3. Use small scraps of dough to fill in crust around edges between lattice strips. Top of crust should be just below top of pan.

7. Gently brush lattice strips with heavy cream and sprinkle with turbinado sugar, if using. Bake tart on baking sheet until crust is deep golden brown, about 50 minutes. Transfer tart with baking sheet to wire rack and let cool to room temperature, about 2 hours. To serve, remove outer metal ring of tart pan, slide thin metal spatula between tart and tart pan bottom, and carefully slide tart onto serving platter or cutting board.

ASSEMBLING A LINZERTORTE

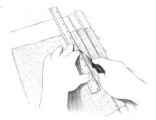

1. After chilling dough square, trim any rough edges, then cut square into 10 strips, each ¾ inch wide, cutting through underlying parchment paper.

2. Place parchment-lined strip of dough over tart and peel off parchment; trim ends of dough. Place 2 more strips parallel to first, spacing them evenly.

3. Place remaining 8 dough strips on tart, rotating pan as needed to form lattice top.

4. Using scraps of dough, fill in crust around edges between lattice strips.

PISSALADIÈRE

Savory Tarts and Quiches

Tomato and Mozzarella Tart

THAWING PUFF PASTRY

Homemade puff pastry is laborious and time-intensive to make, but luckily, convenient frozen puff pastry is readily available in grocery stores. Still, store-bought puff pastry can present the uninitiated with some minor obstacles, particularly when it comes to temperature.

For the perfect puff, the pastry should never come to room temperature. Most cooks thaw puff pastry on the counter, but it can quickly get too warm with this method. We recommend letting the pastry defrost slowly in the refrigerator, where it can't overheat. When rolling or cutting the pastry on the counter, do so as quickly as possible. If the dough becomes too soft, return it to the refrigerator for 5 minutes or so to firm up. Once the puff pastry has been shaped, make sure to chill the dough thoroughly before baking—15 minutes in the freezer or 30 minutes in the refrigerator will do the trick.

✔ WHY THIS RECIPE WORKS

Falling somewhere in between pizza and quiche, a tomato and mozzarella tart shares the flavors of both but features problems unique unto itself. For starters, the moisture in the tomatoes almost guarantees a soggy pastry crust. Also, tomato tarts are often short on flavor. We set out to develop a recipe that could easily be made at home with a solid bottom crust and great vine-ripened flavor.

SALT AND DRAIN A combination of salting and draining on paper towels (with some pressing at the end) extracts much of the moisture from sliced tomatoes destined for a tart. We begin with plum tomatoes here, rather than beefsteak tomatoes, because they have less liquid.

FORM THE PUFF PASTRY CRUST We transform store-bought puff pastry sheets into a rectangular crust with a thin border to contain the topping (tomatoes easily slip off a flat sheet of anything). To do this, we brush egg along one edge of one sheet of puff pastry and overlap it with the second sheet of dough by 1 inch, pressing to seal them together. With a rolling pin, we smooth out the seam. (You can use a pizza cutter to trim the edges straight.) Next, we cut two 1-inch strips from the long side of the dough, and then two 1-inch strips from the short side. After brushing the dough with an egg wash, we gently press the thin strips onto the outer edges of the dough— one per side, creating a well-fitting border. Brushing the strips with more egg wash secures them in place.

PREBAKE THE CRUST We prebake the crust at two different heat levels: a high temperature for initial lift and browning and then a lower temperature to dry out the shell for maximum sturdiness. Starting out at 425 degrees (and held there until puffed and light golden, about 15 minutes) and finishing at 350 degrees (and held there until well browned, 15 minutes longer), the crust emerges flaky yet rigid enough for us to hold it aloft while grasping just one end.

WATERPROOF THE DOUGH The first lines of defense against a soggy tart are a thick coat of egg and a layer of Parmesan cheese applied to the entire tart before prebaking begins. The egg wash creates a deflective but not impermeable layer on the delicate crust. But the Parmesan melts into a solid (and delicious, nutty-tasting) fatty layer that liquid rolls right off, like rain off a duck's back. With these layers intact, we can add mozzarella and tomatoes and still end up with a tart that's firm and crisp, even hours after baking.

TOMATO AND MOZZARELLA TART
SERVES 6 TO 8

Thawing the frozen puff pastry in the refrigerator overnight will help prevent cracking while unfolding it. Be sure to use low-moisture supermarket mozzarella sold in block form, not fresh water-packed mozzarella.

- 2 (9½ by 9-inch) sheets puff pastry, thawed
- 1 large egg, beaten
- 2 ounces Parmesan cheese, grated (1 cup)
- 1 pound plum tomatoes, cored and cut crosswise into ¼-inch-thick slices
  Salt and pepper
- 2 garlic cloves, minced
- 2 tablespoons extra-virgin olive oil
- 8 ounces whole-milk mozzarella cheese, shredded (2 cups)
- 2 tablespoons chopped fresh basil

1. Adjust oven rack to lower-middle position and heat oven to 425 degrees. Line rimmed baking sheet with parchment paper. Dust counter with flour and unfold both pieces of puff pastry onto counter. Brush 1 short edge of 1 sheet of pastry with egg and overlap with second sheet by 1 inch, forming 18 by 9-inch rectangle. Press to seal edges, then use rolling pin to smooth seam. Cut two 1-inch-wide strips from long side of dough and two more from short side. Transfer large piece of dough to prepared baking sheet and brush with egg. Attach long dough strips to long edges of dough and short strips to short edges, then brush dough strips with egg. Sprinkle Parmesan evenly over shell. Using fork, poke evenly spaced holes in surface of shell. Bake for 13 to 15 minutes, then reduce oven temperature to 350 degrees. Continue to bake until golden brown and crisp, 13 to 15 minutes longer. Transfer to wire rack; increase oven temperature to 425 degrees.

2. While shell bakes, place tomato slices in single layer on double layer of paper towels and sprinkle evenly with ½ teaspoon salt; let stand for 30 minutes. Place another double layer of paper towels on top of tomatoes and press firmly to dry tomatoes. Combine garlic, olive oil, and pinch each salt and pepper in small bowl; set aside.

3. Sprinkle mozzarella evenly over baked shell. Shingle tomato slices widthwise on top of cheese (about 4 slices per row); brush tomatoes with garlic oil. Bake until shell is deep golden brown and cheese is melted, 15 to 17 minutes. Let cool on wire rack for 5 minutes. Sprinkle with basil, slide onto cutting board or serving platter, cut into pieces, and serve.

TO MAKE AHEAD: Tart shell can be prebaked through step 1, cooled to room temperature, wrapped in plastic wrap, and kept at room temperature for up to 2 days before being topped and baked with mozzarella and tomatoes.

TOMATO AND SMOKED MOZZARELLA TART

Substitute 6 ounces smoked mozzarella for whole-milk mozzarella.

SUN-DRIED TOMATO AND MOZZARELLA TART

Replacing the plum tomatoes with sun-dried tomatoes turns this into an appetizer you can make any time of year.

Substitute ½ cup oil-packed sun-dried tomatoes, drained, rinsed, and chopped fine, for plum tomatoes.

TOMATO AND MOZZARELLA TART WITH PROSCIUTTO

Place 2 ounces thinly sliced prosciutto in single layer on top of mozzarella before arranging tomato slices.

FORMING THE TART SHELL

1. Brush egg along 1 short edge of 1 sheet of puff pastry. Overlap with second sheet of dough by 1 inch and press to seal pieces together.

2. With rolling pin, smooth out seam. Dough should measure about 18 by 9 inches. Use pizza wheel or knife to trim edges straight, if necessary.

3. With pizza wheel or knife, cut 1-inch strip from 1 long side of dough. Cut another 1-inch strip from same side.

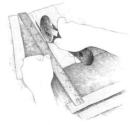

4. Cut 1-inch strip from 1 short side of dough. Cut another 1-inch strip from same side. Transfer large piece of dough to parchment-lined baking sheet and brush with egg.

5. Gently press 1 long strip of dough onto each long edge of dough and brush with egg. Gently press 1 short strip of dough onto each short edge and brush with egg.

6. With pizza wheel or knife, trim excess dough from corners.

Here are some tips for mastering this delicate dough.

1. To help prevent cracking, phyllo must be kept moist until you're ready to work with it. The usual approach is to cover the stack with a damp dish towel. But it's all too easy to overmoisten the towel and turn the dough sticky. We prefer to cover the stack with plastic wrap to protect the phyllo and then place a damp towel on top.

2. Because phyllo is so fragile, some sheets crack and even tear while still in the box. Don't worry about rips; just make sure to adjust the orientation of the sheets as you stack them so that cracks in different sheets don't line up.

3. When phyllo sheets emerge from the box fused at their edges, don't try to separate the sheets. Instead, trim and discard the fused portion.

Weeknight Spanakopita

✓ WHY THIS RECIPE WORKS

The roots of this savory spinach and feta pie, with its trademark layers of flaky, crisp phyllo, run deep in Greek culture, yet most stateside versions are nothing more than soggy layers of phyllo with a sparse, bland filling. We wanted a casserole-style pie with a perfect balance of zesty spinach filling and shatteringly crisp phyllo crust—and we didn't want to spend all day in the kitchen.

CHOOSE THE RIGHT SPINACH Among the various spinach options (baby, frozen, mature curly-leaf), we prefer the bold flavor of fresh curly-leaf spinach. Sautéing, steaming, boiling, and microwaving are all terrific methods for precooking the spinach. For our weeknight pie, we go with the push-button convenience of the microwave.

DRY THE SPINACH We use store-bought phyllo for convenience in our pie. To prevent the crisp phyllo layers from turning soggy from the spinach, we drain the pre-cooked spinach in a colander, pressing on it with the back of a spatula. Then we chop the spinach and squeeze it of excess moisture in a dish towel.

TEMPER THE FETA Rinsing the feta removes some of the salty brine, while the addition of Greek yogurt buffers the assertiveness of the cheese. For creamy tang in every bite, we crumble the feta into fine pieces.

BIND THE PHYLLO—WITH PECORINO Traditional recipes for spanakopita often include a Greek hard sheep's-milk cheese called *kefalograviera* for complexity. Pecorino Romano is a good stand-in. But instead of adding it to the filling, we sprinkle it between the top sheets of phyllo, which not only adds flavor but also helps the flaky layers hold together when the pie is sliced.

BAKE ON A BAKING SHEET Using a baking sheet rather than a baking dish allows excess moisture to easily evaporate from our savory pie, ensuring a browned, crisp crust.

WEEKNIGHT SPANAKOPITA

SERVES 6 TO 8 AS A MAIN COURSE OR
10 TO 12 AS AN APPETIZER

It is important to rinse the feta; this step removes some of its salty brine, which would overwhelm the spinach. Full-fat sour cream can be substituted for whole-milk Greek yogurt. Phyllo dough is also available in larger 18 by 14-inch sheets; if using, cut them in half to make 14 by 9-inch sheets. Do not thaw the phyllo dough in the microwave; let it sit in the refrigerator overnight or on the counter for 4 to 5 hours.

FILLING
- 1¼ pounds curly-leaf spinach, stemmed
- ¼ cup water
- 12 ounces feta cheese, rinsed, patted dry, and crumbled into fine pieces (3 cups)
- ¾ cup whole-milk Greek yogurt
- 2 large eggs, beaten
- 4 scallions, sliced thin
- ¼ cup minced fresh mint
- 2 tablespoons minced fresh dill
- 3 garlic cloves, minced
- 1 teaspoon grated lemon zest plus 1 tablespoon juice
- 1 teaspoon ground nutmeg
- ½ teaspoon pepper
- ¼ teaspoon salt
- ⅛ teaspoon cayenne pepper

PHYLLO LAYERS
- 7 tablespoons unsalted butter, melted
- 8 ounces (14 by 9-inch) phyllo, thawed
- 1½ ounces Pecorino Romano cheese, grated (¾ cup)
- 2 teaspoons sesame seeds (optional)

1. FOR THE FILLING: Place spinach and water in large bowl. Cover bowl with large dinner plate (plate should completely cover bowl and not rest on spinach). Microwave until spinach is wilted and decreased in volume by half, about 5 minutes. Remove bowl from microwave and keep covered for 1 minute. Carefully remove plate and transfer spinach to colander. Using back of rubber spatula, gently press spinach against colander to release excess liquid. Transfer spinach to cutting board and chop coarse. Transfer spinach to clean dish towel and squeeze to remove excess water. Place drained spinach in large bowl. Add feta, yogurt, eggs, scallions, mint, dill, garlic, lemon zest and juice, nutmeg, pepper, salt, and cayenne and mix until thoroughly combined.

2. FOR THE PHYLLO LAYERS: Adjust oven rack to lower-middle position and heat oven to 425 degrees. Line rimmed baking sheet with parchment paper. Using pastry brush, lightly brush 14 by 9-inch rectangle in center of parchment with melted butter to cover area same size as phyllo. Lay 1 phyllo sheet on buttered parchment and brush thoroughly with melted butter. Repeat with 9 more phyllo sheets, brushing each with butter (you should have total of 10 layers of phyllo).

3. Spread spinach mixture evenly over phyllo, leaving ¼-inch border on all sides.

Cover spinach with 6 more phyllo sheets, brushing each with melted butter and sprinkling each with about 2 tablespoons Pecorino. Lay 2 more phyllo sheets on top, brushing each with melted butter (do not sprinkle these layers with Pecorino).

4. Working from center outward, use palms of your hands to compress layers and press out any air pockets. Using sharp knife, score spanakopita through top 3 layers of phyllo into 24 equal pieces. Sprinkle with sesame seeds, if using. Bake until phyllo is golden and crisp, 20 to 25 minutes, rotating baking sheet halfway through baking. Let cool on baking sheet at least 10 minutes or up to 2 hours. Slide spanakopita, still on parchment, onto cutting board. Cut into squares and serve.

TO MAKE AHEAD: Filling can be made up to 24 hours in advance and refrigerated. Freeze assembled, unbaked spanakopita on baking sheet, wrapped well in plastic wrap, or cut spanakopita in half crosswise and freeze smaller sections on plate. Bake spanakopita frozen, increasing baking time by 5 to 10 minutes.

French Onion Tart

✔ WHY THIS RECIPE WORKS
The French elevate a common vegetable to the status of foie gras by gently simmering it in butter, enriching it with custard, and baking it in a buttery crust. The tart is similar to quiche but delivers a more refined slice of pie, with more onions than custard. Trying to make an onion tart at home can produce a tough crust, hardly worth the time carefully cooking onions and making custard. We needed to simplify the crust and shorten the overall preparation time.

PRESS THE CRUST Forget rolling and fitting tart dough for this streamlined tart. We developed an all-butter crust made in a food processor. It's firm enough to simply press into a tart pan.

BACON MAKES IT BETTER For our onion tart, we include bacon, which acts as a crisp foil to the creamy filling. We cut it into small pieces and cook it until browned and crisp. Then, to preserve its crisp texture, we sprinkle it over the top of the filling before baking.

LIGHTEN THE CUSTARD With bacon in the mix, we found a traditional custard just too rich. To solve the issue, we reduce the number of eggs and switch out the cream for half-and-half. Fragrant fresh thyme also cuts through the richness of the custard.

CUT THE ONIONS DIFFERENTLY Onions can take up to an hour to cook until

WHICH ONIONS GIVE THE BEST CARAMELIZED TASTE?

The type of onion you choose when caramelizing onions has a tremendous effect on flavor. Although the caramelizing times of the various onions are consistent, our tasters' preferences were not. Some liked a sweeter, more mellow flavor, while others liked their onions with more bite. Tasters with a sweet tooth gravitated to white and Vidalia onions (the latter being the sweeter of the two). Those who preferred a heartier onion flavor with only moderate sweetness were drawn to Spanish onions.

STEP BY STEP—NO ROLLING REQUIRED

Here's a simple and quick method to ensure an even crust—no rolling pin required.

1. Sprinkle walnut-size clumps of dough evenly into tart pan.

2. Working outward from center, press dough into even layer, sealing any cracks.

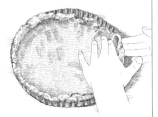

3. Working around edge, press dough firmly into corners of pan with your index finger. Go around edge once more, pressing dough up sides and into fluted ridges.

4. Use your thumb to level off top edge. Use this dough to patch any holes.

meltingly sweet and tender. We found two ways to shorten the cooking time. First, slicing the onions crosswise allows them to soften and break down more readily than slicing them through the root end. Second, covering the onions throughout cooking enables them to cook in half the usual time. Instead of cooking the onions in butter, we use a couple of tablespoons of bacon fat, left from rendering our bacon.

FRENCH ONION AND BACON TART

SERVES 6 TO 8

Either yellow or white onions work well in this recipe, but stay away from sweet onions, such as Vidalias, which will make the tart watery. Use a 9-inch tinned-steel tart pan. This tart can be served hot or at room temperature.

CRUST

1¼	cups (6¼ ounces) all-purpose flour
1	tablespoon sugar
½	teaspoon salt
8	tablespoons unsalted butter, cut into ½-inch cubes and chilled
2–3	tablespoons ice water

FILLING

4	slices bacon, cut into ¼-inch pieces Vegetable oil, if needed
1½	pounds onions, halved through root end and cut crosswise into ¼-inch slices
¾	teaspoon salt
1	sprig fresh thyme
2	large eggs
½	cup half-and-half
¼	teaspoon pepper

1. FOR THE CRUST: Spray 9-inch tart pan with removable bottom with vegetable oil spray. Pulse flour, sugar, and salt in food processor until combined, about 4 pulses. Scatter butter pieces over flour mixture; pulse until mixture resembles coarse sand, about 15 pulses. Add 2 tablespoons ice water and process until large clumps form and no powdery bits remain,

about 5 seconds, adding up to 1 tablespoon more water if dough will not form clumps. Transfer dough to prepared tart pan; pat dough into pan, pressing dough up sides and into fluted edges. Lay plastic wrap over dough and smooth out any bumps or shallow areas. Place tart shell on plate and freeze for 30 minutes.

2. Adjust oven rack to middle position and heat oven to 375 degrees. Place frozen tart shell on baking sheet. Spray piece of extra-wide heavy-duty aluminum foil with vegetable oil spray and gently press against dough and over edges of tart pan. Fill with pie weights and bake until top edge just starts to color and surface of dough no longer looks wet, about 30 minutes. Remove from oven and remove foil and weights. Return sheet with tart shell to oven and bake until golden brown, 5 to 10 minutes. Set sheet with tart shell on wire rack. Do not turn off oven.

3. FOR THE FILLING: Meanwhile, cook bacon in 12-inch nonstick skillet over medium heat until crisp, 5 to 7 minutes. Using slotted spoon, transfer bacon to paper towel–lined plate. Pour off all but 2 tablespoons fat from skillet (or add vegetable oil if needed to make this amount).

4. Add onions, salt, and thyme to skillet. Cover and cook until onions release liquid and start to wilt, about 10 minutes. Reduce heat to low and continue to cook, covered, until onions are very soft, about 20 minutes, stirring once or twice (if after 15 minutes onions look wet, remove lid and continue to cook another 5 minutes). Remove pan from heat and let onions cool for 5 minutes.

5. Whisk eggs, half-and-half, and pepper together in large bowl. Remove and discard thyme sprig from onions. Stir onions into egg mixture until just incorporated. Spread onion mixture over tart shell and sprinkle bacon evenly on top.

6. Bake tart on sheet until center of tart feels firm to touch, 20 to 25 minutes. Let cool on wire rack at least 10 minutes. Remove outer metal ring of tart pan, slide thin metal spatula between tart and tart pan bottom, and carefully slide tart onto serving platter or cutting board. Cut into wedges and serve.

Deep-Dish Quiche

✔ WHY THIS RECIPE WORKS

Typical quiches suffer from one of several classic flaws. Some feel so slight on the plate they're more tart than main-course material, while others are so overaccessorized with add-ins that the carefully bound egg-cream mixture either breaks into a curdled puddle or fades into the background. We wanted a streamlined version of the ultimate quiche: thick-crusted and brimming with creamy custard in which a healthy dose of fillings are perfectly suspended.

CHANGE THE BAKEWARE For us, a real quiche is a tall quiche. But to get a good and tall quiche, you need to use a lot of custard. And a lot of custard does not fit in a traditional tart pan. You could use a springform pan, but the custard has a tendency to leak through the thin gap between the springform's base and ring, not to mention that fitting the pastry dough up the exceptionally tall sides without tearing takes some practice. This is why we use a 9 by 2-inch round cake pan. It's tall enough to contain all the custard we want and won't leak.

MAKE THE CRUST LEAKPROOF For extra insurance against leaks and tearing, we employ three tricks for baking a quiche in a cake pan. First, we line the pan with a foil "sling" to help extract the pastry from this mold. Second, we roll out a 15-inch round of pastry and drape a generous amount of dough up and over the sides of the pan. This helps to anchor the crust in place, preventing it from sagging or shrinking when prebaked. (If any of the crust cracks or forms holes during prebaking, they're easily repaired with reserved dough scraps.) And third, we glaze the baked crust with an egg white wash before adding the filling, which helps seal any would-be cracks. Rich with butter, supremely flaky, and strong enough to resist turning soggy, this crust is the perfect bowl for the satiny custard.

MAKE THE CUSTARD We wanted a quivering, barely set pudding for our quiche custard. But like all gels, custard is a delicate matter, and its success depends on just the right ratio of eggs to liquid (including any excess moisture exuded by watery ingredients like onions), plus gentle, even heat. Too few eggs and the custard is loose and runny, while too many lend it a scrambled-egg flavor and rubbery chew. We settled on eight whole eggs plus the extra yolk left over from sealing the crust and 3 cups of dairy.

USE CORNSTARCH The tricky part comes with adding the fillings: bacon, onions, and cheese for our classic Lorraine quiche (we use leeks and blue cheese for one variation, and sausage, broccoli rabe, and mozzarella for the other). In our quiche Lorraine, when onions enter the equation, the acids they release alter the electrical charges on the egg proteins, causing them to clump together so tightly that they squeeze out the moisture held between them. Starch granules in cornstarch interfere with this clumping by acting as a barrier between the proteins, which prevents them from squeezing out liquid and results in a smooth and creamy custard. Thanks to the cornstarch, this quiche can hold a full 2 cups of onions with no ill effects.

POUR A QUICHE To help the fillings distribute evenly through the custard—rather than clumping in one area of the crust, we scatter the fillings over the crust evenly. Then, we gently pour the custard over the filling ingredients and use a fork to submerge the ingredients down into the custard. Once baked, there will be bites of bacon, onion, and cheese throughout the creamy custard.

DEEP-DISH QUICHE LORRAINE

SERVES 8 TO 10

To prevent the crust from sagging during blind-baking, make sure it overhangs the pan's edge and use plenty of pie weights (3 to 4 cups). Be sure to use a cake pan with at least 2-inch-tall straight sides. To reheat the whole quiche, place it on a rimmed baking sheet on the middle rack of a 325-degree oven for 20 minutes; slices can be reheated in a 375-degree oven for 10 minutes. This recipe uses a total of nine eggs; one egg is separated and the white is used for the crust, while the yolk is used in the filling.

CRUST

1¾	cups (8¾ ounces) all-purpose flour
½	teaspoon salt
12	tablespoons unsalted butter, cut into ½-inch pieces and chilled
3	tablespoons sour cream
4–6	tablespoons ice water
1	large egg white, lightly beaten

CUSTARD FILLING

8	slices thick-cut bacon, cut into ¼-inch pieces
2	onions, chopped fine
1½	tablespoons cornstarch
1½	cups whole milk
8	large eggs plus 1 large yolk
1½	cups heavy cream
½	teaspoon salt
¼	teaspoon pepper
⅛	teaspoon ground nutmeg
⅛	teaspoon cayenne pepper
6	ounces Gruyère cheese, shredded (1½ cups)

1. FOR THE CRUST: Process flour and salt in food processor until combined, about 3 seconds. Add butter and pulse until butter is size of large peas, about 10 pulses.

2. Combine sour cream and ¼ cup ice water in small bowl. Add half of sour cream mixture to flour mixture; pulse 3 times. Repeat with remaining sour cream mixture. Pinch dough with your fingers; if dough is floury, dry, and does not hold together, add 1 to 2 tablespoons more ice water and pulse until dough forms large clumps and no dry flour remains, 3 to 5 pulses.

3. Turn dough out onto counter and flatten into 6-inch disk; wrap disk in plastic wrap and refrigerate until firm but not hard, 1 to 2 hours, before rolling. (Dough can be refrigerated for up to 1 day; let stand at room temperature for 15 minutes before rolling.)

4. Cut two 16-inch lengths of aluminum foil. Arrange foil pieces, perpendicular to each other, in 9-inch round cake pan, pushing them into corners and up sides of pan; press overhang against outside of pan. Spray foil lightly with vegetable oil spray.

5. Roll out dough on generously floured counter to 15-inch circle about ¼ inch thick. Roll dough loosely around rolling pin and unroll into prepared cake pan. Working around circumference, ease dough into pan by gently lifting edge of dough with your hand while pressing into pan bottom with your other hand. Trim any dough that extends more than 1 inch over edge of pan. Patch any cracks or holes with dough scraps as needed. Refrigerate any remaining dough scraps. Refrigerate dough-lined pan until dough is firm, about 30 minutes, then freeze for 20 minutes.

6. Adjust oven rack to lower-middle position and heat oven to 375 degrees. Line dough with foil or parchment paper and fill completely with pie weights, gently pressing weights into corners of shell. Bake on rimmed baking sheet until exposed edges of dough are beginning to brown but bottom is still light in color, 30 to 40 minutes. Carefully remove foil and pie weights. If any new holes or cracks have formed in dough, patch with reserved scraps. Return shell to oven and bake until bottom is golden brown, 15 to 20 minutes longer. Remove shell from oven and brush

DICING ONIONS

A sharp knife and good technique make chopping onions quick and easy.

1. Using chef's knife, halve onion through root end. Lop tops off both halves, leaving root ends intact, and peel onion.

2. Make horizontal cuts, starting with heel of blade and carefully pulling knife toward you, without cutting through root end.

3. Using tip of knife, make several vertical cuts, dragging knife toward you and making sure to keep tip against board.

4. Slice across lengthwise cuts, using your knuckles as guide for knife while holding onion with your fingertips.

MAKING QUICHE IN A CAKE PAN

For a truly deep-dish quiche, forget a pie plate. We use a cake pan lined with aluminum foil for easy removal.

1. Fashion foil sling from 2 lengths of foil to remove quiche.

2. Instead of 12-inch round, roll out dough to 15-inch circle big enough to fit in cake pan with plenty of overhang.

3. Roll dough loosely around rolling pin and unroll it into foil-lined cake pan.

4. Gently ease dough into pan. Trim, leaving generous 1-inch overhang to anchor dough.

interior with egg white. Set aside while preparing filling. Reduce oven temperature to 350 degrees.

7. FOR THE CUSTARD FILLING: Cook bacon in 12-inch skillet over medium heat until crisp, 5 to 7 minutes. Transfer to paper towel–lined plate and pour off all but 2 tablespoons fat from skillet. Return to medium heat, add onions, and cook, stirring frequently, until softened and lightly browned, about 12 minutes. Set aside to cool slightly.

8. Whisk cornstarch and 3 tablespoons milk together in large bowl to dissolve cornstarch. Whisk in remaining milk, eggs and yolk, cream, salt, pepper, nutmeg, and cayenne until smooth.

9. Scatter onions, bacon, and cheese evenly over crust. Gently pour custard mixture over filling. Using fork, push filling ingredients down into custard and drag gently through custard to dislodge air bubbles. Gently tap pan on counter to dislodge any remaining air bubbles.

10. Bake until top of quiche is lightly browned, toothpick inserted in center comes out clean, and center registers 170 degrees, 1¼ to 1½ hours. Transfer to wire rack and let stand until cool to touch, about 2 hours.

11. When ready to serve, use sharp paring knife to remove any crust that extends beyond edge of pan. Lift foil overhang from sides of pan and remove quiche from pan; gently slide thin-bladed spatula between quiche and foil to loosen, then slide quiche onto serving plate. Cut into wedges. Serve warm or at room temperature.

DEEP-DISH QUICHE WITH LEEKS AND BLUE CHEESE

See page 439 for information on cleaning leeks.

Omit bacon and onions. Melt 1 tablespoon unsalted butter in 12-inch skillet over medium heat. Add 4 large leeks, white and light green parts only, halved lengthwise, sliced ¼ inch thick, and washed thoroughly; cook until softened, 10 to 12 minutes. Increase heat to medium-high; continue to cook, stirring constantly, until leeks are beginning to brown, about 5 minutes. Transfer leeks to plate lined with triple layer of paper towels; press with double layer of paper towels to remove excess moisture. Increase salt in filling to 1 teaspoon. Substitute 1½ cups crumbled blue cheese for Gruyère; scatter blue cheese and sautéed leeks evenly over crust before adding custard. Reduce baking time to 1 to 1¼ hours.

DEEP-DISH QUICHE WITH SAUSAGE, BROCCOLI RABE, AND MOZZARELLA

Be sure to use supermarket-style low-moisture mozzarella in this variation; fresh mozzarella will make for a too-wet filling.

Omit bacon and onions. Cook 8 ounces hot or sweet Italian sausage, casings removed, in 12-inch skillet over medium heat, breaking sausage into ½-inch pieces, until no longer pink, 5 to 7 minutes. Transfer to paper towel–lined plate and pour off all but 2 tablespoons fat from skillet. Return skillet to medium heat, add 8 ounces broccoli rabe, trimmed and cut into ½-inch pieces, and cook until slightly softened, about 6 minutes. Transfer broccoli rabe to plate lined with triple layer of paper towels; press with double layer of paper towels to remove excess moisture. Increase salt in filling to 1 teaspoon. Substitute 1½ cups shredded whole-milk mozzarella cheese for Gruyère; scatter mozzarella, cooked sausage, and broccoli rabe evenly over crust before adding custard. Reduce baking time to 1 to 1¼ hours.

Vegetable Galette

✔ WHY THIS RECIPE WORKS

Many free-form vegetable tart recipes simply borrow a standard pastry dough intended for fruit. But not just any old crust will do. Vegetables are more prone to leaking liquid into the crust or falling apart when the tart is sliced. What's more, they don't pack the concentrated, bright flavors of fruit. We needed a crust that was extra-sturdy and boasted a complex flavor of its own. We also wanted a robust-tasting filling featuring the classic combination of meaty mushrooms and sweet leeks bond together to hold together when cut.

MAKE A WHOLE-WHEAT CRUST AND CUT WITH WHITE FLOUR We knew that the earthy flavor and coarser consistency of whole-wheat flour would bring a nice flavor and hearty crumb to our savory filling. But relative to other kinds of flour, whole-wheat contains very little gluten, so it produces a heavier dough that is more prone to falling apart. To ensure that our dough would hold its shape, we needed to add white flour.

GIVE IT A REST With white flour added, our dough turned tough. The problem was water. Whole-wheat flour needs more water to become fully hydrated, so we'd been using more water in the dough than we would have in an all-white flour dough. This extra liquid was being absorbed by the white flour, thereby creating more gluten and making the dough more susceptible to overworking. Instead, we decided to take a hands-off approach to mixing and let the flour absorb the water on its own. We barely mix the dry and wet ingredients together and then chill the dough briefly. Without any effort on our part, this dough is remarkably supple but not floppy.

ROLL AND FOLD To further ensure that the dough is tender and firm (but not tough), we roll the dough into a rectangle and fold it into thirds, then repeat the process twice more.

The result: a tender, moist, wonderfully flaky crust that is less apt to shatter when cut.

PRECOOK THE VEGETABLES Removing moisture from the vegetables is crucial to concentrating flavor and preventing a soggy crust. We microwave and drain the mushrooms and combine them with browned leeks.

ADD BOLD-FLAVORED BINDERS To help the vegetables stay neatly bound and add complexity to the filling, we work in a rich, three-part binder: crème fraîche, Dijon mustard, and crumbled Gorgonzola.

MUSHROOM AND LEEK GALETTE WITH GORGONZOLA

SERVES 6

Cutting a few small holes in the dough prevents it from lifting off the pan as it bakes. A baking stone helps to crisp the crust but is not essential.

DOUGH

1¼	cups (6¼ ounces) all-purpose flour
½	cup (2¾ ounces) whole-wheat flour
1	tablespoon sugar
¾	teaspoon salt
10	tablespoons unsalted butter, cut into ½-inch pieces and chilled
7	tablespoons ice water
1	teaspoon distilled white vinegar

FILLING

1¼	pounds shiitake mushrooms, stemmed and sliced thin
5	teaspoons olive oil
1	pound leeks, white and light green parts only, sliced ½ inch thick and washed thoroughly (3 cups)
1	teaspoon minced fresh thyme
2	tablespoons crème fraîche
1	tablespoon Dijon mustard

1. Trim and discard roots and dark green leaves.

2. Slice trimmed leek in half lengthwise, then cut it into ½-inch pieces.

3. Rinse cut leeks thoroughly in bowl of water to remove dirt and sand.

It's surprisingly simple to
create pleated edges around
free-form tarts.

1. Gently grasp 1 edge of
dough and make 2-inch-wide
fold over filling.

2. Lift and fold another seg-
ment of dough over first fold
to form pleat. Repeat every
2 to 3 inches.

Salt and pepper

3 ounces Gorgonzola cheese, crumbled
(¾ cup)

1 large egg, lightly beaten
Kosher salt

2 tablespoons minced fresh parsley

1. FOR THE DOUGH: Pulse all-purpose flour, whole-wheat flour, sugar, and salt in food processor until combined, 2 to 3 pulses. Add butter and pulse until it forms pea-size pieces, about 10 pulses. Transfer mixture to medium bowl.

2. Sprinkle water and vinegar over mixture. With rubber spatula, use folding motion to mix until loose, shaggy mass forms with some dry flour remaining (do not overwork). Transfer mixture to center of large sheet of plastic wrap, press gently into rough 4-inch square, and wrap tightly. Refrigerate for at least 45 minutes.

3. Transfer dough to lightly floured counter. Roll into 11 by 8-inch rectangle with short side of rectangle parallel to edge of counter. Using bench scraper, bring bottom third of dough up, then fold upper third over it, folding like business letter into 8 by 4-inch rectangle. Turn dough 90 degrees counterclockwise. Roll out dough again into 11 by 8-inch rectangle and fold into thirds again. Turn dough 90 degrees counterclockwise and repeat rolling and folding into thirds. After last fold, fold dough in half to create 4-inch square. Press top of dough gently to seal. Wrap in plastic wrap and refrigerate for at least 45 minutes or up to 2 days.

4. FOR THE FILLING: Place mushrooms in bowl, cover, and microwave until just tender, 3 to 5 minutes. Transfer to colander to drain and return to bowl. Meanwhile, heat 1 tablespoon oil in 12-inch skillet over medium heat until shimmering. Add leeks and thyme, cover, and cook, stirring occasionally, until leeks are tender and beginning to brown, 5 to 7 minutes. Transfer to bowl with mushrooms. Stir in

crème fraîche and mustard. Season with salt and pepper to taste. Set aside.

5. Adjust oven rack to lower-middle position, place baking stone on oven rack, and heat oven to 400 degrees. Line rimmed baking sheet with parchment paper. Remove dough from refrigerator and let stand at room temperature for 15 to 20 minutes. Roll out on generously floured (up to ¼ cup) counter to 14-inch circle about ⅛ inch thick. (Trim edges as needed to form rough circle.) Transfer dough to prepared sheet. With tip of paring knife, cut five ¼-inch circles in dough (one at center and four evenly spaced midway from center to edge of dough). Brush top of dough with 1 teaspoon oil.

6. Spread half of filling evenly over dough, leaving 2-inch border around edge. Sprinkle with half of Gorgonzola, cover with remaining filling, and top with remaining Gorgonzola. Drizzle remaining 1 teaspoon oil over filling. Gently grasp 1 edge of dough and fold up outer 2 inches over filling. Repeat around circumference of tart, overlapping dough every 2 to 3 inches; gently pinch pleated dough to secure but do not press dough into filling. Brush dough with egg and sprinkle evenly with kosher salt.

7. Lower oven temperature to 375 degrees. Bake until crust is deep golden brown and filling is beginning to brown, 35 to 45 minutes. Let tart cool on sheet on wire rack for 10 minutes. Using offset or wide metal spatula, loosen tart from parchment and carefully slide tart off parchment onto cutting board. Sprinkle with parsley, cut into wedges, and serve.

POTATO AND SHALLOT GALETTE WITH GOAT CHEESE

Substitute 1 pound Yukon Gold potatoes, sliced ¼ inch thick, for mushrooms and increase microwave cooking time to 4 to 8 minutes. Substitute 4 ounces shallots, sliced thin, for leeks and rosemary for thyme.

Increase amount of crème fraîche to ¼ cup and substitute ¼ cup chopped pitted kalamata olives and 1 teaspoon finely grated lemon zest for Dijon mustard. Substitute goat cheese for Gorgonzola.

BUTTERNUT SQUASH GALETTE WITH GRUYÈRE

---

1. Microwave 6 ounces baby spinach and ¼ cup water in covered bowl until spinach is wilted and has decreased in volume by half, 3 to 4 minutes. Using potholders, remove bowl from microwave and keep covered for 1 minute. Carefully remove plate and transfer spinach to colander. Gently press spinach with rubber spatula to release excess liquid. Transfer spinach to cutting board and roughly chop. Return spinach to colander and press again with rubber spatula; set aside.

2. Substitute 1¼ pounds butternut squash, peeled and cut into ½-inch cubes, for mushrooms and increase microwave cooking time to about 8 minutes. Substitute 1 thinly sliced red onion for leeks and ½ teaspoon minced fresh oregano for thyme. Substitute 1 teaspoon sherry vinegar for Dijon mustard and stir reserved spinach and 3 ounces shredded Gruyère cheese into filling along with crème fraîche and vinegar in step 4. Omit Gorgonzola.

Pissaladière

✔ WHY THIS RECIPE WORKS
Pissaladière, the classic olive, anchovy, and onion tart from Provence, is easy enough to prepare, but each ingredient must be handled carefully.

MAKE A PIZZALIKE DOUGH We make the dough in a food processor and knead it as little as possible to create a pizzalike dough with the structure to stand up to the heavy toppings. Bread flour works best because its higher percentage of protein translates to a more substantial chew.

CARAMELIZE THE ONIONS We use a combination of high and low heat to caramelize the onions without burning them and we add a bit of water to the onions, which makes it easier to spread them on the crust.

REVERSE THE ORDER OF TOPPINGS To protect the black olives, anchovies, and fresh thyme leaves from burning in the oven, we spread them over the dough and then cover them with the onions. We prefer chopping the anchovies to keep them from being overpowering, but diehard fish lovers can add more as a garnish.

PISSALADIÈRE
MAKES 2 TARTS, SERVING 8 TO 10

If you like, you can slow down the dough's rising time by letting it rise in the refrigerator for 8 to 16 hours in step 1; let the refrigerated dough soften at room temperature for 30 minutes before using.

DOUGH
- 2 cups (11 ounces) bread flour
- 1 teaspoon instant or rapid-rise yeast
- 1 teaspoon salt
- 1 tablespoon olive oil, plus extra as needed
- 1 cup warm water (110 degrees)

CARAMELIZED ONIONS
- 2 tablespoons olive oil
- 2 pounds onions, halved and sliced ¼ inch thick
- 1 teaspoon packed brown sugar
- ½ teaspoon salt
- 1 tablespoon water

OLIVES, ANCHOVIES, AND
GARNISHES
  Olive oil
½ teaspoon pepper
½ cup pitted niçoise olives, chopped
   coarse
8 anchovy fillets, rinsed, patted dry, and
   chopped coarse, plus 12 fillets, rinsed
   and patted dry, for garnish (optional)
2 teaspoons minced fresh thyme
1 teaspoon fennel seeds (optional)
1 tablespoon minced fresh parsley
   (optional)

1. FOR THE DOUGH: Pulse flour, yeast, and salt in food processor (fitted with dough blade if possible) until combined, about 5 pulses. With processor running, slowly add oil, then water; process until dough forms ball, about 15 seconds. Transfer dough to lightly floured counter and form it into smooth, round ball. Place dough in large, lightly greased bowl; cover tightly with greased plastic wrap and let rise at room temperature until doubled in size, 1 to 1½ hours.

2. FOR THE CARAMELIZED ONIONS: While dough is rising, heat oil in 12-inch non-stick skillet over medium-low heat until shimmering. Stir in onions, sugar, and salt. Cover and cook, stirring occasionally, until onions are softened and have released their liquid, about 10 minutes. Remove lid, increase heat to medium-high, and continue to cook, stirring often, until onions are deeply browned, 10 to 15 minutes. Off heat, stir in water, then transfer onions to bowl and set aside.

3. FOR THE TOPPINGS: Thirty minutes before baking, adjust oven rack to lowest position, set baking stone on rack, and heat oven to 500 degrees. Transfer dough to lightly floured counter, divide in half, and cover with greased plastic. Form 1 piece of dough into rough ball by gently pulling edges of dough together and pinching to seal (keep other piece covered). With floured hands, turn dough ball seam side down. Cupping dough with both hands, gently push dough in circular motion to form taut ball. Repeat with second piece of dough. Brush each piece lightly with oil, cover with plastic, and let rest for 10 minutes. Meanwhile, cut two 20-inch lengths of parchment paper and set aside.

4. Coat your fingers and palms generously with oil. Hold 1 piece of dough up and gently stretch it to 12-inch length. Place dough on parchment sheet and gently dimple surface of dough with your fingertips. Using oiled palms, push and flatten dough into 14 by 8-inch oval. Brush dough with oil and sprinkle with ¼ teaspoon pepper. Leaving ½-inch border around edge, sprinkle ¼ cup olives, 1 tablespoon chopped anchovies, and 1 teaspoon thyme evenly over dough, then evenly scatter with half of onions. Arrange 6 whole anchovy fillets, if using, on tart and sprinkle with ½ teaspoon fennel seeds, if using. Slide parchment with tart onto pizza peel, then slide onto baking stone. Bake until deep golden brown, 13 to 15 minutes. While first tart bakes, shape and top second tart.

5. Transfer tart to cutting board and remove parchment; let cool for 5 minutes. While first tart cools, bake second tart. Sprinkle tarts with parsley, if using, and cut each tart into 8 pieces before serving.

SHAPING PISSALADIÈRE

1. Hold dough aloft and stretch.

2. Dimple dough with fingers.

3. Push dough into oval.

4. Add toppings.

DANISH BRAID

Pastry

Pâte à Choux

MAKING CREAM PUFF PASTE

1. Occasionally stir butter mixture until it comes to full boil. Remove pan from heat.

2. Add flour, return pan to low heat, and cook paste for 3 minutes, stirring constantly and using smearing motion.

3. With feed tube open, process paste for 10 seconds, then add eggs in steady stream.

✔ WHY THIS RECIPE WORKS

Pâte à choux, or cream puff pastry, is the most elemental type of French pastry, and it forms the basis for éclairs, gougères, and profiteroles. Pâte à choux should bake up into light, airy, well-puffed pastries with a delicately crispy crust. The inside should be primarily hollow, but lined with a soft, custardy webbing. We aimed to create our own foolproof version.

EMPLOY THE FOOD PROCESSOR The traditional technique of mixing pâte à choux is to bring water or milk, salt, and butter to a boil in a saucepan. Flour is then stirred in to make a paste, the saucepan is returned to low heat and stirred constantly for a few minutes, then eggs are stirred in off the heat. Our only quibble with this method is where the eggs are added, one at a time. The mixture fussily requires vigorous stirring after each addition. If added all at once, the eggs splash about and require patience and a strong arm to incorporate them into the dough. We found that this grunt work was unnecessary when we transferred the paste to a food processor, let the mixture cool briefly, then whirred in all the eggs at once.

TWEAK THE PROPORTIONS For the liquid in our dough, we use a combination of milk and water—during baking, the former helps the pastry brown and the latter keeps it crisp. We also found that puffs made with two whole eggs plus one egg white yield incredibly light, airy pastry with custardy interiors.

DON'T CROWD THE BAKING SHEET We did find that crowding causes the pastry to collapse. Be sure to leave at least an inch of space between portions of the dough.

USE DUAL OVEN TEMPERATURES Pâte à choux is leavened by steam pushing up from the interior, so it requires a blast of heat to get it going. We start the pastries at 425 or 400 degrees (depending on their shape), then turn down the oven for the last several minutes of baking for puffs with tender interiors and a crisp crust.

RELEASE THE STEAM After being baked, the pastries may be crisp externally, but their insides remain moist with residual steam. If the steam isn't released, it will turn the pastries soggy. Immediately following baking, the puffs must be slit to release steam and returned to a turned-off, propped-open oven where they can dry out.

PÂTE À CHOUX (CREAM PUFF PASTRY)

MAKES ENOUGH FOR 8 ÉCLAIRS OR
24 PROFITEROLES

Be sure to sift the flour after measuring.

- 2 large eggs plus 1 large white
- 6 tablespoons water
- 5 tablespoons unsalted butter, cut into 10 pieces
- 2 tablespoons whole milk
- 1½ teaspoons sugar
- ¼ teaspoon salt
- ½ cup (2½ ounces) all-purpose flour, sifted

1. Beat eggs and white together in liquid measuring cup; set aside. Bring water, butter, milk, sugar, and salt to boil in small saucepan over medium heat. Remove saucepan from heat and stir in flour until combined and mixture clears sides of pan. Return saucepan to low heat and cook, stirring constantly, using smearing motion, until mixture is slightly shiny with wet-sand appearance and tiny beads of fat appear on bottom of saucepan, about 3 minutes (mixture should register 175 to 180 degrees).

2. Immediately transfer hot mixture to food processor and process for 10 seconds to cool slightly. With processor running, gradually add beaten eggs in steady stream. Scrape down sides of bowl, then process for 30 seconds until smooth, thick, sticky paste forms.

Éclairs

WHY THIS RECIPE WORKS

In the pastry case, éclairs look tempting, but all too often they are just soggy shells of pastry filled with a starchy pastry cream and topped with a tasteless, waxy glaze. We set out to make éclairs with delicately crisp pastry, a silky-smooth pastry cream, and a glaze that actually tastes of bittersweet chocolate.

PIPE THE DOUGH We start with our recipe for pâte à choux, or cream puff paste, and pipe the dough onto a baking sheet, being sure to leave 1 inch of space between each portion to allow for maximum rise in the oven. If the portions are crowded the rise will be inhibited.

RELEASE STEAM After baking the pastries, we cut a small slit into the side of each one to release steam and then return them to the turned-off oven to dry until the centers are moist (but not wet) and the surface is crisp.

MAKE A SMOOTH, THICKENED PASTRY CREAM We make our pastry cream with plenty of egg yolks, half-and-half, and butter, and just enough cornstarch so that the cream keeps its shape without becoming gummy. To prevent the pastry cream from curdling, we temper, or warm, the yolks with a portion of the hot half-and-half mixture before mixing it all together. In addition to traditional vanilla pastry cream, we also like almond or mocha-flavored pastry cream in our éclairs.

OPEN THREE CHANNELS FOR THE PASTRY CREAM One of the trickiest parts of making éclairs is filling them with pastry cream without mangling the shell. Cutting the éclairs in half horizontally looked sloppy and pastry cream leaked out the sides. Trying to poke a hole at one end and fashioning a path through the pastry was difficult. Instead, we found that cutting three small X-shaped holes across the top of each baked and cooled éclair is the way to go. We then pipe pastry cream into each opening for even distribution.

MIX AND SPOON THE GLAZE OVER THE PASTRIES We make our chocolate glaze with melted semisweet or bittersweet chocolate, half-and-half, and confectioners' sugar. Once glazed, the holes for the pastry cream are camouflaged.

ÉCLAIRS
MAKES 8 ÉCLAIRS

Be sure the pastry cream is thoroughly chilled before filling the pastries. The chocolate glaze should still be warm when glazing the éclairs.

PASTRY

1   recipe Pâte à Choux (page 446)

FILLING AND GLAZE

1   recipe Pastry Cream (recipe follows)
2   ounces semisweet or bittersweet chocolate, chopped fine
3   tablespoons half-and-half
1   cup (4 ounces) confectioners' sugar

1. FOR THE PASTRY: Adjust oven rack to middle position and heat oven to 400 degrees. Spray baking sheet with vegetable oil spray and line with parchment paper.

2. Fit pastry bag with ½-inch plain tip and fill with warm pâte à choux. Pipe pâte à choux into eight 5 by 1-inch logs on prepared sheet, spaced about 1 inch apart. Use back of teaspoon dipped in cold water to even out shape and smooth surface of logs.

3. Bake pastries for 15 minutes (do not open oven door), then reduce oven temperature to 350 degrees and continue to bake until golden brown and fairly firm (pastries should not be soft and squishy), 8 to 10 minutes longer.

4. Remove sheet from oven and cut ¾-inch slit into side of each pastry with paring knife to

QUICK-COOLING PASTRY CREAM AND PUDDINGS

To speed the cooling process, spread out the pastry cream or pudding across a rimmed, parchment paper–covered baking sheet and then cover it with another piece of parchment to prevent a skin from forming. Snip a number of holes in the top layer of parchment to allow for steam to escape.

release steam. Return pastries to oven, turn off oven, and prop oven door open with handle of wooden spoon. Dry pastries in turned-off oven until center is just moist (not wet) and surface is crisp, about 45 minutes. Transfer pastries to wire rack to cool. (Cooled pastries can be stored at room temperature for up to 24 hours or frozen in zipper-lock bag for up to 1 month. Recrisp room-temperature pastries in 300-degree oven for 5 to 8 minutes, or frozen pastries for 8 to 10 minutes.)

5. FOR THE FILLING AND GLAZE: Use tip of small knife to cut 3 small Xs along top of each pastry. Fit clean pastry bag with ¼-inch plain tip and fill pastry bag with pastry cream. Pipe pastry cream into pastries through each X until éclairs are completely filled.

6. Microwave chocolate at 50 percent power for 30 seconds until it melts. Whisk in half-and-half until smooth. Gradually whisk in sugar until smooth. Transfer éclairs to wire rack set over sheet of parchment (for easy cleanup) and spoon warm glaze evenly over tops, being sure to cover holes. Let glaze set, about 20 minutes, before serving. (Filled and glazed éclairs can be stored at room temperature for 4 hours.)

PASTRY CREAM
MAKES ABOUT 2 CUPS

You can substitute 1½ teaspoons vanilla extract for the vanilla bean; stir the extract into the pastry cream with the butter in step 2.

- ½ vanilla bean
- 2 cups half-and-half
- ½ cup (3½ ounces) sugar
-    Pinch salt
- 5 large egg yolks
- 3 tablespoons cornstarch
- 4 tablespoons unsalted butter, cut into 4 pieces

1. Cut vanilla bean in half lengthwise. Using tip of paring knife, scrape out seeds. Bring vanilla bean and seeds, half-and-half, 6 tablespoons sugar, and salt to simmer in medium saucepan over medium-high heat, stirring occasionally.

2. Meanwhile, whisk egg yolks, cornstarch, and remaining 2 tablespoons sugar together in medium bowl until smooth. Slowly whisk 1 cup of simmering half-and-half mixture into egg mixture to temper, then slowly whisk tempered egg mixture into remaining half-and-half mixture. Reduce heat to medium and cook, stirring constantly, until pastry cream is thickened and few bubbles burst on surface, about 30 seconds. Off heat, whisk in butter.

3. Remove vanilla bean and transfer pastry cream to clean bowl. Lay plastic wrap directly on surface of pastry cream and refrigerate until cold and set, about 3 hours. (Pastry cream can be refrigerated for up to 3 days.)

ALMOND PASTRY CREAM

Whisk ¾ teaspoon almond extract into pastry cream with butter.

MOCHA PASTRY CREAM

Add 1 teaspoon instant espresso powder or instant coffee powder to half-and-half mixture before bringing to simmer.

1. Scoop ice cream onto prepared baking sheet, freeze until firm, and cover with plastic wrap.

2. Use paring knife to split puffs about ⅜ inch from bottom. Set 3 bottoms on each dessert plate.

3. Place scoop of ice cream on each bottom and press tops into ice cream. Pour sauce over profiteroles.

Profiteroles

✔ WHY THIS RECIPE WORKS

Profiteroles might just be the most perfect dessert in existence: crisp, tender, and airy pastry encasing cold, creamy ice cream and napped with a dark, luxurious chocolate sauce.

PIPE THE DOUGH AND BAKE We start with our recipe for pâte à choux, or cream puff paste, and pipe the dough into mounds on a baking sheet, being sure to leave 1 inch of space between each portion to allow for maximum rise in the oven. If the portions are crowded the rise will be inhibited. We also smooth the tops of the mounds with a teaspoon dipped in water.

RELEASE STEAM We slit the puffs immediately after baking to release steam and then return them to the oven to dry out to ensure crispness.

ASSEMBLE AND SERVE For easiest assembly, we scoop ice cream onto a chilled baking sheet, then split the puffs and fill them all at once. We make a quick bittersweet chocolate sauce with heavy cream, corn syrup, and butter to drizzle over the ice cream–filled pastries just before serving.

PROFITEROLES

SERVES 6

A serving of profiteroles consists of three baked puffs filled with ice cream and topped with sauce. This recipe makes 24 puffs, technically enough to serve eight, but inevitably a few bake up too awkwardly shaped to serve to guests. For profiteroles, the smooth, dense texture and rich flavor of a high-quality custard-style ice cream is preferable to the light, fluffy texture and milky flavor of Philadelphia-style ice cream, which is made without eggs. If you're serving several guests, prescooping the ice cream makes serving quick and neat, but if you're assembling only a couple servings or your freezer lacks space, you can skip the prescooping step.

PASTRY

1 recipe Pâte à Choux (page 446)

FILLING AND SAUCE

1 quart vanilla or coffee custard-style ice cream
¾ cup heavy cream
3 tablespoons light corn syrup
3 tablespoons unsalted butter, cut into 3 pieces
  Pinch salt
6 ounces bittersweet chocolate, chopped fine

1. FOR THE PASTRY: Adjust oven rack to middle position and heat oven to 425 degrees. Spray baking sheet with vegetable oil spray and line with parchment paper.

2. Fit pastry bag with ½-inch plain tip and fill with warm pâte à choux. Pipe pâte à choux into 1½-inch mounds on prepared sheet, spaced about 1 inch apart (you should have about 24 mounds). Use back of teaspoon dipped in cold water to even out shape and smooth surface of mounds.

3. Bake pastries for 15 minutes (do not open oven door), then reduce oven temperature to 375 degrees and continue to bake until golden brown and fairly firm (pastries should not be soft and squishy), 8 to 10 minutes longer.

4. Remove sheet from oven and cut ¾-inch slit into side of each pastry with paring knife to release steam. Return pastries to oven, turn off oven, and prop oven door open with handle of wooden spoon. Dry pastries in turned-off oven until center is just moist (not wet) and surface is crisp, about 45 minutes. Transfer pastries to wire rack to cool. (Cooled pastries can be stored at room temperature for up to 24 hours or frozen in zipper-lock bag for up to 1 month. Recrisp room-temperature puffs in 300-degree oven for 5 to 8 minutes, or frozen puffs for 8 to 10 minutes.)

5. FOR THE FILLING AND SAUCE: Line clean baking sheet with parchment and freeze until cold, about 20 minutes. Place 2-inch scoops of ice cream onto chilled sheet and freeze until firm, then cover with plastic wrap; keep frozen until ready to serve.

6. Bring heavy cream, corn syrup, butter, and salt to boil in small saucepan. Off heat, stir in chocolate. Cover saucepan and let stand until chocolate is melted, about 5 minutes. Whisk gently until combined. (Sauce can be refrigerated for up to 2 weeks.)

7. To serve, use paring knife to split open 18 pastries about ⅜ inch from bottom; set 3 bottoms on each dessert plate. Place scoop of ice cream on each bottom and gently press tops into ice cream. Pour sauce over profiteroles and serve immediately.

Gougères

✔ WHY THIS RECIPE WORKS

Baked cheese puffs (gougères) are a classic French appetizer. With just a few ingredients, they should be easy enough to make, but many gougères are either dry, brittle, and bitter, or squishy, soft and gooey. We wanted perfect gougères with a crisp, caramel-colored exterior that yielded to a tender, slightly moist interior. And we wanted them to taste a little nutty from the browned cheese.

INCORPORATE GOOD-QUALITY CHEESE Using our Pâte à Choux dough (page 446), minus the sugar, as a base, we simply add cheese to the food processor after the dough has come together, then process a bit longer to incorporate the cheese. Gruyère makes all the difference in our cheese puffs (although Emmentaler or Swiss cheese can be substituted), and a pinch of cayenne pepper (added with the cheese) tastes just right.

PIPE AND BAKE We pipe out mounds that are slightly larger than our profiteroles and, as for our other pastries, we allow for enough space between them on the baking sheet for the best rise in the oven. As with our Profiteroles, we smooth the surface of the mounds with a teaspoon dipped in water.

USE DUAL OVEN TEMPERATURES As we found with our other recipes with pâte à choux, small variations in oven temperature led to wildly different results in both color and texture. We needed a combination method of 425 degrees for 15 minutes and then 375 degrees for another 10 minutes to yield perfect results. Then, to make our puffs perfectly crisp but keep the interior a little softer, we pierce each puff with a paring knife and return them to the cooling oven for just 10 minutes. We dry these puffs in the oven as we do our other pastries for 45 minutes, but we don't cool them once out of the oven. They are best served warm.

GOUGÈRES (CHEESE PUFFS)
MAKES 16

If you prefer smaller gougères, simply use a smaller tip on the piping bag. Pay close attention as they bake because smaller puffs may require a shorter baking time.

- 2 large eggs plus 1 large white
- 6 tablespoons water
- 5 tablespoons unsalted butter, cut into 10 pieces
- 2 tablespoons whole milk
- ¼ teaspoon salt
- ½ cup (2½ ounces) all-purpose flour
- 3 ounces Gruyère cheese, shredded (¾ cup)
- Pinch cayenne pepper

PIPING PROFITEROLES OR GOUGÈRES

1. Pipe paste into 1½-inch mounds on prepared baking sheet.

2. Use back of teaspoon dipped in cold water to even out shape and smooth surface of mounds.

CLEANING A CHEESE GRATER

Graters coated with the sticky residue from soft cheeses can be a chore to clean. Here's an easy way to handle this task.

Rub a hard, stale crust of bread (such as the end of a baguette) over the dirty grater plate to remove most of the mess. Then scrub the grater in hot soapy water to finish the job.

1. Adjust oven rack to middle position and heat oven to 425 degrees. Spray baking sheet with vegetable oil spray and line with parchment paper.

2. Beat eggs and white together in liquid measuring cup; set aside. Bring water, butter, milk, and salt to boil in small saucepan over medium heat. Remove saucepan from heat and stir in flour until combined and mixture clears sides of pan. Return saucepan to low heat and cook, stirring constantly, using smearing motion, until mixture is slightly shiny with wet-sand appearance and tiny beads of fat appear on bottom of saucepan, about 3 minutes (mixture should register 175 to 180 degrees).

3. Immediately transfer hot mixture to food processor and process for 10 seconds to cool slightly. With processor running, gradually add beaten eggs in steady stream. Scrape down sides of bowl, then add cheese and cayenne and process for 30 seconds until smooth, thick, sticky paste forms.

4. Fit pastry bag with ½-inch plain tip and fill with warm cheese mixture and pipe into 2-inch mounds on prepared sheet, spaced about 1 inch apart (you should have about 16 mounds). Use back of teaspoon dipped in cold water to even out shape and smooth surface of mounds.

5. Bake pastries for 15 minutes (do not open oven door), then reduce oven temperature to 375 degrees and continue to bake until golden brown and fairly firm (gougères should not be soft and squishy), 8 to 10 minutes longer.

6. Remove sheet from oven and cut ¾-inch slit into side of each pastry with paring knife to release steam. Return pastries to oven, turn off oven, and prop oven door open with handle of wooden spoon. Dry pastries in turned-off oven until center is just moist (not wet) and surface is crisp, about 45 minutes. Serve warm.

Apple Strudel

✓ WHY THIS RECIPE WORKS

Classic apple strudel is an all-day affair. We wanted to see if we could get full apple flavor, a moist filling, and a crisp, flaky crust in less than an hour.

STREAMLINE WITH STORE-BOUGHT PHYLLO From the outset, we shelved the notion of homemade strudel dough; store-bought phyllo dough provides a good substitute. For a strudel with a crisp, flaky crust that holds its shape and won't dislodge or fly off when approached with a fork, we handle the phyllo dough carefully, sprinkling butter and sugar between its layers to form a cohesive crust.

USE A MIX OF APPLES For the filling, we use a combination of McIntosh and Golden Delicious apples, cut into thin slices, for maximum flavor and tender bites of fruit. Raisins and walnuts add textural interest; plumping the raisins first in apple brandy deepens the apple flavor overall.

LIGHTEN THE FILLING WITH BREAD CRUMBS We incorporate bread crumbs into our filling to help absorb some of the moisture from the filling and prevent the pastry from turning soggy. Browning the bread crumbs in butter also lends rich flavor to the filling.

CUT VENTS IN THE STRUDEL BEFORE BAKING The vents allow steam to escape the pastry during baking—without vents, the pastry will burst open in the oven. Baking takes just 15 minutes in a hot, 475-degree oven. Baking the strudel quickly prevents the delicate phyllo from drying out and cracking apart.

QUICKER APPLE STRUDEL
SERVES 6 TO 8

Phyllo dough is also available in larger 18 by 14-inch sheets; if using, cut them in half to make 14 by 9-inch sheets. Do not thaw the phyllo dough in the microwave; let it sit in the refrigerator overnight or on the counter for 4 to 5 hours. If the phyllo sheets have small cuts or tears in the same location, flip the alternating sheets of phyllo when assembling the strudel in step 4, so that the cuts will not line up and cause a weak spot in the crust. To make fresh bread crumbs, pulse one slice of white sandwich bread (with crust) in a food processor to fine crumbs, about six pulses; you will have 1 cup fresh bread crumbs. Serve the strudel warm with Tangy Whipped Cream (page 280) or Whipped Cream (page 348).

½	cup golden raisins
2	tablespoons Calvados or apple cider
¼	cup fresh white bread crumbs
8	tablespoons unsalted butter, melted and cooled
1	pound Golden Delicious apples, peeled, cored, and sliced ¼ inch thick
1	McIntosh apple, peeled, cored, and sliced ¼ inch thick
⅓	cup walnuts, toasted and chopped fine (optional)
6	tablespoons (2⅔ ounces) granulated sugar
1	teaspoon lemon juice
¼	teaspoon ground cinnamon
⅛	teaspoon salt
10	(14 by 9-inch) phyllo sheets, thawed
1½	teaspoons confectioners' sugar

1. Adjust oven rack to lower-middle position and heat oven to 475 degrees. Line rimmed baking sheet with parchment paper. Combine raisins and Calvados in small bowl, cover, and microwave until simmering, about 1 minute. Let sit, covered, until needed.

2. Toast bread crumbs with 1 tablespoon melted butter in 8-inch skillet over medium heat, stirring often, until golden brown, about 2 minutes; transfer to large bowl.

3. Drain raisins, discarding liquid. Add raisins, apples, walnuts, if using, ¼ cup granulated sugar, lemon juice, cinnamon, and salt to bowl with bread crumbs and toss to combine.

4. Place large sheet of parchment on counter with long side facing you. Lay 1 phyllo sheet on left side of sheet of parchment, then brush with melted butter and sprinkle with ½ teaspoon granulated sugar. Place second phyllo sheet on right side of parchment, overlapping sheets by 1 inch, then brush with butter and sprinkle with ½ teaspoon granulated sugar. Repeat with remaining 8 phyllo sheets, brushing each layer with butter and sprinkling with granulated sugar. Mound filling along bottom edge of phyllo, leaving 2½-inch border on bottom and 2-inch border on sides. Fold dough on sides over apples. Fold dough on bottom over apples and continue to roll dough around filling to form strudel.

5. Gently transfer strudel, seam side down, to prepared baking sheet; brush with remaining butter and sprinkle with remaining 1 teaspoon granulated sugar. Cut four 1½-inch vents on diagonal across top of strudel and bake until golden brown, about 15 minutes, rotating baking sheet halfway through baking. Transfer strudel with baking sheet to wire rack and let cool until warm, about 40 minutes.

6. Dust with confectioners' sugar before serving; slice with serrated knife and serve warm or at room temperature.

QUICKER PEAR STRUDEL

Substitute 2 tablespoons Poire Williams or other pear liqueur for Calvados and 1½ pounds Bosc pears, peeled, cored, and sliced ¼ inch thick for apples. Increase lemon juice to 2 teaspoons.

ASSEMBLING APPLE STRUDEL

1. Brush 1 phyllo sheet with melted butter and sprinkle with sugar. Place second phyllo sheet next to it, overlapping sheets. Brush with more butter and sprinkle with sugar. Repeat this process 4 times.

2. Mound filling along bottom edge of phyllo, leaving 2½-inch border on bottom and 2-inch border on sides.

3. Fold dough on sides over apples. Fold dough on bottom over apples and continue to roll dough around filling to form strudel.

4. After strudel has been assembled and rolled, gently lay it seam side down on prepared baking sheet.

Baklava

✔ WHY THIS RECIPE WORKS

With its copious amounts of butter, sugar, and nuts, baklava is often a lamentable experience; sad, soggy, punishingly sweet, and utterly lifeless specimens are ubiquitous. We wanted crisp, flaky, buttery baklava, filled with fragrant nuts and spices, and sweetened just assertively enough to pair with coffee.

FULLY DEFROST THE PHYLLO There was no question that we would be using store-bought phyllo for a home-baked version of baklava. Our lessons in phyllo began at the grocery store. Avoid packages in the freezer case that are caked with ice—they are almost certain to contain phyllo that is cracked and brittle. Phyllo also needs to be fully defrosted before use. Storing it overnight in the refrigerator requires forethought but it is a good method, as is a 4- to 5-hour thaw at room temperature.

KEEP PHYLLO COVERED DURING ASSEMBLY Phyllo has a reputation for being difficult to work with. Indeed, the paper-thin sheets are quick to dry out and become brittle. We found that during assembly, the phyllo is best kept under a sheet of plastic wrap, then covered with a damp dish towel as added insurance.

CLARIFY THE BUTTER Baklava is made by brushing sheets of phyllo with butter, layering the phyllo with a spiced mixture of ground nuts, baking, then soaking with a sweetened syrup. We wondered if clarifying the butter, which involves removing the milk solids, is really necessary. We used whole butter for our first batch and the surface turned splotchy brown. When made with clarified butter, the pastry browned uniformly. This pastry also had a cleaner, sweeter flavor. Clarifying the butter is key. We also found it is necessary to butter every layer of phyllo. It may seem excessive but if you cut back, the unbuttered sheets will curl and crack.

BUILD THREE LAYERS OF NUTS We started by layering the nut filling (a combination of finely chopped walnuts and almonds) twice between the phyllo, but the pastry lacked cohesion. Instead, we found three thinner layers of nuts between layers of phyllo had superior structure. We flavor the nuts with cinnamon and cloves.

CUT, DON'T SCORE Before baking, it's important to cut the baklava (we do so in a diamond-shaped pattern), not just score it. This ensures neat channels for the honey-sugar syrup to soak into once the hot pastry is out of the oven. We then garnish the baklava with more nuts. The pastry should be cooled completely before serving and we found that both flavor and texture are best when the baklava is allowed to stand for at least 8 hours before serving.

BAKLAVA
MAKES 32 TO 40 PIECES

Phyllo dough is also available in larger 18 by 14-inch sheets; if using, cut them in half to make 14 by 9-inch sheets. Do not thaw the phyllo dough in the microwave; let it sit in the refrigerator overnight or on the counter for 4 to 5 hours. A straight-sided traditional (not nonstick) metal baking pan works best for making baklava. If you don't have this type of pan, a glass baking dish will work. When assembling, use the nicest, most intact phyllo sheets for the bottom and top layers; use sheets with tears or ones that are smaller than the size of the pan in the middle layers, where their imperfections will go unnoticed. If, after assembly, you have leftover clarified butter, store it in an airtight container in the refrigerator; it can be used for sautéing.

ASSEMBLING BAKLAVA

1. Cover phyllo to keep it moist. Place 8 phyllo sheets in buttered baking pan, brushing each sheet with butter.

2. Spread 1 cup of nut filling over bottom layer of phyllo. Place 6 phyllo sheets over nut layer, brushing each sheet with butter. Spread another 1 cup nut filling over phyllo.

3. Repeat with 6 more sheets buttered phyllo and remaining 1 cup nut filling. Finish with 8 to 10 more sheets of buttered phyllo. Using your hands, compress layers to remove air pockets, working from center outward.

4. Cut baklava into diamonds using serrated knife, then bake. Pour syrup over cut lines of baked baklava. Garnish each piece with chopped nuts.

SUGAR SYRUP

1¼ cups (8¾ ounces) sugar
¾ cup water
⅓ cup honey
3 (2-inch) strips lemon zest plus 1 tablespoon juice
1 cinnamon stick
5 whole cloves
⅛ teaspoon salt

NUT FILLING

1¾ cups slivered almonds
1 cup walnuts
2 tablespoons sugar
1¼ teaspoons ground cinnamon
¼ teaspoon ground cloves
⅛ teaspoon salt

24 tablespoons (3 sticks) unsalted butter, cut into 1-inch pieces
1 pound (14 by 9-inch) phyllo, thawed

1. FOR THE SUGAR SYRUP: Bring all ingredients to boil in small saucepan, stirring occasionally to ensure that sugar dissolves. Transfer syrup to 2-cup liquid measuring cup and set aside to cool while making and baking baklava; when syrup is cool, remove spices and lemon zest. (Cooled syrup can be refrigerated for up to 4 days.)

2. FOR THE NUT FILLING: Pulse almonds in food processor until very finely chopped, about 20 pulses; transfer to medium bowl. Pulse walnuts in processor until very finely chopped, about 15 pulses; transfer to bowl with almonds and toss to combine. Measure out 1 tablespoon nuts and set aside for garnish. Add sugar, cinnamon, cloves, and salt to nut mixture and toss well to combine.

3. Adjust oven rack to lower-middle position and heat oven to 300 degrees. Melt butter slowly in small saucepan over medium-low heat until milk solids have separated from butterfat and collected on bottom of saucepan, about 10 minutes. Remove saucepan from heat, let butter settle for 10 minutes, then carefully skim foam from surface with spoon.

4. When all of foam has been removed, slowly pour clear butterfat into bowl, leaving all milk solids behind in the saucepan (you should have about 1 cup clarified butter).

5. Grease 13 by 9-inch baking pan with clarified butter. Keeping phyllo sheets covered with plastic wrap and a damp dish towel to prevent them from drying out, place 1 phyllo sheet in bottom of prepared pan and brush with clarified butter until completely coated. Layer 7 phyllo sheets into pan, brushing each sheet with butter. Sprinkle 1 cup nut filling evenly over phyllo.

6. Layer 6 phyllo sheets into pan, brushing each layer with butter, then sprinkle with 1 cup nut filling. Repeat with 6 phyllo sheets, butter, and remaining 1 cup nut filling.

7. Layer remaining 8 to 10 phyllo sheets into pan, brushing each layer, except final layer, with butter. Working from center outward, use palms of hands to compress layers and press out any air pockets. Spoon 4 tablespoons of butter on top layer and brush to cover surface.

8. Using serrated knife with pointed tip, cut baklava into diamonds. Bake baklava until golden and crisp, about 1½ hours, rotating pan halfway through baking.

9. Immediately pour all but 2 tablespoons of cooled syrup over cut lines (syrup will sizzle when it hits hot pan). Drizzle remaining 2 tablespoons syrup over surface. Garnish center of each piece with pinch of reserved ground nuts. Let baklava cool completely in pan, about 3 hours, then cover with aluminum foil and let sit at room temperature for about 8 hours before serving.

PISTACHIO BAKLAVA WITH CARDAMOM AND ROSE WATER

Omit honey, lemon zest, and cinnamon stick in sugar syrup and increase sugar to 1¾ cups. Substitute 10 whole peppercorns for cloves and stir in 1 tablespoon rose water after discarding peppercorns. Substitute 2¾ cups shelled pistachios for almonds and walnuts and 1 teaspoon ground cardamom for cinnamon and cloves in nut filling.

Puff Pastry Dough

✔ WHY THIS RECIPE WORKS

Puff pastry gets its super-flaky, buttery layers from a process called lamination also known as turning, or folding. Each turn creates paper-thin sheets of butter, and when the dough is baked, the moisture in the butter evaporates into steam, causing the dough to puff and separate into flaky layers.

MIX IN A FOOD PROCESSOR We've tried quick methods for puff pastry dough, which are similar to the process for making pie dough, but these methods (which are hardly quick) lacked the super-flaky layers of the original. We follow tradition and mix flour, sugar, salt, lemon juice, and ice water together in a food processor for even, quick distribution and then we chill the dough to allow it to relax for easier rolling.

MAKE A BUTTER SQUARE While the dough chills, we make a butter square by gently pounding butter sticks into an even layer. We chill the square so that it does not melt when combined with the dough.

FOLD AND ROLL Incorporating the butter into the dough is as easy as placing the chilled butter square over the chilled dough, folding in the corners, and rolling it out. We fold the dough into thirds and then into thirds again, and then repeat this process twice to form multiple sheets of butter and dough that puff into incredibly flaky layers once baked.

PUFF PASTRY DOUGH
MAKES ABOUT 2 POUNDS

If you are making Flaky Apple Turnovers (page 461) or Napoleons (page 458), cut the dough in half (each half will weigh about 1 pound) after it has chilled in step 6; use one piece of dough as directed and refrigerate the rest for up to two days or freeze, wrapped in plastic wrap and aluminum foil, for up to one month.

DOUGH
- 3 cups (15 ounces) all-purpose flour
- 1½ tablespoons sugar
- 1½ teaspoons salt
- 2 teaspoons lemon juice
- 1 cup ice water

BUTTER SQUARE
- 24 tablespoons (3 sticks) unsalted butter, chilled
- 2 tablespoons all-purpose flour

1. FOR THE DOUGH: Process flour, sugar, and salt in food processor until combined, about 5 seconds. With processor running, add lemon juice, followed by ¾ cup water, in slow steady stream. Add remaining ¼ cup water as needed, 1 tablespoon at a time, until dough comes together and no floury bits remain.

2. Turn dough onto sheet of plastic wrap and flatten into 6-inch square. Wrap tightly in plastic and refrigerate for 1 hour.

3. FOR THE BUTTER SQUARE: Lay butter sticks side by side on sheet of parchment paper. Sprinkle flour over butter and cover with second sheet of parchment. Gently pound butter with rolling pin until butter is softened and flour is fully incorporated, then roll it into 8-inch square. Wrap butter square in plastic and refrigerate until chilled, about 1 hour.

4. Roll chilled dough into 11-inch square on lightly floured counter. Place chilled butter square diagonally in center of dough. Fold corners of dough up over butter square so that corners meet in middle and pinch dough seams to seal.

5. Using rolling pin, gently tap dough, starting from center and working outward, until square becomes larger and butter begins to soften. Gently roll dough into 14-inch square, dusting with extra flour as needed to prevent sticking. Fold dough into thirds like business letter, then fold rectangle in thirds to form square. Wrap dough in plastic and let rest in refrigerator for 2 hours.

6. Repeat step 5 twice and let dough rest in refrigerator for 2 hours more before using.

MAKING PUFF PASTRY DOUGH AND TURNING THE DOUGH

1. After rolling dough into 11-inch square, place butter square diagonally on top.

2. Fold dough over butter so that corners meet in middle. Pinch ends of dough together to seal.

3. After rolling dough into 14-inch square, fold it into thirds.

4. Fold ends of dough rectangle over center to form square. Wrap dough in plastic wrap and let rest in refrigerator for 2 hours before repeating step 5.

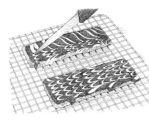

1. Spread chocolate glaze evenly over top of 6 rectangles, then drizzle thin stream of vanilla glaze crosswise over chocolate glaze. Run tip of small knife or toothpick lengthwise through icing to make design.

2. After layering remaining rectangles of pastry with pastry cream to make 6 individual portions, top each portion with glazed pastry rectangle.

✓ WHY THIS RECIPE WORKS

We wanted satiny vanilla pastry cream sandwiched between layers of buttery, crisp, and ultraflaky puff pastry, topped with the design of chocolate and vanilla fondant icing. Just as important, we wanted to bring this recipe out of the pastry kitchen and into the home kitchen.

ENSURE LEVEL LAYERS The puff pastry layers that form Napoleons need to be level so that they can be spread with pastry cream and stacked. We found that the best way to achieve this was to roll the dough into an even layer, poke holes in it with a fork, slide it onto a baking sheet and bake it topped with a second baking sheet, weighted with a large ovensafe dish.

CUT INTO INDIVIDUAL PIECES FOR EVEN STACKING Traditional recipes typically make one large Napoleon and then cut the pastry into individual servings, but this method is fussy, unnecessary, and plagued with issues like the filling squirting out the sides during cutting. Instead, once the pastry is cool, we cut it into individual rectangles before filling and stacking.

ASSEMBLE AND SERVE We use the same luxuriously smooth, rich pastry cream for our Napoleons as we use for our Éclairs (page 447) And for the icings, we skip fussy fondant in favor of a simple confectioners' sugar icing. Once the pastry is filled and glazed, our Napoleons are undeniably elegant.

NAPOLEONS
MAKES 6 NAPOLEONS

If the dough becomes too warm and sticky to work with, cover it with plastic wrap and let it chill in the refrigerator until firm. You can substitute a 1-pound box of store-bought puff pastry dough for homemade puff pastry, if desired. See page 461 for defrosting instructions.

PASTRY
½ recipe Puff Pastry Dough (page 457)

CHOCOLATE GLAZE
1 ounce bittersweet or semisweet chocolate, chopped fine
2 tablespoons milk
¾ cup (3 ounces) confectioners' sugar

VANILLA GLAZE
¼ cup (1 ounce) confectioners' sugar
1½ teaspoons milk
⅛ teaspoon vanilla extract

FILLING
1 recipe Pastry Cream (page 448)

1. FOR THE PASTRY: Adjust oven rack to middle position and heat oven to 325 degrees. Roll dough into 16 by 12-inch rectangle, about ¼ inch thick, between 2 lightly floured sheets of parchment paper. Remove top sheet of parchment and prick pastry with fork every 2 inches.

2. Replace top sheet of parchment and slide dough onto rimmed baking sheet. Place second rimmed baking sheet on top of dough and weight baking sheet with large ovensafe dish. Bake pastry until cooked through and lightly golden, 50 minutes to 1 hour, rotating baking sheet halfway through baking.

3. Remove weight, top baking sheet, and top sheet of parchment and continue to bake pastry until golden brown, 5 to 10 minutes longer. Let pastry cool completely on baking sheet, about 1 hour. (Pastry will shrink slightly.)

4. Cut cooled pastry in half lengthwise with serrated knife and trim edges as necessary to make them straight. Cut each pastry half crosswise into 3 rectangles, then cut each rectangle crosswise into 3 small rectangles (you

Pure almond extract is made from three primary ingredients: alcohol, water, and bitter almond oil. The last is extracted from almonds or (more frequently) their kin, drupes, the botanical term for stone fruits such as peaches and apricots. The almond flavor comes from benzaldehyde, a substance in the kernels of drupes. To find out if brand matters, we tasted four nationally distributed supermarket brands (three pure and one imitation) in pound cake and whipped cream. Interestingly, none of the brands we tasted get their bitter almond oil solely from almonds. One brand uses apricots; a second withheld the exact source but acknowledged that it was from stone fruits; and a third uses a combination of almonds, apricots, peaches, plums, and cherries, according to company spokespeople.

Imitation almond extract also starts with water and alcohol, but it gets its flavor from synthetic benzaldehyde, created in a lab. Our tasters couldn't tell the imitation almond extract from the pure stuff. In fact, McCormick Imitation Almond Extract, came in second, praised for its "nutty" and "buttery" flavor. Our top-rated brand, **Nielsen-Massey Almond Extract**, was "potent" and "bold." It's 90 percent alcohol, by far the highest percentage among the four extracts we tested. The alcohol in almond extract acts as a solvent to extract flavor. Generally, the higher the percentage, the more flavor is extracted, which likely accounts for the "lingering" and "pronounced" taste of this top-rated brand.

will have 18 rectangles). (Puff pastry rectangles can be wrapped tightly in plastic wrap and stored at room temperature for up to 1 day.)

5. FOR THE CHOCOLATE GLAZE: Microwave chocolate at 50 percent power for 15 seconds; stir chocolate, add milk, and continue heating for 10 seconds; stir until smooth. Whisk in confectioners' sugar until smooth.

6. FOR THE VANILLA GLAZE: Whisk sugar, milk, and vanilla together in bowl until smooth.

7. Spread chocolate glaze evenly over top of 6 rectangles of pastry and lay them on wire rack set over sheet of parchment (for easy cleanup). Drizzle thin stream of vanilla glaze crosswise over chocolate glaze. Run tip of small knife or toothpick lengthwise through icing to make design. Let icing set, about 20 minutes.

8. FOR THE FILLING: Meanwhile, spread about 2½ tablespoons of pastry cream evenly over 6 more rectangles of pastry. Gently top each with one of remaining 6 rectangles of pastry and spread remaining pastry cream evenly over tops. Top with glazed pastry rectangles and serve. (Glazed and assembled Napoleons can be stored at room temperature for up to 4 hours.)

ALMOND NAPOLEONS

Substitute Almond Pastry Cream (page 448) for Pastry Cream and add 1 drop almond extract to vanilla glaze.

MOCHA NAPOLEONS

Substitute Mocha Pastry Cream (page 448) for Pastry Cream and add ¼ teaspoon instant espresso powder or instant coffee powder to chocolate glaze before melting.

Flaky Apple Turnovers

✔ **WHY THIS RECIPE WORKS**
Store-bought turnovers are disheartening—the filling is bland and mushy and the dough soggy, making for something more like fast-food pie from a cardboard sleeve than a tantalizing, fruit-laden pastry. We wanted to make the perfect apple turnover, with a flaky, shatteringly crisp crust and firm, not mushy, apples.

DOUBLE UP ON APPLE FLAVOR The tart, full flavor of Granny Smith apples make the best turnover filling. We also like their firm texture, which don't turn to mush once baked. We chop our apples in the food processor with sugar, cinnamon, and lemon juice (for brightness). Draining the apple mixture is important to prevent sogginess. And we combine the apples with applesauce for another layer of apple flavor.

CUT, FILL, AND FOLD For the pastry, we cut out squares from our recipe for Puff Pastry Dough (page 457) and mound the apple mixture in the center. Before folding over the dough to encase the apples, we brush the edges of the dough for a tight seal. The flavor won't be quite as good, but frozen puff pastry can be substituted for homemade. See our defrosting instructions on page 461.

BRUSH, CRIMP, AND BAKE Brushing the sealed and crimped turnovers with some of the drained apple juice and sprinkling them with cinnamon sugar before baking yields flaky, buttery pastry and a filling with knockout apple flavor.

FLAKY APPLE TURNOVERS
MAKES 8 TURNOVERS

If the dough becomes too warm and sticky to work with, cover it with plastic wrap and let it chill in the refrigerator until firm. You can substitute a 1-pound box of store-bought puff pastry dough for homemade puff pastry, if desired. See defrosting instructions at right. If you don't have a food processor, grate the apples on the large holes of a box grater.

1	pound Granny Smith apples, peeled, cored, and chopped coarse
¾	cup (5¼ ounces) sugar
1	tablespoon lemon juice
⅛	teaspoon salt
½	recipe Puff Pastry Dough (page 457), divided into two 8-ounce pieces
½	cup applesauce
1	teaspoon ground cinnamon

1. Adjust oven rack to middle position and heat oven to 400 degrees. Line rimmed baking sheet with parchment paper.

2. Pulse apples, ½ cup sugar, lemon juice, and salt together in food processor until largest pieces of apples are no larger than ½ inch, about 6 pulses. Let mixture sit for 5 minutes, then transfer to fine-mesh strainer set over bowl and let apples drain, reserving juice, until needed.

3. Roll each piece of dough into 10-inch square between 2 lightly floured sheets of parchment. Remove top sheets of parchment and cut each piece of dough into four 5-inch squares (you will have 8 squares total).

4. Toss drained apples and applesauce together in separate bowl. Place 2 tablespoons apple filling in center of each piece of dough. Brush edges of dough with reserved juice, then fold 1 corner of square diagonally over filling.

Crimp edges of dough with fork to seal. Lay turnovers on prepared baking sheet and freeze until firm, about 15 minutes. (Assembled turnovers can be frozen for 1 hour, then transferred to zipper-lock bag and frozen for up to 1 month. Let frozen turnovers sit at room temperature for 20 minutes, then bake as directed.)

5. Combine remaining ¼ cup sugar and cinnamon in bowl. Brush turnovers with more reserved juice and sprinkle generously with cinnamon sugar. Bake turnovers until well browned, 20 to 26 minutes, rotating sheet halfway through baking. Immediately transfer turnovers to wire rack and let cool slightly. Serve warm or at room temperature.

FLAKY CARAMEL-APPLE AND CREAM CHEESE TURNOVERS

Any brand of soft caramels will work here; avoid hard caramel candies.

Substitute 4 ounces cream cheese for applesauce and add 2 caramel candies, quartered, to each turnover before shaping.

FLAKY CRANBERRY-APPLE TURNOVERS

Add ¾ cup dried cranberries to food processor with apples. Substitute ¼ cup thawed frozen orange juice concentrate for ¼ cup of applesauce.

FLAKY CHEDDAR-APPLE TURNOVERS

Substitute ½ cup shredded cheddar cheese for applesauce. Omit cinnamon sugar and sprinkle ¼ cup shredded cheddar over apple juice–brushed turnovers before baking.

SEALING TURNOVERS

Use a fork to crimp the edges of the turnovers.

DEFROSTING STORE-BOUGHT PUFF PASTRY

There's no way around it, puff pastry is time-consuming to make. For those of us who are not up to the project, frozen puff pastry is commonly available in supermarkets and works very well for lots of recipes. Because the dough is frozen, however, it must be defrosted before you can use it; otherwise, it can crack and break apart. We have found that thawing the dough in the refrigerator overnight is the best method, but it takes some forethought. Countertop defrosting works fine too, but don't rush it. Depending on the temperature of your kitchen, it may take between 30 and 60 minutes. The dough should unfold easily once thawed, but still feel firm. If the seams crack, rejoin them by rolling them smooth with a rolling pin. And if the dough warms and softens, place it in the freezer until firm.

Danish

✔ WHY THIS RECIPE WORKS

Tired of the dull-tasting, sticky-sweet Danish you buy at the store? We were, too, so we set out to make a better version at home. We wanted the real thing—flaky, buttery pastry with a not-too-sweet, real fruit filling.

CREATE A TENDER DOUGH Danish dough is similar to croissant dough—it is a rich yeasted dough—but unlike croissants, Danish dough contains eggs. The dough is also sweeter than croissants. We found that just one egg makes a rich, tender dough. Any more and the flavor of the egg is too distinctive.

LAMINATE TO CREATE FLAKINESS Just as we do with croissants we make a butter square that's placed on a relatively lean dough and encased by being rolled out and folded (or turned) a number of times.

PICK YOUR FILLING We find traditional jam fillings too sweet in Danish. Instead, we turn to dried fruit purees, although the fruit (apricots or prunes) needs to be plumped in water to keep it from being too dry. As an alternative to fruit fillings, we also include a sweetened cream cheese filling accented with lemon zest for brightness as well as a second cream cheese filling that we enrich with jarred sour cherries.

SHAPE AND BAKE We use a ruler and pizza wheel (for a Danish braid) to cut the dough into even strips that are surprisingly easy to braid. And for individual Danish, shaping is as easy as cutting out squares and folding over two corners to form a pocket. After baking we give the Danish a light glaze while the pastry is still hot to allow the pastry to soak up the glaze, giving it a final touch of sweetness and a beautiful sheen.

DANISH DOUGH

MAKES ENOUGH FOR 1 LARGE BRAID OR
9 INDIVIDUAL DANISH

If the dough becomes too warm and sticky to work with, cover it with plastic wrap and let it chill in the refrigerator until firm. When rolling the dough out, sprinkle extra flour over the counter and the rolling pin as needed to keep the dough from sticking. For more information on turning the dough, see page 457.

DOUGH

⅓ cup warm whole milk (110 degrees)
1 large egg
1½ cups (7½ ounces) all-purpose flour
¼ cup (1¾ ounces) sugar
1½ teaspoons instant or rapid-rise yeast
¾ teaspoon salt

BUTTER SQUARE

12 tablespoons unsalted butter, cut into 3 equal pieces and chilled
1 tablespoon all-purpose flour

1. **FOR THE DOUGH:** Mix milk and egg together in liquid measuring cup. Using stand mixer fitted with dough hook, combine 1¼ cups flour, sugar, yeast, and salt on low speed. Slowly add milk mixture and mix until dough comes together, about 2 minutes.

2. Increase speed to medium-low and knead dough until it forms sticky ball and becomes elastic, about 8 minutes. If, after 5 minutes, dough appears overly sticky and doesn't come together into ball, add remaining ¼ cup flour, 1 tablespoon at a time. Scrape dough into large, lightly greased bowl, cover with greased plastic wrap, and refrigerate until chilled, about 1 hour.

3. FOR THE BUTTER SQUARE: Lay butter pieces side by side on sheet of parchment paper. Sprinkle flour over butter and cover with second sheet of parchment. Gently pound butter with rolling pin until butter is softened and flour is fully incorporated, then roll it into 5-inch square. Wrap butter square in plastic and refrigerate until chilled, about 1 hour.

4. Roll chilled dough into 9-inch square on lightly floured counter. Place chilled butter square diagonally in center of dough. Fold corners of dough up over butter square so that corners meet in middle and pinch dough seams to seal.

5. Using rolling pin, gently tap dough, starting from center and working outward, until square becomes larger and butter begins to soften. Gently roll dough into 11-inch square, dusting with extra flour as needed to prevent sticking. Fold dough into thirds like business letter, then fold rectangle in thirds to form square. Wrap dough in plastic and let rest in refrigerator for 2 hours.

6. Repeat step 5 and let dough rest in refrigerator for 2 hours more before using.

DANISH BRAID
SERVES 6 TO 8

If the dough becomes too warm and sticky to work with, cover with plastic wrap and let it chill in the refrigerator until firm. The Danish should be brushed with the glaze while hot, but drizzled with the icing after it has cooled.

- 1 recipe Danish Dough (page 462)
- 1 recipe filling (pages 464–465)

GLAZE
- 1½ cups (6 ounces) confectioners' sugar
- 5 teaspoons milk
- 1 teaspoon lemon juice

ICING
- 1 cup (4 ounces) confectioners' sugar
- 1 tablespoon milk

1. Adjust oven rack to middle position and heat oven to 400 degrees. Roll Danish dough into 14-inch square on large sheet of parchment paper. Spread cooled filling down center third of dough, leaving ½-inch border at top and bottom edge.

2. Using pizza wheel, cut dough on either side of filling into diagonal strips about ¾ inch wide (stop cuts ¼ inch shy of filling). Discard top corner of dough on either side, then, starting at top of Danish, crisscross strips over filling to form braid. Slide Danish, still on parchment, onto baking sheet.

3. Cover Danish loosely with greased plastic wrap and let rise at room temperature until puffy, about 30 minutes. Bake Danish until golden brown, 22 to 26 minutes, rotating sheet halfway through baking.

4. FOR THE GLAZE: Transfer baked Danish to wire rack set over sheet of parchment (for easy cleanup). Whisk all ingredients together in bowl and brush it over hot Danish. Let glazed Danish cool completely on rack, about 1 hour.

5. FOR THE ICING: Whisk all ingredients together in bowl. When Danish is completely cool, drizzle icing attractively over top. Let icing set for 20 minutes before serving.

INDIVIDUAL DANISH
MAKES 9 DANISH

If the dough becomes too warm and sticky to work with, cover it with plastic wrap and let it chill in the refrigerator until firm. The Danish should be brushed with the glaze while hot, but drizzled with the icing after they have cooled.

- 1 recipe Danish Dough (page 462)
- 1 recipe filling (recipes follow)
- 1 large egg, lightly beaten

GLAZE
- 1½ cups (6 ounces) confectioners' sugar
- 5 teaspoons milk
- 1 teaspoon lemon juice

MAKING A DANISH BRAID

1. Spread filling or jam onto center third of dough.

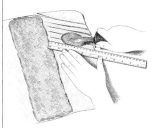

2. Using pizza cutter or paring knife, cut outer thirds into ¾-inch strips (so that cuts are at angle to filling).

3. Alternating sides, fold strips over filling, crisscrossing strips over center and pressing ends to seal, until entire Danish is braided.

MAKING INDIVIDUAL DANISH

1. After cutting dough into 5-inch squares, spoon 1½ tablespoons of filling into center of each square.

2. Fold 2 opposite corners of dough square over filling, brushing dough in center with beaten egg as needed to seal edges together.

ICING
1 cup (4 ounces) confectioners' sugar
1 tablespoon milk

1. Adjust oven rack to middle position and heat oven to 400 degrees. Line baking sheet with parchment paper.

2. Roll Danish dough into 15-inch square on lightly floured counter, dusting with extra flour as needed to prevent sticking. Cut dough into nine 5-inch squares. Place generous 1½ tablespoons cooled filling in center of each square and spread it into 2-inch circle with back of spoon.

3. Fold 2 opposite corners of dough square over center of filling, brushing dough in center with beaten egg as needed to seal edges together. Lay Danish on prepared baking sheet, spaced about 1½ inches apart.

4. Cover Danish loosely with greased plastic wrap and let rise at room temperature until puffy, about 30 minutes. Bake Danish until golden brown, 15 to 20 minutes, rotating sheet halfway through baking.

5. FOR THE GLAZE: Transfer baked Danish to wire rack set over sheet of parchment (for easy cleanup). Whisk all ingredients together in bowl and brush it over hot Danish. Let glazed Danish cool completely on rack, about 1 hour.

6. FOR THE ICING: Whisk all ingredients together in bowl. When Danish are completely cool, drizzle icing attractively over top. Let icing set for 20 minutes before serving.

APRICOT FILLING
MAKES 1½ CUPS

1 cup dried apricots
1 cup (7 ounces) sugar
¾ cup water
2 tablespoons lemon juice

Microwave apricots, sugar, and water together, stirring often, until apricots are softened and puffed, 7 to 10 minutes. Process warm mixture in food processor until smooth, about 15 seconds. Transfer puree to medium bowl and stir in lemon juice. Cover loosely with plastic wrap and refrigerate until filling has set, at least 1 hour or up to 2 days, before using.

PRUNE FILLING
MAKES 1½ CUPS

1 cup pitted prunes
1 cup (7 ounces) sugar
¾ cup water
½ teaspoon vanilla extract

Microwave prunes, sugar, and water together, stirring often, until prunes are softened and puffed, 7 to 10 minutes. Process warm mixture in food processor until smooth, about 15 seconds. Transfer puree to medium bowl and stir in vanilla. Cover loosely with plastic wrap and refrigerate until filling has set, at least 1 hour or up to 2 days, before using.

CHEESE FILLING
MAKES 1 CUP

8 ounces cream cheese, softened
¼ cup (1¾ ounces) sugar
½ teaspoon grated lemon zest

Whisk all ingredients together in medium bowl until combined. Cover with plastic wrap and refrigerate until stiff, at least 1 hour or up to 2 days, before using.

CHEESE AND CHERRY FILLING
MAKES 1½ CUPS

You can substitute 2 cups fresh or thawed frozen raspberries for the cherries (eliminate the cornstarch).

2	cups jarred sour cherries, drained
1¼	cups (8¾ ounces) sugar
1	tablespoon cornstarch
8	ounces cream cheese, softened
½	teaspoon grated lemon zest

1. Simmer cherries, 1 cup sugar, and cornstarch together in medium saucepan over low heat until sugar has melted and mixture thickens, about 10 minutes. Transfer mixture to bowl, cover with plastic wrap, and refrigerate until set, at least 1 hour or up to 2 days, before using.

2. Whisk cream cheese, remaining ¼ cup sugar, and lemon zest in medium bowl until combined. Cover with plastic and refrigerate until stiff, at least 1 hour or up to 2 days, before using. Spoon cherry mixture on top of cheese filling when assembling Danish.

Croissants

✓ WHY THIS RECIPE WORKS

A yeast-raised French classic, a croissant contains the best of both worlds: part pastry, part bread, it has a crisp, deeply golden crust wrapped around tender, pillow-soft, buttery layers—perfect for dipping into a cup of café au lait or hot chocolate. We wanted to create an approachable croissant recipe for home bakers—one that would deliver authentic flavor.

PICK YOUR INGREDIENTS CAREFULLY For the star ingredient, butter, we found that higher-fat European-style butter contains less water than domestic butter, and thus creates flakier layers. The brand of all-purpose flour makes a difference in croissants too, because protein values vary among brands. King Arthur brand all-purpose flour is higher in protein (11.7 percent) than other brands (around 10.5 percent), which means it develops more gluten and is more resistant to tearing—a problem we encountered with lower-protein flours.

LEARN TO LAMINATE The layered structure that characterizes croissants is formed through a process called lamination. First, a basic dough of flour, water, yeast, sugar, salt, and a small amount of butter is made. Then a larger amount of butter is formed into a block and encased in the relatively lean dough. This dough and butter package is rolled out and folded multiple times (each is called a "turn") to form paper-thin layers of dough separated by even thinner layers of butter. Once baked, it's these layers that make croissants so flaky and decadent. To start, we found that more turns didn't necessarily produce more layers—we stopped at three turns, as any more results in a bready texture.

CHILL AND SHAPE We give the dough a 30-minute super chill in the freezer to firm it to the consistency of butter before rolling, cutting, and shaping, thus ensuring perfectly distinct layers.

RISE, BRUSH, AND BAKE After letting the croissants rise until they are doubled in size, we brush them with an egg wash and slide them into a very hot oven. When the croissants emerge from the oven, they possess crisp, delicate tiers of pastry that makes every step of the process worth the effort.

CROISSANTS
MAKES 22

Twelve croissants are baked first; the remaining 10 can be frozen. These croissants take at least 10 hours to make from start to finish, but the process can be spread over 2 days. European-style cultured butters have a higher butterfat content, which makes it easier to fold them into the dough. (Our favorite is from Plugrá.) Any brand of all-purpose flour will produce acceptable croissants, but we recommend using King Arthur All-Purpose Flour, which has a slightly higher protein content. Do not attempt to make these croissants in a room that is warmer than 80 degrees. If at any time during rolling the dough retracts, dust it lightly with flour, fold it loosely, cover it, and return it to the freezer to rest for 10 to 15 minutes.

3	tablespoons unsalted butter plus 24 tablespoons (3 sticks) unsalted European-style butter, very cold
1¾	cups whole milk
4	teaspoons instant or rapid-rise yeast
4¼	cups (21¼ ounces) all-purpose flour
¼	cup (1¾ ounces) sugar
	Salt
1	large egg
1	teaspoon cold water

1. Melt 3 tablespoons butter in medium saucepan over low heat. Remove from heat and immediately stir in milk (temperature should be lower than 90 degrees). Whisk in yeast; transfer milk mixture to bowl of stand mixer. Add flour, sugar, and 2 teaspoons salt. Using dough hook, knead on low speed until cohesive dough forms, 2 to 3 minutes. Increase speed to medium-low and knead for 1 minute. Remove bowl from mixer, remove dough hook, and cover bowl with plastic wrap. Let dough rest at room temperature for 30 minutes.

2. Transfer dough to parchment paper–lined baking sheet and shape into 10 by 7-inch rectangle about 1 inch thick. Wrap tightly with plastic and refrigerate for 2 hours.

3. **TO MAKE THE BUTTER SQUARE:** While dough chills, fold 24-inch length of parchment in half to create 12-inch rectangle. Fold over 3 open sides of rectangle to form 8-inch square with enclosed sides. Crease folds firmly. Place 24 tablespoons cold butter directly on counter and beat with rolling pin for about 60 seconds until butter is just pliable, but not warm, folding butter in on itself using bench scraper. Beat into rough 6-inch square. Unfold parchment envelope. Using bench scraper, transfer butter to center of parchment square, refolding at creases to enclose. Turn packet over so that flaps are underneath and gently roll butter packet until butter fills parchment square, taking care to achieve even thickness. Refrigerate at least 45 minutes.

4. **TO LAMINATE THE DOUGH:** Transfer dough to freezer. After 30 minutes, transfer dough to lightly floured counter and roll into 17 by 8-inch rectangle with long side of rectangle parallel to edge of counter. Unwrap butter and place in center of dough so that butter and dough are flush at top and bottom. Fold 2 sides of dough over butter square so they meet in center. Press seam together with your fingertips. With rolling pin, press firmly on each open end of packet. Roll out dough, perpendicular to edge of counter, to rectangle 24 inches long and 8 inches wide. Bring bottom third of dough up, then fold upper third over it, folding like business letter into 8-inch square. Turn dough 90 degrees counterclockwise. Roll out dough again, perpendicular to edge of counter, into 24 by 8-inch rectangle and fold into thirds. Place dough on baking sheet, wrap tightly with plastic, and return to freezer for 30 minutes.

5. Transfer dough to lightly floured counter so that top flap of dough is facing right. Roll once more, perpendicular to edge of counter, into 24 by 8-inch rectangle and fold into thirds. Place dough on baking sheet, wrap tightly with plastic, and refrigerate for 2 hours.

6. Transfer dough to freezer. After 30 minutes, transfer to lightly floured counter and roll into 18 by 16-inch rectangle with long side

1. Fold 24-inch length of parchment in half to create 12-inch rectangle. Fold over 3 open sides of rectangle to form 8-inch square.

2. Using rolling pin, beat butter until it is just pliable, then fold butter in on itself using bench scraper. Beat butter into rough 6-inch square.

3. Unfold parchment envelope and, using bench scraper, transfer butter to parchment, refolding at creases to enclose.

4. Turn packet over and gently roll butter with rolling pin so butter block fills parchment square, taking care to achieve even thickness. Refrigerate.

LAMINATING THE DOUGH FOR CROISSANTS

1. Roll chilled dough into 17 by 8-inch rectangle. Unwrap butter and place in center of dough, aligning it so that edges of butter and dough are flush at top and bottom. Fold 2 sides of dough over butter so they meet in center of butter square.

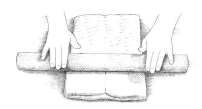

2. Using your fingertips, press seam together. Using rolling pin, press firmly on each open end of packet. Roll dough out lengthwise until it is 24 inches long and 8 inches wide.

3. Starting at bottom of dough, fold into thirds like business letter. Turn dough 90 degrees and roll and fold into thirds again. Place on baking sheet, wrap tightly with plastic wrap, and return to freezer for 30 minutes. Roll and fold into thirds 1 more time.

SHAPING CROISSANTS

1. Transfer dough from freezer to lightly floured counter and roll into 18 by 16-inch rectangle. (If dough begins to retract, fold it loosely in thirds, wrap it, and return it to freezer for 10 to 15 minutes.) Fold upper half of dough over lower half.

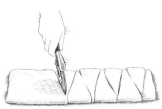

2. Using ruler, mark dough at 3-inch intervals along bottom edge. Move ruler to top of dough, measure in 1½ inches from left, then use this mark to measure out 3-inch intervals. Using pizza wheel or knife, cut dough into triangles from mark to mark.

3. You should have 12 single triangles and 5 double triangles; discard any scraps. Unfold double triangles and cut in half to form 10 single triangles (making 22 triangles in all). If dough begins to soften, return to freezer for 10 minutes.

4. Cut ½-inch slit in center of short side of each triangle. If dough begins to soften, return to freezer for 10 minutes.

5. Grasp triangle by 2 corners on either side of slit and stretch gently, then grasp point and stretch.

6. Place triangle on counter so point is facing toward you. Fold both sides of slit down. Positioning your palms on folds, roll partway toward point.

7. Gently grasp point with 1 hand and stretch; resume rolling, tucking point underneath.

8. Curve ends gently toward one another to form crescent shape.

of rectangle parallel to edge of counter. Fold upper half of dough over lower half. Using ruler, mark dough at 3-inch intervals along bottom edge with bench scraper (you should have 5 marks). Move ruler to top of dough, measure in 1½ inches from left, then use this mark to measure out 3-inch intervals (you should have 6 marks). Starting at lower left corner, use pizza wheel or knife to cut dough into triangles from mark to mark. You will have 12 single triangles and 5 double triangles; discard scraps. Unfold double triangles and cut into 10 single triangles (making 22 equal-size triangles in total). If dough begins to soften, return to freezer for 10 minutes.

7. TO SHAPE THE CROISSANTS: Position 1 triangle on counter. (Keep remaining triangles covered with plastic while shaping.) Cut ½-inch slit in center of short end of triangle. Grasp triangle by 2 corners on either side of slit, and stretch gently, then grasp bottom point and stretch. Place triangle on counter so point is facing toward you. Fold both sides of slit down. Positioning your palms on folds, roll partway toward point. Gently grasp point again and stretch. To finish, continue to roll, tucking point underneath. Curve ends gently toward one another to create crescent shape. Repeat with remaining triangles.

8. Place 12 croissants on 2 parchment-lined baking sheets (6 croissants per sheet), leaving at least 2½ inches between croissants. Lightly wrap sheets with plastic, leaving room for croissants to expand. Let stand at room temperature until nearly doubled in size, 2½ to 3 hours. (Shaped croissants can be refrigerated on baking sheets for up to 18 hours. Remove from refrigerator to rise and add at least 30 minutes to rising time.)

9. After croissants have been rising for 2 hours, adjust oven racks to upper-middle and lower-middle positions and heat oven to 425 degrees. In small bowl, whisk together egg, water, and pinch of salt. Brush croissants with egg wash using pastry brush. Place croissants in oven and reduce temperature to 400 degrees. Bake for 12 minutes, then switch and rotate sheets. Continue to bake until deep golden brown, 8 to 12 minutes longer. Transfer croissants to wire rack and allow to cool until just warm, about 15 minutes. Serve warm or at room temperature.

TO MAKE AHEAD: After shaping, place 10 croissants 1 inch apart on parchment-lined baking sheet. Wrap with plastic wrap and freeze until solid, about 2 hours. Transfer frozen croissants from sheet to zipper-lock bag and return to freezer for up to 2 months. Bake frozen croissants as directed from step 8, increasing rising time by 1 to 2 hours.

EXPONENTIALLY UPPING THE FLAKES IN PASTRY

Croissants, Puff Pastry Dough (page 457), and the flaky pastry we created for our vegetable tart recipes (page 439) all rely on a mathematical phenomenon to achieve their many-layered structure. These so-called laminated pastries, which are made up of alternating layers of dough and fat, are created by repeatedly rolling and folding the dough over itself, typically in thirds (like a business letter). Each set of folds is called a "turn," and with each turn the number of layers increases exponentially rather than linearly. Thus, the first turn gives three (3^1) layers, the next nine (3×3, or 3^2), then 27 ($3 \times 3 \times 3$, or 3^3), then 81, and so on. Just eight turns (in our tests, the highest number possible before the layers got so thin that they melded together) create an astonishing 6,561 layers.

CLASSIC CRÈME BRÛLÉE

CHAPTER 15

Baked Custards, Puddings, and Soufflés

We wondered if the tide had turned since we rated vanilla beans sourced from Madagascar more than a decade ago. At that time, we couldn't recommend any supermarket samples, finding them dried out, with few seeds and even less flavor.

To assess the differences, we sliced open a pod from each brand and scraped out the seeds. We then used the seeds in an uncooked cream cheese frosting and simmered both seeds and pods in cream for use in a simple crème anglaise and in the base of vanilla ice cream.

This time around, in a surprising reversal, we found the supermarket beans not only improved, but also slightly better than the mail-order ones. While some variation can be expected from any agricultural product, most of the differences among beans likely came from how much of the flavor compound vanillin was developed during the curing process. For Madagascar beans, this involves dipping the pods in hot water to halt all growth, drying them in the sun, and placing them (wrapped in cloth and straw mats) in wooden boxes to sweat overnight. This cycle is repeated until a manufacturer decides that the beans are ready to be moved to holding rooms, where they rest until they're shriveled, brown, and fragrant—an indication that they're ready for sorting.

Although all of the brands were acceptable, we recommend **McCormick Madagascar Vanilla Beans** when you want moist, seed-filled pods with complex flavor that tasters called exceptionally "robust" and "vivid."

Crème Brûlée

✓ WHY THIS RECIPE WORKS

Crème brûlée is all about the contrast between the crisp sugar crust and the silky custard underneath. But too often the crust is either skimpy or rock hard, and the custard is heavy and tasteless. We wanted an egg-rich creamy custard topped with a crackly thin crust of caramel.

START WITH HEAVY CREAM There is no point cutting corners here. Heavy cream makes a custard that is thick but not overbearing, luxurious but not death-defying. In short: everything we want.

USE YOLKS ONLY Crème brûlée should be rich and soft—with a puddinglike, spoon-clinging texture—in part because of the exclusive use of egg yolks. Using 4 cups of heavy cream, we played with the number of yolks here. The custard refused to set with as few as six; eight was better, though still slurpy. With 12, however, the custard has a lovely lilting texture, a glossy, luminescent look, and the richest flavor.

KEEP IT COOL Some crème brûlée recipes are based on scalded cream but we found that starting with cold cream allows the eggs to heat more gradually in the oven. If heated quickly, the eggs set only just shortly before they enter the overcooked zone, leaving a very narrow window between just right and overdone. If heated gently, however, they begin to thicken the custard at a lower temperature and continue to do so gradually. Therefore, mixing the eggs with cold cream gives us more time to develop a perfectly textured crème brûlée before we enter the danger zone of overcooked eggs.

PICK VANILLA BEANS The downside to starting with cold cream is that, for this custard, we prefer the use of a vanilla bean over vanilla extract, and it is almost impossible to extract flavor from a vanilla bean in cold liquid. We solve this problem with a hybrid technique: We scald half the cream, along with the vanilla bean and the sugar (to dissolve it), and let it sit for 15 minutes to extract the vanilla flavor. Later, we add the remaining cream cold to lower the temperature before mixing in the eggs. As an added benefit, because the cream is not straight-from-the-fridge cold, the baking time is nicely reduced. The final dish contains the tiny black flecks of vanilla bean seeds that are the signs of added flavor.

BATHE THE RAMEKINS For our water bath (or bain-marie), which prevents the edges of the custard from overcooking while the center saunters to the finish line, we use a large baking dish that can hold all of the ramekins comfortably. (The ramekins must not touch and should be at least ½ inch away from the sides of the dish.) Line the bottom of the dish with a dish towel to protect the floors of the ramekins from the heat of the dish.

PICK THE BEST SUGAR For the crackly caramel crust, we prefer Demerara and turbinado sugars, which are both coarse light brown sugars. They are better than brown sugar, which is moist and lumpy, and granulated sugar, which can be difficult to distribute evenly over the custards. Don't use a broiler to caramelize the crust; it's an almost guaranteed fail with its uneven heat. A torch accomplishes the task efficiently. (And be sure to refrigerate the finished crèmes brûlées—the brûlée can warm up the custard, ruining an otherwise perfect dish.)

CLASSIC CRÈME BRÛLÉE
SERVES 8

Separate the eggs and whisk the yolks after the cream has finished steeping; if left to sit, the surface of the yolks will dry and form a film. A vanilla bean gives the custard the deepest flavor, but 2 teaspoons of vanilla extract, whisked into the yolks in step 4, can be used instead. While we prefer turbinado or Demerara sugar for the caramelized sugar crust, regular granulated sugar will work, too, but use only 1 scant teaspoon on each ramekin or 1 teaspoon on each shallow fluted dish.

1	vanilla bean
4	cups heavy cream
2/3	cup (4 2/3 ounces) granulated sugar
	Pinch salt
12	large egg yolks
8–12	teaspoons turbinado or Demerara sugar

1. Adjust oven rack to lower-middle position and heat oven to 300 degrees.

2. Cut vanilla bean in half lengthwise. Using tip of paring knife, scrape out seeds. Combine vanilla bean pod and seeds, 2 cups cream, sugar, and salt in medium saucepan. Bring mixture to boil over medium heat, stirring occasionally to dissolve sugar. Off heat, let steep for 15 minutes.

3. Meanwhile, place dish towel in bottom of large baking dish or roasting pan; set eight 4- or 5-ounce ramekins (or shallow fluted dishes) on towel (they should not touch). Bring kettle of water to boil.

4. After cream has steeped, stir in remaining 2 cups cream. Whisk egg yolks in large bowl until uniform. Whisk about 1 cup cream mixture into yolks until combined; repeat with 1 cup more cream mixture. Add remaining cream mixture and whisk until evenly colored and thoroughly combined. Strain mixture through fine-mesh strainer into large liquid measuring cup or bowl; discard solids in strainer. Divide mixture evenly among ramekins.

5. Set baking dish on oven rack. Taking care not to splash water into ramekins, pour enough boiling water into dish to reach two-thirds up sides of ramekins. Bake until centers of custards are just barely set and register 170 to 175 degrees, 30 to 35 minutes (25 to 30 minutes for shallow fluted dishes), checking temperature about 5 minutes before recommended minimum time.

6. Transfer ramekins to wire rack and let cool to room temperature, about 2 hours. Set ramekins on baking sheet, cover tightly with plastic wrap, and refrigerate until cold, at least 4 hours.

7. Uncover ramekins; if condensation has collected on custards, blot moisture with paper towel. Sprinkle each with about 1 teaspoon turbinado sugar (1½ teaspoons for shallow fluted dishes); tilt and tap each ramekin to distribute sugar evenly, dumping out excess sugar. Ignite torch and caramelize sugar. Refrigerate ramekins, uncovered, to rechill, 30 to 45 minutes; serve.

ESPRESSO CRÈME BRÛLÉE

Crush the espresso beans lightly with the bottom of a skillet.

Substitute ¼ cup lightly crushed espresso beans for vanilla bean. Whisk 1 teaspoon vanilla extract into yolks in step 4 before adding cream.

TEA-INFUSED CRÈME BRÛLÉE

Substitute 10 Irish Breakfast tea bags, tied together, for vanilla bean; after steeping, squeeze bags with tongs or press into fine-mesh strainer to extract all liquid. Whisk 1 teaspoon vanilla extract into yolks in step 4 before adding cream.

FAMILY-STYLE CRÈME BRÛLÉE

Substitute 11 by 7-inch baking dish for ramekins and bake for 40 to 50 minutes. Let cool to room temperature, 2½ to 3 hours.

MAKE-AHEAD CRÈME BRÛLÉE

Reduce egg yolks to 10. After baked custards cool to room temperature, wrap each ramekin tightly in plastic wrap and refrigerate for up to 4 days. Proceed with step 7.

REMOVING SEEDS FROM A VANILLA BEAN

1. Use small, sharp knife to cut vanilla bean in half lengthwise.

2. Place knife at 1 end of one bean half and press down to flatten bean as you move knife away from you and catch seeds on edge of blade. Add seeds as well as pods to liquid ingredients.

MAKING THE BRÛLÉE

Carefully ignite the torch, then lower it until the end of the flame is about 1 inch from the sprinkled sugar. Hold the flame in place until you see the sugar melt and burn to a caramel color, then move along to the next patch of unburnt sugar repeating the process until the entire custard has a deep golden crust.

Flan

Caramel is extremely hot and can cause serious burns, so care should be taken during this step. Before making the caramel, ready your water bath by placing a dish towel in the bottom of a large baking dish or roasting pan. Place a 9-inch cake pan in the center. Once the caramel is ready, carefully and slowly pour the caramel into the pan, being careful not to splash caramel onto yourself or outside of the cake pan.

✓ WHY THIS RECIPE WORKS

Flan is a deceptively simple, classic Spanish custard. It boasts a slightly lighter texture than a standard baked custard, with an ultracreamy, tender texture. It should taste neither too sweet nor too eggy, and it should be firm enough to unmold on a serving plate without collapsing.

GET THE EGG RATIO RIGHT In our testing, we found that egg whites are what give the flan structure. Too many whites produce a custard that is almost solid and rubbery, while too few whites yield a custard that collapses. Egg yolks provide richness. For a not-too-eggy custard that is soft, yet firm enough to unmold easily, we rely on two egg whites and five egg yolks.

ADD TWO MILKS Using milk alone makes a flan that tastes lean and allows the egg flavor to dominate. Augmenting the milk with heavy cream nudges the dessert into the territory of richer custards like crème caramel. Taking a cue from Spanish and Latin American cookbooks, we add sweetened condensed milk to our low-fat milk. Rich and creamy, without the intense fat of heavy cream—and sweetened to boot—sweetened condensed milk makes for a superior custard.

COAT ONLY THE BOTTOM OF THE PAN Some recipes instruct you to pour the caramel into the pan and then tilt the pan to coat the sides. When we tried this we ended up burning our fingers. Instead we coat only the bottom of the pan, reasoning that the caramel sinks to the bottom during baking anyway. Once unmolded, the caramel pours evenly over the top of the custard.

BAKE IN A WATER BATH Like many custards, we set the pan of flan in a larger baking pan, then fill the baking pan with boiling water until it reaches partway up the sides. This ensures even, gentle heat and creates a moist environment for the custards to bake. And to ensure the bottom of the flan doesn't overbake, we set a dish towel in the bottom of the pan, which keeps the pan in place and cushions it from direct contact with the hot baking pan.

FLAN
SERVES 6

We prefer to use low-fat milk in this recipe, although any type of milk (even skim) can be used, resulting in varying degrees of richness. Note that the custard will look barely set once it is ready to remove from the oven, but it will firm up as it chills in the refrigerator. The best way to clean stuck-on caramel from the cake pan after unmolding the flan is to fill it with boiling water and let it sit for a few minutes until the caramel dissolves. The baked flan, covered tightly with plastic wrap, can be refrigerated for up to 1 day before serving.

- ¼ cup water
- ½ cup (3½ ounces) sugar
- 2 large eggs plus 3 large yolks, room temperature
- 1½ cups 1 or 2 percent low-fat milk
- 1 (14-ounce) can sweetened condensed milk
- ¼ teaspoon grated lemon zest

1. Adjust oven rack to middle position and heat oven to 350 degrees. Place dish towel on bottom of large roasting pan and place 9-inch round cake pan on towel. Bring kettle of water to boil.

2. Pour water into small saucepan, then pour sugar into center of pan (don't let it hit the pan sides). Gently stir sugar with clean

rubber spatula to wet it thoroughly. Bring to boil over medium-high heat and cook, without stirring, until the sugar has dissolved completely and liquid has faint golden color and registers about 300 degrees), 3 to 5 minutes.

3. Reduce heat to medium-low and continue to cook, stirring occasionally, until caramel has dark amber color (about 350 degrees), about 2 minutes longer. Carefully pour caramel into the cake pan. Let caramel cool slightly until hardened.

4. Whisk eggs and yolks together in medium bowl. Whisk in milk, sweetened condensed milk, and zest until thoroughly combined. Pour custard into cake pan.

5. Place roasting pan in oven and carefully pour enough boiling water into pan to reach halfway up sides of cake pan. Bake custard until center is just barely set, 30 to 40 minutes.

6. Carefully remove cake pan from water bath using sturdy spatula and let custard cool to room temperature, about 2 hours. Cover cake pan tightly with plastic wrap and refrigerate until cold, at least 2 hours.

7. To serve, Run thin knife around cake pan to loosen custard. Place inverted serving platter over top and quickly flip custard onto platter, drizzling any extra caramel sauce over top (some caramel will remain stuck in cake pan).

Crème Caramel

✓ WHY THIS RECIPE WORKS

What many people love about crème caramel is the caramel. But while we can't deny its appeal, what most concerned us when we decided to embark on a search for a really great crème caramel was the custard. We wanted custard that was creamy and tender enough to melt in our mouths, yet firm enough to unmold without collapsing on the serving plate. We were also looking for a mellow flavor that was neither too rich nor too eggy.

GET YOUR EGG PROPORTIONS RIGHT We discovered that the proportion of egg whites to yolks in the custard is critical for the right texture. Too many whites cause the custard to solidify too much, and too few leave it almost runny. We prefer a formula of three whole eggs and two yolks.

CHOOSE THE RIGHT MIX OF DAIRY We like our custard made with light cream and milk for the proper amount of richness.

MAKE A NOT-TOO-SWEET CUSTARD To contrast with the sweet caramel, we

keep the amount of sugar in the custard to a minimum.

TWEAK THE CARAMEL-MAKING METHOD In making caramel, sugar and water are heated in a saucepan—the sugar dissolves in the water and simmers until the water evaporates and the sugar caramelizes. This method isn't foolproof and the sugar can sometimes crystallize. We found that adding corn syrup and lemon juice helps break down the sugar, making crystallizing difficult. (Note that crystallization can still occur to any sugar that sticks to the side of the pan. Thus, take care to add the sugar to the center of the pan so it doesn't splash up on the sides.)

BAKE IN A WATER BATH Baking the ramekins in a water bath is essential for even cooking and ensures a delicate custard; a dish towel on the bottom of the pan stabilizes the ramekins and prevents the bottoms of the custards from overcooking.

TWO WAYS TO REMOVE RAMEKINS FROM A WATER BATH

A. We recommend the use of tongs to remove ramekins of custard from a water bath. Cooks who worry about the ramekins slipping in the tongs can try this tip: Slip rubber bands around each of the 2 tong pincers, and the sticky rubber will provide a surer grip.

B. You can skip slipping a rubber band around tongs if you happen to own canning tongs. With their rounded grip designed to curve around jars, canning tongs won't slip.

ALTERNATIVE METHOD FOR MAKING CARAMEL AND CARAMEL SAUCE

Many cooks shy away from making caramel. The process involves nothing more than melting sugar on the stovetop, but it can be tricky nonetheless. The sugar must be heated slowly and carefully to avoid overcooking—an all-too-frequent occurrence even when you're using a thermometer. And there's always the risk of getting splattered by the molten syrup as you stir. We recently learned of an easier, virtually hands-off approach: Use the microwave. Stir 1 cup of sugar, 2 tablespoons of corn syrup (added to help keep the caramel from recrystallizing), 2 tablespoons of water, and ⅛ teaspoon of lemon juice together in a 2-cup microwave-safe measuring cup or glass bowl. Microwave on full power until the mixture is just beginning to brown, 5 to 8 minutes (depending on the strength of your microwave). Remove the caramel from the microwave and let it sit on a dry surface for 5 minutes or until it darkens to a rich honey brown. To make caramel sauce, add ½ cup of hot heavy cream a few tablespoons at a time (so the caramel won't seize up), followed by 1 tablespoon of butter. Caramel doesn't get any easier than this.

CLASSIC CRÈME CARAMEL
SERVES 8

You can vary the amount of sugar in the custard to suit your taste. Most tasters preferred the full ⅔ cup, but you can reduce that amount to as little as ½ cup to create a greater contrast between the custard and the caramel. Cook the caramel in a pan with a light-colored interior, since a dark surface makes it difficult to judge the color of the syrup. Caramel can leave a real mess in a pan, but it is easy to clean; simply boil water in the pan for 5 to 10 minutes to loosen the hardened caramel.

CARAMEL
- ⅓ cup water
- 2 tablespoons light corn syrup
- ¼ teaspoon lemon juice
- 1 cup (7 ounces) sugar

CUSTARD
- 1½ cups whole milk
- 1½ cups light cream
- 3 large eggs plus 2 large yolks
- ⅔ cup (4⅔ ounces) sugar
- 1½ teaspoons vanilla extract
- Pinch salt

1. FOR THE CARAMEL: Combine water, corn syrup, and lemon juice in medium saucepan. Pour sugar into center of pan, taking care not to let sugar crystals touch pan sides. Gently stir with rubber spatula to moisten sugar thoroughly. Bring to boil over medium-high heat and cook, without stirring, until sugar is completely dissolved and liquid is clear, 6 to 10 minutes. Reduce heat to medium-low and continue to cook, swirling occasionally, until mixture darkens to honey color, 4 to 5 minutes longer. Working quickly, carefully divide caramel among eight 6-ounce ramekins. Let caramel cool and harden, about 15 minutes. (Caramel-coated ramekins can be refrigerated for up to 2 days; bring to room temperature before adding custard.)

2. FOR THE CUSTARD: Adjust oven rack to middle position and heat oven to 350 degrees.

Combine milk and cream in medium saucepan and heat over medium heat, stirring occasionally, until steam appears and mixture registers 160 degrees, 6 to 8 minutes; remove from heat. Meanwhile, gently whisk eggs, egg yolks, and sugar in large bowl until just combined. Off heat, gently whisk warm milk mixture, vanilla, and salt into eggs until just combined but not foamy. Strain mixture through fine-mesh strainer into 4-cup liquid measuring cup or bowl; set aside.

3. Bring kettle of water to boil. Meanwhile, place dish towel in bottom of large baking dish or roasting pan and set ramekins on towel (they should not touch). Divide custard evenly among ramekins and set dish on oven rack. Taking care not to splash water into ramekins, pour enough boiling water into dish to come halfway up sides of ramekins; cover dish loosely with aluminum foil. Bake until paring knife inserted halfway between center and edge of custards comes out clean, 35 to 40 minutes. Transfer ramekins to wire rack and let cool to room temperature. (Custards can be refrigerated for up to 2 days.)

4. To unmold, run thin knife around perimeter of each ramekin. Hold serving plate over top of ramekin and invert; set plate on counter and gently shake ramekin to release custard. Repeat with remaining ramekins and serve.

ESPRESSO CRÈME CARAMEL

Espresso beans ground in a coffee grinder would be too fine and impart too strong a coffee flavor to the custard. Instead, crush the beans lightly with the bottom of a skillet.

Heat ½ cup lightly crushed espresso beans with milk and cream mixture until steam appears and mixture registers 160 degrees, 6 to 8 minutes. Off heat, cover and let steep until coffee has infused milk and cream, about 15 minutes. Strain mixture through fine-mesh strainer and proceed as directed, discarding crushed espresso beans. Reduce vanilla extract to 1 teaspoon.

Bread Pudding

✓ WHY THIS RECIPE WORKS

Bread pudding started out as a frugal way to transform stale, old loaves of bread into an appetizing dish. But contemporary versions of this humble dish vary from mushy, sweetened porridge to chewy, desiccated cousins of holiday stuffing. We wanted a dessert cart–worthy dish as refined as any French soufflé: a moist, creamy (but not eggy) interior and a crisp top crust.

PICK THE RIGHT BREAD AND TOAST IT We like challah for its rich flavor. We cut the bread into cubes, then toast them until lightly browned so that they can soak up the custard without turning mushy.

TWEAK THE CUSTARD We started with a basic custard of mostly egg yolks and a few whites, but the eggy flavor was too strong. It turns out that eggy flavor comes from the sulfur compounds in egg whites. So we got rid of the whites and just use the yolks for a luscious, silky custard.

BRUSH AND BAKE Brushing the surface with melted butter and sprinkling the dish with a mix of white and brown sugar prior to baking (at a low temperature to prevent curdling) gives the pudding a crunchy, buttery, sugary crust.

CLASSIC BREAD PUDDING
SERVES 8 TO 10

Challah is an egg-enriched bread that can be found in most bakeries and supermarkets. If you cannot find challah, a firm high-quality sandwich bread such as Arnold Country Classics White or Pepperidge Farm Farmhouse Hearty White may be substituted. If desired, serve this pudding with Whipped Cream (page 348) or with Bourbon–Brown Sugar Sauce (recipe follows). To retain a crisp top crust when reheating leftovers, cut the bread pudding into squares and heat, uncovered, in a 450-degree oven until warmed through, 6 to 8 minutes.

¾ cup (5¼ ounces) plus 1 tablespoon granulated sugar
2 tablespoons light brown sugar
12 ounces challah bread, cut into ¾-inch cubes
9 large egg yolks
4 teaspoons vanilla extract
¾ teaspoon salt
2½ cups heavy cream
2½ cups milk
2 tablespoons unsalted butter, melted

1. Adjust oven racks to middle and lower-middle positions and heat oven to 325 degrees. Combine 1 tablespoon granulated sugar and brown sugar in small bowl; set aside.

2. Spread bread cubes in single layer on 2 rimmed baking sheets. Bake, tossing occasionally, until just dry, about 15 minutes, switching and rotating sheets halfway through baking. Let bread cubes cool for about 15 minutes; set aside 2 cups.

3. Whisk egg yolks, remaining ¾ cup granulated sugar, vanilla, and salt together in large bowl. Whisk in cream and milk until combined. Add remaining cooled bread cubes and toss to coat. Transfer mixture to 13 by 9-inch baking dish and let stand, occasionally pressing bread cubes into custard, until cubes are thoroughly saturated, about 30 minutes.

4. Spread reserved bread cubes evenly over top of soaked bread mixture; gently press into custard. Brush melted butter over top of unsoaked bread cubes. Sprinkle brown sugar mixture evenly over top. Place bread pudding on baking sheet and bake on middle rack until custard has just set, pressing center of pudding with your finger reveals no runny liquid, and center of pudding registers 170 degrees, 45 to 50 minutes. Transfer to wire rack and let cool until pudding is set and just warm, about 45 minutes. Serve.

STALING BREAD

Many recipes that call for stale bread give you two options: using naturally staled, day-old bread, or bread that is "quick staled" by drying in a low oven. Does it matter which technique you use? We staled three types of bread (a French baguette, an egg-enriched challah, and supermarket sliced white bread) in two ways: unwrapped on the counter for three days and in a 225-degree oven for about 35 minutes. We then used the breads to make stuffing, berry puddings, and bread crumbs. Tasters arrived at the same surprising conclusion for all three recipes: The oven-dried versions were the best. The recipes made with oven-dried bread had a fresher taste and a superior structure; the naturally staled bread turned gummy once combined with the other ingredients.

As bread stales naturally, its starch molecules recrystallize in a process called retrogradation, causing the bread to become hard and crumbly, but not necessarily dry. The naturally staled bread was still too moist to produce optimal results. Staling bread quickly in the oven, on the other hand, mostly hardens bread through the removal of moisture, not through retrogradation (which works best at cooler temperatures), ultimately leading to a drier—and better—structure. And though the counter-staled bread produced acceptable results, we'll stick with the faster, more foolproof "oven staling" from now on.

PECAN BREAD PUDDING WITH BOURBON AND ORANGE

See page 9 for information on toasting nuts.

Add ⅔ cup chopped toasted pecans, 1 tablespoon all-purpose flour, and 1 tablespoon softened butter to brown sugar mixture in step 1 and mix until crumbly. Add 1 tablespoon bourbon and 2 teaspoons finely grated orange zest to egg yolk mixture in step 3.

RUM RAISIN BREAD PUDDING WITH CINNAMON

Combine ⅔ cup golden raisins and 5 teaspoons dark rum in small bowl. Microwave until hot, about 20 seconds; set aside to cool, about 15 minutes. Add ⅛ teaspoon ground cinnamon to brown sugar mixture in step 1 and stir cooled raisin mixture into custard in step 3.

BOURBON–BROWN SUGAR SAUCE
MAKES ABOUT I CUP

Rum can be substituted for the bourbon.

½	cup packed (3½ ounces) light brown sugar
7	tablespoons heavy cream
2½	tablespoons unsalted butter
1½	tablespoons bourbon

Whisk sugar and cream together in small saucepan set over medium heat until combined. Continue to cook, whisking frequently, until mixture comes to boil, about 5 minutes. Whisk in butter and bring mixture back to boil, about 1 minute. Remove from heat and whisk in bourbon. Let cool until just warm; serve with bread pudding.

Chocolate Bread Pudding

✔ WHY THIS RECIPE WORKS

Chocolate bread pudding can appear rich and chocolaty, but the chocolate flavor is often disappointing. We wanted a bread pudding with outrageous chocolate flavor and a lush, decadent texture.

START WITH CHALLAH As with our Classic Bread Pudding (page 478), we use rich, toasted challah for our base.

DOUBLE UP ON THE CHOCOLATE The combination of cocoa powder and melted semisweet chocolate provides a solid foundation of chocolate flavor and richness. Instant espresso powder enhances the chocolate flavor without being identifiable.

RETHINK THE SOAKING PROCESS Unlike a basic custard, a custard with melted chocolate is so thick that it doesn't fully soak into the bread. To thin the base, we divide our custard into two liquid mediums: First we make a mixture of heavy cream, milk, and cocoa powder, which is thin enough to soak into the bread. Next we combine more cream with melted chocolate and egg yolks to make a rich custard, which we pour over the soaked bread right in the baking dish.

BAKE AND BLANKET WITH CHOCOLATE Our bread pudding bakes up rich and creamy and to make it even more moist and chocolaty, we pour a warmed mixture of melted chocolate and heavy cream over the pudding just before serving.

CHOCOLATE BREAD PUDDING
SERVES I2

Challah can be found in most bakeries and supermarkets. If you cannot find challah, a firm high-quality sandwich bread such as Arnold Country Classics White or Pepperidge Farm Farmhouse Hearty White may be substituted. It is important to use

Dutch-processed cocoa in this recipe. Natural cocoa powder will make the bread pudding too bitter.

14	ounces challah bread, cut into ½-inch cubes
4	cups heavy cream
2	cups whole milk
1	cup (7 ounces) sugar
½	cup Dutch-processed cocoa powder
1	tablespoon instant espresso powder
8	ounces semisweet chocolate, chopped
10	large egg yolks

1. Adjust oven rack to middle position and heat oven to 300 degrees. Toast bread on rimmed baking sheet, stirring occasionally, until golden and crisp, about 30 minutes. Transfer to large bowl.

2. Increase oven temperature to 325 degrees. Grease 13 by 9-inch baking pan. Heat 1½ cups cream, milk, ½ cup sugar, cocoa, and espresso powder in saucepan over medium-high heat, stirring occasionally, until steaming and sugar dissolves. Pour warm cream mixture over toasted bread and let stand, tossing occasionally, until liquid has been absorbed, about 10 minutes.

3. Meanwhile, bring 1 cup cream to simmer in saucepan over medium-high heat. Remove from heat and stir in chocolate until smooth. Transfer 1 cup chocolate mixture to medium bowl and let cool for 5 minutes (cover pan and reserve remaining chocolate mixture for serving). Add egg yolks, remaining 1½ cups cream, and remaining ½ cup sugar to bowl with chocolate mixture and whisk to combine.

4. Transfer soaked bread mixture to prepared pan and pour chocolate custard mixture evenly over bread. Bake until pudding is just set and surface is slightly crisp, about 45 minutes. Let cool for 30 minutes. Warm reserved chocolate mixture over low heat, then pour over bread pudding. Serve. (Leftover bread pudding should be refrigerated; reheat individual portions in microwave.)

TO MAKE AHEAD: In step 4, once soaked bread mixture has been transferred to prepared pan, pan can be covered with plastic wrap and refrigerated overnight. When ready to bake, remove plastic and proceed with recipe as directed, increasing baking time to 55 minutes to 1 hour. Let reserved chocolate serving sauce cool, then cover with plastic wrap and refrigerate. Heat sauce in microwave when needed.

Grand Marnier Soufflé

✔ WHY THIS RECIPE WORKS

Rising dramatically above the rim of the pan, the perfect soufflé must have a texture that graduates from a crusty exterior to an airy but substantial outer layer to a rich, soft, not completely set center. We wanted to build a light and airy soufflé that also tasted undeniably creamy and we'd build its flavor profile around the orange liqueur Grand Marnier. And knowing the finicky reputation of soufflés, we wanted it to be reliable, too.

MAKE A BASE The base for this soufflé, into which the beaten egg whites are eventually folded, provides flavor and additional moisture to help it all rise. We prepared a blind taste test with three different base options: béchamel, a classic French sauce made with butter, flour, and milk; pastry cream; and *bouillie*, a paste made from flour and milk. The bouillie soufflé had the creamiest, richest texture.

WHIP IT RIGHT The technique used to beat the egg whites is crucial to a successful soufflé. The objective is to create a strong, stable foam that rises well and is not prone to collapse during either folding or baking.

We add sugar to the egg whites as they are whipped. Sugar enhances their stability, making them more resilient to a heavy hand during the folding and less apt to fall quickly after being pulled from the oven. We found that it's best to add most of the sugar after the eggs have become foamy and to do it gradually. If it's added all at once, the soufflé will be uneven, with a shorter rise, and a bit of an overly sweet taste. Don't forget the cream of tartar; it makes for a more stable soufflé with a bigger rise. We also add a little grated chocolate into the whites for another hint of chocolate flavor.

INFUSE WITH FLAVOR For flavor, in addition to Grand Marnier, we include grated orange zest for potent orange flavor. A couple of teaspoons of cocoa powder adds a hint of chocolate flavor.

FOLD IT OVER When combining the voluminous whipped egg whites with the dense batter, vigorous stirring will get you nowhere, quick. The technique we use is called folding. The goal is to incorporate the light egg whites with the heavy batter without deflating the foam.

GIVE THE EDGE A QUICK SWIPE Our Grand Marnier soufflé relies on little beyond eggs, milk, and a little flour for structure and benefits from the following technique: After pouring the batter into the dish, trace a circle in the batter with your finger, ½ inch from the edge of the dish. This breaks the surface tension and helps the ultralight soufflé achieve a high, even rise.

DO NOT OVERCOOK Most important: Never overcook a soufflé. It should be very creamy in the middle and firm around the outside, almost like a pudding cake. Don't wait until the center is completely solid; it will be too late. The center should not be fluid, but it should still be quite loose and very moist. Once you can smell a soufflé baking in the oven, it's about ready to come out. Soufflés should be served immediately.

GRAND MARNIER SOUFFLÉ WITH GRATED CHOCOLATE

SERVES 6 TO 8

Make the soufflé base and immediately begin beating the whites before the base cools too much. Once the whites have reached the proper consistency, they must be used at once. Do not open the oven door during the first 15 minutes of baking time; as the soufflé nears the end of its baking, you may check its progress by opening the oven door slightly. (Be careful here; if your oven runs hot, the top of the soufflé may burn.) A quick dusting of confectioners' sugar is a nice finishing touch, but a soufflé waits for no one, so be ready to serve it immediately.

 2   tablespoons unsalted butter, room temperature, plus 1 tablespoon, softened
 ¾   cup (5¼ ounces) sugar
 2   teaspoons sifted unsweetened cocoa powder
 5   tablespoons (1½ ounces) all-purpose flour
 ¼   teaspoon salt
 1   cup whole milk
 5   large eggs, separated
 3   tablespoons Grand Marnier
 1   tablespoon grated orange zest
 ⅛   teaspoon cream of tartar
 ½   ounce bittersweet chocolate, grated fine

1. Adjust oven rack to upper-middle position and heat oven to 400 degrees. Grease 1½-quart soufflé dish with 1 tablespoon softened butter. Combine ¼ cup sugar and cocoa in small bowl and pour into buttered dish, shaking to coat bottom and sides of dish evenly. Tap out excess and set dish aside.

2. Whisk flour, ¼ cup sugar, and salt in small saucepan. Gradually whisk in milk, whisking until smooth and no lumps remain. Bring mixture to boil over high heat, whisking constantly, until thickened and mixture pulls away from sides of pan, about 3 minutes. Scrape mixture into medium bowl; whisk in

---

FOLDING BEATEN EGG WHITES

If you don't incorporate beaten egg whites properly in your batter, you may be left with eggy patches in your baked goods. Here's our preferred method.

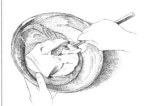

1. Cut through center of batter and egg white mixture with spatula down to bottom of bowl.

2. Pull spatula toward you, scraping along bottom and up side of bowl.

3. Rotate spatula so any mixture clinging to it falls back onto surface of batter.

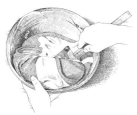

4. Spin bowl quarter turn and repeat process until whites are incorporated and no streaks remain visible.

While testing our soufflé recipe, we decided to find out whether copper bowls are better for whisking egg whites and discovered that they do have a contribution to make: The final baked soufflé has a greater volume, its flavor is less eggy, and it has a crust that has a beautiful light golden color.

Why? When egg whites are whipped in a copper bowl, the copper ions combine with conalbumin, an egg white protein, and as a result slow the coagulation process. This means that the foam takes longer to whip and therefore is more stable. Because the egg foam is more stable, it can better tolerate expansion in the oven. More specifically, the copper of the bowl binds with sulfur atoms contained within some of the egg proteins. And since the eggy flavor comes from the breakdown of these proteins (and the resulting release of sulfur-containing compounds), a soufflé made in a copper bowl is more stable and tastes less eggy. These copper and sulfur bonds also reflect light in a way that allows us to see a golden yellow color in the crust. That said, very good results can also be achieved in stainless-steel bowls, so copper is nice, but not necessary.

remaining 2 tablespoons butter until combined. Whisk in egg yolks until incorporated; stir in Grand Marnier and orange zest.

3. Using stand mixer fitted with whisk, whip egg whites, cream of tartar, and 1 teaspoon sugar on medium-low speed until foamy, about 1 minute. Increase speed to medium-high and whip whites to soft, billowy mounds, about 1 minute. Gradually add half of remaining sugar and whip until glossy, soft peaks form, about 30 seconds; with mixer still running, add remaining sugar and whip until just combined, about 10 seconds.

4. Using rubber spatula, immediately stir one-quarter of whipped whites into soufflé base to lighten until almost no white streaks remain. Scrape remaining whites into base and fold in whites, along with grated chocolate,

with whisk until mixture is just combined. Gently pour mixture into prepared dish and run your index finger through mixture, tracing circumference about ½ inch from side of dish, to help soufflé rise properly. Bake until surface of soufflé is deep brown, center jiggles slightly when shaken, and soufflé has risen 2 to 2½ inches above rim, 20 to 25 minutes. Serve immediately.

KAHLÚA SOUFFLÉ WITH GROUND ESPRESSO

If you do not have espresso beans, substitute an equal amount of instant espresso powder, adding it along with the milk in step 2 so that it dissolves.

Omit orange zest and substitute Kahlúa for Grand Marnier and 1 tablespoon finely ground espresso beans for grated chocolate.

Chocolate Soufflé

✔ WHY THIS RECIPE WORKS

A chocolate soufflé should deliver the best of both worlds: the irresistible flavor of chocolate and the dramatic presentation of a light and creamy soufflé. Too often, the chocolate notes are wan, rather than deep and strong. We wanted to find the secrets behind the perfect chocolate soufflé.

DETERMINE THE RIGHT BASE We began our chocolate soufflé with a béchamel base (a classic French sauce made with equal amounts of butter and flour and whisked with milk over heat) and eggs. But we found that the milk muted the chocolate flavor. We then removed the milk and the flour and separated the eggs; the yolks are beaten with sugar and the whites are whipped separately—the result is a rich base that gives the soufflé plenty of volume.

USE MORE CHOCOLATE We increased the chocolate to a full half pound, and reduced

the butter, which was dulling the chocolate flavor. The result is intense chocolate flavor.

ACCENT THE CHOCOLATE We include vanilla for more depth and a little orange-flavored liqueur for a layer of sophisticated flavor.

DON'T BE AFRAID TO PEEK It's best not to overbake the soufflé, so if you're not sure it's done, use two spoons to gently open up the top of the soufflé. If it's still soupy in the center, simply slide it back in the oven for a few more minutes.

CHOCOLATE SOUFFLÉ
SERVES 6 TO 8

To melt the chocolate using a microwave, heat it at 50 percent power for 2 minutes; stir the chocolate, add the butter, and continue heating until melted, stirring once every additional minute. A soufflé waits for no one so be ready to serve it immediately.

4 tablespoons unsalted butter, cut into ½-inch pieces, plus 1 tablespoon, softened
⅓ cup (2⅓ ounces) plus 1 tablespoon sugar
8 ounces bittersweet or semisweet chocolate, chopped coarse
1 tablespoon orange-flavored liqueur, such as Grand Marnier
½ teaspoon vanilla extract
⅛ teaspoon salt
6 large eggs, separated, plus 2 large whites
¼ teaspoon cream of tartar

1. Adjust oven rack to lower-middle position and heat oven to 375 degrees. Grease 2-quart soufflé dish with 1 tablespoon softened butter, then coat dish evenly with 1 tablespoon sugar; refrigerate until ready to use.

2. Melt chocolate and remaining 4 tablespoons butter in medium heatproof bowl set over saucepan filled with 1 inch of barely simmering water, making sure that water does not touch bottom of bowl, stirring occasionally, until smooth. Stir in liqueur, vanilla, and salt; set aside.

3. Using stand mixer fitted with paddle, beat egg yolks and remaining ⅓ cup sugar on medium speed until thick and pale yellow, about 3 minutes. Fold into chocolate mixture.

4. Using dry, clean bowl and whisk attachment, whip egg whites and cream of tartar on medium-low speed until foamy, about 1 minute. Increase speed to medium-high and whip until stiff peaks form, 3 to 4 minutes.

5. Using rubber spatula, vigorously stir one-quarter of whipped whites into chocolate mixture. Gently fold in remaining whites until just incorporated. Transfer mixture to prepared dish and bake until fragrant, fully risen, and exterior is set but interior is still a bit loose and creamy, about 25 minutes. (Use 2 large spoons to gently pull open top and peek inside.) Serve immediately.

MOCHA SOUFFLÉ

Add 1 tablespoon instant espresso powder dissolved in 1 tablespoon hot water when adding vanilla to chocolate mixture.

INDIVIDUAL CHOCOLATE SOUFFLÉS

Omit 2-quart soufflé dish. Grease eight 8-ounce ramekins with 1 tablespoon butter then coat dishes evenly with 1 tablespoon sugar. In step 5, transfer soufflé mixture to ramekins, making sure to completely fill each ramekin and wipe each rim with wet paper towel. Reduce baking time to 16 to 18 minutes.

MAKE-AHEAD INDIVIDUAL CHOCOLATE SOUFFLÉS

Omit 2-quart soufflé dish. Grease eight 8-ounce ramekins with 1 tablespoon butter then coat dishes evenly with 1 tablespoon sugar. In step 3, bring remaining ⅓ cup sugar and 2 tablespoons water to boil in small saucepan, then reduce heat and simmer until sugar dissolves. With mixer running, slowly add sugar syrup to egg yolks and beat until mixture triples in volume, about 3 minutes. Whip egg whites as directed, beating in 2 tablespoons confectioners' sugar. Stir and fold into chocolate base as directed. Fill each chilled ramekin almost to rim, wiping each rim clean with wet paper towel. Cover each ramekin tightly with plastic wrap and freeze until firm, at least 3 hours or up to 1 month. (Do not thaw before baking.) To serve, heat oven to 400 degrees and reduce baking time to 16 to 18 minutes.

Skillet Soufflé

✔ WHY THIS RECIPE WORKS

Having taken the mystique out of soufflé making, we wondered if we could take our expertise one step further with an everyday lemon soufflé.

WHIP THE YOLKS AND ADD FLOUR We opted for an uncomplicated base of whipped egg yolks (folding beaten whites and sugar in separately). A little flour keeps the soufflé creamy rather than foamy.

INCLUDE LEMON JUICE AND ZEST We didn't want a too-puckery soufflé, but we did want bright, natural citrus flavor. One-third cup of lemon juice and 1 teaspoon of zest deliver bright citrusy flavor.

START IN SKILLET ON THE STOVETOP, FINISH IN THE OVEN We pour the soufflé mixture into a buttered ovensafe skillet. A 10-inch skillet is necessary for the proper height and texture. After a few minutes on the stovetop the soufflé is set around the edges then we move the skillet to the oven to finish. A few minutes later the soufflé is puffed, golden on top, and creamy in the middle.

SKILLET LEMON SOUFFLÉ
SERVES 6

Do not open the oven door during the first 7 minutes of baking, but do check the soufflé regularly for doneness during the final few minutes in the oven. Be ready to serve the soufflé immediately after removing it from the oven. Using a 10-inch traditional (not nonstick) skillet is essential to getting the right texture and height in the soufflé.

5	large eggs, separated
¼	teaspoon cream of tartar
⅔	cup (4⅔ ounces) sugar
⅛	teaspoon salt
1	teaspoon grated lemon zest plus ⅓ cup juice (3 lemons)
2	tablespoons all-purpose flour
1	tablespoon unsalted butter
	Confectioners' sugar

1. Adjust oven rack to middle position and heat oven to 375 degrees. Using stand mixer fitted with whisk, whip egg whites and cream of tartar on medium-low speed until foamy, about 1 minute. Increase speed to medium-high and whip whites to soft, billowy mounds, about 1 minute. Gradually add ⅓ cup sugar and salt and whip until glossy, stiff peaks form, 2 to 3 minutes. Gently transfer whites to clean bowl; set aside.

2. In now-empty mixer bowl, whip egg yolks and remaining ⅓ cup sugar on medium-high speed until pale and thick, about 1 minute. Whip in lemon zest and juice and flour until incorporated, about 30 seconds.

3. Fold one-quarter of whipped egg whites into yolk mixture until almost no white streaks remain. Gently fold in remaining egg whites until just incorporated.

4. Melt butter in 10-inch ovensafe skillet over medium-low heat. Swirl pan to coat it evenly with butter, then gently scrape soufflé batter into skillet and cook until edges begin to set and bubble slightly, about 2 minutes.

5. Transfer skillet to oven and bake soufflé until puffed, center jiggles slightly when shaken, and surface is golden, 7 to 11 minutes. Using potholder (skillet handle will be very hot), remove skillet from oven. Dust soufflé with confectioners' sugar and serve immediately.

SKILLET CHOCOLATE-ORANGE SOUFFLÉ

Grating the chocolate fine is key here; we find it easiest to use either a rasp-style grater or the fine holes of a box grater.

Substitute 1 tablespoon grated orange zest for lemon zest and ⅓ cup orange juice for lemon juice. Gently fold 1 ounce finely grated bittersweet chocolate into soufflé batter after incorporating all whites in step 3.

THE IMPORTANCE OF CREAM OF TARTAR

Recipes that require stiffly beaten egg whites, such as lemon meringue pie, soufflés, and angel food cake often call for potassium acid tartrate, better known as cream of tartar. To find out if this an ingredient you can skip if you don't happen to have it on hand, we made two lemon meringue pies, one with the requisite ½ teaspoon cream of tartar for the four-egg-white meringue and one without.

After a stay in the refrigerator, the meringue without cream of tartar showed beads of moisture on its surface. The pie prepared with cream of tartar emerged in much better shape, with a dry, smooth, bead-free meringue.

The explanation? When egg whites are whipped, the protein strands within begin to unwind and form a network that holds water and air bubbles in place. But egg whites contain sulfur atoms, which form strong bonds that can over-strengthen this network. Acidic cream of tartar slows the formation of the sulfur bonds, preserving the stability of the network so that air and water stay put.

Shopping Guide

Equipment

With a well-stocked kitchen, you will be prepared to tackle any baking project. But the sheer number of equipment choices on the market can be positively overwhelming. How do you know which items are really essential? Or which loaf pan to buy when there are dozens of options? Not to worry—we've done the work for you and cut through the confusion with our comprehensive list. In the chart that follows, we outline the mot important features of all the baking equipment we deem essential for anyone who bakes regularly.

MEASURING EQUIPMENT	ITEM	WHAT TO LOOK FOR	TEST KITCHEN FAVORITES
	DRY MEASURING CUPS	• Stainless-steel cups (hefty and durable) • Measurement markings that are visible even once the cup is full • Evenly weighted and stable • Long handles that are level with the rim of the cup	OXO Good Grips Stainless Steel Measuring Cups $19.99
	LIQUID MEASURING CUP	• Crisp, unambiguous markings that include ¼ and ⅓ cup measurements • Heatproof, sturdy cup with handle • Good to have in a variety of sizes (I, 2, and 4 cups)	Pyrex 2-Cup Measuring Cup $5.99
	ADJUSTABLE MEASURING CUP	• Plungerlike bottom (with a tight seal between plunger and tube) that you can set to correct measurement, then push up to cleanly extract sticky ingredients (such as shortening or peanut butter) • I- or 2-cup capacity • Dishwasher-safe	KitchenArt Pro Adjust-A-Cup Professional Series $12.95
	MEASURING SPOONS	• Long, comfortable handles • Rim of bowl flush with handle • Slim design	Cuisipro Stainless Steel Measuring Spoons Set $11.95
	DIGITAL SCALE	• Easy-to-read display not blocked by weighing platform • At least 7-pound capacity • Accessible buttons • Gram-to-ounce conversion feature • Roomy platform	OXO Good Grips II lb. Food Scale with Pull Out Display $49.99 BEST BUY: Ozeri Pronto Digital Multifunction Kitchen and Food Scale $11.79

MEASURING EQUIPMENT	ITEM	WHAT TO LOOK FOR	TEST KITCHEN FAVORITES
	INSTANT-READ THERMOMETER	• Display auto-rotates • Lights up in low light • Wakes up when unit is picked up • Takes a single AAA alkaline battery • Water resistant	ThermoWorks Thermapen Mk4 $99 BEST BUY: ThermoWorks ThermoPop $29
	OVEN THERMOMETER	• Wide, sturdy base • Clear temperature markings • Fairly easy to read	CDN Pro Accurate Oven Thermometer $6
	CANDY THERMOMETER	• Digital model • Easy-to-read console • Mounting clip (to attach probe to the pan)	ThermoWorks ChefAlarm $59 BEST BUY: Polder Classic Digital Thermometer/Timer $24.99
	KITCHEN TIMER	• Lengthy time range (I second to at least 10 hours) • Ability to count up after alarm goes off • Easy to use and read • Able to track multiple events	OXO Good Grips Triple Timer $19.99 WEARABLE MODEL: ThermoWorks TimeStick $25

BAKEWARE & COOKWARE	ITEM	WHAT TO LOOK FOR	TEST KITCHEN FAVORITES
	RIMMED BAKING SHEET	• Light-colored surface (heats and browns evenly) • Thick, sturdy pan • Dimensions of 18 by 13 inches • Good to have at least two	Nordic Ware Bakers Half Sheet $14.97
	LOAF PAN	• Light gold or dark nonstick surface for even browning and easy release • Good to have both 8½ by 4½-inch and 9 by 5-inch pans	Williams-Sonoma Nonstick Goldtouch Loaf Pan $21
	SQUARE BAKING PAN	• Straight sides • Light gold or dark nonstick surface for even browning and easy release of cakes • Good to have both 9-inch and 8-inch square pans	Williams-Sonoma Nonstick Goldtouch Square Cake Pan $26.95, 8-inch $27.95, 9-inch

BAKEWARE & COOKWARE	ITEM	WHAT TO LOOK FOR	TEST KITCHEN FAVORITES
	ROUND CAKE PAN	• Straight sides • Nonstick coating for even browning and easy release of cakes • Good to have a set of both 9-inch and 8-inch round pans • Light finish ideal for cakes, dark finish ideal for cinnamon buns	BEST ALL-AROUND: Nordic Ware Naturals Nonstick 9-inch Round Cake Pan $14.32 BEST FOR BROWNING: Chicago Metallic Non-Stick 9" Round Cake Pan $10.97
	METAL BAKING PAN	• Dimensions of 13 by 9 inches • Straight sides • Gold nonstick coating for even browning and easy release of cakes and bar cookies	Williams-Sonoma Goldtouch Nonstick Rectangular Cake Pan, 9" x 13" $32.95
	GLASS BAKING DISH	• Dimensions of 13 by 9 inches • Lightweight with large handles for easy grip and safe maneuvering	Pyrex Easy Grab 3-Quart Oblong Baking Dish $7.29
	PIE PLATE	• Golden-hued metal plate bakes crusts without overbrowning • Produces crisp and flaky bottom crusts • Nonfluted lip allows for maximum crust-crimping flexibility • Good to have two	Williams-Sonoma Goldtouch Nonstick Pie Dish $18.95
	SPRINGFORM PAN	• Tall sides for an easy grip • Gold-toned pan produces evenly baked crust • Wide, raised base provides ample support	Williams-Sonoma Goldtouch Springform Pan, 9" $49.95 BEST BUY: Nordic Ware 9" Leakproof Springform Pan $16.22
	TART PAN	• Dark nonstick surface for easy release and deep, even browning • Deep grooves for impressive edges • If you bake a lot, it's good to have multiple sizes, though 9 inches is standard	Matfer Steel Non-Stick Fluted Tart Mold $27

BAKEWARE & COOKWARE	ITEM	WHAT TO LOOK FOR	TEST KITCHEN FAVORITES
	BUNDT PAN	• Heavyweight cast aluminum • Thick, easy-to-grip handles • Clearly defined ridges • 15-cup capacity	Nordic Ware Anniversary Bundt Pan $30.99
	TUBE PAN	• Heavy pan (at least 1 pound) • Heavy bottom for leak-free seal • Dark nonstick surface for even browning and easy release • 16-cup capacity • Feet on rim	Chicago Metallic Professional Nonstick Angel Food Cake Pan with Feet $19.95

	MUFFIN TIN	• Gold nonstick surface for perfect browning
		  and easy release
		• Wide, extended rims and raised lip for
		  easy handling
			OXO Good Grips Non-Stick 12-Cup
			Muffin Pan
			$24.99

	TRADITIONAL SKILLET	• Stainless-steel interior and fully clad for even heat distribution • 12-inch diameter and flared sides • Comfortable, ovensafe handle • Tight-fitting lid included	All-Clad 12-Inch Stainless Steel Fry Pan with Lid $96.85
	NONSTICK SKILLET	• Dark, nonstick surface • 12- or 12½-inch diameter, thick bottom • Comfortable, ovensafe handle • Cooking surface of at least 9 inches • Good to have smaller (8- or 10-inch) skillets too	OXO Good Grips Non-Stick 12-Inch Open Frypan $39.99
	CAST-IRON SKILLET	• Thick bottom and straight sides • Roomy interior (cooking surface of 9¼ inches or more) • Preseasoned	Lodge Classic 12-Inch Cast Iron Skillet $33.31

BAKEWARE & COOKWARE	ITEM	WHAT TO LOOK FOR	TEST KITCHEN FAVORITES
	DUTCH OVEN	• Enameled cast iron or stainless steel • Capacity of at least 6 quarts • Diameter of at least 9 inches • Tight-fitting lid • Wide, sturdy handles	HEAVIER: **Le Creuset 7¼-Quart Round French Oven** $349.95 LIGHTER: **All-Clad Stainless 8-Quart Stockpot** $279.95 BEST BUY: **Cuisinart 7 Qt. Round Covered Casserole** $121.94
	SAUCEPANS	• Large saucepan with 3- to 4-quart capacity and small nonstick saucepan with 2- to 2½-quart capacity • Tight-fitting lids • Pans with rounded corners that a whisk can reach into • Long, comfortable handles that are angled for even weight distribution	LARGE: **All-Clad Stainless 4-Qt Sauce Pan** $179.13 BEST BUY: **Cuisinart MultiClad Unlimited 4 Quart Saucepan with Cover** $65.12 SMALL: **Calphalon Contemporary Nonstick 2½ Quart Shallow Saucepan with Cover** $39.95

BASIC TOOLS	ITEM	WHAT TO LOOK FOR	TEST KITCHEN FAVORITES
	MIXING BOWLS	• Good to have both stainless steel and glass (for mixing, microwaving, and holding prepped ingredients) • Sets of 3 to 4 nesting bowls ranging in capacity from about 1 quart to 4 quarts (for glass) and 1½ quarts to 5 quarts (for stainless steel)	STAINLESS STEEL: **Vollrath Economy Stainless Steel Mixing Bowls** $2.90–$6.90 GLASS: **Pyrex Smart Essentials with Colored Lids** $27.98 for 4-bowl set
	ALL-PURPOSE WHISK	• At least 10 wires • Wires of moderate thickness • Comfortable rubber handle • Balanced, lightweight feel	**OXO Good Grips 11-Inch Balloon Whisk** $9.99
	TONGS	• Scalloped edges • Slightly concave pincers • Length of 12 inches (to keep your hand far from the heat) • Open and close easily	**OXO Good Grips 12-Inch Tongs** $12.95

BASIC TOOLS	ITEM	WHAT TO LOOK FOR	TEST KITCHEN FAVORITES
	SILICONE SPATULA	• Firm, wide blade ideal for efficient scraping and scooping • All-silicone design for easy cleaning	Di Oro Seamless Silicone Spatula—Large $10.97
	ROLLING PIN	• Moderate weight (1 to 1½ pounds) • 19-inch straight barrel • Slightly textured wooden surface to grip dough for easy rolling	J.K. Adams Plain Maple Rolling Dowel $13.95
	OFFSET SPATULAS	• Flexible blade offset to a roughly 30-degree angle • Enough usable surface area to frost the radius of a 9-inch cake • Comfortable handle	LARGE: OXO Good Grips Bent Icing Knife $9.99 SMALL: Wilton 9-Inch Angled Spatula $4.79
	COMPACT SPATULA	• High heat resistance • Comfortable grip • 2-inch wide head	KitchenAid Cookie/Pastry Lifter $8.00
	PASTRY BRUSH	• Silicone bristles (heat-resistant, durable, and easy to clean) • Perforated flaps (to trap liquid) • Angled head to reach tight spots • Comfortable handle	OXO Good Grips Silicone Pastry Brush $6.99
	BOWL SCRAPER	• Curved shape with comfortable grip • Rigid enough to move dough but flexible enough to scrape up batter • Thin, straight edge doubles as dough cutter or bench scraper	iSi Basics Silicone Scraper Spatula $5.99
	BENCH SCRAPER	• Sturdy blade • Beveled edge for easy cutting and scraping • Comfortable handle with plastic, rubber, or nylon grip	Dexter-Russell 6" Dough Cutter/Scraper—Sani-Safe Series $7.01
	SERRATED FRUIT PEELER	• Comfortable grip and nonslip handle • Sharp blade	Messermeister Serrated Swivel Peeler $5.50
	PORTION SCOOP	• Perfect half-sphere shape for easy portioning of batter and dough • Easy-to-squeeze handles to eject dough	OXO Good Grips Large Cookie Scoop $14.97

BASIC TOOLS	ITEM	WHAT TO LOOK FOR	TEST KITCHEN FAVORITES
	CHEF'S KNIFE	• High-carbon stainless-steel knife • Thin, curved 8-inch blade • Lightweight • Comfortable grip and nonslip handle	Victorinox Swiss Army Fibrox Pro 8-Inch Chef's Knife $39.95
	PARING KNIFE	• 3- to 3½-inch blade • Thin, slightly curved blade with pointed tip • Comfortable grip	Victorinox Swiss Army Fibrox Pro 3¼-inch Spear Point Paring Knife $9.47
	SERRATED KNIFE	• 10-inch blade • Broad, deep, pointed serrations • Narrow blade angle • Comfortable grippy handle • Medium weight	Mercer Culinary Millenia 10" Wide Bread Knife $22.10
	KITCHEN SHEARS	• Take-apart scissors (for easy cleaning) • Super-sharp blades • Sturdy construction • Work for both right- and left-handed users	Shun Multi-Purpose Shears/Kershaw Taskmaster Shears $26.30
	RASP GRATER	• Sharp teeth (require little effort or pressure when grating) • Maneuverable over round shapes • Soft, grippy, secure handle	Microplane Premium Classic Zester/Grater $14.95
	GRATER	• Sharp, large holes and generous grating plane • Rubber-lined feet for stability • Comfortable handle	Microplane Specialty Series 4-Sided Box Grater $34.95
	COOKIE CUTTERS	• Metal cutters • Thin, sharp cutting edge and round or rubber-grip top • Depth of at least 1 inch	Little difference among various brands
	BISCUIT CUTTERS	• Sharp edges • A set with a variety of sizes	Ateco 5357 11-Piece Plain Round Cutter Set $14.95

BASIC TOOLS	ITEM	WHAT TO LOOK FOR	TEST KITCHEN FAVORITES
	FINE-MESH STRAINER	• Stiff, tightly woven mesh • Capacity of at least 5 cups with large, durable hooks for support over bowls and pots	Rösle Fine-Mesh Strainer, Round Handle, 7.9 Inches, 20 cm $45
	MANUAL JUICER	• Directs juice in a steady stream with no splattering or overflowing • Large, rounded handles that are easy to squeeze	Chef'n FreshForce Citrus Juicer $23.04
	COOLING RACK	• Grid-style rack with tightly woven, heavy-gauge bars • Should fit inside a standard 18 by 13-inch rimmed baking sheet • Dishwasher-safe	Libertyware Half Size Sheet Pan Cooling Rack $15.99 for set of two
	CUTTING BOARD	• Roomy work surface at least 20 by 15 inches • Teak board for minimal maintenance • Durable edge-grain construction (wood grain runs parallel to surface of board)	Proteak Edge Grain Teak Cutting Board $84.99 BEST BUY: OXO Good Grips Carving & Cutting Board $21.99
	BAKING STONE	• Substantial but not too heavy to handle • Dimensions of 16 by 14 inches • Clay, not cement, for evenly browned crusts	Old Stone Oven Pizza Baking Stone $59.95
	OVEN MITT	• Form-fitting and not overly bulky • Machine washable • Flexible, heat-resistant material	Kool-Tek 15-Inch Oven Mitt by KatchAll $44.95 each
	SPIDER SKIMMER	• Long, well-balanced handle • Easy to maneuver	Rösle Wire Skimmer $41.68 BEST BUY: WMF Profi Plus Spider Strainer 14" (5" dia.) $19.95
	FOOD MILL	• Lightweight but sturdy plastic construction • Easy to turn	RSVP Classic Rotary Food Mill $24.95

SMALL APPLIANCES	ITEM	WHAT TO LOOK FOR	TEST KITCHEN FAVORITES
	FOOD PROCESSOR	• 14-cup capacity • Sharp and sturdy blades • Wide feed tube • Should come with basic blades and discs: steel blade, dough blade, shredding/slicing disc	Cuisinart Custom 14 Food Processor $199.99 MINI FOOD PROCESSOR: Cuisinart Elite Collection 4-Cup Chopper/Grinder $59.95
	STAND MIXER	• Planetary action (stationary bowl and single mixing arm) • Powerful motor • Bowl size of at least 4½ quarts • Slightly squat bowl to keep ingredients in beater's range • Should come with basic attachments: paddle, dough hook, metal whisk	KitchenAid Pro Line Series 7-Qt Bowl Lift Stand Mixer $549.99 BEST BUY: KitchenAid Classic Plus Series Stand Mixer $199.99
	HANDHELD MIXER	• Lightweight model • Slim wire beaters without central post • Variety of speeds	KitchenAid 5-Speed Ultra Power Hand Mixer $69.99 BEST BUY: Cuisinart PowerSelect 3-Speed Hand Mixer $26.77
	BLENDER	• Mix of straight and serrated blades at different angles • Jar with curved base • At least 44-ounce capacity • Heavy base for stability	UPSCALE: Vitamix 5200 $449.00 MIDPRICED: Breville The Hemisphere Control $199.95 INEXPENSIVE: Black + Decker Performance FusionBlade Blender $80.26
	IMMERSION BLENDER	• Easy to maneuver and lightweight with a slim, grippy body • Well-designed blade and cage • Detachable handle for easy cleanup	Braun Multiquick 5 Hand Blender $59.99
	ELECTRIC GRIDDLE	• Large cooking area (about 21 by 12 inches) • Attached pull-out grease trap (won't tip over) • Nonstick surface for easy cleanup	BroilKing Professional Griddle $99.99

SPECIALTY ITEMS	ITEM	WHAT TO LOOK FOR	TEST KITCHEN FAVORITES
	STOVETOP GRIDDLE	• Anodized aluminum for even heating • Nonstick coating • Heat-resistant loop handles • At least 17 by 9 inches (large enough to span two burners) • Pour spout for draining grease	Anolon Advanced Double Burner Griddle $68.99
	APPLE CORER	• Comfortable grip with offset handle • Sharp teeth • Wide blade diameter	CuisiPro Apple Corer $9.95
	PIPING SET	• Contains all of the essentials: twelve 16-inch pastry bags; four plastic couplers; and the following Wilton tips: #4 round, #12 round, #70 leaf, #103 petal, #2D large closed star, #1M open star • All parts available at most craft stores	Test Kitchen Self-Assembled à La Carte Decorating Set $15.32
	PIZZA WHEEL	• Clear plastic wheel to prevent damage to pans • Comfortable, soft-grip handle • Thumb guard to protect fingers	OXO Good Grips 4-Inch Pizza Wheel $12.99
	WAFFLE IRON	• Indicator lights and audible alert • Makes two waffles at a time • Six-point dial for customizing waffle doneness	Cuisinart Double Belgian Waffle Maker $99.95
	RAMEKINS	• Thick, heavy ceramic • Narrow shape • Straight sides	Le Creuset Stackable Ramekin $16.00 for 1 ramekin
	CAKE STAND	• Elevated rotating stand so you can hold the spatula steady for easy frosting • Solid, light construction	Winco Revolving Cake Decorating Stand $29.98

Ingredients

Sometimes brand can make the difference between a baked good that's just OK and one that's truly spectacular. Here are the test kitchen's top-rated brands for ingredients important to baking.

	TEST KITCHEN FAVORITE	WHY WE LIKE IT	RUNNERS-UP
	BUTTER, UNSALTED Plugrá European-Style	• Sweet and creamy • Complex tang and grassy flavor • Enough butterfat (almost 83%) for decadent, but not dense and greasy, baked goods	Land O'Lakes and Vermont Creamery European-Style
	CHOCOLATE, DARK Ghirardelli 60% Cacao Bittersweet Chocolate Premium Baking Bar	• Creamy texture, not grainy or chalky • Complex flavor with notes of cherry and wine with slight smokiness • Balance of sweetness and bitterness	Callebaut Intense Dark L-60-40NV (60% Cacao)
	CHOCOLATE, MILK Dove Silky Smooth	• Intense, full, rich chocolate flavor • Super-creamy texture from abundant milk fat and cocoa butter • Not overwhelmingly sweet	Endangered Species All-Natural Smooth and Green & Black's Organic
	CHOCOLATE, MILK CHIPS Hershey's Kitchens	• Bold chocolate flavor outshines too-sweet, weak chocolate flavor of other chips • Complex with caramel and nutty notes • Higher fat content makes texture creamier than grainy, artificial competitors	
	CHOCOLATE, DARK CHIPS Ghirardelli 60% Premium Baking Chips	• Rich, chocolate flavor • Higher cacao and fat percentages • Dew drop–shaped chips for even distribution	Guittard Extra Dark Chocolate Chips 63%
	CHOCOLATE, UNSWEETENED Hershey's Unsweetened Baking Bar	• Well-rounded, complex flavor • Assertive chocolate flavor and deep notes of cocoa	Valrhona Cacao Pate Extra 100% and Scharffen Berger Unsweetened Dark
	CHOCOLATE, WHITE CHIPS Guittard Choc-Au-Lait	• Creamy texture, not waxy or crunchy • Silky smooth meltability from high fat content • Complex flavor like high-quality real chocolate, no artificial or off-flavors	E. Guittard 31% Cacao Pure White Chocolate Wafers

	TEST KITCHEN FAVORITE	WHY WE LIKE IT	RUNNERS-UP
	CINNAMON Morton & Bassett Spices	• Perfect balance of sweet and spicy • Mellow flavor in baked applications	Penzeys Vietnamese and McCormick
	COCOA POWDER Hershey's Natural Unsweetened	• Full, strong chocolate flavor • Complex flavor with notes of coffee, cinnamon, orange, and spice	Droste
	CORNMEAL Arrowhead Mills Organic Yellow	• Clean, pure corn flavor comes from using whole-grain kernels • Ideal texture resembling slightly damp, fine sand, not too fine or too coarse	
	EXTRACT, ALMOND Nielsen-Massey Pure	• Rich, full-bodied, assertive flavor • Not harsh or artificial • Lovely almond bouquet	McCormick Imitation and McCormick Pure
	EXTRACT, VANILLA McCormick Pure	• Strong, rich vanilla flavor where others are weak and sharp • Complex flavor with spicy, caramel notes and a sweet undertone	CF Sauer Co. Gold Medal Imitation Vanilla Extract, and Rodelle Pure
	FLOUR, ALL-PURPOSE King Arthur Unbleached Enriched	• Fresh, toasty flavor • No metallic taste or other off-flavors • Consistent results across recipes • Made tender, flaky pie crust, hearty biscuits, crisp cookies, and chewy, sturdy bread	Gold Medal Enriched Bleached Presifted, and Gold Medal Unbleached
	Pillsbury Unbleached Enriched	• Clean, toasty, and hearty flavor • No metallic or other off-flavors • Consistent results across recipes • Made flaky pie crust, chewy cookies, and tender biscuits, muffins, and cakes	

TEST KITCHEN FAVORITE	WHY WE LIKE IT	RUNNERS-UP
FLOUR, WHOLE-WHEAT King Arthur Premium	• Finely ground for hearty but not overly coarse texture in bread and pancakes • Sweet, nutty flavor	Bob's Red Mill Organic
MAPLE SYRUP Grade A Dark Amber (little difference among brands)	• Inexpensive • Dark molasses-y color • Rich caramel flavor	Uncle Luke's Pure Maple Syrup, Highland Sugarworks, Coombs Family Farms, Anderson's, Maple Grove Farms, Maple Gold, Spring Tree, Camp Pure
OATS, ROLLED Bob's Red Mill Old Fashioned	• Toasty flavor, even in cookies • Tender texture with just the right amount of chew	Bob's Red Mill Extra Thick
OIL, ALL-PURPOSE Crisco Blends	• Unobtrusive, mild flavor for stir-frying and sautéing and for use in baked goods and in uncooked applications such as mayonnaise and vinaigrette • Neutral taste and absence of fishy or metallic flavors when used for frying	Mazola Canola Oil
OLIVE OIL, EXTRA-VIRGIN, PREMIUM Gaea Fresh Extra Virgin Olive Oil	• Smooth, butter, and balanced flavor • Sweet olive fruitiness with peppery aftertaste	Casa de Santo Amaro Selection
OLIVE OIL, EXTRA-VIRGIN, SUPERMARKET California Olive Ranch Everyday Extra-Virgin Olive Oil	• Fruity, fragrant, and fresh with a complex finish • Flavor rivals winning premium extra-virgin olive oil	Lucini Premium Select

	TEST KITCHEN FAVORITE	WHY WE LIKE IT	RUNNERS-UP
	PEANUT BUTTER, CREAMY Skippy	• Smooth, creamy, and spreadable • Good balance of sweet and salty flavors	Jif
	PRESERVES, RASPBERRY Smucker's	• Clean, strong raspberry flavor, not too tart or sweet • Not overly seedy • Ideal, spreadable texture, not too thick, artificial, or overprocessed	Trappist
	PRESERVES, STRAWBERRY Welch's	• Big, distinct strawberry flavor • Natural-tasting and not overwhelmingly sweet • Thick and spreadable texture, not runny, slimy, or too smooth	Smucker's and Smucker's Simply Fruit Spreadable Fruit
	SALT Maldon Sea Salt	• Light and airy texture • Delicately crunchy flakes • Not so coarse as to be overly crunchy or gritty nor so fine as to disappear	Fleur de Sel de Camargue, Morton Coarse Kosher, and Diamond Crystal Kosher
	SWEETENED CONDENSED MILK Borden Eagle Brand and Nestlé Carnation	• Made with whole milk; creamier in desserts and balances more assertive notes from other ingredients	
	VANILLA BEANS McCormick Madagascar	• Moist, seed-filled pods • Complex, robust flavor with caramel notes	Spice Islands Bourbon
	YOGURT, WHOLE-MILK Brown Cow Cream Top Plain	• Rich, well-rounded flavor, not sour or bland • Especially creamy, smooth texture, not thin or watery • Higher fat content contributes to flavor and texture	Stonyfield Farm Organic Plain

A Note on Conversions

Some say cooking is a science and an art. We would say that geography has a hand in it, too. Flour milled in the United Kingdom and elsewhere will feel and taste different from flour milled in the United States. So, while we cannot promise that the loaf of bread you bake in Canada or England will taste the same as a loaf baked in the States, we can offer guidelines for converting weights and measures. We also recommend that you rely on your instincts when making our recipes. Refer to the visual cues provided. If the bread dough hasn't "come together in a ball," as described, you may need to add more flour—even if the recipe doesn't tell you so. You be the judge.

The recipes in this book were developed using standard U.S. measures following U.S. government guidelines. The charts below offer equivalents for U.S., metric, and imperial (U.K.) measures. All conversions are approximate and have been rounded up or down to the nearest whole number. For example:

1 teaspoon	=	4.929 milliliters, rounded up to 5 milliliters
1 ounce	=	28.349 grams, rounded down to 28 grams

VOLUME CONVERSIONS

U.S.	METRIC
1 teaspoon	5 milliliters
2 teaspoons	10 milliliters
1 tablespoon	15 milliliters
2 tablespoons	30 milliliters
¼ cup	59 milliliters
⅓ cup	79 milliliters
½ cup	118 milliliters
¾ cup	177 milliliters
1 cup	237 milliliters
1¼ cups	296 milliliters
1½ cups	355 milliliters
2 cups	473 milliliters
2½ cups	591 milliliters
3 cups	710 milliliters
4 cups (1 quart)	0.946 liter
1.06 quarts	1 liter
4 quarts (1 gallon)	3.8 liters

WEIGHT CONVERSIONS

OUNCES	GRAMS
½	14
¾	21
1	28
1½	43
2	57
2½	71
3	85
3½	99
4	113
4½	128
5	142
6	170
7	198
8	227
9	255
10	283
12	340
16 (1 pound)	454

CONVERSIONS FOR INGREDIENTS COMMONLY USED IN BAKING

Baking is an exacting science. Because measuring by weight is far more accurate than measuring by volume, and thus more likely to achieve reliable results, in our recipes we provide ounce measures in addition to cup measures for many ingredients. Refer to the chart below to convert these measures into grams.

INGREDIENT	OUNCES	GRAMS
Flour		
1 cup all-purpose flour*	5	142
1 cup cake flour	4	113
1 cup whole-wheat flour	5½	156
Sugar		
1 cup granulated (white) sugar	7	198
1 cup packed brown sugar (light or dark)	7	198
1 cup confectioners' sugar	4	113
Cocoa Powder		
1 cup cocoa powder	3	85
Butter†		
4 tablespoons (½ stick, or ¼ cup)	2	57
8 tablespoons (1 stick, or ½ cup)	4	113
16 tablespoons (2 sticks, or 1 cup)	8	227

* U.S. all-purpose flour, the most frequently used flour in this book, does not contain leaveners, as some European flours do. These leavened flours are called self-rising or self-raising. If you are using self-rising flour, take this into consideration before adding leavening to a recipe.

† In the United States, butter is sold both salted and unsalted. We generally recommend unsalted butter. If you are using salted butter, take this into consideration before adding salt to a recipe.

OVEN TEMPERATURES

FAHRENHEIT	CELSIUS	GAS MARK (IMPERIAL)
225	105	¼
250	120	½
275	135	1
300	150	2
325	165	3
350	180	4
375	190	5
400	200	6
425	220	7
450	230	8
475	245	9

CONVERTING TEMPERATURES FROM AN INSTANT-READ THERMOMETER

We include doneness temperatures in many of our recipes, such as those for poultry, meat, and bread. We recommend an instant-read thermometer for the job. Refer to the table above to convert Fahrenheit degrees to Celsius. Or, for temperatures not represented in the chart, use this simple formula:

Subtract 32 degrees from the Fahrenheit reading, then divide the result by 1.8 to find the Celsius reading.

EXAMPLE:
"Roast until chicken thighs register 175 degrees."
To convert:

175° F − 32 = 143°
143° ÷ 1.8 = 79.44°C, rounded down to 79°C

Index

A

All-Butter Double-Crust Pie Dough, 374–75

All-Butter Single-Crust Pie Dough, 375–76

All-Butter Single-Crust Pie Dough for Custard Pies, 376

All-Purpose Cornbread, 29–30

All-Season Blueberry Cobbler, 352

Almond extract, taste tests on, 460, 497

Almond(s)

Apple Crumble, 354

Apple Upside-Down Cake with, 262

-Apricot Muffins, 39

-Apricot Oatmeal Scones, 61

-Apricot Sour Cream Coffee Cake, 80

Baklava, *454*, 455–56

Big and Chewy Oatmeal-Nut Cookies, 190

Biscotti, 221–22, *223*

blanching, 9

Chocolate Espresso Dacquoise, *326*, 327–30

Chocolate Raspberry Torte, 320–21

Crunch Topping, Blueberry Swirl Muffins with, 41

-Crusted French Toast, 94

decorating cakes with, 289

Granola with Dried Fruit, 98–99

Linzertorte, 426–27

Mexican Chocolate Butter Cookies, 219

Napoleons, 460

-Orange Oatmeal Cookies, Thin and Crispy, 194

and Orange Oatmeal Cookies, Big and Chewy, 190

Pastry Cream, 448

Peach Crumble, 353–54

and Poached Pear Tart, 418–19

Pound Cake, 273

and Raspberries, Skillet Apple Crisp with, 357

and Raspberry Filling, Génoise Layer Cake with, 286–87

-Raspberry Muffins, 39

Ring Coffee Cake, 81–83, *82*

Almond(s) (cont.)

Sablés, 215

Sandies, 198

Spritz Cookies, 218

Toasted

and Honey, Crêpes with, 366

Icing, Fluffy, 292

Meringue Cookies, 227

Triple-Ginger Pear Crisp, 360

Almost No-Knead Bread, 138–39

Cranberry-Pecan, 139

with Olives, Rosemary, and Parmesan, 139

Seeded Rye, 139

Whole-Wheat, 139

American Loaf Bread, 116–17

Anchovies

mincing, 167

Pissaladière, *428*, 442–43

Angel Food Cake, 270–72, *271*

Apple corers, ratings of, 495

Apple(s)

Applesauce Snack Cake, 251–52

Ginger-Cardamom, 252

with Oat-Nut Streusel, 252

Baked, Best, *368*, 369

Cake, French, 262–63

cleaning, 407

Cranberry, and Pecan Topping, 89–90

Crisp, Skillet, 356–57

with Maple and Bacon, 357

with Raspberries and Almonds, 357

with Vanilla, Cardamom, and Pistachios, 357

Crumble, 354

cutting in advance, 356

Dried, Spiced Walnut Granola with, 99

Galette, 408–10, *409*

Modern Mincemeat Pie, 383–84

Pancake, German, 90–92, *91*

Pie

Cranberry-, 382–83

Deep-Dish, 378–81, *379*

Skillet, 355–56

precooking, science behind, 262

Strudel, Quicker, 452–53

Apple(s) (cont.)

Tarte Tatin, 406–7

Turnovers, Flaky, 460–61

Caramel- and Cream Cheese, 461

-Cheddar, 461

-Cranberry, 461

Upside-Down Cake, *260*, 261–62

with Almonds, 262

with Lemon and Thyme, 262

Applesauce Snack Cake, 251–52

Ginger-Cardamom, 252

with Oat-Nut Streusel, 252

Apricot(s)

-Almond Muffins, 39

-Almond Oatmeal Scones, 61

-Almond Sour Cream Coffee Cake, 80

and Corn Muffins with Orange Essence, 49

Crescent-Shaped Rugelach with Raisin-Walnut Filling, 220–21

Filling for Danish, 464

-Orange Ring Coffee Cake, 83

Arugula

Olives, and Ricotta, Chicago-Style Deep-Dish Pizza with, 170

and Prosciutto, Fresh Tomato Pizza with, 162–63

B

Bacon

chopping, tip for, 435

Deep-Dish Quiche Lorraine, 435–38, *436*

Golden Northern Cornbread with, 31

and Maple, Skillet Apple Crisp with, 357

Onion, and Gruyère, Quick Cheese Bread with, 38

and Onion Tart, French, 433–34

Bagels

Cinnamon-Raisin, *149*, 150

cutting safely, 148

Everything, *149*, 150

Plain, 148–50, *149*

Topped, *149*, 150

Kitchen timers, ratings of, **487**
Kiwi
    Classic Fresh Fruit Tart, 415–16
    peeling, 415
Knives, ratings of, **492**

L

Lavender-Honey Zabaglione, Individual Fresh Berry Gratins with, 363
Layer Cakes
    broken layers, remedy for, 296
    cake testers for, 302
    Carrot
        Sheet, Classic, with Cream Cheese Frosting, 312–13
        Sheet, Spiced, with Vanilla Bean–Cream Cheese Frosting, 313
        Ultimate, 310–11
    Chocolate Espresso Dacquoise, *326,* 327–30
    Chocolate Raspberry Torte, 320–21
    Coconut, 296–97
    decorating, simple ideas for, 289
    Devil's Food, Moist and Tender, 305–6
    dry, remedy for, 297
    dusting with confectioners' sugar, 289, 325
    Fallen Chocolate, 335
        Individual, 334–35
        -Orange, 335
    Flourless Chocolate, Ultimate, 325–27
    Fluffy Yellow, with Chocolate Frosting, 284–85
    Foolproof Jelly Roll, 307
    frosting, tips for, 288
    Genoise, with Almond and Raspberry Filling, 286–87
    German Chocolate
        with Banana, Macadamia, and Coconut Filling, 304
        with Coconut-Pecan Filling, 301–4, *303*
        with Coffee, Cashew, and Coconut Filling, 304
        Sheet Cake, 304
    Hot Fudge Pudding Cake, 330–31
    Individual Hot Fudge Pudding Cakes, 331
    Individual Sticky Toffee Pudding Cakes, 331–32, *333*
    leftover, covering, 304
    Lemon, with Fluffy Icing, 290–91

Layer Cakes (cont.)
    leveling and splitting, 287
    Old-Fashioned Chocolate, 299–301
    removing from pans, tips for, 290
    Simple Chocolate Sheet, *308,* 309–10
    soft, slicing, tip for, 322
    Spice, with Cream Cheese Frosting, 314–15
    Spice, with Orange–Cream Cheese Frosting, 315
    Strawberry Cream, *282,* 297–99
    transporting, tips for, 304
    Triple-Chocolate Mousse, 322–24, *323*
    turning into sheet cakes, 299
    Wicked Good Boston Cream Pie, 293–95, *294*
Leaveners, 4
Leek(s)
    and Blue Cheese, Deep-Dish Quiche with, 438
    and Mushroom Galette with Gorgonzola, 439–40, *441*
    preparing, 439
Lemon(s)
    Bars, Perfect, 244–45
    -Blueberry Muffins, 39
    -Blueberry Sour Cream Coffee Cake, 80
    Bundt Cake, 275–77, *276*
    Cheesecake, 341–43
    Chiffon Cake, 269
    Chiffon Pie, 404–5
    -Coconut Chiffon Cake, 269
    Cookies, Glazed, 204–5
        and Crystallized Ginger, 205
        -Orange Cornmeal, 205
    -Cornmeal Blueberry Pancakes, 88
    Essence, Spritz Cookies with, 218
    Glaze, 256
    Glaze, Classic Blueberry Muffins with, 42
    and Goat Cheese Cheesecake with Hazelnut Crust, 343
    juicing, tips for, 245, 342, 403
    Layer Cake with Fluffy Icing, 290–91
    Meringue Pie, 405–6
    –Poppy Seed Angel Food Cake, 272
    –Poppy Seed Muffins, 39
    –Poppy Seed Pound Cake, 275
    Pound Cake, Easy, 274–75
    Sablés, 215
    Soufflé, Skillet, *484,* 485
    and Sugar, Crêpes with, 363–64
    Tart, Classic, 416–18, *417*
    Triple-Citrus Bars, 247

Lemon(s) (cont.)
    Triple-Citrus Cheesecake, 343
    zest, grating, 275
Lightly Sweetened Raspberries, 280
Lime(s)
    -Coconut Cream Pie, 402
    -Glazed Coconut Snowballs, 206–7
    juicing, tip for, 403
    Key, Bars, 245–47, *246*
    Key, Pie, 403
    Triple-Citrus Bars, 247
    Triple-Citrus Cheesecake, 343
Linzertorte, 426–27
Loaf pans, 14, 487

M

Macadamia(s)
    Banana, and Coconut Filling, German Chocolate Cake with, 304
    Tropical Granola with Dried Mango, 99
Make-Ahead Crème Brûlée, 473
Make-Ahead Individual Chocolate Soufflés, 483
Make-Ahead Sticky Buns with Pecans, 75
Malted Milk Frosting, Creamy, 318
Mango, Dried, Tropical Granola with, 99
Maple (Syrup)
    Apple, Cranberry, and Pecan Topping, 89–90
    and Bacon, Skillet Apple Crisp with, 357
    Butter-Pecan, 90
    keeping warm, 93
    -Pecan Cream Scones, Classic, 60
    -Pecan Glazed Oatmeal Scones, 61
    Pecan Pie, 396–97
    taste tests on, 498
Marble Cheesecake, 337
Marbled Blueberry Bundt Cake, 255–56
Measuring cups, 15, 77, 196, 486
Measuring spoons, 15, 486
Meringue Cookies, 225–27, 226
    Chocolate, 227
    Espresso, 227
    Orange, 227
    Toasted Almond, 227
Meringue Pies
    applying topping to, 406
    cream of tartar for, 485
    Lemon, 405–6
Mexican Chocolate Butter Cookies, 219